DISASTER LAW
AND POLICY

ASPEN PUBLISHERS

DISASTER LAW AND POLICY

Second Edition

Daniel A. Farber
University of California, Berkeley

Jim Chen
University of Louisville

Robert R.M. Verchick
Loyola University, New Orleans

Lisa Grow Sun
Brigham Young University

Wolters Kluwer
Law & Business

AUSTIN   BOSTON   CHICAGO   NEW YORK   THE NETHERLANDS

Aspen Publishers
Attn: Permissions Department
76 Ninth Avenue, 7th Floor
New York, NY 10011-5201

To contact Customer Care, e-mail customer.care@aspenpublishers.com, call 1-800-234-1660, fax 1-800-901-9075, or mail correspondence to:

Aspen Publishers
Attn: Order Department
PO Box 990
Frederick, MD 21705

Printed in the United States of America.

1 2 3 4 5 6 7 8 9 0

ISBN 978-0-7355-8834-9

Library of Congress Cataloging-in-Publication Data

Disaster law and policy / Daniel A. Farber . . . [et al.]. — [2nd ed.].
   p. cm.
  Rev. ed. of: Disasters and the law / Daniel A. Farber, Jim Chen. 2006.
  Includes bibliographical references and index.
  ISBN 978-0-7355-8834-9 (perfectbound : alk. paper)
  1. Disaster relief — Law and legislation — United States. 2. Emergency management — Law and legislation — United States. 3. Natural disasters — Law and legislation — United States. 4. Disaster insurance — Law and legislation — United States. 5. Hazard mitigation — Law and legislation — United States. 6. Hurricane protection — Government policy — United States. 7. Disasters — Social aspects. 8. Hurricane Katrina, 2005. I. Farber, Daniel A., 1950- II. Farber, Daniel A., 1950- Disasters and the law.

  KF3750.F37 2010
  344.7305′348 — dc22

2009049655

About Wolters Kluwer Law & Business

Wolters Kluwer Law & Business is a leading provider of research information and workflow solutions in key specialty areas. The strengths of the individual brands of Aspen Publishers, CCH, Kluwer Law International and Loislaw are aligned within Wolters Kluwer Law & Business to provide comprehensive, in-depth solutions and expert-authored content for the legal, professional and education markets.

CCH was founded in 1913 and has served more than four generations of business professionals and their clients. The CCH products in the Wolters Kluwer Law & Business group are highly regarded electronic and print resources for legal, securities, antitrust and trade regulation, government contracting, banking, pension, payroll, employment and labor, and healthcare reimbursement and compliance professionals.

Aspen Publishers is a leading information provider for attorneys, business professionals and law students. Written by preeminent authorities, Aspen products offer analytical and practical information in a range of specialty practice areas from securities law and intellectual property to mergers and acquisitions and pension/benefits. Aspen's trusted legal education resources provide professors and students with high-quality, up-to-date and effective resources for successful instruction and study in all areas of the law.

Kluwer Law International supplies the global business community with comprehensive English-language international legal information. Legal practitioners, corporate counsel and business executives around the world rely on the Kluwer Law International journals, loose-leafs, books and electronic products for authoritative information in many areas of international legal practice.

Loislaw is a premier provider of digitized legal content to small law firm practitioners of various specializations. Loislaw provides attorneys with the ability to quickly and efficiently find the necessary legal information they need, when and where they need it, by facilitating access to primary law as well as state-specific law, records, forms and treatises.

Wolters Kluwer Law & Business, a unit of Wolters Kluwer, is headquartered in New York and Riverwoods, Illinois. Wolters Kluwer is a leading multinational publisher and information services company.

To my mother, Annette Farber Holland.

D.A.F.

To my mother and my father.

J.C.

To Laina and Egon.

R.V.

To my family: May we always be prepared.

L.G.S.

SUMMARY OF CONTENTS

CONTENTS

PREFACE

The significance of disaster law should be self-explanatory. Hurricane Katrina alone has involved many billions of dollars for compensation, insurance, and rebuilding efforts, and lawyers will be heavily involved for years to come in litigating claims to these funds. The loss of life on the Gulf Coast was tragic and in large part avoidable, while the task of rebuilding New Orleans seems stuck in mid-course. Smaller disasters occur on a regular basis, and the United States faces Katrina-scale disaster risk from other possible floods and earthquakes. Internationally, the threats are, if anything, graver. Law has a vital contribution to make in addressing these problems.

Apart from its practical significance, disaster law also deserves more attention because of its intellectual challenges. At first glance, disaster law seems to be nothing but a collection of legal rules of various kinds that happen to come into play when communities have suffered severe physical damage. But at a deeper level, disaster law is about assembling the best portfolio of legal rules to deal with catastrophic risks — a portfolio that includes mitigation, emergency response, compensation and insurance, and rebuilding strategies. Because of this unifying theme, we think that the topic is deserving of serious law school attention even beyond its newsworthy qualities.

The first edition of this book appeared only months after Hurricane Katrina, at a time when disaster issues were just beginning to receive sustained attention from legal scholars. In the years since the first edition was published, courses on disaster issues have begun to spring up around the country, and a small, but growing, body of legal scholarship has emerged.

New legal developments also continue to unfold. Indeed, as this book went to press, a groundbreaking decision from a federal court in Louisiana found the U.S. Army Corps of Engineers liable for its negligent maintenance of a major navigation channel. That failure, the court found, was directly responsible for flood damage in New Orleans' Lower Ninth Ward and the neighboring St. Bernard Parish after Hurricane Katrina. The ruling could pave the way for thousands of lawsuits, or one large class-action suit, that could result in tens of billions of dollars in compensation to flood victims. Or it could prompt a legislative solution that trades future claims against the corps for a broader government compensation package, such as the one that followed the 9/11 attacks. The result depends heavily on what happens when the case is appealed (which the U.S. Department of Justice has already promised to do). This new decision, *In re Katrina Canal Breaches Consolidated Litigation* (E.D. La., No. 05-4182, Nov. 18, 2009), is a good companion to an earlier opinion related to the same litigation, which we have already included in part A in chapter 7.

The intervening years have also provided the opportunity to broaden the focus beyond Katrina and its aftermath. In addition, the original two co-authors have been joined by Lisa Grow Sun and Robert Verchick, providing an infusion of energy and an expansion in expertise.

As a result of all of these developments, we are confident that readers will find deeper analysis, broader coverage, and richer description in this edition than the last. Katrina led to important legal developments: new legislation from Congress and significant judicial decisions on compensation and insurance issues. This edition brings the reader up to date on these significant developments. We have also been able to augment our treatment of the key federal statutes and regulations considerably. In addition, we have added chapters on risk management and on international disaster issues. Finally, most chapters are capped by a problem that calls upon students to apply what they have learned in a realistic setting.

Unfortunately, the problem of natural disasters will always be with us. But the legal system can do more to mitigate the damage, care for and compensate victims, and rebuild sustainable communities. Our hope is that today's law students will take the lead in future efforts to accomplish these critical goals.

Dan Farber
Jim Chen
Robert R.M. Verchick
Lisa Grow Sun

ACKNOWLEDGMENTS

We are grateful to many people for their help in writing this book. We are especially grateful to Steve Errick for his support as a publisher for both editions of this book.

Dan Farber would like to thank Leslie Stone for her deft handling of manuscript corrections and reprint permissions, and Elaine Meckenstock for her research assistance. His work on the book was supported by a grant from National Science Foundation on organizational learning and natural disasters, NSF Grant # CMMI0624296.

Jim Chen would like to thank Mari-Elise Gates and Becky Wimberg for their invaluable assistance.

Rob Verchick would like to thank Erik Christensen, Rob Garda, and John Lovett for the insights they offered during this project. He is also grateful to his assistant Lindsey Reed for her help in the editing stage. Laura Ashley and Sharon Stanley provided excellent research assistance throughout. Helpful financial support was provided by the Loyola University New Orleans College of Law and by the Louisiana Board of Regents Endowed Chairs for Eminent Scholars Program. In addition, Rob Verchick would like to remind readers that the views expressed in this book belong only to the book's authors or the authors of materials excerpted. These views should not be confused with those of his current employer, the U.S. Environmental Protection Agency.

Lisa Grow Sun would like to thank Karl Sun, Robert Grow, Linda Grow, RonNell Andersen Jones, and Brigham Daniels for their insightful feedback and superb advice. She also appreciates generous financial support from the J. Reuben Clark Law School, Brigham Young University; copyright permission assistance from Shawn Nevers; and the outstanding work of her research assistants: Stephanie Barclay, Melinda Bowen, James Dunkelberger, Dustin Glazier, Marcus Hintze, Peachie Jones, Robert Stander, and Reed Willis.

In addition, we thank the following sources for their permission to reprint excerpts of their scholarship:

Action Aid International, *Tsunami Response: A Human Rights Assessment*, www. actionaid.org/docs/tsunami_human_rights.pdf (Jan. 2006). Reprinted with permission.

Anna K. Schwab & David J. Brower, *Increasing Resilience To Natural Hazards: Obstacles And Opportunities For Local Governments Under The Disaster Mitigation Act Of 2000*, in Losing Ground: A Nation on Edge 281, 283-301 (John Nolon & Daniel Rodriguez eds., 2007). Reprinted with permission.

Association of State Floodplain Managers, *A Report Of The 2007 Assembly of the Gilbert F. White National Flood Policy Forum* 33-36 (2007). Reprinted with permission.

B.E. Aguirre, Dialectics of Vulnerability and Resilience, 14 Geo. J. on Poverty L. & Pol'y 39, 41-45 (2007). Reprinted with permission.

Cass R. Sunstein, *Which Risks First?*, 1997 U. Chi. Legal F. 101, 103-105, 112-114 (1997). Reprinted with permission.

Clayton P. Gilette & James E. Krier, *Risk, Court, and Agencies*, 138 U. Pa. L. Rev. 1027, 1027-1029, 1039, 1071-1073, 1076-1079 (1990). Reprinted with permission.

Dan M. Kahan, *Two Conceptions of Emotion In Risk Regulation*, 156 U. Pa. L. Rev. 741 (2008). Reprinted with permission.

Douglas A. Kysar, *It Might Have Been: Risk, Precaution and Opportunity Costs*, 22 J. Land Use & Envtl. L. 1 (2006). Reprinted with permission.

Elaine Enarson, *Women and Girls Last? Averting the Second Post-Katrina Disaster*, available at www.bepress.com/ev/vol2/iss4/art4i. Reprinted with permission.

Erin Ryan, *Federalism and the Tug of War Within: Seeking Checks and Balance in the Interjurisdictional Gray Area*, 66 Md. L. Rev. 503, 522-536 (2007). Reprinted with permission.

Ernest B. Abbott, Otto J. Hetzel & Alan D. Cohn, *State, Local, and First Responder Issues*. Hurricane Katrina Task Force Subcommittee Report, 2006, published by the ABA Standing Committee on Law and National Security, the ABA Section of State and Government, and the ABA Section of Administrative Law & Regulatory Practice. Copyright 2006 by the American Bar Association. Reprinted with permission.

Frank Ackerman & Lisa Heinzerling, *Pricing the Priceless: Cost-Benefit Analysis of Environmental Protection*, 150 U. Pa. L. Rev. 1553 (2002). Reprinted with permission.

Gordon Russell, Rising From the Tide, Times-Picayune (New Orleans), Dec. 11, 2005, A1. Reprinted with permission.

Human Rights Center, University of California, Berkeley, *After the Tsunami: Human Rights of Vulnerable Populations* (October 2005). Reprinted with permission.

Janet Abramovitz, *Unnatural Disasters*, Worldwatch Paper 158, Worldwatch Institute, 5-12 (2001), available at www.worldwatch.Org/Node/832. Reprinted with permission.

Jed Horne, *Carving A Better City*, Times-Picayune (New Orleans), Nov. 13, 2005, A1. Reprinted with permission.

Matthew D. Adler, *Policy Analysis for Natural Hazards: Some Cautionary Lessons From Environmental Policy Analysis*, 56 Duke L.J. 1 (2006). Reprinted with permission.

Metropolitan Policy Program at Brookings, *The New Orleans Index: Tracking the Recovery of New Orleans and the Metro Area* (Aug. 2009), https://gnocdc.s3.amazonaws.com/NOLAIndex/NOLAIndex.pdf. Reprinted with permission.

Mitchell Moss, Charles Schellhamer & David A. Berman, *The Stafford Act and Priorities for Reform*, 6 J. Homeland Security & Emergency Mgmt. 8-16 (2009). Reprinted with permission.

Mtanguliza Sanyika, *Katrina and The Condition Of Black New Orleans: The Struggle For Justice, Equity, and Democracy*, in Race, Place and Environmental Justice After Hurricane Katrina: Struggles To Reclaim, Rebuild, And Revitalize New Orleans And The Gulf Coast, 87, 104-110 (Robert D. Bullard & Beverly Wright eds., 2009). Reprinted with permission.

Nicholas S. Kelley & Michael T. Osterholm, Center for Infectious Disease Research and Policy (CIDRAP), *Pandemic Influenza, Electricity, And The Coal Supply Chain: Addressing Crucial Preparedness Gaps in the United States*, 7-10, 22-24, 43, 47-51 (2008), available at www.cidrapsource.com/content/do/view/marketing/mart/coalreport_landing.html. Reprinted with permission from the University Of Minnesota Board Of Regents.

Oliver A. Houck, *Rising Water: The National Flood Insurance Program and Louisiana*, 60 Tul. L. Rev. 61-164 (1985). Reprinted with permission.

Richard Campanella, Bienville's Dilemma: A Historical Geography of New Orleans 351-354 (2008). Reprinted with permission.

Robert L. Rabin & Suzanne A. Bratis, *Financial Compensation For Catastrophic Loss In The United States*, in Financial Compensation for Victims After Catastrophe (M. Faure & T. Honlief eds., Springer Verlag 2005). Reprinted with permission.

Robert R.M. Verchick, *Facing Catastrophe: Environmental Action for a Post-Katrina World* (forthcoming 2010). Reprinted with permission.

Sean Hecht, *Climate Change and the Transformation of Risk: Insurance Matters*, 55 UCLA L. Rev. 1559 (2008). Reprinted with permission.

Stephen D. Sugarman, "Roles of Government in Compensating Disaster Victims," *Issues in Legal Scholarship*, (2007): Article 1, available at http://www.bepress.com/ils/iss10/art1. Reprinted with permission.

Steve P. Calandrillo, *Responsible Regulation: A Sensible Cost-Benefit, Risk versus Risk Approach to Federal Health and Safety Regulation*, 81 B.U. L. Rev. 957 (2001). Reprinted with permission.

Susan L. Cutter, *The Geography of Social Vulnerability: Race, Class, And Catastrophe*, available at http://understandingkatrina.ssrc.org/Cutter. (Sept. 23, 2005). Reprinted with permission.

Theresa Braine, *Was 2005 the Year of Natural Disasters?*, 84:1 Bull. World Health Org. 4. Reprinted with permission.

CHAPTER 1

INTRODUCTION

A. "SUSPENDED OVER THE ABYSS"

Now I will tell how Octavia, the spider-web city, is made. There is a precipice between two steep mountains: the city is over the void, bound to the two crests with ropes and chains and catwalks. You walk on the little wooden ties, careful not to set your foot in the open spaces, or you cling to the hempen strands. Below there is nothing for hundreds and hundreds of feet: a few clouds glide past; farther down you can glimpse the chasm's bed.

This is the foundation of the city: a net which serves as passage and as support. All the rest, instead of rising up, is hung below: rope ladders, hammocks, houses made like sacks, clothes hangers, terraces like gondolas, skins of water, gas jets, spits, baskets on strings, dumb-waiters, showers, trapezes and rings for children's games, cable cars, chandeliers, pots with trailing plants.

Suspended over the abyss, the life of Octavia's inhabitants is less uncertain than in other cities. They know the net will last only so long.

Italo Calvino, Invisible Cities 75 (1972)

Some of our modern landscapes are, perhaps, not that different from Calvino's fantasy city. From San Francisco to New Orleans to Miami, communities all over the country have operated for years "suspended over the abyss," awaiting the next snapped rope in the form of earthquake, hurricane, or flood. As in Octavia, the dangers in many such cities are obvious and residents are aware (at least when smaller incidents focus the mind) that the place they call home is living on borrowed time. In other communities, the risks posed by natural disaster are less obvious, but often no less significant.

Politicians and civil servants have puzzled over disaster law for centuries. In 1755 an enormous earthquake rocked the city of Lisbon, followed by multiple fires and a devastating tsunami. The city was demolished. As many as 40,000 city residents are believed to have been killed; another 10,000 may have lost their lives in Spain and Morocco.

Often called "the first modern disaster," the event roused many from a complacency that had allowed them to grow too comfortable with the aristocracy and vague notions of fate. During the response and recovery phase, citizens demanded more of government and began seeing themselves as agents of change in their environment. In response, Portugal's prime minister immersed himself in the practical details of reconstruction and launched one of the first scientific inquiries into the mechanics of earthquakes. Zoning rules were imposed, as were Europe's first building codes for seismic events.

In April 1927, the great Mississippi River overflowed its banks from Illinois to the Gulf of Mexico. For six weeks more than 20,000 square miles lay submerged beneath as much as thirty feet of water. An estimated 500,000 to 1,000,000 people lost their homes and nearly 1,000 lost their lives. The consequences would lead Secretary of Commerce Herbert Hoover to take on a massive flood relief effort, establishing a national role for the region's redevelopment and setting the stage for his election to the U.S. presidency. A year after the disaster, the federal government took charge of all flood control projects on the lower Mississippi, and in 1936 it took over projects on *all* federal waterways.

On August 29, 2005, Hurricane Katrina changed the game again. The costliest disaster in American history, the storm's surge plowed across the Gulf coast from central Florida to Texas. New Orleans was the area hardest hit. The surge broke through the federal levee system in more than fifty places, swamping nearly 80 percent of the city. At least 1,836 people lost their lives in the hurricane and subsequent flood (828 in New Orleans), making it one of the deadliest catastrophes in American history. Experts estimate the storm was responsible for more than $81.2 billion in damage.

Hurricane Katrina is often described as a natural event, but the damage in New Orleans was mainly the result of a massive engineering failure. By all expert accounts, Katrina's surge was *within* the federal levee system's intended design specifications. Two professional independent reviews — and one by the U.S. Army Corps of Engineers, itself — attributed much of the flooding to mistakes in levee design and construction stretching back over decades and under the supervision and control of the federal government.[1] The storm and its aftermath caused Americans to question many aspects of hazard protection as well as many aspects of government in general — from environmental protection to race relations, from engineering design to the responsibilities of national government. Many policymakers now wonder what the Katrina disaster might say about the importance of coastal ecosystems, the effects of sea level rise, and the social effects of environmental catastrophe.

It would be one thing if natural hazards threatened only a handful of places. But that is not the case. Disasters come in many varieties and strike in many places, from earthquakes in northern California to wildfires in

---

1. R.B. SEED ET AL., INVESTIGATION OF THE PERFORMANCE OF THE NEW ORLEANS FLOOD PROTECTION SYSTEMS IN HURRICANE KATRINA ON AUGUST 29, 2005 xix (July 31, 2006) (attributing the flood, in part, to "the poor performance of the flood protection system, due to localized engineering failures, questionable judgments, errors, etc. involved in the detailed design, construction, operation and maintenance of the system"), www.ce.berkeley.edu/projects/neworleans/ (Aug. 20, 2009); IVAR L. VAN HEERDEN ET AL., THE FAILURE OF THE NEW ORLEANS LEVEE SYSTEM DURING HURRICANE KATRINA iii-ix (Dec. 18, 2006) (noting failures in worst-case storm analysis, levee design and construction, and levee maintenance), http://www.publichealth.hurricane.lsu.edu/TeamLA.htm (Aug. 20, 2009); U.S. ARMY CORPS OF ENGINEERS, PERFORMANCE EVALUATION OF THE NEW ORLEANS AND SOUTHEAST LOUISIANA HURRICANE PROTECTION SYSTEM: FINAL REPORT OF THE INTERAGENCY PERFORMANCE EVALUATION TASK FORCE, vol. I (June 2009), I-3 (citing poor design and construction as the reason for levee failures), ipet.wes.army.mil (Aug. 20, 2009).

Montana, from massive floods in the Great Plains to hurricanes on the mid-Atlantic coast.

Every year in the United States, events like these cause hundreds of deaths and cost billions of dollars in disaster aid, disruption of commerce, and destruction of homes and critical infrastructure. Although the number of lives lost to natural hazards has generally declined, the economic cost of major disaster response and recovery continues to rise. Every ten years, property damage from natural hazards in the United States doubles or triples in cost. Only Japan suffers more economic damage from natural hazards.

There are many reasons for this trend. Perhaps the most obvious is that the population is growing and expanding into areas that are more prone to natural hazards, such as open coasts, forested areas, or scenic hillsides. Global warming also plays a role, resulting in drier, more fire-prone forests, rising sea levels, and, according to many experts, more powerful storms. As these trends continue, such events will only get worse.

B. DEFINING DISASTER

Disasters can, of course, be understood in many different ways. In this book we focus on disasters triggered mainly by natural forces such as hurricanes, earthquakes, or wildfires. This is similar to the approach taken by many federal disaster laws, which emphasize events tied to geological or meteorological systems. Such calamities are often called "natural disasters," but, strictly speaking, that is a misnomer (even though we will occasionally use the term ourselves as a shorthand). Nearly all "natural disasters" feature some human contribution, whether it be poor construction standards (as in Lisbon), the channeling of a mighty river (as in the 1927 flood), or shoddy levees and urban sprawl (as in New Orleans). As mentioned earlier, human-induced climate change has also changed the game, making it harder to distinguish "Acts of God" from "Acts of Man."

For these reasons, most serious students of disasters have moved from defining a disaster as the hazardous event itself to defining a disaster in terms of the impact that the hazardous event has on people and property—an impact that is determined not only by the magnitude of the event, but also by human interaction with nature, by our choices about where and how we live. Sociologists, for example, tend to define disasters in terms of the social disruption caused by nonroutine, destructive events. *See* What Is a Disaster? New Answers to Old Questions (Ronald W. Perry & E.L. Quarantelli eds., 2005).

For our purposes in elucidating the scope and contours of disaster law, it may be most useful to define disasters, as Professor Dan Farber does, in terms of the governmental and legal responses they demand. On this view, disasters require a "circle of risk management": mitigation, emergency response, compensation, and rebuilding. Rebuilding brings us full circle, as it should occur with an eye toward mitigating impacts of the next disaster. Disasters, then, are those situations or events that require use of this suite of risk management tools.

Understanding disasters in this way focuses us on the legal framework that will best mitigate and respond to disaster risk, as well as the concomitant human suffering. Moreover, this conceptual framework makes clear that disaster law partakes of the bread-and-butter work of many lawyers and lawmakers: mitigating future risk, responding to present damages, and making people and communities whole. At the end of the day, disaster law is an applied field, and the success of various legal tools can be judged by their results in minimizing disaster costs, as a whole, as well as minimizing disparate impacts on vulnerable communities.

C. ORGANIZING DISASTER LAW AND POLICY

The organization of this book reflects this understanding of disasters. Chapter 2, which focuses on the causes of disaster, examines the human contribution to disaster risk and the role of law in shaping the individual and collective choices that increase our exposure to natural hazards. By understanding how our laws (and choices made in the shadow of those laws) exacerbate disaster risk, we begin to see the shape that effective disaster mitigation might take. The chapter also grounds our subsequent discussion in concrete examples of disasters—including both past disasters and potential future disasters that loom on the horizon—to give us a sense of what is at stake if emergency response is ineffective and mitigation efforts are not vigorously pursued.

Chapter 3 focuses on the federal power to respond to disasters. It gives readers the opportunity to use familiar legal principles, such as federalism, and traditional legal tools, such as statutory interpretation, to understand the existing framework for disaster response. The chapter explores federal constitutional powers, gives an overview of the Stafford Act, and considers the military's role in responding to disaster.

Chapter 4 considers the federal emergency response framework in action—examining the federal regulatory scheme for disaster response, with particular focus on catastrophic disasters. Moving beyond the role of the federal government, the chapter turns to the role of state and regional disaster response and, subsequently, to the contributions of private and nongovernmental actors. The chapter ends by examining proposals for reforming the law of emergency response and by giving students a chance to apply their learning in an exercise involving an earthquake.

Before turning in full from disaster response to issues of risk and compensation, we consider in Chapter 5 a critical problem at the intersection of the two issues: the problem of social vulnerability. Too often the poor and other marginalized groups are more acutely affected by disaster. This chapter examines why this is so, taking up issues of poverty, race, gender, immigrant status, and age. Observing how disasters can heighten social tensions and vulnerabilities that already exist, Chapter 5 then urges readers to consider ways in which lawyers and lawmakers might address this problem.

Chapter 6 takes up the issue of risk analysis. Everyone is in favor of taking precautions, but how cautious should we be? And how do we know what risks are really out there? In this chapter, we show how policymakers evaluate risk and examine the underlying assumptions of their techniques. We then ask how societies might respond to disaster risk after a hazard has been evaluated.

Chapter 7 shifts attention to the question of compensation and risk spreading. Should disaster survivors be compensated by the tort system, government programs, or private insurance? The chapter examines the advantages and pitfalls of each of these possibilities in turn, focusing on post-disaster litigation, the national Flood Insurance Program, and the challenges of designing insurance for catastrophic risks.

Chapter 8 then deals with questions of recovery and rebuilding. The chapter considers an array of issues, from city planning to public participation to raising funds. Throughout, readers are encouraged to think about mitigation, risk spreading, social vulnerability, and the tough question of whether or not to even rebuild. To give some context, the chapter examines a few examples of past recovery efforts, including the rebuilding of Kobe, Japan, after the Hanshin earthquake and the resurrection of New Orleans after Katrina.

Finally, Chapter 9 looks at disaster from an international point of view. This provides an opportunity to see how disasters affect countries that are different from the United States — poorer countries, more populous countries, or countries closer to the warm waters of the Equator. The chapter also introduces readers to the wide range of international agreements that have relevance in disaster situations, from the Hyogo Framework, aimed at reducing disaster risk throughout the world, to human rights treaties dealing with racism and sexism. Disasters in poorer parts of the world can differ substantially in terms of lives lost and percentage of the economy affected, when compared with disasters in the United States. Yet Chapter 9 also makes the point that disasters, wherever they occur, have many characteristics in common. Thus all nations have an interest in helping and learning from one another.

D. WEB RESOURCES

The World Wide Web offers an array of resources relevant to disaster law and policy, with topics ranging from emergency management to hazard mitigation to meteorology and geophysics. We have compiled a short list of some of the many fine Web sites now available, concentrating on those that are generally accessible to nonexperts and that have a broad scope.

NATIONAL

Disasters and the Law Database (University of California–Berkeley School of Law) http://www.law.berkeley.edu/library/dynamic/disasters

Disaster Research Center (University of Delaware) http://www.udel.edu/DRC

Federal Emergency Management Agency http://www.fema.gov

GAO Disaster Bibliography (U.S. Government Accountability Office)
http://www.gao.gov/docsearch/featured/dprr.html
Natural Hazards Center (University of Colorado–Boulder)
http://www.colorado.edu/hazards
Natural Hazards Gateway (U.S. Geological Survey)
http://www.usgs.gov/hazards
Wharton Risk Management and Decision Processes Center (University of
Pennsylvania) http://opim.wharton.upenn.edu/risk

INTERNATIONAL

International Strategy for Disaster Reduction (United Nations)
http://www.unisdr.org
ProVention Consortium www.proventionconsortium.org

E. GETTING STARTED

Before turning to the remaining chapters, and with the suite of risk management tools in mind, consider a disaster from recent history: New Mexico's
Cerro Grande fire. Read the short description below and reflect on the questions that follow.

On May 4, 2000, National Park Service fire personnel initiated a prescribed
burn at Bandelier National Monument, a few miles from Los Alamos, New
Mexico. Although the fire plan called for burning about 900 acres to create
a buffer for preventing future fires, the fire quickly burned out of control. The
fire was declared a wildfire on May 5 and — fueled by high winds — eventually
burned some 48,000 acres of forest. BARRY T. HILL, U.S. GEN. ACCOUNTING OFFICE,
FIRE MANAGEMENT: LESSONS LEARNED FROM THE CERRO GRANDE (LOS ALAMOS) FIRE AND
ACTIONS NEEDED TO REDUCE RISKS 1 (2000). Ultimately, the fire destroyed or damaged more than 439 homes, countless businesses, and 7 million trees, causing
an estimated $1 billion in total damages. H.R. REP. NO. 106-710, at 175 (2000)
(Conf. Rep.); HILL, *supra*. More than 1,000 families suffered injury or loss to
person or property, and approximately 18,000 residents of Los Alamos were
forced to evacuate. H.R. REP. NO. 106-710; HILL, *supra*. The spread of the fire was
blamed in large part on the fire plan, which called for initiating the burn in
close proximity to Los Alamos and for setting the fire during a three-year
drought and at the beginning of the southwestern wildfire season, when
winds are particularly strong. HILL, *supra* at 3-5.

Causation and Mitigation. Devastating fires such as the Cerro Grande fire
that ravage communities at the wildland-urban interface are increasingly
common. Why do you think fire losses are increasing and how can we mitigate
these types of disasters? How do you think land use decisions impact the risk of
serious fire losses? How do environmental law and policy influence fire risks?
In some areas, such as Tucson, Arizona, the proliferation of nonnative vegetation such as buffelgrass is transforming fire-resistant desert into highly

flammable grassland. As with the Cerro Grande fire, drought—possibly linked to climate change—is also exacerbating fire risk. What legal response would best meet these challenges?

Emergency Response. Who should be responsible for responding to and fighting this type of fire? The U.S. Forest Service? Local firefighting units? Who should provide needed coordination between different jurisdictions on the ground? Who should be in charge of evacuating residents of at-risk communities? Would your answers change if the fire initially had been sparked by lightning, rather than beginning as a prescribed burn?

Compensation. Who should be liable for the damage caused by fires such as the Cerro Grande fire? The federal government, which developed the flawed plan for the controlled burn? The city council, which approved the building of homes and businesses so close to a national forest, where fire is both an inevitable and a necessary part of the landscape? Private insurers? Individual homeowners who chose not to purchase insurance? What if private insurance is not available to homeowners because of the unpredictable, but potentially high, costs of wildfires? Should some level of government create an insurance pool?

Rebuilding. Should the devastated sections of Los Alamos have been rebuilt? To what extent? Who should have a voice in deciding what rebuilding should occur? What steps should be taken in rebuilding to mitigate future fire risk? Should a comprehensive mitigation and rebuilding plan be in place before homes and businesses are rebuilt?

2

WHY THINGS GO WRONG: CAUSES OF DISASTER

> Floods are acts of nature; but flood losses are largely acts of man.
>   Gilbert White, father of modern floodplain management

In order to analyze the adequacy of our current legal framework for addressing disasters, and to understand how we best mitigate disaster risk, it is important to first understand the sources of disasters—why things go wrong—and how those causal factors have changed over time. No disaster is completely "natural"; human exposure and vulnerability to risk is a product of cultural patterns influenced heavily by law.

In absolute terms, at least, disaster risk is on the rise.[1] From 1990 to 2007, worldwide mortality risk from floods, for example, increased by 13 percent, and the economic risk posed by floods increased by 33 percent. *See* UNITED NATIONS, 2009 GLOBAL ASSESSMENT REPORT ON DISASTER RISK REDUCTION: RISK AND POVERTY IN A CHANGING CLIMATE 5 [hereinafter U.N. 2009 DISASTER RISK REPORT]. Half of the ten most deadly disasters since 1975 occurred between 2003 and 2008. *See id.* at 4. Over the past twenty-nine years, the United States alone has sustained ninety weather-related disasters in which overall damages reached or exceeded $1 billion. Of these ninety disasters, forty have occurred since 2000, and twenty-five since 2005. *See* NATIONAL CLIMATE DATA CENTER, BILLION DOLLAR U.S. WEATHER DISASTERS, http://www.ncdc.noaa.gov/oa/reports/billionz.html#chron (June 17, 2009).

The vast majority of deaths from natural disasters occur in developing countries, *see* CHARLES PERROW, THE NEXT CATASTROPHE: REDUCING OUR VULNERABILITIES TO NATURAL, INDUSTRIAL, AND TERRORIST DISASTERS 15 (2007), but Hurricane Katrina—which claimed some 1,836 lives—is a somber reminder that even the most developed of countries is not immune. Moreover, the economic cost of disasters is rising particularly quickly. The annual total of reported economic damages from natural disasters worldwide was below $25 billion in 1975, but has risen to over $150 billion in 2005. *See* UNITED NATIONS INTERNATIONAL STRATEGY FOR DISASTER REDUCTION, 2005 DISASTERS IN NUMBERS,

---

1. Disaster costs are arguably "fairly stable as percent of GDP." UNITED NATIONS, 2009 GLOBAL ASSESSMENT REPORT ON DISASTER RISK REDUCTION, SUMMARY AND RECOMMENDATIONS 8.

http://www.unisdr.org/disaster-statistics/pdf/2005-disaster-in-numbers.pdf (June 17, 2009).

Why are both the risks and costs of disasters increasing? Several key factors appear to be driving the upward trajectory: (1) modern economic conditions, including the just-in-time economy and the interdependence and privatization of our critical infrastructure; (2) population growth and demographic shifts that increase exposure to hazards; (3) land use planning that exacerbates, rather than mitigates, disaster risk; (4) failure to maintain green and built infrastructure; and (5) climate change. The sections of this chapter will address each of these issues in turn.

All of these drivers of disaster risk are influenced and shaped by the law. In addition to risk, some of these drivers also present opportunities to mitigate that risk. For example, population shifts and aging infrastructure mean that a large percentage of existing infrastructure will need to be replaced in the next fifty years. *See* Report of the Second Assembly of the Gilbert F. White National Flood Policy Forum, Floodplain Management 2050 xi (2007) [hereinafter, Floodplain Management 2050]. Moreover, much additional housing and commercial property will be required to accommodate increased population. Experts estimate that by 2040, the United States will need 70 million more housing units, 40 million of which will be built on new residential lots. (Current housing stock is 125 million units.) *See* Arthur C. Nelson & Robert E. Lane, *The Next 100 Million*, Planning Magazine 73(1): 4 (2007). More than a billion square feet of nonresidential space will also be constructed (30 billion of new square footage and 70 billion of rebuilt footage). *See id.* at 6. The legal structure we have in place during the next few decades will determine, at least in part, whether we capitalize on (or squander) opportunities to rebuild old infrastructure and construct new infrastructure in ways that mitigate disaster risk.

A. MODERN ECONOMIC CONDITIONS

1. THE "JUST-IN-TIME" ECONOMY AND INFRASTRUCTURE INTERDEPENDENCE

Two features of our modern economy — "just-in-time" supply chains and the increasing interconnectedness of a wide array of industries and infrastructure systems — present major challenges in preparing for and responding to disasters. The evolution of just-in-time supply chains, in which businesses seek to reduce inventory and produce goods just as the economy demands them, has eliminated buffers that would minimize the effect of disaster-related supply-chain disruptions. Moreover, the increasing interconnectedness of our critical infrastructure means that a disruption in one industry can cripple a number of other interdependent industries. The risk of pandemic has focused attention on the way that these two major changes in the American business landscape can magnify the effects and costs of disaster, creating a ripple effect through the "life support" system of critical infrastructure on which we depend. Consider the following report on the likely effect of coal-supply disruptions on electricity (and concomitantly, public health) during an influenza pandemic.

NICHOLAS S. KELLEY & MICHAEL T. OSTERHOLM, CENTER FOR INFECTIOUS DISEASE RESEARCH AND POLICY (CIDRAP), *PANDEMIC INFLUENZA, ELECTRICITY, AND THE COAL SUPPLY CHAIN: ADDRESSING CRUCIAL PREPAREDNESS GAPS IN THE UNITED STATES*

7-10, 22-24, 43, 47-51 (2008), http://www.cidrapsource.com/content/
do/view/marketing/mart/coalreport_landing.html
(Copyright University of Minnesota Board of Regents)

The "flattening of the world" (a term coined by New York Times columnist Thomas Friedman) has changed society dramatically since 1968, the year of the last human influenza pandemic. In a flat world, Friedman says, supply chains (all the inputs for a product, from its origin to end use) depend on rapid and reliable communication, and previous demand determines projections of products needed. Stocks of products can be kept to a minimum, thereby reducing costs up and down the supply chain.

The world has never experienced a pandemic during the just-in-time global economy. Today's supply chains lack surge capacity—the ability to quickly scale up to meet demands. During an influenza pandemic, the number of illnesses and deaths worldwide will inevitably cause problems throughout supply chains. Worker absenteeism (whether from illness, fear, need to care for dependents or loved ones, or lack of ability to travel) and disruptions in international and domestic travel will affect every facet of supply chains that deliver the critical products we depend on for immediate health and safety, such as electricity and, in turn, water supplies and sewage systems, food, prescription drugs, and community safety. So interwoven are these products and services in our lives today, their availability is simply taken for granted. Most of the critical lifesaving drugs found in every hospital, for example, are produced outside the United States, particularly in China and India. A pandemic will likely seriously disrupt the international supply chain of these pharmaceutical products, from the synthesis of an active ingredient in a facility in Asia to delivery of the finished drug to a hospital pharmacy in the United States.

Even with this economic backdrop, pandemic planning has focused primarily on public health prevention strategies. But public health planning has not historically included business continuity or critical infrastructure planning. Nor has public health had a statutory authority to require planning and preparedness of the critical infrastructure. . . .

When one considers public health preparedness, the availability of electricity generally is not considered a factor of concern for public health planners. Electricity is typically regarded as reliable and is, in most instances, available for all public health needs. Whether planning for influenza vaccination clinics, investigating outbreaks of a foodborne disease, or responding to a bioterrorism event, public health workers almost always assume that the lights will be on and power available. For disaster scenarios that would compromise electricity, such as after a hurricane, planning activities take into account the loss of power. Most pandemic planning activities, however, do not consider the potential for the loss of electricity. . . .

But electricity truly undergirds the public health infrastructure. It is so vital today that one of us has noted: "Thomas Edison, not John Snow, is really the father of modern public health." Without electricity or the availability or use of backup power sources, safe water treatment and distribution systems, sanitary waste treatment systems, food refrigeration processes, and vaccine manufacturing plants cannot operate. In addition, traffic lights go dark, telecommuting isn't possible, public health surveillance activities are crippled, elevators stop working, and the heating and cooling of buildings cease. . . .

A comprehensive review of government and industry reports and guidance, scientific literature, historical accounts of the 1918-19 pandemic's impact on coal, and hearings about a 2005 train derailment that disrupted coal supply yield[] troubling findings. Despite the nation's massive reliance on the coal industry for electricity generation, little has been done to secure this critical infrastructure and the people who run it during a pandemic. . . .

Coal-fueled power plants maintain coal stocks so that power generation can continue in the event of expected and unexpected short-term disruptions in the supply chain. . . . Over time, coal stocks have gradually become smaller. . . . Coal became a commodity that power companies assumed would be reliably transported with minor disruptions. Power companies became increasingly dependent on the coal transport system, as coal became treated as a just-in-time deliverable commodity. . . .

Industry experts are aware [that major disruptions of coal supply in pandemics could seriously disrupt electricity production in the United States], yet little has been done to remedy [this problem] — not for lack of trying, but primarily because of the costs of increasing coal stocks at power plants in current market conditions. The amount of coal kept on the ground by coal-powered plants has decreased significantly from the 1970s, when keeping 60 to 90 days was the norm. The reduction to 30 days of coal was encouraged by public utility commissions as a way to cut costs. Most public utility commissions will not allow power companies to raise electricity rates solely for the purpose of increasing their coal stocks. Similarly, most power companies will not spend the extra capital to increase coal stocks in the competitive U.S. energy industry.

Based on an understanding of the inextricable link between public health and electricity (and the supply of coal, in particular), decision-makers should consider the following recommendations to reduce the risks posed by an inevitable pandemic:

Recommendation 1: Build coal stocks. First and foremost, every effort must be made to ensure the reliability of electricity supply during a pandemic. With coal plants, the most practical way to ensure a steady supply of fuel during a pandemic is to keep larger stocks at power plants or storage facilities. When the industry prepares for peak electrical demand (the summer in the United States), coal stocks reach their highest for the year. This peak coal stock level should now be maintained as the new minimum level at every coal power plant around the nation. . . . [T]his level will provide a larger buffer against supply-chain disruptions expected during a pandemic. . . .

Recommendation 2: Place coal miners and their supporting infrastructure personnel in the highest priority levels for pandemic response. The United States government should assume primary responsibility for ensuring coal miners and their support infrastructure have priority access to antiviral drugs, pandemic vaccine, and other critical products and services (e.g., critical pharmaceutical drugs, food), because they are not currently identified as a priority in the federal or state plans for supporting the critical infrastructure during a pandemic.

Recommendation 3: Plan for disruptions in the coal supply chain. There will be disruptions in the coal supply chain during a pandemic. In the absence of prior planning, these disruptions will be more severe. It is anticipated that these disruptions will be similar in impact to the disruptions of [Powder River Basin (PRB)] coal in 2005. Coal shipments are likely to be reduced by at least 15% to 25% for periods up to 60 days. This disruption could also occur more than once if, as in other pandemics, illness comes in waves. These disruptions will occur up and down the supply chain; therefore, it is critical that the whole supply chain be involved in pandemic planning. The company that supplies the tires for the dump trucks at the surface mines in the PRB, for example, might have supply or staffing shortages that prevent it from maintaining the trucks' tires, thus reducing the number in operation. Maintaining a larger inventory of critical supplies and cross-training will help these companies continue to function when supply chains are disrupted. At mines, higher absenteeism could lead to a drop in productivity, exacerbating supply disruption with lowered output. To counter this dilemma, larger mine operations might want to consolidate operations temporarily; smaller mine operations might want to consider short-term pooling of resources (staff and equipment) to maintain the higher levels of productivity. . . .

Recommendation 4: Anticipate and develop strategies for responding to disruptions in electrical services. . . . Every power company currently has procedures for such crises as blackouts caused by ice storms, but the procedures typically assume that resources (people, equipment and/or parts) can be rapidly obtained from utilities in unaffected areas. This will not be the case during a pandemic, as no area will be spared. Further, procedures are not typically developed for dealing with fuel shortages, because they are rare and localized. Planners should plan on dealing with and responding to power disruptions during periods when fuel (for power generation and response vehicles) may be scarce. As these plans are developed or modified, care should be taken to ensure that people who receive power when it is scarce are providing the most critical services to the community. These plans should be integrated with community mitigation strategies, such as closings schools and malls that do not need power.

NOTES AND QUESTIONS

1. Many of the recommendations in the preceding report will require increasing inventories (of coal at power plants, tires at trucking companies, etc.) beyond what the market would normally require. Is there an inevitable trade-off between efficiency and disaster preparedness?

2. One barrier to utility companies investing in disaster preparedness is uncertainty about whether such costs can be recovered (by passing them on to customers), or whether they will come out of the utility's bottom line. Immediately after 9/11, the Federal Energy Regulatory Commission stated that it would "approve applications to recover prudently incurred costs necessary to further safeguard the reliability and security of our energy supply infrastructure." 96 FERC ¶61, 299, Docket PL01-6-000 (September 14, 2001). However, a 2003 survey of state public utility commissions found that, although 45 percent of commissions had received applications from utilities for recovery of security-related costs, 85 percent of commissions still lacked standards for determining the prudence of those investments. *See* Joe McGarvey & John D. Wilhelm, National Association of Regulatory Utility Commissioners/National Regulatory Research Institute, 2003 Survey on Critical Infrastructure Security 3-4, nrri.org/pubs/multiutility/04-01pdf. Moreover, according to one industry observer, "Regulators . . . tend to hold prudence hearings after the fact to extract revenues from the utilities," rather than being more involved in evaluating the prudence of taking (or deferring) security measures at the time the decisions are made. Jack Feinstein, *Managing Reliability in Electric Power Companies, in* Seeds of Disaster, Roots of Response: How Private Action Can Reduce Public Vulnerability 164, 178 (Philip E. Auerswald et al. eds., 2006). Is it possible to formulate standards rather than dealing with the issue on an ad hoc basis?

3. What are the risks of interdependent critical infrastructure — both within a critical industry (such as electricity generation) and among industries that provide critical services? The CIDRAP Report highlights some important interdependencies in our critical infrastructure: electricity generation relies on coal mining and transportation, public health relies on electricity, and so forth. The Report can hardly begin, however, to describe the depth and complexity of the interconnectedness of our critical infrastructures and the challenges that interdependence poses for disaster policy.

One of the primary challenges posed by this interconnectedness is the potential for cascading failures in the event of a disaster. Interconnectedness magnifies disaster risk: even a relatively small-scale event could be transformed into a major disaster, as its ripple effects spread. "The efficient function of [interconnected systems that provide key services such as transportation, information, energy, and health care] reflects great technological achievements of the past century, but interconnectedness within and among systems also means that infrastructures are vulnerable to local disruptions, which could lead to widespread or catastrophic failures." National Research Council of the National Academies, Making the Nation Safer: The Role of Science and Technology in Countering Terrorism 1 (2002). Moreover, once a cascading failure has occurred, the interdependence of various critical industries can present a Catch-22 for disaster recovery, as each industry needs other industries to be functioning in order for it, too, to resume services.

Interdependence of critical infrastructure also can conceal a system's true vulnerabilities, thereby complicating disaster planning:

> It is one thing for a single organization to figure out how to operate reliably on its own, and then to carry out the required structural and management reforms successfully. It is another for a *web of interdependent organizations* to do the same thing. In tightly coupled systems, simply identifying vulnerabilities, let alone managing them, is a daunting task. In a sense, risk migrates to the weakest part of the system, but due to overall complexity, the migration occurs without anyone's knowledge, and without a clear understanding of where the weakest links are located. Yet not identifying such vulnerabilities and risks leaves systems unprepared to function during extreme events.

T.M. La Porte, *Managing for the Unexpected: Reliability and Organizational Resilience, in* Seeds of Disaster, *supra*, 71, 73.

Even where vulnerabilities can be accurately identified, responsibility and accountability for addressing them may be diluted by the involvement of multiple, disconnected parties, and collective action problems may arise. Regulators may need to allocate costs to multiple regulated entities to reduce risks. *See* Philip E. Auerswald, *Complexity and Interdependence, in* Seeds of Disaster, *supra*, 157, 157 ("Most pervasive and difficult to manage are the interdependence that exists among firms in different infrastructures — water authorities that depend on electric power for their pumps, or hospitals that depend on transportation providers for the delivery of needed supplies. In all of these cases, accountability for assured continuing of service is limited."); *see also id.* at 162 (describing how the interdependent risk to poultry farms of the avian flu virus might discourage any particular farmer from taking precautions, because farmers who decline to take precautions save the cost of such precautions and can free-ride on the efforts of other farmers).

The interconnectedness of different key infrastructure systems that supply essential services (transportation, electricity, fuel, water, health care, etc.) presents particularly difficult challenges for disaster response and recovery. For example, in many communities, water cannot be distributed unless there is electricity to power pumps. When South Quebec, Canada, suffered a massive ice storm in January 1998 that triggered multiday power outages, Montreal's water distribution was on the brink of shutting down. *See* Patrick Lagadec & Erwann O. Michel-Kerjan, *The Paris Initiative, "Anthrax and Beyond," in* Seeds of Disaster, *supra*, 457, 459. (Many rural Americans get their water from private wells, which also require electricity to bring groundwater to the surface.) In turn, conventional power plants need a continuous influx of makeup water (which replaces water that evaporates in the power generation cycle) both for cooling and for generating steam to turn turbines, transforming heat into mechanical energy. Moreover, the functioning of the electricity grid depends on the operation of the telecommunications network, which allows operators to shift power where it is needed, to avoid overloading (and, ultimately, failure) of power lines, to troubleshoot problems, and to communicate the status of generating systems (especially those with black-start capacity, which can resume operation without an outside source of power). *See* Feinstein, *supra*, at 187-189 (detailing how telecommunications failure could result in electricity grid failure and how recovery efforts would be deadlocked, with each industry needing the other to begin operation first); Michael Kormos & Thomas Bowe, *Coordinated and Uncoordinated Crisis Responses by the Electric Industry*, in SEEDS OF DISASTER, *supra*, at 194, 199 (describing how Y2K fears highlighted the interdependence of electricity and telecommunications).

Intra-industry interdependencies can also pose significant challenges. Most power plants, for example, cannot perform a black-start, in which operations are restored without relying on an external source of power to start the generator. Thus, most plants require some power from elsewhere in the grid in order to resume operations after a major shutdown. Plants without black-start capability can only resume operations by coordinating with the few that have such capacity (very often large, hydroelectric plants, which usually require very little power to resume operations).

4. The August 14, 2003, blackout in the Midwest and northeastern United States and Canada illustrates the challenges posed by both intra- and inter-industry interdependence. The U.S. electric power supply flows through three regional power grids, which together create an electricity system that is "one of the great engineering achievements of the past 100 years." U.S.-CANADA POWER SYSTEM OUTAGE TASK FORCE, FINAL REPORT ON THE AUGUST 14, 2003 BLACKOUT IN THE UNITED STATES AND CANADA: CAUSES AND RECOMMENDATIONS 5 (2004), available at http://www.nerc.com/filez/blackout.html (June 3, 2009). The United States' power system is dependent on the interconnections within each grid, because they allow electricity producers to sell and transport power to distant end users. *See id.* at 6. But interconnection means that an outage in one area may affect many other locations.

The 2003 power outage began near Cleveland, Ohio, when several power transmission lines shut down because trees had grown into the cables. *See id.* at 57. Local power companies had failed to properly trim trees along transmission right-of-ways and to follow other industry reliability guidelines. *See id.* at 17. The Ohio outage caused massive swings in power transmission; the power swings caused sensors in other areas to shut down additional lines, eventually cascading from Ohio to New York to Canada. *See id.* at 73. The blackout left 50 million people without power for up to four days and cost between $4 billion and $10 billion. *See id.* at 1. Amazingly, the entire electrical event lasted only nine or ten seconds. *See* Matthew L. Wald, *The Blackout: What Went Wrong; Experts Asking Why Problems Spread So Far*, N.Y. TIMES, August 16, 2003, at A1. A task force appointed by President George W. Bush concluded that the disaster could have been avoided if power companies had followed reliability regulations promulgated by the North American Electric Reliability Corporation (NERC), a nongovernmental entity responsible for the security and reliability of the power grid. *See* TASK FORCE FINAL REPORT, *supra*, at 131. But NERC was a "voluntary organization, relying on reciprocity, peer pressure and the mutual self-interest of all those involved to ensure compliance with reliability requirements." *Id.* at 9. Ultimately, NERC did not have authority to enforce its standards. In 2005, Congress passed the Energy Policy Act, which authorized enforcement of reliability standards. Pub. L. No. 109-58, 119 Stat. 594. However, the power grid remains a highly interconnected infrastructure, potentially at risk for a cascading disaster capable of rapidly affecting generation, transmission, and distribution of electricity over wide geographic areas.

The 2003 Northeast blackout also illustrates the inter-industry interdependence of critical infrastructure:

> During the one-day blackout, some hospitals and television stations in New York City, Toronto, Cleveland, and Detroit were able to stay open because they had backup generators. Services in other sectors, however, could not be delivered. Elevators in office buildings were stuck between floors, trains stopped between stations, traffic signals went dark, cell phones lost reception, and, in Cleveland, water ceased to flow and sewers overflowed when the electric-powered pumps stopped functioning. If the blackout had persisted for longer than a day, the region's public health and welfare would have begun to suffer from the failures of more and more socially critical missions.

Jay Apt et al., *Electricity: Protecting Essential Services*, in Seeds of Disaster, *supra* 211, 211-212.

5. What is the solution to disaster risks imposed by interdependence of critical services? One strategy for responding to the risks generated by interconnectedness would be to try to minimize interdependence by breaking the system into smaller, more contained parts (by, for example, decentralizing power grids). Is that a good strategy to employ? Decentralizing such services and decreasing interdependence will, in many instances, decrease efficiency and short-term profits. *See* Auerswald, *supra*, at 161. But will it increase disaster security? Consider this argument, made in the context of counterterrorism efforts:

> Our research into the resilience dimension of reliability and especially the world of reliability professionals suggests that this decoupling strategy may be misguided as a means to mitigate vulnerability to terrorism. In fact, redesigns undertaken to decrease interdependence can undermine some of the very features that ensure the operational reliability of these systems in the first place. . . . Complex, interdependent systems convey reliability advantages to those trained professionals who seek to protect or restore them against terrorist attacks. Their complexity allows for multiple strategies of resilience and recovery.

Paul R. Schulman & Emery Roe, *Managing for Reliability in an Age of Terrorism, in* Seeds of Disaster, *supra*, at 132-133. *See also* Kormos & Bowe, *supra*, at 196 ("The electric grid's interdependencies contribute to its resilience. The large, integrated electrical system allows for more flexible response to minute-by-minute changes, such as demand spikes and sags, generator or major transmission failures, or overloads throughout the system.").

6. In some industries, there may be significant legal barriers to decentralization. For example, efforts to decentralize the power grid might include use

of microgrids, in which small local power generators form local grids that can both connect up with the larger grid and operate independently in emergencies. The operation of microgrids appears to be illegal in a number of states and is legally suspect in many other states. (Much turns on whether the microgrid is characterized as a "public utility.") *See* Douglas E. King, Electric Power Micro-grids: Opportunities and Challenges for an Emerging Distributed Energy Architecture 62-65 (May 2006) (Dissertation, Carnegie Mellon University), available at wpweb2.tepper.cmu.edu/ceic/pdfs_other/Doug_King_PhD_Thesis_2006.pdf.

7. If decentralization and decoupling is not the right answer, what is? "Most people assume that the answer to improved reliability lies in better design of complex systems. If we make them more fail-safe or less tightly coupled or more physically dispersed, we will improve their reliability. . . . The key to increased reliability, particularly in relation to resilience, lies not primarily in the design of large technical systems but in their management. Moreover, the preoccupation with design diverts attention from managerial skills and strategies that could improve reliability." Schulman & Roe, *supra*, at 122. Can the law encourage the education and hiring of "reliability professionals," *id.* at 123, who are trained to maximize resilience of our interconnected infrastructure?

8. Are there some disaster-related resources that are so critical that we need to cultivate local or, at least, national capacity to produce them? The 2009 H1N1 (swine) flu pandemic has underscored the difficulties posed by the United States' limited vaccine production capacity. Currently, the United States is incapable of producing sufficient vaccine to protect substantial portions of the U.S. population, and must rely on contracting with foreign firms, whose governments may void such contracts and seize supplies to meet their own countries' needs if the pandemic worsens. Despite ambitious goals set by the U.S. Department of Health and Human Services (HHS) to stockpile at least 40 million doses of swine flu vaccine (enough to inoculate 20 million people) and be capable of vaccinating all 300 million U.S. citizens within six months from the onset of a pandemic, legitimate doubts abound regarding the ability of the HHS to accomplish those goals. Trust for America's Health, Pandemic Flu Preparedness: Lessons from the Front Lines 6 (2009). The Congressional Budget Office reported that U.S. vaccine production capacity is "completely inadequate," and former HHS Secretary Michael Leavitt acknowledged that new production facilities must be built to make the United States independently able to provide necessary vaccines in the event of a pandemic. *Id.* Having the capability to produce new vaccines rapidly and independently is particularly critical when the vaccines cannot be stockpiled long in advance, as is the case for new strains of flu, such as the swine flu. Consequently, the HHS is subsidizing renovation of existing manufacturing plants and construction of new ones, while increasing efforts in research and development, including egg-based production and adjuvants. *See id.* However, lack of adequate funding remains a significant impediment.

9. Maine Senator Susan Collins famously said, "Emergency management officials should not be exchanging business cards during a crisis."

It seems equally true that the CEO of the electricity company should not be exchanging business cards with the CEO of the natural gas company during a crisis. Two commentators have recommended addressing what they describe as the "network factor" ("the increasing dependence of social and economic activities on the operation of networks, combined with increasing interdependencies among these networks") by developing strategic partnerships at the senior-executive level. *See* Lagadec & Michel-Kerjan, *supra*, at 458-462. Recognizing that the difficulty in realizing this solution lies in its implementation, they draw lessons from the Paris Initiative, which culminated in a two-day conference entitled "Anthrax and Beyond," held one year after feared anthrax contamination threatened to paralyze the international postal system. *Id.* at 472. The conference brought together high-level representatives of postal operators from nearly thirty countries, as well as several outside experts, to debrief the crisis, discuss their experiences, consider new approaches to emergency management, and develop a network of contacts that they might rely on in the next crisis. *See id.* The participants were recruited and encouraged to attend by an international team of experts who visited high-level executives in postal organizations. *See id.* at 471. The primary message of the conference was that emergency management "is a challenge for the whole organization, and especially for top-level decision-makers, not only for technical specialists, risk managers, and people in charge of public relations." *Id.* at 472. How can top-level management be encouraged to focus on disaster preparation? The commentators suggest that every large institution should have a "Rapid Reflection Force," with access to top-level management, to develop crisis strategy. *Id.* at 477.

10. Almost certainly, managing the interdependencies of critical infrastructure to mitigate and respond to disasters requires some sharing of information between affected companies, as well as two-way information sharing between affected companies and the government (which continues to own some critical infrastructure and pursues disaster mitigation to protect the public). See Chapter 4, Section C.1 for a discussion of federal efforts to coordinate infrastructure protection.

    a. Private companies are understandably reluctant to share information with each other. Potential barriers to information sharing include fear of losing competitive advantages, confidentiality agreements with customers and suppliers, worries about negligence liability for disclosed vulnerabilities, anxiety about customer reactions to vulnerabilities, and possible antitrust violations. *See* Lewis M. Branscomb & Erwann O. Michel-Kerjan, *Public-Private Collaboration on a National and International Scale, in* Seeds of Disaster, *supra*, at 395, 398. What steps can government take to encourage beneficial exchange of private information? Should Congress carve out a new, specific exemption from antitrust laws for sharing of information necessary for critical infrastructure coordination of disaster planning and response? How would Congress decide which information sharing is truly necessary for disaster coordination? What are the risks that such an exception would swallow the rule?

b. After 9/11, government entities have become more circumspect about the public sharing of information that may reveal critical infrastructure vulnerabilities because of fears that terrorists may exploit that information to identify and target the weak points in our infrastructure systems. *See* David Zocchetti, *Public Disclosure of Information by Emergency Services Agencies: A Post–September 11 Paradigm Shift, in* A LEGAL GUIDE TO HOMELAND SECURITY AND EMERGENCY MANAGEMENT FOR STATE AND LOCAL GOVERNMENTS 1, 4-7 (Ernest B. Abbott & Otto J. Hetzel eds., 2005) (documenting a post-9/11 shift away from public disclosure of information about critical infrastructure vulnerabilities and emergency plans, including several new state laws amending state open-records laws to limit such disclosure). Post-9/11 reluctance to share both government and private information about critical infrastructure vulnerabilities may complicate needed coordination between the private and public sectors and between various private industries, and may also limit public participation in the development of appropriate emergency plans. The 2002 Homeland Security Act exempts from public disclosure under the Freedom of Information Act "critical infrastructure information" submitted to the Department of Homeland Security (DHS) by private entities. 6 U.S.C. §133. Is that exemption justified by the need to encourage private information sharing with the DHS? If less information about critical infrastructure vulnerability is available in the public domain, will private infrastructure owners be able to create disaster plans that accurately account for the possible failure of other infrastructure systems?

c. The creation of the DHS, in response to 9/11, also has complicated information sharing between private industry and government, by splitting information-gathering responsibilities between DHS and the other federal agencies that have traditionally regulated the industry in question:

> This split happened most notably in chemicals and hazardous materials, commercial nuclear plants, and transportation. The fragmentation has contributed to a lack of clarity regarding divisions of responsibility. For example, the Department of Transportation is responsible for regulating transport, but DHS is responsible for transportation security; the Environmental Protection Agency is responsible for regulating chemicals, but DHS is responsible for chemical security. As a result, private sector officials have complained about confusion, contradictory direction, and duplicative information requests and poor coordination between DHS and other federal agencies. Making matters worse, while DHS has lead responsibility for some sectors, it frequently lacks sufficient or comparable technical expertise in those areas traditionally regulated by other federal agencies . . . Lack of deep industry-specific expertise on DHS' part will likely impede robust information sharing between DHS and the private sector.

Daniel B. Prieto III, *Information Sharing with the Private Sector, in* SEEDS OF DISASTER, *supra*, at 404, 411.

2. PRIVATIZATION AND SECURITY EXTERNALITIES

"In recent years, privatization of public facilities and services, particularly at drinking water utilities, has been occurring in the United States at an increasing rate." U.S. General Accounting Office, Water Infrastructure: Information on Financing, Capital, Planning, and Privatization 16 (2002). At least 85 percent of critical infrastructure in the United States is now privately owned. *See* Department of Homeland Security, Critical Infrastructure Sector Partnership, available at http://www.dhs.gov/xprevprot/partnerships/editorial_0206.shtm (June 17, 2009).

Private ownership of these resources has the potential to exacerbate disaster risk and costs. Private infrastructure owners often lack adequate incentives to invest in precautions that lessen the risk of disasters and in measures that allow for optimal disaster response, because the cost to the owner of failure due to disaster does not reflect the total costs experienced by the community at large. Just as with environmental pollution, private costs and social costs diverge. Because private owners do not bear the full costs of critical infrastructure failure, they may not take those costs into account when deciding whether increased investment in disaster mitigation is justified. Disaster scholars have recently begun to identify and discuss these "security externalities":

> A rational company—with no motive other than maximizing the expected present value of net revenues—would spend on infrastructure protection up to the margin where its private value of incremental risk reduction reached its private cost of further security. Yet infrastructure protection is a government challenge, not merely a business challenge, because threats to critical infrastructure have costs, and thus risk reduction has benefits, that extend far beyond private owners of infrastructure assets. . . . Collateral damage can be minor (the hot-dog stand adjacent to the oil pumping station) or major (the metropolis down-wind from the nuclear power plant). . . .
>
> Private arrangements would recognize and respond appropriately to some of these external risks, even in a world without government. For example, a factory that depended on a rail link or pipeline would rationally pay some or most of the security costs for that asset, even if it did not own it. A sufficiently sophisticated insurance industry would lead firms to internalize many external liability costs. Even a rudimentary tort system would stimulate A to enhance safety for B beyond its own pure self-interested level. . . . But transaction costs are likely to be significant, and complex negotiations may degenerate into stalemate. . . . However inventive private arrangements might be, when externalities abound society should still expect an inadequate supply of security absent government participation.

John D. Donahue & Richard J. Zeckhauser, *Sharing the Watch, in* Seeds of Disaster, *supra*, at 429, 448; *see also* Philip E. Auerswald et al., *Where Private Efficiency Meets Public Vulnerability: The Critical Infrastructure Challenge, in* Seeds of Disaster, *supra*, at 3, 9.

Decentralized, private ownership of critical assets and infrastructure systems also presents challenges in terms of coordination and information sharing. *See supra* Section A.1, note 10.

NOTES AND QUESTIONS

1. Professor Jim Salzman has identified five types of standard policy solutions for externality-based market failures in environmental law that he calls the five P's: prescription (prescribing behavior by "command and control" regulation); penalty (imposing financial signals such as taxes and fees); persuasion (providing information so individuals and companies can self-regulate); property rights (bestowing property rights to pollute in certain quantities, which can then be traded in a market system); and payment (providing subsidies). Jim Salzman, *A Field of Green? The Past and Future Ecosystem Services*, 21.2 J. LAND USE & ENVTL. L. 133, 138 (Spring 2006). Which of these policy solutions, if any, might be effective in addressing security externalities? Is the selection of an appropriate remedy complicated by the difficulty in measuring the disaster risk imposed on communities by a business's failure to take particular measures that would foster disaster resilience? By the lack of a common metric for assessing and describing that risk? Are security externalities therefore more difficult to address than environmental externalities? Consider this view:

> In some respects, environmental externalities may provide elements of a model for security externalities. Major business-related environmental disasters, such as large oil spills, burst tank cars of chlorine, or unexpected releases of toxic gases from chemical plants, have been quite infrequent. Predicting how often that might happen, despite efforts to prevent them, is difficult. To that degree, there is a similarity between environmental stewardship and investments to reduce infrastructure vulnerabilities to disaster.
>
> However, while the spatial and temporal scale of impacts make accounting difficult, whatever impacts occur can generally be measured directly in terms of the firm's output—for example, the amount of sulfur dioxide emitted as air pollution. Effluents can be monitored on a minute-to-minute basis. The same does not hold for security externalities, where the consequences of lapses in security may not materialize for months or years. Even more important, environmental compliance, like worker safety, is principally under the control of the firm. Natural disasters are under no one's control, and attacks by terrorists are under the control of attackers. Furthermore, the interdependence of elements of infrastructure makes firms in one sector subject to errors or accidents occurring in another. Thus, firms can focus on recovery from such externally caused disasters, but alone they can do little about their incidence.

Auerswald, *supra*, at 160.

2. Will the analysis of security externalities be different for terrorism risks than for natural disaster risks? Consider the fact that increasing security precautions at one site ("hardening" the site) may cause terrorists to shift to other potential targets.

3. "State and local governments could encourage or require private parties to improve the reliability of important social services in a number of ways. For example, governments could modify electricity tariffs to permit load serving entities to recover costs associated with designing, installing, testing, and maintaining backup on-site power systems for individual customers who sign up for this service." Apt et al., *supra*, at 218.

4. Are there ways in which private companies might actually be better equipped to mitigate disaster risk? Or is privatization only a negative for disaster mitigation?

B. POPULATION GROWTH AND DEMOGRAPHIC TRENDS

Estimates of U.S. population growth by 2050 vary widely—with some estimates as low as 313 million and others as high as 552 million. *See* FLOODPLAIN MANAGEMENT 2050, *supra*, endnote 1 (cataloguing different population estimates). World population also is increasing dramatically. The United Nations estimates that world population will top 9.1 billion by 2050. Press Release, United Nations, World Population to Increase by 2.6 Billion over Next 45 Years with All Growth Occurring in Less Developed Countries (Feb. 24, 2005), available at http://www.un.org/News/Press/docs/2005/pop918.doc.htm.

Population growth will, no doubt, put increasing strains on the environment and increase disaster-related costs. Already, current demographic trends mean that population and economic resources are becoming increasingly concentrated in areas that are particularly vulnerable to natural disasters. Disaster risk itself is "geographically highly concentrated." U.N. 2009 DISASTER RISK REPORT 19. And, like moths to a flame, we seem drawn to high-risk areas, both because disaster risk is often coupled with natural advantages and because of the natural beauty, recreational opportunities, and other amenities of many hazardous locations.

Throughout history, people have settled in places where Mother Nature is both friend and foe. Early human settlements thrived in the alluvial flood plains of the Tigris, Euphrates, and Nile rivers. The settlement of America reflects similar phenomenon. As early Americans moved inland and westward from initial settlements on the eastern seaboard, they were attracted to the banks of America's great rivers—the commercial lifeblood of the nation—which promised fertile soil and easy access to resources and distant markets. Others settled elsewhere on the shores of the great oceans, establishing ports that would service both national and international markets, and fisheries to exploit the ocean's abundance. And many later pioneers would make their homes in the shadow and shelter of the majestic mountains of the West. Of course, the very natural advantages that attracted these settlers also pose great risks: rivers might overflow their banks, low-lying port cities are vulnerable to hurricanes and other storm damage, and the violent geological forces that created the majestic mountains might shake the earth again.

Today, several demographic trends in the United States are putting more people and property in harm's way. These include (1) the increasing concentration of population within cities, (2) the choice of many to live in areas that are particularly prone to natural disasters, and (3) the continuing geographic mobility of households, which results in limited community memory with respect to the risk of disasters and methods for mitigating losses.

The first demographic trend — continuing urbanization — concentrates population and economic resources, which can amplify the costs of even relatively small disasters. *See* DENNIS S. MILETI, DISASTERS BY DESIGN 120 (1999); PERROW, *supra*, at 30. Moreover, because many of our cities were settled, long ago, in risky locations, urbanization means concentrating population in disproportionately hazardous areas that are at risk for potentially catastrophic disasters. Although cities have often been imagined historically as "places of refuge," at least one geographer contends that they are more accurately described today as "hotspots of disaster risk." Mark Pelling, *Urbanization and Disaster Risk*, available at http://www.populationenvironmentresearch.org/papers/Pelling_urbanization_disaster_risk.pdf. More than two-thirds of the U.S. population today live in ten "megapolitan" areas; six are primarily coastal (Northeast, Cascadia, Florida Peninsula, Gulf Coast, Nor-Cal, and Southland (Southern California)), one is expanding toward the coast (Piedmont), one borders the Great Lakes (Midwest), one is in Arizona's Sun Belt (Valley of the Sun), and another is in Tornado Alley (I-35 Corridor). *See* Robert E. Lang & Dawn Dhavale, *Beyond Megalopolis: Exploring America's New "Megapolitan" Geography*, 2005 Metropolitan Institute Census Report Series 05:01 (July 2005) 1, 14, 23. After a city suffers a disaster — even a catastrophic disaster — it is much more likely to be rebuilt than relocated. "Once a city has developed, it rarely disappears, even if it experiences some disastrous flood or earthquake[,] because there are too many individuals, enterprises, and institutions with an interest in that city's economy." David Dodman et al., *Urban Development and Intensive and Extensive Risk* (2008), available at http://www.preventionweb.net/english/hyogo/gar/background-papers. Despite its ongoing struggles, New Orleans stands, nonetheless, as a testament to the resilience of cities.

Urbanization not only concentrates population and economic resources in dangerous areas, but it also can exacerbate those dangers. For example, urban development increases the amount of impermeable surfaces in a region, increasing the quantity and speed of runoff from rain and melting snow and contributing to flood risk. *See* U.N. 2009 DISASTER RISK REPORT 72. Urban development also destroys or degrades floodplains and wetlands that might otherwise mitigate flood damage. *See* discussion *infra*, Section D.1. The urban heat island effect — which can elevate the temperature of "paved over" urban areas more than 22 degrees Fahrenheit over surrounding rural areas, *see* http://www.epa.gov/hiri/ — can increase the risk of heat waves, already one of the most deadly of natural hazards, *see* Kevin A. Borden & Susan L. Cutter, *Spatial Patterns of Natural Hazards Mortality in the United States*, INT'L J. HEALTH GEOGRAPHICS 2008 7:64. Urbanization can also amplify the effects of disasters, because city dwellers are particularly beholden to fragile distribution systems and the just-in-time economy for all basic necessities, and typically do not store provisions or have access to backup sources of food, water, or other resources. *Cf.* CITIZEN CORPS, FEMA, CITIZEN PREPAREDNESS REVIEW: COMMUNITY RESILIENCE THROUGH CIVIL RESPONSIBILITY AND SELF-RELIANCE, ISSUE 5, UPDATE ON CITIZEN PREPAREDNESS RESEARCH 12 (Fall 2007) (reporting findings that rural California residents are most likely to report being "well prepared" for a disaster, whereas Bay Area residents are least likely to report being "well prepared").

The second demographic trend exacerbating disaster risk is that people are increasingly choosing to make their homes in vulnerable areas, such as the coastal regions of the United States and in areas of the South and West that have disproportionately high exposure to natural hazards. Population has risen most quickly in states such as Florida, Maryland, North Carolina, and Texas (which face substantial hurricane risks), as well as states such as California and Washington (which face both flood and seismic risks). *See* G. van der Vink et al., *Why the United States Is Becoming More Vulnerable to Natural Disasters,* Eos, Transactions, American Geophysical Union 79(3) 533, 537 (Nov. 1998). Other environmentally vulnerable regions of the country have also been favorite relocation spots. The West has experienced a population boom, particularly in arid regions such as Arizona and Nevada, where, for example, flood risks—though substantial—are unpredictable and poorly studied, understood, and mitigated.

The natural features that make development simultaneously attractive and risky have influenced not only the siting of cities themselves but also development within cities. Globally, development in risky locations is often driven by poverty, as those with the fewest resources settle in marginal, makeshift housing in hazardous areas; in the United States, however, development in hazardous locations is driven, as often as not, by wealth. In most U.S. communities, oceanfront property—with its attendant beauty and recreational access—is among the most sought-after and valuable property, despite its vulnerability to hurricanes and tsunamis. Similarly, property on the steep grade of cliffs and mountains attracts those seeking sweeping views, despite its vulnerability to landslides. Homeowners also build expensive homes on the edge of majestic forests, where they are vulnerable to wildfires.

The third demographic trend is that the U.S. population continues to be relatively mobile. *See* Alison Stein Wellner, *The Mobility Myth,* Reason Online, April 2006, http://www.reason.com/news/show/33288.html (June 19, 2009) ("[E]ven today, Americans are at least slightly more mobile than people in other countries. For example, 11 percent of U.K. residents moved house in 2001, compared to 14.2 percent of U.S. residents."). This propensity for living in several places in one's lifetime limits "the extent of community and household 'memory' of past disasters." Mileti, *supra,* at 120. A mobile population may feel less stewardship for natural resources, have a less developed social network to turn to in the event of disaster, lack understanding of the risks of settling in hazardous locations, and be less willing to forgo short-term benefits for long-term disaster mitigation. *See* Floodplain Management 2050, *supra,* at 20 ("[B]ecause they tend to move several times during their lifetimes, most people do not develop an intimate understanding of or sense of stewardship for their natural surroundings. The vast majority of coastal dwellers, for instance, are relatively new to the hazards, extreme weather, and fragile ecosystems of that region.").

C. LAND USE DECISIONS

The concentration of population in hazardous areas may appear to be the result of private, individual decisions. In reality, however, those private decisions to live and work in hazardous locations are shaped by local land use policies, and those local land use decisions are, in turn, heavily influenced by state and federal incentives. Effective mitigation of all types of natural hazards — including floods, earthquakes, and wildfires — thus depends heavily on governmental actions and decisions.

1. FLOODS

New Orleans is today, of course, the quintessential example of an American city built to capitalize on the very natural advantages that might prove its undoing. Many other great American urban centers, however, share similar vulnerabilities to Mother Nature. Sacramento is situated at the base of the towering Sierra Nevada range and at the confluence of two major rivers — the Sacramento River and the American River — fed by the abundant rains and snowpack of the Sierras. The abundance of water feeds Sacramento's fertile agricultural land but also presents serious flooding risks to a large, urbanized population living in low-lying regions in the Central Valley. (Most of the Central Valley is near sea level, with some areas below sea level; the Sacramento–San Joaquin Delta includes more than sixty islands below sea level.) Moreover, urban population is continually encroaching on the Central Valley's floodplains.

The entire region is also protected by an aging and poorly maintained network of publicly and privately owned levees, spanning some 1,500 miles. A major flood that overwhelms these levees could inundate some communities with more than twenty feet of water, inflict damages of more than $25 billion in the Sacramento area alone, and cause substantial loss of life. A CALIFORNIA CHALLENGE — FLOODING IN THE CENTRAL VALLEY, A REPORT FROM AN INDEPENDENT REVIEW PANEL TO THE DEPARTMENT OF WATER RESOURCES, STATE OF CALIFORNIA iii (Oct. 15, 2007) [hereinafter FLOODING IN THE CENTRAL VALLEY]. Widespread levee failure also could threaten the drinking-water supply of tens of millions of Californians. (Much of Los Angeles' water supply comes from the Central Valley, via a 444-mile long aqueduct.) These factors, combined with the region's vulnerability to earthquakes that could breach critical levees, has led many to predict that Sacramento could be the next New Orleans.

Most experts agree that current land use policies must be addressed if California is to reduce its flood risks. *See id.* at iv (describing land use planning as "critical to reducing future flood risk in the Central Valley"). A 2005 California State report described the problem as follows:

> California's population growth presents a major challenge to the State's flood management system. In the Central Valley alone, much of the new development is occurring in areas that are susceptible to flooding. In some cases, land use decisions are based on poor or outdated information regarding the seriousness of the flood threat. For example, many flood maps used by public agencies and the general public are decades old and do not reflect the most accurate information regarding potential flooding. Even worse, many maps were made by simply assuming that federal project levees provided protection from 100-year flood events. Unfortunately, recent experience has shown that this assumption is not necessarily valid.

Land use decisions at the local level that allow developments in floodplains protected by the State-federal levee system in the Central Valley greatly increase the risk of State liability for loss of life and property damage. Better coordination is needed between agencies making land use decisions and the parties, often the State, which must bear the burdens and liabilities of those decisions. The State must develop a process that guides regional development with the goal of protecting people and property at risk in floodplains, while connecting the legal liability of ill-advised land use decisions to those making the decisions to approve development in these areas.

Another challenge is that people who live and work behind levees have a false sense of protection. Many believe that the levees will protect them against any level of flooding. Even if a levee was capable of successfully holding back a 100-year flood, a target flood event used by many insurance and public agencies when providing flood protection, it doesn't mean that a larger flood, such as a 110-year or a 150-year flood event, won't flood their property. During a typical 30-year mortgage period, there is a 26 percent chance that a homeowner living behind a levee will experience a flood larger than the 100-year flood. This risk is many times greater than the risk of a major home fire during the same period.

California Department of Water Resources, Flood Warnings: Responding to California's Flood Crisis (Jan. 2005).

Based on the concerns in this report, Governor Schwarzenegger declared a state of emergency for California's floodplains and levees, which allowed exemptions from state environmental laws to permit needed repairs to proceed more quickly. Two years later, in 2007, California passed a suite of floodplain management laws designed to respond to the flood challenges described in this report. Those laws require the California Department of Water Resources (DWR) and the Central Valley Flood Protection Board to promulgate and adopt a Central Valley Flood Protection Plan (CVFPP) by July 2012. Cal. Water Code §9612(b). That plan is supposed to outline a systemic approach for floodplain management in the Central Valley, including "both structural and nonstructural" mechanisms for reducing flood risk. Id. §9616(a). Once the CVFPP is adopted, cities and counties in the Sacramento–San Joaquin Valley are required to develop joint city-county emergency plans, id. §9621, and conform their general plans and zoning ordinances to the CVFPP, Cal. Gov. Code §65302.9; id. §65860.1. After cities and counties make these conforming amendments, they cannot approve development agreements, id. §65865.5, subdivision maps, id. §66474.5, or permits for construction of new residences for property, id. §65962, within "a flood hazard zone" unless they conclude, based on substantial record evidence, that urban or urbanizing property will be protected to the 200-year flood level by existing flood management facilities or conditions imposed on the project, or that a local flood management agency has made "adequate progress on construction of a flood protection system" which will provide at least 200-year protection by 2025. Id.; Cal. Gov. Code §65007(k) (defining "urban level of flood protection" as that necessary to withstanding flooding that "has a 1-in-200 chance of occurring in any given year"). Nonurbanized areas need be protected only to the level required by the Federal Emergency Management Agency (FEMA).

California incentivizes its cities and counties to comply with these requirements by making noncompliant cities and counties liable for contribution to the state, if the state is sued for flood damage, "to the extent that the city or county has increased the state's exposure to liability for property damage by unreasonably approving new development in a previously undeveloped area that is protected by a state flood control project." CAL. WATER CODE §8307(a).

The new floodplain legislation also requires all localities to review local development plans annually for areas subject to flooding, CAL. GOV. CODE §65302(a), and during the next plan revision to "identify rivers, creeks, streams, flood corridors, riparian habits, and land that may accommodate floodwater for purposes of groundwater recharge and stormwater management." *Id.* §65302(d)(3). The next iteration of the plan is also required to identify flood hazards and set comprehensive goals for protecting the community from an unreasonable flooding risk, including evaluating whether new construction should be excluded from flood hazard zones. *See id.* §65302(g). Cities and counties subject to the CVFPP must submit the plan changes to the Central Valley Flood Protection Board and other local flood protection agencies for review and comment. *See id.* §65302.7. In order to make local and state flood management more effective, the DWR was tasked with mapping the 100- and 200-year floodplains protected by project levees, CAL. WATER CODE §9610(a)(1), and mapping levee flood protection zones, *id.* §9130(a). In addition, the 2007 legislation also required the DWR to approve updated code requirements for construction in areas protected by the CVFPP where flood levels might exceed three feet for the anticipated 200-year flood event. CAL. HEALTH & SAFETY CODE §50465.

There is virtual consensus among floodplain managers that current floodplain management relies too much on structural solutions — such as building codes and construction of additional levees — at the expense of nonstructural solutions — such as prohibiting additional development in certain flood-prone areas, and even relocating some existing communities away from flood-prone zones. Although additional investment to maintain existing levees is necessary, flood risk cannot effectively be built away by constructing newer, bigger levees. Indeed, though levees can protect regions from some flood risk, they can also exacerbate risk downstream and in catastrophic events, when levees are overtopped. Stricter, wiser land use restrictions are widely viewed as the most critical and indispensable element of effective floodplain management moving forward.

Consider California's recent legislative attempts in light of the "Action Guidelines" recently issued by a national conference of floodplain managers.

ASS'N OF STATE FLOODPLAIN MANAGERS, FLOODPLAIN MANAGEMENT 2050,
A REPORT OF THE 2007 ASSEMBLY OF THE GILBERT F. WHITE
NATIONAL FLOOD POLICY FORUM

33-36 (2007)

Action Guidelines

Floodplain management professionals and other experts gathered at the Second Assembly of the Gilbert F. White National Flood Policy Forum agreed that sweeping change is urgently needed to avoid the dismal future that awaits if the present course of scattered, short-sighted water-related policies and activities continues. All the essential technical and programmatic steps described in the previous section can be condensed into six action guidelines. These guiding principles capsulize the new ways of thinking and operating that will be needed to achieve safe and sustainable relationships with our water resources. . . .

1. Make room for rivers, oceans, and adjacent lands.

Beginning now, AVOIDANCE of floodprone and/or ecologically sensitive areas should be axiomatic in planning new development. Although a strategy of avoidance cannot erase unwise existing development, it will minimize the cumulative damage, losses, and degradation that otherwise will be felt sorely by 2050.

We need to begin a pattern of gradual and voluntary resettlement of those portions of communities that already have been located in the highest-risk or most ecologically sensitive areas, including areas behind levees and within the downstream influence of dams. At least four lines of attack should be employed in this strategy. First, as we repair and replace infrastructure anywhere in the nation, it should be removed from the floodplain if at all possible or, at a minimum, be brought up to higher standards of safety and environmental protection. Second, states should incorporate into their hazard mitigation plans (and localities into their comprehensive and mitigation plans) strategies to make significant changes to the land uses in certain dangerous or environmentally critical areas. Third, from now on, no state, local, or federal funds (including any type of subsidy in the tax code) should be spent that could foster development or infrastructure in high-risk and/or environmentally sensitive areas or would otherwise conflict with the provisions of Executive Orders 11988 and 11990. Fourth, new and replacement levees should be set farther back from the edges of waterways, which not only will allow more storage space for flood water but also will gradually shift existing and potential development into less hazardous areas.

No adverse impact principles should be applied in all land use and development decisionmaking. The standard of "not causing harm," coupled with the use of future conditions as the basis for hazard and resource identification (as noted below), will result in the protection of people, property, and natural resources and functions now and into the future.

We need widespread measurement of cumulative future conditions in terms of flood flows, flood levels, riverine and coastal erosion, sedimentation, barrier and shoreline migration, sea level rise, subsidence, and other attributes. Then we must establish a policy that limits human actions in watersheds and coastal zones that would alter any of these attributes. This will result in preserving floodplain functions as well as reducing future losses.

2. Reverse perverse incentives in government programs.

An independent, comprehensive review is needed of all federal programs that fund, subsidize, license, or promote development or redevelopment (including disaster relief, the tax code, housing grants, small business loans, and many others). All of these programs should be reformed to eliminate the incentives they unwittingly provide for making unwise decisions and taking inappropriate action with regard to our water resources. In their place, we must create positive incentives for appropriate action anywhere in the watershed, but especially in areas that are floodprone and/or ecologically sensitive.

Federal agencies should adhere closely to E.O. 11988 and 11990 and thereby eliminate federal projects, funding, licenses, permits, loans, grants, or other incentives that foster new or replacement development in floodplains that exposes people, property, and taxpayers to added risk and costs. Public facilities such as causeways, bridges, evacuation routes, and water treatment plants should be treated as additional "critical facilities" under the terms of the Executive Orders.

A sunset date should be established for subsidized and grandfathered flood insurance premium rates, because subsidized rates encourage development in hazardous areas. Exemptions to the flood insurance purchase requirement must be eliminated. We should be moving toward mandatory actuarially based flood insurance (or all-hazards insurance) for all homeowners that drives mitigation and also has a pooling mechanism for coping with catastrophic losses.

3. Restore and enhance the natural, beneficial functions of riverine and coastal areas.

We must make it a national priority to reclaim, over time, our lost riparian and coastal resources wherever possible, including dunes, bottomland forests, estuaries, and marshes. This will help restore natural buffers to storms and floods, supply open space and recreational opportunities for a burgeoning population, and slow the further deterioration of some ecosystems. Generous funding must be sought from all possible sources for this effort. For example, the potential for generating revenue by trading carbon credits should be considered.

Recognition and respect for the natural and beneficial functions of floodprone areas, including the coast, must be incorporated into the programs of all federal, state, and local agencies. . . .

4. Generate a renaissance in water resources governance.

A nationwide vision and policy for water resources sustainability and flood loss reduction are essential. This would require legislation incorporating both a national floodplain management policy and a national riparian and coastal areas policy. The act should establish unequivocally both the value to the nation of these resource areas and their natural functions, as well as their inherent hazards. This policy needs to be supported with a comprehensive legislative package to be coordinated with and implemented through states, local governments, tribes, governors, and others. We need to draw on the leaders and experts of the nation to craft and agree on outcomes and metrics for the year 2050, including how we measure success and failure.

A high-level, central point of coordination and implementation is needed to ensure that water-related laws and programs at all levels are seamlessly aligned and integrated. This could be a new federal agency or other entity but it should be dedicated solely to water-related issues. The wasteful and counterproductive fragmentation and stovepiping of federal (and state) water-related programs and of Congressional oversight of them must be eliminated.

We must consider carefully the central question of whether a national policy of water resources "development" is still relevant for 2050 and beyond or whether a policy of water resources "sustainability" that balances human and ecosystem needs is a wiser approach.

The National Water Assessment, last conducted in 1976, needs to be updated. Up to date data on streamflow, reservoirs, groundwater, and withdrawals are critical to crafting nationwide policy that is both far-seeing and grounded in science.

National programs and investment decisions should be adapted quickly to account for expected trends and impacts associated with the collision of intensified human development and climate change. . . .

5. Identify risks and resources and communicate at public and individual levels.

A thorough, nationwide examination of our water-resources-related risks is the critical first step to understanding and resolving our present and future dilemma. Britain's Foresight Flood and Coastal Defence Project has shown that a scenario-based, comprehensive assessment of risks and resources is feasible even on a very large scale. What is more, the scenarios have proven invaluable in driving home the seriousness of the situation, in fleshing out alternatives, and in communicating with policymakers. Such an assessment should be commenced for the United States at once.

All identification of flood risks and resources should be based on future conditions. In some locales, fully built-out watersheds already are anticipated in comprehensive planning, but the increases in flood risk and the resource depletion that this level of development will bring are not considered in mapping or other management activities. Decisionmaking about all aspects of water resources and water-related hazards must be based on much longer time horizons than are being applied today.

Communication, education, and outreach efforts must be intensified immediately. We need to identify the specific behaviors that must be changed to reduce vulnerability and protect resources. Then we need to work through schools, the media, watershed councils and other local groups, and use any other available means to bring about changes in those behaviors. A communications tool kit for local opinion leaders, industry representatives, homeowners, and others will be a good start.

We must capitalize on technological advances in communication to help people understand flood hazards, the exposure and vulnerability of people to those hazards, and the fragility of water resources. We need to use visual depictions of the impacts of development on flooding and also of the adverse impact of different development scenarios on all properties and on natural resources in the watershed. These should be disseminated digitally to keep pace with other web-based attractions.

Nationwide data on many factors is absolutely critical to determining what the most efficient course will be and when progress is being made. We need to find out who is at risk from flooding and why. We need an inventory of nation's floodprone structures and risk. Existing data feeds need to be monitored so we can determine the impacts of climate change as soon as possible.

Intelligible scenario-based models are needed to help communities grasp and plan for climate change and work towards sustainability of their resources. National databases should be accessible to local governments to assist their decisionmaking.

6. Assume personal and public responsibility.

Actuarially based, all-hazards insurance must become mandatory for all properties, nationwide. The coverage should include a strong loss-reduction (mitigation) component. This will foster individual understanding of risk and acceptance of personal responsibility. If an all-hazards insurance program cannot be developed, then flood insurance under the existing mechanisms should be mandatory for all properties.

Our ethic of land and water stewardship must be revived. We need to provide a framework that will foster local responsibility for dealing with flood risk, sustaining water-related resources, and making wise use of floodprone lands. Incentives need to be institutionalized to ensure that communities that are doing a good job receive benefits related to their efforts and, in contrast, those that do not manage their risks and resources wisely are not allowed to externalize the resulting losses and costs onto the federal taxpayers. These incentives could include a sliding scale for the non-federal share of the cost of disaster relief and recovery; and preference for federal grants and loans given to communities that act to mitigate risks and protect or restore resources.

NOTES AND QUESTIONS

1. Does California's recent legislation go too far or not far enough in restricting land use in floodplains and protecting existing urban areas? Is 200-year protection adequate for urban areas? Does any standard that uses historical records to assess risk adequately take account of the potential for more severe storms caused by climate change? An independent report prepared for the California Department of Water Resources suggests that the level of protection for existing urban areas "should be equivalent to protection against the Standard Project Flood, which represents a flood that can be expected from the *most severe* combination of meteorologic and hydrologic conditions that are considered *reasonably characteristic* of the region." FLOODING IN THE CENTRAL VALLEY, *supra*, at v. For the Central Valley, the Standard Project Flood level falls between the 200- and 500-year protection levels. *See id.* n.6.

2. Why do we continue to develop land that has substantial exposure to natural hazards? One possible explanation mentioned in the above Report is that the artificially maintained flood insurance rates of the National Flood Insurance Program, which are not actuarially based, have subsidized development in hazardous areas, by ensuring that developers can build in floodplains confident that they can obtain relatively low-cost, below-market insurance against any flood risks. Also, numerous programs administered by a variety of federal agencies — including the Department

of Housing and Urban Development, the Department of Agriculture, the U.S. Army Corps of Engineers, the Tennessee Valley Authority, and the Economic Development Administration—subsidize development and have supported development in floodplains. Although Executive Orders 11988 and 11990 (Floodplain Management and Protection of Wetlands, respectively), require federal agencies to consider and pursue practicable alternatives before building on floodplains or wetlands, and to minimize the risk of flood loss or wetland degradation if no alternative exists, critics allege that the Orders have primarily been observed in the breach. Should these Orders be revised to include a more stringent prohibition on federal support of building on floodplains or wetlands? The Obama administration is apparently drafting a new executive order that would prohibit building critical facilities in 500-year floodplains (unless no alternative exists) and would prioritize nonstructural approaches to floodplain management. *See* Taryn Luntz, *Draft Executive Order Aims to Curb Floodplain Development*, N.Y. Times (July 21, 2009), available at http://www.nytimes.com/gwire/2009/07/21/21greenwire-draft-executive-order-aims-to-curb-floodplain-64438.html.

3. Does the availability of federal disaster aid also encourage building in floodplains? Reconsider this question in connection with the readings about federal disaster aid in Chapter 4.

4. Floodplains are attractive to developers for a number of reasons. Floodplains often represent the largest undeveloped, open spaces near existing urban centers; this was certainly true in the St. Louis area after the 1993 floods. Moreover, "floodprone land is relatively less expensive, so developers see that their profit margins can be widened by using that land for development, as long as the costs of future consequences (flood damage and deterioration of the resource) can be passed along to others in the community or to future generations of taxpayers." FLOODPLAIN MANAGEMENT 2050, *supra*, at 9.

5. Are there other obstacles to local government adoption of stricter land use controls? Dennis S. Mileti explains that lack of political will is an important obstacle:

> Few local governments are willing to reduce natural hazards by managing development. It is not so much that they oppose land-use measures (although some do), but rather that, like individuals, they tend to view natural hazards as a minor problem that can take a back seat to more pressing local concerns such as unemployment, crime, housing, and education. Also, the costs of mitigation are immediate while the benefits are uncertain, do not occur during the tenure of current elected officials, and are not visible (like roads or a new library). In addition, property rights lobbies are growing stronger. All of these factors contribute to a lack of political leadership for limiting land use in hazardous areas.

MILETI, *supra*, at 160. Mileti also contends that local governments can be stifled in their efforts to mitigate disasters through land use planning by the expense and complexity of required techniques (such as hazard-zone mapping) and by the regional nature of hazards, which necessitates a coordinated, regional response that can be difficult to achieve. *See id.* Local governments also may lack incentives to deal with regional risks, and may focus on disaster risk—if at all—only through the narrow lens of effects within their own community. Floodplain Management 2050, *supra*, at 12. Moreover, land use decisions in most jurisdictions are made on a parcel-by-parcel basis; regional and long-term planning tools tend to be underutilized and weakened by pressure from developers.

6. Is the solution to land use problems strong federal regulation? Consider this view: "We need a more centralized regulatory system. Local initiative is simply not reliable in the case of mitigation. Localities are reluctant to enforce state standards, national standards are few, and enforcement is lax. This is an area where centralized regulation—standards and enforcement—is needed; given the political influence of growth-oriented city officials and property and building interests, there is bound to be a 'failure' of the private market." Perrow, *supra*, at 37.

7. What does it take for a local community to commit to changes in land use? Does experiencing a serious disaster inspire change? The experience of Missouri after the 1993 Mississippi River flood illustrates the intransigence of current land use policy, at least in some localities. After a particularly cold winter and an unusually wet spring, nine states in the Mississippi River watershed—North Dakota, South Dakota, Nebraska, Kansas, Minnesota, Iowa, Missouri, Wisconsin, and Illinois—suffered record flooding in the summer of 1993. Perrow, *supra*, at 18. The flooding killed approximately fifty people, caused damage in excess of $15 billion, completely inundated seventy-five towns, and destroyed upwards of 10,000 homes. *See id.* at 18. In response to the flooding, the federal government bought 25,000 flooded residential properties at a cost of $1 billion in a voluntary buyout program designed to return floodplains to their natural state. *See* Sara Shipley, *Unprecedented Growth in the Flood Plain Brings Riches and Risks: Business Grows on Land under Water 10 Years Ago*, St. Louis Post-Dispatch, July 27, 2003, at A1. Some midwestern states tightened restrictions on development of flood plains, especially on land flooded in 1993. *See id.*

Missouri, however, did not. Although 4,700 Missouri households participated in the federal buyout, the resulting gains were far outpaced by new development on Missouri's floodplains. During the decade after the 1993 floods, $2.2 billion in new development—including homes, offices, shopping centers, and highways—was built in the St. Louis area on acreage that was underwater during the 1993 floods. This new development occupies some 4,200 acres of Missouri floodplain (75% of which were submerged in 1993) and is either elevated to the 500-year-flood level or protected by 500-year flood earthen levees. Development so protected is exempt from federal flood insurance requirements. *See id.* at A1. Thousands of other acres are slated for future development.

Missouri has no comprehensive floodplain management legislation, so development decisions are left to local officials, who are attracted to the clarion call of tax revenue and job creation. One member of the Bridgeton (Missouri) City Council summarized the race-to-the-bottom mentality of many such floodplain development decisions: "Bridgeton in the past has hugged a lot of trees, and we've lost out on a lot of development. We're going to be surrounded by businesses while we're looking at flood plain." Christopher Carey, *Cities Look to Flood Plains for Jobs, Growth, Tax Dollars*, St. Louis Post-Dispatch, July 29, 2003, at A1 (quoting Councilwoman Barbara Abram). Floodplain development in Missouri is particularly attractive to developers, because floodplains constitute most of the available, undeveloped land in the St. Louis region. Shipley, *supra*, at A1. Moreover, Missouri has enabled new development in flood zones by allowing the building of large, new levees, the costs of which have been subsidized (to the tune of up to 65% for new construction and 80% for repair) by the Army Corps of Engineers. *See id.* A spokesman for the Corps' St. Louis district explained, "We don't make a value judgment on whether that property should be protected. As long as people can show they can meet the requirements, they'll get a permit, whether we like building the flood plain or not." *Id.* (quoting Alan Dooley). In addition to levee subsidization, the federal government continues to pay millions of dollars in disaster aid for Missouri flooding every year. For example, FEMA approved more than $5.3 million in flood-related disaster aid to Missouri residents in 2008. Missouri itself has also subsidized building behind levees by providing "tax-increment financing" to spur economic development. Shipley, *supra*, at A1.

Should we be concerned about this new development in Missouri's floodplains if, indeed, all of the developed land is elevated to the 500-year flood level or protected by 500-year levees?

8. Imagine that you are on the board of a local government. How would you balance local need for jobs and for a growing tax base against the need for flood protection? How would you answer your constituents' questions and concerns? Now imagine yourself having that same conversation in the context in which it most frequently arises: when dealing with a particular property and a particular set of people with a particular plan. Public officials facing development decisions with natural hazards implications rarely make those decisions in the spotlight of the media or with focused attention from the broader public. How does that change the political calculus of floodplain development?

9. The Floodplain Management 2050 Report mentions scenario-based planning as an effective tool for helping the public (and, concomitantly, politicians) make more informed and farsighted land use decisions. In scenario-based planning, experts identify a discrete number of different growth scenarios, based on different land use, transportation, and environmental decisions. The long-term effects in these scenarios (on housing, traffic, economic development, pollution, and other potential axes such as disaster costs) are then modeled and presented to the public, often using computer-aided visualization techniques. Can these techniques help overcome the political logjam that otherwise impedes more disaster-resistant land use decisions? For an overview and example of scenario-based planning, see Envision Utah, http://www.envisionutah. org/envisionprocess.phtml; for an interesting example of scenario-based planning in the aftermath of a disaster, see Louisiana Speaks,

http://www.louisianaspeaks-parishplans.org/PlanningProcess_Louisiana Speaks.cfm. RAND has also developed a computerized version of scenario planning that allows consideration of hundreds of scenarios in order to find robust strategies. *See* http://www.rand.org/ise/projects/improvingdecisions/ water_planning.html.

10. If it is politically infeasible to limit all or most floodplain development, should localities at least limit building of critical infrastructure (such as hospitals, water and sewage treatment plants, and emergency operations centers) and vulnerable facilities (such as nursing homes) in floodplains? The Association of State Floodplain Managers (ASFPM) reported that, as of 2003, nine states have regulations prohibiting construction of critical facilities in certain floodplain areas. *See* Ass'n of State Floodplain Managers, Floodplain Management 2003 at 21.

11. If changes to zoning laws prove difficult to adopt and implement, can information-based solutions, which educate the public and trust them to make wiser land use decisions, be effective? California was the first state to establish a comprehensive natural hazards disclosure requirement in conjunction with the transfer of real estate, requiring disclosure of natural hazards not only when they are within the "actual knowledge" of the seller, but also when a designated local authority has either a list of affected properties or a map of relevant hazards and has posted a notice to that effect. *See* Cal. Civil Code §1103 (requiring seller disclosure if transferred property is in a statutorily defined "special flood hazard area"—FEMA zone "A" or "V"; an "area of potential flooding"—i.e., a dam inundation zone; a "very high fire hazard severity zone"; an "earthquake fault zone"; a "seismic hazard zone"; or a "wildland area that may contain substantial forest fire risks and hazards").

Legislators hoped this law would slow the development of land in hazard zones by decreasing property values in those areas. *See* George Lefcoe, *Property Condition Disclosure Forms: How the Real Estate Industry Eased the Transition from Caveat Emptor to "Seller Tell All,"* 39 Real Prop. Prob. & Tr. J. 193, 242 (2004). Flood zone disclosure has been somewhat successful in lowering property values, as average home prices in California's flood zones dropped 4.3 percent within five years of implementing the law. *See* Austin Troy & Jeff Romm, *Assessing the Price Effects of Flood Hazard Disclosure under the California Natural Hazard Disclosure Law (AB 1195),* 47 J. Envtl. Planning & Mgmt. 137 (Jan. 2004). This data suggests that some home buyers are choosing not to buy properties after learning that the properties are in flood zones. But fire zone disclosure has had little overall effect, and property values have only declined where the property is in close proximity to a recent fire. *See* Austin Troy & Jeff Romm, *Living on the Edge: Economic, Institutional and Management Perspectives on Wildfire Hazard in the Urban Interface, in* 6 Advances in the Economics of Environmental Resources 101 (Austin Troy & Roger G. Kennedy eds., 2007). Based on the limited data available, determining whether the disclosure law is effectively reducing development in hazard zones is very difficult.

California's natural hazard disclosure law also has significant shortcomings. Among them are the costs incurred by sellers who must pay for a professional hazard report; the risk of lulling buyers into assuming that disclosure reports cover every conceivable disaster or are as effective as on-site studies; inaccurate hazard maps and information; and inability to predict when and where disasters will actually occur. *See* Lefcoe, *supra*, at 242. Furthermore, buyers' assessments of risk are often neither objective nor accurate, and they may ignore evidence of low-probability high-risk events. *See id.* at 246; *see also* Daniel Kahneman & Amos Tversky, *Prospect Theory: An Analysis of Decision under Risk*, in CHOICES, VALUES, AND FRAMES 17, 22-25 (Daniel Kahneman & Amos Tversky eds., 2000). Reconsider the effectiveness of disclosure and education-dependent solutions when you read Chapter 6, *infra*.

Other states have enacted a variety of hazard disclosure laws. *See, e.g.,* HAW. REV. STAT. §508D-15 (2006) (requiring disclosure when a property is in a FEMA special flood hazard area, an airport noise exposure area, a military "air installation compatibility use zone," or within an area designated a tsunami inundation zone by the Department of Defense, if the county has provided required hazard zone maps to the public); N.Y. REAL PROP. LAW §14-462 (McKinney 2006) (requiring a "property condition disclosure statement" for residential property that includes whether the property is in a "designated flood plain" or "designated wetland," if the seller has actual knowledge of the designation); OR. REV. STAT. §105.464 (2007) (requiring sellers of previously occupied homes with actual knowledge of hazards to disclose whether the property is "in a designated flood zone," "a designated slide or other geologic hazard zone," or has "been classified as forestland-urban interface").

In addition to disclosure by landowners, beginning in September 2010, the California Department of Water Resources is legally obligated to send yearly notices to landowners whose property is determined to be in "levee flood protection zones." That notice will inform landowners of the residual risk in areas protected by levees (including the risk of catastrophic failure), recommend purchase of flood insurance, and refer landowners to more detailed sources of information. CAL. WATER CODE §9121. "Improving flood risk awareness will help insure that Californians make careful choices when deciding whether to live in Central Valley flood plains, and if so, whether to prepare for flooding and/or maintain flood insurance." CALIFORNIA DEPARTMENT OF WATER RESOURCES, 2007 CALIFORNIA FLOOD LEGISLATION SUMMARY, 4. Do you think such targeted public information campaigns will have an impact on buyer decisions or local decisions about land use or disaster mitigation? Why or why not?

12. How viable a solution is relocation of existing developments? *See, e.g.,* Roger Alford, *Flood-Prone Appalachian Town Seeks Higher Ground*, MIAMI HERALD (June 17, 2009) (describing Army Corps of Engineers plan to relocate the 600-person town of Martin, Kentucky, which has flooded four times in the last decade, to higher ground on an adjacent mountainside); Cornelia Dean, *Some Experts Say It's Time to Evacuate the Coast (for Good)*, N.Y. TIMES, Oct, 4, 2005 (describing the debate over rebuilding Alabama's Dauphin Island after Katrina and one suggestion that Congress establish a commission, like the base-closing commission, to identify coastal areas

that should be denied both federal rebuilding subsidies and access to federal flood insurance). Floodplain Management 2050 suggests that optimal flood plain management would include "planned retreat" from high-hazard and environmentally sensitive areas and "massive buyouts" of "entire parcels of land that are better used as natural open space," or planted with damage-resistant crops. Floodplain Management 2050, *supra*, at 13. Environmental planning expert Dr. Robert Twiss has said that once an area has been developed for housing, it is impossible to reclaim the area for flood control. Nevertheless, California's 2007 floodplain legislation requires cities and counties to provide relocation assistance to economically disadvantaged communities in rural areas at risk for flooding. Cal. Water Code §9622.

13. What legal steps can communities take to reclaim their coastal lands? As hurricanes eat away at Texas's beaches, the state is trying to reclaim some of its coastal lands through a "rolling easement." The Texas Open Beaches Act, enacted in 1959 and amended in 1991, provides in part:

> PROHIBITION. (a) It is an offense against the public policy of this state for any person to create, erect, or construct any obstruction, barrier, or restraint that will interfere with the free and unrestricted right of the public, individually and collectively, lawfully and legally to enter or to leave any public beach or to use any public beach or any larger area abutting on or contiguous to a public beach if the public has acquired a right of use or easement to or over the area by prescription, dedication, or has retained a right by virtue of continuous right in the public. . . .
>
> (c) For purposes of this section, "public beach" shall mean any beach bordering on the Gulf of Mexico that extends inland from the line of mean low tide to the natural line of vegetation bordering on the seaward shore of the Gulf of Mexico, or such larger contiguous area to which the public has acquired a right of use or easement to or over by prescription, dedication, or estoppel, or has retained a right by virtue of continuous right in the public since time immemorial as recognized by law or custom. This definition does not include a beach that is not accessible by a public road or public ferry as provided in Section 61.021 of this code.

Tex. Nat. Res. Code §61.103.

As interpreted by the Texas courts, the Act makes any established public beach easement a dynamic, "rolling easement"—a public right to use the "public beach," defined not in fixed terms, but by reference to the strip of land between the current line of mean low tide and the current natural line of vegetation—lines that will creep inward as the coast itself erodes. *See, e.g.*, Feinman v. State, 717 S.W.2d 106, 110-111 (Tex. App. 1986) (holding that the "public's easement moves with the changing tide" and applying the Act to property that, while previously outside the easement, came within the easement because of coastal erosion caused by Hurricane Alicia). Hurricane Ike's dramatic erosion of the Texas coast means that many oceanfront homes that were outside this public easement before the storm are now within the public beach easement and are obstructions that prevent the "free and unrestricted" right of public use. Many beachfront homes destroyed by Ike therefore arguably cannot be rebuilt, and even those spared by Ike's fury may be subject to removal orders if they are seaward of the post-Ike vegetation line. Should Texas be required (constitutionally or otherwise) to compensate the affected homeowners? *See* Severance v. Patterson, 566 F.3d 490 (5th Cir. 2009) (certifying to the Texas Supreme Court, *inter alia*, the question of whether a landowner ordered to remove a home from property that is newly within the rolling easement is entitled to compensation under the Texas Constitution or other state law). Is Texas taking the homeowners' property or is Hurricane Ike? The takings question is considered more fully below in Section C.4.

Other states have taken different approaches to limit coastal development, but most restrictions do not apply to existing developments. Florida regulates development of hazard areas by establishing "coastal construction control lines along the sand beaches of the state fronting on the Atlantic Ocean, the Gulf of Mexico, or the Straits of Florida." FLA. STAT. ANN. §161.053(1)(a) (2008). These control lines are positioned where the property is "subject to severe fluctuations based on a 100-year storm surge, storm waves, or other predictable weather conditions." *Id.* New construction within control lines is very restricted, and sellers of property located seaward of control lines must disclose that the property is subject to strict regulations. *See id.* §161.57. New York also has a law governing "coastal erosion hazard areas." N.Y. ENVTL. CONSERV. LAW §§34-0101 to 34-0113 (McKinney 1997). This law requires the State Department of Environmental Conservation to designate coastal erosion hazard areas that are then subject to stringent development regulations and permitting requirements.

2. EARTHQUAKES

In 2001, FEMA determined that a major earthquake along the San Andreas fault was one of the three most likely catastrophes to hit the United States. (The other two catastrophes FEMA identified have already come to pass: a terrorist attack on New York City and a major hurricane striking New Orleans.) *See* Jia-Rui Chong & Hector Becerra, *Katrina's Aftermath: California Earthquake Could Be the Next Katrina*, L.A. TIMES, Sept. 8, 2005, at A2. Experts estimate that there is a greater than 99 percent chance that a 6.7-magnitude earthquake will strike one of California's many major faults in the next thirty years. David Perlman, *Sure Bet: Big Quake in Next 30 Years*, S.F. CHRON., April 15, 2008, at A1. One study estimated that a repeat of San Francisco's infamous 1906 earthquake today would kill between 800 and 1,500 people, seriously injure between 4,000 and 6,000 people (depending on the time of day), leave 400,000 people homeless, and cause direct economic losses of more than $93 billion. CHARLES A. KIRCHER ET AL., WHEN THE BIG ONE STRIKES AGAIN: ESTIMATED LOSSES DUE TO A REPEAT OF THE 1906 SAN FRANCISCO EARTHQUAKE (2006), available at www.1906eqconf.org/mediadocs/BigonestrikesReport.pdf (June 7, 2009). Different assumptions about shaking in such an earthquake result in even more horrifying statistics: between 1,800 and 3,400 people dead; between 8,000 and 12,500 seriously injured; 600,000 people homeless; and $120 billion in direct economic losses.

See id. The number of estimated fatalities is actually quite comparable to the estimated 1906 death toll. Although building codes have made buildings much safer, San Francisco and the Greater Bay Area are now home to many more people: the population of San Francisco has more than doubled and that of the Bay Area has increased tenfold. *See id.* That population has also expanded to the west, putting many more people in closer proximity to the San Andreas fault. *See id.*

Moreover, the rubble of the 1906 earthquake may have, quite literally, laid the groundwork for future seismic destruction. As Raymond J. Burby explains,

> San Francisco recovered rapidly from the 1906 catastrophe chiefly because the downtown business district was well insured. . . . However, like London after its fire in 1666, San Francisco declined to alter its basic pattern of streets and land use patterns as it rebuilt. In particular, it ignored Daniel H. Burnham's "City Beautiful" plan for the redesign of the city that had been presented to civic leaders just before the fire: "Few cities ever found themselves demolished, with a ready-made plan for a new and grander city already drawn up, awaiting implementation, and with money pouring in to help realize the plan. San Francisco chose to ignore its Burnham Plan, and decided instead to build at a rate and manner which not only made the city less beautiful than was possible, but more dangerous. The rubble of the 1906 disaster was pushed into the Bay; buildings were built on it. Those buildings will be among the most vulnerable when the next earthquake comes" (Thomas and Witts, 1971, p.274). This statement was prophetic: the city's Marina district, built on 1906 rubble, sustained heavy damage in the 1989 Loma Prieta earthquake.

RAYMOND J. BURBY, COOPERATING WITH NATURE 34 (1998).

The U.S. Geological Survey continues to report that, in the San Francisco Bay Area, "[t]he highest [liquefaction] hazard areas . . . are concentrated in regions of man-made landfill, especially fill that was placed many decades ago in areas that were once submerged bay floor. Such areas along the Bay margins are found in San Francisco, Oakland and Alameda Island, as well as other places around San Francisco Bay." http://earthquake.usgs.gov/regional/nca/qmap. (Liquefaction occurs when earthquake shaking of water-saturated, sandy soil causes that soil to liquefy and lose its strength; in essence, liquefaction results in earthquake-induced quicksand.) The Oakland approach to the San Francisco–Oakland Bay Bridge — which collapsed during the 1989 Loma Prieta earthquake, killing forty-two people — was built on soft bay mud that shook much more strongly than other ground in the vicinity. *See id.*

In response to the 1971 San Fernando earthquake, the California Legislature passed the Alquist-Priolo Earthquake Fault Zoning Act. CAL. PUB. RES. CODE §§2621-2630. The Act prohibits subdivisions and "structures for human occupancy" across or within fifty feet of active faults. *See id.* §2621.5. The Act requires the state geologist to create Earthquake Fault Zone Maps depicting Earthquake Fault Zones and distribute them to all affected localities and state agencies. *See id.* §2 622. Any project within an Earthquake Fault Zone, with a few limited exceptions, is then subject to regulation by the Alquist-Priolo Act and local agencies. *See id.* §2621.5. For example, any project proposal within an Earthquake Fault Zone must have an accompanying geologic investigation and report outlining the potential for surface fault displacement. Policies and

Criteria of the State Mining and Geology Board with Reference to the Alquist-Priolo Earthquake Fault Zoning Act, CAL. ADMIN. CODE tit. 14, §3603 (West 1984). The Act also authorizes local governments to implement stricter zoning standards, CAL. PUB. RES. CODE §2624, and many localities choose to do so.

NOTES AND QUESTIONS

1. Avoiding building within close proximity to known active faults seems like a prudent zoning approach. Can zoning otherwise be useful in mitigating potential earthquake damage? Should development on landfill or in lique-faction zones be restricted? Earthquake damage is often unpredictable and does not always occur along or near identified faults. The 1994 Northridge earthquake, for instance, occurred along a previously unknown fault and caused billions of dollars of damage to unsuspecting homeowners.

2. Should homeowners in earthquake-prone areas be required to purchase earthquake insurance? "Hurricane Katrina . . . has had a dual effect on homeowners in the Bay Area. . . . Some Californians called their insurance agents and signed up for quake coverage. But for many others, watching billions of dollars in federal aid pour into the Gulf Coast merely bolstered the sense that the government would come to the rescue after a big earthquake." Scott Lindlaw, *Homeowners Willing to Gamble*, HOUSTON CHRON., March 20, 2006. Reconsider the question in connection with Chapter 7.

3. FIRE

Like floods, wildfires have a dual nature: they are both a potentially devastating and lethal natural force and an important ecological process. Since 2000, many western states have suffered their worst fire losses on record. Review the description of the 2000 New Mexico Cerro Grande fire in Chapter 1.

The Cerro Grande fire demonstrates the increasing difficulties for wildfire management posed by the growing wildland-urban interface (WUI), the area where urban development and wildlands meet. The proximity of communities to wildlands puts those communities at risk for catastrophic fires and limits options for wildland fire management by increasing the riskiness of prescribed burns and by pressuring the Forest Service to suppress all fires on wildlands that threaten urban development, even when good forest management practices dictate allowing the fire to burn to reduce the risk of more catastrophic fires. One recent Office of Inspector General report found that 87 percent of federal wildfire suppression was undertaken for the purpose of protecting private property in the WUI. U.S. DEP'T OF AGRIC., OFFICE OF INSPECTOR GEN. W. REGION, AUDIT REPORT: FOREST SERVICE LARGE FIRE SUPPRESSION COSTS, Report. No. 08601-44-SF, at ii (Nov. 2006).

For wildfires, the costs of holding disaster at bay may be as significant as the costs of disaster-inflicted damage. A recent study found that only 14 percent of the forested wildland interface was currently developed in the United States, and that if even 50 percent of the remaining 86 percent of the wildland interface were developed, annual federal firefighting costs to protect private property would increase from the current range of $630 million to $1.2 billion per year to an estimated $2.3 to 4.3 billion per year. *See* Patricia Gude et al., *Potential for Future Development on Fire-Prone Lands*, J. FORESTRY, 106(4) 198, 202 (June 2008). Despite these costs, the potential for wildland interface development is immense.

Do local governments have sufficient incentives to regulate zoning in the WUI? Do homeowners have sufficient incentives to take recommended precautions for fire-proofing their homes and land? Consider this report from the Office of Inspector General.

U.S. DEP'T OF AGRIC., OFFICE OF INSPECTOR GEN. W. REGION, AUDIT REPORT: FOREST SERVICE LARGE FIRE SUPPRESSION COSTS

Report No. 08601-44-SF at 5-9 (Nov. 2006) (citations and footnotes omitted)

[The U.S. Forest Service (FS)] has not consistently followed guidance designed to ensure that it equitably allocates financial responsibility for its fire suppression activities. First, FS managers have not renegotiated wildfire protection agreements between FS and non-Federal entities to equitably apportion State and local wildland urban interface (WUI) protection responsibilities. Second, FS, without considering the relative values at risk, continues to give the protection of privately-owned property a higher priority than the protection of natural resources. These circumstances exist because FS perceives States as unwilling to voluntarily expand their protection responsibilities to include a greater share of WUI protection costs and because political and public expectations compel FS to make protecting property its highest priority. Consequently, FS has borne much more than its share of the expenses associated with fighting wildfires, which causes its costs to escalate while losing valuable natural resources in favor of private structures. Some FS estimates would put the cost of WUI protection at between $547 million to $1 billion in FYs 2003 and 2004.

The 1995 Federal Wildland Fire Management Policy and its 2001 update defines the operational role of Federal agencies in the WUI as assisting non-Federal entities in wildland firefighting but makes Tribal, State, and local governments responsible for structural fire protection. The policy also directs Federal agencies to ensure that WUI areas are covered by fire protection agreements. These agreements are to be renegotiated as needed to ensure that they remain compatible with Federal policy and that they equitably apportion State and local responsibilities.

The Federal Wildland Fire Management Policy also directed Federal wildland fire management agencies to give public and firefighter safety first priority, and to suppress fires at minimum cost, giving due consideration to the values of both property and natural/cultural resources at risk. Making natural resources and properties equal protection priorities was a shift in wildfire suppression direction. Prior to 1995, FS policy had prioritized wildfire protection objectives in the order of life, property, and natural resources. Consequently, wildfire suppression resources were often diverted to protect private properties while more valuable natural resources burned. In effect, the current Federal policy no longer gives private property automatic priority over the protection of natural resources.

Together, these criteria allow FS to adopt a more cost effective approach to fighting fires. By sharing financial responsibility for WUI protection with State, Tribal, and local governments, FS should bear only that portion of the costs related to its protection efforts for Federal property. By weighing the relative value of the natural resources endangered against that of private property, FS should be able to utilize strategies that are cost effective. However, since this guidance has not been consistently implemented, FS continues to pay more than its share of fire suppression costs. . . .

The protection of homes and other property in the WUI is an escalating fire problem. WUI development has been steadily increasing with housing starts in the WUI being three times greater than elsewhere. In the fire-prone areas of the western Rocky Mountains, 2.2 million homes are expected to exist in the WUI by the year 2030 — a 40 percent increase over current levels. . . .

Under FS directives, cooperative wildland fire protection agreements must be reviewed and updated on an annual basis to maintain compatibility with Federal policies. These agreements with Federal and non-Federal fire management agencies are to improve the efficiency and effectiveness of fire management and protection of State, private, and Federal lands. Wildfire protection responsibilities may be delineated on the basis of jurisdictional boundaries or through the negotiation of direct protection areas (DPAs) that are defined by boundaries based on logical protection responsibilities rather than ownership patterns. Once responsibility for protecting lands is determined, the protecting agency assumes full financial responsibility for associated firefighting costs. . . .

We reviewed cooperative wildland fire protection agreements negotiated between FS regions 1, 5, and 6 and the States of Oregon, Washington, California, Montana, and Idaho and concluded that FS is subject to an inequitable wildfire protection burden because the agreements had not been renegotiated to reflect appropriate WUI protection responsibilities. For example, the Region 6 master agreement defined wildfire protection responsibilities based on jurisdictional boundaries rather than DPAs. The Region 1 and 5 master agreements defined protection responsibilities based on DPAs but the defined protection areas had not been significantly altered or updated for an average of 12 years. The combination of these two circumstances has the potential to significantly increase the FS' wildfire suppression costs by expanding the agency's role in WUI protection beyond that directed by the 2001 Federal Wildland Fire Management Policy.

In addition, when FS protection responsibilities are directly adjacent to WUI development, FS line officers feel compelled to aggressively suppress wildfires because the fires threaten privately-owned structures, even if the fires pose no threat to FS resources. [Such wildfire suppression for the purpose of protecting privately-owned structures is contrary to established federal policy.]

In order to reflect the fact that the Federal Government is not primarily responsible for structure protection in the WUI, FS managers need to delineate Federal protection responsibilities using DPAs that are annually reviewed and updated. Renegotiating the wildfire protection agreements would not impact wildfire operations or suppression effectiveness. FS would still be committed to participating in mutual aid agreements that dispatched Federal resources to wildfire incidents to protect life and public safety. The updated protection agreements would serve only to more equitably allocate financial responsibility for WUI protection to States and local governments.

Assigning the financial responsibility for WUI wildfire protection to State and local government is critical because Federal agencies do not have the power to regulate WUI development. Zoning and planning authority rests with State and local government. Unregulated WUI development increases FS wildfire suppression costs. Under the terms of current protection agreements, FS and Federal taxpayers bear the wildfire cost implications of development decisions made by local governments about where and how structures will be built in the WUI. The inequity of this situation is further exacerbated by the fact that only a small portion of the WUI is in FS or Federal ownership. A recent study conducted by the Wilderness Society estimated that most WUI acreage is owned by private, State, or Tribal entities.

With current wildfire suppression funding levels nearing $1 billion annually, the cost of protecting private property in the WUI has significant financial implications. However, while FS spends record amounts protecting private landowners from advancing wildfires, these individuals have done little to protect themselves. According to a July 2000 report by the National Association of State Foresters, people moving into the WUI give little thought to the threat posed by wildfires, expecting to be provided with urban type emergency services if and when a wildfire occurs. Other WUI residents believe that insurance companies or Federal disaster assistance will cover any property losses.

Homeowner reliance on the Federal government to provide wildfire suppression services places an enormous financial burden on FS, as the lead Federal agency providing such services. It also removes incentives for landowners moving into the WUI to take responsibility for their own protection and ensure their homes are constructed and landscaped in ways that reduce wildfire risks. FS research has found that it is the fuel conditions within 200 feet of structures that determine whether or not those structures will burn. Other FS research concluded that home losses in the WUI are largely independent of both FS wildfire suppression efforts and fuel reduction activities because effective wildfire protection depends almost solely on the fuel reduction activities that take place on privately-owned land.

Linking wildfire suppression responsibility to jurisdictional authority is important because studies have shown that Federally-sponsored voluntary programs have not been sufficient in changing landowner behavior. Mandatory zoning and building regulations may be needed to compel landowners to take the actions necessary to protect their homes and property from wildfire. If State and local agencies became more financially responsible for WUI protection, it would likely encourage these agencies to more actively implement land use regulations that minimize the risk to people and structures from wildfire. Once State and local agencies enact and enforce appropriate zoning and building regulations, much of the cost associated with protecting WUI areas incurred by Federal, State, and local firefighting agencies will be reduced. . . .

While recognizing the current financial inequality of WUI protection, FS officials believe that States will not renegotiate protection agreements that increase States' WUI protection costs. FS officials added that States generally believe the FS is responsible for all fire suppression costs incurred on FS lands even when fires are suppressed in order to protect private property on sometimes distant State and county lands.

NOTES AND QUESTIONS

1. Forest Service officials blame the inequity of existing protection agreements in part on states' unwillingness to renegotiate such agreements. How might the federal government incentivize states to come to the table?
2. Most western states — which are experiencing the greatest growth at the wildland interface — have some legislation addressing construction in the WUI, though the content of the legislation varies widely:

   > Within Arizona, New Mexico, Idaho, and Colorado, the language in the states' legislation addressing the WUI is rather adaptable: recommending building standards or encouraging counties to prepare plans that would reduce wildfire problems. In Oregon, California, Utah, and Montana, state laws clarify that counties can legally deny subdivisions that do not mitigate or avoid threats to public health and safety from wildland fire. The state laws within Oregon, California, and Utah go beyond this to set minimum standards for development in high wildfire hazard areas. For example, California state law requires that homeowners in the WUI clear and maintain vegetation-specific distances around structures; Utah sets minimum standards for ordinance requirements based on the 2003 International Urban Wildland Interface-Code; and Oregon sets standards for defensible space, fuel breaks, building materials, ingress and egress, and open burning on the property.

   Gude, *supra*, at 203. Should local communities create special districts when subdivisions are approved to pass on the costs of fire suppression to those who build in high-risk areas?
3. "The law of fire is in its infancy," Keiter, *supra*, at 378, and consists today of an "uncoordinated and fragmented welter of organic statutory provisions, environmental protection mandates, annual budget riders, site-specific legislation, judicial decisions, policy documents, management plans, and diverse state statutory prohibitions," *id*. at 303-304. The only significant federal statute directed at fire policy is the 2003 Healthy Forests Restoration Act (HFRA), which focuses primarily on reducing fuel loading that resulted from prior reliance on a policy of total fire suppression. Pub. L. No. 108-148, 117 Stat. 1887 (2003) (codified at 16 U.S.C. §§ 6501-6591 (2003)). At least one critic charges that this focus has encouraged more homeowners to build in the WUI, by "conveying a sense of security and federal approval" for WUI development and ignoring underlying land use issues. *See* Jamison Colburn, *The Fire Next Time: Land Use Planning in the Wildland/Urban Interface*, 28 J. LAND RESOURCES & ENVTL. L. 223, 242-243 (2008).
4. The definition of the WUI is fluid and debatable. How close to public forest (or other forest) should construction be to be considered WUI development? By some definitions, 38 percent of all homes are located in the WUI (and more than 60% of new home construction in the 1990s took place

there). *See* Lauren Wishnie, Student Article, *Fire and Federalism: A Forest Fire Is Always an Emergency*, 17 N.Y.U. ENVTL. L.J. 1006, 1012-1013 (2008). Is a definition that includes nearly 40 percent of existing homes a legally useful category?

5. Like floodplain mapping, accurate mapping of fire zones is expensive, technologically complex, and potentially subject to local political pressures. Gude et al., *supra*, at 204. Should the federal government map wildfire hazards, as it does with special flood hazard areas? The Forest Service and Department of Interior are already engaged in some fire mapping through the joint LANDFIRE project (Landscape Fire and Resource Management Planning Tools Project). The Federal Land Assistance, Management, and Enhancement (FLAME) Act—passed by the House and being considered by the Senate—would require the secretaries of the Interior and Agriculture Departments to create regional maps of communities most at risk of wildfire and identify priority areas for fuels reduction projects. *See* S. 561, 111th Cong. (2009) (as referred to the Senate Committee on Energy and Natural Resources).

6. The FLAME bill also encourages communities within priority areas to become "fire-ready" (meaning that they have cooperative fire agreements, effective local fire codes, and community wildfire protection plans, and that they are "engaged in a successful collaborative process," such as a resource advisory committee) by making such communities eligible for federal cost-share grants to educate, train, equip, and implement wildfire protection. The secretaries are also directed to develop firefighting cost-sharing agreements with states that encourage community readiness. The bill also charges the secretaries with creating a cohesive wildland fire management strategy, including a cost-effective firefighting plan, a risk assessment system, and a fuels-reduction system. Additionally, the bill would create the "federal land assistance, management, and enhancement" fund (FLAME), for fighting unpredicted catastrophic wildfires (separate from amounts annually appropriated for predicted firefighting workload). *See id.* Critics worry that creating a separate fund for catastrophic fires (rather than requiring the Forest Service to find the money in its existing budget) will remove any remaining disincentives to fighting all fires near the WUI.

7. Should firefighting policy encourage individual homeowners to shoulder some of the responsibility for protecting their homes by allowing them to decline evacuation and stay to defend their homes? The Australian-pioneered Leave Early or Stay and Defend approach, which encourages homeowners either to evacuate early or to make an educated choice to stay and defend their homes, was gaining some currency in Southern California, until the Black Saturday brush fires in Victoria, Australia, on February 7, 2009, claimed nearly 200 lives, including some homeowners who were actively defending their homes. *See* Catherine Saillant, *Australian Fires Give State Pause*, L.A. TIMES, Mar. 6, 2009.

8. Scientists have suggested that climate change may have contributed to the devastating Black Saturday brush fires that claimed so many lives and destroyed two Australian towns, incinerating at least 750 homes. *See* Meraiah Foley, *Death Toll in Australian Fire Climbs to 131*, N.Y. TIMES, Feb. 8,

2009, at A8. While acknowledging that it is impossible to definitively ascribe any individual fire to climate change, Australia's Commonwealth Scientific and Industrial Research Organization (CSIRO) has attributed "[t]he extreme fire weather conditions" that fueled the fire "to the very high temperatures following a 50 year warming trend, and very dry conditions following 12 years of below-average rainfall." CSIRO, *Q & A: Victorian Bushfires*, http://www.csiro.au/resources/Victorian-Bushfires-QA.html#9. Scientists have also suggested that severe wildfires will likely increase in frequency because of climate change.

9. One in five homes in the WUI is a second home. Gude, *supra*, at 200. Does this affect the equities of asking federal taxpayers to bear a substantial burden for fire suppression? Should the income of the homeowner or the value of the home matter?

10. When it comes to protecting homes from wildfire, the layout of communities may be as important as their location:

> There are . . . a number of very poorly planned subdivisions [in the Malibu–Santa Monica mountains] which were divided in the late 1920s and 30s with lot sizes of less than an acre and many more typically 5,000 to 10,000 sq. ft. in size. These subdivisions were primarily designed for weekend cabin type[s] of use. However, today the expensive homes built on these parcels are occupied on a year-round basis. There are approximately 6,000 of these ill-conceived small parcels in the Santa Monica Mountains. These subdivisions have very narrow winding roads which cannot accommodate fire equipment and are for the most part very heavily wooded with both natural and exotic plant species. These types of subdivisions are disasters just waiting to happen.
>
> Proper site design on a large parcel can reduce fire danger to some extent. [H]owever, in these small lot subdivisions it is impossible in many cases to significantly reduce the fire hazards given the very steep site topography, lack of adequate water supply, proximity to other structures and limited access for fire equipment.

Jack Ainsworth & Troy Alan Doss, Cal. Coastal Comm'n, Presentation to the Post-Fire Hazard Assessment Planning and Mitigation Workshop at the University of California, Santa Barbara: Natural History of Fire & Flood (Aug. 18, 1995). Firefighting can also be complicated in areas with very large lot sizes, because firefighters must defend large areas to protect a few homes.

4. TAKINGS DOCTRINE AS A LIMIT ON LAND USE DECISIONS

In the United States, property rights have a great deal of political weight. They also have some degree of constitutional protection. Blocking development of land can sometimes be an unconstitutional taking of property. The Takings Clause of the Fifth Amendment provides that private property shall not "be taken for public use, without just compensation." The seminal decision was Pennsylvania Coal v. Mahon, 260 U.S. 393 (1922). This case involved a Pennsylvania statute making it unlawful for coal companies to cause the collapse or subsidence of any overlaying structure, such as a residence. In the case before the

Court, the coal company contended that the effect would be to make mining completely infeasible, wiping out the value of the mining rights that they had purchased from the owner of the surface rights. In an opinion by Justice Holmes, the Court held that this was a taking of property because the statute had "very nearly the same effect for constitutional purposes as appropriating or destroying it." *Id.* at 414. Since then, courts have struggled to determine when a regulation "goes too far" and becomes a taking. The most important modern case, Penn Central Transportation Co. v. New York, 438 U.S. 104 (1978), attempted to provide a synthesis of the law. According to *Penn Central*, except where a regulation physically invades property (as by providing public access), the test is whether the regulation unreasonably "interfered with distinct investment-backed expectations." *Id.* at 123. In the following case, however, the Court attempted to provide more of a bright-line test.

LUCAS v. SOUTH CAROLINA COASTAL COUNCIL

Supreme Court of the United States, 1992, 505 U.S. 1003,
112 S. Ct. 2886, 120 L. Ed. 2d 798

Justice SCALIA delivered the opinion of the Court.

In 1986, petitioner David H. Lucas paid $975,000 for two residential lots on the Isle of Palms in Charleston County, South Carolina, on which he intended to build single-family homes. In 1988, however, the South Carolina Legislature enacted the Beachfront Management Act, which had the direct effect of barring petitioner from erecting any permanent habitable structures on his two parcels. A state trial court found that this prohibition rendered Lucas's parcels "valueless." This case requires us to decide whether the Act's dramatic effect on the economic value of Lucas's lots accomplished a taking of private property under the Fifth and Fourteenth Amendments requiring the payment of "just compensation." . . .

[O]ur decision in *Mahon* [an early takings decision by Justice Holmes] offered little insight into when, and under what circumstances, a given regulation would be seen as going "too far" for purposes of the Fifth Amendment. In 70-odd years of succeeding "regulatory takings" jurisprudence, we have generally eschewed any "'set formula'" for determining how far is too far, preferring to "engag[e] in . . . essentially ad hoc, factual inquiries." We have, however, described at least two discrete categories of regulatory action as compensable without case-specific inquiry into the public interest advanced in support of the restraint. The first encompasses regulations that compel the property owner to suffer a physical "invasion" of his property. . . .

The second situation in which we have found categorical treatment appropriate is where regulation denies all economically beneficial or productive use of land. As we have said on numerous occasions, the Fifth Amendment is violated when land-use regulation "does not substantially advance legitimate state interests *or denies an owner economically viable use of his land.*"[4]

---

4. Regrettably, the rhetorical force of our "deprivation of all economically feasible use" rule is greater than its precision, since the rule does not make clear the "property interest" against which

We have never set forth the justification for this rule. Perhaps it is simply, as Justice Brennan suggested, that total deprivation of beneficial use is, from the landowner's point of view, the equivalent of a physical appropriation. . . . Surely, at least, in the extraordinary circumstance when *no* productive or economically beneficial use of land is permitted, it is less realistic to indulge our usual assumption that the legislature is simply "adjusting the benefits and burdens of economic life," [*Penn Central*], in a manner that secures an "average reciprocity of advantage" to everyone concerned. And the *functional* basis for permitting the government, by regulation, to affect property values without compensation — that "Government hardly could go on if to some extent values incident to property could not be diminished without paying for every such change in the general law" — does not apply to the relatively rare situations where the government has deprived a landowner of all economically beneficial uses.

On the other side of the balance, affirmatively supporting a compensation requirement is the fact that regulations that leave the owner of land without economically beneficial or productive options for its use — typically, as here, by requiring land to be left substantially in its natural state — carry with them a heightened risk that private property is being pressed into some form of public service under the guise of mitigating serious public harm. *See, e.g.,* Annicelli v. South Kingstown, 463 A.2d 133, 140-141 (R.I. 1983) (prohibition on construction adjacent to beach justified on twin grounds of safety and "conservation of open space"); Morris County Land Improvement Co. v. Parsippany–Troy Hills Township, 40 N.J. 539, 552-553, 193 A.2d 232, 240 (1963) (prohibition on filling marshlands imposed in order to preserve region as water detention basin and create wildlife refuge). As Justice Brennan explained: "From the government's point of view, the benefits flowing to the public from preservation of open space through regulation may be equally great as from creating a wildlife refuge through formal condemnation or increasing electricity production through a dam project that floods private property." The many statutes on the books, both state and federal, that provide for the use of eminent domain to impose servitudes on private scenic lands preventing developmental uses, or

---

the loss of value is to be measured. When, for example, a regulation requires a developer to leave 90% of a rural tract in its natural state, it is unclear whether we would analyze the situation as one in which the owner has been deprived of all economically beneficial use of the burdened portion of the tract, or as one in which the owner has suffered a mere diminution in value of the tract as a whole. (For an extreme — and, we think, unsupportable — view of the relevant calculus, see Penn Central Transportation Co. v. New York City, 42 N.Y.2d 324, 333-334, 397 N.Y.S.2d 914, 920, 366 N.E.2d 1271, 1276-1277 (1977), *aff'd*, 438 U.S. 104, 98 S. Ct. 2646, 57 L. Ed. 2d 631 (1978), where the state court examined the diminution in a particular parcel's value produced by a municipal ordinance in light of total value of the taking claimant's other holdings in the vicinity.) Unsurprisingly, this uncertainty regarding the composition of the denominator in our "deprivation" fraction has produced inconsistent pronouncements by the Court. The answer to this difficult question may lie in how the owner's reasonable expectations have been shaped by the State's law of property — i.e., whether and to what degree the State's law has accorded legal recognition and protection to the particular interest in land with respect to which the takings claimant alleges a diminution in (or elimination of) value. In any event, we avoid this difficulty in the present case, since the "interest in land" that Lucas has pleaded (a fee simple interest) is an estate with a rich tradition of protection at common law, and since the South Carolina Court of Common Pleas found that the Beachfront Management Act left each of Lucas's beachfront lots without economic value.

to acquire such lands altogether, suggest the practical equivalence in this setting of negative regulation and appropriation.

We think, in short, that there are good reasons for our frequently expressed belief that when the owner of real property has been called upon to sacrifice *all* economically beneficial uses in the name of the common good, that is, to leave his property economically idle, he has suffered a taking. . . .

It is correct that many of our prior opinions have suggested that "harmful or noxious uses" of property may be proscribed by government regulation without the requirement of compensation. For a number of reasons, however, we think the South Carolina Supreme Court was too quick to conclude that that principle decides the present case. The "harmful or noxious uses" principle was the Court's early attempt to describe in theoretical terms why government may, consistent with the Takings Clause, affect property values by regulation without incurring an obligation to compensate — a reality we nowadays acknowledge explicitly with respect to the full scope of the State's police power. . . .

The transition from our early focus on control of "noxious" uses to our contemporary understanding of the broad realm within which government may regulate without compensation was an easy one, since the distinction between "harm-preventing" and "benefit-conferring" regulation is often in the eye of the beholder. It is quite possible, for example, to describe in *either* fashion the ecological, economic, and aesthetic concerns that inspired the South Carolina legislature in the present case. One could say that imposing a servitude on Lucas's land is necessary in order to prevent his use of it from "harming" South Carolina's ecological resources; or, instead, in order to achieve the "benefits" of an ecological preserve. Whether one or the other of the competing characterizations will come to one's lips in a particular case depends primarily upon one's evaluation of the worth of competing uses of real estate. . . .

Where the State seeks to sustain regulation that deprives land of all economically beneficial use, we think it may resist compensation only if the logically antecedent inquiry into the nature of the owner's estate shows that the proscribed use interests were not part of his title to begin with.[5] This accords, we think, with our "takings" jurisprudence, which has traditionally been guided by the understandings of our citizens regarding the content of, and the State's power over, the "bundle of rights" that they acquire when they obtain title to property. It seems to us that the property owner necessarily

---

5. Drawing on our First Amendment jurisprudence, Justice Stevens would "loo[k] to the *generality* of a regulation of property" to determine whether compensation is owing. The Beachfront Management Act is general, in his view, because it "regulates the use of the coastline of the entire state." There may be some validity to the principle Justice Stevens proposes, but it does not properly apply to the present case. The equivalent of a law of general application that inhibits the practice of religion without being aimed at religion, is a law that destroys the value of land without being aimed at land. Perhaps such a law — the generally applicable criminal prohibition on the manufacturing of alcoholic beverages challenged in *Mugler* [*v. Kansas*, 123 U.S. 623, 8 S. Ct. 273, 31 L. Ed. 205] (1887), comes to mind — cannot constitute a compensable taking. But a regulation *specifically directed to land use* no more acquires immunity by plundering landowners generally than does a law specifically directed at religious practice acquire immunity by prohibiting all religions. Justice Stevens' approach renders the Takings Clause little more than a particularized restatement of the Equal Protection Clause.

expects the uses of his property to be restricted, from time to time, by various measures newly enacted by the State in legitimate exercise of its police powers; "[a]s long recognized, some values are enjoyed under an implied limitation and must yield to the police power." [*Mahon.*] And in the case of personal property, by reason of the State's traditionally high degree of control over commercial dealings, he ought to be aware of the possibility that new regulation might even render his property economically worthless (at least if the property's only economically productive use is sale or manufacture for sale). In the case of land, however, we think the notion pressed by the Council that title is somehow held subject to the "implied limitation" that the State may subsequently eliminate all economically valuable use is inconsistent with the historical compact recorded in the Takings Clause that has become part of our constitutional culture. . . .

The "total taking" inquiry we require today will ordinarily entail (as the application of state nuisance law ordinarily entails) analysis of, among other things, the degree of harm to public lands and resources, or adjacent private property, posed by the claimant's proposed activities, *see, e.g.,* Restatement (Second) of Torts §§ 826, 827, the social value of the claimant's activities and their suitability to the locality in question, *see, e.g., id.,* §§ 828(a) and (b), 831, and the relative ease with which the alleged harm can be avoided through measures taken by the claimant and the government (or adjacent private landowners) alike, *see, e.g., id.,* §§ 827(e), 828(c), 830. The fact that a particular use has long been engaged in by similarly situated owners ordinarily imports a lack of any common-law prohibition (though changed circumstances or new knowledge may make what was previously permissible no longer so, *see id.,* §827, Comment g.) So also does the fact that other landowners, similarly situated, are permitted to continue the use denied to the claimant.

It seems unlikely that common-law principles would have prevented the erection of any habitable or productive improvements on petitioner's land; they rarely support prohibition of the "essential use" of land. The question, however, is one of state law to be dealt with on remand. We emphasize that to win its case South Carolina must do more than proffer the legislature's declaration that the uses Lucas desires are inconsistent with the public interest, or the conclusory assertion that they violate a common-law maxim such as *sic utere tuo ut alienum non laedas.* As we have said, a "State, by *ipse dixit,* may not transform private property into public property without compensation. . . ." Instead, as it would be required to do if it sought to restrain Lucas in a common-law action for public nuisance, South Carolina must identify background principles of nuisance and property law that prohibit the uses he now intends in the circumstances in which the property is presently found. Only on this showing can the State fairly claim that, in proscribing all such beneficial uses, the Beachfront Management Act is taking nothing.[6]

---

6. . . . We stress that an affirmative decree eliminating all economically beneficial uses may be defended only if an *objectively reasonable application* of relevant precedents would exclude those beneficial uses in the circumstances in which the land is presently found.

Justice KENNEDY, concurring in the judgment.

In my view, reasonable expectations must be understood in light of the whole of our legal tradition. The common law of nuisance is too narrow a confine for the exercise of regulatory power in a complex and interdependent society. The State should not be prevented from enacting new regulatory initiatives in response to changing conditions, and courts must consider all reasonable expectations whatever their source. The Takings Clause does not require a static body of state property law; it protects private expectations to ensure private investment. I agree with the Court that nuisance prevention accords with the most common expectations of property owners who face regulation, but I do not believe this can be the sole source of state authority to impose severe restrictions. Coastal property may present such unique concerns for a fragile land system that the State can go further in regulating its development and use than the common law of nuisance might otherwise permit.

The Supreme Court of South Carolina erred, in my view, by reciting the general purposes for which the state regulations were enacted without a determination that they were in accord with the owner's reasonable expectations and therefore sufficient to support a severe restriction on specific parcels of property. The promotion of tourism, for instance, ought not to suffice to deprive specific property of all value without a corresponding duty to compensate. Furthermore, the means as well as the ends of regulation must accord with the owner's reasonable expectations. Here, the State did not act until after the property had been zoned for individual lot development and most other parcels had been improved, throwing the whole burden of the regulation on the remaining lots. This too must be measured in the balance.

Justice BLACKMUN, dissenting.

[T]he Court justifies its new rule that the legislature may not deprive a property owner of the only economically valuable use of his land, even if the legislature finds it to be a harmful use, because such action is not part of the "long recognized" "understandings of our citizens." These "understandings" permit such regulation only if the use is a nuisance under the common law. Any other course is "inconsistent with the historical compact recorded in the Takings Clause." It is not clear from the Court's opinion where our "historical compact" or "citizens' understanding" comes from, but it does not appear to be history.

The principle that the State should compensate individuals for property taken for public use was not widely established in America at the time of the Revolution. . . .

Even into the 19th century, state governments often felt free to take property for roads and other public projects without paying compensation to the owners. As one court declared in 1802, citizens "were bound to contribute as much of [land], as by the laws of the country, were deemed necessary for the public convenience." . . .

. . . In short, I find no clear and accepted "historical compact" or "understanding of our citizens" justifying the Court's new taking doctrine. Instead, the Court seems to treat history as a grab-bag of principles, to be adopted where they support the Court's theory, and ignored where they do not. If the Court decided that the early common law provides the background principles for interpreting the Taking Clause, then regulation, as opposed to physical confiscation, would not be compensable. If the Court decided that the law of a later period provides the background principles, then regulation might be compensable, but the Court would have to confront the fact that legislatures regularly determined which uses were prohibited, independent of the common law, and independent of whether the uses were lawful when the owner purchased. What makes the Court's analysis unworkable is its attempt to package the law of two incompatible eras and peddle it as historical fact.

Justice STEVENS, dissenting.

In considering Lucas' claim, the generality of the Beachfront Management Act is significant. The Act does not target particular landowners, but rather regulates the use of the coastline of the entire State. Indeed, South Carolina's Act is best understood as part of a national effort to protect the coastline, one initiated by the Federal Coastal Zone Management Act of 1972. . . . Moreover, the Act did not single out owners of undeveloped land. The Act also prohibited owners of developed land from rebuilding if their structures were destroyed, and what is equally significant, from repairing erosion control devices, such as seawalls. In addition, in some situations, owners of developed land were required to "renouris[h] the beach . . . on a yearly basis with an amount . . . of sand . . . not . . . less than one and one-half times the yearly volume of sand lost due to erosion." In short, the South Carolina Act imposed substantial burdens on owners of developed and undeveloped land alike. This generality indicates that the Act is not an effort to expropriate owners of undeveloped land.

Admittedly, the economic impact of this regulation is dramatic and petitioner's investment-backed expectations are substantial. Yet, if anything, the costs to and expectations of the owners of developed land are even greater: I doubt, however, that the cost to owners of developed land of renourishing the beach and allowing their seawalls to deteriorate effects a taking. The costs imposed on the owners of undeveloped land, such as petitioner, differ from these costs only in degree, not in kind.

NOTES AND QUESTIONS

1. After Hurricane Hugo, so many structures were damaged in the area that the state relented on its ban on rebuilding existing houses. After further negotiations, South Carolina eventually bought the lots for over $1.5 million. The area has been flooded many times since the Supreme Court's ruling, and the inhabitants have constructed walls of two-ton and three-ton sandbags. Carol M. Rose, *The Story of* Lucas *: Environmental Land Use Regulation Between Developers and the Deep Blue Sea, in* RICHARD J. LAZARUS & OLIVER A. HOUCK, ENVIRONMENTAL LAW STORIES 268-269 (2005).

2. One noteworthy aspect of *Lucas* is Justice Scalia's use of a narrowly construed "nuisance exception," at least in total takings cases. This is in

sharp contrast to the call by some for an expansive new land ethic focusing on ecological interdependency. Justice Scalia's use of nuisance law has attracted attention from commentators, who have suggested that nuisance law has been far more fluid and adaptable than Scalia suggests. *See, e.g.,* Christine A. Klein, *The New Nuisance: An Antidote to Wetland Loss, Sprawl, and Global Warming*, 48 B.C. L. Rev. 1155, 1155, 1233 (2007) (arguing that *Lucas*, with its explicit recognition that "changed circumstances or new knowledge may make what was previously permissible no longer so," has spurred the development of a new nuisance doctrine with renewed emphasis on balancing public and private interests); *see also* Richard J. Lazarus, *The Measure of a Justice: Justice Scalia and the Faltering of the Property Rights Movement within the Supreme Court*, 57 Hastings L.J. 759, 823-824 (2006) (contending that the *Lucas* rule that Justice Scalia "hoped to serve as a per se takings rule proves, in its practical operation, to work more often as a per se no takings rule").

3. What type of restrictions on land development might survive scrutiny under *Lucas?* Applying *Lucas*'s nuisance exception, "a number of state and federal courts have held that governmental efforts to protect wetlands do not constitute regulatory takings because wetland destruction constitutes a nuisance." Klein, *supra*, at 1202; *see also* Edward A. Thomas & Sam Riley Medlock, *Mitigating Misery: Land Use and Protection of Property Rights Before the Next Big Flood*, 9 Vt. Envtl. L. 155, 171 (2008) (arguing that the trend is to sustain government "hazard-based" land use regulations, particularly floodplain regulations, against takings challenges). Is it easier to see how *Lucas*'s nuisance exception might be invoked to justify floodplain or wetlands regulation than to justify earthquake zoning?

D. GREEN AND BUILT INFRASTRUCTURE

1. GREEN INFRASTRUCTURE

As Professor Rob Verchick has written, although we usually think of our infrastructure (such as roads, bridges, and dams) as gray, most of our infrastructure is, in fact, green. Robert R.M. Verchick, Facing Catastrophe: Environmental Action for a Post-Katrina World (2010). And much of that natural, green infrastructure can provide some protective buffering effect against natural disasters. Mangrove forests may play a role in coastal defense, as may coral reefs, both of which can help dissipate wave intensity and storm surge under certain conditions. Wetlands can likewise dissipate storm surge and absorb flood waters. Vegetative cover and forests help prevent landslides and avalanches. Indeed, more than a decade ago, in 1997, researchers estimated the global value of the ecosystem's role in "disturbance regulation"—including storm protection, flood control, and drought recovery—at $1.8 trillion a year. Robert Costanza et al., *The Value of the World's Ecosystem Services and Natural Capital*, Nature, vol. 387 (May 15, 1997) 253, 259.

a. Wetlands and Other Coastal Infrastructure

The role of natural infrastructure in mitigating the effects of natural disasters garnered national attention in the aftermath of Katrina, as Gulf Coast residents wondered to what extent homes and lives would have been spared but for the loss of so much of the region's wetlands:

ROBERT R.M. VERCHICK, FACING CATASTROPHE: ENVIRONMENTAL
ACTION FOR A POST-KATRINA WORLD

(forthcoming 2010) (internal citations and footnotes omitted)

Louisiana's coastal plain contains one of the largest expanses of coastal wetlands in the contiguous United States. In fact, a quarter of *all* coastal wetlands in the Lower 48 are in Louisiana. . . . Louisiana's coastal plain hosts an extraordinary diversity of coastal habitats, ranging from natural levees and beach ridges to large swaths of forested swamps, to freshwater, intermediate, brackish, and saline marshes. These features, which nourish wildlife, filter water, and dampen storm surges, help make the coastal plain, to quote from the Army Corps of Engineers, one of "the most productive and important natural assets" in the country.

While most people do not realize it, one of the most important services provided by coastal marshes involves storm protection. Imagine blasting water through a garden hose at full force onto a cement driveway. The water splashes and surges, fanning out in many directions. Now imagine spraying water from the same hose onto a thick, dense lawn. The difference between the cement and the lawn is the difference between a storm path composed of open water and denuded coast and one composed of lush forests and marsh. Louisiana's coastal wetlands act as vast sponges, absorbing billions of gallons of rainfall and shielding people and property from storms. The effect is impressive, even for city dwellers who have never seen a marsh: by some estimates, every two miles of wetlands south of New Orleans reduces tropical storm surges there by half a foot. For this reason, local environmentalists sometimes refer to the coast as a "horizontal levee." Coastal wetlands also help shield an internationally significant commercial-industrial complex from the destructive forces of storm-driven waves and tides. . . .

Unbelievably, this titan among wetlands, this biotic and commercial treasure, is disappearing before our very eyes. Since Percy Viosca's enlightened plea for wetlands protection, Louisiana has lost more than *1.2 million acres* of its "trembling prairie." Today, the Army Corps of Engineers believes Louisiana is losing about 6,600 acres of coastal wetlands per year. Why is this happening? The effect is partly due to natural subsidence. The soft soils of the coastal plain naturally shift and sink over time. But this phenomenon, at best, explains only a small fraction of the loss. The real culprits are human-made: Louisiana's vast network of levees, navigational channels, and oil-and-gas infrastructure. The levee system accelerates coastal land loss by reducing the natural flow of a river's freshwater and sediment to wetland areas where lost land would then naturally be replenished. Instead, that valuable water and sediment is funneled down the Mississippi and shot into the Gulf, toward the outer continental shelf, where the formation of barrier islands is impossible.

Louisiana's coastal plain is crisscrossed with a vast matrix of navigational canals, including ten major navigational channels and literally thousands of smaller access canals serving navigation, allowing oil-rig access, and cradling oil and gas pipelines. Recall that up close, those swamps seemed lusty and vital. But from a helicopter or plane, the view is more depressing—like green shag carpet being eaten by a Pac Man. Those channels mean death to nearby marshlands. They cut the land off from the natural flow of water and starve them of nutrients. Often the banks of these channels (which are seldom maintained) crumble and fall away, expanding waterways by many yards over time. The major navigational channels pose their own special threat to flood control by sometimes acting as "hurricane highways," allowing storms to sweep inland, past marshland, like liquid bulldozers.

In the 1980s, local groups made up of environmentalists, shrimpers, scientists, and business people began pushing for plans to save the coast. One result was the federal Coastal Wetlands Planning, Protection and Restoration Act of 1990 (the "Breaux Act"), which created a federal and state task force to implement wetlands restoration projects with annual funds of around $40 million. In 1998, state and federal agencies, with the participation of a diverse group of local churches, scientists, environmentalists, and fishermen, developed a book length plan called "Coast 2050: Toward a Sustainable Coastal Louisiana," which offered a host of ecosystem restoration strategies. The underlying principles of the Coast 2050 Plan were to restore or mimic the natural processes that built and maintained coastal Louisiana. The complete plan, to be implemented over the next 50 years, carried a price tag of $14 billion, nearly twice as much as the Everglades restoration project. Though expensive, Coast 2050 actually seemed a bargain, considering the costs of doing nothing threatened to exceed $100 billion in lost jobs, lost infrastructure, lost fishing, and increased hurricane damage. But Coast 2050 was never funded. In 2004, hamstrung by climbing deficits, the Bush Administration suggested the Corps lower its sights and focus on only a few projects totaling between $1 to 2 billion. In the end, the Corps did not even receive that amount. The President's 2005 Energy Bill provided only $540 million for Louisiana's coastal restoration over four years.

Hurricanes Katrina and Rita changed all this—first by tearing its own chunks of wetlands out of the Louisiana coast, making coastal erosion an even more serious problem, and second by highlighting for the public the essential role that wetlands play in storm protection. I mentioned that the Army Corps estimates that Louisiana loses 6,600 acres, which is around 25 square miles, of its coast every year under "normal" circumstances. Over night, hurricanes Katrina and Rita destroyed *four times* that amount of wetlands, transforming 217 square miles of productive swamp and marsh into open water. Some of the most heavily damaged marshland was located south and east of Lake Borgne, wetlands that once offered protection to St. Bernard Parish, a white working-class community, and to New Orleans' own Lower Ninth Ward. In 2008 Hurricanes Ike and Gustav again raked through this fragile coast, threatening coastal protection and commerce. . . . Talking to a local reporter, Dave Cvitanovich, an oyster grower, says "By far, coastal erosion is our biggest problem now." "I'm out on the water every day and, God, it's accelerating. There's no slowdown. It's like watching an ice cube melt on your table."

The good news is that public awareness of the problem is at an all-time high. Even school children will tell you that we are losing a football field's worth of land every half hour and that those football fields are one of the first shields against bad storms. For the first time, the federal government is getting serious about plans to restore the coast, understanding that it will take billions not millions of dollars. There is still a very long way to go, and many pitfalls along the way. . . . But the storms of 2005 sent a clear message: in addition to *goods*, the Louisiana coast provides *services* too, most significantly storm protection. We can't afford to kill the goose that lays *that* golden egg.

NOTES AND QUESTIONS

1. Can restoration of Louisiana's coastal wetlands play an important role in protecting New Orleans from future floods? Even some who acknowledge that restoring the wetlands is a "worthy goal" worry that there is "almost no scientific evidence that suggests that we will be able to put the wetlands back on the scale and nature needed to reduce storm impacts." *See* Soil Science Society of America, Wetlands Restoration Not a Panacea for Louisiana Coast (Sept. 30, 2008), ScienceDaily, available at http://www.sciencedaily.com/ releases/2008/09/080924190637.htm (quoting Robert Young, Director of the Program for the Study of Developed Shorelines at Western Carolina University, summarizing the findings of a white-paper coauthored by twenty-six coastal scientists and engineers).

2. As with wetlands, there are limited empirical data about the protective effect of other green infrastructure and the wisdom of relying heavily (or exclusively) on that infrastructure for disaster protection. Nevertheless, initial reports after the devastating 2004 Indian Ocean tsunami suggested that mangrove forests provided substantial protection from the tsunami:

> The scale of the 26 December 2004 Indian Ocean tsunami was almost unprecedented. In areas with the maximum tsunami intensity, little could have prevented catastrophic coastal destruction. Further away, however, areas with coastal tree vegetation were markedly less damaged than areas without. Mangrove forests are the one most important coastal tree vegetation in the area and are one of the world's most threatened tropical ecosystems.
>
> Measurements of wave forces and modeling of fluid dynamics suggest that tree vegetation may shield coastlines from tsunami damage by reducing wave amplitude and energy. . . .
>
> Our results suggest that mangroves and *Casuarina* plantations attenuated tsunami-induced waves and protected shorelines against damage. . . . Conserving or replanting coastal mangroves and greenbelts should buffer communities from future tsunami events.

Finn Danielsen et al., *The Asian Tsunami: A Protective Role for Coastal Vegetation*, 310 Science 643 (2005). Other scientists have contested this conclusion and warn against relying on coastal vegetation to protect against tsunamis. *See, e.g.*, Papri Sri Raman, *Mangroves "Do Not Protect against Tsunamis,"* Sci-DevNet (Jan. 14, 2009), http://www.scidev.net/en/news/mangroves-do-not-protect-against-tsunamis-.html (discussing a forthcoming report from the UN Environment Programme that concludes that "there is no compelling evidence that coastal forests — such as mangroves — can act as 'bioshields' to adequately protect against tsunamis or cyclone storm surges").

3. Like coastal wetlands, riparian wetlands along rivers, lakes, and streams, may play an important role in flood protection. Studies estimate that the destruction of forest riparian wetlands along the Mississippi River has reduced flood storage capacity along the Mississippi's banks from approximately sixty days of river discharge to a mere twelve days. 2005 WORLD RESOURCES INSTITUTE MILLENNIUM ECOSYSTEM ASSESSMENT REPORT, ECOSYSTEMS AND HUMAN WELL-BEING: WETLANDS AND WATER 47. This loss of wetland storage capacity may have exacerbated the 1993 Mississippi floods. *See id.*

4. The federal government can control development of wetlands under Section 404 of the Clean Water Act. There has been considerable controversy over the scope of this jurisdiction. In United States v. Riverside Bayview Homes, Inc., 474 U.S. 121 (1985), the Court held that federal jurisdiction extended to wetlands that are adjacent to navigable waters or their tributaries. In Solid Waste Agency v. U.S. Army Corps of Engineers, 531 U.S. 159 (2001), the Court held that the statute did not apply to "isolated" wetlands that are not linked to navigable waters; the Court intimated that regulating those wetlands might exceed Congress's power under the Constitution. More recently, a plurality held in Rapanos v. United States, 547 U.S. 715, 742 (2006), that the government's power to regulate wetlands is confined to those wetlands that are both adjacent to, and a have a "continuous surface connection" with, "relatively permanent waters" of the United States. However, Justice Kennedy, concurring in the judgment, believed the federal jurisdiction over wetlands is limited instead to wetlands with a "significant nexus" (either physical or ecological) to navigable waters of the United States. *Id.* at 779 (Kennedy, J., concurring in judgment). Because the dissenters argued for complete deference to the Army Corps of Engineers, *id.* at 807 (Stevens, J., dissenting), Justice Kennedy's test is likely to hold sway with lower courts.

b. Forest as Green Infrastructure

Forests are also an important component of green infrastructure that can help to prevent both avalanches and mudslides. "[F]orests in potential avalanche release areas can reduce the risk of avalanches because trees break up snow cover, prevent wind-blown snow drifts, keep snow under shade and therefore colder and firmer, and their fallen boles and boughs tend to anchor snow and prevent it from moving." PROACT, THE ROLE OF ENVIRONMENTAL MANAGEMENT AND ECO-ENGINEERING IN DISASTER RISK REDUCTION AND CLIMATE CHANGE ADAPTATION 9 (2008). The economic value of the avalanche-suppression effect of forests in the Swiss Alps has been estimated at approximately $100/hectare/year in open areas and as much as $170,000/hectare/year in areas surrounding significant economic assets. *Id.* at 9-10. Switzerland therefore provides federal monetary incentives for management of such protective forests. *See id.* at 28. Moreover, studies in Pakistan and Japan have demonstrated that vegetative cover — particularly dense trees — helps prevent landslides (triggered by earthquakes or otherwise), particularly relatively small landslides, which are the most common. *See id.* at 24-28.

China is hoping that forests can provide a buffering effect against a different type of natural disaster: dust storms. During the spring of 2006, Beijing experienced record dust storms, which have been aggravated in recent years by desertification. China now intends to build the Green Wall of China — a 4,500-kilometer-long forest, which it hopes will help protect settled areas from windstorms that sweep in from the Gobi Desert. *See id.* at 43.

Congress has also recognized that forests can play an important role in reducing floods. In fact, one of the primary reasons Congress authorized the creation of national forests in the 1800s was because of the fear that ravaged forests might disappear, taking with them critical watersheds that "encourage stream flows while preventing floods." United States v. New Mexico, 438 U.S. 696, 705 (1978).

Interfering with natural processes that shape our green infrastructure also can have unintended consequences for disaster risk. For fifty years, the U.S. Forest Service engaged in a total fire suppression policy and allowed forests to grow unchecked by natural fires that normally remove small vegetation and dead wood. *See* Evan N. Turgeon, Federal Forests, *Biomass, and Ethanol: Energy Security Sabotaged*, 39 ENVTL. L. REP. NEWS & ANALYSIS 10140, 10141 (2009). Fire suppression eventually created older, denser forests containing extremely high quantities of fuel and posing a much higher risk of catastrophic fire. *See id.* When the number of forest acres burned annually nearly quadrupled in the 1990s, the U.S. General Accounting Office reported that "[s]cientists and agency officials believe that this increase in large, intense, uncontrollable, and catastrophically destructive wildfires is in large part the result of the Forest Service's decades-old policy of putting out wildfires on national forests." U.S. GENERAL ACCOUNTING OFFICE, REPORT TO THE SUBCOMMITTEE ON FORESTS AND FOREST HEALTH, COMMITTEE ON RESOURCES, HOUSE OF REPRESENTATIVES, WESTERN NATIONAL FORESTS: A COHESIVE STRATEGY IS NEEDED TO ADDRESS CATASTROPHIC WILDFIRE THREATS 4 (1999). Furthermore, logging, road building, and livestock grazing have altered natural forest structure and consequently increased the risk of wildfires. *See* Rebecca K Smith, *War on Wildfire: The U.S. Forest Service's Fire Suppression Policy and Its Legal, Scientific, and Political Context*, 15 U. BALT. J. ENVTL. L. 25, 38 (2007).

c. Strategies for Protecting Green Infrastructure

Why have we underinvested in green infrastructure protection and what strategies could be employed to correct this market failure? Consider this approach, from a recent United Nations Report:

UNITED NATIONS, 2009 GLOBAL ASSESSMENT REPORT ON
DISASTER RISK REDUCTION: RISK AND POVERTY IN A CHANGING CLIMATE

162-165

The management of ecosystem services

6.4.1 Approaches to ecosystem management

Resilient ecosystems are not only important for reducing disaster risks. They are critical to providing for sustainable livelihoods, in securing a reliable flow of goods and services, and in reducing vulnerability to an increasingly unpredictable climate. Building ecosystem resilience requires actions at different scales, with a wide array of stakeholders, and an understanding that different bodies of knowledge, including scientific, technical and local and traditional, are needed to understand the effects of global environmental change on local ecosystems.

The global decline in many regulating and provisioning ecosystem services contributes to increasing hazard for poor urban and rural households as well as declining livelihood resilience. From this perspective, ecosystem management is an emerging practice that can potentially contribute both to the regulation of weather-related hazards as well as to the strengthening of livelihoods. . . .

In the case of ecosystem restoration, the avoided costs may significantly exceed the restoration costs. For example, planting and protecting 12,000 ha of mangroves by the IFRC in Viet Nam cost approximately US$ 1 million but reduced the costs of sea dyke maintenance by US$ 7.3 million per year. At the same time, the co-benefits may also greatly exceed the opportunity costs. For example, the Millennium Ecosystem Assessment estimated that the value of healthy coastal mangroves as nurseries, pollution filters and coastal defences is US$ 1,000 to US$ 36,000 for mangrove value versus US$ 200 per hectare for shrimp farming. In Malaysia, the economic value of mangroves as coastal defences has been estimated at US$ 300,000 per kilometre, taking into account the costs of hard engineering work to achieve the same protective effect. In Switzerland, the economic value of forests in preventing avalanches is valued at US$ 100 per hectare per year in open areas but up to US$ 170,000 in areas with high-value assets.

At the same time, ecosystems often provide important co-benefits if properly managed. Some of the most fertile agricultural land on the planet depends on regular flooding to recharge the soil with nutrients. Flooding can also recharge aquifers in semi-arid areas or transport vital sediments and nutrients to sustain coastal fisheries in other areas. Periodic fire is vital to the health of some forest ecosystems. In these cases the co-benefits of protecting the ecosystem usually outweigh the opportunity costs. The best examples of ecosystem management are win-win strategies that simultaneously reduce hazard and increase livelihood viability for poor households, while providing broader global co-benefits in areas such as water and energy supply, air quality and climate regulation.

Managing the provision of ecosystem services is complicated for many reasons. While the benefits may appear obvious they are often shared by many people over the long term. Ensuring that private interests do not degrade these social benefits requires effective and long-term institutional, legal and administrative systems backed up with the resources and political support to be respected. There are many opportunities to engineer ecosystems to provide multiple ecosystem services. However, engineering ecosystems to ensure that they optimally produce services that are produced and consumed by different social groups and economic and political interests at different scales is usually a daunting governance challenge. Nevertheless, there are a number of different practices that applied appropriately or in combination can facilitate ecosystem management in a way that does reduce hazard and strengthen livelihoods.

6.4.2 Environmental governance

The broad area of environmental governance involves creating policy and regulatory frameworks and institutional structures to promote environmental sustainability. Often these frameworks specify levels of environmental protection and call for means to monitor and enforce that protection. One of the best known and most widely applied tools is the use of Environmental Impact Assessments (EIA) in project and investment planning and approval. Disaster risk considerations are now increasingly factored into EIAs. . . .

6.4.3 Integrated planning

Integrated planning, in which both environmental and disaster risk considerations are factored into land use and development planning, is another mechanism that can facilitate the management of ecosystems. This includes integrated coastal zone management, integrated water resource management, as well as specific initiatives such as the Mangroves for the Future initiative — a multi-country, multi-agency, multi-stakeholder initiative aimed at improving coastal zone management. The success of integrated planning is closely associated with the quality of governance and in most countries success has depended, as in other areas, on innovative partnerships between national agencies, local governments and civil society.

6.4.4 Protected areas

Protected areas legislation, and other methods of natural resource management to conserve and restore ecosystems, is another relevant tool. The promotion of natural floodplains and wetlands as cost effective measures for flood hazard mitigation is becoming increasingly accepted in a number of countries as an alternative to expensive hard-engineering measures such as canalizing rivers and building flood defence walls. Protected forests regulate the water cycle, can mitigate flood and drought hazard and contribute to the sustainability of rural livelihoods both through the provision of forest products as well as eco-tourism. Coastal afforestation and the protection and restoration of mangroves can complement sea walls to protect erosion prone coastlines.

6.4.5 Environmental technology

A range of new environmental technologies and innovations is being introduced by the private sector, NGOs and public sector initiatives that offer new soft or eco-engineering approaches to the management of ecosystems and hazards and of energy, as well as to the strengthening of rural and urban livelihoods. Examples include technologies for water harvesting in drought prone areas, for managing temperature extremes in housing, fuel efficient stoves aimed to limit deforestation, decentralized microhydro and solar energy, and countless others. While the potential of technological innovation is enormous, major cultural and economic barriers often exist to their adoption by risk-averse poor rural and urban communities. As a result, while pilot projects abound, cases of mainstreaming and up-scaling are still the exception.

6.4.6 Payment for ecosystem services

Payment for ecosystem services (PES) is an environmental management tool that has been in existence since the 1990s. It involves placing a monetary value upon ecosystem services and then finding both 'buyers' and 'sellers.' The costs and benefits of the different kinds of provisioning, regulatory and cultural ecosystem services are valued and systems are designed so that users pay for the services provided. For example, a protected watershed provides water for domestic consumption and hydro-energy for a nearby city but if the watershed were deforested for logging this would provide benefits for those who sold the wood. If logged, the costs in terms of reduced availability and more expensive water and electricity would be paid for by the residents of the city. Using a PES approach, the opportunity costs of protecting the watershed would be paid for by water and electricity consumers (predominantly from peri-urban and urban areas), who receive co-benefits in terms of a secure and cheap supply of water and energy. PES could therefore potentially play a major role in supporting efforts to reduce hazard both in urban and rural areas as well as to increase rural livelihood sustainability. . . .

However, the mainstreaming of PES is still in its infancy and many current PES programmes present serious obstacles to the inclusion of poor households, given that they were originally designed to meet conservation rather than poverty reduction goals. The policy attention in many countries is indeed now shifting to identifying reforms needed to increase the potential of PES for poverty reduction and even in their current imperfect form, PES programs have managed to deliver some important benefits to low-income households, including the penetration of new markets for sustainable timber, organic coffee and other agroforestry products. Like other forms of environmental income, PES may not be sufficient in itself to raise rural households out of poverty, but it can become an important contributor to livelihood security due to the regularity of the payments and the incentive they provide to manage sustainable ecosystems. . . .

NOTES AND QUESTIONS

1. As the report mentions, the benefits of preserving natural infrastructure may be obvious, but they are often long-term benefits shared by a diffuse group of people. What challenges are posed when the benefits of preserving a resource are widely shared by many who do not own the resource but the costs of preserving the resource (or refraining from exploiting it) are concentrated on the owner? See the discussion of externalities in the privatization section, *supra*, and the built infrastructure section, *infra*. Which of these strategies for protecting green infrastructure might make sense in the United States?

2. To what extent do U.S. laws requiring Environmental Impact Statements mandate that agencies consider the effect of natural infrastructure loss on disaster risk? The National Environmental Policy Act (NEPA) requires that a federal agency undertaking a "major Federal action significantly affecting the quality of the human environment" provide an Environmental Impact

Statement. 42 U.S.C. §4332(C) (2009). The agency is required to determine both direct and indirect effects that are "reasonably foreseeable," Metro Edison Co. v. People Against Nuclear Energy, 460 U.S. 766, 774 (1983); "[i]ndirect effects may include growth inducing effects and other effects related to induced changes in the pattern of land use, population density or growth rate, and related effects on air and water and other natural systems, including ecosystems." 40 C.F.R. §1508.8. Do these requirements adequately focus the agency's attention on disaster mitigation? *Cf.* Katherine Hausrath, *Tough Love: Should We Analyze Federal Emergency Management Agency Disaster Planning under the National Environmental Policy Act?*, 13 Hastings W.-Nw. J. Envtl. L. & Pol'y 161 (2007), 178-182 (arguing that the National Flood Insurance Program and the National Hurricane Program should require EISs, because FEMA's planning is a major federal action significantly affecting the environment; the programs do not meet an established exception; and preparing an EIS would fulfill the purposes of NEPA by allowing the public the benefit of a full analysis before moving into hurricane- or flood-prone areas). After a disaster has already occurred, some federal actions are exempted from EIS requirements by the Stafford Act, *see, e.g.,* 42 U.S.C. §5159 (2009) (exempting from NEPA an action that restores a "facility substantially to its condition prior to the disaster or emergency"), or by regulatory procedures, *see, e.g.,* 44 C.F.R. §10.8 (2009); FEMA, Alternative Arrangements to Meet NEPA Requirements for Reconstruction of New Orleans 1, available at http://www.fema.gov/pdf/plan/ehp/noma/alt_arr_nepa.pdf (providing "alternative arrangements" for numerous post-Katrina grant applications, which truncated the NEPA process).

3. One of the problems of preserving green infrastructure is that a wide number of resource users will want to use it for other purposes (and often using it means consuming it). Compare this to other infrastructure that is generally built for a specific purpose. *See* Brigham Daniels, *Emerging Commons and Tragic Institutions*, 37 Envtl. L. 515 (2007) ("It is somewhat troubling—a paradox of preservation—that the more a commons is preserved for less consumptive uses, the more attractive it might seem to those who would use the commons for more consumptive uses: the more a commons is preserved, the more it becomes a target."). For example, if a community is successful in preventing development of floodplains in the short term, over time they may become particularly attractive for development because they constitute large, contiguous open tracts of lands, which may otherwise be in short supply.

2. BUILT INFRASTRUCTURE

Like our green infrastructure, much of the infrastructure built to protect us against disaster—such as levees—has been neglected and poorly maintained. Some levees, including those that were supposed to protect New Orleans, were poorly designed and constructed in the first instance. Others have deteriorated over time. In addition, other infrastructure whose failure could result in disaster—such as dams—has likewise been poorly maintained.

a. Levees

The failure of the flood protection system of levees and floodwalls surrounding New Orleans has been described as a catastrophic engineering failure. The Interagency Performance Evaluation Task Force (IPET), created by the U.S. Army Corps of Engineers and staffed by distinguished government, academic, and private sector scientists and engineers, concluded that approximately half of the direct losses from Katrina flooding could have been avoided if levees and floodwalls had not breached. IPET, PERFORMANCE EVALUATION OF THE NEW ORLEANS AND SOUTHEAST LOUISIANA HURRICANE PROTECTION SYSTEM: FINAL REPORT OF THE INTERAGENCY PERFORMANCE EVALUATION TASK FORCE, Volume 1, Executive Summary and Overview, June 1, 2008, I-5, available at ipet.wes.army.mil (June 5, 2009); *see also* R.B. Seed et al., *Investigation of the Performance of the New Orleans Flood Protection Systems in Hurricane Katrina on August 29, 2005* xix-xx (Final Report), July 31, 2006, (explaining that one of the root causes of the flooding was "poor performance of the flood protection system, due to localized engineering failures, questionable judgments, errors, etc. involved in the detailed design, construction, operation and maintenance of the system"), available at http://works.bepress.com/rmoss/17.

The Army Corp of Engineers, which constructed the levees, has itself acknowledged that design and construction flaws contributed to the levees' failure. *See* John Schwartz, *Army Corps Admits Flaws in New Orleans Levees*, N.Y. TIMES, June 1, 2006. Consider this excerpt from the IPET Report:

IPET, PERFORMANCE EVALUATION OF THE NEW ORLEANS AND SOUTHEAST LOUISIANA HURRICANE PROTECTION SYSTEM: FINAL REPORT OF THE INTERAGENCY PERFORMANCE EVALUATION TASK FORCE, VOLUME 1, EXECUTIVE SUMMARY AND OVERVIEW

(June 1, 2008), I-2 to I-3, ipet.wes.army.mil (June 5, 2009)

The System

The system did not perform as a system. In some areas it was not completed, and in others, datum misinterpretation and subsidence reduced its intended protective elevation. The capacity for protection varied because of some structures that provided no reliable protection above their design elevations and others that had inadequate designs leaving them vulnerable at water elevations significantly below the design intent. The designs of the levee-floodwall structures along the outfall canals were particularly inadequate. A series of incremental decisions . . . systematically increased the inherent risk in the system without recognition or acknowledgment.

The Storm

Katrina created record surge and wave conditions along the east side of New Orleans and the coast of Mississippi. Peak water levels along the Plaquemines and St. Bernard levees and within the Inner Harbor Navigation Canal (IHNC) were significantly higher than the structures leading to massive overtopping and eventually breaching. Wave heights during Katrina were typically similar to those assumed for the design of the structures, except for Plaquemines

Parish where they were higher than the design assumptions. Wave periods, however, were three times longer than the design assumptions, particularly along the east side of St. Bernard and Plaquemines Parishes. The longer period, more energetic waves created much greater potential for runup and overtopping. Conditions within Lake Pontchartrain were roughly equal to the design criteria for the shoreline structures. The Mississippi River Gulf Outlet (MRGO) channel, presumed to be a major factor in propagating storm surge into the IHNC, was demonstrated to have little impact on storm water levels for large storms.

The Performance

With the exception of four foundation design failures, all of the major breaches were caused by overtopping and subsequent erosion. Reduced protective elevations increased the amount of overtopping, erosion, and subsequent flooding, particularly in Orleans East. Ironically, the structures that ultimately breached performed as designed, providing protection until overtopping occurred and then becoming vulnerable to catastrophic breaching. The levee-floodwall designs for the 17th Street and London Avenue Outfall Canals and IHNC were inadequate for the complex and challenging environment. In four cases the structures failed catastrophically prior to water reaching design elevations. A significant number of structures that were subjected to water levels beyond their design limits performed well. Typically, in the case of floodwalls, they represented more conservative design assumptions and, for levees, use of higher quality, less erodible materials.

The Consequences

Approximately 80% of New Orleans was flooded, in many areas with depth of flooding exceeding 15 ft. The majority, approximately two-thirds overall in areas such as Orleans East Bank and St. Bernard, of the flooding and half of the economic losses can be attributed to water flowing through breaches in floodwalls and levees. There were at least 727 fatalities in the five parishes in and around New Orleans, and over 70% of the fatalities were people over age 70. The poor, elderly, and disabled, the groups least likely to be able to evacuate without assistance, were disproportionately impacted. Direct property losses exceeded $20 billion, and 78% of those losses were in residential areas. There was an additional loss of over $7 billion in public structures and utilities. . . . Where water depths were small, recovery has been almost complete. In areas where water depths were greater, little recovery or reinvestment has taken place.

The Army Corps of Engineers is now rebuilding New Orleans' levee system to provide 100-year protection to New Orleans, a level that many experts feel is wholly inadequate for an urban area. *See* Report: Post-Katrina Levees Not Strong Enough (April 24, 2009), http://www.msnbc.com/id/30391989/. Most of the country's other levees are receiving even less attention and are also in dire need of renovation, repair, or replacement. In 2009, the American

Society of Civil Engineers Report Card for America's Infrastructure gave America's more than 100,000 miles of levees a "D" (poor) grade and estimated that it will cost more than $100 billion to rehabilitate the nation's levees. *See* ASCE 2009 REPORT CARD FOR AMERICA'S INFRASTRUCTURE 40-41 [hereinafter 2009 REPORT CARD]. Moreover, as of 2009, the Army Corps of Engineers lists 114 levees participating in its levee safety program that pose an unacceptable risk of failure. *See* http://www.usace.army.mil/CEPA/FactSheets/Pages/LeveeSafetyProgram. aspx. This list does not include levees that previously failed inspections and either did not make necessary repairs or did not do so quickly enough to maintain eligibility for the levee safety program (and concomitant eligibility for federal rehabilitation funds for levee repair after flooding occurs). *See id.*

A number of factors contribute to the wholly unsatisfactory state of the nation's levees. First, there is neither a comprehensive inventory of existing levees nor any systematic program for assessing the condition of the more than 85 percent of levees that are locally owned. *See id.* at 40, 42. The Water Resources Development Act of 2007, passed by Congress in response to Hurricane Katrina, requires the U.S. Army Corps of Engineers, FEMA, and DHS to develop a joint database, inventorying all federal levees, as well as non-federal levees for which state and local governments voluntarily provide information. *See* Pub. L. No. 110-114, §9004, 121 Stat. 1041, 1290 (codified at 33 U.S.C. §3303). Little information has been reported about non-federal levees. Just ten states inventory levees within their borders, and only twenty-three states have tasked an agency to manage levee safety. *See id.* at 42. Of the inventoried federal levees, 177 (approximately 9%) "are expected to fail in a flood event." *Id.* at 42.

Second, the National Flood Insurance Program requires mandatory flood insurance for federally backed mortgages on properties located in Special Flood Hazard Areas, defined as those with a 1% annual chance of a flood event (also referred to as a "100-year flood"); properties protected by "100-year flood" levees are exempt from the mandatory insurance requirements. *Id.* at 43. Thus, the "100-year flood" standard, which was not intended as a safety standard, "became the target design level for many levees because it allowed development to continue while providing relief from mandatory flood insurance purchase for homeowners living behind accredited levees." *Id.* at 43-44. This level of protection not only is arguably inadequate (and based on insufficient, old data), but also creates a false sense of security about flood risk for those who live behind the levees and are unaware of the significant (even catastrophic) residual risk they would face if the levees were overtopped or breached. Many people believe that a "100-year flood" is likely to be a rare event, when — in fact — there is a 26 percent chance that it will occur in the span of a 30-year mortgage. *Id.* at 43.

Third, most existing levees were originally designed and engineered to protect cropland from flooding; development and population has exploded in the shadow of many such levees, which now are the fragile bulwark between floods and people. In 1997 alone, more than fifty California levees failed, leading to eight fatalities, damaging or destroying 24,000 homes, and forcing the evacuation of over 100,000 people. *See* John Ritter, *Several Cities Dependent on Vulnerable Levees*, U.S.A. TODAY, Sept. 11, 2005. Lester Snow, Director of the

California Department of Water Resources characterized California's network of levee as "an old, aging system that instead of protecting farmland is actually protecting small cities" and reported that "levees of questionable integrity [are] protecting higher value real estate." *Id.*

Although most levees that protect significant urban populations are owned by federal, state, or local governments, some are privately owned. As described *supra*, private levee owners often lack adequate incentives to maintain (or strengthen) their levees because many of the risks posed by unsafe levees are external to the owner — that is, a levee failure will likely impose costs on many community members, not just the levee owner. These security externalities result in insufficient investment in levee safety.

b. Dams

As with levees, we neglect dam design and maintenance at our peril. The 1976 Teton Dam disaster — described as "one of the most colossal and dramatic failures in our national history" — demonstrates the deadly and costly consequences of dam failure. The disaster claimed 11 lives, killed approximately 13,000 head of livestock, and caused damages estimated as high as $2 billion. Eric A. Stene, The Teton Basin Project (Bureau of Reclamation History Program 1995), available at http://www.usbr.gov/dataweb/html/teton.html (quoting *Teton Dam Disaster: Hearings before a Subcomm. of the Comm. on Government Operations, H.R.*, 94th Cong. 1 (1976) (statement of Congressman Leo J. Ryan, Subcomm. Chairman)). The dam breached on June 5, 1976, less than seven months after the U.S. Department of Interior's Bureau of Reclamation completed its construction and before it was ever filled to capacity. *See id.* Once the reservoir broke through, the earthen dam released 250,000 acre-feet of water within six hours, Timothy J. Randle et al., Geomorphology and River Hydraulics of the Teton River Upstream of Teton Dam, Teton River, Idaho 6 (2000), washing away the embankment and damaging 427,000 acres of farmland. Stene, *supra*. The following day, President Gerald Ford declared the five surrounding counties to be a federal disaster area. *Id.* In addition to repair costs, the federal government eventually paid out more than $300 million in claims to flood survivors. *Id.*

Whatever the cause of the dam's breach — experts cite design flaws, inadequate planning, "goal-oriented" risk assessments, and poor site selection as likely contributors, *id.* — the disaster underscores the need for vigilance in dam construction and maintenance. Like levees, U.S. dams received a "D" rating from the American Society of Civil Engineers 2009 Report Card for America's Infrastructure, which estimated that the United States needs to invest more than $12.5 billion in dam infrastructure over the next five years, 2009 Report Card, *supra*, at 15, a number which nevertheless falls far short of the $50 billion the Association of State Dam Safety Officials has estimated is necessary to repair the nation's dams, *id.* at 20. A primary driver of this near-failing grade is the ever-increasing number of "high hazard potential" dams (failure of which is anticipated to cause loss of life) that are deficient and in need of repair. In 2001, there were 498 high-hazard dams judged to be deficient; by 2007, that number had risen to 1,826. *Id.* at 17 (chart). Moreover, the report concludes that the total number of high-hazard-potential dams "is also increasing at an alarming rate, now totaling 15,237," largely as a result of new development beneath dams. *Id.* at 16. Indeed, as is the case with levees, many aging dams originally built to shelter (and provide irrigation water for) agricultural lands are now being pressed into service to protect large population centers. *See id.* at 21-22. The number of newly designated high-hazard-potential dams in need of repair is thus far outpacing the rate at which dam repairs are being made.

The U.S. Army Corps of Engineers maintains a national inventory of the more than 85,000 dams in the United States. *See id.* at 16. However, only 11 percent of dams are regulated or owned by the federal government, and thus the primary onus for dam maintenance and repair falls to the states. *See id.* In 1996, Congress established the National Dam Safety Program, administered by FEMA, to provide grants and technical assistance to establish state dam safety programs. *See* Pub. L. No. 104-303, §8, 110 Stat. 3658, 3658 (codified at 33 U.S.C. 467(f) (2006)); 2009 Report Card, *supra*, at 18. Although every state except Alabama now has a formal dam safety program, most are insufficiently funded and staffed. *See id.* at 16. Additionally, some states have laws which exempt many dams from inspection. Missouri, for example, exempts 740 high-hazard dams because they are less than thirty-five feet high. *Id.* Although modest improvements have been made in state programs, some 30 percent of high-hazard dams have not been inspected in the last five years, and 50 percent of high-hazard dams lack Emergency Action Plans, which specify actions to be taken in the event of dam failure. *See id.* at 18.

In addition to dams and levees, other aging infrastructure originally built for agricultural purposes now threatens growing communities. On January 5, 2008, a century-old irrigation canal burst in Fernley, Nevada, flooding more than 600 homes with frigid water. When the canal was built in 1903, Fernley's population was 654; in 2008, it was approximately 20,000. See Scott Sonner, *Floods Prompt Review of Canals*, Hayward Daily Rev., April 5, 2008.

c. Buildings and Building Codes

States have the power to enact building codes setting forth minimum standards for building construction or rehabilitation. States have exercised this power in divergent ways: Some have exercised the authority themselves to enact state building codes; many have delegated the power to local governments. See http://www.disastersafety.org/building_codes/map.asp?state= AR#results (cataloguing state and local adoption of building codes). Even those states that have statewide building codes may allow local modification of the codes. Whether it is the state or a local entity doing the regulating, most jurisdictions adopt a model building code and may tailor it, by amendment, to the particular hazards of the area. Prior to 1994, there were three primary model building codes; now those codes have been merged into the model International Building Code.

There is much debate about the need for state-led code adoption and enforcement. Proposed legislation would amend the Stafford Act to encourage states to adopt and actively enforce federally approved, statewide building codes by making states that do so eligible for more post-disaster hazard mitigation grant money. *See, e.g.*, Disaster Response, Recovery, and Mitigation Enhancement Act of 2009, H.R. 3377, 111th Cong. §201.

Recent earthquakes have demonstrated the close connection between the quality and design of buildings and earthquake mortality. On May 12, 2008, a 7.9-magnitude earthquake struck China's southwestern Sichuan province, killing more than 68,000 people (nearly 18,000 were still officially listed as missing one year later). At least 5,335 of the dead were schoolchildren, who were attending class in shoddily built schools at the time the earthquake hit. *See The Sichuan Earthquake: Salt in Their Wounds*, Economist, May 16, 2009, at 48. Other structures—including hospitals and factories—that shot up during China's recent building boom also collapsed, calling into question the enforcement of earthquake building codes instituted after more than 240,000 died in the 1976 Tangshan earthquake. Chinese law now requires that hospitals and schools be built to withstand 8.0-magnitude earthquakes. *See id.* (The Sichuan earthquake may, in fact, have been caused by other built infrastructure: a growing number of scientists believe the quake was triggered by the four-year-old Zipingpu Reservoir, which housed more than 320 million tons of water less than a mile from the fault. *See* Sharon LaFraniere, *Possible Link between Dam and China Quake*, N.Y. Times, Feb. 6, 2009, at A1.) On April 6, 2009, a 6.3-magnitude quake in L'Aquila, Italy, claimed nearly 300 lives, left some 50,000 homeless, and destroyed not only storied medieval churches but also modern buildings, including a University of L'Aquila dormitory and L'Aquila's new hospital, completed in 2000. *See* Silvia Aloisi, *Italy Quake Exposes Poor Building Standards*, Reuters, Apr. 7, 2009, available at http://www.alertnet.org/thenews/newsdesk/L7932819.htm (June 7, 2009).

Seismic building codes were widely adopted in the western United States in the 1970s and gained traction in the eastern United States in the 1990s. Much of the current controversy over the disaster resilience of U.S. buildings focuses on the extent to which older buildings should be retrofitted to meet current building standards. Certain types of older buildings are particularly vulnerable to collapse in earthquakes. For example, structures with bearing walls constructed from unreinforced masonry (bricks or blocks held together by mortar only, with no steel or other reinforcement) have performed poorly in past earthquakes. Although California banned construction of unreinforced masonry buildings (URMs) after 1933, California has approximately 25,900 existing URMs in its highest earthquake zone (Seismic Zone 4). California Seismic Safety Commission, 2006 Report to the Legislature, Status of the Unreinforced Masonry Building Law (Nov. 2006) 2, available at http://www.seismic.ca.gov/pub.html, June 10, 2009. The cost of retrofitting these buildings was estimated in the 1980s at approximately $4 billion. *See id.* at 3.

In 1986, California passed the Unreinforced Masonry Building Law, which required local building departments in Seismic Zone 4 to (1) inventory unreinforced masonry construction buildings built before adoption of local building codes requiring earthquake resistant design, Cal. Gov. Code §§ 8875, 8875.2(a); (2) establish a mitigation program for those buildings, *id.* §8875.2(b); and (3) report progress to the California Seismic Commission. Although the mitigation program may include strengthening and demolishing buildings, and other measures, the only mandatory measure is notifying the building's owner of the hazard. *See id.* Overall, the law has been quite effective in encouraging retrofitting of URMs: as of 2006, 70 percent of California's URMs had been either retrofitted or demolished. 2006 REPORT TO THE LEGISLATURE, *supra*, at 9. Some California localities have been very proactive in retrofitting unreinforced masonry buildings. For instance, by 2005, all but one of Los Angeles' 8,700 URMs had been retrofitted or demolished. *See* Chong & Becerra, *supra*, at A2. Rates of retrofitting/demolition are unsurprisingly much higher in local jurisdictions that mandate retrofitting (86% of URMS retrofitted/demolished), as compared to those jurisdictions that require owners to assess earthquake risk but make retrofitting voluntary (24%) or to jurisdictions that provide notice only (13%). 2006 REPORT TO THE LEGISLATURE, *supra*, at 7.

Many other western states with high seismicity have been less proactive in pursuing retrofitting. (According to the U.S. Geological Survey, the ten states with the most earthquakes are: Alaska, California, Hawaii, Nevada, Washington, Idaho, Wyoming, Montana, Utah, and Oregon. See http://earthquake.usgs.gov/regional/states/top_states.php [June 10, 2009]). For example, as of 2006, Utah had some 200,000 unreinforced masonry buildings (including single family homes, which were largely excluded from California's retrofitting efforts). Lee Davidson, *Shaken to Pieces*, DESERET NEWS, April 25, 2006. More than 80 percent of Utah's population is clustered along the Wasatch Front, "an extremely active seismic zone." FEMA, HAZUS-MH Used in Support of Utah Seismic Safety Legislation, www.fema.gov/plan/prevent/hazus (June 10, 2009). Modeling of a 7.0-magnitude daytime earthquake along the Wasatch Front predicted more than 6,000 deaths, 80 percent of which were caused by URMs. *Id.* In response, Utah's legislature passed a 2008 joint resolution "urging" Utah's Seismic Safety Commission to inventory unreinforced masonry buildings and recommend mitigation priorities, *see* Utah H.J.R. 7 (2008 General Session), but it has not taken any more definitive action. As of June 2009, Seattle, which has an estimated 1,000 URMs, was considering adoption of a city ordinance that would require retrofitting. *See* http://www.seattle.gov/dpd/Emergency/UnreinforcedMasonryBuildings/default.asp (June 10, 2009). The Nevada legislature passed a bill that would have required inventorying URMs, but the governor vetoed it on the grounds that it would be an unfunded mandate to cities. Assem. 326, 2007 Leg., 74th Sess. (Nev. 2007); NEVADA EARTHQUAKE SAFETY COUNCIL, 2007 ANNUAL REPORT, available at www.nbmg.unr.edu/nesc/2007annualreport.pdf (June 10, 2009).

Other types of structures — including those made from "non-ductile reinforced concrete" and "soft story wood-frame buildings" also are at serious risk during earthquakes. "In terms of the relative risk factor, URM and non-ductile buildings (without seismic retrofit) are at least 20 times more 'risky' than other buildings, on average." KIRCHER ET AL., *supra*. Past earthquakes have also exposed the vulnerability of "soft-story" buildings, which have a weak, inadequately braced lower story, such as homes or apartment buildings built over garages. Of the 16,000 housing units rendered uninhabitable by the Loma Prieta earthquake, 7,700 were soft-story residential buildings. CAL. HEALTH & SAFETY CODE §19160(g). The 1994 Northridge earthquake destroyed 34,000 soft-story housing units, *id.*, many of them multistory residential buildings with tuck-under garages.

NOTES AND QUESTIONS

1. To what standard should older buildings, such as URMs, be retrofitted? Only to the level that protects human life and safety? Or to a level that preserves the building and limits economic loss? In making this calculation, does it matter what percentage of the city's housing or building stock is made up of vulnerable buildings? For example, one survey found that approximately 50 percent of San Francisco single-family wood residences and 70 percent of multifamily wood residences had a soft story. KIRCHER ET AL., *supra*. Another report suggests that a major earthquake could destroy 25 percent of San Francisco's building stock. Is there some danger that loss of housing in a major San Francisco earthquake would reach a "tipping point," such that the city would have great difficulty recovering? *See* Memorandum, Advisory Committee, Community Action Plan for Seismic Safety, Incentives to Encourage Seismic Retrofits: Options for San Francisco (Sept. 5, 2008), available at http://www.seattle.gov/dpd/Emergency/UnreinforcedMasonryBuildings/ ReportsandMaterials/default.asp (June 10, 2009). How should historic preservation be taken into account when establishing retrofit standards? *Cf.* Michael Wines, *To Protect an Ancient City, China Moves to Raze It*, N.Y. TIMES, May 27, 2009 (reporting China's plans to raze the ancient Silk Road city of Kashgar, ostensibly to protect residents from earthquake risks posed by centuries-old buildings).

2. Florida's experience with Hurricane Andrew in 1992 demonstrates that even the strictest of building codes will do little good if it is not vigorously enforced. Although the South Florida Building Code had some deficiencies, it was thought to be one of the most hurricane resistant in the country, requiring design standards that would withstand a 120–mile-per-hour wind. Nevertheless, even though Andrew's wind speeds did not significantly exceed 120 miles per hour, Florida's homes and buildings suffered massive damage. Investigations lay much of the blame on insufficient inspections (Dade County employed so few building inspectors that each was required to inspect approximately thirty-five buildings a day), concessions to builders in the enforcement of code provisions, building styles that were not well suited to hurricanes, and poor workmanship (which was not adequately regulated). MILETI, *supra*, at 128-131.

E. CLIMATE CHANGE

When political satirist Bill Maher interviewed Stanford climate scientist Stephen Schneider, Maher queried: "Did we put our hurricanes on steroids?" Schneider agreed it was an apt question. What will be the effects of climate change on disaster risk and costs? One important consequence of climate change for disaster risk is the increase in weather extremes:

> Changes in extreme weather and climate events have significant impacts and are among the most serious challenges to society in coping with a changing climate.

Many extremes and their associated impacts are now changing. For example, in recent decades most of North America has been experiencing more unusually hot days and nights, fewer unusually cold days and nights, and fewer frost days. Heavy downpours have become more frequent and intense. Droughts are becoming more severe in some regions, though there are no clear trends for North America as a whole. The power and frequency of Atlantic hurricanes have increased substantially in recent decades, though North American mainland land-falling hurricanes do not appear to have increased over the past century. Outside the tropics storm tracks are shifting northward and the strongest storms are becoming even stronger.

It is well established through formal attribution studies that the global warming of the past 50 years is due primarily to human-induced increases in heat-trapping gases. Such studies have only recently been used to determine the causes of some changes in extremes at the scale of a continent. Certain aspects of observed increases in temperature extremes have been linked to human influences. The increase in heavy precipitation events is associated with an increase in water vapor; and the latter has been attributed to human-induced warming. No formal attribution studies for changes in drought severity in North America have been attempted. There is evidence suggesting a human contribution to recent changes in hurricane activity as well as in storms outside the tropics, though a confident assessment will require further study.

In the future, with continued global warming, heat waves and heavy downpours are very likely to further increase in frequency and intensity. Substantial areas of North America are likely to have more frequent droughts of greater severity. Hurricane wind speeds, rainfall intensity, and storm surge levels are likely to increase. The strongest cold season storms are likely to become more frequent, with stronger winds and more extreme wave heights.

Current and future impacts resulting from these changes depend not only on the changes in extremes, but also on response by human and natural systems.

U.S. CLIMATE CHANGE SCIENCE PROGRAM 2008 REPORT: WEATHER AND CLIMATE EXTREMES IN A CHANGING CLIMATE 1, available at http://www.climatescience.gov/Library/sap/sap3-3/final-report/(June 15, 2009).

NOTES AND QUESTIONS

1. Although it seems likely that climate change will increase variability and weather extremes, uncertainty about how climate change may affect any given locality may make planning for climate change effects difficult. For example, two of the major modeling centers for climate change impacts have predicted opposite trajectories for the U.S. Southwest: one model predicts that the Southwest will get wetter, whereas the other predicts that it will get drier. *See* Soroosh Sorooshian, Presentation to Straw Bale Forum, Hat Ranch, Williams, AZ, Climate Variability, Water Resources, and Urban Growth in the Southwest (July 16, 2008).

2. Another impact of climate change that will substantially affect disaster risk is sea level rise. As a U.S. Climate Change Science Program Report explains, "Projections of sea-level rise for the twenty-first century vary widely, ranging from several centimeters to more than a meter. Rising sea level can

inundate low areas and increase flooding, coastal erosion, wetland loss, and saltwater intrusion into estuaries and freshwater aquifers." U.S. CLIMATE CHANGE SCIENCE PROGRAM AND THE SUBCOMMITTEE ON GLOBAL CHANGE RESEARCH REPORT, COASTAL SENSITIVITY TO SEA-LEVEL RISE: A FOCUS ON THE MID-ATLANTIC REGION IX (2009), available at http://www.climatescience.gov/Library/sap/sap4-1/final-report/default.htm#finalreport (June 15, 2009). More intense storms plus sea level rise could deliver a serious one-two punch to America's coastal regions.

3. As of June 2009, the United States did not have specific greenhouse gas regulation. The United States failed to ratify the Kyoto Protocol, an international treaty requiring emission reduction of six greenhouse gases: carbon dioxide, methane, nitrous oxide, sulfur hexafluoride, hydrofluorocarbons, and perfluorocarbons, Kyoto Protocol to the United Nations Framework Convention on Climate Change, Dec. 11, 1997, 2303 U.N.T.S. 148, in part because developing countries that are also major polluters, such as China and India, were not required to meet similar reduction standards. *See* Todd M. Lopez, *A Look at Climate Change and the Evolution of the Kyoto Protocol*, 43 NAT. RESOURCES J. 285, 298 (2003).

However, greenhouse gases are likely to be regulated soon, either under the Clean Air Act or under a future law aimed specifically at greenhouse gases. The Supreme Court held in 2007 that carbon dioxide is an "air pollutant" under the Clean Air Act. Massachusetts v. E.P.A., 549 U.S. 497, 528 (2007). Accordingly, the EPA must regulate carbon dioxide emissions from motor vehicles if it finds that motor vehicle carbon dioxide emissions "contribute[] to air pollution which may reasonably be anticipated to endanger public health or welfare." *Id.* at 532. The Court ultimately instructed the EPA to determine whether greenhouse gases endanger the public. *See id.* at 533.

In April, 2009, the EPA implemented the Court's instructions by making a proposed "endangerment" finding. If finalized, this finding will require the EPA to regulate greenhouse gas emissions. *See* Proposed Endangerment and Cause or Contribute Findings for Greenhouse Gases under Section 202(a) of the Clean Air Act, 74 Fed. Reg. 18886-01 (Apr. 24, 2009). However, the Obama administration has publicly stated that the Clean Air Act is not the right vehicle for regulating greenhouse gases, and the proposed finding did not include specific regulations, which could take months or years to formulate.

Congress is currently considering legislation that may preempt the Clean Air Act's newfound authority over greenhouse gases. The House Committee on Energy and Commerce has proposed the American Clean Energy and Security Act, H.R. 2454, 111th Cong. (2009). If passed, it will be the United States' first comprehensive greenhouse gas legislation, and will create (1) standards for "clean" energy sources and energy efficiency; (2) a federal greenhouse gas cap-and-trade program; and (3) measures offering some protection to consumers, and to energy-intensive industries that may be hurt by a U.S. transition to carbon controls. *See* Svend Brandt-Erichsen et al., *EPA Proposes Regulating Greenhouse Gases under Clean Air Act: Hearing in Seattle on May 21, 2009*, MARTEN LAW GROUP ENVIRONMENTAL NEWS, April 17, 2009, http://www.martenlaw.com/news/?20090417-epa-proposes-regulating-ghg (June 15, 2009). Some Congressional action to regulate greenhouse gases seems likely.

CHAPTER 3

WHO'S IN CHARGE? FEDERAL POWER TO RESPOND TO DISASTER

Disasters present important governance challenges because they rarely respect political and regulatory boundaries. A single disaster can affect multiple localities, states, and even countries. The interjurisdictional nature of disaster problems poses an important question for disaster responders: who is in charge? This chapter and the following one consider some answers to this question, exploring the roles of various actors (federal, state, regional, local, and nongovernmental) in disaster response and highlighting questions of power, capacity, and obligation. This chapter takes up the question of federal constitutional and statutory authority to respond to disasters. Section A begins by considering what constitutional powers the federal government may employ in disaster response. Section B considers the challenges federalism poses for effective disaster response and discusses which levels of government should have responsibility for responding to disasters. Finally, Section C turns to the federal statutory scheme for disaster response, including statutes authorizing federal civilian disaster aid (primarily the Stafford Act), as well as those authorizing—and limiting—the role of the military in disaster response.

A. THE U.S. CONSTITUTION: FEDERAL AND STATE POWER TO RESPOND TO DISASTERS

1. THE CONSTITUTION AND EMERGENCIES

The Constitution makes some provision for emergency situations. Article I, section 8, clause 12 grants Congress the power to raise armies, and Article II, section 2 appoints the President Commander and Chief of those armies. Article IV, section 4 obligates the United States to protect states against invasion and, when requested, against domestic violence. Article I, section 8, clause 15 empowers Congress to call out the militia to repel invasions, quell insurrections, and enforce federal law. Moreover, some provisions of the Constitution explicitly contemplate emergency situations that warrant special rules. For example, Article I, section 10, clause 3 provides: "No State shall, without the Consent of Congress, lay any Duty of Tonnage, keep Troops, or Ships of War in time of Peace . . . or engage in War, *unless actually invaded, or in such imminent Danger as will not admit of delay*" (emphasis added). Article I pledges that "[t]he privilege of the Writ of Habeas Corpus shall not be suspended, *unless when in Cases of Rebellion or Invasion the public Safety may require it.*" U.S. CONST. art. I, §9, cl. 2 (emphasis added). The Third Amendment promises that "[n]o Soldier shall, *in time of peace* be quartered in any house, without the consent of the Owner," but allows quartering soldiers "*in time of war*" according to "a manner to be prescribed by law" (emphases added). Finally, the Fifth Amendment's promise of "presentment or indictment of a Grand Jury" applies neither to "cases arising in the land or naval forces" nor to cases "in the Militia, *when in actual service in time of War or public danger*" (emphasis added).

For the most part, however, the Constitution does not explicitly place emergencies outside of the normal constitutional order. Indeed, the American constitutional tradition has long suspected that "emergency powers . . . tend to kindle emergencies." Youngstown Sheet & Tube Co. v. Sawyer, 343 U.S. 579, 650 (1952) (Jackson, J., concurring). Disasters are thus to be addressed within the ordinary constitutional scheme of government.

That ordinary constitutional scheme is a federal system of government, in which sovereignty is divided between the federal and state governments. As Justice Kennedy observed, "The Framers split the atom of sovereignty." United States Term Limits v. Thornton, 514 U.S. 779, 838 (1995) (Kennedy, J., concurring). The federal government is a government of enumerated powers: it may only exercise those powers that are granted to it by the Constitution. The Tenth Amendment explicitly confirms that "[t]he powers not delegated to the United States by the Constitution, nor prohibited by it to the States, are reserved to the States respectively, or to the people." The states, in contrast, have police power to protect the health, safety, and welfare of their citizens. States therefore have plenary authority to respond to disaster in almost any way, so long as they do not violate constitutional rights and are not legitimately preempted by Congress.

Because the federal government is one of limited powers, federal authority to respond to emergencies must be derived from one of the specific constitutional grants of authority to the federal government. Both political branches of the federal government have general powers that can be invoked in disaster preparedness, mitigation, and response, as well as specific powers that come into play only during a time of crisis. In addition to the constitutional grants of power enumerated below, Congress has the power "[t]o make all Laws which shall be necessary and proper for carrying into Execution the foregoing Powers and all other Powers vested by this Constitution." U.S. CONST. art. I, §8, cl. 18.

2. CONGRESSIONAL AUTHORITY TO RESPOND TO DISASTERS

Commerce Clause Authority. Article I, Section 8, Clause 3 of the Constitution grants Congress the power "[t]o regulate Commerce with foreign Nations, and among the several States." Since the New Deal, Congress's power to regulate interstate commerce has been sweeping. As part of the Rehnquist Court's federalism revival, however, the Supreme Court in the 1990s recognized some limits on Congress's ability to regulate local, noneconomic activity pursuant to its Commerce Clause authority. *See* United States v. Lopez, 514 U.S. 549 (1995) (striking down the Gun Free School Zones Act, which prohibited possession of a firearm in a school zone); United States v. Morrison, 529 U.S. 598 (2000) (striking down a provision of the Violence Against Women Act that granted a civil remedy for victims of private, gender-motivated violence). When Congress is regulating neither the channels nor the instrumentalities of interstate commerce, then Congress may properly exercise its Commerce Clause authority only when "the regulated activity 'substantially affects' interstate commerce." Lopez, 514 U.S. at 559. If the regulated activity is economic in nature, then the "aggregate effect" of similar conduct may be considered when judging the substantiality of the activity's effect on interstate commerce; if the regulated activity is noneconomic, then aggregation may not be allowed. *See* Morrison, 529 U.S. at 617; *see also* Gonzales v. Raich, 545 U.S. 1, 25 (2005) (defining economic activity as the production, distribution, and consumption of commodities). Most major federal statutes that impact disaster mitigation and response (including the major federal disaster statute — the Stafford Act — and federal environmental statutes) can be justified, at least in part, as exercises of Congress's Commerce Clause authority.

Spending Clause Authority. Article I, Section 8, Clause 1 of the Constitution grants Congress "Power To lay and collect Taxes, Duties, Imposts and Excises, to pay the Debts and provide for the common Defense and general Welfare of the United States." It is well established that, pursuant to this Spending Clause power, Congress can spend federal funds to promote the general welfare and does not have to point to another enumerated power to justify federal expenditures. United States v. Butler, 297 U.S. 1 (1936). Pursuant to its Spending Clause authority, then, Congress has broad power to spend in response to disasters.

When exercising its Spending Clause power, Congress can condition the receipt of federal funds on a state's agreement to comply with particular standards or undertake particular activities so long as the condition is unambiguously expressed in the statute and is sufficiently related to the federal purpose for the spending. *See* South Dakota v. Dole, 483 U.S. 203 (1987). Congress has frequently conditioned federal disaster spending on state adoption of emergency preparedness plans. *See, e.g.,* Pet Evacuation and Transportation Standards Act of 2006, Pub. L. No. 109-308, 120 Stat. 1725 §2 (codified at 42 U.S.C. §5196) (conditioning emergency shelter funds on states sufficiently planning for the disaster relief needs of households with pets); Disaster Mitigation Act of

2000, Pub. L. No. 106-390, 114 Stat. 1552 §322 (codified at 42 U.S.C. §5165) (conditioning hazard mitigation funds on states developing approved natural disaster mitigation plans).

In addition, Congress sometimes uses its Spending Clause authority as a more politically palatable alternative to Commerce Clause authority when regulating areas of traditional state concern as, for example, when it passed the Coastal Zone Management Act, which offers federal funding for state land use plans that protect coastal environments. *See* 16 U.S.C. §§ 1456, §§ 1455(d)-1455(2)(I) (offering financial support to coastal states implementing approved state management programs that define and protect coastal zones by, inter alia, designating appropriate land and water use, and controlling and planning for shoreline erosion).

Militia Clause Authority. Congress's Article I powers include the authority "[t]o provide for calling forth the Militia to execute the Laws of the Union, suppress Insurrections and repel Invasions," Art. 1, §8, cl. 15, and the related power "[t]o provide for organizing, arming, and disciplining the Militia, and for governing such Part of them as may be employed in the Service of the United States, reserving to the States respectively, the Appointment of Officers, and the Authority of training the Militia according to the discipline prescribed by Congress," Art. 1, §18, cl. 16. Thus, if a disaster impedes execution of federal law (or either causes or results from an insurrection or invasion), Congress may claim authority to federalize state militias to respond to the crisis.

Fourteenth Amendment, Section 5 Enforcement Power. Section 5 of the Fourteenth Amendment grants Congress the power "to enforce, by appropriate legislation" the guarantees of the Fourteenth Amendment, which include equal protection and due process of law. When congressional legislation is prophylactic in nature (regulating behavior that does not itself violate the Fourteenth Amendment but that might conceal, encourage, or lead to a violation), then the legislative response must be congruent and proportional to an identified pattern of injury to constitutional rights. *See* City of Boerne v. Flores, 521 U.S. 507, 520 (1997). If the constitutional right Congress is protecting receives only rational basis scrutiny, then in applying this requirement, the Court has required strong record evidence of past rights violations by states or their political subdivisions before prophylactic legislation will be allowed. *See, e.g.,* Kimel v. Florida Board of Regents, 528 U.S. 62 (2000) (age discrimination). If the right (or classification) in question commands heightened scrutiny, then the Court has required much less justification from Congress. *See* Nevada Dept. of Human Resources v. Hibbs, 538 U.S. 721 (2003) (gender discrimination). Section 308 of the Stafford Act prohibits government bodies from discriminating on the basis of race, color, nationality, or gender (as well as other characteristics) when distributing federal disaster aid, *see* 42 U.S.C. §5151; using its Section 5 authority, Congress presumably could go farther, prohibiting state and local discrimination on the basis of race and sex in the provision of all disaster services, not just those that are federally funded.

NOTES AND QUESTIONS

1. Given the interdependence of local activities and the national (or, indeed global) economy, is there any disaster that would not "substantially affect" interstate commerce? Of course, the disaster is not precisely what is being regulated, is it? What if Congress decided, in advance of a disaster, to mitigate disaster risk by regulating local land use? Would it have Commerce Clause authority, for instance, to create federal zoning laws prohibiting building within 100 feet of an earthquake fault?

2. *Lopez* arguably represents an anomaly — at least within a twentieth-century constitutional tradition since the New Deal, marked by tolerance of an ever-larger degree of federal involvement in local affairs. The scope of federal involvement transcends the strictly commercial and readily embraces matters, such as civil rights, that nonlawyers might regard as moral rather than economic. Has the public understanding of the constitutionally mediated balance of power between the federal government and the states shifted so dramatically since the New Deal that the presumptive leadership of state and local governments in emergency response has actually reversed? In other words, do ordinary Americans expect the federal government, rather than state or local governments, to take the lead role in responding to natural disasters and other emergencies? If so, does such an expectation justify wholesale reconsideration of federalism during disasters?

3. Even if the activity Congress seeks to regulate falls squarely within its Commerce Clause powers, federalism may nonetheless constrain the ways in which Congress can achieve its regulatory objectives. Printz v. United States, 521 U.S. 898 (1997), established the proposition that principles of federalism and federal separation of powers bar the federal government from "commandeering" state executive officers for the purpose of enacting or implementing federal law. "The power of the Federal Government would be augmented immeasurably if it were able to impress into service — and at no cost to itself — the police officers of the 50 States." *Id.* at 922. The *Printz* dissenters expressed concern that the inability to conscript state officers to enforce federal law could hamstring federal disaster response: "[S]ince the ultimate issue is one of power, we must consider its implications in times of national emergency. Matters such as the enlistment of air raid wardens, the administration of a military draft, the mass inoculation of children to forestall an epidemic, or perhaps the threat of an international terrorist, may require a national response before federal personnel can be made available to respond." *Id.* at 940 (Stevens, J., dissenting). The majority countered that "[n]o comparative assessment of the various interests" at stake "can overcome [the] fundamental defect" of allowing the federal commandeering of state executive officers to "offend[]" the "very principle of separate state sovereignty." *Id.* at 932. Does this principle mean that state and local officials would be free to disregard any command or instructions from Federal Emergency Management Agency (FEMA) officials or other federal disaster responders?

4. Some scholars, arguing from originalist premises, have contended that Congress's Spending Clause power should be limited to "the power to

spend for the 'general' welfare and not for the special welfare of particular regions or states." John C. Eastman, *Restoring the "General" to the General Welfare Clause*, 4 Chap. L. Rev. 63, 65 (2001). Professor Eastman argues, for example, that "the Fourth Congress did not even believe it had the power to provide relief to the citizens of Savannah, Georgia after a devastating fire destroyed the entire city," because that expenditure would not have been for the "general welfare." *Id.* at 79. In today's interconnected world, where would one draw a meaningful line between spending that benefits particular localities and spending that furthers the general welfare? *See also* Michele L. Landis, *Let Me Next Time Be "Tried by Fire": Disaster Relief and the Origins of the American Welfare State 1789-1874*, 92 Nw. U. L. Rev. 967, 972 (1998) (contending that the historical evidence demonstrates that "during the period from 1789 to 1875, the Constitution provided no serious impediment to the development of disaster relief into the first sustained, organized social welfare program of the federal government").

5. Do the Militia Clause grants of authority imply that Congress may use only state militias (called into federal service), and not regular federal troops, when it wants to use military force domestically and, concomitantly, that the only purposes for which military forces can be used domestically are those enumerated in Clause 15 ("execut[ing] the Laws of the Union, suppress[ing] Insurrections and repel[ling] Invasions")? *See* Stephen I. Vladeck, *The Domestic Commander in Chief*, 29 Cardozo L. Rev. 1091, 1100 (2008) (arguing that the Militia Clauses were intended to designate state militias as the exclusive military forces that could be called upon to act domestically but concluding that the Supreme Court has read the Clauses as imposing no limits on Congress's use of federal regulars). *Contrast* Jason Mazzone, *The Security Constitution*, 53 UCLA Law Rev. 29, 63 (2005) (contending that Article IV obligates the federal government to protect states from invasion or domestic violence and that Congress can choose to fulfill that obligation either by deploying federal military personnel or by employing state militias). If the Militia Clauses were interpreted to mean that only state militias could be deployed domestically and only for the purposes specified in Clause 15, would Congress have had the power to deploy state militia troops to respond to reports of civil unrest in New Orleans in Katrina's aftermath?

6. Congress has, historically, exercised its "calling forth" power by delegating it to the president. In a series of acts dating back to 1792, Congress has delegated to the president the power to call forth the militia (and, beginning in 1799, federal troops) to act in times of domestic crisis in at least some of the circumstances outlined in the First Militia Clause (art. I, §8, cl. 15). *See* Stephen I. Vladeck, Note, *Emergency Power and the Militia Acts*, 114 Yale L.J. 149 (2004), 159-164. The current incarnation of this power is the Insurrection Act, 10 U.S.C. §§ 331-334, discussed *infra*.

7. Article IV, Section 4 of the Constitution pledges that "[t]he United States shall guarantee to every State in this Union a Republican Form of Government, and shall protect each of them against Invasion; and on Application of the Legislature, or of the Executive (when the Legislature cannot be

convened) against domestic Violence." In Luther v. Borden, 48 U.S. (7 How.) 1 (1849), the Supreme Court declined to decide which of two competing factions represented the lawful government of Rhode Island, reasoning that the responsibility "rests with congress to decide what government is the established one in a State." *Id.* at 42 ("Congress must necessarily decide what government is established in the State before it can determine whether it is republican or not."); *see also* Pacific Tel. Co. v. Oregon, 223 U.S. 118 (1912). Although *Luther* is regarded as foreclosing judicial enforcement of the Republican Guaranty Clause, *see* Baker v. Carr, 369 U.S. 186, 218-224 (1962), does this provision of the Constitution empower the political branches of the federal government to "guarantee to every State . . . a Republican Form of Government" and to "protect [the states] against Invasion" or "domestic Violence"? Does it obligate the federal government to do so? Reconsider this question in connection with the Insurrection Act, 10 U.S.C. §§ 331-334. *See infra.*

8. Who is "the Militia"? In District of Columbia v. Heller, 128 S. Ct. 2783 (2008), which held that the Second Amendment confers an individual right to keep and bear arms, the majority defined "militia" to include not only organized state militias but also the unorganized militia, historically defined as all able-bodied men within a certain age range. *See id.* at 2791, 2799. Some commentators have argued that, pursuant to its Calling Forth authority, Congress could respond to a disaster by placing state and local first responders—who are part of the unorganized state militia—under federal command, even without the consent of state officials:

> The solution [to the problems of federalism in times of emergency] is to allow the national government, when it responds to certain kinds of emergencies, to call into periods of mandatory federal service the emergency response personnel of the state in which the emergency occurs and, where necessary, emergency response personnel from other states. During emergencies, these state employees—police, firefighters, emergency medical technicians, urban search and rescue teams, and public health specialists—would serve with compensation under the command of the President, as Commander in Chief. With the power to place in federal service these state and local personnel, the federal government would be able to direct the response effort without being stymied by the vagaries of state and local bureaucracies.

Jason Mazzone, *The Commandeerer in Chief*, 83 NOTRE DAME L. REV. 265, 273 (2007). *See also* Brian C. Brook, Note, *Federalizing the First Responders to Acts of Terrorism via the Militia Clauses*, 54 DUKE L.J. 999, 1024 (2005). Do the Militia Clauses provide Congress an alternative path for "commandeering" state and local officials to implement federal disaster response? If so, would the federal government be required to pay those "called forth" for their services? Wouldn't individuals so "called forth" be limited to executing the laws of the United States, suppressing insurrections, and repelling invasions? *See* Mazzone, *The Commandeerer in Chief, supra*, at 277 (arguing that this emergency commandeering power would be limited to "times of invasion, insurrection, and opposition to federal law," but that "many emergencies will trigger the commandeering power because of their secondary effects: as events in New Orleans following Katrina showed, natural disasters frequently produce riots and other forms of lawlessness that satisfy the Constitution's conditions for federal deployment of state personnel").

9. Are National Guard troops part of the Militia? As the Supreme Court explained in Perpich v. Department of Defense, 496 U.S. 334, 345 (1990), since 1933 Congress has required by statute that all members of state National Guard units enlist, simultaneously, in the U.S. National Guard, which consists of the Army National Guard and the Air National Guard (reserve components of the U.S. Army and Air Force, respectively). This "dual enlistment" means that "a member of the Guard who is ordered to active duty in the federal service is thereby relieved of his or her status in the State Guard for the entire period of federal service." Id. at 346. Thus, members of State Guard units must "[k]eep three hats in their closets — a civilian hat, a state militia hat, and an army hat — only one of which is worn at any particular time." Id. at 348. Accordingly, when Congress federalizes state National Guardsmen by calling them into federal service, it does so pursuant to its separate Article I power to "raise armies," see U.S. Const. art. 1, §8, cl. 13, not pursuant to the Militia Clauses. Based on this reasoning, the Court held that it was permissible for Congress to deploy federalized National Guard troops abroad for training purposes. Does this mean that when Congress federalizes state National Guard units they can be deployed domestically for purposes other than executing federal law, suppressing insurrections, and repelling invasions? See Vladeck, The Domestic Commander in Chief, supra at 1102.

10. Can you imagine a situation in which Congress might wish to invoke its Fourteenth Amendment, Section 5 powers in the context of disaster preparation or response? Reconsider your answer in light of the reading in Chapter 5 on social vulnerability.

11. In addition to prohibiting discrimination on the basis of race, color, nationality, or sex in the provision of federal disaster relief, Section 308 of the Stafford Act forbids discrimination on the basis of religion, age, disability, English proficiency, or economic status. See 42 U.S.C. §5151. Could Congress use its Section 5 authority to impose similar standards on the provision of state disaster relief, or would such standards have to be justified by some other congressional power?

3. EXECUTIVE AUTHORITY TO RESPOND TO DISASTERS

Article II of the Constitution vests the president with the "executive power," Art II, Section 1, clause 1, and provides that the "President shall be the Commander in Chief of the Army and Navy of the United States, and of the Militia of the several States, when called into the actual Service of the United States," art. II, §2, cl. 1. Moreover, the president is also charged with the responsibility that "he shall take Care that the Laws be faithfully executed." Art. II, §3.

One of the great constitutional debates of our day is over the existence and extent of presidential inherent authority to respond in times of emergency, acting either without congressional authorization or — in even more aggressive and controversial formulations — in disregard of congressionally imposed limits. For a recent overview of some of the contours of this debate, *see* David J. Barron & Martin S. Lederman, *The Commander in Chief at the Lowest Ebb — A Constitutional History*, 121 Harv. L. Rev. 941 (2008). *See also* Candidus Dougherty, *"Necessity Hath No Law": Executive Power and the Posse Comitatus Act*, 31 Campbell L. Rev. 1 (2008). Much of the contemporary debate has occurred in the context of presidential wartime powers (whether a traditional ground war or a more nebulous War on Terror), but that debate has implications for the president's inherent authority to respond to domestic crises as well. For instance, would the president have the authority, without authorization from Congress, to declare martial law in the aftermath of a catastrophic disaster? "Martial law" is an imprecise term without clear legal meaning and might take many different forms — for example, enlisting the military to enforce civilian laws, suspending the writ of habeas corpus, or trying civilians in military courts. President Lincoln employed all of these forms of martial law during the Civil War. *See* Dan Farber, Lincoln's Constitution (2003) 144-175. More recently, some of President George W. Bush's top legal advisors argued that the president had the authority to deploy the military to arrest terrorist suspects (who were U.S. citizens) on U.S. soil, in upstate New York. *See* Mark Mazzetti & David Johnston, *Bush Weighed Using Military in U.S. Arrests*, N.Y. Times, July 25, 2009, at A1.

B. FEDERALISM: FRIEND OR FOE?

Hurricane Katrina took an inestimable toll in human lives, suffering, and property damage; it also took a significant toll on public confidence in the ability of government at all levels — federal, state, and local — to respond effectively to natural disasters, terrorist attacks, and other emergencies. Many have laid a significant portion of the blame for the failed Katrina response squarely at the feet of jurisdictional uncertainty caused by federalism. Indeed, in the aftermath of Katrina, one commentator calls on us to "stop federalism before it kills again!" Stephen M. Griffin, *Stop Federalism Before It Kills Again: Reflections on Hurricane Katrina*, 21 St. John's J. Legal Comment 527 (2007).

There is little doubt that federalism poses some challenges for emergency response. Disasters will often require quick, decisive action. Division of power and resources between the federal government and states and localities, however, means that disaster response will also require coordination and communication, which can be difficult to achieve in real time under disaster conditions. Failure to coordinate may mean that limited resources are wasted in duplicative efforts, while other pressing matters fall through the cracks. Additionally, the existence of shared, overlapping power to plan for and respond to disasters may encourage each level of government to shirk its own responsibilities, assuming (or hoping) that the other level of government is taking the required action. This shirking might be compounded by the possibility that federalism will cloud accountability for government failures in the event of a disaster, allowing each actor to blame the botched response on the others and thereby evade the political consequences of failure. Federalism has the potential to confuse lines of accountability not only among constituents but also among decision makers, who may consequently fail to learn the lessons of past disasters.

These challenges, of course, are not unique to federalism (in the disaster context or otherwise). They occur whenever power is divided, horizontally as well as vertically. Federal agencies that have some shared responsibility and jurisdiction in disaster response may encounter many of these same dynamics. Similarly, division of responsibility among private and public actors may also create many of these challenges.

How much of the tragically inept government response to Katrina can fairly be blamed on federalism? Has federalism become a convenient scapegoat to explain away other government failings? Consider this account of federalism's role in the failed Katrina response.

Erin Ryan, Federalism and the Tug of War Within: Seeking Checks and Balance in the Interjurisdictional Gray Area

66 Md. L. Rev. 503, 522-536 (2007) (internal citations and footnotes omitted)

According to eyewitness accounts and primary documents cataloging the relevant events, the response to Katrina was characterized by failures in coordinated command and communications between local, state, federal, and volunteer responders, as authorities struggled to determine what the federalism directives in applicable federal laws mandated regarding whom should be responsible for which parts of the response. Revised after the 9/11 attacks and issued in 2004, the new National Response Plan (NRP) recognizes that saving lives and protecting the health of the public are top priorities of incident management. However, the NRP also demarcates that, in emergency situations, states will be responsible for the implementation of police powers traditionally within their purview (such as local law enforcement, fire protection, and delivery of food and shelter), and the federal government will act in a supportive capacity, responding to specific requests by state authorities for assistance.

Although the Federal Emergency Management Agency's (FEMA) seeming paralysis in the face of the post-Katrina crisis may suggest incompetent leadership, it is also attributable to a federalism-related "operating system crash" under the NRP, which faltered just as software does when unable to parse unanticipated inputs. According to the NRP's federalism directive, federal authorities could not act preemptively, lest they tread in the protected realm of state sovereign authority. However, state authorities were unable to make the specific requests for assistance anticipated under the NRP. Local infrastructure was so damaged by the storm that communications were down, and state and local authorities were apparently so overwhelmed themselves that they did not know what to ask for. It may also be that state authorities were simply unprepared or incompetent to play the role anticipated of them by the NRP. But as former FEMA Director Michael Brown would later testify before Congress in defense of his agency's decisionmaking: "The role of the federal government in emergency management is generally that of coordinator and supporter . . . [a role] fully supported by the basic concept of federalism, recognizing that the sovereign states have primary responsibility for emergency preparedness and response in their jurisdictions." Thus, as Katrina bore down on the Gulf Coast, these departures from the NRP's script left regulatory responders struggling to decipher, in essence, which parts of the response effort were the proper purview of the state, and which the proper purview of the federal government. . . .

Federalism concerns were not limited to managerial choices in the field but pervaded the response effort up to the highest levels. News reports indicated that "[f]or days, Bush's top advisers argued over legal niceties about who was in charge," that "[i]nterviews with officials in Washington and Louisiana show that as the situation grew worse, they were wrangling with questions of federal/ state authority," and that "the crisis in New Orleans deepened because of a virtual standoff between hesitant federal officials and besieged authorities in Louisiana." The issues that most snarled the response effort were uncertainty about the point at which the federal government should stop waiting for instructions on how to assist the state and take initiative via its superior command capacity (through the deployment of U.S. military or federalized National Guard troops), and after that, confusion about who would then be in charge.

Even as it became clear that federal assistance was necessary, uncertainty unfolded among all three levels of government as to who should be in control of the troops to be deployed. Apparently desperate for results, New Orleans Mayor Ray Nagin supported federalizing the response, while Louisiana Governor Kathleen Babineaux Blanco balked, and President George W. Bush, hesitant to offend federalism principles in this interjurisdictional no man's land, waited for clarity. In one infamous exchange four days into the crisis at a strategy session aboard Air Force One, the distraught Mayor slammed the conference table with his hand and asked the President "to cut through this and do what it takes to have a more-controlled command structure. If that means federalizing it, let's do it." Mayor Nagin recommended the Pentagon's "on-scene commander," Lieutenant General Russel Honoré, to lead the flailing relief effort on behalf of the federal government. According to another meeting participant, President Bush turned to Governor Blanco and said, "[w]ell, what do you think of that, Governor?" But Governor Blanco declined to discuss the matter except in a private meeting with the President, which apparently followed the strategy session. However, there was still no agreement over one week later, leaving idle the assistance of an estimated 100,000 National Guard troops accessible on short notice in neighboring states. News accounts suggest that Governor Blanco did ask the President for 40,000 federal troops, but did not agree to surrender oversight of the relief effort to the federal government.

Had Governor Blanco surrendered her claim to control over the relief effort, President Bush would have been able to reconcile the urgency of providing needed federal assistance with the federalism principles that he believed foreclosed such authorization in the interim. Nevertheless, contemporaneous news accounts indicate that the Justice Department's Office of Legal

Counsel researched the matter and "concluded that the federal government had authority to move in even over the objection of local officials."

. . . [W]hat is most significant about the President's decision is why he declined to exercise the potential Stafford Act authority in the first place, given such overwhelming political pressure to do so and his demonstrated confidence asserting untested federal executive authority in other realms. One patent explanation for the President's hesitancy to explore all potential avenues of authority during the most devastating natural disaster in U.S. history is the profound influence of strict-separationist idealism. Federalizing the Louisiana National Guard and subjecting state and city police to federal command would have blurred the very lines of regulatory authority that New Federalism so endeavors to preserve. The best alternative explanation — and one equally troubling — is that the White House relied on New Federalism rhetoric for political cover in avoiding any involvement with the unfolding mess. Either way, that New Federalism ideals could stall effective governance at such a key moment or provide reliable cover to so monumental an abdication suggests their infirmity.

In the end, reasonable people may disagree on how best to apportion blame between the amply culpable local, state, and federal authorities for the failed response, subsequently heralded as "a national disgrace." That said, it remains difficult to digest the confirmed reports that after fifteen-foot floodwaters swept through the Jackson Barracks headquarters of the Louisiana National Guard Headquarters — severing communication lines, flooding high-water trucks, and converting the entire nerve center force into 375 more New Orleans refugees in need of a water rescue — White House officials stalled in Washington, debating how the finer principles of constitutional federalism dictated the scope of federal intervention. In their defense, the debate was at least warranted by a faithful interpretation of the federalism model advanced by the sitting Supreme Court. But it raises the fair question, in light of the stakes and the results that can flow from that model — is this really the federalism we intended? . . .

While the President's senior advisers fiddled with federalism, New Orleans drowned. The details of the debacle are by now painfully well-known to most Americans, but they bear repeating to highlight the scope of the failed response. Over a thousand residents perished in their homes and neighborhoods, and up to thirty-four died in the makeshift mass shelters at the New Orleans Superdome and convention center, where some 39,000 evacuees were encamped without adequate food, water, power, or sanitary facilities for up to seven days. Two-thirds of the occupants were women, children, or elderly, many of them infirm, and they huddled in darkness and 100-degree temperatures amidst the unbearable stench of human waste covering the floors and the ceiling debris fallen from holes torn from the roof by the storm. Unchecked lawless behavior terrorized citizens and local law enforcement alike, both within the emergency shelters and on the flooded city streets. The near total collapse of landline, satellite, and cell phone communications hindered the ability of local law enforcement and the Louisiana National Guard to coordinate a response — even available radio channels were so jammed with traffic that they became useless.

The chaotic rescue and evacuation efforts impacted families as well, as the National Center for Missing and Exploited Children reported in mid-September 2005 that 1,831 children from Louisiana, Alabama, and Mississippi were reported as missing in the aftermath of the storm, and that, weeks later, only 360 of these cases had been resolved. At least a million evacuees took shelter in other cities and states, and by March 2006 the federal government had committed $6.9 billion in shelter and direct financial assistance to Gulf Coast residents affected by the hurricane. Countless thousands of starving and injured companion animals continued to roam the streets or languish trapped within the homes of evacuated owners for weeks following the storm, most perishing before rescue but not before ghastly suffering.

Damage to oil infrastructure was the worst ever experienced by the industry. More than nine million gallons were reported spilled, and gas prices skyrocketed to as high as $6 per gallon in the following weeks. Chemical spills, rotting remains, and flooding resulted in environmental hazards ranging from land-based toxic sludge to poisoned water supplies that will continue to threaten human health and safety into the foreseeable future. Approximately $88 billion in federal aid has already been allocated toward relief, recovery, and rebuilding efforts, and an additional $20 billion has been requested to assist a variety of federal agencies in their continuing relief efforts. These moneys have been earmarked for programs including unemployment assistance, community disaster loans to local governments, housing assistance, and public assistance projects. Separate grants have also been awarded, including a $1.6 billion special congressional appropriation to the Department of Education for public and private schools where relocated students enrolled. . . .

Of course, much of the devastation that Gulf Coast residents suffered from the winds and rain of Katrina cannot be blamed on bad disaster management. Setting aside the degree to which anthropogenic climate change contributes to the intensity of hurricanes like Katrina, hurricanes are a force of nature that we have long learned to fear. River and wetland management choices along the Mississippi Delta exacerbated the flooding that proved the worst of New Orleans's battles, and Americans are right to ask for better long-term planning from the local, state, and federal authorities responsible for these activities. Still, it was the bungled humanitarian relief effort—the disorganized response that stranded the sick and injured, separated young children from their parents, and left the most vulnerable members of society struggling to survive amidst prolonged "Lord of the Flies" conditions—that triggered public outrage.

NOTES AND QUESTIONS

1. Is the poor Katrina response (at all levels of government) an indictment of federalism itself, the model of federalism in use, or the particular leaders who failed to negotiate federalism's potential pitfalls and cooperate for the good of New Orleans? Are there advantages to having a federalist system that are manifest during disaster response? Is it beneficial to have expertise and resources available at multiple levels of government? Are disaster survivors more likely to trust and take direction from federal or local officials?

2. If divided power is the problem, is federal control over major — or at least catastrophic — disasters the answer? Will state personnel respond well to being commanded by federal authorities? Do federal authorities have the capacity to mount an effective response without state and local input and resources? A wholly federal response to even a catastrophic disaster would appear nearly impossible, as federal officials lack the intimate knowledge of the area and its conditions that local officials possess.

3. In addition to issues of power and capacity, the question of who is in charge of disaster response implicates notions of responsibility and obligation. Historically, states have been charged with ensuring the health and safety of their citizens. Although this obligation has not abated, perhaps it is increasingly shared with federal authorities.

> Most of us have grown up in a world in which federal assistance in time of disaster is taken for granted. Consider the primary conclusion of the House Select Committee: "Our investigation revealed that Katrina was a national failure, an abdication of the most solemn obligation to provide for the common welfare." This conclusion implies that the nation fell short on a key constitutional commitment. But is this conclusion consistent with historic understandings of federalism? To put this in a more pointed way, when did the national government formally commit itself to having primary responsibility for the welfare of the people of the states? Of course, the Committee could not point to a constitutional amendment or a widely understood legal commitment originating from the Preamble to the Constitution.
>
> The Committee report is quite revealing on this score. As noted above, the Committee argued that the federal government must respond "proactively" to a disaster like Katrina. Yet when discussing the military's role, the Committee made this general remark: "The Select Committee does not believe there is a simple answer to improving state and federal integration. Local control and state sovereignty are important principles rooted in the nation's birth that cannot be discarded merely to achieve more efficient joint military operations on American soil." Thus, the Committee's report points ultimately in two directions — both toward greater federal responsibility in time of national catastrophe and toward a continued essential role for state and local governments. How could it be otherwise? The Committee could not by itself surmount the conflicts inherent in American federalism.
>
> Why was the Committee confused in this way? The answer lies in the process of constitutional change. When it criticized the national response, the Committee invoked a value system that was a product of informal twentieth century constitutional change and was not implied by anything in the text of the Constitution. This kind of criticism would not have occurred to anyone in the eighteenth or nineteenth centuries. During the twentieth century and especially during the New Deal, the constitutional order changed in a somewhat helter-skelter unplanned fashion. Certainly no constitutional amendment was approved that might have provided firm legitimacy and guidance to the federal government's new power. The formal structure of American federalism remained intact.

Stephen M. Griffin, *Stop Federalism Before It Kills Again: Reflections on Hurricane Katrina*, 21 St. John's J. Legal Comment 527, 536-538 (2007) (citations omitted).

4. Why would the federal government be obligated to respond to disasters? Because it has committed itself to do so? Because it has the capacity to respond when states and localities are overwhelmed? Because citizens expect it to fill that role? In the aftermath of Hurricane Andrew, a Category 5 hurricane that devastated southern Florida in August 1992, the Director of the Dade County (Florida) Office of Emergency Management voiced a common reaction when he asked, "Where in the hell is the cavalry?" Mary Jordan, *President Orders Military to Aid Florida*, WASH. POST, Aug 28, 1992, at A1.

5. Throughout the twentieth century, especially after the Mississippi River flood of 1927, the federal government became progressively more involved in emergencies. The "role of the Federal government in disaster response has evolved significantly throughout the past 200 years":

> In 1803, in what is widely seen as the first instance of Federal intervention in a disaster scenario, Congress approved the use of Federal resources to assist the recovery of Portsmouth, New Hampshire, following a devastating urban fire. Between 1803 and 1950, the Federal government intervened in over 100 incidents (earthquakes, fires, floods, and tornados), making Federal resources available to affected jurisdictions. These interventions were limited and were delivered in an ad hoc manner without an established Federal role or coordinated response plan. The Federal government also quickly recognized the role that private non-profit organizations can play. In 1905, Congress chartered the American Red Cross as a charitable organization to provide disaster relief support during crises. . . .
>
> During the Great Depression, the approach of the Federal government became more proactive. For example, Congress endowed the Bureau of Public Roads with the authority to provide continuous grants to States for the repair of disaster-damaged infrastructure and charged the Army Corps of Engineers with the task of mitigating flood-related threats. This piecemeal legislative approach was eventually replaced by the Civil Defense Act of 1950[,] the first comprehensive legislation pertaining to Federal disaster relief.
>
> In 1952, President Truman issued Executive Order 10427, which emphasized that Federal disaster assistance was intended to supplement, not supplant, the resources of State, local, and private sector organizations. This theme was echoed two decades later [by] President Nixon. . . . "Federal disaster assistance is intended to supplement individual, local and state resources." . . .
>
> Th[e] piecemeal approach to disaster assistance was problematic and it prompted legislation that required greater cooperation between Federal agencies and authorized the President to coordinate these activities.
>
> The 1960s and early 1970s brought massive disasters requiring major Federal response and recovery operations by the Federal Disaster Assistance Administration, established within the Department of Housing and Urban Development (HUD). Hurricane Carla struck in 1962, Hurricane Betsy in 1965, Hurricane Camille in 1969 and Hurricane Agnes in 1972. The Alaskan Earthquake hit in 1964 and the San Fernando Earthquake rocked Southern California in 1971. These events served to focus attention on the issue of natural disasters and brought about increased legislation. In 1968, the National Flood Insurance Act offered new flood protection to homeowners, and in 1974 the Disaster Relief Act firmly established the process of Presidential disaster declarations.

However, emergency and disaster activities were still fragmented. When hazards associated with nuclear power plants and the transportation of hazardous substances were added to natural disasters, more than 100 Federal agencies were involved in some aspect of disasters, hazards and emergencies. Many parallel programs and policies existed at the State and local level, compounding the complexity of Federal disaster relief efforts. The National Governor's Association . . . asked President Jimmy Carter to centralize Federal emergency functions.

President Carter's 1979 executive order merged many of the separate disaster-related responsibilities into a new Federal Emergency Management Agency (FEMA). Among other agencies, FEMA absorbed: the Federal Insurance Administration, the National Fire Prevention and Control Administration, the National Weather Service Community Preparedness Program, the Federal Preparedness Agency of the General Services Administration and the Federal Disaster Assistance Administration activities from HUD. Civil defense responsibilities were also transferred to the new agency from the Defense Department's Defense Civil Preparedness Agency.

THE WHITE HOUSE, THE FEDERAL RESPONSE TO HURRICANE KATRINA: LESSONS LEARNED 11-12, 158-159 n.11 (2006). FEMA itself was absorbed in 2002 into a new bureaucracy that united emergency response and defense against terrorism within the Department of Homeland Security. For a detailed history of the expansion of the federal role in emergency management, *see* EMERGENCY MANAGEMENT: THE AMERICAN EXPERIENCE 1900-2005 (Claire B. Rubin ed., 2007).

C. THE FEDERAL STATUTORY SCHEME

Constitutional provisions and Supreme Court case law on federalism represent only the first step in understanding the relationship between federal, state, and local authorities during disasters. Of far greater practical significance are the statutes that organize and implement federal power, defining the federal role in emergency response, disaster relief, and law enforcement. Chief among these laws is the Robert T. Stafford Disaster Relief and Emergency Assistance Act, 42 U.S.C. §§ 5121-5208 (2009), which is administered by FEMA.

1. THE STAFFORD ACT: DEPLOYMENT OF FEDERAL CIVILIAN AID AND RESOURCES

a. Triggers for Federal Aid: Emergencies and Major Disasters

The basic premise of the Stafford Act is that the federal government will step in to provide disaster aid to affected states when the disaster is of sufficient magnitude and severity that it overwhelms state and local capacity to respond. Accordingly, most relief provisions of the Act are not triggered until a state governor requests, and the president provides, a disaster (or emergency) declaration. The accompanying graphic, taken from FEMA's National Response Framework Overview Document, outlines the process for states obtaining aid under the Stafford Act.

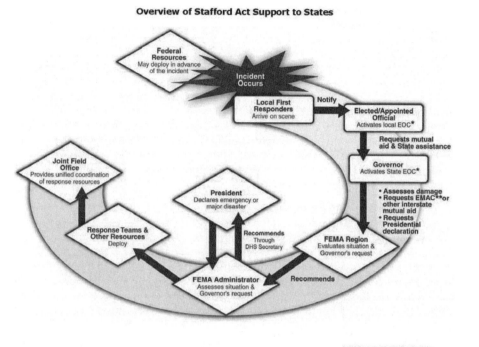

Overview of Stafford Act Support to States

* Emergency Operations Center
** Emergency Management Assistance Compact

Moreover, the Stafford Act distinguishes between two disaster incident levels—emergencies and major disasters—and establishes parallel, though not identical, procedures for obtaining the requisite declarations. Section 401 of the Stafford Act, 42 U.S.C. §5170, governs major disaster declarations. Section 501, 42 U.S.C. §5191, governs emergency declarations.

§5122. Definitions
As used in this Act—

(1) "Emergency" means any occasion or instance for which, in the determination of the President, Federal assistance is needed to supplement State and local efforts and capabilities to save lives and to protect property and public health and safety, or to lessen or avert the threat of a catastrophe in any part of the United States.

(2) "Major Disaster" means any natural catastrophe (including any hurricane, tornado, storm, high water, wind-driven water, tidal wave, tsunami, earthquake, volcanic eruption, landslide, mudslide, snowstorm, or drought), or, regardless of cause, any fire, flood, or explosion, in any part of the United States, which in the determination of the President causes damage of sufficient severity and magnitude to warrant major disaster assistance under this Act to supplement the efforts and available resources of States, local governments, and disaster relief organizations in alleviating the damage, loss, hardship, or suffering caused thereby.

§5170. Procedure for [major disaster] declaration.
All requests for a declaration by the President that a major disaster exists shall be made by the Governor of the affected State. Such a request shall be based on

a finding that the disaster is of such severity and magnitude that effective response is beyond the capabilities of the State and the affected local governments and that Federal assistance is necessary. As part of such request, and as a prerequisite to major disaster assistance under this chapter, the Governor shall take appropriate response action under State law and direct execution of the State's emergency plan. The Governor shall furnish information on the nature and amount of State and local resources which have been or will be committed to alleviating the results of the disaster, and shall certify that, for the current disaster, State and local government obligations and expenditures (of which State commitments must be a significant proportion) will comply with all applicable cost-sharing requirements of this chapter. Based on the request of a Governor under this section, the President may declare under this chapter that a major disaster or emergency exists.

§5191. Procedure for [emergency] declaration.

(a) Request and declaration

All requests for a declaration by the President that an emergency exists shall be made by the Governor of the affected State. Such a request shall be based on a finding that the situation is of such severity and magnitude that effective response is beyond the capabilities of the State and the affected local governments and that Federal assistance is necessary. As a part of such request, and as a prerequisite to emergency assistance under this chapter, the Governor shall take appropriate action under State law and direct execution of the State's emergency plan. The Governor shall furnish information describing the State and local efforts and resources which have been or will be used to alleviate the emergency, and will define the type and extent of Federal aid required. Based upon such Governor's request, the President may declare that an emergency exists.

NOTES AND QUESTIONS

1. Does the definition of "major disaster" cover a disease outbreak, such as an influenza pandemic? Does your analysis depend on whether the influenza is a naturally occurring strain or a biologically engineered strain released in a bioterrorist attack? Historically, FEMA has taken the position that "biological disasters" do not qualify as Stafford Act "major disasters." Department of Homeland Security, *A Review of the Top Officials 3 Exercise* (Nov. 2005), available at http://www.dhs.gov/xoig/assets/mgmtrpts/ OIG_06-07_Nov05.pdf. However, the Homeland Security Council asserted in its Implementation Plan for the National Strategy for Pandemic Influenza that "the President could declare either an emergency or a major disaster with respect to an influenza pandemic." *See* Homeland Security Council, *Implementation Plan for the National Strategy for Pandemic Influenza* 212, available at www.lib.umich.edu/govdocs/pdf/fluplan.pdf. For a discussion of statutory arguments as to whether pandemic influenza can qualify as a "major disaster," *see* Edward C. Liu, *Would an Influenza Pandemic Qualify as a Major Disaster under the Stafford Act?* (CRS Report for Congress, Order Code RL34724, Oct. 20, 2008) (concluding that the president could reasonably interpret "major disaster" to cover a flu pandemic).

2. Would the definition of "major disaster" cover a nonnatural event, such as an electronic attack on the Internet, not attributable to fire, flood, or

explosion? *See* Ernest B. Abbott, *Representing Local Governments in Cata-strophic Events: DHS/FEMA Response and Recovery Issues*, 37 Urb. Law. 467, 471 (2005) (suggesting it does not).

3. Do these definitional difficulties suggest that, rather than defining "major disaster" by reference to specific hazard events, the Act should instead define disaster in terms of some other referent, such as societal or community disruption? For example, the International Disaster Response Guidelines, adopted unanimously by the International Conference of the Red Cross and Red Crescent in 2007, define "disaster" as a "serious disruption of the functioning of society, which poses a significant, widespread threat to human life, health, property or the environment, whether arising from accident, nature or human activity, whether developing suddenly or as a result of long-term processes, but excluding armed conflict." The Secretariat of the United Nations International Strategy for Disaster Reduction defines disaster as "a serious disruption of the functioning of a community or a society causing widespread human, material, economic or environmental losses which exceed the ability of the affected community or society to cope using its own resources." Would one of these definitions better serve the purposes of the statute? Is the solution instead for Congress to amend the Act whenever any new threat seems to warrant inclusion as a "major disaster"?

4. In the run-up to President Obama's inauguration, Washington, D.C., Mayor Adrian Fenty requested, and President Bush granted, an emergency declaration for Washington, D.C., for the days immediately prior to and including the inauguration. The request was prompted, in part, by Congress's allocation of only $15 million to cover D.C.'s inauguration costs, which was some $2.3 million less than the District had spent on security for President Bush's (smaller) second inauguration. *See* Dan Leaderman & John Ward, *Inauguration Declared "Emergency,"* Wash. Times, Jan. 14, 2009. Was this a proper declaration of "emergency" or an improper end run around Congress's appropriation process?

5. Should the president's decision to grant or withhold an emergency or major disaster declaration be subject to judicial review? Section 305 of the Act (42 U.S.C. §5148) provides that "[t]he Federal Government shall not be liable for any claim based upon the exercise or performance of or the failure to exercise or perform a discretionary function or duty on the part of a Federal Agency or an employee of the Federal Government in carrying out the provisions of the Act." This provision would seem to immunize the president's decision from review. *See* Kansas v. United States, 748 F. Supp. 797, 799-800 (D. Kan. 1990) (holding that the "President's decision on a request for a declaration of major disaster is not subject to [judicial] review"). More generally, Section 305's language is almost identical to the Federal Tort Claims Act's (FTCA) exception for "[a]ny claim . . . based upon the exercise or performance or the failure to exercise or perform a discretionary function or duty" by a federal employee. 28 U.S.C. §2680(a). The Stafford Act's immunity provision is interpreted *in pari materia* with the FTCA's frequently litigated "discretionary function" exception. *See* Freeman v. United States, 556 F.3d 326, 336-337 (5th Cir. 2009) (holding that the Stafford Act's "discretionary function" exception, as interpreted by reference to the FTCA's exception, precluded

liability for the federal government's failure to provide Katrina survivors with adequate food, water, shelter, and medical assistance in accordance with provisions of the Catastrophic Index Annex of the National Response Plan); Graham v. FEMA, 149 F.3d 997, 1006 (9th Cir. 1998).

6. When can the federal government respond to a disaster or potential disaster without a request from the affected state? Section 501(b) of the Stafford Act (42 U.S.C. §5191(b)) provides that the president may exercise his authority to provide federal emergency assistance pursuant to sections 5192 and 5193 without a state request for an emergency declaration when the president "determines that an emergency exists for which the primary responsibility for response rests with the United States because the emergency involves a subject area for which, under the Constitution or laws of the United States, the United States exercises exclusive or preeminent responsibility and authority." Although the section directs the president to "consult with the Governor of any affected State, if practicable," the president can proceed without the governor's consent. Presumably, this authority enables the president to declare an emergency in the event of disasters or attacks affecting military installations and other federal properties. This authority was first invoked by President Clinton in the aftermath of the Oklahoma City bombings. *See* Jim Winthrop, *The Oklahoma City Bombing: Immediate Response Authority and Other Military Assistance to Civil Authority (MACA)*, 1997-JUL Army Law 3, 10-11. Might this provision also authorize the federal government to declare an emergency and respond without a state request to a catastrophic disaster that cripples state and local government? *See* Ryan, *supra*, at 530 (concluding that "the question is unsettled").

b. Federal Aid Available for Major Disasters

The president's issuance of a major disaster declaration authorizes (but does not require) the president to provide various types of federal disaster assistance to affected states, localities, and individuals. Major disaster assistance can include (1) response and recovery aid to states and localities (including General Federal Assistance, Essential Assistance, other Public Assistance (to permanently repair infrastructure), and Community Disaster Loans); (2) hazard mitigation assistance; and (3) individual assistance.

i. RESPONSE AND RECOVERY AID TO STATES AND LOCALITIES

§5170a. General Federal assistance.
In any major disaster, the President may—
  (1) direct any Federal agency, with or without reimbursement, to utilize its authorities and the resources granted to it under Federal law (including personnel, equipment, supplies, facilities, and managerial, technical, and advisory services) in support of State and local assistance response and recovery efforts, including precautionary evacuations;
  (2) coordinate all disaster relief assistance (including voluntary assistance) provided by Federal agencies, private organizations, and State and local governments, including precautionary evacuations and recovery;

(3) provide technical and advisory assistance to affected State and local governments for—

    (A) the performance of essential community services;

    (B) issuance of warnings of risks and hazards;

    (C) public health and safety information, including dissemination of such information;

    (D) provision of health and safety measures;

    (E) management, control, and reduction of immediate threats to public health and safety; and

    (F) recovery activities, including disaster impact assessments and planning;

(4) assist State and local governments in the distribution of medicine, food, and other consumable supplies, and emergency assistance; and

(5) provide accelerated Federal assistance and Federal support where necessary to save lives, prevent human suffering, or mitigate severe damage, which may be provided in the absence of a specific request and in which case the President

    (A) shall, to the fullest extent practicable, promptly notify and coordinate with officials in a State in which such assistance or support is provided; and

    (B) shall not, in notifying and coordinating with a State under subparagraph (A), delay or impede the rapid deployment, use, and distribution of resources to victims of a major disaster.

§5170b. Essential assistance

(a) In general—Federal agencies may on the direction of the President, provide assistance essential to meeting immediate threats to life and property resulting from a major disaster, as follows:

    (1) Federal resources, generally—Utilizing, lending, or donating to State and local governments Federal equipment, supplies, facilities, personnel, and other resources, other than the extension of credit, for use or distribution by such governments in accordance with the purposes of this chapter.

    (2) Medicine, durable medical equipment, food, and other consumables—Distributing or rendering through State and local governments, the American National Red Cross, the Salvation Army, the Mennonite Disaster Service, and other relief and disaster assistance organizations medicine, durable medical equipment, food, and other consumable supplies, and other services and assistance to disaster victims.

    (3) Work and services to save lives and protect property—Performing on public or private lands or waters any work or services essential to saving lives and protecting and preserving property or public health and safety, including—

        (A) debris removal;

        (B) search and rescue, emergency medical care, emergency mass care, emergency shelter, and provision of food, water, medicine, durable medical equipment, and other essential needs, including movement of supplies or persons;

        (C) clearance of roads and construction of temporary bridges necessary to the performance of emergency tasks and essential community services;

(D) provision of temporary facilities for schools and other essential community services;

(E) demolition of unsafe structures which endanger the public;

(F) warning of further risks and hazards;

(G) dissemination of public information and assistance regarding health and safety measures;

(H) provision of technical advice to State and local governments on disaster management and control;

(I) reduction of immediate threats to life, property, and public health and safety; and

(J) provision of rescue, care, shelter, and essential needs—

(i) to individuals with household pets and service animals; and

(ii) to such pets and animals.

(4) Contributions—Making contributions to State or local governments or owners or operators of private nonprofit facilities for the purpose of carrying out the provisions of this subsection.

(b) Federal share—The Federal share of assistance under this section shall be not less than 75 percent of the eligible cost of such assistance.

(c) Utilization of DOD resources

(1) General rule—During the immediate aftermath of an incident which may ultimately qualify for assistance under this subchapter [major disaster assistance] or subchapter IV-A of this chapter [emergency assistance], the Governor of the State in which such incident occurred may request the President to direct the Secretary of Defense to utilize the resources of the Department of Defense for the purpose of performing on public and private lands any emergency work which is made necessary by such incident and which is essential for the preservation of life and property. If the President determines that such work is essential for the preservation of life and property, the President shall grant such request to the extent the President determines practicable. Such emergency work may only be carried out for a period not to exceed 10 days.

(2) Rules applicable to debris removal—Any removal of debris and wreckage carried out under this subsection shall be subject to section 5173(b) of this title, relating to unconditional authorization and indemnification for debris removal.

(3) Expenditures out of disaster relief funds—The cost of any assistance provided pursuant to this subsection shall be reimbursed out of funds made available to carry out this chapter.

(4) Federal share—The Federal share of assistance under this subsection shall be not less than 75 percent.

(5) Guidelines—Not later than 180 days after November 23, 1988, the President shall issue guidelines for carrying out this subsection. Such guidelines shall consider any likely effect assistance under this subsection will have on the availability of other forms of assistance under this chapter.

(6) Definitions—For purposes of this section

(A) Department of Defense—The term "Department of Defense" has the meaning the term "department" has under section 101 of Title 10.

(B) Emergency work—The term "emergency work" includes clearance and removal of debris and wreckage and temporary restoration of essential public facilities and services.

Public Assistance Grant Program. Under the foregoing provisions, federal disaster aid can take two forms: either emergency measures can be taken by the federal government itself, or the federal government can reimburse states and localities for debris removal and other "emergency protective measures" (such as search and rescue and sheltering) taken by the state and local governments to respond to the disaster. Federal reimbursement for state and local "emergency measures" takes place pursuant to FEMA's Public Assistance Grant Program. *See* FEMA, Public Assistance Guide 44-53 (1999), available at http://www.fema.gov/government/grant/pa/paguided.shtm.

Another critical component of the Public Assistance Grant Program for major disasters is outlined in Section 406 of the Stafford Act, which authorizes the president to make contributions "to a State or local government for the repair, restoration, reconstruction, or replacement of a public facility damaged or destroyed by a major disaster," 42 U.S.C. 5172(a)(1)(A), and — under certain circumstances — to make similar grants to private nonprofit facilities, including facilities that provide "critical services . . . in the event of a major disaster," *id.* §5172(a)(3)(i), or facilities that have already sought the maximum Small Business Act disaster loan for which they are eligible, *id.* §5172(a)(3)(ii). The federal government will bear at least 75 percent of eligible costs, unless the facility has previously been damaged in the preceding ten years by a similar event and the owner failed to "implement appropriate mitigation measures to address the hazard," *id.* §5172(b)(2), in which case the minimum federal share is 25 percent. If the owner decides not to repair or replace the facility, it can elect instead to receive a grant equal to 90 percent of the federal share of eligible costs (for public entities) or 75 percent of the federal share (for private nonprofits). *Id.* §51724(c).

Community Disaster Loans. Section 417 of the Stafford Act, 42 U.S.C. §5184, authorizes the president to make loans to local governments affected by major disasters:

§5184. Community Disaster Loans

(a) In General — The President is authorized to make loans to any local government which may suffer a substantial loss of tax and other revenues as a result of a major disaster, and has demonstrated a need for financial assistance in order to perform its government functions.

(b) Amount — The amount of any such loan shall be based on need, shall not exceed

(1) 25 percent of the annual operating budget of that local government for the fiscal year in which the major disaster occurs, and shall not exceed $5,000,000; or

(2) if the loss of tax and other revenues of the local government as a result of the major disaster is at least 75 percent of the annual operating budget of that local government for the fiscal year in which the major disaster occurs, 50 percent of the annual operating budget of that local government for the fiscal year in which the major disaster occurs, and shall not exceed $5,000,000.

Repayment of the loan is cancelled if, for the three years subsequent to the disaster, local government revenues are insufficient to meet the operating budget of that local government. §417(c), 42 U.S.C. §5184(c).

Other Response and Recovery Aid to States and Localities. Other provisions of the Stafford Act also authorize the federal government to provide direct aid to communities affected by major disasters, by supplying food "for emergency mass feeding," §413, 42 U.S.C. §5180 (authorizing and "direct[ing]" the president to assure an adequate food stock); emergency public transportation, §419, 42 U.S.C. §5186; temporary emergency communications systems in anticipation of a major disaster or emergency, §418, 42 U.S.C. §5185; and debris removal (or grants for debris removal) from publicly and privately owned lands, §407, 42 U.S.C. §5173.

NOTES AND QUESTIONS

1. The provisions outlined above reflect a number of changes prompted by FEMA's response to Katrina. One of the most significant additions is §5170a(5), which allows FEMA, in a declared "major disaster," to provide accelerated federal assistance and support, without a state request, when necessary to save lives, prevent suffering, and mitigate severe damage. This provision explicitly confirms authority that FEMA has long claimed but exercised only sporadically: the power to implement a proactive federal response utilizing a "push" system for deploying assets to devastated areas, rather than a traditional "pull" system:

   What is a push system? In response to most disasters, the federal government provides assistance in response to state requests. This reactive approach is often referred to as a "pull" system in that it relies on states knowing what they need and being able to request it from the federal government. States may make these requests either before disasters strike because of the near certainty that federal assistance will be necessary after such an event, e.g., with hurricanes, or afterwards, once they have conducted preliminary damage assessments and determined their response capabilities are overwhelmed.

   Unlike the bulk of the disasters requiring FEMA's response, catastrophic disasters require the federal response to be more proactive. This proactive response is referred to as a "push" system, in which federal assistance is provided and moved into the affected area prior to a disaster or without waiting for specific requests from the state or local governments. . . .

   . . . [P]re-positioning of disaster supplies and assets is not in and of itself a push of commodities. Once assets are pre-positioned to go into the field, they still need to be mobilized and deployed into the field either proactively by pushing the commodities to the state or reactively by waiting for a request from the state.

   Operational procedures for a push are not well exercised, practiced, or utilized. The majority of declared disasters are not catastrophic. Because of this, the pull system is most commonly used during disasters and training exercises and, therefore, is more familiar to disaster response personnel. In fact, the NRP-CIA [National Response Plan Catastrophic Incident Annex] has never been appropriately exercised. As a result, federal personnel have little experience or comfort with instituting a proactive response.

   Additionally, if the Homeland Security Secretary does not invoke the NRP-CIA, federal personnel have no clear instruction to switch from a reactive approach to a proactive approach. Without this clear direction, federal personnel can be uncomfortable pushing resources into the state because of the inherent risks, such as complicating the disaster response by diverting needed resources from other areas or wasting millions of dollars in a duplication of effort.

U.S. HOUSE OF REPRESENTATIVES, A FAILURE OF INITIATIVE, FINAL REPORT OF THE SELECT BIPARTISAN COMMITTEE TO INVESTIGATE THE PREPARATION FOR AND RESPONSE TO HURRICANE KATRINA 136-137 (2006) [hereinafter HOUSE KATRINA REPORT]. Is this new authority sufficient to allow a fully effective federal response to a catastrophic disaster? Should there be a separate, explicit federal power to push resources into a devastated area even without a major disaster declaration (which requires a state request), when a disaster incapacitates the state's chain of command and continuity of government? (For example, if a major earthquake destroyed a state's historic capitol building while the governor was there and the legislature was in session?) Should there be federal power to push resources into devastated areas where lives are at stake when the governor is not incapacitated, but is either incompetent or unwilling to request a federal disaster declaration?

2. Section 5170a has also been amended to make clear that the federal government has the authority to support and coordinate precautionary evacuations. *See* 42 U.S.C. §5170(a)(1)-(2).

3. Another new addition is section 5170b(a)(3)(J), which allows the federal government to provide assistance for rescuing, sheltering, and caring for individuals with pets and service animals (as well as the animals themselves). Many residents of New Orleans apparently refused to evacuate because doing so would have forced them to abandon their pets:

> In hurricane-ravaged New Orleans, the lack of planning added to the burden and stress of both rescuers and residents. In a city of 500,000 as many as 69 percent of the people are pet owners and, by some estimates, there are as many as 600,000 pets and animals affected by the devastation of hurricane Katrina. Private rescue organizations estimate they have saved about 5,000 animals so far and have reunited only 600 animals with their owners. Estimates indicate there are an equal percentage of pet owners nationwide.

Introduction of the Pets Evacuation and Transportation Standards (PETS) Act of 2005, 151 Cong. Rec. E1943, E1943 (Sept. 22, 2005) (statement of Rep. Tom Lantos, D-Cal.); *see also Pets Evacuation and Transportation Standards Act of 2005*, 152 Cong. Rec. H2985, H2986 (May 22, 2006) (statement of Rep. Christopher Shays, R-Conn.). According to an animal search and rescue expert, "There is a direct correlation between people risking their lives in a disaster and the presence of pets in the home." Jay Romano, *Protecting Pets in a Disaster*, N.Y. TIMES, Sept. 25, 2005, at 14 (quoting Joseph Buttito). In addition to expanding essential assistance to encompass the needs of households with animals, the Pet Evacuation and Transportation Standards Act of 2006 requires, as a condition of federal funding, that state and local preparedness plans address those needs. Pub. L. No. 109-38, 120 Stat. 1725 §2, codified at 42 U.S.C. §5196b(g). How hard will it be to provide shelters that accommodate pets and service animals? Given the possibility of allergies, will separate shelters be required for pet owners? The Red Cross generally has responsibility for shelters, but its policies forbid allowing pets in its shelters.

4. Other revisions to emergency response law enacted in response to Katrina include the creation of the National Emergency Child Locator Center and the National Emergency Family Registry and Locator System. *See* Post-Katrina Emergency Management Reform Act of 2006, Pub. L. No. 109-295, §§ 689b(b)-689c, 120 Stat. 1394, 1449 (2006), codified at 6 U.S.C. §§ 774-775. During a major disaster or emergency, the National Emergency Child Locator Center serves as a clearinghouse for information about displaced children: it assists law enforcement in locating children and in reuniting children with their families. *See* 6 U.S.C. §774(b)(2)(C). The Center provides a toll-free number to receive reports about displaced children, creates a Web site to provide information about children to those who might be looking for them, and deploys staff to gather necessary information. *See id.* §§ 774(b)(3)(A)-774(b)(3)(C). Similarly, the National Emergency Family Registry and Locator System is designed to help reunify families separated after an emergency or major disaster. *See id.* §775(b). Displaced adults register voluntarily by submitting personal information to the database, and this information is accessible to individuals named by the displaced adult as well as law enforcement officials. *See id.* §§ 775(c)(1)-775(c)(2).

A recent report card by Save the Children, issued in June 2009, suggests that, despite these changes, children are still extremely vulnerable during disasters, in part because states remain poorly prepared to meet the disaster-related needs of children. *See* SAVE THE CHILDREN, THE DISASTER DECADE: LESSONS UNLEARNED FOR THE U.S. (June 2009), available at http://www.savethechildren.org/programs/us-literacy-and-nutrition/disaster-decade-lessons.html, June 28, 2009. The report found that only seven out of fifty states met all four of the report's minimum preparedness standards, which are having a state law or regulation (1) mandating that all licensed child care facilities have a written evacuation plan; (2) facilitating reunification of families by requiring all child care facilities to notify parents of an emergency; (3) requiring that child care facilities' plans make specific accommodation for children with special needs; and (4) requiring a multihazard disaster plan for grades K-12. Over half of the states only met one standard, and eleven states met none of the standards. In addition, the report found that many emergency shelters do not count children separately from adults, which makes it difficult to provide services that meet the needs of children and keep them safe. Furthermore, families are not separated from the rest of the population in emergency shelters, so families may be sharing space with sexual offenders. This leaves children vulnerable to possible violence, abuse, and even rape. *See id.* Should federal law be amended to address any of these concerns?

ii. FEDERAL HAZARD MITIGATION ASSISTANCE

Section 404 of the Stafford Act (42 U.S.C. §5170c) authorizes the president to contribute to hazard mitigation efforts in the wake of a major disaster. Pursuant to this authority, FEMA created the Hazard Mitigation Grant Program

(HMGP). After the president has made a major disaster declaration, the HMGP provides grants to states and local governments to implement long-term hazard mitigation measures within a presidentially declared disaster area. The HMGP allows communities to implement disaster mitigation measures during the immediate recovery period, when destruction occasioned by the disaster already necessitates repair or replacement of infrastructure, and when communities are most amenable to mitigation. (The Disaster Mitigation Act of 2000, Pub. L. No. 106-390, 114 Stat. 1552, amended the Stafford Act to provide for pre-disaster hazard mitigation as well, by authorizing pre-disaster mitigation grants to fund cost-effective hazard mitigation measures before disaster strikes. *See* 42 U.S.C. §5133.)

Although FEMA has the authority to provide HMGP grants, certain limitations apply, including applicant and project eligibility requirements and ceilings on federal contributions. Eligible applicants include state and local governments, Indian tribes or other tribal organizations, and certain nonprofit organizations. Individuals may not apply, but state or local governments may apply on their behalf. Though FEMA may administer HMGP grants, under 42 U.S.C. §5170c(c)(1), a state wishing to administer grants may submit an application for delegation of the authority to administer the program. Eligible projects include those that will reduce or eliminate losses from future disasters. Section 5170c(a) states that FEMA "may contribute up to 75 percent of the cost of hazard mitigation measures which the President has determined are cost-effective and which substantially reduce the risk of future damage, hardship, loss, or suffering in any area affected by a major disaster." FEMA's total contributions must not exceed a certain percentage of the grant, which varies based on the total aggregate amount of the grant. *See* 42 U.S.C. §5170c(a). However, states may receive increased funding by submitting a mitigation plan, which must be approved by the president. *See* 42 U.S.C. §5165.

iii. FEDERAL ASSISTANCE TO INDIVIDUALS AND HOUSEHOLDS

Pursuant to §408 of the Stafford Act (42 U.S.C. §5174), the president is authorized "in consultation with the Governor of a State," to "provide financial assistance and, if necessary, direct services, to individuals and households in the State who, as a direct result of a major disaster, have necessary expenses and serious needs in cases in which the individuals and households are unable to meet such needs through other means."

Specifically, §408 authorizes "housing assistance" to respond to "disaster-related housing needs" (including financial assistance for rent, direct provision of temporary housing units where the housing stock would otherwise be inadequate, and financial assistance for the repair or replacement of "owner-occupied private residences"). 42 U.S.C. §5174(b)-(c). Section 408 also authorizes financial assistance for "disaster-related medical, dental, and funeral expenses," as well as "personal property, transportation, and other necessary expenses or serious needs resulting from the major disaster." *Id.* §5174(e)(1)-(2). The maximum amount of financial assistance an individual or household can receive under §408 was capped at $30,300 in 2009 (the cap is adjusted annually based on the Consumer Price Index).

FEMA administers §408 through its Individuals and Households Program. After a disaster incident, affected individuals may apply for aid directly to FEMA through its disaster helpline or Web site. http://www.fema.gov. Once an individual files an application, one of FEMA's ten regional offices sends an inspector to the damaged property to make a decision regarding eligibility for aid. Eligible individuals must live in a presidentially declared disaster area and have losses that are not otherwise covered by insurance. Details of the application process for individual aid are available at http://www.fema.gov/pdf/ assistance/process/help_after_disaster_english.pdf.

Other sections of the Stafford Act also authorize aid to individuals affected by major disasters. For example, §410, 42 U.S.C. §5177, authorizes the president "to provide to any individual unemployed as a result of a major disaster such benefit assistance as he deems appropriate." Section 412, 42 U.S.C. §5179, authorizes the president to distribute food coupons, pursuant to the 1964 Food Stamp Act, if he determines that "low-income households are unable to purchase adequate amounts of nutritious food" due to a major disaster. The president is also authorized to provide professional counseling services (or training), §416, 42 U.S.C. §5182, and to oversee legal services, §415, 42 U.S.C. §5182, for victims of major disasters.

c. Federal Aid Available for "Emergencies"

In a presidentially declared "emergency," the Stafford Act provides for more limited aid to states, localities, and individuals. Section 501, 42 U.S.C. §5192, governs "federal emergency assistance."

§5192. **Federal emergency assistance**
(a) Specified — In any emergency, the President may —

(1) direct any Federal agency, with or without reimbursement, to utilize its authorities and the resources granted to it under Federal law (including personnel, equipment, supplies, facilities, and managerial, technical and advisory services) in support of State and local emergency assistance efforts to save lives, protect property and public health and safety, and lessen or avert the threat of a catastrophe, including precautionary evacuations;

(2) coordinate all disaster relief assistance (including voluntary assistance) provided by Federal agencies, private organizations, and State and local governments;

(3) provide technical and advisory assistance to affected State and local governments for —
(A) the performance of essential community services;
(B) issuance of warnings of risks or hazards;
(C) public health and safety information, including dissemination of such information;
(D) provision of health and safety measures; and
(E) management, control, and reduction of immediate threats to public health and safety;

(4) provide emergency assistance through Federal agencies;

(5) remove debris in accordance with the terms and conditions of section 5173 of this title;

(6) provide assistance in accordance with section 5174 of this title [federal assistance to individuals and households];

(7) assist State and local governments in the distribution of medicine, food, and other consumable supplies, and emergency assistance; and

(8) provide accelerated Federal assistance and Federal support where necessary to save lives, prevent human suffering, or mitigate severe damage, which may be provided in the absence of a special request and in which case the President—

(A) shall, to the fullest extent practicable, promptly notify and coordinate with a State in which such assistance or support is provided; and

(B) shall not, in notifying and coordinating with a State under subparagraph (A), delay or impeded the rapid deployment, use and distribution of critical resources to victims of an emergency.

(b) General—Whenever the Federal assistance provided under subsection (a) of this section with respect to an emergency is inadequate, the President may also provide assistance with respect to efforts to save lives, protect property and public health and safety, and lessen or avert the threat of a catastrophe, including precautionary evacuations.

(c) Guidelines—The President shall promulgate and maintain guidelines to assist Governors in requesting the declaration of an emergency in advance of a natural or man-made disaster (including for the purpose of seeking assistance with special needs and other evacuation efforts) under this section by defining the types of assistance available to affected States and the circumstances under which such requests are likely to be approved.

The federal share of emergency assistance provided must be at least 75 percent of eligible costs. *See* 42 U.S.C. §5193(a).

Much of this aid is identical to that provided for major disasters. Recall, too, that the president has 10-Day Authority under 42 U.S.C. §5170b to use DOD resources to perform "emergency work" in advance of an emergency declaration. Perhaps the most important limitation on federal assistance in an emergency (as opposed to a major disaster), however, is that the total amount of emergency assistance provided under the foregoing provisions is capped at $5 million, *see id.* §5193(b)(1), unless the president determines that "(A) continued emergency assistance is immediately required; (B) there is a continuing and immediate risk to lives, property, public health or safety; and (C) necessary assistance will not otherwise be provided on a timely basis," *id.* §5193(b)(2). Moreover, in contrast to a major disaster declaration, an emergency declaration does not trigger public assistance grants (for emergency work and for repairing or replacing damaged public facilities or private nonprofit facilities), grants for hazard mitigation, community disaster loans, emergency public transportation, unemployment assistance, food stamps, legal services, or crisis counseling assistance and training.

2. OTHER STATUTES AUTHORIZING FEDERAL CIVILIAN DISASTER RESPONSE

A number of specific statutory schemes supplement the Stafford Act when the nation confronts certain types of disasters. *See, e.g.,* Defense Against

Weapons of Mass Destruction Act, 50 U.S.C. §§ 2301-2368 (2008) (providing federal aid to state and local emergency agencies responding to terrorist incidents involving weapons of mass destruction). One of the most important of these statutes is the Public Health Service Act, 42 U.S.C. §§ 201-300hh-11, which gives the secretary of Health and Human Services broad emergency authority to respond to public health disasters, including the power to deploy the U.S. Public Health Service Commissioned Corps and other instruments of the Department of HHS, such as the Centers for Disease Control, the Food and Drug Administration, and the National Institutes of Health. The secretary's primary authority under the Act is found in 42 U.S.C. §247d(a), which allows the secretary to declare a public health emergency and then take appropriate steps to respond:

> If the Secretary determines, after consultation with such public health officials as may be necessary, that (1) a disease or disorder presents a public health emergency; or (2) a public health emergency, including significant outbreaks of infectious diseases or bioterrorist attacks, otherwise exists, the Secretary may take such action as may be appropriate to respond to the public health emergency, including making grants, providing awards for expenses, and entering into contracts and conducting and supporting investigations into the cause, treatment, or prevention of a disease or disorder as described in [other sections of the Act].

On April 26, 2009, the acting HHS secretary exercised this authority to declare a nationwide public health emergency for influenza A (H1N1), the so-called swine flu virus.

The Public Health Service Act also outlines a variety of other powers the secretary has for preparing for, and responding to, public health emergencies. These include:

* *Establishing international and interstate isolation and quarantine.* Although the primary authority of the states over public health includes the power to isolate and quarantine individuals, the federal government regulates individuals who are entering the United States or crossing state boundaries. Under 42 U.S.C. §264, the secretary of HHS has the power "to prevent the introduction, transmission, or spread of communicable diseases from foreign countries into the States or possessions, or from one State or possession into any other State or possession." The secretary's isolation and quarantine authority is limited to those communicable diseases listed in a presidential Executive Order. *See* 42 U.S.C. §246(b); E.O. 13295 (April 2003); E.O.13375 (April 2005). The secretary may issue regulations for the apprehension and examination of "any individual reasonably believed to be infected with a communicable disease" who is moving or about to move from one state to another or who poses a probable source of infection to individuals who will be moving from one state to another. The secretary has broader authority to issue regulations providing for the apprehension and detention of individuals entering the United States from foreign countries in order to prevent the spread of disease, and may also inspect, disinfect, or destroy infected animals or articles that pose a danger to humans. The HHS secretary has delegated

interstate and foreign quarantine authority to the director of the Centers for Disease Control (CDC). *See* 42 C.F.R. Part 70-71. Substantial changes to these regulations have been proposed.

The federal government is directed to cooperate with and aid state and local authorities in the enforcement of their quarantines and health regulations, and the federal government may accept assistance from state and local authorities in enforcement of federal quarantine regulations. *See* 42 U.S.C. §243(a). Generally, federal authority does not supersede state law; however, to the extent that state measures conflict with an exercise of federal quarantine authority under 42 U.S.C. §264 (granting federal authority over international and interstate quarantines) or under §266 (granting federal authority over quarantines conducted in times of war), federal authority may supersede state provisions. *See* 42 U.S.C §264(e). Federal regulations implement the power to override state measures in order to control the interstate transmission of a communicable disease by vesting in the director of the CDC the authority to take control of state efforts (and implement such measures as he or she deems reasonably necessary to prevent the spread of the disease) when the director determines that measures taken by state health authorities are insufficient to prevent the disease's spread. *See* 42 C.F.R. §70.2. A recent U.S. attorney general memorandum to the secretaries of DHS, HHS, and other relevant agencies notes that "[t]he authority to implement an intrastate federal quarantine is less clear [than that for interstate quarantine], although the statutes and regulations provide some authority for HHS and CDC to take some intrastate measures." Office of the Attorney General, Memorandum to the President, Summary of Legal Authorities for Use in Response to an Outbreak of Pandemic Influenza (April 25, 2009), available at http://www.ncsl.org/IssuesResearch/Health/H1N1FluSwineFluPublicHealthAlert/tabid/17089/Default.aspx (June 19, 2009).

* *Maintaining the Strategic National Stockpile (SNS).* The Public Health Service Act directs the secretary of HHS to collaborate with the Centers for Disease Control and Prevention and to coordinate with the Department of Homeland Security in maintaining a stockpile of "drugs, vaccines and other biological products, medical devices and other supplies" needed to protect the nation during a bioterrorist attack or other public health emergency. *See* 42 U.S.C. §247d-6b(a)(1). A "stockpile" may consist of either a physical accumulation of supplies or a contractual agreement with vendors to deliver the needed supplies. *See id.* §247d-6b(e).

* *Credentialing of health professionals.* The Public Health Service Act directs the secretary of HHS to link existing state verification systems to maintain a single, national, interoperable network for verifying the credentials and licenses of health care professionals who volunteer to provide health services during a public health emergency. 42 U.S.C. §247d-7b(a). The secretary may also "encourage" states to adopt mechanisms for waiving state licensing requirements for health professionals seeking to provide medical services during a state health emergency, upon verification that the professional is licensed and in good standing in another state. *Id.* §247d-7b(i).

In addition to the authority granted to the secretary pursuant to the Public Health Service Act, federal law also provides for the waiver of a wide variety of regulatory requirements in cases of public health emergency. For instance, the Food, Drug, and Cosmetics Act permits the emergency use of an unapproved new drug, an unlicensed biological product, or a medical device that has not been approved or cleared for commercial distribution in the event of an emergency involving a biological, chemical, radiological, or nuclear agent. *See* 21 U.S.C. §360bbb-3(a). The secretary may declare such an emergency in the event of a domestic or military emergency, or of a significant potential for such emergency, involving heightened risk of attack with a specified biological, chemical, radiological, or nuclear agent. *See* 21 U.S.C. §360bbb-3(b)(1)(A)-(B). Emergency use of an unapproved drug may also be permitted if the secretary of HHS has declared a public health emergency pursuant to 42 U.S.C. §247d that affects national security and that involves a specified biological, chemical, radiological, or nuclear agent, or a specified disease or condition that may be attributable to such agent. *See* 21 U.S.C. §360bbb-3(b)(1)(C). In 2004 a federal district court enjoined the Department of Defense's mandatory anthrax vaccination program based on the FDA's failure to solicit additional public comments before certifying the safety and efficacy of the anthrax vaccine. *See* Doe v. Rumsfeld, 341 F. Supp. 2d 1, 16 (D.D.C. 2004). The HHS responded by issuing its first authorization for emergency use so that the Defense Department could continue anthrax vaccinations. *See* Determination and Declaration Regarding Emergency Use of Anthrax Vaccine Absorbed for Prevention of Inhalation Anthrax, 70 Fed. Reg. 5450 (Feb. 2, 2005). This waiver authority seems geared primarily toward terrorist attacks. Does it extend to a naturally occurring pandemic virus? On April 27, 2009, pursuant to this emergency authority, the FDA authorized use of a new swine flu diagnostic test, as well as widespread distribution of the antiviral drugs Relenza and Tamiflu, without compliance with label requirements. *See* FDA News Release (April 27, 2009), available at http://www.fda. gov/NewsEvents/Newsroom/PressAnnouncements/ucm149571.htm (June 19, 2009).

The federal government also has two statutory tools for shielding health care professionals when they volunteer services during emergencies. First, the Volunteer Protection Act, 42 U.S.C. §§ 14501-14505, immunizes individuals providing volunteer services to nonprofit or governmental organizations. The institutions themselves, however, are not immunized. *See id.* §14503(c). Second, the federal government may also protect health care providers by hiring them directly. *See* Public Health Security and Bioterrorism Preparedness and Response Act of 2002, Pub. L. No. 107-188, §102, 116 Stat. 594, 599-603 (amending 42 U.S.C. §300hh-11(d) to authorize the secretary of Homeland Security to appoint intermittent employees "in accordance with applicable civil service laws and regulations"); 42 U.S.C. §5149(b)(1) (enabling federal agencies, for purposes of carrying out the Stafford Act, to appoint temporary personnel without regard to federal civil service requirements); 42 U.S.C. §209(f) (authorizing the secretary of HHS to hire public health consultants without regard to civil service rules).

3. DEPLOYMENT OF FEDERAL MILITARY FORCES AND THE POSSE COMITATUS ACT

a. The Posse Comitatus Act

Federal military forces can, and often do, play an important role in disaster relief. In the aftermath of Katrina, for example, 50,116 National Guard personnel and 22,670 federal troops were deployed to aid in disaster relief. *See* HOUSE KATRINA REPORT, *supra*, at 202 (chart). Under the Stafford Act, the Department of Defense (DOD) is a "federal agency," that can be called upon by the president in a declared major disaster to provide "general federal assistance" under §5170a or "essential assistance" under §5170b. *See* 42 U.S.C. §5122(8) (" 'Federal agency' means any department, independent establishment, Government corporation, or other agency of the executive branch of the Federal Government, including the United States Postal Service, but shall not include the American National Red Cross."). Similarly, in a declared emergency, the DOD is one of the federal agencies the president can call upon to provide "federal emergency assistance" under §5192.

Moreover, pursuant to §5170b(c) of the Stafford Act, the DOD is singled out as the agency on whom the president may call in the "immediate aftermath of an incident which may ultimately qualify" as a major disaster or emergency, but has not yet been declared as such. Upon the request of the governor of the affected state, the president may — for a period of ten days in advance of a major disaster or emergency declaration — direct the DOD "for the purpose of performing on public and private lands any emergency work which is made necessary by the incident and which is essential for the preservation of life and property." *Id.* §5170b(c)(1). For purposes of the 10-Day Authority, " 'emergency work' includes clearance and removal of debris and wreckage and temporary restoration of essential public facilities and services." *Id.* §5170b(c)(6)(B). This provision allows the president to put the DOD to work meeting critical public needs even if communication failures or other difficulties prevent the governor from immediately transmitting all of the information necessary for a major disaster or emergency declaration.

Despite these clear authorizations to use DOD resources, President Bush — in the immediate aftermath of Katrina — professed uncertainty about his ability to send federal troops into Louisiana. The president's reluctance to commit federal military personnel hinged, at least in part, on an old law, the Posse Comitatus Act, 18 U.S.C. §1385, and its exceptions. The Posse Comitatus Act provides that "[w]hoever, except in cases and under circumstances expressly authorized by the Constitution or Act of Congress, willfully uses any part of the Army or the Air Force as a posse comitatus or otherwise to execute the laws shall be fined under this title or imprisoned not more than two years, or both." *Id.*

"The phrase 'posse comitatus' is literally translated from Latin as the 'power of the county' and is defined at common law to refer to all those over the age of 15 upon whom a sheriff could call for assistance in preventing any type of civil disorder." United States v. Hartley, 796 F.2d 112, 114 n.3 (5th Cir. 1986); *accord* United States v. Yunis, 681 F. Supp. 891, 891 n.1 (D.D.C.

1988); *see also* H.R. Rep. No. 97-71, Part II, 97th Cong., 1st Sess. 4 (1981) (citing 1 William Blackstone, Commentaries *343-344), *reprinted in* 1981 U.S.C.C.A.N. 1781, 1786. Before states and localities had sizable police forces, the sheriff would supplement his numbers by calling for local citizens to aid him—as a posse comitatus—in pursuing and apprehending criminals. The first significant (and very controversial) use of posse comitatus to enforce federal law was the notorious 1850 Fugitive Slave Law, which required citizens to aid federal marshals in pursuing and detaining fugitive slaves. *See* Gautham Rao, *The Federal Posse Comitatus Doctrine: Slavery, Compulsion, and Statecraft in Mid-Nineteenth Century America*, 26 Law & Hist. Rev. 1, 24 (2008). In 1854, Attorney General Caleb Cushing issued an opinion concluding that military troops (including militia and federal regulars) could be enlisted in the posse comitatus. *See id.* at 36.

The use of the federal military as a posse comitatus to enforce the laws came to full fruition during military reconstruction of the South. During the fiercely contested presidential election of 1876, President Ulysses S. Grant sent federal troops to police federal polling places in Florida, Louisiana, and South Carolina, whose electoral votes were the subject of partisan disputes over the popular vote. An electoral commission, controlled by the Republican Congress that appointed it, awarded all of the contested electoral votes to Republican candidate Rutherford B. Hayes, who prevailed by a single electoral vote over Democrat Samuel J. Tilden. *See* H.W.C. Furman, *Restrictions upon Use of the Army Imposed by the Posse Comitatus Act*, 27 Mil. L. Rev. 85, 94-95 (1960). *See generally* David E. Engdahl, *Soldiers, Riots and Revolution: The Law and History of Military Troops in Civil Disorders*, 57 Iowa L. Rev. 1 (1971). The Posse Comitatus Act was then passed in response to Southern objections that federal military power was being abused and civil authority subordinated to military might.

Despite its ugly roots in Reconstruction politics, the Posse Comitatus Act has often been viewed as embodying the broader notion that using military troops as a domestic police force risks both individual rights and civilian supremacy over the military. This understanding still requires policymakers and courts to delineate those situations in which the military's role in law enforcement is substantial enough to constitute a violation of the Act.

Of course, the Posse Comitatus Act does not forbid all use of federal military troops to respond to natural or other disasters. The Act, by its terms, forbids deploying federal troops only when they are to be used "as a posse comitatus or otherwise to execute the laws." If "execute the laws" were read very broadly—as coincident, for instance, with the president's constitutional charge to see that the laws are faithfully executed—then the Act would forbid all but expressly authorized use of the federal military to implement or carry into effect any state or federal law, including disaster relief programs. In context, however, it is clear that "execute the laws" has the narrower meaning of enforcing laws against civilians and compelling citizens to comply with the law, such that the Act only forbids assigning civilian law enforcement functions to federal troops.

Prosecutions under the Act itself have been virtually nonexistent, so most of the judicial interpretation of the Act has occurred when an individual is prosecuted for another crime and defends on the ground that federal military involvement in his investigation or apprehension rendered the actions of law enforcement officers illegal. Consider the *Red Feather* case below, which arose out of military involvement in the federal response to the February 1973 occupation of Wounded Knee, South Dakota, by followers of the American Indian Movement. The defendant was charged under 18 U.S.C. §231(a)(3) with interfering with law enforcement officers engaged in the lawful performance of their official duties — officers who had received federal military assistance in the form of equipment, supplies, advice, and aerial reconnaissance.

United States v. Red Feather

392 F. Supp. 916, 921-924 (D.S.D. 1975), *aff'd sub nom.*
United States v. Casper, 541 F.2d 1275 (8th Cir. 1976)

Bogue, District Judge. . . .

Upon careful examination of the legislative history of 18 U.S.C. §1385, this Court has reached several conclusions of law. First, the clause contained in 18 U.S.C. §1385 "uses any part of the Army or the Air Force as a posse comitatus or otherwise" means the direct active use of Army or Air Force personnel and does not mean the use of Army or Air Force equipment or materiel. 18 U.S.C. §1385 was intended by Congress . . . to eliminate the direct active use of federal troops by civil law enforcement officers. The prevention of the use of military supplies and equipment was never mentioned in the debates, nor can it reasonably be read into the words of the Act. Only the direct active use of federal [troops is] forbidden, unless expressly authorized by the Constitution or by Act of Congress. An Act of Congress, 10 U.S.C. §331, has authorized the President of the United States to order use of the militia and armed forces, but no such order was issued by the President as to the Wounded Knee occupation. The Congressional debates clearly reveal that . . . Congress intended to prohibit the direct active use of any unit of federal military troops of whatever size or designation to include one single soldier or large units such as a platoon or squadron, to execute the laws. . . . [W]hen 18 U.S.C. §1385 was enacted, many Southerners resented the use of federal troops in places in which government had been reestablished, especially since such use was often directed, in their view, toward altering the outcome of elections in Southern states. For example, in the disputed Tilden-Hayes election of 1876, Rutherford B. Hayes obtained the necessary electoral votes only because the disputed votes of South Carolina, Louisiana, and Florida were all awarded to him. In each of these states the elections were accomplished by the use of federal troops, ostensibly to preserve the peace, and in each state when elections were contested, the troops supported the reconstruction candidates. Of primary concern was the prospect of United States marshals, on their own initiative, calling upon troops to form a posse or to otherwise perform direct law enforcement functions to execute the law. Thus, . . . the act was intended to stop army troops, whether one or many, from answering the call of any marshal or deputy marshal to perform direct law enforcement duties to aid in execution of the law. . . .

[T]he intent of Congress in enacting this statute and by using the clause "uses any part of the Army or the Air Force as a posse comitatus or otherwise," was to prevent the direct active use of federal troops, one soldier or many, to execute the laws. Congress did not intend to prevent the use of Army or Air Force materiel or equipment in aid of execution of the laws. Moreover, through enactment of the Economy Act of 1932, 31 U.S.C. §686, Congress has provided extremely broad authorization for any executive department or independent establishment to place orders with any other willing department for materials, supplies, equipment, work, or service. . . .

[T]his Court concludes that 18 U.S.C. §1385 may be violated only through the direct active use of troops for the purpose of executing the laws and 18 U.S.C. §1385 is not violated by the use of Army or Air Force materiel, supplies, or equipment of any type or kind in execution of the law. . . .

[T]his holding is not only dictated by the statute and its legislative history, but from a practical economic standpoint, this holding is supported by common sense. During and after any natural disaster in this country whether due to flood, heavy snowstorms, earthquake, tornado or otherwise, there is always the possibility of looting and other acts of civil disorder. Most of this nation's smaller governmental units simply cannot maintain an inventory of emergency vehicles and other equipment adequate to meet such a crisis. If the affected municipality or county requests and receives, and law enforcement officers are using Department of Defense equipment or supplies to aid in enforcing the laws, . . . it would violate common sense and do violence to the intent of Congress in passing 18 U.S.C. §1385 to hold that those arrested for criminal acts must be released because law enforcement officers were using military equipment to aid in executing the law. . . .

In order to more fully establish what evidence of military involvement would constitute unlawful conduct under 18 U.S.C. §1385 and thus be relevant to disprove the third element of the charge against the defendants under 18 U.S.C. §231(a)(3), the clause "to execute the laws" contained in 18 U.S.C. §1385 must be construed. It is the opinion of this Court that Congress intended, by use of the clause "to execute the laws," to make unlawful the direct active participation of federal military troops in law enforcement activities. Congress did not intend to make unlawful the involvement of federal troops in a passive role in civilian law enforcement activities. . . .

Activities which constitute an active role in direct law enforcement are: arrest; seizure of evidence; search of a person; search of a building; investigation of crime; interviewing witnesses; pursuit of an escaped civilian prisoner; search of an area for a suspect and other like activities. . . . Activities which constitute a passive role which might indirectly aid [law enforcement include] aerial photographic reconnaissance[;] military personnel under orders to report on the necessity of military intervention; preparation of emergency contingency plans to be used if military intervention is ordered; advice or recommendations given to civilian law enforcement officers by military personnel on tactics or logistics; presence of military personnel to deliver military material, equipment or supplies, to train local law enforcement officials on the proper use and care of such material or equipment, and to maintain such material or equipment. . . .

[Therefore,] any evidence that United States marshals or agents of the Federal Bureau of Investigation used Army or Air Force Troops, one soldier or many, in an active role of direct law enforcement by performing one or more of the specific acts set forth above during the occupation of Wounded Knee, is admissible. Such [activity] is unlawful under 18 U.S.C. §1385 and therefore relevant and material to disprove the third element of the 18 U.S.C. §231(a)(3) charge against defendants, i.e., that law enforcement officers were lawfully performing their official duties. . . .

NOTES AND QUESTIONS

1. The Department of Defense has interpreted the Posse Comitatus Act as generally prohibiting "direct" military involvement in civilian law enforcement but permitting "indirect" assistance such as the transfer of information obtained during normal military operations, as well as other actions that "do not subject civilians to [the] use [of] military power that is regulatory, prescriptive, or compulsory." DOD Directive 5525.5 §E4.1.7.2; *accord* United States v. Hitchcock, 286 F.3d 1064, 1069, *amended on other grounds*, 298 F.3d 1021 (9th Cir. 2002). Specifically, the DOD has interpreted the prohibition on using military personnel "as a posse comitatus or otherwise to execute the laws" to include, inter alia, "[i]nterdiction of a vehicle, vessel aircraft or other similar activity"; "[a] search or seizure"; "[a]n arrest, apprehension, stop and frisk, or similar activity"; and "[u]se of military personnel for surveillance or pursuit of individuals, or as undercover agents, informants, investigators, or interrogators." DOD Directive 5525.5 §E4.1.3.1-4.1.3.4.

2. Federal courts typically classify potential violations of the Act by using three tests to determine when military involvement in law enforcement transcends the presumptively permissible zone of "indirect" assistance: (1) whether civilian law enforcement officials have made "direct active use" of military personnel (as in *Red Feather*), (2) whether military involvement has "pervaded the activities" of civilian authorities, and (3) whether the military has become so entangled in civilian law enforcement as to subject citizens to the "exercise of military power that is regulatory, proscriptive, or compulsory in nature." *See* United States v. Kahn, 35 F.3d 426, 431 (9th Cir. 1994); United States v. Yunis, 924 F.2d 1086, 1094 (D.C. Cir. 1991); United States v. Hartley, 678 F.2d 961, 978 n.24 (11th Cir. 1982).

3. Would it violate the Posse Comitatus Act for federal troops to enforce an evacuation order? To provide security for distribution of food and other essential supplies? To direct traffic? To police the perimeter of a disaster scene? To operate a checkpoint allowing residents (but excluding nonresidents) from reentering a disaster area? To enforce a quarantine or isolation order? To administer compelled vaccination during a pandemic? *See* James Balcius & Bryan A Liang, *Public Health Law & Military Medical Assets: Legal Issues in Federalizing National Guard Personnel*, 18 ANNALS HEALTH L. 35, 55-57 (2009).

4. Even without the express statutory authority granted in the Stafford Act, President Bush could have deployed federal troops to provide every type of assistance outlined under the Stafford Act (search and rescue, food distribution, debris removal, etc.) without running afoul of the Posse Comitatus

Act, because those activities do not involve federal military participation in law enforcement. What, then, was the source of the president's reluctance to send federal troops to New Orleans? Apparently, "Pentagon and military officials [believed] that no active-duty forces could have been sent into the chaos of New Orleans on Wednesday or Thursday [immediately after the hurricane made landfall] without confronting law-and-order challenges." Eric Lipton et al., *Storm and Crisis: Military Response; Political Issues Snarled Plans for Troop Aid*, N.Y. TIMES, Sept. 9, 2005, at A1. Thus, federal officials were reluctant to send federal troops to New Orleans because they believed the troops necessarily would have to engage in law enforcement functions in order to protect themselves and carry out their mission. They feared that federal troops would therefore be forced to violate the Posse Comitatus Act, unless they could be deployed under the Insurrection Act, an exception to the Posse Comitatus Act. *See infra.*

5. Consider one author's contention that the behavior of military troops responding to Katrina underscores the necessity of the Posse Comitatus Act:

> Soon after troops began arriving in New Orleans, television news broadcasts repeatedly showed footage of General Honoré yelling at a group of soldiers in the back of a pickup truck who were training their M-16s on haggard-looking civilian men, women, and children. The General said: "Point your weapons to the ground, this is not Iraq." The soldiers epitomized a posse comitatus and appeared to be playing out a scene from a developing country run by aberrant gangs.
>
> Scenes like this were precisely why the PCA was passed: to enforce civilian authority over the military in order to maintain a democratic form of government. Unfortunately, Congress and the courts have created so many exceptions that the PCA has lost its teeth. The modern PCA appears to be nothing more than a legacy law.

Candidus Dougherty, *While the Government Fiddled Around, The Big Easy Drowned: How the Posse Comitatus Act Became the Government's Alibi for the Hurricane Katrina Disaster*, 29 N. ILL. U. L. REV. 117, 146 (2008). Dougherty contends that the PCA presented no real obstacle to the government's provision of humanitarian aid and was simply a convenient scapegoat to justify the government's inadequate response. *See id.*

6. Courts typically take a benign view of the origins and purposes of the Posse Comitatus Act: "The purpose of this statute is to prevent use of the federal army to aid civil authorities in the enforcement of civilian laws. Congress adopted the Act's precursor in 1878 in response to abuses resulting from such use in former Confederate States after the Civil War. The Act reflects a concern, which antedates the Revolution, about the dangers to individual freedom and liberty posed by use of a standing army to keep civil peace." Gilbert v. United States, 165 F.3d 470, 472 (6th Cir. 1999).

7. By contrast, some scholars vehemently condemn what they consider the whitewashing of the Posse Comitatus Act's odious origins:

> This nineteenth century remnant from the Reconstruction period has been mischaracterized from its very beginnings, at times deliberately. One initial deception was to hide the Act's racist origins by linking the Act with the

principles surrounding the founding of the United States, without accounting for the passage of the Constitution or the Civil War. To compound
matters, the Act's most vocal nineteenth century supporters incorporated
by reference the controversial, yet somewhat contrived, arguments against
a standing U.S. army from the revolutionary period. The Act's supporters
also hid their unsavory agenda behind patriotic phrases and ideas
of the Anti-Federalists that the founders themselves had not put into
practice. In short, the Act was carefully disguised in two levels of deliberate
misinformation.

The effort to disguise the Act's true origins in Reconstruction bitterness
and racial hatred was overwhelmingly successful. The language of mis-
direction grew over the years by frequent repetition that eventually transformed a hate law into the respected shorthand for the general principle
that Americans do not want a military national police force. Additionally,
just about everyone examining the law focused on the false historical arguments instead of carefully analyzing the law's actual text and historical
context. . . .

Many of the courts analyzing the Act also wrote about the law as if it was
the only law or principle that limited the use of the armed forces in a law
enforcement role. Some, therefore, have claimed to discern a broader policy
or "spirit" behind the Act that is not supported by the historical record or
the statute's text. While these wider policies are sound, they are embodied
in federalism, the law concerning federal arrest authority, election law, and
especially fiscal law. The portion of the Posse Comitatus Act that survived
the nineteenth century doesn't have to do all the work, a view that even the
Act's original proponents appeared to recognize. Trying to force-fit all these
other principles into the surviving part of the Act has only created a need to
"discover" a number of implied exceptions and has sowed a great deal of
confusion.

Further muddying the waters, much of the commentary about this topic
has been infected with a now thoroughly discredited, and racist, historical
analysis of the Reconstruction period. Other commentators, and courts,
have simply avoided or minimized the Act's brutal racist origins. . . .

Gary Felicetti & John Luce, *The Posse Comitatus Act: Setting the Record
Straight on 124 Years of Mischief and Misunderstanding before Any More
Damage Is Done*, 175 MIL. L. REV. 86, 88-92 (2003).

8. Regardless of its origins, is the Posse Comitatus Act justified by the fact that
   military troops are not trained to deal with the nuances of civilian law
   enforcement, including the difficulties of crowd control, restraints on
   the use of deadly force, and respect for constitutional rights?

   Modern combat is very fast-paced: decisions are made quickly in the heat
   and stress of a life-and-death struggle. Soldiers are highly trained to use force
   in the furtherance of the mission. They are trained to respond with force
   when facing an adversary because the adversary is likely to do the same.
   Being under fire changes the landscape and changes the stakes. . . . Military
   personnel have different approaches to tactical situations than what is
   required in a law enforcement situation. The appropriate reaction to an
   adversarial law enforcement situation is not necessarily the use of deadly
   force; a more deliberative approach may be more appropriate. Conversely,
   military personnel involved in a combat situation need to quickly decide

when deadly force should be used. Moving military personnel between these two situations may cause the soldier to misread or misunderstand a situation and use the wrong kind of force.

Michael T. Cunningham, *The Military's Involvement in Law Enforcement: The Threat Is Not What You Think*, 26 SEATTLE U. L. REV. 699, 715-716 (2003). *See also* Christopher H. Lytton, *America's Borders and Civil Liberties in a Post–September 11th World*, 12 J. TRASNAT'L L. & POL'Y 197, 204 (2003) ("Soldiers are taught to violently and effectively destroy the enemy and their training does not include sensitivity to constitutional limitations on search, seizure, and the use of reasonable force."); Dan Bennett, Note, *The Domestic Role of the Military in America: Why Modifying or Repealing the Posse Comitatus Act Would Be a Mistake*, 10 LEWIS & CLARK L. REV. 935, 944 (2006) ("[T]here is no reason to assume that the military is often, or even ever, suited to the tasks of domestic law enforcement. As Lawrence Korb, the former Assistant Secretary of Defense puts it, the armed forces are 'trained to vaporize, not Mirandize.'"); Sean J. Kealy, *Reexamining the Posse Comitatus Act: Toward a Right to Civil Law Enforcement*, 21 YALE L. & POL'Y REV. 383, 434 (2003) (arguing that a "right to civil law enforcement is grounded in a long tradition that antedates the Revolution and the ratification of the Constitution, is reflected in several of the protections guaranteed by the Constitution, and has been reaffirmed in statutes and case law").

9. Does allowing the military to assume responsibility for civilian law enforcement in the aftermath of disasters present any real risk that civilian institutions will be subordinated to military control? *See* Bennett, *supra*, at 935, 943-944 (describing the Posse Comitatus Act as a "crucial bulwark for liberty" and arguing that increased use of military in domestic law enforcement presents a "very real, if remote, danger that the military will seek to gain supremacy over the civilian institutions of government," threatens "universal trust in the military as a non-political body," and is "inherently repugnant to most Americans"). Would the risk be greater in a disaster that spanned many months or even years, such as a virulent flu pandemic? Is the notion that the military threatens civilian rule outdated?

> The change in Americans' perception of the military . . . warrants a change in the PCA. Present-day Americans view the military much more favorably than [they] did at the dawn of the Revolution. American troops no longer symbolize suppression; instead to some they represent "beacons of freedom" at home and abroad. The rise of American nationalism post–September 11th causes citizens to perceive soldiers as heroes, not villains, and to perceive the Army as protector of safety, not an imposer of threat. Consequently, Americans no longer mandate the artificial construct separating civilian law enforcement from military operations when the immediacy of a disaster requires otherwise.

Jessica DeBianchi, Note, *Military Law: Winds of Change—Examining the Present-Day Propriety of the Posse Comitatus Act after Hurricane Katrina*, 17 U. FLA. J.L. & PUB. POL'Y 473, 500 (2006).

10. Are Posse Comitatus Act restrictions justified by the effect on military readiness of domestic disaster deployments? Consider this component of

Cunningham's critique, which is rooted in the belief that the military is neither "the tool of oppression feared by liberal legal scholars and pundits" nor "the 'always successful' organization that those on the right think it is":

> The real issue . . . is not whether the military's involvement in law enforcement can be reconciled under both the PCA and our concept of civil liberties; that is likely possible. The real concern with widening the military's participation in law enforcement (as well as other nontraditional military missions) is not an erosion of civil liberties, but an erosion of military capabilities. . . . [Is] the use of military forces in counter-drug operations, or law enforcement in general, . . . a good or bad thing[?] In the end, the use of the military in law enforcement is somewhere in the middle. On the one hand, there are good points. For example, the military's logistical and power projection capabilities increase the reach of American law enforcement. On the other hand, there are bad points. The military tends to think in terms of "complete victory" over an opponent through the use of overwhelming force, which may not be a useful mindset in law enforcement operations. Additionally, using military units for direct or indirect law enforcement degrades those units' readiness for combat operations. . . . The real threat posed by increasing military participation in law enforcement is that use of the military in law enforcement operations will dull the critical war-fighting skills the military services need. Fundamentally, the nation must think and choose wisely, using the military in law enforcement judiciously, when its capabilities can be of most use, of greatest success, and complementary to the skills the military needs to be effective in a modern combat environment.

Cunningham, *supra*, at 701-702. Many of the troops sent to relieve conditions in the wake of Hurricane Katrina had returned from or were en route to foreign tours of duty (particularly in Iraq and Afghanistan). Does the liberal use of military personnel and material during disasters effectively open an additional front for these troops at the very moment when American forces are stretched to their limits by active military engagements across the globe? Or is it the overseas deployment of National Guard troops that unduly drains state military (militia) resources that should be available for domestic disaster response? *See Hurricane Katrina: The Role of the Governors in Managing the Catastrophe: Hearing before the S. Comm. on Homeland Sec. and Governmental Affairs*, 109th Cong. 25 (2006) (statement of Kathleen Blanco, Gov., State of Louisiana) (explaining that some 6,000 of Louisiana's 11,000 National Guardsmen were not available to respond to Katrina because they were deployed overseas).

11. As a matter of policy, just how desirable — or objectionable — is the Posse Comitatus Act? Does your answer depend on whether military involvement in law enforcement is considered in the abstract, or whether it is considered in the specific context of disasters and other emergencies that overwhelm state and local officials?

12. What personnel are covered by the Posse Comitatus Act?

    a. Does the Posse Comitatus Act apply to the Navy (including the Marine Corps)? Although the statute does not name those branches of the military, courts have debated whether this omission, by operation of the interpretive canon *expressio unius est exclusio alterius*, confines the Act to the Army and the Air Force, the branches that *are* named in 18 U.S.C. §1385. *Compare* United States v. Kahn, 35 F.3d 426, 431 (9th Cir. 1994) (concluding that plain language excludes the Navy); United States v. Yunis, 924 F.2d 1086, 1093 (D.C. Cir. 1991) (same); *and* State v. Short, 113 Wash. 2d 35, 775 P.2d 458 (1989) (same) *with* United States v. Walden, 490 F.2d 372, 374-375 (4th Cir.), *cert. denied*, 416 U.S. 983 (1974) (suggesting that although the Act does not apply "by its terms" to the Marines, "consideration of the legislative history of the Act and interpretive opinions reveals a policy applicable to all of the armed services"); People v. Blend, 175 Cal. Rptr. 263, 267 (Cal. Ct. App. 1981) (concluding that the Act "applies to all branches of the federal military").

This theoretical interpretive question has little practical significance. The Department of Defense has applied the proscriptions of the Posse Comitatus Act to the Navy (including the Marine Corps), as well as the Army and the Air Force. Congress has directed the secretary of Defense to "prescribe such regulations as may be necessary to ensure that any activity (including the provision of any equipment or facility or the assignment or detail of any personnel) under this chapter does not include or permit direct participation by a member of the Army, Navy, Air Force, or Marine Corps in a search, seizure, arrest, or other similar activity unless participation in such activity by such member is otherwise authorized by law." 10 U.S.C. §375. In response to this directive, the Department of Defense has subjected the Navy to the same restrictions on direct participation in law enforcement applicable to Army and Air Force personnel. *See* U.S. Dept. of Defense, Directive No. 5525.5, DoD Cooperation with Civilian Law Enforcement Officials encl. 4, at 4.3 (Jan. 15, 1986), available at http://www.dtic.mil/whs/directives/corres/html/552505.htm and http://www.fas.org/irp/dod-dir/dod/d5525_5.pdf. Despite its application to the other military branches, the Posse Comitatus Act does not apply to the Coast Guard — which is charged by statute with certain law enforcement functions — unless the Coast Guard is operating under the DOD's command and control. 14 U.S.C. §2; 1 Center for Law & Military Operations, Domestic Operational Law (DOPLAW) Handbook for Judge Advocates 16 (2006) [hereinafter DOPLAW].

b. Does the Posse Comitatus Act apply to National Guard troops? National Guard troops can be activated in three different legal capacities. First, a state governor can activate National Guard troops to "state active duty status." When acting in this capacity, National Guard troops are commanded by the state governor and compensated with state funds. Second, pursuant to Title 32 of the U.S. Code, a state governor may, with the permission of the secretary of the Army or Air Force, activate National Guard troops to "full-time National Guard duty" status. *See* 32 U.S.C. §§ 328, 502(f). Title 32 troops are under the direction of the state governor, who acts as commander in chief; however, they are paid by the federal government. 32 U.S.C. §§ 902, 905. Third, under Title 10, the president may call National Guard troops into federal "Active Duty." 10 U.S.C. §12406 authorizes the president to call the National Guard into federal service to repel an invasion, suppress a rebellion, or to aid in the execution of federal law, when those laws cannot be executed with federal regular forces alone. The president is the commander in chief of these federal active duty troops (who are considered regular federal Army or Air Force), and the troops are paid federal salaries.

> The PCA . . . applies to Reserve members of the Army, Navy, Air Force, and Marine Corps who are on active duty, active duty for training, or inactive duty training in a Title 10 duty status. Members of the National Guard performing active duty for training or inactive duty training in a Title 32 duty status are not subject to the PCA. Only when members of the National Guard are in a Title 10 duty status (federal status) will they be subject to the PCA. Members of the National Guard also perform additional duties in a State Active Duty (SAD) status and are not subject to PCA in that capacity. Civilian employees of the Department of Defense are only subject to the prohibitions of the PCA if they are under the direct command and control of a military officer."

DOPLAW, *supra*, at 17 (emphases and footnotes omitted) (citing DOD Cooperation with Civilian Law Enforcement Officials, Department of Defense Directive 5525.5, ¶E4.2). *See also* Gilbert v. United States, 165 F.3d 470, 473 (6th Cir 1999) ("The [Posse Comitatus] Act does not apply to members of the National Guard unless they have been called into 'federal service.' ").

After Katrina, Louisiana Governor Blanco refused to consent to federalization of the Louisiana National Guard. In an attempted compromise, President Bush proposed a hybrid structure, in which one National Guard commander would have been authorized to command both Title 10 and Title 32 personnel, and would have been required to report both to the president and the governor. 2006 A.B.A. Hurricane Katrina Task Force Rep. 66. Governor Blanco rejected this alternative.

13. Does the Posse Comitatus Act restrict the use of armed forces in law enforcement outside the United States? Most courts, finding no congressional intent to restrict uses of American troops abroad, have given the Act no extraterritorial effect. *See, e.g.,* D'Aquino v. United States, 192 F.2d 338, 351 (9th Cir. 1951), *cert. denied*, 343 U.S. 935 (1952); Chandler v. United States, 171 F.2d 921, 936 (1st Cir. 1948), *cert. denied*, 336 U.S. 918 (1949). More recently, however, the Ninth Circuit has suggested that the extraterritorial applicability of the Posse Comitatus Act remains an open question, citing other statutory restrictions on the use of American troops abroad. Kahn, 35 F.3d at 431 n.6 (citing 10 U.S.C. §§ 371-381). The DOD has indicated that it will consider requests for extraterritorial use of the military as law enforcement on a case-by-case basis, and will grant such requests only when justified by "compelling and extraordinary circumstances." Department of Defense Directive 5525.5, ¶8.1.

14. No person appears ever to have been successfully prosecuted for a violation of the Posse Comitatus Act. *See, e.g.,* Matthew Carlton Hammond, Note,

The Posse Comitatus Act: A Principle in Need of Renewal, 75 Wash. U. L.Q. 953, 961 (1997). Two Army officers were indicted in 1879, a year after the Act's passage, for sending troops to a U.S. marshal for the purpose of enforcing revenue laws. It is not known whether these officers were prosecuted. *See id.* at 961 n.53. That said, violations of the Act may yield "[o]ther adverse consequences":

> In many criminal cases, defendants have argued that a violation renders their arrest unlawful; therefore, evidence seized incident to the arrest must be suppressed under the Exclusionary Rule. A review of the cases, however, reveals no federal cases and only one state case in which the Exclusionary Rule was actually applied. In egregious cases, a violation may warrant a civil claim against the military department or the individual service member. A review of these cases, however, reveals only one federal case in which a court supported a tort claim.

Matthew J. Gilligan, *Opening the Gate? An Analysis of Military Law Enforcement Authority over Civilian Lawbreakers on and off the Federal Installation*, 161 Mil. L. Rev. 1, 11 (1999). In addition, the Posse Comitatus Act remains "available in criminal or administrative proceedings to punish a lower-level commander who uses military forces to pursue a common felon or to conduct sobriety checkpoints off of a federal military post," and military officers accused of "misusing federal military assets to support a purely civilian criminal matter" have seen "their careers abruptly brought to a close." Craig T. Trebilcock, *The Myth of Posse Comitatus*, J. Homeland Security (October 2000), available at http://www.homelandsecurity.org/journal/articles/Trebilcock.htm. The most important and far-reaching consequences of the Act, however, have been in the formulation of DOD policy about military involvement in civil law enforcement functions.

b. Statutory Exemptions to the Posse Comitatus Act

The prohibitions of the Posse Comitatus Act do *not* apply "in cases and under circumstances expressly authorized by the Constitution or Act of Congress." 18 U.S.C. §1385. A number of statutes expressly authorize the federal military to engage in civilian law enforcement. *See* DOPLAW, *supra*, at 31-32.

Several of the exceptions are of particular interest in disaster (or potential disaster) situations. For example, in an emergency situation in which civilian law enforcement officers lack capacity to enforce the law, the DOD, upon request by the attorney general, is permitted to deploy military forces to assist in enforcing federal restrictions on the handling of nuclear materials; such assistance may include conducting searches and seizures and arresting suspects. 18 U.S.C. §831(e). DOD may likewise provide assistance, at the request of the attorney general, in "an emergency situation involving a biological or chemical weapon of mass destruction,"10 U.S.C. §382(a), but participation in arrest and search and seizure are authorized—if at all—under only the most limited of emergency circumstances, *id.* §382(d). In addition, the secretary of Health and Human Services can authorize military officers stationed at seacoast posts (and Coast Guard personnel) to aid states in executing state quarantines and health laws, "respecting any vessel arriving in, or bound to, any port or district thereof." 42 U.S.C. §97.

One of the most important exceptions to the Posse Comitatus Act is the Insurrection Act, 10 U.S.C. §§ 331-335. When invoked, the Insurrection Act authorizes the president to invest members of federalized state militias or federal regulars with broad civil law enforcement powers. The Insurrection Act—originally enacted during the Civil War, *see* Act of July 29, 1861, ch. 25, 12 Stat. 281—is the most recent in a long series of statutes, dating back to 1792, delegating Congress's power "[t]o provide for calling forth the Militia to execute the Laws of the Union, suppress Insurrections and repel Invasions," U.S. CONST. art. I, §8, cl. 15, *see* Vladeck, Note, *supra*, at 159, to implement Article IV, Section 4 of the Constitution, and (post–Civil War) to enforce the Fourteenth Amendment.

INSURRECTION ACT

10 U.S.C. §§ 331-334

§331. Federal aid for State governments.

Whenever there is an insurrection in any State against its government, the President may, upon the request of its legislature or of its governor if the legislature cannot be convened, call into Federal service such of the militia of the other States, in the number requested by that State, and use such of the armed forces, as he considers necessary to suppress the insurrection.

§332. Use of militia and armed forces to enforce Federal authority.

Whenever the President considers that unlawful obstructions, combinations, or assemblages, or rebellion against the authority of the United States, make it impracticable to enforce the laws of the United States in any State by the ordinary course of judicial proceedings, he may call into Federal service such of the militia of any State, and use such of the armed forces, as he considers necessary to enforce those laws or to suppress the rebellion.

§333. Interference with State and Federal law.

The President, by using the militia or the armed forces, or both, or by any other means, shall take such measures as he considers necessary to suppress, in a State, any insurrection, domestic violence, unlawful combination, or conspiracy, if it—

(1) so hinders the execution of the laws of that State, and of the United States within the State, that any part or class of its people is deprived of a right, privilege, immunity, or protection named in the Constitution and secured by law, and the constituted authorities of that State are unable, fail, or refuse to protect that right, privilege, or immunity, or to give that protection; or

(2) opposes or obstructs the execution of the laws of the United States or impedes the course of justice under those laws.

In any situation covered by clause (1), the State shall be considered to have denied the equal protection of the laws secured by the Constitution.

§334. Proclamation to disperse.

Whenever the President considers it necessary to use the militia or the armed forces under this chapter, he shall, by proclamation, immediately order the insurgents to disperse and retire peaceably to their abodes within a limited time.

NOTES AND QUESTIONS

1. What constitutes an insurrection? Consider the following jury charge, issued by the federal district court that tried members of the American Railway Union for their role in the legendary Pullman Strike of 1894:

> Insurrection is a rising against civil or political authority, the open and active opposition of a number of persons to the execution of law in a city or state. Now, the laws of the United States forbid, under penalty, any person from obstructing or retarding the passage of the mail, and make it the duty of the officers to arrest such offenders, and bring them before the court. If, therefore, it shall appear to you that any person or persons have willfully obstructed or retarded the mails, and that their attempted arrest for such offense has been opposed by such a number of persons as would constitute a general uprising in that particular locality, then the fact of an insurrection, within the meaning of the law, has been established; and he who by speech, writing, or other inducement assists in setting it on foot, or carrying it along, or gives it aid or comfort, is guilty of a violation of law. It is not necessary that there should be bloodshed; it is not necessary that its dimensions should be so portentous as to insure probable success, to constitute an insurrection. It is necessary, however, that the rising should be in opposition to the execution of the laws of the United States, and should be so formidable as for the time being to defy the authority of the United States. When men gather to resist the civil or political power of the United States, or to oppose the execution of its laws, and are in such force that the civil authorities are inadequate to put them down, and a considerable military force is needed to accomplish that result, they become insurgents; and every person who knowingly incites, aids, or abets them, no matter what his motives may be, is likewise an insurgent. The penalty for the offense is severe, and, as I have said, is designed to protect the government and its authority against direct attack.

   In re Charge to Grand Jury, 62 F. 828, 830 (N.D. Ill. 1894). *See generally* William Cawardine, The Pullman Strike (1973).

2. Much of the Fourteenth Amendment was aimed at imposing special disabilities on the losers of the Civil War. Sections 2, 3, and 4 of that amendment continue to serve notice that those who engage in insurrection or rebellion against the United States do so at their peril. *See, e.g.*, U.S. Const. amend. XIV §3 (disqualifying from federal office any person "who, having previously taken an oath, as a member of Congress, or as an officer of the United States, or as a member of any State legislature, or as an executive or judicial officer of any State, to support the Constitution of the United States, shall have engaged in insurrection or rebellion against the same, or given aid or comfort to the enemies thereof"). Does the stigma of the word "insurrection," as reflected in the punitive provisions of the Fourteenth Amendment and court decisions such as the Pullman Strike case, impede the

contemporary use of the Insurrection Act? Is there some other word without this stigma that would convey the same meaning?

3. Recall Article IV, Section 4 of the Constitution: "The United States shall guarantee to every State in this Union a Republican Form of Government, and shall protect each of them against Invasion; and on Application of the Legislature, or of the Executive (when the Legislature cannot be convened), against domestic Violence." *See* discussion, *supra*, Section A.2.

   a. Does this provision represent an affirmative power vested in Congress and the president? A responsibility that the United States must discharge vis-à-vis its constituent states? Both?

   b. Consider the term "domestic violence." How does this term compare to the term "insurrection," as it is used (1) within the Insurrection Act and (2) within Article I, Section 8 of the Constitution?

4. Recall that the National Guard may be called into the service of the United States "[w]henever — (1) the United States, or any of the Commonwealths or possessions, is invaded or is in danger of invasion by a foreign nation; (2) there is a rebellion or danger of a rebellion against the authority of the Government of the United States; or (3) the President is unable with the regular forces to execute the laws of the United States." 10 U.S.C. §12406. The Insurrection Act has been used to deploy National Guard units in support of desegregation orders that met "massive resistance" during the 1950s and 1960s. Perhaps the most prominent use of this power took place in September 1957, when President Eisenhower ordered the National Guard and Air National Guard of Arkansas to remove "obstruction of justice . . . with respect to . . . enrollment and attendance at public schools in the Little Rock School District." Order No. 10,730, 22 Fed. Reg. 7628 (Sept. 24, 1957); *see also* Exec. Order No. 11,053, 27 Fed. Reg. 9681 (Sept. 30, 1962) (Mississippi public schools); Exec. Order No. 11,111, 28 Fed. Reg. 5709 (June 11, 1963) (University of Alabama); Exec. Order No. 11,118, 28 Fed. Reg. 9863 (Sept. 10, 1963) (Alabama public schools).

   These executive orders were preceded by presidential proclamations, issued under 10 U.S.C. §334, commanding private citizens engaged in an insurgency to disperse and retire peaceably to their homes. *See* Proc. No. 3204, 22 Fed. Reg. 7628 (Sept. 23, 1957) (Little Rock public schools, particularly Central Little Rock High School); Proc. No. 3497, 27 Fed. Reg. 9681 (Sept. 30, 1962) (Mississippi public schools); Proc. No. 3542, 28 Fed. Reg. 5707 (June 11, 1963) (University of Alabama); Proc. No. 3554, 28 Fed. Reg. 9861 (Sept. 10, 1963) (Alabama public schools). Similar proclamations were issued in connection with Martin Luther King Jr.'s peace march from Selma to Montgomery, *see* Proc. No. 3645, 30 Fed. Reg. 3739 (March 23, 1965), and urban riots throughout 1967 and 1968, *see, e.g.*, Proc. No. 3795, 32 Fed. Reg. 10,905 (July 26, 1967) (Detroit).

5. The Insurrection Act enabled the first President Bush to send troops to quell civil unrest in the U.S. Virgin Islands after Hurricane Hugo in 1989. *See* Proc. No. 6023, 54 Fed. Reg. 39,151 (Sept. 20, 1989); Exec. Order No. 12,690, 54 Fed. Reg. 39, 153 (Sept. 20, 1989). Three years later, President Bush again invoked the Insurrection Act in response to the Rodney King riots in Los

Angeles. *See* Proc. No. 6427, 57 Fed. Reg. 19,359 (May 1, 1992); Exec. Order No. 12,804, 57 Fed. Reg. 19,361 (May 1, 1992).

6. If President George W. Bush and his advisors believed that lawlessness in New Orleans was so prevalent that federal troops necessarily would be required to engage in some law enforcement functions, why didn't he invoke the Insurrection Act to justify his deployment of troops to New Orleans to put down looting and lawlessness? Governor Blanco did not make the requisite request under §331 (and, in fact, was anxious to retain control over National Guard troops and objected to any suggestion that they be federalized). Could President Bush have invoked §332 or §333? It appears that politics, as much as legal uncertainty, made President Bush reluctant to invoke the Insurrection Act. Said one senior administration official, "Can you imagine how it would have been perceived if a president of the United States of one party had pre-emptively taken from the female governor of another party the command and control of her forces, unless the security situation made it completely clear that she was unable to effectively execute her command authority and that lawlessness was the inevitable result?" Lipton et al., *supra*, at A1. Indeed, given the history of the Posse Comitatus Act itself and the historic use of federalized National Guard troops to enforce school desegregation orders over Southern state objections, any attempt to federalize National Guard troops over the objection of a Southern governor might be politically risky. Couldn't President Bush have invoked the Insurrection Act but then sent federal regular troops, rather than federalizing the National Guard? Apparently, Defense Secretary Donald Rumsfeld actively resisted the deployment of federal active-duty troops to New Orleans and relented only under direct presidential order. *See* Stephanie Grace, *Defiant Rumsfeld Left City to Suffer*, TIME-PICAYUNE, May 21, 2009.

7. If a pandemic were to overwhelm the ability of state and local civilian authorities to enforce quarantine and other public health measures such as those suggested in the Model State Emergency Health Powers Act, *see* THE CENTER FOR LAW AND THE PUBLIC'S HEALTH, THE MODEL STATE EMERGENCY HEALTH POWERS ACT (2001), could the Insurrection Act be invoked to authorize military officials to enforce those measures? *See* Jennifer Elsea & Kathleen Swendiman, *Federal and State Quarantine and Isolation Authority* 20-21 (CRS Report for Congress, Order Code RL33201, Aug. 16, 2006) (yes).

c. Nonstatutory Exceptions to the Posse Comitatus Act

In addition to exceptions "expressly authorized by . . . Act of Congress," the Posse Comitatus Act is suspended also "in cases and under circumstances expressly authorized *by the Constitution*." 18 U.S.C. §1385 (emphasis added). Relying on the "inherent legal right of the U.S. Government—a sovereign national entity under the Federal Constitution—to insure the preservation of public order and the carrying out of governmental operations within its territorial limits, by force if necessary," the DOD has long asserted two "constitutional exceptions" to the Posse Comitatus Act. *See* 32 C.F.R. §215.4(c)(1). First, the DOD claims authority to protect federal property and functions when local authorities cannot or will not. *See id.* §215.4(c)(1)(ii). Second, the DOD claims nonstatutory emergency response authority to respond in the immediate aftermath of natural disasters, when local capacity is overwhelmed, to save lives, prevent human suffering, mitigate serious property damage, and restore government functioning and public order. *See id.* §215.4(c)(1)(i). This authority is neither subject to the limitations of the Posse Comitatus Act nor conferred by the Stafford Act or other federal statute.

The DOD's emergency response authority can take one of two forms: Military Support to Civil Authorities and Military Assistance for Civil Disturbances. Military Support to Civil Authorities (MSCA) is governed by DOD Directive 3025.1, "Military Support to Civil Authorities (MSCA)," which sets forth DOD policy applicable to disaster-related civil emergencies (as well as civil emergencies occasioned by attacks on the United States), *see* ¶1.1. Paragraph 4.5.1 provides that

> [i]mminently serious conditions resulting from any civil emergency [defined as "[a]ny natural or manmade disaster or emergency that causes or could cause substantial harm to the population or infrastructure, E2.1.4] or attack may require immediate action by military commanders, or by responsible officials of other DoD Agencies, to save lives, prevent human suffering, or mitigate great property damage. When such conditions exist and time does not permit prior approval from higher headquarters, local military commanders and responsible officials of other DoD Components are authorized by this Directive . . . to take necessary action to respond to requests of civil authorities. All such necessary action is referred to in this Directive as "Immediate Response."

DOD Directive 3025.1,"Military Support to Civil Authorities (MSCA) (Jan. 15, 1993), available at www.dtic.mil/whs/directives/corres/pdf/302501p.pdf.

The aid that the military can provide to civil authorities as part of MSCA — either through Immediate Response ordered by military commanders at the scene or when FEMA (or another federal agency designated as the lead agency for emergency response) determines that the required response is beyond the capability of civil authorities, *see* ¶4.4.4.2 — includes many of the same types of assistance that are otherwise available under the Stafford Act. DOD Directive 3025.1 details that "Immediate Response may include DOD assistance to civil agencies in meeting the following types of need":

- Rescue, evacuation, and emergency medical treatment of casualties, maintenance or restoration of emergency medical capabilities, and safeguarding the public health.
- Emergency restoration of essential public services (including fire-fighting, water, communications, transportation, power, and fuel).
- Emergency clearance of debris, rubble, and explosive ordnance from public facilities and other areas to permit rescue or movement of people and restoration of essential services.
- Recovery, identification, registration, and disposal of the dead.
- Monitoring and decontaminating radiological, chemical, and biological effects; controlling contaminated areas; and reporting through national warning and hazard control systems.

- Roadway movement control and planning.
- Safeguarding, collecting, and distributing food, essential supplies, and material on the basis of critical priorities.
- Damage assessment.
- Interim emergency communications.
- Facilitating the reestablishment of civil government functions.

3025.1 ¶¶4.5.4.1-4.5.4.10. The military is directed *not* to "perform any function of civil government unless absolutely necessary on a temporary basis." *Id.* §4.4.10. Any military commander who is directed to perform or does undertake to perform "such functions shall facilitate the reestablishment of civil responsibility at the earliest time possible." *Id.*

Much of this aid does not constitute executing the law and thus could be provided without violating the Posse Comitatus Act, even without invoking a purported "constitutional exception." Indeed, MSCA explicitly excludes "military support to civil law enforcement," DOD 3025.1 ¶¶2.6, 4.2, which is governed instead by DOD Directive 3025.12. Nevertheless, the foregoing list does include some activities — "controlling contaminated areas," "roadway movement control and planning," and "safeguarding . . . food" and other essential supplies — that appear to constitute "direct active use" of military personnel in civilian law enforcement.

DOD provision of "Military Assistance for Civil Disturbances (MACDIS) is much more likely to involve military participation in civil law enforcement and thus more likely to necessitate invocation of an exception to the Posse Comitatus Act. Authorization for express military support to civil law enforcement is outlined in DOD Directive 3025.12, "Military Assistance for Civil Disturbances (MACDIS)," which specifically invokes the Congress's constitutional authority under the First Militia Clause — as delegated to the president — to justify use of federal armed forces "to suppress insurrections, rebellions, and domestic violence." DOD 3025.12 ¶4.1.1, available at http://www.dtic.mil/whs/directives/corres/html/302512.htm. The Directive specifies that "[a]ny employment of Military Forces in support of law enforcement operations shall maintain the primacy of civilian authority" and that requests to the DOD shall be made by the attorney general "in response to an official request by State or Federal civil law enforcement or Executive authorities." DOD 3025.12 ¶4.1.5.

MACDIS operations are to be taken in response to civil disturbances, which are defined as "[g]roup acts of violence and disorders prejudicial to public law and order." E2.1.4. Thus, MACDIS presumably should be invoked in response to a natural disaster only when that disaster triggers civil unrest. Consider the following paragraphs of the MACDIS directive:

> 4.2.2. Military Forces shall not be used for MACDIS unless specifically authorized by the President, except in the following emergency circumstances. In these circumstances, responsible DOD officials and commanders will use all available means to seek Presidential authorization through the chain of command while applying their emergency authority under this Directive.
>
> 4.2.2.1. When the use of Military Forces is necessary to prevent loss of life or wanton destruction of property, or to restore governmental functions and

public order. That "emergency authority" applies when sudden and unexpected civil disturbances (including civil disturbances incident to earthquake, fire, flood, or other such calamity endangering life) occur, if duly constituted local authorities are unable to control the situation and circumstances preclude obtaining prior authorization by the President.

4.2.2.2. When duly constituted State or local authorities are unable or decline to provide adequate protection for Federal property or Federal government functions, Federal action (including the use of Military Forces) is authorized, as necessary, to protect the Federal property or functions.

Despite the apparent restriction of MACDIS under DOD 3025.12 to those natural disaster situations that trigger civil unrest (or threaten federal property or federal government functions), DOD Directive 5525.5, "DOD Cooperation with Civilian Law Enforcement Officials," which deals most forthrightly with the Posse Comitatus Act, arguably interprets Emergency Authority — which it views as exempt from the Act's restrictions — more broadly:

E.4.1.2.3. [Permissible direct assistance includes actions] that are taken under the inherent right of the U.S. Government, a sovereign national entity under the U.S. Constitution, to ensure the preservation of public order and to carry out governmental operations within its territorial limits, or otherwise in accordance with applicable law, by force, if necessary. This authority is reserved for unusual circumstances, and will be used only under DoD Directive 3025.12, which permits use of this power in two circumstances:

E.4.1.2.3.1. The emergency authority authorizes prompt and vigorous Federal action, including use of military forces, to prevent loss of life or wanton destruction of property and to restore governmental functioning and public order when sudden and unexpected civil disturbances, disaster, or calamities seriously endanger life and property and disrupt normal governmental functions to such an extent that duly constituted local authorities are unable to control the situation.

E.4.1.2.3.2. Protection of federal property and functions authorizes Federal action, including the use of military forces, to protect Federal property and Federal Government functions when the need for protection exists and duly constituted local authorities are unable or decline to provide adequate protection.

DOD Directive 5525.5, available at http://www.dtic.mil/whs/directives/corres/html/552505.htm.

NOTES AND QUESTIONS

1. To the extent that DOD claims emergency response authority to engage in civil law enforcement functions (without constraint by the Posse Comitatus Act) to "prevent loss of life or wanton destruction or property" in the aftermath of natural disasters, can that authority be grounded in the Constitution? Is it expressly authorized? Does your answer depend on whether the natural disaster has triggered civil unrest? If constitutional authority is found in a constitutional power granted to the president (such as inherent commander-in-chief authority) or a power granted to

Congress (such as calling forth the militia), how could immediate response actions taken by low-level military officers — without presidential authorization — be justified? Are these actions justified by some extraconstitutional notion of necessity? *Cf.* Mitchell v. Harmony, 54 U.S. (13 How.) 115, 134 (1851) (reasoning that an emergency can vest a military officer with "discretionary power" to take private property for the public good if the officer had reasonable grounds to believe that the necessity was imminent).

2. Should historical practice be enough to justify a nonstatutory exception to the Posse Comitatus Act, even if it does not rise to the level of an express constitutional authorization? The immediate response authority, derived from no statute, appears to stem from the historical practice of the armed forces. During the 1906 San Francisco earthquake and fire, for instance, the commander of the Army's Pacific Division unilaterally directed all troops under his command to help civilian law enforcement officers in their effort to stop looting, fight fires, and protect federal buildings. *See* Winthrop, *supra*, at 5.

3. Does the DOD's assertion of inherent emergency authority and immediate response authority upset the balance of powers established through the Posse Comitatus Act, Stafford Act, Insurrection Act, and other statutes governing the deployment of federal troops and resources in civilian law enforcement?

d. Reforming the Posse Comitatus Act

Does the Insurrection Act strike the right balance with the Posse Comitatus Act? In the aftermath of Hurricane Katrina, President Bush asserted that "a challenge on this scale requires greater federal authority and a broader role for the armed forces — the institution of our government most capable of massive logistical operations on a moment's notice." Julian E. Barnes & Kenneth T. Walsh, *A Uniform Response?*, U.S. NEWS & WORLD REP., Oct. 3, 2005, at 28. In response to President Bush's call for greater authority to use the military in disaster response, Congress passed Section 1076 of the John Warner National Defense Authorization Act of 2007, 109 P.L. 364, 120 Stat. 2083, which changed the title of the Insurrection Act to "Enforcement of the Laws to Restore Public Order" and amended §333 as follows:

§333. **Major public emergencies; interference with State and Federal law**
    (a) USE OF ARMED FORCES IN MAJOR PUBLIC EMERGENCIES. —

(1) The President may employ the armed forces, including the National Guard in Federal service, to —
    (A) restore public order and enforce the laws of the United States when, as a result of a natural disaster, epidemic, or other serious public health emergency, terrorist attack or incident, or other condition in any State or possession of the United States, the President determines that —
        (i) domestic violence has occurred to such an extent that the constituted authorities of the State or possession are incapable of maintaining public order; and

(ii) such violence results in a condition described in paragraph (2); or

(B) suppress, in a State, any insurrection, domestic violence, unlawful combination, or conspiracy if such insurrection, violation, combination, or conspiracy results in a condition described in paragraph (2).

(2) A condition described in this paragraph is a condition that —

(A) so hinders the execution of the laws of a State or possession, as applicable, and of the United States within that State or possession, that any part or class of its people is deprived of a right, privilege, immunity, or protection named in the Constitution and secured by law, and the constituted authorities of that State or possession are unable, fail, or refuse to protect that right, privilege, or immunity, or to give that protection; or

(B) opposes or obstructs the execution of the laws of the United States or impedes the course of justice under those laws.

(3) In any situation covered by paragraph (1)(B), the State shall be considered to have denied the equal protection of the laws secured by the Constitution.

(b) NOTICE TO CONGRESS. — The President shall notify Congress of the determination to exercise the authority in subsection (a)(1)(A) as soon as practicable after the determination and every 14 days thereafter during the duration of the exercise of that authority.

This provision — which was embedded in a massive appropriations bill — passed over the objection of all fifty state governors, who claimed that the amendment was an unwarranted expansion of the president's power to federalize the National Guard without the consent of the affected state governor. *See* Letter from Janet Napolitano et al., to Bill Frist, Majority Leader, et al. (Aug. 31, 2006), available at http://www.nga.org/portal/site/nga/menuitem.cb6e7818 b34088d18a278110501010a0/?vgnextoid=0a05e362c5f5d010VgnVCM1000001 a01010aRCRD. Senator Patrick Leahy also objected on the ground that the "constructive friction in existing law when it comes to martial law declarations" is beneficial because "[u]sing the military for law enforcement goes against one of the founding tenets of our democracy." 152 Cong. Rec. S10808-09 (daily ed. Sept. 29, 2006).

The amendment had an extremely short shelf life: it was overturned and the Insurrection Act restored to its previous form by the 2008 Defense Appropriations Bill. *See* National Defense Authorization Act for Fiscal Year 2008, 110 Pub. L. No. 181, 122 Stat. 3 §1068.

NOTES AND QUESTIONS

1. Which version of the Insurrection Act do you prefer? Is there a major substantive difference between the two versions in terms of the conditions that allow the president to use military troops for civilian law enforcement? Or did the Amendments simply clarify that the requisite conditions could occur as the result of natural disasters? *See* Michael Greenberger, *Yes,*

Virginia, the President Can Deploy Federal Troops to Prevent the Loss of a Major American City from a Devastating Natural Catastrophe, 26 Miss. C. L. Rev. 107, 108 (2006) (arguing that the Warner Act's amendment of §333 "merely codifie[d] and clarifie[d] the federal power that existed prior to its enactment"). Would changing the name of the Act, alone, have been enough to make invocation of the Act's authority more politically palatable for the president? (The 2008 bill reinstated the title "Insurrection Act.") Does the repeal of the Warner Act's amendment to the Insurrection Act imply that the now reinstated Act should be read narrowly (and perhaps read not to apply in natural disaster situations at all)?

2. Some commentators have argued that, rather than amending the Insurrection Act to better account for disaster situations, Congress should create a new, distinct disaster relief exception to the Posse Comitatus Act as part of the Stafford Act:

> As the name suggests, the Insurrection Act contemplates heavy-handed military tactics in order to quell threats to the legitimacy of state and federal governments. The primary objective of the military under the Stafford Act is disaster relief. The Insurrection Act pits the military directly against the citizens in a situation where humanitarian relief should take precedence over law enforcement. For these reasons, political officials shy away from invoking the Insurrection Act when it might be legally permissible, and would find it hard to invoke the Act for the purpose of traffic control or securing shelters of disaster victims. Ironically, by granting the military so much power, the Insurrection Act grants them too little, as it suggests overkill and often fits poorly into primarily disaster relief missions. . . . Instead of relying on ill-fitted exceptions [like the Insurrection Act] and fine distinctions, necessary military activities should fall under the statutory framework of the Stafford Act. . . . The military's primary focus remains humanitarian relief, but providing relief may necessitate the exercise of power that is regulatory, proscriptive, or compulsory in nature. . . . [Without such authority,] the military may be reluctant to take on relief missions where it foresees a high probability of having to set up road blocks, control traffic, or restore order. Scenarios like this, which do not always fit easily into the Insurrection Act, could be met by allowing state officials the statutory option of coupling essential law enforcement with the [humanitarian] mission."

Isaac Tekie, Note, *Bringing the Troops Home to a Disaster: Law, Order, and Humanitarian Relief*, 67 Ohio St. L.J. 1227, 1261-1262 (2006). If such an exception were created, what particular law enforcement activities should the military be allowed to undertake? Providing security at emergency shelters? Directing traffic? Enforcing quarantines? Arresting looters?

3. Other commentators have suggested that, rather than creating new Posse Comitatus Act exceptions, Congress should cut back on existing exceptions:

> The struggle to define the appropriate role of the military in domestic life comes at a critical juncture in our nation's development. With an increased emphasis on homeland security following the 9/11 attack, the government and the public have yielded to the military's growing involvement in domestic affairs. Such acquiescence is not surprising. Following 9/11, public confidence in the military reached record highs. But even before that, the

U.S. military had consistently rated as the most trustworthy of public and private institutions—even more trustworthy than churches, universities, hospitals, the U.S. Supreme Court, and any other part of the government. In the last two decades, the military has been steadily used to aid law enforcement in a variety of domestic situations. . . . The government's and public's reliance on the military is only magnified by concerns regarding another terrorist attack. The line between civil disorder and national security—between domestic law enforcement and military necessity—is continually blurred.

By increasing the military's presence in the domestic sphere, however, the federal government is obscuring the traditional lines between military and civilian roles. Even when sanctioned by civil leaders, the increased role of the armed forces in the domestic life endangers civil liberties and the democratic process. . . . A fundamental tenet of our society, first reflected in the Declaration of Independence, is the desire of civilian supremacy over military power. . . .

[Sections 331 to 334] should be combined and new language inserted that restricts the President's discretion, increases the states' role in the decision-making process, and provides the National Guard—not the standing Army—with the primary domestic security responsibilities.

Jackie Gardina, *Toward Military Rule? A Critique of Executive Discretion to Use the Military in Domestic Emergencies*, 91 MARQ. L. REV. 1027, 1029-1031, 1073 (2008).

EMERGENCY RESPONSE

The prior chapter considered the federal constitutional and statutory framework for disaster response. Section A of this chapter examines that federal framework in action, as implemented through the federal regulatory scheme for disaster response, focusing in particular on catastrophic disasters (those that cause extraordinary levels of casualties or damage) and the flawed federal response to Hurricane Katrina. Moving beyond the role of the federal government, Section B turns to state and regional disaster response, considering state disaster laws and the multijurisdictional Emergency Management Assistance Compact (EMAC). Section C explores the role of private and nongovernmental actors (including individual citizens) in disaster response. The penultimate section of the chapter, Section D, then takes up proposals for reform of disaster response law. Finally, Section E sets forth a disaster scenario tabletop exercise to facilitate consideration of the chapter's issues — including negotiating a chain of command — in a simulated disaster situation.

A. THE FEDERAL EMERGENCY REGULATORY SCHEME

In times of disaster, even the soundest legal structure is only as effective as its implementation. When Katrina struck, "the System did not perform as a system"; "the hurricane protection in New Orleans and Southeast Louisiana was a system in name only." 1 ARMY CORPS OF ENGINEERS, FINAL REPORT OF THE INTERAGENCY PERFORMANCE EVALUATION TASKFORCE (IPET) 3 (June 1, 2006). As it was with infrastructure, so, too, with personnel: by most accounts, the federal and state agencies charged with coordinating the response to Hurricane Katrina performed abysmally. The federal framework, for its part, had been developed in response to the terrorist attacks of September 11, 2001. The four-year cycle from September 11 to Hurricane Katrina — from the worst mass crime to the worst natural disaster in American history — severely tested the law of emergency response. Unfortunately, the federal response system — with some notable exceptions such as the Coast Guard — did not perform well.

This section begins by exploring the evolution of the Federal Emergency Management Agency (including the creation of the Department of Homeland Security) and the implementation of Homeland Security Presidential Directive 5 (HSPD-5). It focuses on the two most important components of HSPD-5: the National Response Plan (now the National Response Framework) and the National Incident Management System. Next, the section considers how the system functioned during Katrina and whether it is better equipped today to deal with catastrophic disasters.

1. EVOLUTION OF THE FEDERAL EMERGENCY MANAGEMENT AGENCY

The Federal Emergency Management Agency (FEMA) was created as an independent agency by President Carter to forge a comprehensive, federal approach to emergency management. *See* Reorganization Plan No. 3, 43 Fed. Reg. 41,943 (June 19, 1978); Exec. Order No. 12,127, 44 Fed. Reg. 19,369 (March 31, 1979); Exec. Order No. 12,148, 44 Fed. Reg. 43,239 (July 20, 1979). The new agency assumed responsibility for emergency functions that previously had been distributed among a variety of federal agencies (including the Department of Housing and Urban Development's Federal Disaster Assistance Administration and the Department of Defense, which had responsibility for civil defense).

Even before the terrorist attacks of September 11, 2001, President Bush began reorganizing FEMA to focus on terrorist threats. *See* Keith Bea, *Federal Emergency Management Policy Changes after Hurricane Katrina: A Summary of Statutory Provisions* (CRS Report for Congress, Order Code RL33729, Dec. 15, 2006). After 9/11, Congress passed the Homeland Security Act of 2002, Pub. L. No. 107-296, 116 Stat. 2135 (codified at 6 U.S.C. §§101-557), which created the Department of Homeland Security (DHS). The Department's "primary mission" is described principally in terms of terrorism; the first three responsibilities of the DHS are to "prevent terrorist attacks within the United States," to "reduce the vulnerability of the United States to terrorism," and to "minimize the damage, and assist in the recovery, from terrorist attacks that do occur within the United States." 6 U.S.C. §111(b)(1). Only then does the Homeland Security Act direct DHS to "act[] as a focal point regarding natural and man-made crises and emergency planning." *Id.* §111(b)(1)(D).

The Homeland Security Act consolidated the functions of FEMA within DHS and made FEMA a subordinate organization within DHS, subject to the secretary of Homeland Security's broad power to reorganize the Department. The Act thus represented the most comprehensive reorganization of federal emergency authority since FEMA's creation. The Homeland Security Act assigned the secretary of Homeland Security a wide range of responsibilities for emergency preparedness and response. In addition to "helping to ensure the effectiveness of emergency response providers to terrorist attacks, major disasters, and other emergencies," the secretary must manage "the Federal Government's response to terrorist attacks and major disasters" and "coordinat[e] . . . Federal response resources . . . in the event of a terrorist attack or major disaster." *Id.* §312(1), (3). The secretary is also directed to "aid[] the recovery from terrorist attacks and major disaster." *Id.* §312(4).

The reorganized FEMA retained all of its Stafford Act "functions and authorities," and was directed to "lead[] and support[] the Nation in a comprehensive, risk-based emergency management program" for all hazards, centered around mitigation, preparedness planning, response, recovery, and coordination of emergency management to increase efficiency. *See* Pub. L. No. 107-296, §507(a)(1)-(2). In the years following the Homeland Security Act's enactment, however, the secretary of Homeland Security used his reorganizational authority to transfer some former FEMA functions to other components of the DHS. These changes culminated in a Department-wide reorganization by Secretary Michael Chertoff, announced on July 13, 2005 (before Katrina) and effective on October 1, 2005, which transferred most preparedness functions of the Directorate of Emergency Preparedness and Response (of which FEMA was a part) to a newly created Preparedness Directorate. *See* Henry B. Hogue, *Federal Emergency Management and Homeland Security Organization: Historical Developments and Legislative Options* 20-21 (CRS Report for Congress, Order Code RL33369, June 1, 2006).

In the aftermath of Hurricane Katrina, many blamed FEMA's anemic response on FEMA's submersion in a sprawling bureaucracy focused primarily on terrorism, as well as the accelerating reassignment of many of FEMA's preparedness functions to other DHS divisions. In response to these and other criticisms, Congress enacted the Post-Katrina Emergency Management Reform Act of 2006. Pub. L. No. 109-295, 120 Stat. 1355 (2006) [hereinafter Post-Katrina Act]. The Act transferred back to FEMA most (but not all) of the preparedness functions that had been reassigned to the Preparedness Directorate of the DHS, 6 U.S.C. §315, and imposed qualifications for the newly created head (administrator) of FEMA, *id.* §313(c). Moreover, the Post-Katrina Act elevated FEMA's status in the Department, by establishing it as a "distinct entity" within the DHS, *id.* §316; exempting it from the secretary's reorganization authority, *id.*; giving the newly created FEMA administrator direct access to the president and Congress, *id.* §313(c); designating the FEMA administrator as the principal advisor to the president, the secretary, and the Homeland Security Council on all emergency management matters, *id.* §313(c)(4); authorizing the president to designate the administrator to serve as a member of the Cabinet during disasters, *id.* §313(c)(5)(A); and limiting the secretary's ability to reduce FEMA's authority or divert its assets, *id.* §316(c)(1).

The Post-Katrina Act affirmed that FEMA's primary mission "is to reduce the loss of life and property and protect the Nation from all hazards, including natural disasters, acts of terrorism, and other man-made disasters, by leading and supporting the Nation in a risk-based, comprehensive emergency management system of preparedness, protection, response, recovery, and mitigation." 6 U.S.C. §313(b)(1). Accordingly, the Act reiterates that the responsibilities of the FEMA administrator include:

> (8) [a]ssisting the President in carrying out the functions under the Robert T. Stafford Disaster Act . . . and carrying out all functions and authorities given to the Administrator under that Act;

(9) [c]arrying out the mission of the Agency to reduce the loss of life and property and protect the Nation from all hazards by leading and supporting the Nation in a risk-based, comprehensive emergency management system of —

(A) mitigation, by taking sustained actions to reduce or eliminate long-term risks to people and property from hazards and their effects;

(B) preparedness, by planning, training, and building the emergency management profession to prepare effectively or mitigate against, respond to, and recover from any hazard;

(C) response, by conducting emergency operations to save lives and property through positioning emergency equipment, personnel, and supplies, through evacuating potential victims, through providing food, water, shelter, and medical care to those in need, and through restoring critical public services; and

(D) recovery, by rebuilding communities, so individuals, businesses, and governments can function on their own, return to normal life, and protect against future hazards[.]

6 U.S.C. §314(a).

NOTES AND QUESTIONS

1. In carrying out his or her responsibilities, the FEMA administrator is instructed to "coordinate the implementation of a risk-based, all-hazards strategy that builds those common capabilities necessary to prepare for, protect against, respond to, recover from, or mitigate against natural disasters, acts of terrorism, and other man-made disasters, while also building the unique capabilities necessary to prepare for, protect against, respond to, recover from, or mitigate against the risks of specific types of incidents." 6 U.S.C. §314. Is this "all-hazards approach" the most efficient and effective way to organize emergency management authority or would we do better to establish separate agencies tasked with responding to specific types of emergencies? More specifically, how compatible are the tasks of combating terror and responding to other emergencies, especially natural disasters?

2. Despite FEMA's newly elevated status within the DHS, there are continuing calls to return FEMA to its status as an independent agency outside of DHS. *See, e.g.*, Federal Emergency Management Advancement Act, S. 412, 111th Cong. (2009). Would removing FEMA from the DHS be beneficial? Does continued focus on FEMA's organizational structure divert attention from more important substantive questions about FEMA's mission performance?

3. Does the addition of "protection" to FEMA's primary mission add anything to the Agency's authority or responsibilities?

4. As FEMA fumbled and New Orleans suffered, President Bush's chummy praise for FEMA Director Michael Brown ("Brownie, you're doing a heckuva job!") came to exemplify much of what was wrong with out-of-touch presidential and inexperienced FEMA leadership during the disaster. Brown, it appeared, had been elevated to the post despite his lack of any substantial emergency management experience. The Post-Katrina Act requires that the FEMA administrator have "a demonstrated ability in and knowledge of emergency management and homeland security" and "not less than

5 years of executive leadership and management experience in the public or private sector." 6 U.S.C. §313. In a Signing Statement to the law, President Bush objected to this provision on the grounds that it eliminated too many qualified individuals from the pool. Statement on Signing the Department of Homeland Security Appropriations Act, 2007, 42 WEEKLY COMP. PRES. DOC. 1742 (Oct. 4, 2006). The Post-Katrina Act also aims to increase the professionalism and expertise of FEMA staff by requiring FEMA to develop a "strategic human capital plan," and establish "appropriate career paths"—including requisite training, education, and experience—for agency personnel. 5 U.S.C. §§10102, 10103. The Act also authorizes recruitment and retention bonuses, *id.* §§10104, 10105, and directs the establishment of a "graduate-level Homeland Security Education program" to educate senior federal officials (and state and local officials) with emergency management responsibilities, 6 U.S.C. §415.

2. FEDERAL EMERGENCY RESPONSE PLANS

In addition to the other emergency management responsibilities assigned to the secretary of the DHS by the Homeland Security Act of 2002, the Act also directed the secretary to perform two specific tasks to coordinate and plan multijurisdictional response to disasters and terrorism. First, the Act directed the secretary to "build[] a comprehensive *national incident management system* with Federal, State, and local government personnel, agencies, and authorities, to respond to such attacks and disasters." 6 U.S.C. §312(5) (emphasis added). Second, the Act required the secretary to "consolidat[e] existing Federal Government emergency response plans into a single, coordinated *national response plan.*" *Id.* §312(6) (emphasis added).

In 2003 President Bush issued Homeland Security Presidential Directive 5 (HSPD-5), a blueprint for the "management of domestic incidents." *See* Homeland Security Presidential Directive/HSPD-5, 39 WEEKLY COMP. PRES. DOC. 263 (March 7, 2003). The directive was designed to facilitate cooperation between all levels of government by "using a national approach to domestic incident management." *Id.* ¶(3). It also designates the secretary of Homeland Security as the principal federal official (PFO) for domestic incident management. *See id.* ¶(4) Specifically, the directive provides:

> [T]he Secretary is responsible for coordinating Federal operations within the United States to prepare for, respond to, and recover from terrorist attacks, major disasters, and other emergencies. The Secretary shall coordinate the Federal Government's resources utilized in response to or recovery from terrorist attacks, major disasters, or other emergencies if and when any one of the following four conditions applies: (1) a Federal department or agency acting under its own authority has requested the assistance of the Secretary; (2) the resources of State and local authorities are overwhelmed and Federal assistance has been requested by the appropriate State and local authorities; (3) more than one Federal department or agency has become substantially involved in responding to the incident; or (4) the Secretary has been directed to assume responsibility for managing the domestic incident by the President.

Id. The directive also recognizes the primary role of states in responding to disasters, specifying that the secretary would coordinate with the states to ensure adequate planning and that the federal government would "assist State and local authorities when their resources are overwhelmed, or when Federal interests are involved." *Id.* ¶(6). The guidance also acknowledges the role of nongovernmental entities in disaster response, and directs the secretary to coordinate with the private sector. *See id.* ¶(7).

HSPD-5 implemented the requirements of the 2002 Homeland Security Act by directing the secretary to establish two complementary components of a plan for managing "domestic incidents": a National Incident Management System (NIMS) and a National Response Plan (NRP). Together, the NIMS and the NRP (now the National Response Framework (NRF)) represent the heart of the post–September 11 framework for federal emergency response. The directive encourages states to adopt the NIMS, by conditioning federal preparedness assistance to the states (including grants, contracts, and other activities) on state NIMS adoption. *See id.* ¶(20).

The first iteration of the NRP—adopted by the federal government in December 2004—suffered from several infirmities, which became painfully clear in Katrina's aftermath. First, it was unclear what triggered the NRP (both substantively and procedurally). The NRP was designed to deal with "Incidents of National Significance," but those incidents were not clearly defined, nor was the procedure for invoking the Plan clearly specified. Perhaps more importantly, the NRP did not specify what actions were to be taken once an Incident of National Significance was declared. *See* THE WHITE HOUSE, THE FEDERAL RESPONSE TO HURRICANE KATRINA: LESSONS LEARNED 13-15 (2006) [hereinafter LESSONS LEARNED].

Consider how the newly minted National Response Framework, effective March 22, 2009, deals with these difficulties.

FEMA, NATIONAL RESPONSE FRAMEWORK

7-11 (Jan. 2008)

RESPONSE: THE *WHAT* AND THE *HOW* The *National Response Framework* is always in effect, and elements can be implemented at any level at any time. The *Framework* is capabilities based, which is to say that local governments, tribes, States, and the Federal Government all develop functional capabilities and identify resources that may be required based on hazard identification and risk assessment, threats, and other potential incidents such as those represented by the National Planning Scenarios.

The *Framework* describes *what we do* and *how we respond.* In short, the *National Response Framework* explains how, at all levels, the Nation effectively manages all-hazards response consistent with the *National Strategy for Homeland Security.* . . .

SCOPE The *Framework* provides structures for implementing nationwide response policy and operational coordination for all types of domestic incidents. It can be partially or fully implemented in the context of a threat, in anticipation of a significant event, or in response to an incident.

Selective implementation allows for a scaled response, delivery of the resources needed, and an appropriate level of coordination. . . .

It is not always obvious at the outset whether a seemingly minor event might be the initial phase of a larger, rapidly growing threat. The *Framework* incorporates standardized organizational structures that promote on-scene initiative, innovation, and sharing of essential resources drawn from all levels of government, NGOs, and the private sector. Response must be quickly scalable, flexible, and adaptable. The *Framework* is also intended to accelerate the assessment and response to incidents that may require Federal assistance. In practice, many incidents require virtually reflexive activation of interagency coordination protocols to forestall the incident from becoming worse or to surge more aggressively to contain it. A Federal department or agency acting on independent authority may be the initial and the primary Federal responder, but incidents that require more systematic Federal response efforts are now actively coordinated through the appropriate *Framework* mechanisms described in this document and in its supporting annexes. This initial coordination of Federal incident assessment and response efforts is intended to occur seamlessly, without the need for any formal trigger mechanism.

This *Framework*, therefore, eliminates the Incident of National Significance declaration. No such declaration is required by the *Framework* and none will be made. The authorities of the Secretary of Homeland Security to coordinate large-scale national responses are unaltered by this change. Elimination of this declaration will, however, support a more nimble, scalable, and coordinated response by the entire national emergency management community.

RESPONSE DOCTRINE Response doctrine defines basic roles, responsibilities, and operational concepts for response across all levels of government and with NGOs and the private sector. The overarching objective of response activities centers upon saving lives and protecting property and the environment. . . .

Response doctrine is comprised of five key principles: (1) engaged partnership, (2) tiered response, (3) scalable, flexible, and adaptable operational capabilities, (4) unity of effort through unified command, and (5) readiness to act. An introductory word about each follows.

ENGAGED PARTNERSHIP Leaders at all levels must communicate and actively support engaged partnerships by developing shared goals and aligning capabilities so that no one is overwhelmed in times of crisis. Layered, mutually supporting capabilities at Federal, State, tribal, and local levels allow for planning together in times of calm and responding together effectively in times of need. Engaged partnership includes ongoing communication of incident activity among all partners to the *Framework*, and shared situational awareness for a more rapid response. In particular, the potential for terrorist incidents requires *a heightened state of readiness* and nimble, practiced capabilities baked into the heart of our preparedness and response planning. . . . Preparedness activities should be coordinated among all involved agencies within the jurisdiction, as well as across jurisdictions. Integrated planning, described later in this *Framework*, will assist in identifying gaps in capability and developing strategies to fill those gaps. Nationwide preparedness is described in the

National Preparedness Guidelines and the *National Exercise Program*. These documents lay out 15 National Planning Scenarios that form the basis of the newly coordinated national exercise schedule and priorities, and identify 37 core capabilities that are needed to support response across the Nation. The *Guidelines* identify core local, tribal, community, and State capabilities that will be supported by the DHS homeland security grant programs.

TIERED RESPONSE Incidents must be managed at the lowest possible jurisdictional level and supported by additional capabilities when needed. It is not necessary that each level be overwhelmed prior to requesting resources from another level.

Incidents begin and end locally, and most are wholly managed at the local level. Many incidents require unified response from local agencies, NGOs, and the private sector, and some require additional support from neighboring jurisdictions or the State. A small number require Federal support. National response protocols recognize this and are structured to provide additional, tiered levels of support when there is a need for more resources or capabilities to support and sustain the response and initial recovery. All levels should be prepared to respond, anticipating resources that may be required.

SCALABLE, FLEXIBLE, AND ADAPTABLE OPERATIONAL CAPABILITIES As incidents change in size, scope, and complexity, the response must adapt to meet requirements. The number, type, and sources of resources must be able to expand rapidly to meet needs associated with a given incident. The *Framework*'s disciplined and coordinated process can provide for a rapid surge of resources from all levels of government, appropriately scaled to need. Execution must be flexible and adapted to fit each individual incident. For the duration of a response, and as needs grow and change, responders must remain nimble and adaptable. Equally, the overall response should be flexible as it transitions from the response effort to recovery. This *Framework* is grounded in doctrine that demands a tested inventory of common organizational structures and capabilities that are scalable, flexible, and adaptable for diverse operations. Adoption of the *Framework* across all levels of government and with businesses and NGOs will facilitate interoperability and improve operational coordination.

UNITY OF EFFORT THROUGH UNIFIED COMMAND Effective *unified command* is indispensable to response activities and requires a clear understanding of the roles and responsibilities of each participating organization. Success requires ***unity of effort***, which respects the chain of command of each participating organization while harnessing seamless coordination across jurisdictions in support of common objectives.

Use of the Incident Command System (ICS) is an important element across multijurisdictional or multiagency incident management activities. It provides a structure to enable agencies with different legal, jurisdictional, and functional responsibilities to coordinate, plan, and interact effectively on scene. As a team effort, unified command allows all agencies with jurisdictional authority and/or functional responsibility for the incident to provide joint support through mutually developed incident objectives and strategies established at the command level. Each participating agency maintains its own authority, responsibility, and accountability. This *Framework* employs the

NIMS standardized structures and tools that enable a unified approach to be effective both on scene and at the emergency operations centers. . . . The *NIMS* supports response through the following elements of unified command: (1) developing a single set of objectives; (2) using a collective, strategic approach; (3) improving information flow and coordination; (4) creating common understanding of joint priorities and restrictions; (5) ensuring that no agency's legal authorities are compromised or neglected; and (6) optimizing the combined efforts of all agencies under a single plan.

READINESS TO ACT Effective response requires readiness to act balanced with an understanding of risk. From individuals, households, and communities to local, tribal, State, and Federal governments, national response depends on the instinct and ability to act. A forward-leaning posture is imperative for incidents that have the potential to expand rapidly in size, scope, or complexity, and for no-notice incidents.

Once response activities have begun, on-scene actions are based on *NIMS* principles. To save lives and protect property and the environment, decisive action on scene is often required of responders. Although some risk may be unavoidable, first responders can effectively anticipate and manage risk through proper training and planning. Command, single or unified, is responsible for establishing immediate priorities for the safety of not only the public, but the responders and other emergency workers involved in the response, and for ensuring that adequate health and safety measures are in place. The Incident Commander should ensure that each incident has a designated safety officer who has been trained and equipped to assess the operation, identify hazardous and unsafe situations, and implement effective safety plans.

Acting swiftly and effectively requires clear, focused communication and the processes to support it. Without effective communication, a bias toward action will be ineffectual at best, likely perilous. An effective national response relies on disciplined processes, procedures, and systems to communicate timely, accurate, and accessible information on the incident's cause, size, and current situation to the public, responders, and others. Well-developed public information, education strategies, and communication plans help to ensure that lifesaving measures, evacuation routes, threat and alert systems, and other public safety information are coordinated and communicated to numerous diverse audiences in a consistent, accessible, and timely manner.

In addition to these sweeping (and somewhat vague) principles, the NRF attempts to define — in much more detail than the NRP — the roles and responsibilities of local, tribal, state, and federal governments (as well as individuals, NGOs (nongovernmental organizations), and the private sector). Indeed, it even outlines specific roles for particular state-level officials, including governors, state Homeland Security advisors, and directors of state Emergency Management agencies. *See id.* at 21-22.

The NRF also emphasizes the importance of developing "detailed, robust, all-hazards response plans" at all levels of government. *See id.* at 28. Additionally, the NRF emphasizes a preparedness cycle for building government capability, consisting of the following steps: (1) planning; (2) organizing response structures and equipping and training responders; (3) conducting multijurisdictional exercises; and (4) evaluating and improving the plans based on exercise experiences. *See id.* at 28-32.

The NRF also designates the National Operations Center (NOC) as the "primary national hub for situational awareness and [incident management] operations coordination across the Federal Government." *Id.* at 55. The NOC, a "continuously operating multiagency operations center," *id.*, collects and synthesizes all relevant data, and then communicates that information to senior federal officials (including the DHS secretary) and federal operations centers. The NOC includes two distinct operations centers: the National Response Coordination Center (NRCC), which is FEMA's primary operations management center, and the National Infrastructure Coordinating Center (NICC), which monitors critical infrastructure and key resources. *Id.* at 56.

In organizing governmental response at all levels, the NRF builds on the principles of the National Incident Management System (NIMS). Consider the key concepts of NIMS, which provides a "consistent template for managing incidents," NRF at 1, as described in the National Response Framework.

FEMA, National Response Framework

4, 48-49 (Jan. 2008)

The **National Incident Management System (NIMS)** is a companion document that provides standard command and management structures that apply to response activities. This system provides a consistent, nationwide template to enable Federal, State, tribal, and local governments, the private sector, and NGOs to work together to prepare for, prevent, respond to, recover from, and mitigate the effects of incidents regardless of cause, size, location, or complexity. This consistency provides the foundation for utilization of the NIMS for all incidents, ranging from daily occurrences to incidents requiring a coordinated Federal response. . . .

NIMS provides a core set of common concepts, principles, terminology, and technologies in the following areas:

Incident Command System (ICS). Much of NIMS is built upon ICS, which was developed by the Federal, State, and local wildland fire agencies during the 1970s. ICS is normally structured to facilitate activities in five major functional areas: command, operations, planning, logistics, and finance/administration. In some circumstances, intelligence and investigations may be added as a sixth functional area.

Multiagency Coordination System (MACS). The primary function of MACS is to coordinate activities above the field level and to prioritize the incident demands for critical or competing resources, thereby assisting the coordination of the operations in the field. MACS consists of a combination of elements: personnel, procedures, protocols, business practices, and communications integrated into a common system. For the purpose of coordinating resources and support between multiple jurisdictions, MACS can be implemented from a fixed facility or by other arrangements outlined within the system. Examples of multiagency coordination include a State or county emergency operations center, a State intelligence fusion center, the National Operations Center, the Department of Homeland Security/Federal Emergency Management Agency (FEMA) National Response Coordination Center, the Department of Justice/Federal Bureau of Investigation (FBI) Strategic Information and Operations Center, the FBI Joint Operations Center, and the National Counterterrorism Center.

Unified Command. Unified command is an important element in multijurisdictional or multiagency incident management. It provides guidelines to enable agencies with different legal, geographic, and functional responsibilities to coordinate, plan, and interact effectively. As a team effort, unified command allows all agencies with jurisdictional authority or functional responsibility for the incident to jointly provide management direction to an incident through a common set of incident objectives and strategies and a single Incident Action Plan. Each participating agency maintains its authority, responsibility, and accountability.

Training. Leaders and staff require initial training on response principles, as well as ongoing training to provide updates on current concepts and procedures.

Identification and Management of Resources. Classifying types of resources is essential to ensure that multiple agencies can effectively communicate and provide resources during a crisis, including implementing a plan to inventory, mobilize, and track resources prior to, during, and after an incident.

Mutual Aid and Assistance. Executing mutual aid and other agreements established prior to an incident with appropriate entities at the local, tribal, State, and Federal levels is an important element of preparedness, along with the readiness to develop/implement new agreements during the life cycle of an incident.

Situational Awareness. Situational awareness is the ability to identify, process, and comprehend the critical information about an incident. More simply, it is knowing what is going on around you. Situational awareness requires continuous monitoring of relevant sources of information regarding actual incidents and developing hazards.

Qualifications and Certification. Competent staff is a requirement for any leader managing an incident. During a crisis there will not be time to determine staff qualifications, if such information has not yet been compiled and available for review by leaders. To identify the appropriate staff to support a leader during a crisis, qualifications based on training and expertise of staff should be identified and evidenced by certification, if appropriate.

Collection, Tracking, and Reporting of Incident Information. Information today is transmitted instantly via the Internet and the 24/7 news channels. While timely information is valuable, it also can be overwhelming. For an effective response, expertise and experience must be leveraged to support decisionmaking and to summarize and prioritize information rapidly. Information must be gathered accurately at the scene and effectively communicated to those who need it. To be successful, clear lines of information flow and a common operating picture are essential.

Crisis Action Planning. Deliberative planning during nonincident periods should quickly transition to crisis action planning when an incident occurs. Crisis action planning is the process for rapidly adapting existing deliberative plans and procedures during an incident based on the actual circumstances of an event. Crisis action planning should also include the provision of decision tools for senior leaders to guide their decisionmaking.

NOTES AND QUESTIONS

1. The NRF's elimination of "Incidents of National Significance" and its "always in effect" approach obviate questions about when the NRF, as a whole, is triggered, but does it go any distance in clarifying when particular actions are to be taken under the NRF? In particular, does the NRF provide sufficient clarity about when the DHS should assume the responsibility for coordinating federal response? Consider the NRF's more specific attempts to clarify these triggers:

> **Incident Management.** The Secretary of Homeland Security is the principal Federal official for domestic incident management. By Presidential directive and statute, the Secretary is responsible for coordination of Federal resources utilized in the prevention of, preparation for, response to, or recovery from terrorist attacks, major disasters, or other emergencies. The role of the Secretary of Homeland Security is to provide the President with an overall architecture for domestic incident management and to coordinate the Federal response, when required, while relying upon the support of other Federal partners. . . .
>
> The FEMA Administrator, as the principal advisor to the President, the Secretary, and the Homeland Security Council on all matters regarding emergency management, helps the Secretary in meeting these HSPD-5 responsibilities.
>
> Federal assistance for incidents that do not require DHS coordination may be led by other Federal departments and agencies consistent with their authorities. The Secretary of Homeland Security may monitor such incidents and may activate specific Framework mechanisms to provide support to departments and agencies without assuming overall leadership for the Federal response to the incident.
>
> The following four HSPD-5 criteria define situations for which DHS shall assume overall Federal incident management coordination responsibilities within the Framework and implement the Framework's coordinating mechanisms: (1) a Federal Department or agency acting under its own authority has requested DHS assistance, (2) the resources of State and local authorities are overwhelmed and Federal assistance has been requested, (3) more than one Federal department or agency has become substantially involved in responding to the incident, or (4) the Secretary has been directed by the President to assume incident management responsibilities. . . .
>
> [S]everal Federal departments and agencies have their own authorities to declare disasters or emergencies. For example, the Secretary of Health and Human Services can declare a public health emergency. These declarations may be made independently or as part of a coordinated Federal response. Where those declarations are part of an incident requiring a coordinated

Federal response, those Federal departments or agencies act within the over-all coordination structure of the Framework.

NRF at 25-26.

The four HSPD-5 criteria were also referenced in the definition of "Incidents of National Significance." Does the approach taken by the current NRF replicate much of the earlier confusion about when the NRP was triggered in the context of deciding when DHS is required to assume federal incident management and implement the NRF's "coordinating mechanisms"?

2. The NRF refers to a "bias toward action" and a "forward-leaning posture." Is a bias toward action desirable? What specific steps would the federal government take to implement this "forward-leaning posture"? The NRF suggests that such actions by Federal and State governments include engaging in "advanced readiness contracting" with private sector entities for procurement of emergency resources, locating "pre-positioned resources" in vulnerable areas, and developing "pre-scripted mission assignments." *Id.* at 29-30.

3. The explicit formulation of the "Response Doctrine" and its five principles — engaged partnership; tiered response; scalable, flexible, and adaptable operational capabilities; unity of effort through unified command; and readiness to act — is a new addition to the NRF. However, most of the principles themselves were also found in the NRP. For example, both the NIMS and the NRF — like the earlier NRP — proceed on the premise that "incidents are generally handled at the lowest jurisdictional level possible." NRF at 10. Should the potential scope of modern disasters — hurricanes bearing down on major population centers, pandemics that can spread across the globe in days or weeks — cause us to reconsider this fundamental proposition? Consider this opinion expressed by the Bush Administration:

> Disaster response in America traditionally has been handled by State and local governments, with the Federal government playing a supporting role. Limits on the Federal government's role in disaster response are deeply rooted in American tradition. State and local governments — who know the unique requirements of their citizens and geography and are best positioned to respond to incidents in their own jurisdictions — will always play a large role in disaster response. The Federal government's supporting role respects these practical points and the sovereignty of the States as well as the power of governors to direct activities and coordinate efforts within their States. While we remain faithful to basic constitutional doctrine and time tested principles, we must likewise accept that events such as Hurricane Katrina and the terrorist attacks of September 11, 2001, require us to tailor the application of these principles to the threats we confront in the 21st Century.

LESSONS LEARNED, *supra*, at 11. One commentator has suggested that the presumption that incidents should be handled at the lowest level possible incorporates an important principle which is often overlooked in application — that determining the lowest possible level requires an adequate assessment of capacity to deal with the problem at hand: "[T]he federalism premise of as-localized-as-possible governance (or "subsidiarity") incorporates an often overlooked problem-solving value. Directing that public decision-making take place at the most local level possible implies the most local level with capacity — or the most local level of government that may actually be able to solve the problem." Ryan, *supra*, at 51. Does the NRF contain adequate mechanisms for determining the lowest level of government capable of responding to a disaster situation?

4. The NRF contains a new section that describes planning at all levels of government "as the cornerstone of national preparedness." NRF at 71. In accordance with Homeland Security Presidential Directive 8, "National Preparedness," the NRF describes three levels of federal plans (Strategic Guidance Statement and Strategic Plan; National-Level Interagency Concept Plan; and Federal Department and Agency Operations Plans) that should exist for each of fifteen National Planning Scenarios. Three of the fifteen scenarios deal primarily with naturally occurring disasters (Scenario 9: Natural Disaster — Major Earthquake; Scenario 10: Natural Disaster — Major Hurricane; and Scenario 3: Biological Disease Outbreak — Pandemic Influenza). The others are various nightmare terrorism scenarios, ranging from the detonation of improvised nuclear devices to the release of pneumonic plague in a major metropolis. NRF at 75.

5. What exactly is the Incident Command System (ICS)?

> ICS was developed and refined over many years by incident commanders at the Federal, State, and local levels and was being successfully implemented throughout the country prior to being included in the NIMS. The ICS provides a means to coordinate the efforts of individual responders and agencies as they respond to and help manage an incident. The ICS organization, the structure and size of which can be tailored to the complexity and size of any given incident, comprises five major functional areas — Command, Planning, Operations, Logistics, and Finance/Administration. This system grew out of the challenges of interagency coordination experienced when fighting wildfires in western states. . . . Recognizing that most incidents are managed locally, the command function under ICS is set up at the lowest level of the response, and grows to encompass other agencies and jurisdictions as they arrive.

LESSONS LEARNED, *supra*, at 13. There are several key roles defined by ICS: an Incident Commander (who has authority and responsibility for managing all incident operations at the incident site), and the Command Staff (a Public Information Officer, Safety Officer, Liaison Officer, and other positions). NRF at 50. In an incident involving "multiple command authorities," the incident can be led by "a unified command comprised of officials who have jurisdictional authority or functional responsibility for the incident under an appropriate law, ordinance, or agreement," rather than by a single Incident Commander. *Id.*

6. What is "unified command"? Compare "unity of command" with "unified command":

> Unity of command: The concept by which each person within an organization reports to one and only one designated person. The purpose

of unity of command is to ensure unity of effort under one responsible commander for every objective.

Unified command: An application of the Incident Command System used when there is more than one agency with incident jurisdiction or when incidents cross political jurisdictions. Agencies work together through the designated members of the Unified Command, often the senior person from agencies and/or disciplines participating in the Unified Command, to establish a common set of objectives and strategies and a single incident action plan.

LESSONS LEARNED, *supra*, at 13. NIMS and the NRF apparently aspire to unified command, but not unity of command. Can unity of command be achieved in a program for emergency response? Should it?

7. How well is unified command — which admittedly requires a "team effort" — likely to work in an emergency situation that involves federal, state, and local responders (and potentially responders from a number of states and localities)? Reconsider, in this regard, the conflict between President Bush and Louisiana Governor Blanco over the control of National Guard troops in Katrina's aftermath. *See* Chapter 3, Section B, *supra*. Is the NRF's expectation that "unity of effort" will produce "seamless coordination across jurisdictions in support or common objectives" wishful thinking or a reasonable goal that can be implemented through concrete actions?

8. The NRF and NIMS attempt to facilitate "unified command" by coordinating federal incident support to states through a Joint Field Office (JFO), which provides a common physical location for the members of the "Unified Coordination Group." The Unified Coordination Group "is comprised of senior officials from the State and key Federal Departments and Agencies," NRF at 52, and is charged with developing common objectives and strategies. State officials represented in the Unified Coordination Group include two key figures appointed by the governor: the State Coordinating Officer and the Governor's Authorized Representative. *Id.* The role of the JFO is not to "manage on-scene operations," but rather to "support . . . on-scene efforts and conduct[] broader support operations." *Id.* at 62. On-scene operations are managed by the local incident command.

9. In addition to difficulties in coordinating federal and state response, disputes between different federal agencies with overlapping jurisdiction may challenge notions of "unified command." Another manifestation of the tension between FEMA and larger DHS control of emergency functions was conflict over the relationship between FEMA's Federal Coordinating Officer (FCO), appointed in Stafford Act incidents, and the principal federal official (PFO), appointed by the secretary of DHS (subdelegating the secretary's authority as principal federal official for emergency management as described in note 1). The FCO position arises from the Stafford Act's command that the president appoint a federal coordinating officer immediately upon declaring a major disaster or emergency. *See* 42 U.S.C. §5143. Under the Stafford Act, the FCO appraises the most urgent needs, establishes field offices, coordinates relief efforts, and takes other appropriate action to guide citizens and public officials. *See id.* By contrast, the NRP created the new position of principal federal officer, "personally

designated" by the secretary of Homeland Security as his or her representative as "the lead federal official." DEPARTMENT OF HOMELAND SECURITY, NATIONAL RESPONSE PLAN 33 (2004). The PFO, a nonstatutory post, holds no "directive authority" over the FCO or other officials and does not replace the incident command structure. *Id.*

The Post-Katrina Act reaffirmed FEMA's primary role by requiring that the NRP provide an appropriate role, consistent with the Stafford Act, for the FCO, and prohibiting the PFO from exercising "directive authority" over the FCO. 6 U.S.C. §319(c). The NRF attempts to clarify the roles of the PFO and FCO, in accordance with the new statutory guidance:

> What are the roles and responsibilities of the Principal Federal Officer (PFO) and the Federal Coordinating Officer (FCO)? The [DHS] Secretary may elect to designate a single individual to serve as his or her primary representative to ensure consistency of Federal support as well as the overall effectiveness of the Federal incident management. When appointed, such an individual serves in the field as the PFO for the incident. The Secretary will only appoint a PFO for catastrophic or unusually complex incidents that require extraordinary coordination. When appointed, the PFO interfaces with Federal, State, tribal, and local jurisdictional officials regarding the overall Federal incident management strategy and acts as the primary Federal spokesperson for coordinated media and public communications.
>
> For Stafford Act incidents (i.e., Presidentially declared emergencies or major disasters), upon the recommendation of the FEMA Administrator and the Secretary of Homeland Security, the President appoints an FCO. The FCO is a senior FEMA official trained, certified, and well experienced in emergency management, and specifically appointed to coordinate Federal support in the response to and recovery from emergencies and major disasters. The FCO executes Stafford Act authorities, including commitment of FEMA resources and the mission assignment of other Federal departments or agencies. The same individual will not serve as the PFO and the FCO at the same time for the same incident.

DHS, National Response Framework: Frequently Asked Questions 6, available at http://www.fema.gov/emergency/nrf/aboutNRF.htm. Does this division of responsibilities make sense? The NRF also reiterates that the PFO does not have "directive authority" over the FCO and clarifies that the PFO's role is to promote collaboration and resolve any federal interagency conflict, not to "direct or replace the incident command structure." NRF at 67. If both an FCO and PFO are appointed for one incident, then the two officials are colocated at the JFO. *See id.* at 63.

10. Another way the federal government coordinates and delivers disaster aid is through rapidly deployable "strike teams" with specific skill sets. The Post-Katrina Act directed FEMA to establish Incident Management Assistance Teams (IMATs) to support local incident command and facilitate establishment of unified command. 42 U.S.C. §5144. Designed to activate in two hours and arrive on-site within twelve hours, IMATs are staffed by full-time emergency management personnel and tasked with providing leadership in delivering federal aid, coordinating interjurisdictional response, and supplying decision makers with initial situational awareness. *See* FEMA Fact Sheet: IMAT (2009), http://www.fema.gov/pdf/

media/factsheets/2009/dod_inc_mgmt_asst_teams.pdf. IMATs consolidate and streamline federal first-response and presence, and will eventually absorb existing Emergency Response Teams (ERT) and Federal Incident Response Support Teams (FIRST).

11. Another of FEMA's primary mechanisms for coordinating federal support is calling up one of the fifteen Emergency Support Functions (ESFs) outlined in the NRF. "ESFs are organized groups of government and private sector entities that provide support, resources, and services. An ESF is staffed by specialists from multiple Federal departments, agencies, and the private sector. The purpose of the ESFs is to integrate skills and capabilities that reside in disparate organizations to coordinate support to State and local response agencies, including both physical resources and staff." LESSONS LEARNED, *supra*, at 15. Each ESF covers one functional area and is headed by a lead agency.

12. The following table classifies Emergency Support Functions according to ESF number, function, and primary implementing department or agency:

ESF #	Emergency Support Function	Primary Department or Agency
ESF #1	Transportation	DOT
ESF #2	Communications	DHS (NCS)
ESF #3	Public Works and Engineering	DOD (USACE)
ESF #4	Firefighting	USDA (Forest Service)
ESF #5	Emergency Management	DHS (FEMA)
ESF #6	Mass Care, Emergency Assistance, Housing, and Human Services	DHS (FEMA)
ESF #7	Logistics Management & Resource Support	GSA and DHS (FEMA)
ESF #8	Public Health and Medical Services	HHS
ESF #9	Search and Rescue	DHS (FEMA)
ESF #10	Oil and Hazardous Materials Response	EPA
ESF #11	Agriculture and Natural Resources	USDA
ESF #12	Energy	DOE
ESF #13	Public Safety and Security	DOJ
ESF #14	Long-Term Community Recovery	DHS (FEMA)
ESF #15	External Affairs	DHS

NRF at 58-59.

13. Among the functions laid out in the NRF, ESF #8 (Public Health and Medical Services) figures very prominently. Because natural disasters often destroy hospitals and strain infrastructure in every respect, disease looms large as a source of secondary casualties after a catastrophe. Moreover, the 2009 H1N1 pandemic has heightened interest in strategies for combating public-health risks such as pandemic flu and bioterrorism. ESF #8 provides the general "mechanism for coordinated Federal assistance . . . in response to a public health and medical disaster." FEMA, Emergency Support Function #8 — Public Health and Medical Services Annex (2008), available at http://www.fema.gov/pdf/emergency/nrf/nrf-esf-08.pdf. Some of the core functional areas for which ESF #8 provides assistance are assessment of public health/medical needs; health surveillance; medical care personnel; health/medical/veterinary equipment and supplies; patient evacuation; food safety and security; agricultural safety and security; potable water/wastewater and solid waste disposal; and mass fatality management, victim identification, and decontamination of remains. *Id.* at 8-1. The primary agency of ESF #8 is the Department of Health and Human Services (HHS), which leads the federal effort to provide public health and medical assistance to affected areas by giving instructions to fifteen federal agencies and the American Red Cross, and by coordinating national preparedness, response, and recovery actions. *Id.* at 8-2. "Throughout operations, ESF #8 coordinates and communicates with federal (at the headquarters and regional levels), state, local, and tribal partners to determine the ongoing public health and medical needs." Brian Kamoie, *The National Response Plan: A New Framework for Homeland Security, Public Health, and Bioterrorism Response*, 38 J. Health L. 287, 300-304 (2005).

The Biological Incident Annex is another mechanism aimed at preventing the possibility of widespread disease outbreak. FEMA, Biological Incident Annex (2008), available at http://www.fema.gov/pdf/emergency/nrf/nrf_BiologicalIncidentAnnex.pdf. Again, HHS is the primary federal agency for public health, medical preparation, and response to a biological terrorism attack or naturally occurring outbreak. *Id.* at BIO-2. Once HHS is notified of a threat or disease outbreak that requires federal assistance, HHS will request activation of ESF #8 from FEMA. *Id.* at BIO-8. The Annex then outlines "actions, roles, and responsibilities associated with response to a human disease outbreak," as well as response actions, such as threat assessment notification procedures, laboratory testing, joint investigative/response procedures, and activities related to recovery. *Id.* at BIO-1. Some of the federal government's objectives in response to a biological terrorism event or a naturally occurring disease outbreak are to "detect the event through disease surveillance and environmental monitoring; identify and protect the population(s) at risk; determine the source of the disease; assess the public health, law enforcement, and international implications; control and contain any possible epidemic (including providing guidance to State, tribal, territorial, and local public health authorities); augment and surge public health and medical services;

identify the cause and prevent the recurrence of any potential resurgence, additional outbreaks, or further spread of disease; and assess the extent of residual biological contamination and conduct response, restoration, and recovery actions as necessary." *Id.* The Annex provides for "environmental surveillance systems," which detect agents that could cause a biological incident and allow for rapid mobilization of a public health response if necessary. *Id.* at BIO-2, BIO-6. An incident may also be detected by "clinical or hospital presentation." *Id.* at BIO-4.

14. In addition to the ESFs, the National Response Framework also has "incident annexes," such as the Biological Incident Annex discussed in the prior note, that outline response for different types of disasters. Currently, there are separate annexes for biological incidents, catastrophic incidents, food and agriculture incidents, mass evacuation incidents, nuclear/radiological incidents, cyber incidents, and terrorism incidents. One of the most important of these annexes — and one that has received extensive attention post-Katrina — is the Catastrophic Incident Annex, discussed below.

3. HURRICANE KATRINA AND CATASTROPHIC DISASTERS: THE POST-9/11 FRAMEWORK IN ACTION

Hurricane Katrina posed the first serious test of HSPD-5 and the twin cornerstones of its approach to managing disasters, the NIMS and the NRP. The post–September 11 framework for emergency response failed many aspects of this initial challenge. Most of these failures were related to the catastrophic magnitude of the Katrina disaster — both the extraordinary number of casualties and the extraordinary amount of damage inflicted on the Gulf Coast. As you read the following congressional report on the failure of crucial aspects of the HSPD-5 system, consider whether the new NRF and NIMS might perform better than the old iterations in catastrophic circumstances such as those presented by Katrina, or whether some new, more drastic alternative approach is required.

U.S. House of Representatives, A Failure of Initiative

Final Report of the Select Bipartisan Committee to Investigate the
Preparation for and Response to Hurricane Katrina 131-132 (2006)

With the creation of the Department of Homeland Security (DHS) and the development of the National Response Plan (NRP), an additional layer of management and response authority was placed between the President and FEMA, and additional response coordinating structures were established. The Secretary of Homeland Security became the President's principal disaster advisor responsible for enabling the President to effectively utilize his authority under the Stafford Act to direct all federal agencies, particularly the Department of Defense (DOD), to respond in a coordinated and expeditious fashion. As part of these changes, critical response decision points were assigned to the Secretary of Homeland Security. Secretary [Michael] Chertoff executed these responsibilities late, ineffectively, or not at all. These secretarial authorities include:

The designation of an incident of national significance (INS);
The authority to convene the Interagency Incident Management Group (IIMG);
The designation of the principal federal official (PFO); and
The invocation of the national response plan's catastrophic incident annex (NRP-CIA).

There was plenty of advance warning by the National Weather Service, and the consequences of a category 4 hurricane striking New Orleans were well-documented. Fifty-six hours prior to landfall, Hurricane Katrina presented an extremely high probability threat that 75 percent of New Orleans would be flooded, tens of thousands of residents may be killed, hundreds of thousands trapped in flood waters up to 20 feet, hundreds of thousands of homes and other structures destroyed, a million people evacuated from their homes, and the greater New Orleans area would be rendered uninhabitable for several months or years. An August 28 report by the department's National Infrastructure Simulation and Analysis Center concluded: "Any storm rated Category 4 or greater . . . will likely lead to severe flooding and/or levee breaching, leaving the New Orleans metro area submerged for weeks or months."

Under these conditions it seems reasonable to expect the criteria for designating an INS would have been met, the appointment of a PFO would be necessary to coordinate an unprecedented federal response, the IIMG would be convened to provide strategic guidance and recommendations to the Secretary and the President, and the NRP-CIA would be invoked to shift the federal response posture from a reactive to proactive mode in order to save lives and accelerate assistance to overwhelmed state and local systems. According to a recent letter submitted by DHS . . . in response to the preliminary observations of the Comptroller General . . . , DHS viewed the NRP-CIA as applicable only to no-notice or short-notice events. And the Select Committee acknowledges that the State of Louisiana expressed its satisfaction with the supplies and that former FEMA Director Michael Brown directed that commodities be "jammed up" the supply chain.

While the NRP-CIA may be particularly applicable to a no-notice event, the Annex itself reflects only that a catastrophic incident may occur with little or no warning. And the pre-positioning of supplies to the satisfaction of state and local authorities, while an appropriate measure for a disaster without catastrophic consequences, was clearly not sufficient for the catastrophic consequences of Hurricane Katrina.

Instead, absent a catastrophic disaster designation from Chertoff, federal response officials in the field eventually made the difficult decisions to bypass established procedures and provide assistance without waiting for appropriate requests from the states or for clear direction from Washington. These decisions to switch from a "pull" to a "push" system were made individually, over several days, and in an uncoordinated fashion as circumstances required. The federal government stumbled into a proactive response during the first several days after Hurricane Katrina made landfall, as opposed to the Secretary making a clear and decisive choice to respond proactively at the beginning of the disaster. The White House Homeland Security Council (HSC), situated at the apex of the policy coordination framework for DHS issues, itself failed to proactively de-conflict varying damage assessments. One example included an eyewitness account of a levee breach supplied by a FEMA official at 7:00 p.m. on August 29. The White House did not consider this assessment confirmed for 11 more hours, when, after 6:00 a.m. the next morning, it received a Homeland Security Operations Center (HSOC) Situation Report confirming the breach.

The catastrophic nature of Katrina confirmed once again that the standard "reactive" nature of federal assistance, while appropriate for most disasters, does not work during disasters of this scale. When local and state governments are functionally overwhelmed or incapacitated, the federal government must be prepared to respond proactively. It will need to anticipate state and local requirements, move commodities and assets into the area on its own initiative, and shore up or even help reconstitute critical state and local emergency management and response structures.

The need for assistance is extreme during the initial period of a catastrophic hurricane, yet the ability of state and local responders to meet that need is limited. That is why it is so important for the federal government, particularly DOD resources, to respond proactively and fill that gap as quickly as possible. Because it takes several days to mobilize federal resources, critical decisions must be made as early as possible so that massive assistance can surge into the area during the first two days, not several days or weeks later. The NRP-CIA was drafted to meet this specific and well known requirement, yet Chertoff never invoked it for Katrina.

NOTES AND QUESTIONS

1. "The Catastrophic Incident Annex of the NRP includes the assumption that large-scale evacuations, whether spontaneous or directed pursuant to authorities, may be more likely to occur after attacks than natural disasters, and that the maintenance of public health will 'aggravate attempts to implement a coordinated evacuation management strategy.'" Keith Bea, *Disaster Evacuation and Displacement Policy: Issues for Congress* 5 (CRS Report for Congress, Order Code RS22235, Sept. 2, 2005). Did this planning assumption demonstrate that the NRP was "skewed toward . . . terrorist attacks" and therefore less well suited for "address[ing] the complications evident in the evacuation of New Orleans"? *Id.* Nearly four years after September 11, 2001, Katrina posed the question as squarely as possible: did the United States fundamentally err in assigning responsibility for all emergency response, including relief and rebuilding efforts in connection with natural disasters, to an agency whose principal mission is directed toward detecting and preventing terrorist attacks? The current iteration of the Catastrophic Incident Annex has eliminated this planning assumption.

2. Scholars in many fields distinguish between failures of capacity and failures of performance. For example, tort law distinguishes sharply between design defects and manufacturing defects. *Compare* RESTATEMENT (THIRD) OF TORTS: PRODUCTS LIABILITY §2(b) *with* RESTATEMENT (SECOND) OF TORTS §402A. *See*

generally Frank J. Vandall & Joshua F. Vandall, *A Call for an Accurate Restatement (Third) of Torts: Design Defect*, 33 U. MEM. L. REV. 909 (2003). Linguists distinguish between competence and performance, between the innate capacity to speak and speech as it actually occurs. *See, e.g.*, NOAM CHOMSKY, LANGUAGE AND MIND 4 (enlarged ed. 1972). Was the failure of the NRP during Katrina one of design and capacity, or was it one of execution and performance? The former suggests that the proper remedy lies in legislative reform, perhaps to the point of overhauling the entire law of emergency response. The latter suggests that fault is more appropriately assigned to individual actors: FEMA Director Michael Brown, Secretary of Homeland Security Michael Chertoff, or perhaps even President George W. Bush.

3. The Senate assigned blame at all levels, describing Katrina's relief effort as one plagued by "failures in design, implementation, and execution of the National Response Plan." UNITED STATES SENATE, COMMITTEE ON HOMELAND SECURITY AND GOVERNMENTAL AFFAIRS, HURRICANE KATRINA: A NATION STILL UNPREPARED 27-1 (2006) [hereinafter SENATE KATRINA REPORT]. The Senate's report identified the following as some of the major failures of the Katrina response, *see generally id.* at 27-1 to 27-17:

   a. *Insufficient training and exercises.* The NRP "is a complex, ambitious, 400-plus-page high-level plan," a "very detailed, acronym-heavy document that is not easily accessible to the first-time user." Beyond an initial wave of training for headquarters staff of component agencies, DHS evidently made no further efforts to "ensur[e] that the NRP would be well implemented."

   b. *The roles of the principal federal official and the federal coordinating officer.* The NRP's failure to "define the role of the PFO or distinguish it from that of the FCO" posed "an obstacle to an effective, coordinated response to Katrina."

   c. *Potentially overlapping agency roles.* The NRP "fail[ed] to delineate areas of potentially overlapping responsibility among federal agencies." For instance, the NRP assigned responsibility for Emergency Support Function 8, Public Health and Medical Services, to HHS, even though one of the response mechanisms, the National Disaster Medical System, answers to FEMA and DHS. Consequently, "[i]n the response to Katrina, FEMA and HHS engaged in minimal coordination on pre-positioning and deploying Disaster Medical Assistance Teams."

   d. *Contingency and catastrophic planning.* As "a high-level plan, with a core set of principles meant to apply to a wide range of possible events," the NRP "was not designed to address specific scenarios or geographic areas, or to provide operational details." The plan simply failed to " 'contemplate' an event on the massive scale of Katrina."

   e. *Mistakes in declaring an Incident of National Significance.* According to the NRP, "every event that provokes a Presidential declaration under the Stafford Act automatically becomes an Incident of National Significance." President Bush's August 27, 2005, emergency declaration for portions of Louisiana automatically transformed Hurricane Katrina into an INS. Nevertheless, three days later, Secretary of Homeland Security Chertoff issued another "declaration" designating Katrina an INS. "At minimum, the Secretary's redundant declaration of an Incident of National Significance confused an already difficult situation and suggested a lack of familiarity with core concepts of the NRP within the Secretary's Office."

f. *The appointment of Michael Brown as principal federal official.* Apart from the wisdom of appointing a principal federal official "who had no experience as an emergency manager," Secretary Chertoff's appointment of FEMA Director Michael Brown as PFO for Katrina "violated the literal requirements of the NRP." The NRP prohibits the PFO "from occupying another position or having another set of conflicting or distracting obligations at the same time."

g. *Non-implementation of the Catastrophic Incident Annex.* "In failing to implement the National Response Plan's Catastrophic Incident Annex (NRP-CIA), Secretary Chertoff ignored a potentially powerful tool that might have alleviated difficulties in the federal response to Katrina." Though not accompanied by changes in the Stafford Act or other legislation (and therefore unable to provide new emergency response authority to federal officials), the NRP-CIA does "set a policy and tone for an urgent and proactive response that moves beyond the usual procedures in responding to an 'ordinary' disaster."

4. Recall that "the NRP-CIA turns what is traditionally a 'pull' system, in which the federal government waits to receive requests from state and local officials, or from other federal agencies, into a 'push' system, where federal authorities proactively deploy resources to mobilization centers close to the disaster or, in certain circumstances, directly to the incident scene to assist in responding to the incident." SENATE KATRINA REPORT, *supra,* at 27-9. Because Secretary Chertoff did not invoke the NRP-CIA after Katrina to provide clear authority for pushing resources into affected areas, the "pull" system evolved into a "push" system over a number of days because of individual decisions of FEMA personnel on the ground. A similar evolution had occurred after Hurricane Iniki in Hawaii. The House Final Report on Katrina concluded:

> [The efforts behind] the switch to a push response [illustrate] important principles of effective emergency management. First, they demonstrate the importance of having qualified and experienced professionals in charge of operations. Second, these officials need to have the authority to commit resources as they see fit without waiting to seek approval from above. And, third, federal officials need to have good working relationships with their state counterparts. . . .

U.S. HOUSE OF REPRESENTATIVES, A FAILURE OF INITIATIVE, FINAL REPORT OF THE SELECT BIPARTISAN COMMITTEE TO INVESTIGATE THE PREPARATION FOR AND RESPONSE TO HURRICANE KATRINA 138-139 (2006) [hereinafter HOUSE KATRINA REPORT]. Does this analysis suggest that disaster planning should not be so detailed and specific that it precludes experienced emergency management personnel on the ground from making informed choices about what measures the particular situation demands?

5. The ad hoc evolution of the push system (in the absence of clear legal authority, let alone coordinated direction from a hierarchical command structure) epitomizes "emergent" behavior, as identified by complexity theory, in which uncoordinated actors following small-scale rules generate systemic effects transcending any one actor's local conduct. *See* JOHN H. HOLLAND, EMERGENCE: FROM CHAOS TO ORDER (1998); STEVEN JOHNSON, EMERGENCE: THE CONNECTED LIVES OF ANTS, BRAINS, CITIES, AND SOFTWARE (2001). The ability of on-site officials to make quick judgments, informed by firsthand observations not available to faraway supervisors, might have greater potential to effect good outcomes in emergencies than the designation of a federal coordinating officer under the Stafford Act or the designation of a principal federal official under the NRF.

6. The 2006 Post-Katrina Act defines "catastrophic incident" as "any natural disaster, act of terrorism, or other man-made disaster that results in extraordinary levels of casualties or damage or disruption severely affecting the population (including mass evacuations), infrastructure, environment, economy, national morale, or government functions in an area." *See* 6 U.S.C. §701(4). This definition is virtually identical to that then in use in both the NRP and the NRP-CIA. It is unclear why Congress felt it necessary to include this definition at all, although the Act does direct FEMA to make specific provision for catastrophic incidents when undertaking certain preparedness functions, including establishing adequate Surge Capacity Force to deal with catastrophic incidents, *see* Pub. L. No. 109-295, §624(a)(1), codified at 6 U.S.C. §711(a)(1), and training regional office Strike Teams to respond to catastrophic disasters, *see* Pub. L. No. 109-295, §507(f)(5), codified at 6 U.S.C. §317(f)(5). *See also* Mitchell Moss et al., *The Stafford Act and Priorities for Reform*, 6 J. HOMELAND SECURITY & EMERGENCY MGMT. 8-9 (2009) (arguing that this definition of catastrophic incident should have been integrated into the Stafford Act, rather than simply included in new sections of law dealing with national emergency management).

7. If another catastrophic hurricane were to strike the Gulf coast today, would the new NRF function better than the NRP did during Katrina? The current NRF, like the NRP, calls specifically for proactive response to catastrophic incidents: "Prior to and during catastrophic incidents, especially those that occur with little or no notice, the State and Federal governments may take proactive measures to mobilize and deploy assets in anticipation of a formal request from the State for Federal assistance." NRF at 42. These proactive measures would likely be taken for "catastrophic events involving chemical, biological, radiological, nuclear, or high-yield explosive weapons of mass destruction, large-magnitude earthquakes, or other catastrophic incidents affecting heavily populated areas," and are to be coordinated with state, tribal, and local governments "when possible." *Id.* As you read the following excerpt from the current Catastrophic Incident Annex, think about whether, if properly invoked, it would help avoid some of the problems that plagued the Katrina response.

FEMA, National Response Framework, Catastrophic Incident Annex

(2008), available at http://www.fema.gov/emergency/nrf/incidentannexes.htm

Coordinating Agency: Department of Homeland Security/Federal Emergency Management Agency

Cooperating Agencies: All Federal departments and agencies (and other organizations) with assigned primary or supporting Emergency Support Function responsibilities

Introduction

Purpose

The Catastrophic Incident Annex to the National Response Framework (NRF-CIA) establishes the context and overarching strategy for implementing and coordinating an accelerated, proactive national response to a catastrophic incident.

A more detailed and operationally specific National Response Framework Catastrophic Incident Supplement (NRF-CIS) is published independently of the NRF and annexes.

Scope

A catastrophic incident, as defined by the NRF, is any natural or manmade incident, including terrorism, that results in extraordinary levels of mass casualties, damage, or disruption severely affecting the population, infrastructure, environment, economy, national morale, and/or government functions. A catastrophic incident could result in sustained nationwide impacts over a prolonged period of time; almost immediately exceeds resources normally available to State, tribal, local, and private-sector authorities in the impacted area; and significantly interrupts governmental operations and emergency services to such an extent that national security could be threatened. These factors drive the urgency for coordinated national planning to ensure accelerated Federal and/or national assistance.

Recognizing that Federal and/or national resources are required to augment overwhelmed State, tribal, and local response efforts, the NRF-CIA establishes protocols to preidentify and rapidly deploy key essential resources (e.g., medical teams, search and rescue teams, transportable shelters, medical and equipment caches, etc.) that are expected to be urgently needed/required to save lives and contain incidents.

Upon the occurrence of a catastrophic incident, or in advance if determined by the Secretary of Homeland Security, the Government will deploy Federal resources, organized into incident-specific "packages," in accordance with the NRF-CIS and in coordination with the affected State and incident command structure.

Where State, tribal, or local governments are unable to establish or maintain an effective incident command structure due to catastrophic conditions, the Federal Government, at the direction of the Secretary of Homeland Security, may establish a unified command structure, led by the Unified Coordination Group (UCG), to save lives, protect property, maintain operation of critical infrastructure/key resources (CIKR), contain the event, and protect national security. The Federal Government shall transition to its role of coordinating and supporting the State, tribal, or local government when they are capable of reestablishing their incident command.

The NRF-CIA is primarily designed to address no-notice or short-notice incidents of catastrophic magnitude, where the need for Federal assistance is obvious and immediate, where anticipatory planning and resource pre-positioning were precluded, and where the exact nature of needed resources and assets is not known. Appropriately tailored assets and responses identified in the NRF-CIS, as well as other select Federal resources and assets, may also be deployed in support of a projected catastrophic event (e.g., a major hurricane) with advance warning in support of the anticipated requests of State, tribal, and local governments.

Policies

A catastrophic incident will likely trigger a Presidential major disaster declaration and result in the Secretary of Homeland Security or a designee implementing the NRF-CIA/CIS.

All deploying Federal resources remain under the control of their respective Federal department or agency during mobilization and deployment. Some Federal departments and agencies have the authority, under their own statutes, to deploy directly to the incident scene.

Federal resources arriving at a National Logistics Staging Area (NLSA) remain there until requested by State/local incident command authorities, when they are integrated into the response effort.

Federal assets unilaterally deployed to the NLSA in accordance with the NRF-CIS do not require a State cost share. However, in accordance with the Stafford Act, State requests for use of deployed Federal assets may require cost-sharing.

For no-notice or short-notice catastrophic incidents, Federal resources identified in the execution schedule of the NRF-CIS will be mobilized and deployed, unless it can be credibly established that an action listed is not needed at the catastrophic incident venue.

If during a response, it is determined that the incident is catastrophic in nature, any remaining actions not originally initiated from the execution schedule will be initiated.

States are encouraged to conduct planning in collaboration with the Federal Government for catastrophic incidents as part of their steady-state preparedness activities.

The Federal Government, in collaboration with States, tribes, local governments, the private sector, and nongovernmental organizations (NGOs), develops proactive plans for activation and implementation of the NRF-CIA, to include situations where the need exceeds or challenges the resources and/or capabilities of State and local governments to respond and where the Federal Government may temporarily assume roles typically performed by State, tribal, and local governments.

The occurrence or threat of multiple or successive catastrophic incidents may significantly reduce the size, speed, and depth of the Federal response. If deemed necessary or prudent, the Federal Government may reduce the allocation of finite resources when multiple venues are competing for the same resources.

Situation

The initial response to a catastrophic incident starts on a local level with the local, tribal and/or State responders. However, there may be circumstances that exceed the capabilities of State, local, or tribal authorities in which they are unable to initially establish or maintain a command structure for incident response. In these instances, accelerated Federal response may be warranted, and the Department of Homeland Security (DHS)/Federal Emergency Management Agency (FEMA) will coordinate response activities until local, tribal, and/or State authorities are capable or have re-established their incident command structure.

Continuity of Operations (COOP)/Continuity of Government (COG): Following a catastrophic event, segments of State, tribal, and local governments as well as NGOs and the private sector may be severely compromised. The Federal Government and its national partners must be prepared to fill potential gaps to ensure continuity of government and public- and private-sector operations. The incident may cause significant disruption of the impacted area's CIKR, such as energy, transportation, telecommunications, law enforcement, and public health and health care systems.

Incident Condition: Normal procedures for certain Emergency Support Functions (ESFs) may be expedited or streamlined to address the magnitude of urgent requirements of the incident. All ESFs must explore economies of scale to maximize utilization and efficiency of limited resources. In the case of a catastrophic incident, it is expected that the Federal Government or other national entities will provide expedited assistance in one or more of the following areas: [mass evacuations (ESF #5); mass care, housing, and human services (ESF #6); search and rescue (ESF #9); victim decontamination (ESF #8); environmental assessment and decontamination (ESF #10); public health and medical support (ESF #8); medical equipment and supplies (ESF #8); casualty transportation (ESF #8); public safety and security (ESF #13); public information (ESF #15); and critical infrastructure (CIKR Support Annex).] . . .

Planning Assumptions

A catastrophic incident will result in large numbers of casualties and/or displaced persons, possibly in the tens to hundreds of thousands. During a catastrophic incident response, priority is given to human life-saving operations.

The nature and scope of a catastrophic incident will immediately overwhelm State, tribal, and local response capabilities and require immediate Federal support.

A detailed and credible common operating picture will not be achievable for 24 to 48 hours (or longer) after the incident. As a result, response activities may have to begin without the benefit of a detailed or complete situation and critical needs assessment.

The nature and scope of the catastrophic incident will include major natural or manmade hazards including chemical, biological, radiological, nuclear, or high-yield explosive attacks, and cyber attacks.

A catastrophic incident has unique dimensions/characteristics requiring that response plans/strategies be flexible enough to effectively address emerging needs and requirements.

A catastrophic incident will occur with little or no warning. Some incidents may be well underway before detection.

Multiple incidents will occur simultaneously or sequentially in contiguous and/or noncontiguous areas. Some incidents, such as a biological WMD attack, may be dispersed over a large geographic area and lack a defined incident site.

A catastrophic incident will produce environmental impacts that severely challenge the ability and capacity of governments and communities to achieve a timely recovery.

Federal resources must be capable of mobilization and deployment before they are requested via normal NRF protocols.

Large-scale evacuations, organized or self-directed, may occur.

Existing health care systems in the impacted area are expected to be quickly overwhelmed, requiring evacuation of existing patients from these facilities to accommodate increased patient workload if the facility remains operational. Additionally, those persons with special needs, including residents of nursing homes and extended care facilities, will require special attention during evacuation.

Large numbers of people will be left temporarily or permanently homeless and may require prolonged temporary housing. Some displaced people will require specialized attention, healthcare assistance, and assistance with activities of daily living based on their special needs.

A large number of household pets and service animals will require appropriate care, sheltering, medical attention, and transportation.

A catastrophic incident will have significant international dimensions, including impacts on the health and welfare of border community populations, cross-border trade, transit, law enforcement coordination, and others. . . .

Federal Response

In accordance with NRF provisions for a proactive Federal response to catastrophic incidents, the NRF-CIA employs an expedited approach to the provision of Federal resources to save lives and contain the incident.

Guiding principles for a proactive Federal catastrophic incident response include the following:

* The primary mission is to save lives, protect property and critical infrastructure, contain the event, and protect the national security.
* Standard procedures outlined in the NRF regarding requests for assistance may be expedited or, under extreme circumstances, temporarily suspended in the immediate aftermath of an incident of catastrophic magnitude, pursuant to existing law.
* Preidentified Federal response resources are mobilized and deployed, and, if required, begin emergency operations to commence life-safety activities.

* Notification and full coordination with States occur, but the coordination process should not delay or impede the rapid mobilization and deployment of critical Federal resources.
* Upon recognition that a catastrophic incident condition (e.g., involving mass casualties and/or mass evacuation) exists, the Secretary of Homeland Security immediately begins implementation of the NRF-CIA. Upon notification from the National Operations Center (NOC) that the NRF-CIA has been implemented, Federal departments and agencies immediately:
  * Take actions to activate, mobilize, and deploy incident-specific resources in accordance with the NRF-CIS.
  * Take actions to protect life, property, and critical infrastructure under their jurisdiction, and provide assistance within the affected area.
  * Commence those hazard-specific activities established under the appropriate and applicable NRF Incident Annex(es), including the NRF-CIA.
  * Commence functional activities and responsibilities established under the NRF ESF Annexes.

NRF-CIA actions that the Federal Government takes in response to a catastrophic incident include:

* For no-notice or short-notice catastrophic events resulting in little or no time to assess the requirements of the State, tribal, and local governments, all Federal departments and agencies initiate actions to mobilize and deploy resources by scenario type as planned for in the NRF-CIS.
* For those potential catastrophic incidents where there is time to coordinate with State, tribal, and local governments, as well as private-sector and NGO authorities, Federal departments and agencies will pre-deploy appropriately tailored elements specified in the NRF-CIS, as well as other Federal resources as required to meet the anticipated demands of the specific incident scenario.
* For no-notice/short-notice catastrophic events when there is little or no time to assess the requirements of the State, tribal, and local governments, Federal departments and agencies initiate actions to mobilize and deploy resources by scenario type as planned for in the NRF-CIS. To that end, the Department of Defense (DOD) is prepared to provide capabilities in the following support categories: aviation, communication, defense coordinating officer/defense coordinating element, medical treatment, patient evacuation, decontamination, and logistics.

All Federal departments and agencies and organizations assigned primary or supporting ESF responsibilities immediately begin implementation of those responsibilities, as appropriate or when directed by the President.

Incident-specific resources and capabilities (e.g., medical teams, search and rescue teams, equipment, transportable shelters, preventive and therapeutic pharmaceutical caches, etc.) are activated and prepared for deployment to an NLSA near the incident site. The development of site-specific catastrophic incident response strategies (as detailed in the NRF-CIS) that include the pre-identification of incident-specific critical resource requirements and corresponding deployment/employment strategies accelerate the timely provision of critical capabilities.

Regional Federal facilities are activated and prepared to receive and treat casualties from the incident area. Federal facilities are directed to reprioritize services (in some cases possibly reducing or postponing certain customary services) until life-saving activities are concluded. The development of site-specific catastrophic incident response plans that include the preidentification of projected casualty and mass care support requirements and potentially available facilities expands the response architecture and accelerates the availability of such resources.

Supplementary support agreements with NGOs and the private sector are activated. Given the projected high demand for Federal support, as well as the potential national security implications of a catastrophic incident, Federal departments and agencies may be asked to redirect efforts from their day-to-day responsibilities to support the response effort. . . .

NOTES AND QUESTIONS

1. The NRF-CIA continues to emphasize that the Annex is primarily for "no-notice or short-notice events." Does that language make it less likely that the Annex will be invoked in events such as major, predicted hurricanes, even if the hurricane has catastrophic effects? Or is it likely that Katrina sufficiently impressed on federal leaders the importance of invoking the Annex?

2. One of the Katrina response shortcomings identified by the Senate was failure to adequately delineate the potentially overlapping roles of federal agencies. Does the NRF-CIA's statement that "[a]ll deploying Federal resources remain under the control of their respective Federal department or agency" answer or compound this problem? The Senate also criticized the NRP's lack of operational details. A supplement to the annex (which was in draft form when Katrina occurred) — the NRF-CIS — is undergoing revision as of June 2009. It is intended to supply detailed operational instructions and timelines for catastrophic disaster response.

3. The NRF-CIA, like the NRP-CIA, establishes an alternative "push" system for catastrophic incidents, identifying the conditions under which federal emergency response may proceed proactively and prescribing expedited and streamlined protocols for performing Emergency Support Functions. How can the government know *ex ante* which events should be handled with the default "pull" system and which events qualify for the NRF-CIA's "push" treatment? Compounding the difficulty is the way in which hurricanes, earthquakes, and other natural disasters follow a right-skewed distribution characteristic of complex systems rather than the usual Gaussian ("bell curve") distribution. *See generally* Daniel A. Farber, *Probabilities Behaving Badly: Complexity Theory and Environmental Uncertainty*, 37 U.C. DAVIS L. REV. 145 (2003).

B. STATE AND REGIONAL EMERGENCY RESPONSE

Notwithstanding the elaborate legal structures of the Stafford Act, the Homeland Security Act, HSPD-5, and the National Response Framework, emergency response remains in the first instance the responsibility of state and local governments. For example, although the federal response to Katrina has attracted intense scrutiny in the popular press and by the federal government itself, much of the success or failure of the response to Katrina hinged on the actions—and omissions—of state and local officials such as Louisiana Governor Kathleen Blanco and New Orleans Mayor Ray Nagin. This section therefore turns to state and regional emergency response authority. After reviewing Louisiana's response to Katrina, we will examine a representative state emergency management statute and then the interstate Emergency Management Assistance Compact (EMAC), which won praise for its effectiveness in delivering relief during Katrina.

1. STATE EMERGENCY RESPONSE

Ernest B. Abbott, Otto J. Hetzel & Alan D. Cohn,
State, Local, and First Responder Issues

The Hurricane Katrina Task Force Subcommittee Report," 2006, published
by the ABA Standing Committee on Law and National Security,
ABA Section of State and Government, and the ABA Section of Administrative
Law & Regulatory Practice. ©2006 by the American Bar Association.
Reprinted with permission. This information or any or portion thereof
may not be copied or disseminated in any form or by any means
or stored in an electronic database or retrieval system without
the express written consent of the American Bar Association.

The authority of state and local elected officials to act under a state's police powers is at its apex during a disaster. Governors are given broad discretion under state constitutions and statutes to take actions deemed necessary to reduce imminent threats to life, property, and public health and safety. They have extraordinary powers, upon declaration of a state of emergency, to commandeer resources, control property, order evacuations, suspend laws and administrative requirements, and take other measures necessary to respond to the emergency. State and local authorities are of course the "first responders" to every emergency, since in all instances the event occurs initially in one or more local jurisdictions.

States devolve authority to local units of government in various ways. Some cities possess "home rule" authority, either by reason of predating the establishment of the state, or by operation of a state's constitution or law. Local governments in general may also possess authority specifically delegated by the state through charter or operation of state law. Virtually all states have also codified their emergency response powers in some combination of statutes and executive orders, and have developed plans and procedures for responding to catastrophic incidents that derive from these expressions of state authority. Most local governments have taken similar steps. . . .

[F]our questions should guide an examination of the adequacy and use of state and local government authority to respond to catastrophic incidents: how did the state *express or clarify* its authority through statutes or executive orders; how was that authority *implemented* through plans, procedures, and protocols; in what manner did the state *execute* that authority during incidents; and how did the state *delegate* its authority to local units of government? . . . [These questions place] certain heavily reported aspects of the Louisiana response to Hurricane Katrina . . . in context, and . . . suggest[] how to examine whether that State's, and any state's, authorities are sufficient to respond to a disaster of this magnitude.

One example is the question of evacuation. Could Louisiana Governor Blanco have ordered a mandatory evacuation of Orleans Parish prior to Mayor Ray Nagin's evacuation order on Sunday, August 28, 2005, and was the decision not to do so due to a lack of authority?

The Louisiana Homeland Security and Emergency Assistance and Disaster Act ("Louisiana Disaster Act") [LA. REV. STAT. §§29:721-733] empowers the governor to address emergencies and disasters, including those caused by flood or other natural disasters such as hurricanes. On Friday, August 26, 2005 — three days before landfall of Hurricane Katrina and while there was still considerable uncertainty as to where Katrina would hit — Governor Blanco declared a state of emergency.

The Louisiana Disaster Act specifically empowers the Governor, upon the declaration of an emergency or disaster, to "[d]irect and compel the evacuation of all or part of the population from any stricken or threatened area within the state if he [or she] deems this action necessary for the preservation of life or other disaster mitigation, response, or recovery." [LA. REV. STAT. §29:724(D)(5).] Thus, the Louisiana Disaster Act clearly authorizes the Governor to order a mandatory evacuation of any parish.

However, the Southeast Louisiana Hurricane Evacuation and Sheltering Plan ("Evacuation Plan") states that each parish, and not the state, will determine whether to issue a voluntary or mandatory evacuation order with respect to that parish. The Evacuation Plan has three phases: Precautionary/Voluntary; Recommended; and Mandatory. During these phases, the "Risk Area Parish" declares a state of emergency, marshals transportation resources, implements public transportation plans, coordinates evacuation orders with the state and other Risk Area Parishes, and instructs people to evacuate. The state plays only a supporting and consulting role, aside from the implementation of the contra-flow plan.

The Louisiana State Police initiated contra-flow on interstate highways running up from coastal Louisiana beginning on Saturday, August 27, 2005. However, the Governor did not order a mandatory evacuation of Orleans Parish at that time. The Evacuation Plan contemplates that the state "prepare proclamations for the State to intervene in local situations if local government fails to act." There is no indication in the official timelines of the State of Louisiana, however, that the State sought to override any parish's judgment as to whether or when to order a mandatory evacuation.

It cannot be known whether the Governor's action to order the mandatory evacuation of a parish prior to the parish government ordering such an evacuation would have resulted in a more complete evacuation, given the structure of the Evacuation Plan and the questions that existed until the last minute concerning the ultimate path of the hurricane. It is clear, however, that the Governor possessed the authority to order such an evacuation, although the state apparently chose, in making that authority operational in the form of the Evacuation Plan, to delegate that authority to local units of government (in this case, the parishes) without specifying the degree to which the State retained that authority, and criteria under which the State would exercise that retained authority.

A related example relates to the use of buses for evacuation. Aerial footage of floodwaters covering dozens of inoperative yellow school buses was shown repeatedly on news channels. Could the State or parish governments have forcibly commandeered these and other buses (and drivers) prior to the hurricane's landfall to help in evacuating residents who lacked other means of transportation to use for evacuation, and was the decision not to do so due to a lack of authority?

The Louisiana Disaster Act gives the Governor authority, under a declaration of emergency or disaster, to "[u]tilize all available resources of the state government and of each political subdivision of the state as reasonably necessary to cope with the disaster or emergency"; to "[t]ransfer the direction, personnel, or functions of state departments and agencies or units thereof for the purpose of performing or facilitating emergency services"; and to "commandeer or utilize any private property if he [or she] finds this necessary to cope with the disaster or emergency." [LA. REV. STAT. §29:724(D)(2)-(4).] The Act gives parish presidents the same authority with respect to instruments of parish government and private property. [*See id.* §29:727(F)(2)-(4).] Thus, both the State and parish governments had expressed [sic] authority to commandeer buses and drivers. . . . [Likewise, disaster] plans contemplate[d] commandeering buses and drivers, if necessary, in support of evacuation efforts.

The timelines provided by the State of Louisiana make no mention of state authority being exercised to commandeer either school district or private resources, or to reassign or direct state employees holding appropriate driving credentials in the hours and days prior to landfall. It was not until August 31, 2005, that the Governor issued an Executive Order requiring each school district in Louisiana to make its school buses available to the Louisiana Office of Homeland Security and Emergency Preparedness, and authorized that office to commandeer those buses. . . .

In the crucible of a catastrophic incident response, it is very difficult, and indeed often inadvisable, to reverse the ways in which authority was previously implemented and delegated in plans, procedures, and protocols, since such reversal in the midst of crisis response can result in operational chaos. Failure to exercise authority as set forth in plans, procedures, and protocols can result in confusion and paralysis of decision-making. Thus, the time to ensure the adequacy of implementation of authority and its delegation, and the comprehension of such authority and its implementation by state and local government decision-makers, is prior to the onset of such an event. . . .

NOTES AND QUESTIONS

1. The Louisiana state legislature has amended the Louisiana Homeland Security and Emergency Assistance and Disaster Act over twenty times since Hurricane Katrina. Three changes are particularly relevant to the above report. First, in 2006, the Office of Homeland Security was brought within the office of the governor and specifically charged to "[i]nclude a proposed evacuation component in the homeland security and state emergency operations plan that includes specific regional and interregional planning provisions and promotes intergovernmental coordination of evacuation activities." Act of Feb. 23, 2006, No. 39, Sec. 1, §726, 2006 La. Sess. Law Serv. (West) (codified as amended at LA. REV. STAT. §29:726(E)(13)(a) (2009)). In a separate bill, passed the same day, the legislature set a May 31, 2006, deadline to promulgate regulations to guide local governments in utilizing all available transportation resources. *See* Act of Feb. 23, 2006, No. 36, Sec. 1, §726, 2006 La. Sess. Law Serv. (West) (codified as amended at LA. REV. STAT. §29:726(E)(17) (2009)). The legislature emphasized that school and city buses, as well as government and other relief vehicles, should be used with special consideration for the elderly, the infirm, tourists, those without personal transportation, and those that refuse to leave. *See id.* Finally, in 2008, the legislature clarified the concurrent authority of the parish president and the governor to order evacuation, providing that "[the governor] may order a forced evacuation order for one or more parishes or parts thereof if a forced evacuation is not issued by the parish president." Act effective June 16, 2008, No. 214, sec. 1, §730.3, 2008 La. Sess. Law Serv. (West) (codified as amended at LA. REV. STAT. §29:730.3 (2009)). Will these changes help Louisiana deal with future hurricanes, or is the real problem failure to utilize existing authority?

2. On Saturday, August 27, 2005, Mayor Ray Nagin issued the first mandatory evacuation in the history of New Orleans. Aided by contraflow, the practice of converting all highway lanes outbound, more than a million people evacuated southeastern Louisiana within twenty-four hours. Nearly 100,000 New Orleanians, however, remained in the city. Though some residents sought refuge at "shelters of last resort" — the Louisiana Superdome, the Convention Center, and the I-10 "cloverleaf" — others rode out the storm at home. *See* SENATE KATRINA REPORT, *supra*, at 1-4 to 1-5, 16-1 to 16-14.

   Why did so many New Orleanians play "hurricane roulette"? Many did so out of necessity. Lacking cars to leave, let alone the estimated $1,000 needed to shelter a family of four, the poorest residents of the city had no choice. City, state, and federal officials failed to coordinate bus evacuations until after the storm had struck and the levees had been breached. Still others elected to stay home. Snarled traffic associated with previous evacuations evidently persuaded some residents to stay, as did the experience of surviving earlier storms (particularly Camille, a Category 5 hurricane that struck the Gulf Coast in 1969). It also appears that many residents of New Orleans refused to evacuate because they did not want to abandon their pets. See discussion *supra*, Chapter 3, Section C.1.b., note 3.

How effective can any evacuation order be, at any level of government, if it is not backed by (1) transportation for those who lack the means to evacuate themselves and (2) perhaps some measure of coercion for those who might otherwise risk staying?

3. What measures should states take to enforce mandatory evacuations? Should police attempt to impress on evacuation resisters the gravity of the situation by asking them to provide next-of-kin information or write their social security numbers on their arms for possible identification purposes? Should those who ignore evacuation orders face monetary penalties or criminal prosecution? *See, e.g.,* N.C. Stat. §166A-15.1. (imposing civil liability for the cost of rescue on a person who willfully ignores a disaster-related warning about personal safety); Utah Crim. Code §76-8-317 (making failure to obey an evacuation order a class B misdemeanor, punishable by up to six months in prison and a fine of up to $1,000).

4. Many of the issues that plague the coordination of federal relief efforts with state-level efforts reappear in the coordination of statewide relief with local governments. Others, such as the Posse Comitatus Act's attempt to resolve the inherent tension between military and civilian authority, are noticeably absent in the relationship between state governments and their subdivisions. Some of the common issues involve questions of governmental structure. Traditional distinctions in local government law—between "Dillon's Rule" that local governments have only those powers that are explicitly assigned to them, on one hand, and "home rule" approaches that empower local governments absent contrary directions from their states—correspond to competing visions of federalism. Structural issues aside, questions of finance and competence are even more salient at the state level than they are in the relationship between the federal government and the states. Apart from granting money to local governments and conducting extensive training for local officials, which most states would gladly do if only they had unlimited resources, what concrete measures can help states coordinate emergency response efforts with their constituent localities?

5. One area in which state disaster laws have undergone significant revision in recent years is public health authority to respond to pandemics. After the 2001 anthrax attacks in the United States, many public health experts were concerned that state health laws were antiquated and inadequate for potential modern public health emergencies, including pandemics and bioterrorism. In late 2001, legal experts at the Center for Law and the Public's Health at Georgetown and Johns Hopkins universities drafted the Model State Emergency Health Powers Act (MSEHPA). The Center for Law and the Public's Health, The Model State Emergency Health Powers Act (2001), available at http://www.publichealthlaw.net/ModelLaws/MSEHPA.php (June 22, 2009).

MSEHPA addresses planning for public health emergencies; surveillance, and reporting measures (to detect and track public health emergencies); management of public and private property (including establishing decontamination facilities, acquiring medical supplies, and using private property for quarantine); power over persons (including power to vaccinate, test, treat, isolate, and quarantine individuals); liability of government and private medical workers during public health emergencies; and public communication. Under MSEHPA, during a "public health emergency" declared by the state governor, public health authorities can issue mandatory isolation orders (for infected individuals) and mandatory quarantine orders (for exposed individuals), violation of which constitutes a misdemeanor. *Id.* §604(a). Although individuals may refuse vaccination, testing, or treatment, those who do are subject to involuntary isolation or quarantine. *See id.* §§601-604. MSEHPA does provide some due process protections before quarantine or isolation (including a court order), although most pre-quarantine/pre-isolation procedures may be suspended where immediate action is needed to protect the public health. *See id.* §605. Other controversial provisions allow public health authorities to condition a health worker's continuing license to practice medicine on rendering of requested aid during the public health emergency, *see id.* §608, and limit state (and most private) liability to "gross negligence or willful misconduct," *see id.* §804. As of July 2006, thirty-eight states had adopted at least some provisions from (or based on) the MSEHPA. *See* MSEHPA State Legislative Surveillance Table (summarizing state activity) and MSEHPA State Legislative Activity Table (detailing state bills based on the Act), both available at http://www.publichealthlaw.net/ModelLaws/MSEHPA.php (June 22, 2009).

In 2003, representatives from five states and numerous public health experts, organizations, and agencies, collaborated to produce the more comprehensive Turning Point Model State Public Health Act (MSPHA), which includes some provisions from the MSEHPA. The MSPHA provides for compulsory testing, treatment, and vaccination under certain circumstances, *see* MSPHA §§5-106 to 5-107, 5-109, and, like the MSEHPA, provides for temporary quarantine and isolation before a court hearing is held, if delay would jeopardize the public health, *see id.* §5-108[d]. It also sets standards for quarantine and isolation (including using the least restrictive means necessary to prevent spread of disease and requiring competent medical care for those detained). The full text of the MSPHA is available at http://www.hss.state.ak.us/dph/improving/turningpoint/MSPHA.htm (June 22, 2009). As of August 2007, thirty-three states had passed bills incorporating at least some provisions of the Turning Point MSPHA. *See* The Turning Point Model State Public Health Act: State Legislative Matrix Table (showing provisions adopted by each state), available at http://www.publichealthlaw.net/Resources/ResourcesPDFs/MSPHA%20Matrix%20Table.pdf (June 22, 2009). Overall, James Hodge, executive director of the Center for Law and the Public's Health, reports that more than half of the states have adopted some version of one of the two model laws. *See* Debra Cassens Weiss, *Will Swine Flu Merit Quarantines? If So, New Laws Give States Authority*, ABAJournal, Apr. 27, 2009, available at http://www.abajournal.com/news/will_swine_flu_merit_quarantines_if_so_new_laws_give_states_authority/ (June 22, 2009). For a detailed cataloguing of state isolation and quarantine laws, see http://www.ncsl.org/?TabId=17104 (June 19, 2009).

6. How does due process constrain a state's ability to force treatment or isolate or quarantine individuals during a pandemic or other public health

emergency? *See* George J. Annas, *Blinded by Bioterrorism: Public Health and Liberty in the 21st Century*, 13 HEALTH MATRIX 33, 58 (2003) (criticizing MSEHPA for allowing a person to be quarantined on the basis of a "written directive by a public health official" for fifteen days before a hearing is required and allowing group rather than individual quarantine hearings); *cf.* Jacobson v. Massachusetts, 197 U.S. 11, 12, 27 (1905) (upholding a Massachusetts statute that permitted local boards of health to require compulsory vaccination—on pain of a $5 fine—when they deemed it "necessary for the public health or safety"). Are compulsory measures likely to be effective or can quarantine succeed only if most people willingly comply?

7. State laws adopting public health authority triggered by the governor's declaration of a "public health emergency" often overlap with more general state emergency management laws, most of which are triggered by a governor's declaration of a "disaster" or a "general emergency," in accordance with statutory definitions and procedures. Every state currently has a law authorizing the declaration of a "general emergency," a "disaster," or both. *See* James G. Hodge, Jr. & Evan D. Anderson, *Principles and Practice of Legal Triage during Public Health Emergencies*, 64 N.Y.U. ANN. SURV. AM. L. 249, 264 (2008). The declaration typically triggers extraordinary powers vested in the state's governor. Consider the Texas version of a state emergency management law.

TEXAS DISASTER ACT OF 1975

codified at Texas Gov Code Section 418

Sec. 418.004. DEFINITIONS. In this chapter:

(1) "Disaster" means the occurrence or imminent threat of widespread or severe damage, injury, or loss of life or property resulting from any natural or man-made cause, including fire, flood, earthquake, wind, storm, wave action, oil spill or other water contamination, volcanic activity, epidemic, air contamination, blight, drought, infestation, explosion, riot, hostile military or paramilitary action, other public calamity requiring emergency action, or energy emergency.

. . .

Subchapter B. Powers and Duties of Governor

Sec. 418.011. RESPONSIBILITY OF GOVERNOR. The governor is responsible for meeting:

(1) the dangers to the state and people presented by disasters; and

(2) disruptions to the state and people caused by energy emergencies.

Sec. 418.012. EXECUTIVE ORDERS. Under this chapter, the governor may issue executive orders, proclamations, and regulations and amend or rescind them. Executive orders, proclamations, and regulations have the force and effect of law.

Sec. 418.013. EMERGENCY MANAGEMENT COUNCIL. (a) The governor by executive order may establish an emergency management council to advise and assist the governor in all matters relating to disaster mitigation, preparedness, response, and recovery. . . .

Sec. 418.014. DECLARATION OF STATE OF DISASTER. (a) The governor by executive order or proclamation may declare a state of disaster if the governor finds a disaster has occurred or that the occurrence or threat of disaster is imminent.

(b) Except as provided by Subsection (c), the state of disaster continues until the governor:

(1) finds that:

(A) the threat or danger has passed; or

(B) the disaster has been dealt with to the extent that emergency conditions no longer exist; and

(2) terminates the state of disaster by executive order.

(c) A state of disaster may not continue for more than 30 days unless renewed by the governor. The legislature by law may terminate a state of disaster at any time. On termination by the legislature, the governor shall issue an executive order ending the state of disaster.

(d) An executive order or proclamation issued under this section must include:

(1) a description of the nature of the disaster;

(2) a designation of the area threatened; and

(3) a description of the conditions that have brought the state of disaster about or made possible the termination of the state of disaster.

(e) An executive order or proclamation shall be disseminated promptly by means intended to bring its contents to the attention of the general public. An order or proclamation shall be filed promptly with the division of emergency management, the secretary of state, and the county clerk or city secretary in each area to which it applies unless the circumstances attendant on the disaster prevent or impede the filing.

Sec. 418.015. EFFECT OF DISASTER DECLARATION. (a) An executive order or proclamation declaring a state of disaster:

(1) activates the disaster recovery and rehabilitation aspects of the state emergency management plan applicable to the area subject to the declaration; and

(2) authorizes the deployment and use of any forces to which the plan applies and the use or distribution of any supplies, equipment, and materials or facilities assembled, stockpiled, or arranged to be made available under this chapter or other law relating to disasters.

(b) The preparedness and response aspects of the state emergency management plan are activated as provided by that plan.

(c) During a state of disaster and the following recovery period, the governor is the commander in chief of state agencies, boards, and commissions having emergency responsibilities. To the greatest extent possible, the governor shall delegate or assign command authority by prior arrangement embodied in appropriate executive orders or plans, but this chapter does not restrict the governor's authority to do so by orders issued at the time of the disaster.

Sec. 418.016. SUSPENSION OF PROCEDURAL LAWS AND RULES. The governor may suspend the provisions of any regulatory statute prescribing the procedures for conduct of state business or the orders or rules of a state agency if strict compliance with the provisions, orders, or rules would in any way prevent, hinder, or delay necessary action in coping with a disaster.

Sec. 418.017. USE OF PUBLIC AND PRIVATE RESOURCES. (a) The governor may use all available resources of state government and of political subdivisions that are reasonably necessary to cope with a disaster.

(b) The governor may temporarily reassign resources, personnel, or functions of state executive departments and agencies or their units for the purpose of performing or facilitating emergency services.

(c) The governor may commandeer or use any private property if the governor finds it necessary to cope with a disaster, subject to the compensation requirements of this chapter.

Sec. 418.018. MOVEMENT OF PEOPLE. (a) The governor may recommend the evacuation of all or part of the population from a stricken or threatened area in the state if the governor considers the action necessary for the preservation of life or other disaster mitigation, response, or recovery.

(b) The governor may prescribe routes, modes of transportation, and destinations in connection with an evacuation.

(c) The governor may control ingress and egress to and from a disaster area and the movement of persons and the occupancy of premises in the area.

Sec. 418.019. RESTRICTED SALE AND TRANSPORTATION OF MATERIALS. The governor may suspend or limit the sale, dispensing, or transportation of alcoholic beverages, firearms, explosives, and combustibles.

Sec. 418.020. TEMPORARY HOUSING. (a) The governor may enter into purchase, lease, or other arrangements with an agency of the United States for temporary housing units to be occupied by disaster victims and may make units available to any political subdivision. . . .

(c) Under regulations prescribed by the governor, the governor may temporarily suspend or modify for a period of not more than 60 days any public health, safety, zoning, intrastate transportation, or other law or regulation if by proclamation the governor considers the suspension or modification essential to provide temporary housing for disaster victims. . . .

Sec. 418.021. FEDERAL AID FOR LOCAL GOVERNMENT. (a) On the governor's determination that a local government of the state has suffered or will suffer a substantial loss of tax and other revenue from a major disaster and has demonstrated a need for financial assistance to perform its governmental functions, the governor may apply to the federal government on behalf of the local government for a loan and may receive and disburse the proceeds of an approved loan to the local government. . . .

Sec. 418.022. AID FOR INDIVIDUALS. (a) On the governor's determination that financial assistance is essential to meet disaster-related necessary expenses or serious needs of individuals or families adversely affected by a major disaster that cannot be otherwise adequately met from other means of assistance, the governor may accept a grant by the federal government to fund the financial assistance, subject to the terms and conditions imposed on the grant. The governor may agree with the federal government or any officer or agency of the United States pledging the state to participate in funding not more than 25 percent of the financial assistance.

(b) The governor may make financial grants to meet disaster-related necessary expenses or serious needs of individuals or families adversely affected by a major disaster that cannot otherwise adequately be met from other means of assistance. The grants may not exceed an aggregate amount in excess of that established by federal statute for an individual or family in any single major disaster declared by the president of the United States.

(c) The governor may designate in the state emergency management plan the Department of Human Services or another state agency to carry out the functions of providing financial aid to individuals or families qualified for disaster relief. The designated agency may employ temporary personnel for those functions to be paid from funds appropriated to the agency, from federal funds, or from the disaster contingency fund. The merit system does not apply to the temporary positions. The governor may allocate funds appropriated under this chapter to implement the purposes of this chapter.

Sec. 418.023. CLEARANCE OF DEBRIS. (a) Through the use of any state agency or instrumentality, the governor, acting through members of the Emergency Management Council, may clear or remove debris or wreckage from public or private land or water if it threatens public health or safety or public or private property in a state of disaster declared by the governor or major disaster declared by the president of the United States.

(b) The governor may accept funds from the federal government and use the funds to make grants to a local government for the purpose of removing debris or wreckage from public or private land or water.

(c) Debris or wreckage may not be removed from public or private property until the affected local government, corporation, organization, or individual presents to the governor or member of the Emergency Management Council an unconditional authorization for removal. Debris or wreckage may not be removed from private property until the state is indemnified against any claim arising from removal. In instances where it is not practical and further delay would create a greater risk to public health or safety, the governor, acting through the Emergency Management Council, may remove debris or wreckage from public or private property without an unconditional authorization or indemnification.

(d) If the governor provides for clearance of debris or wreckage under this chapter, state employees or other individuals acting by authority of the governor may enter on private land or water to perform tasks necessary to the removal or clearance operation. Except in cases of willful misconduct, gross negligence, or bad faith, a state employee or agent performing his duties while complying with orders of the governor issued under this chapter is not liable for the death of or injury to a person or for damage to property. . . .

NOTES AND QUESTIONS

1. Why do you think the Texas act chooses not to adopt the Stafford Act's definition of "major disaster"? Does having a different state trigger for emergency powers create confusion?
2. Does this statute give the Texas governor sufficient powers to respond to disasters? Given that the governor is charged with protecting Texas citizens from disaster-related danger, should he have the power to mandate evacuation, rather than simply recommend evacuation?
3. How should the governor determine whether (and how) to exercise his authority to recommend evacuation and to restrict access to the affected area?
4. Are there adequate legislative checks on the governor's exercise of disaster-triggered powers? What role, if any, should the state legislature play in the immediate aftermath of a major disaster?

2. REGIONAL EMERGENCY RESPONSE

The structure of federal disaster relief suggests that, for most non-catastrophic events, affected communities should rely initially on state and local resources. It follows that some emergencies, even those affecting more than one state, may not warrant full federal involvement. In the antiterrorism context, the Justice Department has fostered multijurisdictional partnerships for meeting regional threats. *See generally* DEPARTMENT OF JUSTICE, BUREAU OF JUSTICE ASSISTANCE, MUTUAL AID: MULTIJURISDICTIONAL PARTNERSHIPS FOR MEETING REGIONAL THREATS (September 2005). Even in circumstances meriting aggressive federal intervention, interstate cooperation can supplement federal aid. The Emergency Management Assistance Compact (EMAC), an interstate compact ratified by Congress in 1996, provides the framework for mutual cooperation:

EMERGENCY MANAGEMENT ASSISTANCE COMPACT

Pub. L. No. 104-321, 110 Stat. 3877 (1996)

Article I Purpose and Authorities

This compact is made and entered into by and between the participating member states which enact this compact, hereinafter called party states. For the purposes of this compact, the term "states" is taken to mean the several states, the Commonwealth of Puerto Rico, the District of Columbia, and all U.S. territorial possessions.

The purpose of this compact is to provide for mutual assistance between the states entering into this compact in managing any emergency disaster that is duly declared by the Governor of the affected state, whether arising from natural disaster, technological hazard, man-made disaster, civil emergency aspects of resources shortages, community disorders, insurgency, or enemy attack.

This compact shall also provide for mutual cooperation in emergency-related exercises, testing, or other training activities using equipment and personnel simulating performance of any aspect of the giving and receiving of aid by party states or subdivisions of party states during emergencies, such actions occurring outside actual declared emergency periods. Mutual assistance in this compact may include the use of the states' National Guard forces, either in accordance with the National Guard Mutual Assistance Compact or by mutual agreement between states.

Article II General Implementation

Each party state entering into this compact recognizes that many emergencies transcend political jurisdictional boundaries and that intergovernmental coordination is essential in managing these and other emergencies under this compact. Each state further recognizes that there will be emergencies which require immediate access and present procedures to apply outside resources to make a prompt and effective response to such an emergency. This is because few, if any, individual states have all the resources they may need in all types of emergencies or the capability of delivering resources to areas where emergencies exist.

The prompt, full, and effective utilization of resources of the participating states, including any resources on hand or available from the federal government or any other source, that are essential to the safety, care, and welfare of the people in the event of any emergency or disaster declared by a party state, shall be the underlying principle on which all articles of this compact shall be understood.

On behalf of the Governor of each state participating in the compact, the legally designated state official who is assigned responsibility for emergency management will be responsible for formulation of the appropriate interstate mutual aid plans and procedures necessary to implement this compact.

Article III Party State Responsibilities

A. It shall be the responsibility of each party state to formulate procedural plans and programs for interstate cooperation in the performance of the responsibilities listed in this article. In formulating such plans, and in carrying them out, the party states, insofar as practical, shall:

1. Review individual state hazards analyses and, to the extent reasonably possible, determine all those potential emergencies the party states might jointly suffer, whether due to natural disaster, technological hazard, man-made disaster, emergency aspects of resources shortages, civil disorders, insurgency, or enemy attack;
2. Review party states' individual emergency plans and develop a plan which will determine the mechanism for the interstate management and provision of assistance concerning any potential emergency;
3. Develop interstate procedures to fill any identified gaps and to resolve any identified inconsistencies or overlaps in existing or developed plans;
4. Assist in warning communities adjacent to or crossing the state boundaries;

5. Protect and assure uninterrupted delivery of services, medicines, water, food, energy and fuel, search and rescue, and critical lifeline equipment, services, and resources, both human and material;
6. Inventory and set procedures for the interstate loan and delivery of human and material resources, together with procedures for reimbursement or forgiveness; and
7. Provide, to the extent authorized by law, for temporary suspension of any statutes or ordinances that restrict the implementation of the above responsibilities.

B. The authorized representative of a party state may request assistance to another party state by contacting the authorized representative of that state. The provisions of this compact shall only apply to requests for assistance made by and to authorized representatives. Requests may be verbal or in writing. If verbal, the request shall be confirmed in writing within thirty days of the verbal request. Requests shall provide the following information:

1. A description of the emergency service function for which assistance is needed, including, but not limited to, fire services, law enforcement, emergency medical, transportation, communications, public works and engineering, building, inspection, planning and information assistance, mass care, resource support, health and medical services, and search and rescue;
2. The amount and type of personnel, equipment, materials and supplies needed, and a reasonable estimate of the length of time they will be needed; and
3. The specific place and time for staging of the assisting party's response and a point of contact at that location.

C. There shall be frequent consultation between state officials who have assigned emergency management responsibilities and other appropriate representatives of the party states with affected jurisdictions and the United States Government, with free exchange of information, plans, and resource records relating to emergency capabilities.

Article IV Limitations

Any party state requested to render mutual aid or conduct exercises and training for mutual aid shall take such action as is necessary to provide and make available the resources covered by this compact in accordance with the terms hereof; provided that it is understood that the state rendering aid may withhold resources to the extent necessary to provide reasonable protection for such state.

Each party state shall afford to the emergency forces of any party state, while operating within its state limits under the terms and conditions of this compact, the same powers, except that of arrest unless specifically authorized by the receiving state, duties, rights, and privileges as are afforded forces of the state in which they are performing emergency services. Emergency forces will continue under the command and control of their regular leaders, but the organizational units will come under the operational control of the emergency services authorities of the state receiving assistance. These conditions may be activated, as needed, only subsequent to a declaration of a state emergency or disaster by the governor of the party state that is to receive assistance or upon commencement of exercises or training for mutual aid and shall continue so long as the exercises or training for mutual aid are in progress, the state of emergency or disaster remains in effect, or loaned resources remain in the receiving state, whichever is longer.

Article V Licenses and Permits

Whenever any person holds a license, certificate, or other permit issued by any state party to the compact evidencing the meeting of qualifications for professional, mechanical, or other skills, and when such assistance is requested by the receiving party state, such person shall be deemed licensed, certified, or permitted by the state requesting assistance to render aid involving such skill to meet a declared emergency or disaster, subject to such limitations and conditions as the Governor of the requesting state may prescribe by executive order or otherwise.

Article VI Liability

Officers or employees of a party state rendering aid in another state pursuant to this compact shall be considered agents of the requesting state for tort liability and immunity purposes. No party state or its officers or employees rendering aid in another state pursuant to this compact shall be liable on account of any act or omission in good faith on the part of such forces while so engaged or on account of the maintenance or use of any equipment or supplies in connection therewith. Good faith in this article shall not include willful misconduct, gross negligence, or recklessness.

Article VII Supplementary Agreements

Inasmuch as it is probable that the pattern and detail of the machinery for mutual aid among two or more states may differ from that among the states that are party hereto, this compact contains elements of a broad base common to all states, and nothing herein shall preclude any state entering into supplementary agreements with another state or affect any other agreements already in force between states. Supplementary agreements may comprehend, but shall not be limited to, provisions for evacuation and reception of injured and other persons and the exchange of medical, fire, police, public utility, reconnaissance, welfare, transportation and communications personnel, and equipment and supplies.

Article VIII Compensation

Each party state shall provide for the payment of compensation and death benefits to injured members of the emergency forces of that state and representatives of deceased members of such forces in case such members sustain injuries or are killed while rendering aid pursuant to this compact, in the same manner and on the same terms as if the injury or death were sustained within their own state.

Article IX Reimbursement

Any party state rendering aid in another state pursuant to this compact shall be reimbursed by the party state receiving such aid for any loss or damage to or expense incurred in the operation of any equipment and the provision of any service in answering a request for aid and for the costs incurred in connection with such requests; provided, that any aiding party state may assume in whole or in part such loss, damage, expense, or other cost, or may loan such equipment or donate such services to the receiving party state without charge or cost; and provided further, that any two or more party states may enter into supplementary agreements establishing a different allocation of costs among those states. Article VIII expenses shall not be reimbursable under this article.

Article X Evacuation

Plans for the orderly evacuation and interstate reception [*sic*] of portions of the civilian population as the result of any emergency or disaster of sufficient proportions to so warrant, shall be worked out and maintained between the party states and the emergency management/services directors of the various jurisdictions where any type of incident requiring evacuations might occur. Such plans shall be put into effect by request of the state from which evacuees come and shall include the manner of transporting such evacuees, the number of evacuees to be received in different areas, the manner in which food, clothing, housing, and medical care will be provided, the registration of the evacuees, the providing of facilities for the notification of relatives or friends, and the forwarding of such evacuees to other areas or the bringing in of additional materials, supplies, and all other relevant factors. Such plans shall provide that the party state receiving evacuees and the party state from which the evacuees come shall mutually agree as to reimbursement of out-of-pocket expenses incurred in receiving and caring for such evacuees, for expenditures for transportation, food, clothing, medicines, and medical care, and like items. Such expenditures shall be reimbursed as agreed by the party state from which the evacuees come. After the termination of the emergency or disaster, the party state from which the evacuees come shall assume the responsibility for the ultimate support of repatriation of such evacuees.

Article XI Implementation

A. This compact shall become effective immediately upon its enactment into law by any two states. Thereafter, this compact shall become effective as to any other state upon enactment by such state.

B. Any party state may withdraw from this compact by enacting a statute repealing the same, but no such withdrawal shall take effect until thirty days after the Governor of the withdrawing state has given notice in writing of such withdrawal to the Governors of all other party states. Such action shall not relieve the withdrawing state from obligations assumed hereunder prior to the effective date of withdrawal.

C. Duly authenticated copies of this compact and of such supplementary agreements as may be entered into shall, at the time of their approval, be deposited with each of the party states and with the Federal Emergency Management Agency and other appropriate agencies of the United States Government.

Article XII Validity

This compact shall be construed to effectuate the purposes stated in Article I. If any provision of this compact is declared unconstitutional, or the applicability thereof to any person or circumstances is held invalid, the constitutionality of the remainder of this compact and the applicability thereof to other persons and circumstances shall not be affected.

Article XIII Additional Provisions

Nothing in this compact shall authorize or permit the use of military force by the National Guard of a state at any place outside that state in any emergency for which the President is authorized by law to call into federal service the militia, or for any purpose for which the use of the Army or the Air Force would in the absence of express statutory authorization be prohibited under §1385 of Title 18 of the United States Code.

NOTES AND QUESTIONS

1. Mutual aid as a tool for emergency management traces its origins to global instability in 1949, when President Truman responded to the Soviet Union's explosion of its first nuclear device and North Korea's invasion of South Korea by establishing the Federal Civil Defense Administration. In 1950 Congress passed the Federal Civil Defense Act, the Defense Production Act, and the Disaster Relief Act. (Only the Disaster Relief Act addressed both natural and military disasters.) In connection with these statutes, Congress also ratified the Civil Defense Compact of 1950.

   Nearly half a century later, EMAC became the first interstate compact since the Civil Defense Compact to facilitate interstate cooperation as a way to supplement federal emergency response. After Hurricane Andrew struck Florida in 1992, the Southern Governors' Association formed the Southern Regional Emergency Management Assistance Compact (SREMAC) in 1993. In 1995 the SREMAC opened membership to any state or territory that wished to join; one year thereafter, Congress ratified the broadened agreement as EMAC.

2. All fifty states, the District of Columbia, Guam, Puerto Rico, and the U.S. Virgin Islands have passed the requisite legislation to become members of EMAC. The National Emergency Management Association has also drafted Model Intrastate Mutual Aid Legislation, based on the interstate compact, to facilitate mutual aid agreements between political subdivisions of a state. *See* http://www.emacweb.org/?150 (June 20, 2009).

3. Whether implemented on a regional or an intrastate basis, EMAC actively pursues a decentralized approach to emergency response. Does decentralization of response authority to states or to counties and municipalities supply a viable alternative to prevailing systems such as the Stafford Act

and the NRF? Consider the performance of EMAC in the aftermath of Katrina:

U.S. House of Representatives, A Failure of Initiative

Final Report of the Select Bipartisan Committee to Investigate
the Preparation for and Response to Hurricane Katrina 144-145 (2006)

Finding: Once activated, the Emergency Management Assistance Compact (EMAC) enabled an unprecedented level of mutual aid assistance to reach the disaster area in a timely and effective manner

EMAC provided invaluable interstate mutual aid in support of Hurricane Katrina by deploying more than 67,891 personnel (19,481 civilians and 48,477 National Guard) to Louisiana and Mississippi. EMAC facilitated mutual assistance from 48 states, the District of Columbia, the Virgin Islands and Puerto Rico.

In support of Hurricane Katrina, more than 2,188 resource requests (missions) were filled. Record numbers of National Guard troops, local responders, and health/medical personnel were deployed through the compact. EMAC also works in cooperation with the federal government by co-locating personnel, when requested, in the NRCC or Regional Response Coordination Center (RRCC) in order to share information on EMAC activities in the affected states, monitor the availability of needed resources being offered by assisting states, and facilitate overall emergency response and recovery activities.

Through state statute, EMAC addresses the legal issues of liability, workers compensation, reimbursement, and professional licensure — prior to a disaster or emergency when resource needs and timing are critical. State and territory members must pre-designate personnel with the authority to request and commit resources. Standard operating procedures exist for compact members and training and exercise of state personnel is required. While formalized protocols are in place, EMAC is designed to be adaptable and scaleable to meet the changing needs of each event.

Following each large scale activation of the compact, a review and evaluation of the response is conducted and standard operating procedures revised and updated to reflect lessons learned and best practices. For example, lessons learned from the 2004 Florida hurricanes led to an overhaul of some operational procedures related to mobilization and deployment of resources, an enhanced automation system to provide more accurate data and electronic tracking of resources, and a new standardized EMAC training curriculum and updated operations manual. These enhancements were either in progress or completed prior to Hurricane Katrina.

In Mississippi, EMAC assistance was considered a success. The assistance in Mississippi included help from other states' security agencies (such as their state police) as well as various states' National Guards (troops and hard assets). . . . Louisiana state officials also viewed EMAC assistance as very successful. One state official said there were almost 900 EMAC agreements for assistance. Although the EMAC response from surrounding states varied, state officials applauded EMAC for successfully getting law enforcement manpower assistance. According to state police officers Ralph Mitchell and Joseph Booth, Arkansas, Tennessee, New Jersey, and California all sent law enforcement officers through EMAC.

FEMA officials also noted the general success of EMAC. Because of the magnitude of the disaster, however, Louisiana was unable to handle all of the EMAC requests, requiring FEMA to become more involved in the process than normal. In particular, FCO Scott Wells noted some state offers of assistance through FEMA were rejected by Louisiana. He said these offers were rejected by SCO Smith because of concerns about the costs to the state.

NOTES AND QUESTIONS

1. Why did EMAC succeed where so many other response systems failed either partially or catastrophically? What distinguished EMAC, an interstate compact, from counterparts that covered either a smaller geographic footprint (local and state plans) or the entire United States (HSPD-5 and its components, especially the NIMS and the NRP)?
2. By the same token, EMAC did not perform flawlessly. Louisiana affirmatively rejected some offers of assistance from other states, evidently concerned that Louisiana would bear the eventual costs. Articles VIII and IX of EMAC, respectively, address "compensation" and "reimbursement." What is the distinction between these categories? Did EMAC offer Louisiana some alternative to refusing aid on grounds of cost? Article IX stipulates "that any aiding party state may assume in whole or in part such loss, damage, expense, or other cost, or may loan such equipment or donate such services to the receiving party state without charge or cost." It also provides "that any two or more party states may enter into supplementary agreements establishing a different allocation of costs among those states." "Compensation" under article VIII, however, may not be "reimbursable" under article IX.
3. Multijurisdictional emergency response systems, whether implemented through federal law (such as HSPD-5) or through an interstate compact (such as EMAC) may be viewed as a form of insurance among participating governments. Increasing the geographic footprint of an emergency response system has the effect of deepening an insurance pool: it allows participants to spread risks across a deeper and therefore more stable source of financial resources. The simultaneous presence of HSPD-5 and EMAC can be analogized to the presence of multiple layers of insurance against risk that defies any single state's ability to manage.
4. Of course, the insurance analogy suggests a fundamental weakness of these arrangements within a country with persistent differences along two dimensions. First, states have predictably different risk profiles. For instance, states with seashores are more vulnerable to hurricanes and typhoons, whereas states near geologically active faults, such as the San Andreas and New Madrid faults, are more prone to earthquakes. Second, states also have different levels of income and wealth. Environmental and economic differences impair the management of HSPD-5, EMAC, and other

multijurisdictional emergency response systems. These schemes strongly resemble a health insurance system in which some beneficiaries are predictably poorer and sicker than others.

5. Reconsider article VII of EMAC:

> Inasmuch as it is probable that the pattern and detail of the machinery for mutual aid among two or more states may differ from that among the states that are party hereto, this compact contains elements of a broad base common to all states, and nothing herein shall preclude any state entering into supplementary agreements with another state or affect any other agreements already in force between states.

Is this provision an adequate tool for overcoming persistent differences in the economic and risk profiles among states?

C. PRIVATE AND NONGOVERNMENTAL RESPONSE

1. PRIVATE ENTITIES

When the Mississippi River valley was inundated by massive flooding in 1927, the federal government response relied heavily on private-sector resources. Secretary of Commerce Herbert Hoover served as disaster czar, but the federal government supplied little else by way of muscle or materiel. As discussed in Chapter 2, nongovernmental actors remain crucial today, especially in restoring critical infrastructure and services after a disaster. See Lee M. Zeichner, *Private Sector Integration, in* AMERICAN BAR ASSOCIATION, HURRICANE KATRINA TASK FORCE SUBCOMMITTEE REPORT 33, 34-38 (Feb. 2006). Almost all communications and energy facilities in the United States are privately controlled. *See* Jim Chen, *The Nature of the Public Utility: Infrastructure, the Market, and the Law,* 98 Nw. U. L. REV. 1617, 1633-1640 (2004). Ensuring the continued supply of fuel and health care likewise demands more comprehensive interaction with the private sector. *Cf.* HOMELAND SECURITY COUNCIL, NATIONAL STRATEGY FOR PANDEMIC INFLUENZA (2005); U.S. DEPARTMENT OF HEALTH & HUMAN SERVICES, HHS PANDEMIC INFLUENZA PLAN (2005). The Department of Homeland Security's blueprint for protecting "critical infrastructure and key resources (CI/KR)," DEPARTMENT OF HOMELAND SECURITY, INTERIM NATIONAL INFRASTRUCTURE PROTECTION PLAN 1 (2005), acknowledges the importance of the private entities that "own[] and operate[] the vast majority of the Nation's CI/KR," *id.* at 4. DHS contemplates "CI/KR Sector Coordinating Councils" that would engage private owners and operators of infrastructure with their public-sector counterparts in emergency planning and response. *See id.* at 5, 33-34.

Nonetheless, although the United States is dependent on privately owned infrastructure, the Stafford Act does not explicitly authorize private-sector involvement in emergency response. Thus, although the current statutory framework may not preclude federal assistance to private, for-profit companies engaged in disaster relief efforts, it does not specifically authorize such support.

Indeed, legal confusion impaired efforts by private entities to restore communications and other critical services in areas crippled by Katrina:

> Many companies turned to the Federal Government for support because the civil unrest, coupled with the unprecedented level of damage from the storm and subsequent flooding, hindered their access to the disaster site and to necessary resources, thus impairing their ability to repair the damaged critical infrastructure on their own. When requesting support from the Federal Government, many companies were unable to receive assistance because Federal agencies indicated that they did not have the authority to provide them support under the Stafford Act, and the NRP did not guide an interpretation that would enable that support. . . .
>
> Congress stated that its intent in creating the [Stafford] Act was "to provide an orderly and continuing means of assistance by the Federal Government to State and local Governments in carrying out their responsibilities to alleviate the suffering and damage which result from such disasters by," among other things, "achieving greater coordination and responsiveness of disaster preparedness and relief programs." [42 U.S.C. §5121.] The Act acknowledges the need for robust coordination; however, it does not clearly address coordination with the private sector. The Stafford Act provides assistance to "State or local Governments for the repair, restoration, reconstruction, or replacement of a public facility damaged or destroyed by a major disaster and for associated expenses incurred by the Government." [*Id.* §5172(a)(1)(A).]
>
> Although the language of the statute does not specifically preclude the private sector from receiving resources under the Act, it does not clearly grant the Federal Government authority to provide assistance to private entities, apart from nonprofit organizations. It states that the president can provide resources to "a person that owns or operates a private non-profit facility damaged or destroyed by a major disaster for the repair, restoration, reconstruction, or replacement of the facility and for associated expenses incurred by the person." [*Id.* §5172(a)(1)(B).] In addition, the law states that the president can "coordinate all disaster relief assistance (including voluntary assistance) provided by Federal agencies, private organizations, and State and local Governments." [*Id.* §5170(a)(2).] Section 5170(b)(3) of the Act also allows Federal departments and agencies to "provide assistance essential to meeting immediate threats to life and property resulting from a major disaster."
>
> This permission to "render assistance" to prevent loss of life or other serious harm stems from a long-standing tradition embodied in policy, regulation, statute, and international obligation. Indeed, the focus of this discussion is properly on the existence of present authority to assure participation by necessary private sector infrastructure stewards in actions directed at such life saving activity, rather than eligibility of private sector entities for reimbursement. . . .
>
> Absent from the Stafford Act is any direct reference to Federal assistance to "for-profit" entities, and it does not recognize that [telecommunications infrastructure providers], which own about 80 percent of the Nation's critical infrastructure, play a critical recovery role in disasters to address the threats to public health and safety, life, and property.

The president's National Security Telecommunications Advisory Committee, Legislative and Regulatory Task Force, *Federal Support to Telecommunications Infrastructure Providers in National Emergencies: Designation as "Emergency Responders (Private Sector)"* 7-9 (Jan. 31, 2006). Should the Stafford Act be amended to authorize emergency response actions by private-sector, for-profit entities and to authorize federal aid to private responders? If so, what measures can best facilitate voluntary relief efforts by the private parties who supply vital infrastructure and services? (The NRF does acknowledge that the private sector and NGOs play an "essential role" in disaster response, NRF at 6-7, and NIMS defines "emergency responder" to include "Federal, State, territorial, tribal, substate regional, and local governments, NGOs, private sector-organizations, critical infrastructure owners and operators, and all other organizations and individuals who assume an emergency management role," NIMS at 139.)

The Task Force report quoted above advocates the creation of a new legal category, "emergency responders (private sector)," that would enable private owners of infrastructure to secure governmental protection and other "non-monetary" assistance as their employees work to restore service. Thus far, this recommendation has not been implemented. The only post-Katrina amendment to the Stafford Act to address the role of private disaster responders was contained in the Safe Ports Act, enacted October 13, 2006. *See* Pub. L. No. 109-347, §607, 120 Stat. 1941. The new provision adds to the Stafford Act a requirement that, absent exceptional circumstances, federal agencies shall not "deny or impede access to the disaster site to an essential service provider whose access is necessary to restore and repair an essential service" or otherwise "impede the restoration or repair" of essential services. *See* 42 U.S.C. §5189e(b). The definition of "essential service provider" specifically includes "a private, for profit entity," contributing to disaster response efforts, that provides telecommunications service, electrical power, natural gas, water and sewer services, or any other essential service, as determined by the president. *See id.* §5189(a). Thus, though the Stafford Act now prohibits federal agencies from actively denying or impeding private utility companies' access to the disaster area, it does not specifically authorize federal agencies to help private infrastructure companies gain access to the site, secure safe working conditions for employees, or give other nonmonetary aid to companies working to restore essential services.

Moreover, the current statutory scheme does not recognize the disaster response role that may be played by private companies that are not necessarily "essential service providers." Much of the critical assistance supplied to devastated areas in the aftermath of Hurricane Katrina was provided voluntarily by various private companies. For instance, Wal-Mart donated more than $18 million to emergency relief efforts, delivered 150 Internet-ready computers to shelters to help family members find one another, dispatched over 2,450 truckloads of supplies, filled prescriptions free of charge to evacuees with emergency medical needs, and donated more than twenty-five vacant facilities to impacted states for relief efforts. Wal-Mart, Fact Sheets, available at http://walmartstores.com/FactsNews/FactSheets, June 24, 2009. Home Depot dispatched more than 800 truckloads of supplies to impacted areas and also used buses to transport 1,000 employees into the region from other areas. Steven Horwitz, *Making Hurricane Response More Effective: Lessons from the Private Sector and the Coast Guard during Katrina* (March 2008), http://www.mercatus.org/uploadedFiles/Mercatus/Publications/PDF_20080319_MakingHurricaneReponseEffective.pdf. Budweiser delivered truckloads of water and ice, and Ford provided vehicles for search and rescue. Mary L.G.

Theroux, *Public and Private Responses to Katrina: What Can We Learn?* (October 2005), available at http://www.independent.org/newsroom/article.asp?id= 1589 (June 24, 2009).

Beyond the sheer magnitude of the private relief effort was the swiftness with which supplies reached the public. Professor Steven Horwitz observed that "Wal-Mart and Home Depot were able to get . . . assistance to the disaster areas almost immediately after the storm had passed, in comparison to the days — in some cases weeks — that residents waited for government agencies to provide relief." Horwitz, *supra.* Sheriff Harry Lee of Jefferson Parish (which borders New Orleans) opined that "if the American government would have responded like Wal-Mart has responded, we wouldn't be in this crisis." *Id.* One particularly interesting comparison of private versus public relief efforts comes from contrasting the disaster response of a private hospital, HCA, with that of a government-owned hospital, Charity, across the street. *See* Theroux, *supra.* In the immediate aftermath of Katrina, HCA executives determined that they would need to lease twenty helicopters to safely evacuate their patients. HCA acted quickly on these plans and was able to evacuate its critically ill patients without one mishap. Charity Hospital, on the other hand, was completely without emergency supplies and unable to get government help in evacuating. *See id.* Charity's patients were finally rescued by privately leased helicopters on HCA's tab. *See* Hospital Corporation of America, *HCA Completes Airlift Evacuation at Tulane University Hospital and Clinic; Assists Nearby Hospitals,* available at http://phx.corporate-ir.net/phoenix.zhtml?c=63489&p=irol-newsArticle&ID=752385&highlight= (June 24, 2009). Why were private actors arguably more adept at responding to Katrina than the government?

Many utility companies also were extremely effective at reestablishing services for their customers. Even though all 195,000 Mississippi Power customers were without power, nearly two-thirds of the company's transmission and distribution system was damaged or destroyed, and its second-largest electric generating plant was flooded, Southern Power was able to restore power in just twelve days, thanks in large part to the aid of many other utility companies throughout the country. *See* Transmission & Distribution, *Southern Company CEO Shares Details of Successful Hurricane Katrina Response with Senate Committee,* available at http://tdworld.com/hurricane-katrina-relief/Southern-Company-response (June 24, 2009). In Louisiana, Cleco Power was able to restore power to 80 percent of its customers in just three weeks. *See* Terry Wildman, *Cleco Faces the Beast,* available at http://tdworld.com/katrina_reflections_supp/Cleco-Katrina-reflection (June 24, 2009).

2. THE RED CROSS

Perhaps the most important nongovernmental organization involved in emergency response and disaster relief is the American Red Cross. When originally chartered by Congress in 1900, the American Red Cross was assigned the role of "carry[ing] on a system of national and international relief in time of peace . . . in mitigating the sufferings caused by pestilence, famine, fires, floods, and other great national calamities." See Kevin R. Kosar, *The Congressional Charter of the American National Red Cross: Overview, History, and Analysis* 19, Table 2 (CRS Report for Congress, Order Code RL33314, March 15, 2006) (quoting the 1900 charter). Six years later, in 1906, when an earthquake struck San Francisco and an ensuing fire engulfed the city, President Theodore Roosevelt announced that all federal aid would be channeled through the Red Cross. *See* NATIONAL ACADEMY OF PUBLIC ADMINISTRATION, COPING WITH CATASTROPHE: BUILDING AN EMERGENCY MANAGEMENT SYSTEM TO MEET PEOPLE'S NEEDS IN NATURAL AND MANMADE DISASTERS 10 (1993). The American Red Cross continues to play a unique and critical role in U.S. disaster response:

> The Red Cross is an independent, non-governmental organization . . . that operates as a nonprofit, tax-exempt, charitable institution pursuant to a charter granted by the United States Congress. [*See* 36 U.S.C. §300101.] It has the legal status of a "federal instrumentality" due to its charter requirements to carry out responsibilities delegated by the federal government.
>
> [The Red Cross has the responsibility] to perform all duties incumbent upon a national society in accordance with the spirit and conditions of the Geneva Conventions to which the United States is a signatory, to provide family communications and other forms of assistance to members of the U.S. military, and to maintain a system of domestic and international disaster relief, including mandated responsibilities under the Federal Response Plan coordinated by the Federal Emergency Management Agency.
>
> The Red Cross is not a federal agency, nor does it receive federal funding on a regular basis to carry out its services and programs. It receives financial support from voluntary public contributions and from cost recovery charges for some services. Its stated mission is to "provide relief to victims of disasters and help people prevent, prepare for, and respond to emergencies."
>
> To meet its mandated responsibilities under the NRP, the Red Cross functions as an ESF primary organization in coordinating the use of mass care resources in a presidentially declared disaster or emergency. As the lead agency for ESF #6, dealing with Mass Care, Housing and Human Services, the Red Cross assumes the role of providing food, shelter, emergency first aid, disaster welfare information and bulk distribution of emergency relief items.

HOUSE KATRINA REPORT, *supra*, at 42. In the current ESF #6, the Red Cross is a support agency, while DHS/FEMA is the lead. Relying on a nongovernmental entity to carry out critical components of federal disaster relief policy has both advantages and disadvantages. For example, as a well-respected charitable organization, the Red Cross has significant fund-raising capacity. On the other hand, federal and Red Cross policies may sometimes conflict. Implementation of new federal policy favoring accommodation of pets in shelters may founder on the Red Cross's reluctance (for liability and other reasons) to accept pets at its shelters, which are often the only shelters provided when disaster strikes.

3. CITIZENS AND CITIZEN GROUPS

In addition to the Red Cross and private-sector corporations, individual citizens can play an important role in disaster response. Indeed, sociological literature commonly recognizes that the true first responders in any disaster tend to be the survivors themselves, as they extricate themselves from danger and begin to aid their family members and neighbors. To capitalize on the post-9/11 national spirit of volunteerism and in recognition of the critical role that local citizens play in the aftermath of disasters, President Bush, in January 2001, established the Citizen Corps, which is coordinated by FEMA. According to the Citizen Corps Web site, its mission is to "harness the power of every individual through education, training, and volunteer service to make communities, safer, stronger, and better prepared to respond to threats of terrorism, crime, public health issues, and disasters of all kinds." Consider the following description of the role of the Citizen Corps in community disaster preparedness and response.

> The Citizen Corps mission is accomplished through a national network of state, local, and tribal Citizen Corps Councils. These Councils build on community strengths to implement the Citizen Corps programs and will carry out a local strategy to have every American participate.
>
> Everyone can do something to help make our families and our communities safer through:
>
> Personal responsibility: Developing a household preparedness plan and disaster supplies kits, observing home health and safety practices, implementing disaster mitigation measures, and participating in crime prevention and reporting.
>
> Training: Taking classes in emergency preparedness, response capabilities, first aid, CPR, fire suppression, and search and rescue procedures.
>
> Volunteer service: Engaging individuals in volunteer activities that support first responders, disaster relief groups, and community safety organizations. Everyone can do something to support local law enforcement, fire, emergency medical services, community public health efforts, and the four stages of emergency management: prevention, mitigation, response and recovery efforts.
>
> Local Citizen Corps Councils will:
> * promote and strengthen the Citizen Corps programs at the community level, such as Volunteers in Police Service programs, CERT teams, Medical Reserve Corps units, and Neighborhood Watch groups;
> * provide opportunities for special skills and interests;
> * develop targeted outreach for the community, including special needs groups;
> * provide opportunities of training in first aid and emergency preparedness;
> * organize special projects and community events;
> * encourage cooperation and collaboration among community leaders; and
> * capture smart practices and report accomplishments; and
> * create opportunities for all residents to participate.

See http://www.citizencorps.gov/councils.

Of particular interest to disaster response are local Community Emergency Response Teams (CERT) teams. The CERT concept was first developed by the Los Angeles City Fire Department in 1985, and has now been implemented in more than 1,100 communities. CERT teams are sponsored by state, county, or local emergency management agencies and provide classroom and simulation training to interested citizens (on a voluntary basis) in disaster preparedness, fire suppression, medical operations, light search and rescue, disaster psychology, and team building. FEMA supports CERT teams by providing training materials for local entities. *See* https://www.citizencorps.gov/cert/about.shtm (June 22, 2009).

In the aftermath of Katrina, a morbid joke that made the rounds of the emergency management community suggested that FEMA's new disaster policy was "YOYO (You're on your own.)." Regardless of any post-Katrina improvements made to government's capacity to respond to disasters, there remains some truth in this assessment. In the immediate aftermath of disasters, local citizens are well advised to have their own disaster plans and resources at the ready. Despite public information campaigns urging people to have an emergency supply of food and water, a portable seventy-two-hour survival kit, and a written plan in case of emergency, most citizens have not complied with these recommendations. In a recent study, only 53 percent reported having any sort of specifically designated emergency supplies. *See* FED. EMERGENCY MGMT. AGENCY, PERSONAL PREPAREDNESS IN AMERICA: FINDINGS FROM THE CITIZEN CORPS NATIONAL SURVEY 7 (2009), available at http://www.citizencorps. gov/pdf/Personal_Preparedness_In_America-Citizen_Corps_National_Survey.pdf [hereinafter *Findings*]. Of those who reported having emergency supplies, only 40 percent reported including a flashlight in their emergency kit and only 34 percent included a first aid kit. *See id.*

Indeed, even those who report that they are prepared for disasters admit to being less prepared when asked more specific questions. For example, one study found that only 55 percent of those reporting that they had an emergency kit reported that they had enough food, and only 36 percent reported having enough water. *See* FED. EMERGENCY MGMT. AGENCY, CITIZEN PREPAREDNESS REVIEW, UPDATE ON CITIZEN PREPAREDNESS RESEARCH 5 (2007), available at http://www.citizencorps.gov/pdf/citizen_prep_review_issue_5.pdf. In a separate study, among those who reported that they "have been prepared for at least the past six months," 40 percent did not have a household plan, 80 percent had not conducted a home evacuation drill, and nearly 60 percent did not know their community's evacuation routes. *Findings, supra*, at 15. Barriers to individual preparedness include the public's low perception of community risk and the fact that 57 percent of those surveyed "expected to rely on emergency responders in the first 72 hours following a disaster." *Id.* at 25, 59. One report suggests that education specifically targeting the public's underestimation of community risk and unrealistic expectations of outside assistance could help motivate greater individual preparedness. *See id.* at 54-55.

NOTES AND QUESTIONS

1. How can state and local governments integrate private resources more fully into disaster planning? If efforts focus on low- to mid-level private company employees (rather than high-level management), will such efforts be effective?
2. How much are CERT teams likely to contribute to disaster response? For a listing of some ways in which CERT teams have responded to disasters, see https://www.citizencorps.gov/cert/certinaction/index.shtm (June 22, 2009).

3. How can government (or other organizations) more effectively encourage personal disaster preparedness? Is it unrealistic to expect that more citizens could comply with the hallmarks of disaster preparedness: a written family disaster plan, a seventy-two-hour kit, and an emergency supply of food and water? How much food and water can individuals and families reasonably be urged to store? Consider that experts recommend at least a seventy-two-hour supply of water, which includes — at a minimum — one gallon per person per day.

D. REFORMING THE LAW OF EMERGENCY RESPONSE

The response to Katrina was so roundly denounced that proposals for reform arose almost immediately. The perceived failure of the law of emergency response prompted a long season of political introspection. Many of the proposed statutory reforms were adopted by the 2006 Post-Katrina Act and incorporated into the new National Response Framework. As the notes throughout this chapter reveal, however, many questions remain about the effectiveness of individual reforms, as well as other incremental changes that might be made. This chapter concludes by examining two reform proposals. The first reading presents, as a possible model for reform, the federal government's concentration of authority in a single "recovery czar" in response to the Mississippi River flood of 1927. A second reading proposes a number of more incremental changes to the existing statutory and regulatory scheme. Comparing the two proposals, consider whether what we need is wholesale reform of our approach to disaster law or more limited reforms that leave the basic structure intact.

KEVIN R. KOSAR, DISASTER RESPONSE AND APPOINTMENT OF A RECOVERY CZAR: THE EXECUTIVE BRANCH'S RESPONSE TO THE FLOOD OF 1927

(Oct. 25, 2005) (CRS Order Code RL33126)

In the wake of the destruction caused by Hurricanes Katrina and Rita, the press and policymakers have looked to the past for examples of federal responses to natural disasters that might serve as models for emulation today. A number of newspaper articles have referred to the executive branch's response to the 1927 Mississippi River flood. Some Members of Congress have expressed an interest in creating a cabinet-level "czar" to administer Hurricane Katrina and Hurricane Rita relief programs. Since the federal response to the flood of 1927 featured Secretary of Commerce Herbert Hoover as the director of the flood response and wielding immense executive powers, this episode . . . may be of particular interest. . . .

[The federal response to the 1927 flood] was primarily an executive branch response. President Calvin Coolidge created a quasi-governmental commission that included members of his Cabinet and the American National

Red Cross. This commission encouraged the public to donate funds to the relief effort and utilized federal resources, American National Red Cross volunteers, and the private sector to carry out the relief and recovery program. The commission also gave Secretary of Commerce Herbert Hoover near-absolute authority.

The concentration of power and the blending of the governmental and private sectors in Hoover's hands enabled the relief effort to be carried out expeditiously and creatively. President Coolidge's empowerment of Hoover alone as director of the flood response clarified to federal, state, and local officials and the public who was in charge. As will be seen, historical accounts and assessments of the federal flood response failed to locate any instances of jurisdictional confusion or power struggles between agencies.

However, this administrative structure was not without costs. There was little direct federal oversight of actual relief provision. . . . Furthermore, the concentration of power in a single set of hands enabled Secretary Hoover to undertake inadvisable actions with nearly no constraints.

The Mississippi River Flood of 1927

. . . From late August 1926 through the spring of 1927, unusually heavy precipitation fell upon the Mississippi River Valley. "From January 1 to April 30, 1927, enough rain fell in various sections of [the Mississippi River basin] to cover the entire territory to a depth of 10.79 inches." . . .

In April 1927, the Mississippi River began bursting levees. The first was at Dorena, MO, where on April 16, 1,200 feet of levee crumbled. Five days later, massive crevasses opened in levees in Mounds Landing, MS, and then Pendleton, AR; hundreds of millions of gallons of water violently washed over the land. The flood had begun and its end was not declared until late July. People were drowned in the fields and in their homes. The rush of the water was so immense and violent that it permanently altered the topography in areas. Near the levee break at Mounds Landing, for example, the flood left a 65 acre lake that remains to this day.

In all, levees in Arkansas, Louisiana, Mississippi, and Missouri broke in 145 places. Over 26,000 square miles of land in seven states inhabited by some 930,000 persons were flooded. The damage was immense — 41,487 buildings were destroyed, 162,017 homes flooded, and over $100 million [about $1.12 billion in 2005 dollars] in crops and farm animals destroyed. It is unclear how many persons were killed — accounts vary widely — but, it seems clear that at least 246 died. . . .

Federal Disaster Response, Relief, and Reconstruction

The federal government's response to the disaster was a mixture of pre-New Deal minimalist federal governance and, to use recent parlance, "governing by network." The federal government would make no immediate appropriations to the affected area. Instead, it would utilize federal resources and coordinate networks of federal, state, private, and not-for-profit organizations to deliver relief services. The President's Cabinet would direct the relief effort in close consultation with the American National Red Cross. Thus, flood response policy was centralized, but, its execution was decentralized.

In 1927, there was no federal disaster-response agency. Instead, the federal government had a partnership with the Red Cross, a congressionally chartered quasi-governmental entity, established for a number of purposes, including the carrying out of "a system of national and international relief in time of peace, and to apply the same in mitigating the suffering caused by pestilence, famine, fire, floods, and other great national calamities, and to devise and carry out measures for preventing the same." Under the charter, the President of the United States was to appoint six members, one of whom was to serve as chairman, of the eighteen-person central committee. The other five members were to be "named by him from the Departments of State, War, Navy, Treasury, and Justice." While the law did not provide a position for the President himself, Coolidge had been asked and agreed to serve as President of the Red Cross.

On April 22, 1927, President Calvin Coolidge issued a proclamation to the nation. He declared, "The Government is giving such aid as lies within its powers. . . . But the burden of caring for the homeless rests upon the agency designated by Government charter to provide relief in disaster — the American National Red Cross." He made no mention of emergency appropriations. Rather, Coolidge, as President of the United States and the Red Cross, asked for the public to donate $5 million [$55.9 million in 2005 dollars] to the Red Cross. Additionally, the President created a quasi-governmental commission to assist the Red Cross in the relief effort. Coolidge appointed Herbert Hoover, Secretary of Commerce, as chairman.

Hoover was an apt choice — he had been elected to the Central Committee of the Red Cross by the incorporators and he had experience managing post–World War I relief and reconstruction efforts in Europe. Hoover was directly assisted by James L. Fieser, acting chairman of the Red Cross. The remainder of the commission, whose roles, according to President Coolidge, were to lend expert advice and expedite resource provision, included the secretaries of the Departments of the Treasury, War, and Navy, and the members of the Red Cross Central Committee.

That same day — April 22 — [the "Hoover Flood Commission"] met for the first time and made three major decisions. First, it effectively turned over direction of the Red Cross's relief effort to Secretary Hoover. Second, it appointed Henry M. Baker, disaster relief director for the Red Cross, as the actual administrator of the response effort. As "dictator," Baker would do the work to execute Hoover's directions. Third, the Flood Commission agreed that each of the affected states should appoint a "dictator"; this individual would serve as the point-person for the state, and who would see to it that state resources were provided to the centrally directed response. These decisions made Hoover, to use recent nomenclature, the "czar" for federal disaster response, likely the first.

This concentration of a wide array of governmental powers in a single set of hands enabled the federal government to respond rapidly without bureaucratic impediments. If Hoover asked for a federal resource, the Hoover Flood Commission would see that it was provided. The Memphis flood response headquarters served as an "administrative pump." A hodgepodge of resources from the many partners in the relief effort flowed in, as did advice from the

Hoover Flood Commission and local relief workers. The headquarters, which was divided into operational units, including purchase and supply, river transportation and rescue work, rail transportation, and so forth, served as a processor. . . . Out of the pump flowed streams of coordinated responses. A single, official channel of communication — "Field Operations Letters" — was established; through it, the headquarters delivered relief plan directions to local personnel and groups by telephone calls and radio communications directed to regional Red Cross offices.

Furthermore, coordinating the federal response with the Red Cross gave the relief effort the power to draw upon thousands of already-trained Red Cross volunteers in affected areas. These volunteers on the scene provided information to the [Hoover Commission's] headquarters for use in planning and coordinating the response, and utilized relationships they had with affected residents and governments to help execute the response. Federal, state, and quasi-governmental entities and private citizens and businesses were linked to form an "administrative machine."

The President, for his part, let the Hoover Flood Commission run relief administration. He issued a further plea for another $5 million in donations to the Red Cross on May 2. Hoover, though, directed the expenditure of the funds, often shipping allotments to local Red Cross chapters to expend according to their directions.

The scale of the relief effort was massive. Approximately 640,000 displaced persons were aided by the Red Cross; 307,208 stayed in over 150 Red Cross camps, many for up to four months; the remainder of evacuees stayed elsewhere, but, received food from the Red Cross. The Red Cross provided those in the camps with food, tobacco, medical care, clothing, and some entertainment. Evacuees, typically, lived in tents donated by the Department of War, and had access to simple bathing and toilet facilities. They received rudimentary medical care; some entertainment and courses in home economics were provided.

While the relief operations were of considerable breadth, federal recovery and reconstruction efforts were quite modest. The Army Corp of Engineers, after some delay, repaired the levees. Hoover encouraged affected states to incorporate state reconstruction corporations. He also strongly encouraged banks in affected areas and the captains of industries of the day to provide working capital for the banks by buying stock in them. His plan was for state reconstruction corporations to lend money to farmers, sell these loans to the Federal Intermediate Credit Corporation, and use the proceeds to make more loans. The Red Cross, meanwhile, helped citizens rebuild some of their homes, and provided them with seeds, farm implements, basic household furnishings, and other items to help them regain the ability to sustain themselves. . . .

An Assessment of the Executive Branch's Response

The public donated and the Red Cross delivered over $21 million [$234.9 million] in aid. The federal government provided, perhaps, $10 million [$111.8 million] in resources and manpower — nearly $32 million [$346.7 million] in all.

On the whole, the response and relief provided by the federal government and Red Cross appear to have been well executed. The concentration of great power in the person of Secretary Hoover enabled quick and creative responses. By April 23, 1927, U.S. Coast Guard boats were rescuing citizens trapped in trees and on rooftops, bridges, and high grounds, the U.S. Army had shipped thousands of tents, cots, and blankets to areas where Red Cross camps were being set up, and the Navy had received Hoover's request to dispatch boats and rescue crews. . . .

The blending of governmental and private resources enabled creative responses. For example, the Red Cross Rescue Fleet was cobbled together from privately owned yachts, commercial barges, boats belonging to federal agencies such as the U.S. Army, Navy, Coast Guard, and river steamships. Railroads were employed to move . . . materials, manpower, and evacuees. Hoover also brought into the mix the Rockefeller Foundation, which provided public health assistance to affected counties.

Additionally, President Coolidge's employment of a Cabinet-based commission helped clarify to the public and local, state, and federal officials who was in charge of the flood response. Secretary Hoover was widely known throughout the nation, and the President made sure that everyone got the message that Hoover was in charge by utilizing the bully pulpit — he issued a presidential proclamation to the press. That same day — April 23 — Hoover and Fieser made contact with governors to let them know that the federal government and Red Cross would jointly direct all activities. The scholarly and press accounts on the flood response cited above reveal no jurisdictional disputes between federal agencies or between federal and state agencies. Again, Hoover created an "administrative machine."

That said, the federal response has been faulted on at least four points. First, while the employment of governmental and private sector resources allowed for creative responses, it also opened the door to potential abuses. For example, Hoover, reportedly, empowered Baker to order the seizure of privately owned boats by relief workers. Thus, with no executive order or statute, private individuals were authorized to take the property of others. To whom individuals affected and aggrieved by civilian exercise of federal powers would protest or appeal is simply unclear.

Second, decentralized execution meant that the federal government had little oversight of the actual operations of the relief camps. Two significant incidents illustrate the limitations of this method of administration. First, critics accused the Red Cross of being slow to respond to the spread of venereal diseases among camp residents. Second, in some Red Cross camps, local officials brutalized Black evacuees and disallowed them to leave the camps.[2] . . . [T]he

---

2. Under the sharecropper relationship, a farmer would work land owned by another person and turn over to the landowner the products thereof. The landowner would sell the agricultural products and give the farmer a "share" of the proceeds. Under such an arrangement, many Blacks in the South had fallen into near or outright peonage. Farmers fell into debt when landowners would charge them for various items and services — such as loans for seed — and provided small returns. Bound by debt, farmers could not leave the land. After the flood of 1927, landowners had a strong interest in seeing that their sharecroppers returned to their fields. Therefore, they often employed threats of violence and called upon state and local governments to help them force farmers to return to work.

federal government had no one at these sites to provide accurate reports on the conditions or put a halt to these actions.[3]

Third, directions from headquarters and Hoover to field operations were very explicit as to the goals desired. In one instance, Hoover [ordered] a regional representative . . . to erect a camp to hold 10,000 persons and gave instructions on the proper construction and installation of the facilities, including tent platforms, latrines, pipelines, wells, and power lines. However, these same directions provided little direction as to the appropriate means. Locals were to figure it out themselves. Free to use whatever means they felt necessary to achieve these ends, local relief workers, in many instances, forced Black males, sometimes at gun point, to participate in flood response work. In short, workers carrying out ostensibly federal work were not federal workers, and did not have to follow federal administrative laws.

Finally, there is the matter of power concentration in the hands of a Cabinet-level czar. As head of the Hoover Flood Commission, head of the Red Cross flood relief effort, and the public face of flood relief—thanks to his tireless public relations efforts—Secretary Hoover held an immense amount of administrative and political power. . . . While this empowered him to do much good work, Hoover also made glaring mistakes, and made matters worse by refusing to admit his errors and make amends. Critically, nobody, the President excepted, could force Hoover to change course. For example,

> [t]here is evidence that Hoover was aware of the mistreatment of Blacks in the camps and the shortcomings of his credit provision plan. Yet, he did little to fix these problems.
>
> In late May of 1927, the Secretary decided that the farmers of the area should plant soybeans, instead of cotton. He directed the Red Cross, which received public donations for the flood response, to buy enough soybean seed for 400,000 acres. When informed by agricultural scientists that soybeans were not an advisable crop choice for the affected areas, Hoover disregarded this counsel and contacted banks to urge them to loan monies to farmers for soybean crops.
>
> A destitute victim departing a relief camp might receive no more than "tickets that entitled him to railway fare . . . , and to a tent if his house was gone, tickets that gave him lumber, seeds, implements [for gardening], and a mule or cow." Many newspapers . . . argued that the federal government, which was running a massive surplus, should provide direct aid to flood victims in order to help them regain self-sustenance. Hoover disagreed—he thought flood victims had received enough to get back on their feet. Unfortunately, even these modest resources did not reach those in need. Red Cross officials distributed some evacuees' allotments to the planters for whom they worked. Some planters charged evacuees for the goods.

In summation, President Coolidge's version of a disaster response and recovery czar enabled quick and apparently efficient utilization of

---

3. . . . President Coolidge empowered Hoover to issue reports on the progress of flood recovery. With an eye on a run for the presidency in 1928, this gave Hoover a strong incentive to be less than objective about inadequate results. Thus, he would often claim that six or fewer persons died once he was put in control of flood response. This figure is not deemed credible.

governmental and private sector resources and personnel. It also, though, gave a single administrator a large quantity of power with only presidential oversight, and, in some instances, that power appears to have been used inadvisably.

NOTES AND QUESTIONS

1. The definitive book on the 1927 flood is JOHN M. BARRY, RISING TIDE: THE GREAT MISSISSIPPI FLOOD OF 1927 AND HOW IT CHANGED AMERICA (1998). Kevin Kosar's CRS report draws heavily from Barry's book.
2. John Barry notes that the displacement of African Americans from flooded homes and their mistreatment in Hoover's camps pushed thousands of Blacks out of the Mississippi Delta. *See* BARRY, *supra*, at 417. Coupled with the invention of the mechanical cotton picker and the boll weevil infestation, *see* NICHOLAS LEMANN, THE PROMISED LAND: THE GREAT BLACK MIGRATION AND HOW IT CHANGED AMERICA 5-6 (1991); Jim Chen, *Of Agriculture's First Disobedience and Its Fruit*, 48 VAND. L. REV. 1261, 1302-1312 (1995), the flood of 1927 sparked the eventual movement of more than 6 million Americans of African descent from the rural South to the urban North between the Great War and the Great Society. Do disasters often have the capacity to trigger major societal movements?
3. How would the federal government appoint a "disaster czar"? He or she would surely "exercis[e] significant authority pursuant to the laws of the United States," Buckley v. Valeo, 424 U.S. 1, 126 (1976), and be subject to the Appointments Clause, U.S. CONST. art II, §2, cl. 2. Unless the czar's mission can be characterized as limited in time and scope, *cf.* Morrison v. Olson, 487 U.S. 659, 671-673 (1988) (describing the traits of an "inferior" officer), or unless the czar is already a principal officer of the United States, the Senate must confirm his or her appointment.
4. Given the scale and scope of federal involvement in emergencies, especially its escalation since 1927, a straightforward restoration of the Mississippi River flood's "disaster czar" approach seems fanciful. The experience of 1927 nevertheless retains enough allure to prompt a congressional inquiry after Katrina. Insofar as today's federal emergency response system aspires to "unified command" across jurisdictions and to a more rational coordination of fifteen emergency support functions, in what respects does Herbert Hoover's 1927 experience remain pertinent?
5. Another recent proposal for disaster reform draws on the Hoover-as-disaster-czar experience to suggest creating a statutory basis for a "Presidential Officer-in-Charge," who would have flexibility to respond to megadisasters that, the authors contend, are essentially "unplannable":

> We recommend stand-by federal legislation to enable the president to appoint an officer-in-charge, not to take over state and local responsibilities, but to do two essential things. First, to provide the authority and resources to mobilize the federal establishment (and, by virtue of being able to do this, being in a stronger position to influence major institutions on the scene to get their act together). Second, to enable the national government to adopt extraordinary measures. A major charge to the person assigned as this "presidentially

designated driver" would be to report to the president and the Congress within a prescribed period of time on whether extraordinary national action is needed, and if so what it should be. In doing so, the officer-in-charge and the staff of this office would draw on the expertise of federal, state, and local officials and agencies, voluntary groups, and outside experts.

Proposals that emerge out of this process would be time sensitive. At the discretion of the officer-in-charge, we suggest that these proposals be subject to special Congressional procedures like those for international trade agreements and, at the discretion of the officer-in-charge, that they could be considered en bloc under processes like those for base-closing commissions. Such authority to put forward legislative proposals for fast, special action would not infringe on the authority of the president and the Congress to reject them, nor on the powers and responsibilities that policymakers and first responders at the state and local levels must retain. What such authority would accomplish — in government jargon — is provide the officer-in-charge with the capacity to collaborate and facilitate — and in plain English, to lead.

Richard P. Nathan & Marc Luncy, *Who's in Charge? Who Should Be? The Role of the Federal Government in Megadisasters: Based on Lessons from Hurricane Katrina* (June 2, 2009), available at http://www.rockinst.org/pdf/disaster_recovery/gulfgov/gulfgov_reports/2009-06-02-Whos_in_Charge.PDF.

Consider now a more incremental reform proposal that suggests numerous changes that could be made within the existing statutory framework:

MITCHELL MOSS, CHARLES SCHELLHAMER & DAVID A. BERMAN, *THE STAFFORD ACT AND PRIORITIES FOR REFORM*

6 J. HOMELAND SECURITY & EMERGENCY MGMT. 8-16 (2009)

To improve response, the Post Katrina Act establishes a new level for "Catastrophic Incidents," defined as:

"Any natural disaster, act of terrorism, or other man-made disaster that results in extraordinary levels of causalities [*sic*] or damage or disruption severely affecting the population (including mass evacuations), infrastructure, environment, economy, national morale, or government functions in an area."

This new level of catastrophic incidents is designed to improve the immediate federal response following a catastrophe and provides "Regional Strike Teams" and a "Surge Capacity Force" to ensure that FEMA arrives as soon as possible and is backed up by enough staff to provide an effective response.

Changes were also made to the Stafford Act to develop a national disaster housing strategy, provide more money for pre-disaster mitigation, create programs to facilitate family reunions, and the location of displaced children. However, the catastrophic incident provisions of the 2006 Post Katrina Act were not included in the Stafford Act — they are included in sections of law that deal with national emergency management — thus effectively adding a new layer of regulation and meaning that a disaster can now simultaneously be declared a "Major Disaster" under the Stafford Act, an "Incident of National Significance" under the National Response Framework [before its most recent revision], and a "Catastrophic Incident" under the Post Katrina Act.

Shortcomings

While the designation of a "catastrophe" under the Post Katrina Act brings additional resources to bear in the days following a catastrophe, it does not change the underlying concepts upon which federal disaster policy is built, nor does it guide long-term recovery.

Current federal disaster policy is designed with smaller scale disasters in mind — such as floods, tornadoes, and winter storms. No distinction is made between a blizzard that strikes Buffalo and a hurricane the magnitude of Katrina — both can be declared a "major disaster" under the Stafford Act.

Well intended federal regulations and policies designed to meet the needs of smaller-scale disasters become roadblocks that hamper both initial response and long term recovery when they are deployed to deal with a catastrophe such as Hurricane Katrina or the September 11 attacks. As Gil Jamieson, FEMA's deputy administrator for Gulf Coast recovery explained, "There was a tendency in the early days to think we could run this as we might run a garden-variety disaster, but you just can't push that big of a pig through the pipe."

Two years after Hurricane Katrina, 43,000 families in Louisiana still live in temporary trailers. Crime has skyrocketed in New Orleans, but the police superintendent continues to work out of a trailer, and the city's DNA lab has not been rebuilt. Fewer than half of the public schools have reopened. Only 20% of the levees are as high as they should be.

The definition of a "catastrophic incident" from the Post Katrina Act should be added to the Stafford Act to bring coordination between the two laws. Several changes, outlined below, should also be made to the Stafford Act to ensure its provisions do not again hamper response and recovery efforts.

Local Government Financing

After Hurricane Katrina, the City of New Orleans was forced to lay off nearly half its workforce because there was not enough cash on hand to meet payroll obligations. The Stafford Act authorizes federal disaster assistance to cover the overtime of local government workers for work related to responding to the disaster, but not regular salaries.

The Act also authorizes loans of up to $5 million to cover forgone tax revenues lost in the wake of disasters, but when faced with the loss of a significant proportion of the local tax base following a catastrophe, state and local governments do not have an adequate means to quickly recover forgone revenue and continue government services without supplemental appropriations from Congress. After the September 11 attacks, New York City lost approximately $2.5 to $2.9 billion in tax revenue for FY 2002 and 2003. According to a Congressional Research Service report, almost three-quarters of Louisiana state personal income and retail sales (72.8 percent and 72.2 percent, respectively) were generated in the declared disaster parishes, with 24.3 percent of personal income and 22.3 percent of all retail sales generated in the New Orleans metropolitan statistical area (MSA).

The Stafford Act should be amended to abolish the $5 million cap on loans to reimburse for lost tax revenue. In addition, sections of the Stafford Act that allow the federal government to fund overtime pay of public employees should be amended to allow the federal government to, in part or in full, pay the salaries of state and local public employees in areas stricken by a catastrophe for a limited amount of time. This will ensure that areas affected by a catastrophe do not face the dual challenge of overwhelming devastation and a bankrupt local government forced to lay off workers.

Insurance

An underlying assumption of federal policy is that assistance to business and individuals should first come from insurance. The Stafford Act states, "The President . . . shall assure that no such person, business concern, or other entity will receive such assistance with respect to any part of such loss as to which he has received financial assistance under any other program or from insurance or any other source."

It is essential for businesses and individuals to have insurance, and for the government to encourage insurance coverage in order to minimize the amount of taxpayer money spent following a disaster. The problem is that, following a catastrophe, important documents needed by businesses and individuals to document ownership and proof of insurance may have been lost, making it difficult for people to apply and receive government assistance in a timely fashion. As Don Wilson, president of the national Association of Small Business Development Centers explained following Katrina, "Even if your CPA has copies of your records, their records may have been destroyed."

Even more troubling, insurance companies have moved to minimize loses, leaving victims in difficult financial positions. In a bid to avoid payouts to those who had hurricane — but not flood — coverage following Katrina, insurance companies argued that the damage in New Orleans was caused by flooding, not the hurricane, and that the devastation along the Gulf Coast was caused by surge flooding, not hurricane winds. In February 2007, State Farm was found by a federal judge in Mississippi to have acted in a "grossly negligent way" after denying a homeowner's claim following the hurricane. Numerous other Katrina related lawsuits against insurance companies are making their way through the courts, and in time judgments will be levied and settlements reached, resulting in payouts — but this may not come until years after the hurricane.

Even when insurance companies act to make payments, the devastation that follows a catastrophe can overwhelm the company and result in multi-month delays for insurance payments. Nearly 9 months after the hurricane hit, the insurance modeling firm ISO estimated that Louisiana had $24.3 billion in insured losses, but records from the Louisiana Department of Insurance showed that only half that amount — $12.5 billion — had been paid out by April 2006. A year after Katrina, thousands in Mississippi were also still waiting for insurance payments.

Government policy must continue to encourage insurance coverage so that insurance companies, not taxpayers, absorb the majority of the bill following a catastrophe. However, the Stafford Act and its regulations should be modified to allow cash assistance — which is capped at $28,800 per household, and further subdivided with caps on repairs, temporary housing assistance, and other items — to flow to qualified homeowners and renters following a catastrophe without having to provide proof of insurance coverage. This will provide devastated families with immediate assistance in order to begin the recovery process. This assistance could later be reimbursed to the government when insurance coverage is received, or though income taxes.

Utilities

Following a catastrophe, the resumption of utilities — electricity, water, sewer, and telecommunications — is critical. Lives can be saved and suffering minimized with functioning utilities. According to the Federal Communications Commission, Hurricane Katrina destroyed more than 3 million customer phone lines, and more than a thousand cell phone sites. Private telecommunications firms were among the first to repair destroyed communications lines, patching their way into New Orleans in the wake of Hurricane Katrina well ahead of the federal government. However, utility workers are not treated as emergency responders. As recounted in news reports, "BellSouth found a soggy, unhappy crowd of people outside its main downtown New Orleans switching facility soon after Katrina blew over. Company executives said they feared the crowd would try to forcibly enter the building to seize the food and water supplies inside — which could have disrupted the fragile telecommunications network even more."

Fearing for their safety, and with gun shots being fired, BellSouth was forced to evacuate the building, shutting down phone lines in New Orleans that were still functional. BellSouth had requested security escorts and "priority" access to food, fuel, water and shelter from the federal government, but were denied because the Stafford Act does not recognize utility workers as "emergency responders."

The Stafford Act should be amended so that, following a catastrophe, utility workers are recognized as "emergency responders," thus enabling them to receive security escorts and priority access to food, fuel, water, and shelter.

Distribution of Funds

To make up for limitations within the Stafford Act, Congress historically has appropriated billions of dollars and established special programs that provide additional assistance following a catastrophe. After the 1994 Northridge (Los Angeles) Earthquake, Congress appropriated $11 billion. $40 billion was appropriated following the September 11 attacks, and $110 billion after Hurricanes Katrina and Rita.

The distribution of this funding, along with Stafford Act assistance, is governed by an elaborate set of procedures. The result is that it takes months, if not years, for the responsible federal agencies to process and distribute the assistance. For example, nearly a year and half after Katrina, of the $42 billion given to FEMA, $25 billion has been distributed. The Army Corps of Engineers had spent $1.3 billion out of $5.8 billion for levee repairs, and the Department of Housing and Urban Development had distributed $1.7 billion out of $17 billion received.

With the bulk of immediate rescue and recovery work, along with long-term planning and rebuilding resting in the hands of state and local governments, a system that provides federal assistance to state and local governments as quickly as possible is paramount.

Often delays are not caused by provisions of the law, but exist within regulations and interpretations. During the 1990s, FEMA successfully responded to catastrophes and major disasters like the 1993 Midwest floods and the 1994 Oklahoma City bombing by relaxing the regulations that implement the Stafford Act. A similar result could occur if FEMA designed its Public Assistance Program in a fashion such that one damage survey and estimate was written for each affected community or state. This would allow FEMA to quickly provide assistance to state and local governments in a form similar to a block grant. Where possible, money appropriated by Congress following a catastrophe should also be provided directly to state and local governments in the form of block grants. This will eliminate the burden and associated time delays placed on federal agencies as they distribute the assistance, and it will give state and local governments flexibility in using the money as they see fit.

A general rider within the Stafford Act for catastrophic events, giving the President, in consultation with Congress, the authority to wave Stafford Act provisions and regulations following a catastrophe represents another effective means of providing regulatory flexibility following a catastrophe. To prevent an open ended mandate, the rider could also require the President, after an initial damage assessment, and in coordination with Congress, to set a cap on the amount of immediate and long term recovery assistance that will be provided for the catastrophe.

21st Century Threats

Looking to the future, Congress specifically exempted chemical, biological, and nuclear attacks and accidents from the Stafford Act in response to President Carter's use of disaster regulations to respond to the Three Mile Island accident. However, with the possibility of a terrorist attack involving a chemical, biological, or nuclear agent, the Stafford Act should be amended to include these types of disasters.

The President possesses power under other laws, including the National Emergencies Act, and the Comprehensive Environmental Response, Compensation, and Liability Act of 1980 to respond to major disturbances of the public order, environmental disasters, and incidents that result in the release of hazardous substances. Title V of the Homeland Security Act of 2002 also gives Department of Homeland Security the power to act in the event of a nuclear or public health incident.

Beyond causing a large number of causalities [sic], a chemical, biological, radiological, or nuclear attack or accident has the potential to devastate local economies, wreck [sic] havoc on infrastructure, and generate the need for temporary housing. Recovering from such attacks or accidents could require extensive, long-term investment, which the major disaster assistance programs of the Stafford Act are designed to facilitate — but do not cover because a major disaster is defined to exclude these types of events. If needed, the President may declare an emergency under the Stafford Act, but this limits federal assistance to $5 million, unless expanded by the President. The definition of a major disaster should be amended to allow the full range of Stafford

Act options to come into play during a chemical, biological, radiological, or nuclear attack or accident. If the incident is of sufficient magnitude to qualify as a catastrophe, the catastrophic assistance provisions recommended by this paper could also come into effect.

Conclusion

Throughout the history of American disaster policy, existing federal government agencies with their own policies, objectives, and constituencies have been cobbled together to create new agencies, and layers of law have been added on top existing regulations without amending previous laws or revisiting the assumptions upon which they rest. This has produced a system where disasters are governed by multiple regulations — the Stafford Act, the Homeland Security Act of 2002, the Post Katrina Emergency Management Reform Act of 2006, and the National Response Framework — meaning a disaster can simultaneously be declared a Major Disaster, a Catastrophic Incident, and an Incident of National Significance, and be responded to in accordance with the provisions of all of those laws. Any future attempts to modify the disaster management system in the United States must be conscious of this tendency and instead work to produce a system that harmoniously blends old and new elements.

By failing to account for catastrophes, current American disaster policy has been unable to meet the challenges of large-scale events such as Hurricane Katrina. Well meaning limitations designed with blizzards and tornadoes in mind have been transformed into roadblocks that hamper the ability of the government and private sector to respond and rebuild.

In an era in which the United States faces unprecedented challenges and threats to the safety and well being of its citizens, the Stafford Act must be amended. State and local governments should not be forced to contend with an outdated federal disaster policy that does not recognize twenty-first century threats, does not address catastrophic incidents, and that delays long term recovery by channeling funds through an array of federal agencies proving [*sic*] assistance directly to state and local governments.

NOTES AND QUESTIONS

1. Which of the many reform proposals suggested in the foregoing reading seem most pressing? How practical are the solutions proposed in the article? For example, would state and local governments coping with the aftermath of a major disaster be more efficient and prompt in administering federal disaster aid than FEMA? Can recovery costs be estimated accurately enough to rely on a block grant system instead of reimbursements?

2. How much of a concern is it if an incident is designated both a "catastrophic incident" within the meaning of the Post-Katrina Act and a "major disaster"? (Recall that the most recent 2009 iteration of the NRF eliminates the category "Incidents of National Significance.") What would adding a "catastrophic incident" level to the Stafford Act achieve? If a catastrophic incident level is added to the Act, should Congress also add new powers or procedures that would be triggered by declaration of a catastrophic

event? The Stafford Act gives the president authority to deploy federal resources without further congressional action. Are catastrophic events so outside the norm that Congress cannot realistically decide in advance what additional resources ought to be committed, such that post hoc, event-specific legislation—rather than a Stafford Act amendment—is required?

E. A SIMULATION EXERCISE: MAJOR EARTHQUAKE

This scenario is based, in part, on one of the fifteen National Planning Scenarios (Scenario 9: Natural Disaster—Major Earthquake). *See* NATIONAL PLANNING SCENARIOS: EXECUTIVE SUMMARIES. For interesting visual depictions of the consequences of a large-scale earthquake along the San Andreas fault, see http:// www.shakeout.org/resources/videos.html (cataloguing videos prepared for the 2008 Great California Shakeout earthquake drill) (June 25, 2009).

At 9:15 A.M. on Tuesday, February 7, a 7.2-magnitude earthquake struck the major metropolitan area of Fault City. Located in the Intermountain West, the Fault City metropolitan area is home to some 3 million people (10 million people live in the six-county area). Although scientists had long predicted a moderate to catastrophic earthquake in the region, there were no specific seismic changes in the days and weeks leading up to the event that indicated that a major quake was imminent. Approximately three hours after the initial quake, at 12:03 P.M., a massive aftershock—registering 8.0 on the Richter Scale—shook the already devastated region. Subsurface faulting has occurred along sixty miles of the fault zone; the areas of greatest destruction are densely populated urban and suburban areas. It is now 1:10 P.M.; further aftershocks (perhaps in the 7.0-8.0 range) are expected and could continue for months.

Damage reports are beginning to trickle in. No one can say for sure how reliable the reports are, as telecommunications networks are functioning sporadically, at best. Extrapolating from initial reports, the State's Head of Emergency Management estimates that there may be 1,400 fatalities, 100,000 injuries requiring medical care, and more than 18,000 people in need of hospitalization for serious and life-threatening injuries. Many of the city's largest hospitals have suffered extensive damage and cannot care for existing patients, much less the surge of injured who are flooding emergency rooms.

Hundreds of thousands of homes—and some 150,000 other buildings—have been destroyed, as a result of the shaking and concomitant liquefaction (earthquake-induced quicksand). Many of those homes shifted off their foundations. Several tall buildings in the downtown area—including one recently completed high-rise apartment building—collapsed completely, "pancaking" as floors collapsed down onto one another. As many as 20,000 people may be trapped in collapsed homes and buildings.

Additionally, most of the homes and buildings in the area that are still standing have neither electricity nor natural gas (and most homes and buildings in the area require both electricity and natural gas in order for their heating systems to work). The downtown area (including the State Capitol, which houses the State Emergency Management Department's Emergency Response Center) and the closest suburbs have gone completely dark. The State Capitol's emergency generator, which had not been tested in several years, has malfunctioned and will not start. Natural gas leaks have sparked a number of fires throughout the city, at least one of which is threatening a large hospital and several adjacent long-term care facilities. A large number of fire stations and fire trucks have been destroyed.

Many water mains have broken; wastewater treatment plants have been heavily damaged, and raw sewage is leaking into the streets in many neighborhoods. (The city's water distribution system also requires electric pumps to function.) The infrastructure damage is particularly extensive because the area's geography dictates that nearly every major natural gas and water pipeline in the city crosses over the major fault line. It is now 39 degrees outside, and weather forecasts indicate that snow or sleeting rain can be expected as evening approaches. Lows in the 20s are expected overnight.

Reports of serious environmental threats are also beginning to surface. Fuel pumps at several gas stations have ruptured, leaking thousands of gallons of gasoline onto city streets. Several large chemical facilities in the city have sustained serious damage. One unsubstantiated report indicates that there may be a small chlorine gas leak at a municipal water treatment center. (Chlorine gas was used as a weapon during World War I.)

Estimates suggest that at least 500,000 people are already planning to evacuate (including some who must evacuate to seek shelter and those who will choose to self-evacuate regardless of official evacuation advice). Both evacuations and transport of needed emergency supplies will be hampered by the state of major highways and bridges: many have buckled, making them all but impassable, and others are completely blocked by debris. Many freeway overpasses have also collapsed. The city's underground commuter system is in shambles, and many are feared trapped in underground stations and trains. An entire section of the city located along the eastern mountain range — home to 35,000 people — has been all but cut off from the surrounding area by a new twelve-foot-high fault scarp. Thousands of skiers are potentially trapped in the city's many ski resorts, which are also located primarily in the eastern mountains.

Ten miles northeast of the city, Hill Side Reservoir has suffered major damage. Although the dam has not yet ruptured, experts on site are concerned that even another small aftershock could cause a catastrophic failure. The dam is relatively small in comparison to others in the area — holding back only 300 million gallons of water — but its rupture could nonetheless flood 30,000 houses, and floodwaters could reach the downtown area.

Communities some seventy miles outside of the city also felt significant shaking, but damage there is much less extensive. Most homes and buildings appear to be intact. Unfortunately, the CEO of the natural gas company — Intermountain Gas — has received numerous reports from the company's emergency call center that many homeowners in these less damaged areas are following advice (widely repeated on the radio) to turn off their natural gas. Those homes are now without heat as well. The CEO reports that once a customer's natural gas is turned off, it can only be turned back on by a power company technician; the unnecessary gas shutoffs are going to create a huge additional burden on the relatively small Intermountain Gas repair crew.

The governor has gathered his core staff, the head of the state's Emergency Management Department, and Fault City's mayor, in a makeshift emergency center at a military base on the outskirts of the city. Officials from the Army Corps of Engineers, EPA, Red Cross, and FEMA's Regional Office (also located in Fault City) are on their way. The governor is also in touch by satellite phone with the CEO of Intermountain Gas, the CEO of MountainWest Construction (a large, regional construction company headquartered in Fault City), the president of Charity Hospital (a large nonprofit hospital with moderate damage), and the heads of several local water districts.

Assign individuals to play some of the different roles outlined above. For purposes of this exercise, assume that the state has the same emergency response law as Texas. Working together, negotiate a chain of command and establish emergency response priorities and plans.

Consider at least the following questions as you work on this table-top exercise:

1. In your assigned role, consider what actions you should take first. What actions will you suggest to others as priorities? Who will be in charge of setting priorities? Will priorities be set by negotiation? By dictate (by the governor or someone else)?

2. How will communication be established and maintained? In making your decisions, how will you account for uncertainties about what is happening on the ground in different areas of the city? How will you improve situational awareness?

3. What steps does the governor need to take to ensure that the state gets necessary federal aid? Are there any obstacles to fulfilling those responsibilities?

4. What would an evacuation look like under these circumstances and how could it be accomplished? Where will shelters be established? How will the displaced (particularly those with special needs) be located and transported?

5. Consider how the dynamic at this makeshift emergency center changes as federal officials become involved. What will the chain of command look like? How will it be negotiated? How will it evolve over time? Beyond the assigned roles, who else needs to be involved at this early stage of response?

6. What is the role of private actors in the immediate aftermath of the disaster? How will questions of liability affect private- (and public-) actor behavior?

CHAPTER 5

SOCIAL VULNERABILITY

Sometime that night the winds came back. Everything in the world had a strong rattle, sharp and short. . . . [Janie] saw the drifting mists gathered in the west—that cloud field of the sky—to arm themselves with thunders and march forth against the world. Louder and higher and lower and wider the sound and motion spread, mounting, sinking, darking.

It woke up old Okechobee and the monster began to roll in his bed. Began to roll and complain like a peevish world on a grumble. The folks in the quarters and the people in the big houses further around the shore heard the big lake and wondered. The people felt uncomfortable but safe because there were the seawalls to chain the senseless monster in his bed. The folks let the people do the thinking. If the castles thought themselves secure, the cabins needn't worry. Their decision was already made as always. Chink up your cracks, shiver in your wet beds and wait on the mercy of the Lord. The bossman might have the thing stopped before morning anyway. It is so easy to be hopeful in the day time when you can see the things you wish on. But it was night, it stayed night. Night was striding across nothingness with the whole round world in his hands. . . .

They huddled closer and stared at the door. They just didn't use another part of their bodies, and they didn't look at anything but the door. The time was past for asking the white folks what to look for through that door. Six eyes were questioning God.

Zora Neale Hurston[1]

"The moral test of government," said Hubert H. Humphrey, "is how it treats those who are in the dawn of life, the children; those who are in the twilight of life, the aged; and those who are in the shadows of life, the sick, the needy and the handicapped." Arnold v. Arizona Dept. of Health Servs., 160 Ariz. 593, 775 P.2d 521, 537 (1989) (quoting Humphrey). Natural disaster puts government to an extreme version of this test. This chapter addresses the relationship between social vulnerability and natural disasters. It begins with a global overview. Disasters are never strictly "natural"; they invariably stem from social as well as environmental factors.

---

1. ZORA NEALE HURSTON, THEIR EYES WERE WATCHING GOD 158-159 (Harper Perennial 2006; 1st ed. 1937).

Hurricane Katrina and the societal heartbreak associated with that storm inspired the first edition of this book. Although the present edition as a whole looks beyond Katrina, that event continues to loom prominently in this chapter. No previous natural disaster in the nation's history exacted a grimmer toll. More than a thousand Americans died; another million evacuated the Gulf Coast. The legendary city of New Orleans all but sank when its levees failed and the resulting storm surge drowned many of the city's feeblest, most vulnerable residents. The flood waters consumed the forlorn hope that the United States could rescue its citizens during their darkest and neediest hour.

Precisely because Katrina unfolded as a tragedy of race and class, of official incompetence and social injustice, the story of that disaster, in its often gruesome detail, continues to provide the ideal backdrop against which to examine the racial and class-based dimensions of social vulnerability during and after natural disasters. This chapter then addresses other vectors of discrimination laid bare by disaster: sex, age, disability, and immigrant status. A discussion of price-gouging laws rounds out this chapter's exploration of economic exploitation during disaster.

A. DISASTERS AS A FUNCTION OF INJUSTICE

Natural disaster supposedly does not discriminate; it putatively strikes everyone in its path, without regard to race, class, sex, age, or disability. In other words, "poverty is hierarchic, smog is democratic." Ulrich Beck, Risk Society: Toward a New Modernity 36 (1986); *accord* Scott Frickel, *Our Toxic Gumbo: Recipe for a Politics of Environmental Knowledge,* http://understandingkatrina.ssrc.org/Frickel (June 11, 2009). Closer examination of the natural and social factors in any disaster, however, belies this assumption. Disaster does not so much erase as expose social vulnerability. Though " '[n]atural disasters' such as hurricanes, earthquakes, and floods are sometimes viewed as 'great social equalizers' " that "strike unpredictably and at random, affecting black and white, rich and poor, sick and well alike," harms from disasters "are not visited randomly or equally in our society." Center for Progressive Reform, An Unnatural Disaster: The Aftermath of Hurricane Katrina 34 (2005). Around the world, social injustice contributes so heavily to the incidence and intensity of natural disasters that the quest for equality may be regarded as a valuable tool for improving disaster preparedness, response, mitigation, compensation, and rebuilding.

This section begins with a global view of the relationship between natural disasters and social injustice. Losses from catastrophic events will not be stemmed until the law honestly confronts the contribution of "civilized" society to "natural" disasters:

Theresa Braine, Was 2005 the Year of Natural Disasters?

84:1 Bull. World Health Org. 4 (Jan. 2006)

The year 2005 saw the aftermath of the 26 December 2004 earthquake and tsunami waves in Asia, hurricanes in central and north America, notably

Katrina, . . . and the 8 October earthquake in Pakistan and India. The year also saw famine after crops were destroyed by locusts in Niger. Virtually unnoticed by the outside world was tiny El Salvador where the country's highest volcano, Ilamatepec, erupted on 1 October, displacing more than 7,500 people and killing two. A few days later Hurricane Stan swept through and killed about 70 people with floods and mudslides.

From January to October 2005, an estimated 97,490 people were killed in disasters globally and 88,117 of them in natural disasters. . . . [T]he number of natural disasters—floods, windstorms, droughts and geological disasters—recorded since 1900 have increased and the number of people affected by such disasters has also increased since 1975.

Is this as bad as it gets, or could it get worse? Why do natural disasters appear to be increasingly frequent and increasingly deadly?

Today's disasters stem from a complex mix of factors, including routine climate change, global warming influenced by human behaviour, socioeconomic factors causing poorer people to live in risky areas, and inadequate disaster preparedness and education on the part of governments as well as the general population.

Some disasters experts reject the term "natural disasters," arguing that there is almost always a man-made element. . . . Dr Ciro Ugarte [of the Pan American Health Organization (PAHO)], explain[ed] that natural disasters would not have such a devastating effect on people's lives if they were not exposed to such risks in the first place.

Natural phenomena do not always generate human disasters. Ugarte noted that in 2005, several earthquakes that struck in South America were of a higher magnitude than the one that devastated northern Pakistan and parts of India in October, but these hit sparsely populated areas and therefore caused less damage. The same goes for several tsunamis in 2005 which were not deemed "disasters" because they didn't endanger anyone, Ugarte said.

Natural phenomena are likely to affect more people because Earth's population has increased. According to the United Nations Population Fund, this stands at about 6.5 billion people and is projected to reach 9.1 billion people in 2050.

Marko Kokic, spokesperson for WHO's Health Action in Crisis department, said that some communities are more vulnerable to the effects of natural disasters than 100 years ago because of ecological degradation. He said that, for example, when tropical storms hit the Caribbean in September 2004, there was nothing to stop storm waters gathering and wreaking devastation in Haiti because of deforestation. "We need to tackle the underlying issues, such as poverty and inequity," Kokic said, adding: "In many countries, people cut down trees because wood is the cheapest fuel."

Disasters are also a consequence of development and industrialization. In Europe, experts believe that countries such as France and Germany are more adversely affected by floods today because major rivers, such as the Rhine, have been straightened to ease commercial traffic.

Global warming as well as routine, cyclical climate changes are causing a higher number of strong hurricanes in the Caribbean, meteorologists say. Add to that the increasing number of people living in areas such as coastlines, in substandard housing and the destruction in a crisis of essential infrastructure, such as hospitals, and you have the potential for more devastating disasters than a few decades ago.

There have always been disasters. The bubonic plague wiped out more than 25 million people, or 37% of Europe's population, in the 1300s. More recently, the 1918-19 flu pandemic killed between 20 and 40 million people worldwide. One of the earliest recorded disasters, the eruption of Vesuvius in 79 AD, buried the ancient Roman city of Pompeii killing about 10,000 people. Today, two million people live within its possible range, illustrating one major difference between then and now.

About 75 disasters were reported globally in 1975. . . . In 2000 the figure peaked at 525 and dropped to just under 400 in 2004. By far the highest number of fatalities—about 450,000—occurred in 1984. In 2004 nearly 300,000 died in disasters, but the number of people affected has soared since 1975 with about 600 million people affected by disasters of all kinds in 2002.

So complex and intertwined are the factors behind these disasters that some experts believe the most practical approach to preparedness may be to focus on reducing the risks rather than factors behind the risks.

Dave Paul Zervaas, regional coordinator for Latin America and the Caribbean at the United Nations' International Strategy for Disaster Reduction, argued that preparation should focus on making people less vulnerable to disasters. "We think it's much more important now to look at vulnerabilities, because you have factors you can control," Zervaas said. "You can work to lower vulnerability [to disasters]."

Hurricane Katrina in the United States is a good example, Zervaas said. A number of factors contributed to the damage and loss of life. The storm was huge. It struck a city whose levees had not been maintained or strengthened for years, and government agencies' response to the emergency was at first inadequate.

In Central America storms such as hurricanes Mitch and Stan have wrought damage with rain and landslides rather than wind. "The poverty issue and the social inequity situation have not become much better in most places," said Zervaas, adding that migration to cities conspires with a lack of urban planning to put people in danger.

Clearly, climate change—whether helped by human behaviour or not—is playing a role. Hurricane experts say the world is in the midst of a routine, cyclical climate change that causes the Caribbean to heat up, increasing the frequency of powerful storms. The effect of this is greater than that of global warming. . . .

Experts agree that the poor are disproportionately hit. "In several of these countries, the poor people are looking for spaces to build their houses or their communities [and] they find spaces that are not already used," Ugarte said. "And those spaces that are not already used are usually the spaces at higher risk for natural phenomena. There's a huge relationship between this kind of damage and poverty."

For this reason financial services play a role in both prevention, and damage limitation and recovery. . . . [T]he risks generated by climate change [include] . . . "blows to the world economy sufficiently severe to cripple the resilience that enables affluent countries to respond to catastrophes." . . . While it is important to encourage people, governments and companies to buy insurance, not everyone can afford it or see the need.

Microfinancing is another avenue, giving poor people the means to improve their economic situation so that a disaster does not hit them as hard as it would otherwise, and also by lending them money to use in recovering from it. . . .

PAHO has expanded its programmes to focus not only on preparedness but also on mitigation. This involves reducing secondary deaths and destruction that can occur in the aftermath of a disaster, and implementing building codes that require hospitals, schools, military bases, and other vital structures to be built to withstand such disasters.

Many countries say they can't afford more preparation, but some measures are simple and can be inexpensive, such as a tsunami warning system, Ugarte said. "But from there to Banda Aceh, that is another step," Ugarte said, referring to the capital of the Indonesian province that was worst hit by the earthquake and tsunami of December 2004. "And from Banda Aceh to all the little communities on the coast, that's another issue. That last link of the chain is not in place. And that is the system that we need to build."

Disaster experts say early warning systems and education are essential to prevent and mitigate against the effects of natural disasters. . . . [A] simple phone call saved thousands of lives when the giant tsunami waves hit India in 2004. A fisherman's son named Vijayakumar Gunasekaran, who lives in Singapore, heard about the tsunami early on the radio and phoned relatives living on the east coast of India. Following his warning, all 3,630 residents evacuated their village there before the waves arrived.

NOTES AND QUESTIONS

1. The increase in the frequency and intensity of natural disasters depends on a complex web of interrelated factors. Climate change, environmental degradation, population growth, social and economic inequality, and governmental policy all contribute. These factors span a spectrum that can be calibrated according to the degree of putative control that governments can exert.
a. *Climate change.* Though "environmental geographers [say] there is no such thing as a natural disaster," Neil Smith, *There's No Such Thing as a Natural Disaster,* http://understandingkatrina.ssrc.org/Smith (June 11, 2009), the factors that contribute to disasters do vary in the degree of effective control that humans can exert. Perhaps the most complex and therefore most unmanageable natural phenomenon, climate change is affected by a staggering range of factors. Since the Industrial Revolution, however, the earth's climate has begun to exhibit two disturbing trends. First, overall temperature has risen. Second, departures from "normal" conditions are becoming more frequent and more intense. Storms and temperature extremes—in both directions—are rapidly becoming the norm rather than the exception. *See generally, e.g.,* INTERGOVERNMENTAL PANEL ON

CLIMATE CHANGE, CLIMATE CHANGE 2001: WORKING GROUP II, IMPACTS, ADAPTATION AND VULNERABILITY (2001); SPENCER WEART, THE DISCOVERY OF GLOBAL WARMING (2003).

Assume, at least for argument's sake, that the principal drivers of climate change are anthropocentric. Greenhouse gas emissions represent the very sort of "diffuse, cross-jurisdictional" crises that defy "haphazard local encouragement" and require cooperative solutions. Stephen M. Nickelsburg, Note, *Mere Volunteers? The Promise and Limits of Community-Based Environmental Protection*, 84 VA. L. REV. 1371, 1409 (1998); *see also* Daniel A. Farber, *Stretching the Margins: The Geographic Nexus in Environmental Law*, 48 STAN. L. REV. 1247, 1271 (1996). Because individual contributions to climate change are hard to quantify and even harder to control, whether through incentives or coercive regulation, governments will have great difficulty fashioning satisfactory *ex post* remedies, let alone effective *ex ante* prevention.

b. *Localized environmental degradation.* Environmental conditions on a smaller footprint also affect the probability and impact of natural disasters. Wealth and poverty are each capable of degrading the environment and thereby contributing to disaster. Whereas poverty and desperation have driven deforestation in Haiti, the urge to move more barge traffic in western Europe has driven the straightening of the Rhine. For strikingly different reasons, both regions find themselves more vulnerable to storms, flooding, and other putatively natural phenomena.

c. *Population growth and distribution.* The mere existence of more humans increases the number of potential casualties. *See generally* JOEL COHEN, HOW MANY PEOPLE CAN THE EARTH SUPPORT? (1995); PAUL EHRLICH & ANNE EHRLICH, THE POPULATION EXPLOSION (1990). These population increases are not distributed evenly. The rich and the poor alike are crowding seashores and other environmentally vulnerable areas. Poverty arguably poses a greater challenge for disaster management, since the poor often have no choice but to live in risky areas. The inability of the poor to heed evacuation orders, examined in Chapter 4, finds a distressing corollary in the continued presence of the poor in areas prone to storms, flooding, earthquakes, and other disasters.

d. *Governmental policies.* Katrina represented merely one prominent instance of legal failure. The federal government and the most directly affected states shared responsibility for failure on at least three distinct levels. First, these governments fell short of optimal *preparedness,* in the sense of educating themselves and the public on ways to minimize risk and on the division of authority in the event of disaster. Early warning systems and evacuation protocols had to be improvised, even though the probability of a strong hurricane hitting New Orleans was substantial and anticipated, and even though officials at all levels of government knew that such a strike could inflict many casualties. Second, once Katrina struck, officials did not carry out the best available plans for *response and mitigation.* For instance, Secretary of Homeland Security Michael Chertoff failed to invoke the National Response Plan's Catastrophic

Incident Annex. Finally, the Gulf Coast sustained intense *secondary damage* to hospitals and other elements of public infrastructure that contribute most to mitigation and recovery. Governments should strive to minimize secondary casualties attributable more directly to these losses than to the disaster itself.

e. *Idiosyncratic barriers to perceiving problems and prescribing change.* Decision makers are heavily influenced by their personal experiences. Walter Isaacson, vice-chairman of the Louisiana Recovery Authority, was initially an advocate of aggressive, top-down urban planning as a precondition to the disbursement of Community Block Development Grants and other publicly controlled funds set aside for recovery efforts after Katrina. He reversed field when he learned that his family's neighborhood, Broadmoor, had been targeted for bulldozing and conversion into green space. Perhaps belatedly, Walter Isaacson came to appreciate that a planning official's preferred "urban footprint" may demand the bulldozing of someone else's neighborhood. *See* Jim Chen, *Law among the Ruins, in* LAW AND RECOVERY FROM DISASTER: HURRICANE KATRINA 1, 3 (Robin Paul Malloy ed., 2009).

To be sure, failed policies are more readily remedied than broader social and environmental problems, such as economic inequality or global climate change. The structure of this chapter and of this book as a whole reflects this instinct. We have focused so far on the initial allocation of governmental authority and the actual implementation of emergency response measures, leaving to later chapters more diffuse issues of compensation, risk spreading, prevention, mitigation, and long-term environmental protection. The immediate subject of social vulnerability and its contribution to a natural disaster illustrates the interplay of governmental, economic, social, and environmental forces. Precisely because there is no such thing as a strictly natural disaster, government should focus in the first instance on matters more within its control, hopeful that success in overcoming economic and social injustice will lessen the suffering from disasters.

2. Consider this summary of human factors that contribute to the "mortality, displacement, [and] economic destruction" wrought by disasters:

> The first of these is pre-disaster preparedness and mitigation. From constructing housing (or levees) to withstand natural [shocks] to pre-positioning adequate relief supplies and preparing realistic evacuation plans, the ability of communities and societies to plan ahead to resist disaster is critical.
>
> Second, the in-disaster coping capacities of affected populations: are there resources on which they are able to fall back? In some hunger-prone regions of the world, for example, 'famine foods' — not eaten in good times but growing wild and freely available — can provide some meager support in periods of scarcity. In developed ones, have communities been able to build up and ensure access to stockpiles of canned goods, drinking water and first aid supplies? Or has their ability to build up a margin of safety been whittled away by poverty and marginalisation?
>
> Third, the immediacy, quantity, efficiency and coverage of the disaster response: each element is critical. Response may be timely but insufficient,

ignoring key communities; or, as is all too frequent in the case of major "CNN catastrophes" which creep onto the world's television screens, the response may eventually be large but months too late. . . .

Finally, the longer term commitment of governments and other actors to post-disaster recovery: long after the flood waters and the TV cameras both recede, reconstruction and rehabilitation are critical in rebuilding shattered lives and livelihoods. But continued commitment (and investment) at this point can capitalise on a unique opportunity to build towards the reduction of future disasters.

Stephen Jackson, *Un/natural Disasters, Here and There*, http://understanding katrina.ssrc.org/Jackson (June 11, 2009).

3. Katrina capped a global year of misery that began with a natural disaster of even greater geographic and social scale. Roughly a quarter of a million people died in the Indian Ocean tsunami of December 26, 2004. Another million people were displaced. Though spread across three continents, the populations most directly affected by the tsunami were united in poverty and their vulnerability to one of the most destructive disasters in history:

HUMAN RIGHTS CENTER, UNIVERSITY OF CALIFORNIA, BERKELEY

After the Tsunami: Human Rights of Vulnerable Populations 1 (October 2005)

The tsunami of December 26, 2004, devastated thousands of communities along the coastline of the Indian Ocean. More than 240,000 people were killed. Tens of thousands went missing and are presumed dead, and more than a million people were displaced. Those most affected by the tsunami were the poor, including fisher folk, coastal workers with small retail or tourist businesses, workers in the tourism industry, migrants, and those who farmed close to coastal areas. The majority of those who died were women and children.

Immediately following the tsunami, international aid agencies feared that human traffickers might seize the opportunity to compel those most vulnerable (women, children, and migrant workers) into situations of forced labor. . . . [O]ther human rights problems, including arbitrary arrests, recruitment of children into fighting forces, discrimination in aid distribution, enforced relocation, sexual and gender-based violence, loss of documentation, as well as issues of restitution, and land and property tenure soon emerged in certain tsunami-affected areas.

As we have seen in the aftermath of hurricane Katrina, which devastated coastal areas in the southern United States, natural disasters often catch national and local governments and relief agencies unprepared to deal with the massive exigencies of emergency relief and management, and can expose victims of these catastrophes to violations of human rights.

Victims of natural disasters are protected by a host of human rights treaties and agreements. Both the UN Guiding Principles on Internal Displacement and the Sphere Project's Humanitarian Charter and Minimum Standards in Disaster Response protect victims of natural disaster and guide relief efforts to ensure that those displaced receive access to adequate and essential relief — including food, shelter, and medical care. These guiding principles maintain that internally displaced persons (IDP) have the right to request and to receive protection and assistance from national authorities who, in turn, have the primary duty and responsibility to protect and assist populations within their jurisdiction.

Natural disasters can exacerbate pre-existing vulnerabilities of populations already at risk. Poverty-stricken groups living in substandard housing, on unstable ground, or in flood plains are usually the principal victims of these disasters. Often these groups have experienced ongoing discrimination because of their ethnicity, religion, class, or gender, which has left them living in fragile physical environments. Moreover, pre-existing civil war or a history of ongoing human rights abuses can complicate or interfere with aid relief and reconstruction.

In countries where corruption and bureaucratic incompetence are rife, certain individuals and groups may manipulate their political connections to receive or distribute aid at the expense of others. Still other groups may receive little or no aid because of their ethnicity, religion, gender, age, or social standing. These abuses can leave individuals and families at risk and prolong the time they have to stay in poorly built and even dangerous camps and shelters for internally displaced people.

Isolated in camps, the internally displaced often are sidelined as government officials in distant towns and cities formulate and implement resettlement and rebuilding programs, sometimes in favor of special interests. Uncoordinated relief efforts run the risk of exacerbating these problems, especially where there is weak government oversight of the activities of international agencies and aid organizations. A tension can develop between government appropriating all decision-making to itself or allowing nongovernmental organizations to carry out their missions as they see fit. Lack of a middle ground leaves survivors with no one to turn to for assistance.

NOTES AND QUESTIONS

1. Compare Hurricane Katrina with the Indian Ocean tsunami. What might American policy makers learn from an even greater tragedy that spanned the entire Indian Ocean rim? Conversely, can global efforts against staggering losses to natural disaster learn from domestic failures in one of the world's wealthiest nations? The parallels between Katrina and the tsunami are fairly obvious: catastrophic loss of life and property, disparate impact based on social and economic status, and a distressing degree of official incompetence. Some salient differences, however, do distinguish the two disasters:

    a. *Preexisting human rights violations.* Whatever else might be said of inequality, civil rights, and human dignity in the United States, none of Katrina's victims were exposed to conscription into civil wars or opportunistic human trafficking. North America, to put it mildly, knows nothing of the misery that afflicts less developed parts of the world.

    b. *Corruption and lack of transparency and accountability in government.* Again, official fecklessness in America falls short of the sheer ineptitude of governments in many of the world's poorest countries. Katrina's impact on New Orleans and the Gulf Coast was the subject of extensive public discussion. The House of Representatives, the Senate, and the White House all delivered scathing reports on the failures of the response effort, complete with concrete platforms for reform. Some officials perceived as having performed poorly during Katrina, such as former FEMA chairman Michael Brown, lost power.

c. *Wealth, poverty, and inequality.* According to the World Bank's gauges of absolute poverty, the world's poorest subsist on $1 per day in purchasing power parity (relative to the value of U.S. dollars in 1985). Such extreme levels of poverty are unknown — and politically unthinkable — in the United States. By the same token, *relative* poverty exists everywhere, and by this standard the United States fares poorly, at least as compared with other industrialized countries. According to the United Nations, *see* UNITED NATIONS, HUMAN DEVELOPMENT INDICATORS 270 (2005), the United States reported a Gini coefficient of 40.8, which corresponds to a higher level of economic inequality than either India (32.5) or Bangladesh (31.8), two significantly poorer countries that suffered mightily during the 2004 tsunami, *see id.* at 272.[2]

d. *War.* Nearly a century and a half after Appomattox Court House, every American combat veteran is eligible for membership in the Veterans of Foreign Wars. Many other countries, sadly, continue to experience war as a thoroughly domestic phenomenon. Most Americans have no personal experience with the conscription of children or the exploitation of civilians as human shields against organized violence.

2. In the end, Katrina and the Indian Ocean tsunami should not be compared as part of an exercise to determine which victims suffered more, but rather as part of a learning experience by which policymakers might minimize future suffering. Taking account of geographic, social, economic, and political differences represents an important step in that learning process. "If the Indian Ocean Tsunami and Hurricane Katrina can be said to have any 'lessons' for us, it is to suggest that western developed countries may have as much to learn about disaster preparedness, management and recovery from non-western developing countries in terms of community-based assistance and the integrated flexible use of technology as the latter do from the former in terms of technocratic know-how and scientific expertise." Greg Bankoff, *The Tale of the Three Pigs: Taking Another Look at Vulnerability in the Light of the Indian Ocean Tsunami and Hurricane Katrina,* http://understandingkatrina. ssrc.org/Bankoff (June 11, 2009).

3. The Berkeley tsunami report identifies two sources of international norms that might govern disaster relief efforts. One of these is the United Nations' Guiding Principles on Internal Displacement, which will receive more consideration in Chapter 9 (international law). The other is the handbook of the Sphere Project, a collaborative effort of the Red Cross, Red Crescent, and other humanitarian organizations. A substantial portion of the Sphere Project's handbook outlines the "Humanitarian Charter" to which participating organizations aspire. The handbook's "Minimum Standards," by

---

2. The Gini coefficient is a measure of economic inequality; a higher score on this gauge indicates greater disparities in income within a country. *See* Philip M. Dixon, Jacob Weiner, Thomas Mitchell-Olds & Robert Woodley, *Bootstrapping the Gini Coefficient of Inequality,* 68 ECOLOGY 1548 (1988).

contrast, "are based on agencies' experience of providing humanitarian assistance":

> Though the achievement of the standards depends on a range of factors, many of which may be beyond our control, we commit ourselves to attempt consistently to achieve them and we expect to be held to account accordingly. We invite other humanitarian actors, including states themselves, to adopt these standards as accepted norms. . . .
>
> [W]e commit ourselves to make every effort to ensure that people affected by disasters have access to at least the minimum requirements (water, sanitation, food, nutrition, shelter and health care) to satisfy their basic right to life with dignity. To this end we will continue to advocate that governments and other parties meet their obligations under international human rights law, international humanitarian law and refugee law.

The Sphere Project Handbook: Humanitarian Charter and Minimum Standards in Disaster Response 19 (2004).

4. Social vulnerability in times of disaster raises questions of human rights. How can international human rights law balance the proposition that environmental quality is "essential to . . . the enjoyment of human rights," Stockholm Declaration, Report of the United Nations Conference on the Human Environment, U.N. Doc. A/Conf.48/14, 11 I.L.M. 1416, 1416 (1972) (preamble), with the equally solemn pronouncement that economic development is also a "universal and inalienable right and an integral part of fundamental human rights"? Vienna Declaration and Programme of Action, U.N. Doc. A/CONF.157/24, *adopted at* Vienna, June 14-25, 1993, *reprinted in* 32 I.L.M. 1661 (1993). Environmental sustainability may hinge on a global transition from poverty to affluence and from authoritarianism to democracy rather than the suppression of economic development. *See* Jack M. Hollander, The Real Environmental Crisis: Why Poverty, Not Affluence, Is the Environment's Number One Enemy (2003). Of the world's myriad environmental problems, "persistent poverty may turn out to be the most aggravating and destructive." Patrick Low, *Trade and the Environment: What Worries the Developing Countries?*, 23 Envtl. L. 705, 706 (1993).

5. Katrina and the tsunami exposed serious flaws in several nations' capacity for preparedness, response, mitigation, and recovery in the event of natural disaster. Many of those flaws are attributable to—or at least exacerbated by—social, economic, and political inequalities expressed by the catchall phrase, "social vulnerability." To what extent is the global community willing to engage problems of social vulnerability once a single, catastrophic event has subsided? Or is the world doomed to remain inherently unequal and unjust—and correspondingly unprepared for the next tragedy that blends natural calamity with human injustice?

B. THE SCARS OF RACE, CLASS, AND INJUSTICE

Among Hurricane Katrina's first casualties was any expectation that the storm and the governmental response to it would deal equally with all victims, without regard to race or class. In a survey of Katrina evacuees living in Houston, "68 percent of respondents thought the federal government would have responded more quickly if people trapped in the floodwaters were 'wealthier and white rather than poorer and black.'" U.S. HOUSE OF REPRESENTATIVES, A FAILURE OF INITIATIVE: FINAL REPORT OF THE SELECT BIPARTISAN COMMITTEE TO INVESTIGATE THE PREPARATION FOR AND RESPONSE TO HURRICANE KATRINA 19 (2006). At its worst, the storm exposed longstanding racial, social, and economic inequities. To be effective and legitimate, the legal response to disasters must address these injustices.

SUSAN L. CUTTER, THE GEOGRAPHY OF SOCIAL VULNERABILITY:
RACE, CLASS, AND CATASTROPHE

---

http://understandingkatrina.ssrc.org/Cutter (June 11, 2009)

The revelations of inadequate response to the hurricane's aftermath are not just about failures in emergency response at the local, state, and federal levels or failures in the overall emergency management system. They are also about failures of the social support systems for America's impoverished — the largely invisible inner city poor. The former can be rectified quickly (months to years) through organizational restructuring or training; the latter requires much more time, resources, and the political will to redress social inequities and inequalities that have been sustained for more than a half century and show little signs of dissipating.

How did we arrive at such a confluence of natural and social vulnerabilities manifested as the Hurricane Katrina disaster? This complex emergency began with geography — the spatial interaction of humans and their environment over time. Officially founded in 1718 by Jean-Baptiste Le Moyne de Bienville, New Orleans was strategically located at the crossroads of three navigable water bodies, Lake Pontchartrain, the Gulf of Mexico, and the Mississippi River. Important primarily as a trading depot for French fur trappers, the city evolved into one of the most important ports in America providing a gateway to the nation's agricultural riches.

The original settlement was on the highest ground in the bayou, Vieux Carré (the French Quarter), which later became the heart and soul of the modern city. How prescient for the early settlers to build on the highest ground available. As the settlement grew in the ensuing decades, New Orleans became a major American port city and a sprawling metropolis sandwiched between and surrounded by water. . . .

To reduce the natural risks of flooding, the physical environment surrounding New Orleans was re-engineered, spawning an era of structural river control. Levees were built to control the flow of the mighty Mississippi, but they were also built to contain flooding from Lake Pontchartrain, especially useful during hurricane season. . . . Instead of seeing the deposition of alluvium that one expects in a deltaic coastline, the levees channeled the river and its sediment, destroying protective wetlands south and east of the city. With many areas of the city below sea level, even heavy rainfall became a problem filling the city with water just like a giant punchbowl. An elaborate pumping system was required to keep the city dry during heavy rains, let alone tropical storms. What would happen during a hurricane, a levee failure, or an intentional levee breach used to divert floodwaters away from the city as was done in 1927?

Concurrent with the physical transformation of the city, a new social geography was being created as well. The South's segregated past was best seen in the spatial and social evolution of southern cities, including New Orleans. Migration from the rural impoverished areas to the city was followed by white flight from urban areas to more suburban communities. Public housing was constructed to cope with Black population influxes during the 1950s and 1960s and in a pattern repeated throughout America, the housing was invariably located in the most undesirable areas — along major transportation corridors, on reclaimed land, or next to industrial facilities. Employment opportunities were limited for inner city residents as jobs moved outward from the central city to suburban locations, or overseas as the process of globalization reduced even further the number of low skilled jobs. The most impoverished lived in squalor-like conditions concentrated in certain neighborhoods within cities, with little or no employment, poor education, and little hope for the future for their children or grandchildren. It is against this backdrop of the social geography of cities and the differential access to resources that we can best understand the Hurricane Katrina disaster.

Socially created vulnerabilities are largely ignored in the hazards and disaster literature because they are so hard to measure and quantify. Social vulnerability is partially a product of social inequalities — those social factors and forces that create the susceptibility of various groups to harm, and in turn affect their ability to respond, and bounce back (resilience) after the disaster. But it is much more than that. Social vulnerability involves the basic provision of health care, the livability of places, overall indicators of quality of life, and accessibility to lifelines (goods, services, emergency response personnel), capital, and political representation.

Race and class are certainly factors that help explain the social vulnerability in the South, while ethnicity plays an additional role in many cities. When the middle classes (both White and Black) abandon a city, the disparities between the very rich and the very poor expand. Add to this an increasing elderly population, the homeless, transients (including tourists), and other special needs populations, and the prospects for evacuating a city during times of emergencies becomes a daunting challenge for most American cities. What is a major challenge for other cities became a virtual impossibility for New Orleans. Those that could muster the personal resources evacuated the city. With no welfare check (the hurricane struck near the end of the month), little food, and no help from the city, state, or federal officials, the poor were forced to ride out the storm in their homes or move to the shelters of last resort. This is the enduring face of Hurricane Katrina — poor, black, single mothers, young, and old — struggling just to survive; options limited by the ineffectiveness of preparedness and the inadequacy of response. . . .

As a nation, we have very little experience with evacuating cities from natural hazards. . . . Crisis relocation planning was the norm during the height of the Reagan administration, but many social scientists scoffed at the implausibility of the effort as a precautionary measure against a nuclear attack.

Our collective experience with evacuations is based on chemical spills or toxic releases, planning for nuclear power plant accidents, and hurricanes. In most cases, but certainly not all, the evacuations have been in rural or suburban places, not a major U.S. city. . . . The potential differences in response are critical and highlight the difficulties in emergency preparedness for major cities. The number of large urban hospitals, the dependence on public transportation, and the need for mass sheltering all complicate preparedness efforts in these dense multi-ethnic and multi-racial cities. In addition to the sheer number of people at risk, emergency managers have the additional task of identifying those residents who may be the most vulnerable — the poor, the infirm, the elderly, the homeless, women, and children. The nescient result is an ever-widening disparity in society's ability to cope with more persistent social and economic problems in urban areas, let alone a potential mass impact event of unknown origin. This is the story of Hurricane Katrina and its aftermath. . . .

Just as there is variation in the physical landscape, the landscape of social inequity has increased the division between rich and poor in this country and has led to the increasing social vulnerability of our residents, especially to coastal hazards. Strained race relations and the seeming differential response to the disaster suggest[] that in planning for future catastrophes, we need to not only look at the natural environment in the development of mitigation programs, but the social environment as well. It is the interaction between nature and society that produces the vulnerability of places. While physical vulnerability is reduced through the construction of disaster-resistant buildings, changes in land use, and restoration of wetlands and floodways, a marked reduction in social vulnerability will require an improvement in the overall quality of life for the inner city poor. We should not have the equivalent of developing world conditions in a nation as wealthy as the United States. This is the tragedy of Hurricane Katrina. . . .

Disasters will happen. To lessen their impacts in the future, we need to reduce our social vulnerability and increase disaster resilience with improvements in the social conditions and living standards in our cities. We need to build (and rebuild) damaged housing and infrastructure in harmony with nature and design cities to be resilient to environmental threats even if it means smaller, more livable places, and fewer profits for land and urban developers and a smaller tax base for the city. Disasters are income neutral and color-blind. Their impacts, however, are not.

NOTES AND QUESTIONS

1. Reconsider this statement by Susan Cutter: "Social vulnerability is partially a product of social inequalities — those social factors and forces that create the susceptibility of various groups to harm, and in turn affect their ability to respond, and bounce back (resilience) after the disaster." This pivotal passage suggests that social vulnerability consists of two distinct components: the *susceptibility* of certain groups to harm and the *resilience* of these groups. *See generally* Susan L. Cutter, Bryan. J. Boruff & W. Lynn Shirley, *Social Vulnerability to Environmental Hazards*, 84 Soc. Sci. Q. 242 (2003).

a. *Susceptibility* is an *ex ante* quality; it is already in place when disaster strikes. Inequality in New Orleans and other parts of the South has taken hundreds of years to build. Differences in living conditions, wealth, and power rendered the poorest, often black victims of Katrina susceptible to disproportionate loss.

b. *Resilience,* by contrast, assumes importance after the fact. Rebuilding destroyed communities demands extraordinary human and material resources. Capital available — and often taken for granted — for recovery in more affluent communities may simply not exist in poorer communities. Crucial physical and social infrastructure, often strained or undermined by disaster and its aftermath, is not as readily reestablished.

2. Consider also this definition of vulnerability:

> By vulnerability we mean the characteristics of a person or group in terms of their capacity to anticipate, cope with, resist, and recover from the impact of a natural hazard. It involves a combination of factors that determine the degree to which someone's life and livelihood is put at risk by a discrete and identifiable event in nature or in society.

PIERS BLAIKIE, TERRY CANNON, IAN DAVIS & BEN WISNER, AT RISK: NATURAL HAZARDS, PEOPLE'S VULNERABILITY AND DISASTERS 9 (1994).

B.E. AGUIRRE, DIALECTICS OF VULNERABILITY AND RESILIENCE

14 Geo. J. on Poverty L. & Pol'y 39, 41-45 (2007)

The complexity inherent in the concepts of vulnerability and resilience is in part due to the multiple systems in which they operate simultaneously . . . and from the interactions and inter-effects that take place among these systems. Resilience is an example of morphostasis — that is, a process directed to preserve the social system. Vulnerability is a type of morphogenesis, for it facilitates changes in the system, at times by becoming more differentiated. Vulnerability is a synonym of exhaustion, impotence, weakness, or exposure to harm. [There are] three types of vulnerabilities: a pre-existing condition in a social organization; a social product, in which vulnerability is the outcome of the differential distribution of power and privilege in society; and bio-physical risks associated with specific geographical sites. [An even more] comprehensive list of vulnerabilities . . . includes natural, physical, economic, social, political, technical, ideological, cultural, educational, ecological, and institutional risks, all of these subsumed in the concept of global vulnerability. It is seldom noted, however, that from an open system dialectic perspective, a state of vulnerability of social organization reveals the presence and operation of risks and may constitute a window of opportunity calling for mitigations, which may improve its resilience and its adaptive capacity in the face of crises and disasters. The absence of an awareness of vulnerability may also be associated with the presence of unknown risks. Known vulnerability illuminates the need of social organizations to change so as to minimize risks and increase their capability to adjust to their environment, and may bring about efforts at mitigation. . . .

Resilience has been defined in many ways, including an ability to "bounce back" and continue to function; predict and prevent potential problems; improvise and recombine resources in new ways; develop a collective and shared vision of dangers and what to do about them; and constantly monitor threatening contextual conditions. . . . [R]esilience "is also about the opportunities that disturbance opens up in terms of recombination of evolved structures and processes, renewal of the system and emergence of new trajectories." Resilience is partly a recursive function of conscious awareness, planning, and training that anticipates or responds to the presence of vulnerabilities and tries to mitigate and provide solutions to them. These are all dimensions of resilient systems. Resilient actions do not merely reflect the capacity of systems to reconstitute themselves as they existed prior to the crisis, but show a system's ability to absorb, respond, recover, and reorganize from an internally or externally induced set of demands which reveal the presence of vulnerability and bring about mitigation efforts. As indicated previously, it is a never-ending open process, for multiple sources of often unanticipated demands create changes in the known dynamics of the systems. Past experiences cannot be used as the only source of information to anticipate new risks. Imagination, creativity, and careful historical reconstructions of past disastrous events, including both cross national and international scientific assessments of major crises and disasters, are needed to attempt to anticipate and prevent new risks' effects. Inherent in the very solution meant to bring about temporary adaptation is the creation of new and frequently unanticipated vulnerabilities, resulting in the need for new efforts at mitigation and resilience. This is due in part to the incomplete nature of human knowledge, our inability to foresee the multilevel and contradictory impacts of our actions regardless of our intent, and the weight of traditions which limit creative adaptation, as well as exogenous changes in the natural and social environments. . . .

Resilience is also the ability to take action in anticipation of demands and known vulnerabilities to forestall or minimize them, although . . . the effectiveness of such efforts is always open to the vagaries of limited human knowledge, entrenched interest, and inability to come up with solutions outside prevailing cultural practices. [A] study of Sydney, Australia, [has] demonstrated that the city so far has escaped major disasters mostly because of a relatively benign natural environment even as other vulnerabilities, such as environmental degradation and poverty, are largely ignored. What could happen in less benign environments is evidenced by Katrina, for it was an announced catastrophe that revealed the rigidities of political interests and narrow-minded public service. Local scientists for at least a decade earlier had outlined what would happen in the absence of adaptive change, and how to bring such change about, which involved learning to live with the Mississippi River rather than against it. A contrasting example is the "growing with the sea" strategy of the Netherlands, in which the Dutch recognized that their coastal mitigation measures were not working and adopted a system that allows for occasional extreme flooding while minimizing the damages. These cases show that often disasters are the indirect effects of political traditions, entrenched economic and social power, and the presence or lack of leadership, rather than a lack of scientific knowledge about what needs to be done. These processes of political economy often determine whether or not societies recognize their risks and associated vulnerabilities, and whether they engage in mitigation efforts that enhance their resilience and their adaptive capacity.

Resilience of social organizations is one of a number of factors that determine their adaptive capacity. Changes which enhance resilience take place neither in a linear fashion nor without conflicting objectives: policy changes are often contentious, technological changes have unintended consequences, demographic transitions can bring their own pressures through changes in resource needs, and the built environment is subject to constant maintenance needs and changes in usage. The challenge for the incorporation of resiliency is to identify what enhances the ability of social organizations to rebound effectively, taking into account the actual physical, biological, personality, social, and cultural systems that are present and the limited amount of economic and other resources that may be available to lessen vulnerability.

In an immediate sense, disasters are the outcome of the interaction between a hazard and a social organization with a portfolio of risks, vulnerabilities, and resilience. Disasters are disturbances that have the "potential to create opportunity for doing new things, for innovation and for development." They are not solely caused by vulnerabilities, but also, counter-intuitively, by previous efforts at mitigation and enhancement of resilience. Disasters are moments of rupture in the "normal" or taken-for-granted operations of social organizations. They reveal the critical balance existing among vulnerability, mitigation, resilience, and community recovery, and the extent to which the social organization has not been able to adapt effectively to its environments. Both vulnerability and resilience fluctuate over time and space, allowing for the differential impacts of hazards on the built and social systems. A dialectical approach to vulnerability and resilience to disaster necessitates a shift in our conceptualizations from discrete strategies to reduce disaster-related risks and vulnerability to more dynamic, holistic, and integrated approaches to enhance societal adaptation.

NOTES AND QUESTIONS

1. May disaster victims seek legal relief from the officials who supervised an emergency preparedness and response effort that appears not only to have been wholly inadequate but also arguably to have exposed blacks to greater harm than similarly situated whites? Aside from the question of whether government had a duty to act, *cf.* DeShaney v. Winnebago County Dept. of Soc. Servs., 489 U.S. 189 (1989), formidable barriers block the path to relief. A direct claim that government inaction violates disaster victims' civil rights seems remote at best.

   a. Constitutional law does not recognize an equal protection claim based solely on the claim that otherwise neutral conduct has a racially disparate impact. *See* Washington v. Davis, 426 U.S. 229, 242 (1976). An equal protection violation typically hinges on "[p]roof of racially discriminatory intent or purpose." Village of Arlington Heights v. Metropolitan Housing Dev. Corp., 429 U.S. 252, 265 (1977); *accord, e.g.,* City of Cuyahoga Falls v. Buckeye Community Hope Found., 538 U.S. 188, 194 (2003). The government must have chosen a particular course "because of" and not merely "in spite of" the decision's adverse impact on "an identifiable group." Personnel Adm'r v. Feeney, 442 U.S. 256, 279 (1979); *accord* McCleskey v. Kemp, 481 U.S. 279, 298 (1987).

b. On the other hand, when even neutral legislation or governmental conduct produces a clear pattern that cannot be explained except on racial grounds, a constitutional violation may lie. *See* Gomillion v. Lightfoot, 364 U.S. 339 (1960); Yick Wo v. Hopkins, 118 U.S. 356 (1886); *cf.* Lane v. Wilson, 307 U.S. 268 (1939); Guinn v. United States, 238 U.S. 347 (1915). The appearance of "a clear pattern, unexplainable on grounds other than race," makes the "evidentiary inquiry . . . relatively easy." *Arlington Heights,* 429 U.S. at 266. Because cases presenting "a pattern [this] stark" are "rare," however, "impact alone is [seldom] determinative, and [a reviewing] Court must look to other evidence." *Id.*

c. In most cases, evidence of "invidious discriminatory purpose" demands a deeper inquiry into the "historical background" underlying official conduct. *Arlington Heights,* 429 U.S. at 267. "The specific sequence of events leading up the challenged decision also may shed some light on the decisionmaker's purposes." *Id.* Departures from "the normal procedural sequence" or from substantive decisionmaking criteria "also might afford evidence that improper purposes are playing a role." *Id.* Finally, "[t]he legislative or administrative history may be highly relevant, especially where there are contemporary statements by members of the decisionmaking body, minutes of its meetings, or reports." *Id.* at 268. What evidence can be found in the record of official conduct during the preparation for a hypothetical hurricane hitting New Orleans, during Katrina itself, and throughout recovery after the storm?

d. The use of legislative or administrative history gives rise to another basis for relief, albeit one rarely encountered. The Supreme Court has invalidated an otherwise facially neutral law that disenfranchised all persons convicted of crimes of moral turpitude, citing statements showing that the law's proponents intended to prevent blacks from voting. *See* Hunter v. Underwood, 421 U.S. 222 (1985). *But cf.* Palmer v. Thompson, 403 U.S. 217, 224 (1971) ("[N]o case in this Court has held that a legislative act may violate equal protection solely because of the motivations of the men who voted for it.").

e. "In many instances, to recognize the limited probative value of disproportionate impact is merely to acknowledge the 'heterogeneity' of the Nation's population." *Arlington Heights,* 429 U.S. at 266 n.15 (quoting Jefferson v. Hackney, 406 U.S. 535, 548 (1972)).

f. Notwithstanding *Washington v. Davis* and *Arlington Heights,* the Supreme Court is more willing in certain contexts to infer discriminatory purpose from disparate impact. *See, e.g.,* Shaw v. Reno, 509 U.S. 630 (1993) (gerrymandering); Batson v. Kentucky, 476 U.S. 79 (1986) (peremptory jury challenges); Rogers v. Lodge, 458 U.S. 613 (1982) (vote dilution); Swann v. Charlotte-Mecklenburg Bd. of Educ., 402 U.S. 1 (1971) (school desegregation). Does anything about natural disasters, the nature of social vulnerability during disaster, or the role of government warrant a comparable judicial willingness to infer purpose from effect? Or, as in the context of selective prosecution, must a claim alleging a racially uneven response to a disaster "draw on 'ordinary equal protection standards'"? United States v. Armstrong, 517 U.S. 456, 465 (1996).

2. The Eighth Amendment supplies another constitutional analogy by which policy vis-à-vis vulnerable populations during a disaster may be judged. A prison official's "deliberate indifference" to a substantial risk of serious harm to an inmate violates the prohibition on "cruel and unusual punishments." *See, e.g.,* Helling v. McKinney, 509 U.S. 25 (1993); Wilson v. Seiter, 501 U.S. 294 (1991); Estelle v. Gamble, 429 U.S. 97 (1976).

a. "Deliberate indifference" demands that an official have a state of mind more blameworthy than negligence. In considering a claim that inadequate medical care violated the Eighth Amendment, the Supreme Court has distinguished "deliberate indifference to serious medical needs of prisoners," *Estelle,* 429 U.S. at 104, from mere "negligen[ce] in diagnosing or treating a medical condition," *id.* at 106. Transcending the "ordinary lack of due care for the prisoner's interests or safety," Whitley v. Albers, 475 U.S. 312, 319 (1986), deliberate indifference ultimately requires subjective intent:

> [A] prison official cannot be found liable under the Eighth Amendment for denying an inmate humane conditions of confinement unless the official knows of and disregards an excessive risk to inmate health or safety; the official must both be aware of facts from which the inference could be drawn that a substantial risk of serious harm exists, and he must also draw the inference.

Farmer v. Brennan, 511 U.S. 825, 837 (1994).

b. Perhaps the officials in charge of preparing for and responding to Katrina can be accused of *passive* rather than deliberate indifference:

> [R]acial exclusion . . . today happens not so much through active bigotry as it does through the tacit exclusions created by these sorts of unstated, unconsidered social habits. . . . [I]f your social network is, for purely historical reasons, defined by color lines that were drawn long ago in a different and undeniably widely bigoted age, then you don't have to be a bigot yourself to be perpetuating the institutional structures of racial exclusion. . . . This was exactly Illinois Senator Barack Obama's point when he declared on the Senate floor that the poor response to Katrina was not "evidence of active malice," but merely the result of "a continuation of passive indifference." These structural exclusions matter very much for one's total life opportunities, including crucially one's economic opportunities—and thus greatly affect one's opportunities to, say, escape from deadly hurricanes.

Nils Gilman, *What Katrina Teaches about the Meaning of Racism,* http://understandingkatrina.ssrc.org/Gilman (June 11, 2009). Is "passive indifference" less blameworthy than its deliberate counterpart?

3. For yet another legal perspective on vulnerability, consider U.S. Sentencing Guidelines §3A1.1, which instructs judges to enhance the sentence of a federal criminal defendant who "intentionally selected any victim or any property as the object of the offense of conviction because of the actual or perceived race, color, religion, national origin, ethnicity, gender, disability, or sexual orientation of any person" or who "knew or should have known that a victim of the offense was a vulnerable victim."

a. The Guidelines are structured so that the presence of "race, color, religion, national origin, ethnicity, gender, disability, or sexual orientation" automatically qualifies a defendant for an enhanced sentence, independent of any inquiry into the victim's vulnerability.

b. With respect to the sentencing enhancement for a "vulnerable victim," the following three-pronged test applies:

> The enhancement may be applied where: (1) the victim was particularly susceptible or vulnerable to the criminal conduct; (2) the defendant knew or should have known of this susceptibility or vulnerability; and (3) this vulnerability or susceptibility facilitated the defendant's crime in some manner; that is, there was "a nexus between the victim's vulnerability and the crime's ultimate success."

United States v. Iannone, 184 F.3d 214, 220 (3d Cir. 1999); *accord, e.g.,* United States v. Zats, 298 F.3d 182, 186 (3d Cir. 2002). At least the first two prongs of this test can be applied by analogy to officials accused of failing to address social vulnerabilities during a natural disaster. Certain victims are "particularly susceptible or vulnerable" in times of disaster, and public officials "kn[o]w or should have known of this susceptibility or vulnerability." Because the Sentencing Guidelines are an artifact of criminal law, the analogy degrades somewhat with respect to the third prong. But some connection remains. The presence of a "nexus between the victim's vulnerability" and the social harm attributable to a natural disaster arguably should bear on the degree of official responsibility for shortcomings in remedying social vulnerabilities through preparation, response, mitigation, or recovery.

4. In assessing the moral (if not legal) culpability that should be assigned for the socially lopsided effects of natural disasters, consider the following account:

> It is society's most vulnerable who were "left behind" by government efforts to assess, to plan for, and to respond to a storm of Katrina's magnitude. And this was predictably so. A host of government decisions were made — each of which had the potential to mitigate or exacerbate the effects of a hurricane for the people of New Orleans — against a social, economic, and political backdrop that made the disproportionate impacts of certain government choices virtually inevitable. Where the choice was to forego the basic services and protections typically provided by a government, it should have been clear to decision makers precisely who would be left to fend for themselves.
>
> Twenty-eight percent of people in New Orleans live in poverty. Of these, 84 percent are African American. Twenty-three percent of people five years

and older living in New Orleans are disabled. An estimated 15,000 to 17,000 men, women, and children in the New Orleans area are homeless. The lowest lying areas of New Orleans tend to be populated by those without economic or political resources. The city's Lower Ninth Ward, for example, which was especially hard hit and completely inundated by water, is among its poorest and lowest lying areas. Ninety-eight percent of its residents are African American. . . . "[I]n New Orleans, water flows away from money. Those with resources who control where the drainage goes have always chosen to live on the high ground. So the people in the low areas were the hardest hit."

Of the households living in poverty, many have no access to a car: 21,787 of these households without a car are black; 2,606 are white. This lack of access became crucial, given an evacuation plan premised on the ability of people to get in their cars and drive out of New Orleans.

CENTER FOR PROGRESSIVE REFORM, AN UNNATURAL DISASTER: THE AFTERMATH OF HURRICANE KATRINA 34-35 (2005).

5. The Congressional Research Service has quantified the unequal social impact of Hurricane Katrina:

Hurricane Katrina disproportionately impacted communities where the poor and minorities, mostly African Americans, resided. The three states where communities were damaged or flooded by the hurricane rank among the poorest in the nation. According to the 2000 Census, Mississippi ranked second only to the District of Columbia in its poverty rate; Louisiana was right behind it ranking third, and Alabama ranked sixth. CRS estimates that about one-fifth of the population most directly impacted by the storm was poor. That poverty rate (21%) was well above the national poverty rate of 12.4% recorded in the 2000 Census. . . . In addition, over 30% of the most impacted population had incomes below one-and-one-half times the poverty line and over 40% had income below twice the poverty line. . . .

The hurricane's impact on New Orleans also took a disproportionate toll on African Americans. An estimated 310,000 black people were directly impacted by the storm, largely due to flooding in Orleans Parish. Blacks are estimated to have accounted for 44% of storm victims. In Orleans Parish, an estimated 272,000 black people were displaced by flooding or damage, accounting for 73% of the population affected by the storm in the parish. In contrast, an estimated 101,000 non-black people in Orleans Parish were displaced by flooding or damage, accounting for about 63% of the non-black population living in the parish; still a high proportion affected, but somewhat less than that experienced by blacks.

Among blacks living in Orleans Parish who were most likely displaced by the storm, over one-third (89,000 people, or 34.0% of displaced blacks) were estimated to have been poor, based on 2000 Census data. Among non-black (predominantly white) persons living in the parish who were likely displaced by the storm, an estimated 14.6% (14,000) were poor.

Thomas Gabe, Gene Falk & Maggie McCarty, *Hurricane Katrina: Social-Demographic Characteristics of Impacted Areas* 14, 16-17 (Nov. 4, 2005) (CRS Order Code RL33141).

6. Katrina's disparate impact on poor and non-white individuals has been characterized as part of a larger pattern of "environmental injustice":

> Katrina . . . was an exceptionally large echo of a socioeconomic political condition known popularly as environmental injustice, the longstanding pattern whereby people of color and the poor are exposed to greater environmental risk while receiving fewer environmental amenities. Between the two, race has a statistically stronger link than class, and recent reports reveal that the association between race and environmental hazards is increasing. If we examine the background policies and decisions that ultimately led to the devastation in the wake of Katrina, we begin to see the event as part of this larger pattern.
>
> For example, planners anticipated that approximately 100,000 transit-dependent residents of New Orleans, mostly poor and black, would have no private transportation out of the city in an emergency. The federal, state and local governments made no provision for them. Instead, evacuation plans relied on private automobiles. Environmental justice activists, citing Hurricane Hugo in 1989 and the 2005 release of chlorine gas from a train crash in South Carolina, note that this is not the first time people of color have been overlooked by emergency planners and then received slower assistance afterwards.

Eileen Gauna, *Katrina and Environmental Injustice,* http://jurist.law.pitt.edu/forumy/2005/10/katrina-and-environmental-injustice.php (Oct. 10, 2005). Other critics have argued that Katrina's indignities are "part of a pattern of environmental disasters in which low-income communities and communities of color are overlooked in the preparations before such disasters occur and receive less rapid assistance afterwards." CENTER FOR PROGRESSIVE REFORM, AN UNNATURAL DISASTER: THE AFTERMATH OF HURRICANE KATRINA 35-36 (2005). *See generally* ROBERT D. BULLARD, DUMPING IN DIXIE: RACE, CLASS AND ENVIRONMENTAL QUALITY (3d ed. 2000); LUKE W. COLE & SHEILA FOSTER, ENVIRONMENTAL RACISM AND THE RISE OF THE ENVIRONMENTAL JUSTICE MOVEMENT (2000).

7. In addition to environmental injustice, racial bias manifested itself in the New Orleans housing market before and after Katrina:

> [M]any residents lacked the insurance and assets needed to recover from the storm. New Orleans had a relatively low homeownership rate—just 47 percent compared to 67 percent nationally. . . . And much of the housing stock was old (though not necessarily in bad condition), with 45 percent of the units constructed before 1950, more than twice the national figure (21 percent). Without mortgages, many low-income longtime home-owners opted out of costly homeowners insurance or flood insurance. Moreover, FEMA had designated many of these areas to be at "low" flood risk, so lenders did not require flood insurance.
>
> Like most cities across the country, New Orleans already had an affordable housing crisis before Katrina. According to the 2000 Census, two-thirds (67 percent) of extremely low income households in New Orleans bore excessive housing cost burdens (by federal standards, housing costs that exceed 30 percent of income), a figure slightly higher than average for Louisiana and slightly lower than that for the nation as a whole. More than half (56 percent) of very low income households in New Orleans were paying more than half their income for housing, also comparable to national

figures. Both owners and renters were equally disadvantaged, with majorities of both groups facing excessive housing cost burdens.

Only a small proportion of needy households received federal housing assistance — a public housing apartment, other federally subsidized housing, or Housing Choice Voucher (Section 8). Those that did receive assistance had lower housing costs, but many had to cope with living in some of the nation's worst public housing. . . .

Historically, the city's public housing projects were sited in low-income neighborhoods, isolating low-income residents from the rest of the city and exacerbating both racial segregation and the concentration of black poverty. Decades of neglect and mismanagement had left these developments in severe distress. Residents of projects like Desire, Florida, and Iberville endured intolerable physical conditions, high levels of violent crime, rampant drug trafficking, and myriad other social ills. These distressed public housing communities blighted the surrounding neighborhoods and exacerbated the overall racial and economic segregation in the city.

Susan J. Popkin, Margery A. Turner & Martha Burt, *Rebuilding Affordable Housing in New Orleans: The Challenge of Creating Inclusive Communities* 2-3 (Jan. 2006) (available at http://www.urban.org/UploadedPDF/900914_affordable_housing.pdf).

8. Destruction of housing stock poses especially pointed issues of social injustice. Of the more than $20 billion in direct property damage caused by Katrina, nearly four-fifths ($16 billion) involved residential property. *See* 1 ARMY CORPS OF ENGINEERS, FINAL REPORT OF THE INTERAGENCY PERFORMANCE EVALUATION TASKFORCE (IPET) 8 (June 1, 2006). In Katrina's immediate aftermath, FEMA placed an estimated 125,000 evacuees in hotels; "an untold number" of additional evacuees "stay[ed] with friends and family or liv[ed] in cars, tents, or damaged homes." National Fair Housing Alliance, *No Home for the Holidays: Report on Housing Discrimination against Hurricane Katrina Survivors* 4-5 (Dec. 20, 2005) (available at http://newreconstruction.civilrights.org/LinkClick.aspx?fileticket=dhpik3cZYgc=&tabid=2555&mid=5418).

9. Nearly half the persons displaced by Katrina were renters. *See* Olympia Duhart & Eloisa C. Rodriguez-Dod, *Legislation and Criminalization Impacting Renters Displaced by Katrina, in* LAW AND RECOVERY FROM DISASTER, *supra*, at 141, 141-142. For three months in 2006, St. Bernard Parish banned the renting of residential property to anyone besides blood relatives. *See* St. Bernard Parish (La.) Ord. 670-09-06 (Sept. 16, 2006), *amended*, Ord. 697-12-06 (Dec. 19, 2006). *See generally* Duhart & Rodriguez-Dod, *supra*, at 143-148.

10. "The longer-term challenge" is to rebuild New Orleans "without recreating intense concentrations of minority poverty and distress":

Instead of isolating needy families in pockets of extreme poverty, affordable housing should be provided throughout the metropolitan area so low-income households choosing to return to New Orleans have safe and secure places to live, along with access to the good jobs and schools needed to get ahead. And for those who do not return, affordable housing policies should help ensure that people left homeless by Katrina enjoy the same opportunities in their new communities, do not wind up concentrated in the poorest neighborhoods, and receive the supports they need so they do not end up even worse off than they were in New Orleans.

To expand the stock of moderately priced rental and for-sale housing, while allowing returning residents flexibility and choice about where to live, we recommend a strategy that addresses both the supply side and the demand side of the housing market. More specifically, regulatory incentives and capital subsidies should be used to encourage and support the construction of affordable housing units throughout the metropolitan region (by both for-profit and nonprofit developers). At the same time, low-income households returning to the area should receive vouchers to supplement what they can afford to pay to rent or buy modest housing in neighborhoods of their choice. . . .

Whatever decisions are ultimately made about how to move forward, reconstruction should be based on what is known about how to incorporate high-quality, affordable housing into healthy mixed-income communities that offer real opportunities for low-income families. . . . [T]he city may not be able to recover economically unless its low-wage workforce returns — both the reconstruction effort itself and the city's tourism industry depend on them. And much of what creates the unique and vibrant New Orleans culture grows directly out of its lower-income and minority communities with their many deeply rooted families.

Popkin et al., *supra,* at 8-9. *See generally* Myron Orfield, *Land Use and Housing Policies to Reduce Concentrated Poverty and Racial Segregation,* 33 Fordham Urb. L.J. 877 (2006). On the other hand, in what might be regarded as a form of creative destruction, *see generally* Joseph A. Schumpeter, Capitalism, Socialism and Democracy (1975) (1st ed. 1942), disaster enables government to remedy past segregation through integrative reconstruction. *See* Michèle Alexandre, *Navigating the Topography of Inequality Post-Disaster: A Propose for Remedying Past Geographic Segregation during Rebuilding, in* Law and Recovery from Disaster, *supra,* at 157.

11. One proactive way to assimilate lessons from disasters is to think of ways that the government and other parties involved in preparing for, responding to, and recovering from disasters can develop greater cultural competence in order to minimize the effects of social vulnerability. The "cultural competence continuum" developed in Terry L. Cross et al., Towards a Culturally Competent System of Care, Volume I: A Monograph of Effective Services for Minority Children Who Are Severely Emotionally Disturbed (1989) describes a spectrum ranging from least to greatest cultural competence: (1) destructiveness, (2) incapacity, (3) blindness, (4) precompetence, (5) competence, and finally (6) proficiency.

The following excerpt, though aimed at the narrower question of mental health services, illustrates how greater cultural competence can improve disaster assistance of all kinds:

U.S. Department of Health and Human Services, Developing Cultural Competence in Disaster Mental Health Programs: Guiding Principles and Recommendations

(DHHS Pub. No. SMA 3828), 14-17 (2003)

Culture as a source of knowledge, information, and support provides continuity and a process for healing during times of tragedy. Survivors react to and recover from disaster within the context of their individual racial and ethnic backgrounds, cultural viewpoints, life experiences, and values. Culture offers a protective system that is comfortable and reassuring. It defines appropriate behavior and furnishes social support, identity, and a shared vision for recovery. For example, stories, rituals, and legends that are part of a culture's fabric help people adjust to catastrophic losses by highlighting the mastery of communal trauma and explaining the relationship of individuals to the spiritual. Despite the strengths that culture can provide, responses to disaster also fall on a continuum. Persons from disadvantaged racial and ethnic communities may be more vulnerable to problems associated with preparing for and recovering from disaster than persons of higher socioeconomic status.

Because of the strong role that culture plays in disaster response, disaster mental health services are most effective when survivors receive assistance that is in accord with their cultural beliefs and consistent with their needs. As disaster mental health service providers seek to become more culturally competent, they must recognize three important social and historical influences that can affect the success of their efforts. These three influences are the importance of community, racism and discrimination, and social and economic inequality.

The Importance of Community

Disasters affect both individuals and communities. Following a disaster, there may be individual trauma, characterized as "a blow to the psyche that breaks through one's defenses so suddenly and with such brutal force that one cannot react to it effectively." There also may be collective trauma — "a blow to the basic tissues of social life that damages the bonds attaching people together and impairs the prevailing sense of community." Cultural and socioeconomic factors contribute to both individual and community responses to the trauma caused by disaster.

The culture of the community provides the lens through which its members view and interpret the disaster. . . . [A] disrupted and fragmented [community] will be able to provide less support than a cohesive community.

A classic example is . . . the devastating 1972 flood in Buffalo Creek, West Virginia. The flood led to relocation of the entire community [and] a "loss of community," in which people lost not only their sense of connection with the locale but also the support of people and institutions. Results of this community's fragmentation included fear, anger, anxiety, and depression.

Other studies have emphasized positive effects that can result from disaster experiences in communities that perform a protective role and cushion the stress of the disaster. Compared with non-disaster-related suffering, which is isolating and private, the suffering of disaster survivors can be collective and public. However, devastating disasters can have positive outcomes. They can bring a community closer or reorient its members to new priorities or values. Individuals may exhibit courage, selflessness, gratitude, and hope that they may not have shown or felt before the disaster.

Community often is extremely important for racial and ethnic minority groups, and it may dramatically affect their ability to recover from disaster. For example, a racial or ethnic minority community may provide especially strong social support functions for its members, particularly when it is surrounded by a hostile society. However, its smaller size may render it more fragile and more subject to dispersion and destruction after a disaster. Members of some racial and ethnic minority groups, such as refugees, previously have experienced destruction of their social support systems, and the destruction of a second support system may be particularly difficult.

Racism and Discrimination

Many racial and ethnic minority groups, including African Americans, American Indians, and Chinese and Japanese Americans, have experienced racism, discrimination, or persecution for many years. . . . [R]acial discrimination persists in housing rentals and sales, hiring practices, and medical care. Racism also takes the form of demeaning comments, hate crimes, and other violence by institutions or individuals, either intentionally or unintentionally.

As a result of past or present experiences with racism and discrimination, racial and ethnic minority groups may distrust offers of outside assistance at any time, even following a disaster. They may not be accustomed to receiving support and assistance from persons outside of their own group in non-disaster circumstances. Therefore, they may be unfamiliar with the social and cultural mechanisms of receiving assistance and remain outside the network of aid. . . . For example, following the 1994 California earthquake, . . . many immigrants' distrust of government posed a barrier to their use of disaster services. Likewise, some of the survivors of a hurricane in Alabama were immigrants from Asian Communist countries who did not trust any government and were not accustomed to receiving Government assistance.

Social and Economic Inequality

Poverty disproportionately affects racial and ethnic minority groups. For example, in 1999, 8 percent of whites, 11 percent of Asian Americans and Pacific Islanders, 23 percent of Hispanic Americans, 24 percent of African Americans, and 26 percent of American Indians and Alaska Natives lived in poverty. Significant socioeconomic differences also exist within racial and ethnic minority groups. For example, although some subgroups of Asian Americans have prospered, others remain at low socioeconomic levels.

Social and economic inequality also leads to reduced access to resources, including employment; financial credit; legal rights; and education, health, and mental health services. Poor neighborhoods also have high rates of homelessness, substance abuse, and crime.

Poverty makes people more susceptible than others to harm from disaster and less able to access help. Low-income individuals and families typically lose a much larger part of their material assets and suffer more lasting negative effects from disaster than do those with higher incomes. Often, disadvantaged persons live in the least desirable and most hazardous areas of a community, and their homes may be older and not as sound as those in higher income areas. . . .

[S]ome groups cannot readily access [disaster relief] services. Negative perceptions derived from pre-disaster experiences may serve as a barrier to seeking care. Lack of familiarity with sources of community support [and] lack of transportation are common barriers for many immigrants and unwillingness to disclose their immigration status is a major barrier.

Middle-class disaster survivors are more likely than lower-income people . . . to know how to complete forms, communicate adequately, talk to the "right" people, or otherwise maneuver within the system. Thus, they may be more likely to receive aid than survivors with fewer means or those from different cultures. On the other hand, affluent groups . . . may fear a loss of control and find it humiliating to accept emergency assistance such as clothing, food, loans, and emotional support from disaster workers.

In some instances, people of lower socioeconomic status exhibit strong coping skills in disaster situations because they have seen difficult times before and have survived. In other instances, the loss of what little one had may leave an individual feeling completely hopeless.

NOTES AND QUESTIONS

1. Mental health experts have identified certain characteristics of disasters that bear heavily on the emotional distress felt by survivors and on health professionals' efforts to assist in their recovery. *See* Robert Bolin & Lois Stanford, *The Northridge Earthquake: Community-Based Approaches to Unmet Recovery Needs,* 22 DISASTERS 21 (1998); Department of Health & Human Services, *Assuring Cultural Competence in Health Care: Recommendations for National Standards and an Outcomes-Focused Research Agenda* 6 (2000):

a. *Intensity of the impact.* Disasters that effect intense destruction within a brief period are more likely to cause emotional distress than slower, less destructive disasters.

b. *Impact ratio.* When a significant proportion of a community sustains losses, there are fewer survivors available to lend material and emotional support to others.

c. *Potential for recurrence.* The threat of recurrence, real or perceived, of the disaster or of associated hazards can increase stress in survivors.

d. *Cultural and symbolic aspects.* Survivors may be deeply disturbed by disaster-related changes in their lives, even in their routines. Natural and human-caused disasters can have great symbolic effects.

e. *Extent and type of loss.* Deaths of loved ones, personal injury, property damage or loss, and job loss can affect emotional recovery.

2. How did Katrina measure on these gauges? Consider the Corps of Engineers' assessment of the storm's physical and social consequences:

> The most serious direct impact of Katrina was the high number of deaths. While large numbers of people were able to evacuate, the groups least likely to be able to do so on their own, the poor, elderly, and disabled, were hardest hit. . . . [F]looding was highly correlated to land elevation, and the areas with the lowest elevations were largely residential. This places the residential population who cannot readily evacuate at the greatest risk.
>
> Katrina caused direct property losses (excluding Plaquemines Parish) of over $20 billion, approximately 78 percent ($16 billion) of which was attributed to residential losses. The next largest component was the 11.5 percent

($2.4 billion) attributed to commercial losses. There was an additional $6.0 to $6.7 billion in losses attributed to public infrastructure, including the hurricane protection system itself. The most significant infrastructure impact was incurred by the hurricane protection system (1.8 to 2.08 billion) followed by roadway networks and assets of the regional electrical distribution/transmission grid. Together, the damages to these categories of infrastructure totaled approximately $2.0 billion. This estimate is followed by damages to public transit assets of approximately $690 to $730 million followed by damages to rail lines, airport facilities, gas and water distribution, telecommunications assets, and assets for waterborne transportation totaling an additional $1.7 to $1.9 billion. Approximately half of the direct economic losses, excluding public and utilities infrastructure, can be associated with breaching of levees and floodwalls. The remaining losses alone, attributable to rainfall and overtopping, constitute the largest losses experienced in any disaster in the New Orleans vicinity.

Combined with the significant and far-reaching impact of Hurricane Katrina regarding initial displacement of population, workforce, and businesses, the impacts to infrastructure and affiliated public welfare and services will contribute to slowed phasing of recovery with regard to return of populace and business activities. Orleans Parish alone is estimated to have lost over 60 percent of its population and St. Bernard Parish nearly 80 percent. On the other hand, St. Charles and Tammany Parishes have increased in population since before the storm. . . .

[T]he social organization of the community and region has been compromised by the mass exodus of the population, the structural damage, and the demands to respond and rebuild. The flooding caused a breakdown in New Orleans' social structure, a loss of cultural heritage, and dramatically altered the physical, economic, political, social, and psychological character of the area. . . .

The immediate physical damage made large portions of the city uninhabitable, with thousands of residential, commercial, and public structures destroyed. Basic infrastructure facilities, such as power, water, sewer, and natural gas lines, were made inoperable and continued to be out of service for months after the event. Many victims not only lost their homes, but also their schools, health care, places of worship, places of trade, and jobs. The forced relocations disrupted family and friend networks. As a result, the event not only had an immediate impact on the well being of the population of those living and working in the metropolitan area, but also resulted in basic changes in the social organization of all aspects of that population.

1 ARMY CORPS OF ENGINEERS, FINAL REPORT OF THE INTERAGENCY PERFORMANCE EVALUATION TASKFORCE (IPET) 8-9 (June 1, 2006). "These impacts are unprecedented in their social consequence and unparalleled in the modern era of the United States." *Id.* at 9.

C. SEX, AGE, DISABILITY, AND IMMIGRANT STATUS

Bias has many manifestations. Women, children, the elderly, persons with disabilities, and immigrants (documented and otherwise) all suffer from disaster in ways that other victims do not. *See generally* Daniel A. Farber, *Disaster Law and Inequality*, 25 Law & Ineq. 297, 302-308 (2007). Justice John Paul Stevens's frequent admonition, that there indeed "is only one . . . Equal Protection Clause," serves as a reminder that the aspiration to equality persists no matter what the source of injustice.[3] This section therefore examines social vulnerability by sex, age, disability, and immigration status.

1. SEX: WOMEN AND WOMEN'S CONTRIBUTIONS TO POSTDISASTER RECOVERY

Although Katrina is most often framed as a tragedy of race and class, at least one commentator argues that it should also be regarded as a tragedy of sex:

Elaine Enarson, Women and Girls Last? Averting the Second Post-Katrina Disaster

http://understandingkatrina.ssrc.org/Enarson (June 11, 2009)

The fault lines of American society, as much as the failings of its infrastructure, are shamefully on display in the aftermath of Hurricane Katrina. Race, class, age and (dis)ability are now at the heart of the public debate about vulnerability, preparedness and emergency response, but this is also a story, as yet untold, about women and men.

It was low-income African American women, many single mothers among them, whose pleas for food and water were broadcast around the world from the Superdome, women more than men who were evacuated from nursing homes, and women more than men whose escape of sorts was made with infants, children and elders in tow. Now we see on nightly TV the faces of exhausted women standing in seemingly endless lines seeking help of any kind. In the long run, as we have learned from studies of past disasters, women will be at the heart of this great city's rebirth, and the emotional center of gravity for their families on the long road to the "new normal." They will stitch the commemorative quilts, organize community festivals and hurricane anniversary events, support their schools and faith-based organizations and relief agencies, and compose and sing many of the Katrina songs to come. Though not this simple, it is often said that men rebuild buildings while women reweave the social fabric of community life.

We are transfixed now by images of needy women and strong men (a few with female partners) wearing badges, carrying weapons and riding in armored vehicles, and will soon be treated to endless photos of hardworking men hauling garbage, replacing roofs, making speeches and decisions. Behind the scenes (taking nothing away from others), women labor, too. In the dreary months ahead, after the nation's attention wanes, the burdens on women will be exceptional and exceptionally invisible. Imagine cleaning just one flooded

---

3. Adarand Constructors, Inc. v. Pena, 515 U.S. 200, 246 (1995) (Stevens, J., dissenting); *see also* City of Richmond v. J.A. Croson Co., 488 U.S. 469, 514 n.5 (1989) (Stevens, J., concurring in part and concurring in the judgment); Karcher v. Daggett, 462 U.S. 725, 749 (1983) (Stevens, J., concurring); Craig v. Boren, 429 U.S. 190, 211 (1976) (Stevens, J., concurring).

room, helping just one toddler or teen to sleep well again, restoring the sense of security to a widowed mother's life. The basic domestic chores of "homemaking" gain new significance and are vastly more difficult in a FEMA trailer, a friend's apartment or the basement of a church — and parents will call upon daughters more than sons for help. Nothing will change in a hurry as women pack and unpack, moving from place to place across the nation with distracted partners, bewildered children, pets and whatever possessions remain or are gathered piecemeal. The demands on the women who take them in and make them at home are incalculable, and displaced families will stay longer than anyone now imagines. Women across the nation are also the lifeblood of voluntary organizations of all descriptions, now being pulled inexorably into relief work. They will continue to do this work when the funds dry up and women (and to a lesser extent men) marginalized by race and class fall between the (gaping) cracks of the relief system. Long after we think Katrina over and done with, women whose jobs and professions in teaching, health care, mental health, crisis work, and community advocacy bring them into direct contact with affected families will feel the stress of "first responders" whose work never ends.

NOTES AND QUESTIONS

1. As women go during and after disaster, so goes society at large:

> The hallmark of such a mega-disaster as Hurricane Katrina is that it shreds the social networks and institutions, which provide a modicum of stability and coherence in people's lives. Women are particularly vulnerable when these social institutions deteriorate, particularly in their role as caregivers. Nearly forty percent of children in Mississippi had either not completed their school year or had missed a significant amount of class time. Combined with unsafe housing and neighborhoods, and unreliable systems of criminal justice and police protection, women often find themselves in a volatile home environment — the children are at home, disengaged from school; their spouse or partner is unemployed, with little economic opportunity available; their material possessions have mostly been destroyed; and they are living in extremely close quarters — often four or five family members in a 250 square foot trailer, for over a year, with no certain housing solution in sight. Many respondents spoke to us of the enormous strain on personal relationships, and it is not surprising that mental health disability is so endemic.

Irwin Redlener, David M. Abramson & Richard Garfield, *Lessons from Katrina: What Went Wrong, What Was Learned, Who's Most Vulnerable*, 13 Cardozo J.L. & Gender 783, 786-787 (2008).

2. Disaster affects women and men differently. *Compare, e.g.*, Jane C. Ollenburger & Graham A. Tobin, *Women and Postdisaster Stress, in* The Gendered Terrain of Disaster: Through Women's Eyes 95 (Elaine Enarson & Betty Hearn Morrow eds., 1998) *and* Jane C. Ollenburger & Graham A. Tobin, *Women, Aging, and Post-Disaster Stress: Risk Factors,* 17 Intl. J. Mass Emergencies & Disasters 65 (1999) *with, e.g.*, Lawrence A. Palinkas et al., *Social, Cultural, and Psychological Impacts of the Exxon Valdez Oil Spill,* 52 Human Org. 1 (1993). The very condition

of "being female is a risk factor for experiencing post-disaster psychological trauma." Farber, *supra,* 25 Law & Ineq. at 305-306. Nor have observers failed to account for differences in women's vis-à-vis men's contributions to disaster relief and recovery. *See, e.g.,* Ayse Yonder, Sengul Akcar & Prema Gopalan, Women's Participation in Disaster Relief and Recovery (2005). Enarson transcends these first-order differences. Unless women recover on terms equivalent to men after a disaster, the area's social fabric will suffer long-term secondary damage.

3. Recall how *susceptibility* and *resilience* represent distinct components of vulnerability. The disproportionate number of women trapped inside New Orleans suggests that women were more *susceptible* during the hurricane. Enarson argues that New Orleans will not be as *resilient* unless women contribute significantly to the recovery. Women play a pivotal role in combating poverty and other social ills. "Teach a man to fish, and he eats. Teach a woman to fish, and everyone eats." Elizabeth Palmberg, *"Teach a Woman to Fish . . . and Everyone Eats." Why Women Are Key to Fighting Global Poverty,* Sojourners Mag., June 2005 (quoting Ritu Sharma of the Women's Edge Coalition). *See generally* Elizabeth M. King & Andrew D. Mason, Engendering Development — Through Gender Equality in Rights, Resources, and Voice (2001).

4. Are there other groups or individuals whose postdisaster welfare heavily affects a community's resilience? How might the law recognize "keystone" actors who are most likely to make the greatest contribution to recovery? Social capital, the often fickle and fragile fabric of a community, holds the key to a population's vulnerability to disaster and its ability to bounce back. *See* Eric Klinenberg, Heat Wave: A Social Autopsy of Disaster in Chicago 19 (2002).

2. AGE AND DISABILITY

Thomas Gabe, Gene Falk & Maggie McCarty, Hurricane Katrina: Social-Demographic Characteristics of Impacted Areas

(CRS Order Code RL33141), 17-19 (Nov. 4, 2005)

The Aged. The aged may have been especially affected by Katrina. Many had close ties to their communities, having resided there for years, and for some, their entire lifetimes. Some may have found it more difficult than others to evacuate. The elderly are more likely to live alone, and less likely to own a car, or be able to drive. Some may have been more isolated, living alone, or homebound due to frailty or disability.

Home Ownership Status and Community Ties. Among households headed by persons age 65 or older who were likely displaced by the storm, 70% are estimated to have owned their own home — an ownership rate higher than any other age group. Among aged homeowners likely displaced by the storm, over 70% had lived in their homes for over 20 years, and 47% over 30 years, in the year 2000. Among likely displaced aged renters, an estimated

55% had lived in their rental units for over 20 years, and 36% over 30 years, based on 2000 Census data.

Living Arrangements. An estimated 88,000 persons age 65 and older were likely displaced by Hurricane Katrina, or 12.4% of the population affected by flooding and/or storm damage. Among the aged population affected, an estimated 27,000 lived alone, in one-person households, which accounted for 41% of households with an aged member.

The hurricane likely displaced an estimated 45,000 persons age 75 and older, a population prone to frailty. Among this group, nearly 15,000 are estimated to have lived alone, in one-person households, which accounted for 45% of the households with a member age 75 or older.

Disability Status. Nearly half (48%) of all persons age 65 or older living in flooded or damage-affected areas reported having a disability, and over one-quarter (26%) reported two or more types of disability. Reported disabilities included sensory disabilities (blindness, deafness, or severe hearing impairment), and other disabilities reflecting conditions lasting more than six months that limit various activities. These activity-limiting disabilities include mental disabilities (difficulty learning, remembering, or concentrating); self-care disabilities (difficulty dressing, bathing, or getting around inside the home); and, going outside disabilities (difficulty going outside the home alone to shop or visit a doctor's office). An estimated 13% of persons age 65 and older in the flood or damage-affected areas reported a self-care disability, and 19% of those age 75 and older; one-quarter of those age 65 and older reported a disability that made it difficult to go outside, unassisted, and of those age 75 and older, one-third reported such a disability.

Poverty Status. Among aged persons likely displaced by the storm, an estimated 12,600, based on 2000 Census data, were poor, or about 14.7% of the aged displaced population, and nearly 23,600 (27.6%) had incomes below 150% of the poverty line.

Vehicle Availability. Among all households living in the flood or damage-affected areas, an estimated 19% had no vehicle available to the household. Among households with heads age 65 or older, over one-quarter (26%) were without a vehicle, and among those age 75 or older, one-third (33%). In order to evacuate from the storm, these households would have been dependent on other nonresident family members, friends, neighbors, or public or specially arranged transportation.

Children. About one-fourth of the people who lived in areas damaged or flooded by Hurricane Katrina were children (under age 18). Hurricane Katrina struck at the beginning of the school year, potentially displacing an estimated 183,000 children, . . . including an estimated 136,000 children who were of school age. An estimated 47,000 children under the age of 5 lived in neighborhoods that experienced flooding or damage from the hurricane.

Child Poverty Rates in Areas Acutely Affected by Hurricane Katrina. The characteristics of the children in the damaged and flooded areas reflect greater disadvantage compared with the characteristics of children in the nation as a whole. Many of the children in affected areas were poor. [Among 180,102 children in areas flooded or damaged by Hurricane Katrina, 54,646, or 30.3 percent, were poor. Among children aged 0-4, 32.8 percent, or 15,079 out of 46,025, were poor.] . . . The poverty rate of 30% for children in hurricane-flooded or damaged areas is almost twice the 2000 Census child poverty rate for the nation as a whole of 16.6%. . . .

[A]bout 15,000 children of preschool age (age 0-4), or about one-third of all children in that age group, were poor. Another 40,000 school age children who lived in flooded or hurricane-damaged areas were poor. Over half (55%) of the children most likely to have been displaced by the hurricane were African American. . . . Approximately 45% of the displaced black children were estimated to have been poor (about 45,000 children), accounting for 25% of all children displaced by the storm, and 82% of all poor displaced children.

Living Arrangements of Children in Hurricane-Affected Areas. Children in the areas damaged and flooded by Hurricane Katrina were more likely than children nationwide to live in female-headed families. . . . Overall, 38% of children under the age of 18 in the hurricane-affected areas lived with a female head; nationally, this percentage is 20%. Children in female-headed families are more likely to be poor than children living in married couple or other families. . . . [N]ationwide, 41% of children in female-headed families were in poverty versus an overall poverty rate of 16%. Further, a single mother often needs child care to enter the workforce or remain working. In the Hurricane Katrina-damaged and flooded areas, there were 12,000 preschool children living in families headed by a single mother. The high rate of children living with single mothers also is consistent with the hurricane having disproportionately affected African Americans, as African American children are more likely than children of other racial and ethnic groups to be raised by a single mother.

NOTES AND QUESTIONS

1. Age classifications warrant no special scrutiny as a matter of equal protection jurisprudence. *See* Massachusetts Bd. of Retirement v. Murgia, 427 U.S. 307 (1976). Limits on constitutional relief do not necessarily govern other sources of law. Should problems of age — whether applied to the elderly or to children — warrant special attention during disasters? In what ways are the aged and the young especially *susceptible?* To what extent are these groups less *resilient* than others during recovery? You may find it helpful to distinguish between the general difficulties posed by poverty (which disproportionately affect children and the elderly) and unique problems associated with youth or old age.
2. In political, social, and physical terms, children face drastically different challenges in times of disaster than do the elderly. Even if the very young

and the very old posed challenges of precisely the same difficulty, however, the law could be more responsive to one class at the apparent expense of the other. Because children cannot vote, whereas the elderly represent a politically potent constituency, children rarely secure as much legal protection as do their elders. How seriously does American society take its nominal commitment to "the upbringing and education of children"? Pierce v. Society of Sisters, 268 U.S. 510, 534-535 (1925).

3. Certain types of bias, though expressed along some vector besides age, reap their heaviest toll from the very young and the very old. Discrimination in health care is one example. *See, e.g.*, Lindsey J. Hopper, Note, *Striking a Balance: An Open Courts Analysis of the Uniform Emergency Volunteer Health Practitioners Act,* 92 MINN. L. REV. 1924 (2008). Another is housing. *See, e.g.*, Alexandre, *supra;* Duhart & Rodriguez-Dod, *supra.* What both types of bias have in common is their disparate impact on the physically vulnerable, a condition that corresponds (roughly) with youth and senescence. Laws against health care and housing discrimination target the use of race as an illicit factor in allocating these scarce, potentially life-saving resources. The primary beneficiaries, however, tend to be the youngest and oldest members of the protected groups.

4. Like classifications based on age, classifications based on disability do not trigger heightened constitutional scrutiny. *See* Heller v. Doe, 509 U.S. 312 (1993); City of Cleburne v. Cleburne Living Center, 473 U.S. 432 (1985). Nearly half of the elderly victims of Katrina had one disability; more than a quarter reported multiple disabilities. The disabled are uniquely vulnerable to disaster. *See generally* Debra Lyn Bassett, *Place, Disasters, and Disabilities, in* LAW AND RECOVERY FROM DISASTER, *supra,* at 51, 61-69. Although accounting for persons with disabilities "when planning disaster relief in the first instance minimizes harm and reduces (re)development costs in the future," Janet E. Lord, Michael E. Waterstone & Michael Ashley Stein, *Natural Disasters and Persons with Disabilities, in* LAW AND RECOVERY FROM DISASTER, *supra,* at 71, 72, this call for prescient preparation goes unheeded:

> Emergency situations arising from natural disasters invariably cause human suffering. It is the responsibility of domestic governments and international humanitarian assistance organizations to minimize this anguish to the greatest extent possible, especially for vulnerable populations. Almost by definition, advance planning is crucial. Yet all too often governments, humanitarian assistance agencies, and other policy makers fail to adopt a disability perspective in natural disaster humanitarian crisis situations. With distressing frequency, the disability experience is either neglected completely or lost when cast among other vulnerable groups.

Id. Put bluntly, "poor people with chronic health conditions" in times of disaster "suffer[] disproportionately—and unnecessarily." Leah J. Tulin, Note, *Poverty and Chronic Conditions during Natural Disaster: A Glimpse at Health, Healing and Hurricane Katrina,* 14 GEO. J. ON POVERTY L. & POL'Y 115, 115 (2007).

3. ALIENAGE AND IMMIGRATION

Immediately after Hurricane Katrina, the Department of Homeland Security announced that it would "refrain from initiating employer sanction enforcement actions for the next 45 days for civil violations, under Section 274A of the Immigration and Nationality Act [8 U.S.C. §1324a], with regard to individuals who are currently unable to provide identity and eligibility documents as a result of the hurricane." Department of Homeland Security, *Notice Regarding I-9 Documentation Requirements for Hiring Hurricane Victims* (Sept. 6, 2005). The decision to suspend enforcement of the immigration laws triggered an uptick in Latino immigration:

> In the weeks following the storm, the construction industry quickly became a magnet for Latino immigrants who were lured by the promise of paychecks and an emergency federal decree temporarily suspending immigration-enforcement sanctions. . . .
>
> The media picked up on the trend in early October 2005 and described how employers were seeking Latino immigrants to help rebuild the affected areas. Together with a cartoon in the *Los Angeles Times* that depicts an African American walking out of New Orleans holding two suitcases and a Mexican laborer walking in holding tools to repair a broken levee, articles with titles such as "Illegal Workers Eying the Gulf Coast," "Big Easy Uneasy about Migrant Wave," "La Nueva Orleans" and "A New Spice in the Gumbo" all signal the role that immigrants, many of them Latino laborers, will play in the efforts to rebuild.
>
> Yet Latinos responding to labor-market demand have not been all that welcome. New Orleans Mayor Ray Nagin famously asked at a forum with business leaders, "How do I make sure New Orleans is not overrun with Mexican workers?" Although he quickly distanced himself from the remark — which provoked a joint statement about unity by civil rights and Latino organizations — many in the region believe contractors favor cheap, foreign labor over local, native workers.

Katharine Donato & Shirin Hakimzadeh, *The Changing Face of the Gulf Coast: Immigration to Louisiana, Mississippi, and Alabama,* http://www.migrationinformation. org/Feature/display.cfm?id=368 (June 11, 2009).

Conflict with Latino newcomers illustrates merely one of the many legal issues surrounding immigrants, immigration, and Hurricane Katrina:

RUTH ELLEN WASEM, KATRINA-RELATED IMMIGRATION ISSUES AND LEGISLATION

(Sept. 19, 2005) (CRS Order Code RL33091)

Caught in the web of [Katrina's] tragedy and its sweeping dilemmas are a unique subset of immigration-related issues. The loss of livelihood, habitat, and life itself has very specific implications for foreign nationals who lived in the Gulf Coast region. . . .

This report focuses on four immigration policy implications of Hurricane Katrina. It opens with a discussion of employment verification and other documentary problems arising for those who have lost their personal identification documents. It follows with an overview of the rules for noncitizen

eligibility for federal benefits. Issues pertaining to how the loss of life or livelihood affects eligibility for immigration visa benefits are discussed next. The
report closes with . . . background on relief from removal options for Katrina-
affected aliens. . . .

Personal Identification and Employment Eligibility. Many of the victims
of Hurricane Katrina lack personal identification documents as a result of being
evacuated from their homes, loss or damage to personal items and records, and
ongoing displacement in shelters and temporary housing. As a result of the
widespread damage and destruction to government facilities in the area
affected by the hurricane, moreover, many victims will be unable to have
personal documents re-issued in the near future. Lack of adequate personal
identification documentation . . . has specific consequences under immigration law, especially when it comes to employment.

The Immigration and Nationality Act (INA) requires employers to verify
employment eligibility and establish identity through specified documents
presented by the employee—citizens and foreign nationals alike. Specifically,
§274(a)(1)(B) of the INA makes it illegal for an employer to hire any person—
citizen or alien—without first verifying the person's authorization to work in
the United States. . . .

Noncitizen Eligibility for Federal Assistance. Lack of sufficient documentation to confirm eligibility for federal programs and assistance is a core issue
for all victims, not merely those who are noncitizens. The eligibility of noncitizens for public assistance programs, moreover, is based on a complex set of
rules that are determined largely by the type of noncitizen in question and the
nature of services being offered. The Personal Responsibility and Work Opportunity Reconciliation Act of 1996 [Pub. L. No. 104-193] is the key statute that
spells out the eligibility rules for noncitizens seeking federal assistance. . . .

Legal Permanent Residents. Under current law, noncitizens' eligibility
for the major federal means-tested benefit programs largely depends on
their immigration status and whether they arrived in the United States (or
were on a program's rolls) before August 22, 1996, the enactment date of
the Personal Responsibility and Work Opportunity Reconciliation Act of
1996. . . . Several bills that would waive the categorical [eligibility] requirements for various federal programs in the case of Hurricane Katrina victims
have been introduced, but most are silent on the issue of noncitizens. On
September 13, however, legislation to provide the Secretary of Agriculture
with additional authority and funding to provide emergency relief to victims
of Hurricane Katrina (S. 1695) was introduced, and, among other provisions,
this bill would treat legal immigrants in the United States who are victims of
Hurricane Katrina as refugees for the purposes of food stamps.

Unauthorized Aliens. The PRWOR of 1996 . . . also denies most federal
benefits, regardless of whether they are means tested, to unauthorized
aliens. . . . The class of benefits denied is broad and covers: (1) grants, contracts, loans, and licenses; and (2) retirement, welfare, health, disability,
housing, food, unemployment, postsecondary education, and similar benefits.

So defined, this bar covers many programs whose enabling statutes do not individually make citizenship or immigration status a criterion for participation. Thus, programs that previously were not individually restricted — the earned income tax credit, social services block grants, and migrant health centers, for example — became unavailable to unauthorized aliens, unless they fall within the act's limited exceptions. These programmatic exceptions include: treatment under Medicaid for emergency medical conditions (other than those related to an organ transplant); short-term, in-kind emergency disaster relief; immunizations against immunizable diseases and testing for and treatment of symptoms of communicable diseases; [certain] services or assistance (such as soup kitchens, crisis counseling and intervention, and short-term shelters). . . .

P.L. 104-193 also permits unauthorized aliens to receive Old Age, Survivors, and Disability Insurance benefits under Title II of the Social Security Act (SSA), if the benefits are protected by that title or by treaty or are paid under applications made before August 22, 1996. Separately, the P.L. 104-193 states that individuals who are eligible for free public education benefits under state and local law shall remain eligible to receive school lunch and school breakfast benefits. (The act itself does not address a state's obligation to grant all aliens equal access to education under the Supreme Court's decision in Plyler v. Doe, 457 U.S. 202 (1982).) P.L. 104-193 expressly bars unauthorized aliens from most state and locally funded benefits. The restrictions on these benefits parallel the restrictions on federal benefits.

Disaster Assistance. . . . [N]oncitizens — regardless of their immigration status — are not barred from short-term, in-kind emergency disaster relief and services or assistance that deliver in-kind services at the community level, provide assistance without individual determinations of each recipient's needs, and are necessary for the protection of life and safety. Moreover, the [Stafford Act] . . . requires nondiscrimination and equitable treatment in disaster assistance:

> The President shall issue, and may alter and amend, such regulations as may be necessary for the guidance of personnel carrying out Federal assistance functions at the site of a major disaster or emergency. Such regulations shall include provisions for insuring that the distribution of supplies, the processing of applications, and other relief and assistance activities shall be accomplished in an equitable and impartial manner, without discrimination on the grounds of race, color, religion, nationality, sex, age, or economic status.

FEMA assistance provided under the Stafford Act includes (but is not limited to) grants for immediate temporary shelter, cash grants for uninsured emergency personal needs, temporary housing assistance, home repair grants, unemployment assistance due to the disaster, emergency food supplies, legal aid for low-income individuals, and crisis counseling. . . .

Relief from Removal. At various times in the past, the Attorney General has provided, under certain conditions, discretionary relief from deportation so that aliens who have not been legally admitted to the United States or whose temporary visa has expired nonetheless may remain in this country temporarily. . . . The Attorney General has provided blanket relief by means of the suspension of enforcement of the immigration laws against a particular group of individuals. In addition to Temporary Protected Status (TPS) which may be provided by the Secretary of DHS, the two most common discretionary procedures to provide relief from deportation have been deferred departure or deferred enforced departure (DED) and extended voluntary departure (EVD). Unlike TPS, aliens who benefit from EVD or DED do not necessarily register for the status with [U.S. Citizenship and Immigration Services], but they trigger the protection when they are identified for deportation. . . .

NOTES AND QUESTIONS

1. Migrants rarely come from the poorest sectors of society. The truly abject have too few resources to move. Migrants typically have at least modest resources and social networks at their disposal. *See* Elizabeth Fussell, *Leaving New Orleans: Social Stratification, Networks, and Hurricane Evacuation,* http://understandingkatrina.ssrc.org/Fussell (June 11, 2009); Douglas S. Massey & Kristin Espinosa, *What's Driving Mexico-US Migration? A Theoretical, Empirical and Policy Analysis,* 102 AM. J. SOCIOLOGY 939 (1997); J. Edward Taylor, *Differential Migration, Networks, Information and Risk, in* MIGRATION THEORY, HUMAN CAPITAL AND DEVELOPMENT 147 (Oded Stark ed., 1986).

2. Section 308 of the Stafford Act, 42 U.S.C. §5151, as amended by the Post-Katrina Emergency Management Reform Act of 2006, Pub. L. No. 109-295, §689a, 120 Stat. 1335, 1449, now prohibits discrimination on the basis of "English proficiency." The Post-Katrina Act also instructs the director of FEMA to "identify, in coordination with State and local governments, population groups with limited English proficiency and take into account such groups in planning for an emergency or major disaster." *Id.* §616(a)(1), *codified at* 42 U.S.C. §5196f.

D. PRICE GOUGING AFTER NATURAL DISASTERS

Natural disasters routinely create shortages. High prices are the predictable response of markets to shortages. Although price gouging affects all survivors of a disaster, policymakers often worry that it falls most heavily upon the most vulnerable survivors. In the immediate aftermath of a disaster, legislatures often restrict the ability of vendors to charge what the market will bear for food, water, medicine, and other essential supplies. This section reviews those laws, their constitutionality, and their efficacy.

ANGIE A. WELBORN & AARON M. FLYNN, PRICE INCREASES IN THE AFTERMATH
OF HURRICANE KATRINA: AUTHORITY TO LIMIT PRICE GOUGING

(CRS Order Code RS22236), 1-4 (Sept. 2, 2005)

There are no federal laws that specifically address price gouging. Price gouging laws exist at the state level and are generally applicable in situations arising from a declared emergency. An increase in prices alone does not necessarily constitute price gouging, and technically, price gouging only occurs when the trigger event has been met in a particular state. If there exists evidence of collusive activity among retailers, suppliers, or manufacturers, federal antitrust laws could be applicable. The Federal Trade Commission monitors gas prices and investigates possible antitrust violations in the petroleum industry. . . .

While there is no federal price gouging law, many states have enacted some type of prohibition or limitation on price increases during declared emergencies. All of the affected states — Louisiana, Mississippi, Alabama, and Florida — have price gouging laws that are triggered by the declaration of an emergency in the state. Generally, the laws prohibit the sale of goods and services in the designated emergency area at prices that exceed the prices ordinarily charged for comparable goods or services in the same market area at or immediately before the declaration of an emergency. However, there exists a general exemption for increased prices that are the result of additional costs incurred for procuring the goods or services in question, or "national or international market trends."

The Florida statute [FLA. STAT. §501.160] is the most detailed of the four. It establishes a prima facie case of unconscionable pricing, if:

1) The amount charged represents a gross disparity between the price of the commodity or rental or lease of any dwelling unit or self-storage facility that is the subject of the offer or transaction and the average price at which that commodity or dwelling unit or self-storage facility was rented, leased, sold, or offered for rent or sale in the usual course of business during the 30 days immediately prior to a declaration of a state of emergency, and the increase in the amount charged is not attributable to additional costs incurred in connection with the rental or sale of the commodity or rental or lease of any dwelling unit or self-storage facility, or national or international market trends; or

2) The amount charged grossly exceeds the average price at which the same or similar commodity was readily obtainable in the trade area during the 30 days immediately prior to a declaration of a state of emergency, and the increase in the amount charged is not attributable to additional costs incurred in connection with the rental or sale of the commodity or rental or lease of any dwelling unit or self-storage facility, or national or international market trends.

Commodity is broadly defined to include "any goods, services, materials, merchandise, supplies, equipment, resources, or other article of commerce," and specifically includes, "without limitation, food, water, ice, chemicals, petroleum products, and lumber necessary for consumption or use as a direct result of the emergency." . . .

Typically, state price gouging laws are triggered only when there has been a declaration of emergency in the state. The laws, therefore, are only applicable in areas affected by the declared emergency. Thus, in other parts of the country, not directly affected by Hurricane Katrina, state price gouging laws, where they exist, are not likely to be generally applicable to any price increases occurring subsequent to the hurricane. While price increases may not fall within the definition of price gouging, if the raising of prices by retailers, suppliers, or manufacturers is the result of collusive activity, the federal anti-trust laws could be applicable.

Under special circumstances and depending on the scope of the statute in question, state price gouging laws could be triggered by the declaration of an emergency not specifically related to a natural disaster occurring in the state. For example, Georgia's price gouging statute can be triggered by the declaration of an "energy emergency," which is defined as "a condition of danger to the health, safety, welfare, or economic well-being of the citizens of this state arising out of a present or threatened shortage of usable energy resources." [GA. CODE ANN. §§ 10-1-393, 38-3-3.] The Governor of Georgia declared such an emergency on August 31, 2005, triggering the state's price gouging statute.

NOTES AND QUESTIONS

1. At least fifteen states and Guam have statutes that specifically address price gouging during emergencies. *See* ALA. CODE §8-31-3 to -6; ARK. CODE ANN. §4-88-301 to -305; CAL. BUS. & PROF. CODE §7123.5; CAL. CIV. CODE §§ 1689.5-.14; CAL. PENAL CODE §396; CONN. GEN. STAT. §42-232; FLA. STAT. ANN. §§ 501.160, .201-.213; GA. CODE ANN. §10-1-393; GUAM CODE ANN. §32201; IND. CODE §§ 4-6-9.1-1 to -7; LA. REV. STAT. ANN. §29:732; MISS. CODE ANN. §75-24-25; N.Y. GEN. BUS. LAW §396-r; N.C. GEN. STAT. ANN. §75-37; S.C. CODE 1976 §39-5-145; TEX. BUS. & COM. CODE ANN. §1746(25); VA. CODE ANN. §59.1-525 to -529; W. VA. CODE §46A-6J-1 to -6. Ordinary trade regulation laws may also address price increases during disasters and other emergencies. For an evaluation of Florida's price-gouging statute, see Gary E. Lehman, *Price Gouging: Application of Florida's Unfair Trade Practices Act in the Aftermath of Hurricane Andrew,* 17 NOVA L. REV. 1029 (1993). For a study of California's legislation, see Sean P. Lafferty, *Consumer Protection, Emergencies—Protection against Price Gouging,* 26 PAC. L.J. 215 (1995).

2. Tennessee and Virginia regulate price gouging in vaccines during medical emergencies. *See* TENN. CODE ANN. §47-18-2801 to -2805; VA. CODE ANN. §59.1-533 to -37. California penalizes an engineer who offers to practice engineering without legal authority, impersonates or uses the seal of another practitioner, or uses an expired or revoked certificate in connection with repairing structures damaged by natural disasters. *See* CAL. BUS. & PROF. CODE §6788.

3. On June 28, 2005, two months before Hurricane Katrina, Louisiana very presciently amended its price-gouging statute. 2005 La. Sess. Law Serv. Act No. 149 (S.B. No. 162) reenacted LA. REV. STAT. ANN. §29:732 and added the following italicized language:

   During a state of emergency as declared by the governor or as declared by the parish president, *or during a named tropical storm or hurricane in or threatening the Gulf of Mexico,* the value received for goods and services sold within the designated emergency area may not exceed the prices ordinarily charged for comparable goods and services in the same market area at, or immediately before, the time of the state of emergency. However, the value received may include reasonable expenses and a charge for any attendant business risk, in addition to the cost of the goods and services which necessarily are incurred in procuring the goods and services during the state of emergency.

4. Retail gasoline prices, already a subject of political concern, often rise after a disaster. The federal government has occasionally imposed price controls on petroleum products. *See generally* Welborn & Flynn, *supra,* at 4-6. The Economic Stabilization Act of 1970, Pub. L. No. 91-379, 84 Stat. 796, authorized the President to control commodity prices, including crude oil and refined petroleum. President Nixon exercised this authority in 1971 before it expired in 1974. The Emergency Petroleum Allocation Act of 1973 (EPAA), Pub. L. No. 93-159, 87 Stat. 627 (codified at 15 U.S.C. §§ 751-760), directed the President to adopt temporary measures "to deal with shortages of crude oil, residual fuel oil, and refined petroleum products or dislocations in their national distribution system" and to "minimiz[e] the adverse impacts of such shortages or dislocations on the American people and the domestic economy." Until it expired in 1981, the EPAA authorized the President to allocate oil and to set its price. Finally, the federal government can influence oil supplies and prices by manipulating the Strategic Petroleum Reserve (SPR). *See* Energy Policy and Conservation Act of 1975, Pub. L. No. 94-163, 89 Stat. 871 (codified as amended at 42 U.S.C. §§ 6231-6247).

5. Scholars have speculated that price-gouging laws emerge in response to recent, salient experiences with calamity. *See* Christine Jolls, Cass R. Sunstein & Richard Thaler, *A Behavioral Approach to Law and Economics,* 50 STAN. L. REV. 1471, 1513 (1998). Of the sixteen jurisdictions with all-purpose price-gouging statutes, nine are prone to hurricanes: Alabama, Florida, Georgia, Louisiana, Mississippi, North Carolina, South Carolina, Texas, and Virginia. Guam is prone to typhoons. So is California, although earthquakes probably figure more prominently in that state's political consciousness. Of the remaining five states, Connecticut and New York are marginally susceptible to hurricanes. The presence of landlocked Arkansas, Indiana, and West Virginia counsels "[m]ore in-depth empirical research . . . to determine" whether behavioral considerations provide the most convincing explanation, or "whether conventional interest-group theories provide an alternative account." *Id.*

6. Price-gouging laws are rationalized as a tool for correcting a temporary market failure. The market's ordinary ability to allocate goods and services to buyers who value them most is thought to be impaired by a temporary spike in prices. Price-gouging statutes and their functional equivalents (such as state trade regulation laws and federal antitrust laws) are thought to strip sellers of a windfall attributable solely to high prices that cannot spur further output within an emergency's time frame. *See, e.g.,* United States v. Eli Lilly & Co., 1959 Trade Cas. (CCH) ¶69,536 (D.N.J. 1959); Almarin Phillips & George R. Hall, *The Salk Vaccine Case: Parallelism, Conspiracy and Other Hypotheses,* 46 VA. L. REV. 717 (1960). Conventional economic wisdom, however, disfavors price-gouging statutes. During shortages, high prices are the most efficient market-clearing mechanism. Suppressing prices serves solely to discourage vendors of essentials from entering the market. *See, e.g.,* RICHARD G. LIPSEY & PETER O. STEINER, ECONOMICS 83-88

(5th ed. 1978); P.D. Byrnes, W.J. Lowry & E.J. Bondurant II, *Product Shortages, Allocation and the Antitrust Laws,* 20 ANTITRUST BULL. 713 (1975); James I. Serota, *Monopoly Pricing in a Time of Shortage,* 33 LOY. U. CHI. L.J. 791 (2002). One study concludes that federal price control legislation, such as the proposed (but never enacted) Federal Price Gouging Prevention Act,[4] would have increased the economic damage from hurricanes Katrina and Rita by $1.5 to $2.9 billion. W. David Montgomery, Robert A. Baron & Mary K. Weinkopf, *Potential Effects of Proposed Price Gouging Legislation on the Cost and Severity of Gas Supply Interruptions,* 3 J. COMPET. L. & ECON. 357 (2007).

7. Notwithstanding conventional economic objections to price gouging statutes, they may play a limited role during catastrophic breakdowns of ordinary commercial conditions:

> Natural disasters . . . have the potential to cause mass market failures in this era of electronic consumerism. Price gouging may be fine so long as consumers can access their financial assets or credit markets to pay according to their reservation price. But where payment mechanisms have broken down and uncertainty prevents the development of alternative measures, anti-gouging laws may actually be necessary to facilitate a minimum level of commerce. Because postdisaster commercial transactions often help reduce the negative externalities that natural disasters and terrorist attacks might produce, the result of facilitating a minimal level of commerce may actually be more optimal than what a free market would yield.
>
> This analysis reveals, however, the efficiency limits of anti-gouging laws. Only where the payment systems supporting consumer markets have collapsed is the enforcement of such laws appropriate. Non-coordinated price hikes in areas unaffected by the actual physical impact or secondary consequences of disasters should be permitted without government interference. Because existing state anti-gouging laws do not distinguish adequately between affected and unaffected areas, legislative reform is required.
>
> Moreover, anti-gouging laws may make sense where markets price inefficiently. To the extent that a product is affected by an "availability" or "anchoring" heuristic, the result of a supply-or demand-shock may be an increase in price beyond the market optimum. Price increases may become "sticky." If such heuristics are widespread, it may take too much time for a market to correct naturally. Anti-gouging laws, by preventing rapid price hikes, help avoid this problem of asymmetric market correction.

Geoffrey C. Rapp, *Gouging: Terrorist Attacks, Hurricanes, and the Legal and Economic Aspects of Post-Disaster Price Regulation,* 94 KY. L.J. 535, 538-539 (2005-06); *cf.* David Skarbeck, *Market Failure and Natural Disasters: A Reexamination of Anti-Gouging Laws,* 37 PUB. CONTRACT L.J. 771 (2008) (rejecting Rapp's hypotheses by defending the role of the market as a facilitator of discoveries about the elasticity of demand for commodities in shortage).

---

4. H.R. 1252, 110th Cong., 1st Sess. (May 24, 2007). The Federal Price Gouging Prevention Act passed the House on May 23, 2007, but never reached a Senate vote. *See* http://www.govtrack.us/congress/bill.xpd?bill=h110-1252.

8. To what extent does the Constitution constrain the regulation of price gouging? The Supreme Court has addressed this question in the context of laws designed to curb windfall profits during wartime:

UNITED STATES v. COMMODITIES TRADING CORP.

Supreme Court of the United States, 339 U.S. 121, 70 S. Ct. 547,
94 L. Ed. 707 (1950)

Mr. Justice BLACK delivered the opinion of the Court.

Commodities Trading Corporation brought this suit in the Court of Claims to recover "just compensation" for about 760,000 pounds of whole black pepper requisitioned by the War Department in 1944. . . . The United States contended that the [Office of Price Administration] ceiling price of 6.63 cents per pound was just compensation. Commodities denied this, claiming 22 cents per pound. It argued that Congress did not and could not constitutionally fix the ceiling price as a measure for determining what is just compensation under the Constitution. . . .

[This case is] controlled by the clause of the Fifth Amendment providing that private property shall not be "taken for public use, without just compensation." This Court has never attempted to prescribe a rigid rule for determining what is "just compensation" under all circumstances and in all cases. Fair market value has normally been accepted as a just standard. But when market value has been too difficult to find, or when its application would result in manifest injustice to owner or public, courts have fashioned and applied other standards. Since the market value standard was developed in the context of a market largely free from government controls, prices rigidly fixed by law raise questions concerning whether a "market value" so fixed can be a measure of "just compensation." . . .

The word "just" in the Fifth Amendment evokes ideas of "fairness" and "equity," and these were the primary standards prescribed for ceiling prices under the Emergency Price Control Act. As assurance that prices fixed under its authority by the administrative agency would be "generally fair and equitable," Congress provided that price regulations could be subjected to judicial review. All legitimate purchases and sales had to be made at or below ceiling prices. And most businessmen were compelled to sell because, for example, their goods were perishable or their businesses depended on continuous sales. Thus ceiling prices of commodities held for sale represented not only market value but in fact the only value that could be realized by most owners. Under these circumstances they cannot properly be ignored in deciding what is just compensation.

The extent to which ceiling prices should govern courts in such a decision is another matter. Congress did not expressly provide that prices fixed under the Price Control Act should constitute the measure of just compensation for property taken under the Fifth Amendment. And §4(d) provides that the Act shall not be construed as requiring any person to sell. But §1(a) declared the Act's purposes "to assure that defense appropriations are not dissipated by excessive prices" and to "prevent hardships . . . to the Federal, State, and local governments, which would result from abnormal increases in prices. . . ." Congress thus plainly contemplated that these governments should be able to buy goods fulfilling their wartime needs at the prices fixed for other purchasers. The crucial importance of this in the congressional plan for a stabilized war economy to limit inflation and prevent profiteering is shown by the fact that during the war approximately one-half of the nation's output of goods and services went to federal, state and local governments. And should judicial awards of just compensation be uniformly greater in amount than ceiling prices, expectations of pecuniary gains from condemnations might prompt many owners to withhold essential materials until the Government requisitioned them. We think the congressional purpose and the necessities of a wartime economy require that ceiling prices be accepted as the measure of just compensation, so far as that can be done consistently with the objectives of the Fifth Amendment.

[Dissenting opinions by Justices Frankfurter and Jackson are omitted.]

NOTES AND QUESTIONS

Commodities Trading appears to foreclose takings clause objections to price-fixing statutes adopted in response to war, disaster, or other emergency. Suppose that the government, as an alternative to regulating prices, purchased supplies for distribution on some basis other than willingness and ability to pay. If the government is the primary or exclusive purchaser of a commodity, vendors may respond by raising prices. This issue arose in United States v. Cors, 337 U.S. 325 (1949), a case involving the pricing of tugboats purchased by the federal government during wartime:

> The special value to the condemner as distinguished from others who may or may not possess the power to condemn has long been excluded as an element from market value. In time of war or other national emergency the demand of the government for an article or commodity often causes the market to be an unfair indication of value. The special needs of the government create a demand that outruns the supply. The market, sensitive to the bullish pressure, responds with a spiraling of prices.
>
> The normal market price for the commodity becomes inflated. And so the market value of the commodity is enhanced by the special need which the government has for it. . . . [A]t the time of the requisition there was "a rising market and a strong demand for tugs of all types" in and around the Port of New York, due in part at least to the shortage of tugs resulting from the government's requisitioning program.
>
> It is not fair that the government be required to pay the enhanced price which its demand alone has created. That enhancement reflects elements of the value that was created by the urgency of its need for the article. It does not reflect what "a willing buyer would pay in cash to a willing seller" in a fair market. It represents what can be exacted from the government whose demands in the emergency have created a sellers' market. In this situation, as in the case of land included in a proposed project of the government, the enhanced value reflects speculation as to what the government can be compelled to pay. That is a hold-up value, not a fair market value. That is a value which the government itself created and hence in fairness should not be required to pay.

Id. at 333-334. For an analysis of *Commodities Trading* and *Cors,* see Gregory R. Kirsch, Note, *Hurricanes and Windfalls: Takings and Price Controls in Emergencies,* 79 VA. L. REV. 1235 (1993).

E. CONCLUSION: LAW AMONG THE RUINS

At first glance, disaster law may appear to be nothing more than a collection of rules that happen to come into play when localities suffer severe physical damage. Upon deeper examination, especially of the social dimensions of catastrophic loss, disaster law emerges as the enterprise of assembling the best portfolio of legal rules to deal with catastrophic risks.

To prevent or at least to mitigate future disasters, we must confront social vulnerability in all its forms, from racial and class-based vectors of discrimination to sex, age, disability, and immigrant status. These factors contribute to the susceptibility of specific individuals and groups to disaster. In addition to recognizing these sources of susceptibility to harm during disasters and ameliorating their impacts, government owes its weakest citizens a corresponding responsibility to maximize their resilience in a disaster's wake.

Recovery from disaster almost invariably generates a narrative of personal survival, suffering, and heroism. The time eventually comes when "the needles thick on the ground" destroyed by a storm, tsunami, or earthquake "will deaden the footfall so that we shall move among trees as soundlessly as smoke." ROBERT PENN WARREN, ALL THE KING'S MEN 438 (Harvest 1996, 1st ed. 1946). "But that will be a long time from now, and soon now we shall go . . . into the convulsion of the world, out of history into history and the awful responsibility of Time." *Id.*

In the meanwhile, those of us charged with debating, designing, and deploying the entire battery of legal tools designed to prevent and mitigate disaster face a twofold challenge. First, law must seek to minimize social susceptibility before the next natural event becomes a social catastrophe. Second, during times of relative tranquility, the law should strive to improve resilience within vulnerable communities so that they might recover more rapidly and effectively should disaster strike. Addressing both of these dimensions of social justice in times of disaster fulfills the highest calling in public governance, that of law among the ruins.

6
EVALUATING AND RESPONDING TO RISK

This chapter is devoted to the concept of risk. Precautions and planning about disasters must be geared to the risk of a disaster. But how should we measure risk, and once we have measured it, how should we decide on the appropriate level of precautions?

One standard approach to risk analysis is based on expected utility theory. Here is how it works. We begin with the probability of an event — for example, the odds that a tossed coin will come up heads or tails, which is 0.5. Suppose that you can win $10 if the coin comes up heads, but lose $5 if it comes up tails. The question is whether to take the bet. If you repeated a bet of this type many times, on average you would expect to win $10 half the time and lose $5 half the time. So your expected return is $[(.5 \times 10) - (.5 \times 5)] = 2.50$. Thus, if you played this game often enough, on average you would expect to win a two dollars and fifty cents each time. It's a good bet so long as you do not have to pay more than two dollars and fifty cents to play.

We used the term "expected utility" earlier and this requires a small revision in the analysis. People are often risk averse — that is, they prefer not to gamble. For instance, they may strongly prefer a sure thing of losing $1,000 in the form of paying an insurance premium rather than take a 1 percent chance of losing $100,000. Yet, if you do the arithmetic, you will see that in expected value terms, the two are equivalent. $(1 \times 1,000 = .01 \times 100,000)$. Economists explain this by saying that the utility of an additional dollar declines as wealth rises. This seems intuitively right — a homeless person would surely care far more than Bill Gates about the loss of $20. Because of declining marginal utility, the dollars in the premium are less "valuable" than the dollars the person would lose if the gamble was unsuccessful. So what people care about is the not the expected dollar value of the loss, but its expected-utility value.

In practice, of course, finding the correct probabilities is not as easy as it is with coin tosses. For further discussion of the techniques used by risk analysts, you may want to consult a standard text such as Daniel M. Kammen & David M. Hassenzahl, SHOULD WE RISK IT? EXPLORING ENVIRONMENTAL, HEALTH, AND TECHNOLOGICAL PROBLEM SOLVING (1999), or M. Granger Morgan & Max Henrion,

Uncertainty: A Guide to Dealing with Uncertainty in Quantitative Risk and Policy Analysis (1990).

Partly because of risk aversion, it is important to know the probabilities associated with the full range of possible harms, not just the most likely level of harm. In other words, we should not consider merely the "typical" California earthquake or the "typical" Gulf Coast hurricane. (Using the term "typical" may actually be misleading, as we will see.)

A graph of the probability of harm as against the extent of that harm can take various shapes. When an event is caused by a large number of random factors, the resulting probability distribution is often the famous bell-shaped curve (also called the normal or Gaussian distribution). A lot of statistical analysis is based on normal distributions.

Even people who have never heard of a bell curve have an intuitive sense of its properties, with most events bunched near the average and extreme outcomes fading away quickly. If the average cat weighs 10 pounds, we can expect that most cats will be within a few pounds of the average, and we can safely disregard the possibility of a 200-pound tabby.

Complex systems, however, are often characterized by a different type of statistical distribution called a "power law."[1] If feline weight were subject to a power law, we would find that the vast majority of cats were tiny or even microscopic but that 1,000-pound housecats would cross our paths now and then. Under a power law, the possibility of freak outcomes, a one-ton Siamese, weighs heavily in the analysis, often more heavily than the far more numerous "routine" outcomes, the tiny micro-cats. Indeed, a power law probability distribution makes it somewhat misleading to even talk about "typical" outcomes. This is definitely not true of the sizes of cats, but it may well be true of CATs (hurricane strengths).

The difference between complexity and randomness is that random factors operate independently of each other whereas complexity involves interactive systems. In statistical terms, this difference is reflected in the difference between a normal distribution and a power law distribution. In practical terms, the difference is that extreme events are more likely in complex systems — obviously something that's very relevant to disaster issues.

In this chapter, we will begin by looking closely at the question of how to evaluate risks. The quantitative methods used by risk analysts and economists are at odds with the intuitive reactions of people to hazards. We will probe these differences in depth. We will then consider approaches to deciding on the proper response. Knowing the risk that an earthquake will occur does not directly tell us how much we should spend on precautions. That determination may be made in terms of standard engineering practices, cost-benefit analysis, or the precautionary principle.

In this analysis, in order to determine the seriousness of a risk, we only need to know the odds that it will materialize and the amount of "utility" that will be lost. We will see in Section A, however, that human beings do not necessarily conform to this model, which raises the question of whether the

---

1. For an introduction to power laws, *see* Manfred Schroeder, *Fractals, Chaos, Power Laws: Minutes from an Infinite Paradise* 103-119 (1991).

economist approach is a more rational alternative to ordinary attitudes toward risk.

A. EVALUATING RISKS

CLAYTON P. GILETTE & JAMES E. KRIER, RISK, COURT, AND AGENCIES

138 U. PA. L. REV. 1027, 1027-1029, 1039, 1071-1073, 1076-1079 (1990)[2]

. . . What does "risk" *mean?* To anticipate our argument, suppose that the concept signifies different things to different people — more particularly, one thing to agency experts and another to the lay public. . . . The resulting contest is, at bottom, one of competing rationalities, and its resolution is a matter of ethics and politics, not technical expertise. Nothing in the training, credentials, or legitimacy of risk assessors or bureaucrats qualifies them to settle the issue. Hence deference to agencies would grant them ground they have no right to claim. Deference would beg a central question in the control of public risk. . . .

. . . [G]enerally speaking "experts appear to see riskiness as synonymous with expected annual mortality [and morbidity]."[3] So, for example, when technical experts are asked to rank the risks of various activities and technologies, "their responses correlate highly with technical estimates of annual fatalities."[4] When experts write about relative risk, they implicitly or explicitly use body counts as the relevant measure. And, in a way seemingly consistent with the logic of their method, they insist that a death is a death is a death — 1,000 lives lost in a single anticipated annual catastrophe, or through many accidents expected every year, or lost ten-fold but only once every decade on average, or lost in a single community or across the country, are all the same to them.

In the view of experts, then, risk is a one-dimensional phenomenon. . . .

For the lay person, risk is *n*-dimensional, as William Lowrance suggested in an early study. He observed that a variety of considerations in addition to expected fatalities and injuries affect people's judgments about risk: involuntary exposure, delayed effects, scientific uncertainty about the hazard in question, "dreaded" versus common hazards (for example, the threat of death from invisible radiation as opposed to an auto accident), irreversible consequences, and others. Since the time of Lowrance's work, any number of studies have found "that many attributes other than death rates determine judgments of riskiness" by lay people, whose "model of what constitutes risk

---

2. Copyright © 1990, University of Pennsylvania Law Review. Reprinted by permission.

3. Slovic, *"Perception of Risk,"* 236 SCI. 280, 283 (1983) (citation omitted); *see also* Slovic, Fischhoff & Lichtenstein, *Facts and Fears: Understanding Perceived Risk, in* SOCIETAL RISK ASSESSMENT: HOW SAFE IS SAFE ENOUGH? 181, 191-192 (R. Schwing & W. Albers, Jr., eds. 1980) (experts view risk as synonymous with technical fatality estimates).

4. Slovic, Fischhoff & Lichtenstein, *Regulation of Risk: A Psychological Perspective, in* REGULATORY POLICY AND THE SOCIAL SCIENCES 241, 263 (R. Noll ed., 1985) [hereinafter Slovic, Fischhoff & Lichtenstein, *Regulation of Risk*]; *see also id.* at 266 (Fig. 4) (showing that experts' risk judgments are closely associated with annual fatality rates). . . .

appears to be much richer than that held by most technical experts." Thus the public is known to be concerned about risks that have catastrophic potential, that are unfamiliar, uncontrollable, or involuntary, that threaten future generations, that would concentrate fatalities in time or space, that are distinctively threatening as opposed to widespread and shared by the general population, that are manmade as opposed to natural. . . .

Return, then, to the public's rich image of risk, and reflect for a moment on its many dimensions. People have a lower tolerance for involuntary than for voluntary exposure.[5] Even on its surface, the concern here is easily understood, and closely related to the dimensions of uncontrollability and uncertainty. Voluntary exposure presupposes knowledge. Knowledge coupled with freedom of action facilitates individual choice and efforts to control events bearing on the choice. To be forced to face a risk, on the other hand, or to be ignorant of it, or to sense that no one is really in command of it, leaves one's well-being in the hands of others, or of no one. Either alternative is obviously inferior, under most circumstances, to being in charge.

Upon deeper examination, this sense of voluntariness might trivialize the true concern. Suppose my situation (say I am an unskilled worker) "forces" me to "choose" a risky occupation, in exchange for some wage premium. Is my exposure to the risk "voluntary"? Suppose, more generally, that I rightly see life as full of difficult choices. Is it sensible to say that, given my power to choose — given that any choice is "voluntary" — I should accept without complaint whatever consequences follow? The answer might be yes if the world were organized in a way consistent with ideal values and principles, but it is not. Behind the notion of voluntariness, then, there may lurk more fundamental concerns about autonomy and equality and power among individuals in the society, for it is the pre-existence of these that lets free choice be morally interesting. People perhaps are saying that some risks seem consistent with such ideals and others not, and registering the view by showing a greater acceptance of risks that they regard as "voluntary" in fundamentally important ways, as opposed to "chosen" in some narrower sense.

The foregoing account enlightens us about other popular dimensions of risk, such as the enhanced dislike of delayed (latent) effects, and of irreversible ones. Latency frustrates knowledge, and irreversibility frustrates control. They make it more difficult for us to govern our own circumstances — and also to govern our governors. How do we hold accountable officials whose mistakes or misdeeds manifest themselves only decades after a term of office? And how do we correct for what they have done, if what they have done is uncorrectable? Latency and irreversibility practically deny us the fruits of trial-and-error, perhaps the best means yet devised by which to resolve uncertainty.

What of the special dislike of manmade as opposed to natural hazards? Once again, a story grows out of what has been said thus far: Humans might treat each other with motives that Nature could never have, and this matters. . . . First, people are responsible for artificial risks, but not for

---

5. There is some indication that the voluntary-involuntary distinction actually serves as a proxy for other concerns, such as catastrophic potential, dread, uncontrollability, and like factors. . . .

natural ones, and the government's job is to regulate what people do. Second, only manmade risks can, in any meaningful sense, threaten autonomy, an additional reason to be especially wary of them. Third, the harms we suffer because of the acts of others carry special injury; we mourn the deaths from a natural flood but resent, deeply, the ones from a broken dam. We "are concerned not simply with safety but with responsibility and guilt as well."

These same concerns arise in the case of those manmade risks we and others classify as "public": risks generated by highly centralized high technologies. This is especially so because public risks entail so much uncertainty (given their complexity), imply such considerable power, and are capable of such calamitous effects. The last consideration, in particular, implicates the public's aversion to the possibility of disastrous consequences and brings us to the cluster of factors that enter into what is termed "dread." Dread correlates significantly with some aspects of risk that we have already discussed, such as involuntariness and uncontrollability, but also with such others as inequitable distributions, threats to future generations, and catastrophic potential — each of which speaks almost for itself.

The idea of inequitable distributions, for example, reflects the view that just as a right thinking society should concern itself with the distribution of wealth, so too should it do so with the distribution of risk. For example, risks that might result in death or disease are often considered worth taking because they confer significant benefits not otherwise available. This risk burden may be regarded as equitably distributed only if it is borne by those who simultaneously enjoy the benefits. Burdens imposed on others, or diverted to future generations, generate worries about exploitation. Alternatively, risks concentrated in time and space might be regarded as inequitable or otherwise unacceptable because concentration can result in losses that are avoided by broader distributions. This suggests, then, a link between inequitable distributions and catastrophic potential. Concentrated risks can threaten whole communities, and the loss of a community is the loss of a valued thing distinct and apart from the disaggregated bodies of a community's citizens.

NOTES AND QUESTIONS

1. Cognitive psychologists have developed a descriptive theory of how people make decisions under conditions of risk and uncertainty. A dominant theme in the theory is that most people do not evaluate risky circumstances in the manner assumed by conventional decision theory: specifically, they do not seek to maximize the expected value of some function such as utility when selecting among actions with uncertain outcome. This cognitive theory has implications for regulatory policies designed to control risk to life, health, and the environment. For further discussion, *see* Roger G. Noll & James E. Krier, *Some Implications of Cognitive Psychology for Risk Regulation*, 19 J. Legal Stud. 747 (1990).

2. For more discussion of how and why experts and lay persons assess environmental risks differently, *see* Howard Margolis, Dealing with Risk: Why the Public and the Experts Disagree on Environmental Issues (1996);

Cass R. Sunstein, *The Laws of Fear*, 115 HARV. L. REV. 1119 (2002); Howard Margolis, *A New Account of Expert/Lay Conflicts of Risk Intuition*, 8 DUKE ENVTL. L. & POL'Y F. 115 (1997). Cognitive bias can adversely affect decision making. For instance, millions of Americans substituted driving for air travel in the months after September 11, 2001. This change in behavior caused an estimated 353 deaths in the final months of 2001. *See* Rerd Gigerenzer, *Dread Risk, September 11, and Fatal Traffic Accidents*, 15 PSYCH. SCI. 286 (2004).

3. The analysis above suggests that a number of factors besides probabilities and estimated harms may affect public response to disaster risks: risks will get the most attention if they have catastrophic potential, are unfamiliar or uncontrollable, or result in geographically concentrated fatalities. This suggests that potentially catastrophic events may get more attention than more routine disasters, even if the routine disasters are cumulatively quite damaging. Also, natural disasters get less attention than man-made events — imagine if the New Orleans levees had been blown up by terrorists, or on the other hand, if the Twin Towers had been hit by a meteor.

4. Gillette and Krier focus on the different aspects of risk that are relevant to the public. In the next excerpt, Dan Kahan considers how emotion affects perception of risk and how this may lead different individuals to divergent perceptions. The two excerpts can be considered complementary: one focuses on risk characteristics and the other on the individual characteristics of the person assessing the risk. They have in common an interest in the distinction between expert and lay opinions about risk.

DAN M. KAHAN, TWO CONCEPTIONS OF EMOTION IN RISK REGULATION

156 U. PA. L. REV. 741 (2008)

Recent work in cognitive and social psychology makes it clear that emotion plays a critical role in public perceptions of risk, but doesn't make clear exactly what that role is or why it matters. This Article examines two competing theories of risk perception, which generate two corresponding understandings of emotion and its significance for risk regulation. The "irrational weigher" theory asserts that laypersons' emotional apprehensions of risk are heuristic substitutes for more reflective judgments, and as such lead to systematic errors. It therefore counsels that risk regulation be assigned to politically insulated experts whose judgments are free of emotion's distorting impact. The "cultural evaluator" theory, in contrast, asserts that emotional apprehensions of risk reflect persons' expressive appraisals of putatively dangerous activities. It implies that emotional apprehensions of risk should at least sometimes be afforded normative weight in law and also generates distinctive strategies for reconciling sound risk regulation with genuinely participatory, democratic policymaking. . . .

Recent advances in the study of risk perception seem to furnish decisive evidence of emotion's antagonism to reason. A growing body of empirical research supplies compelling proof of the critical role that emotions play in the apprehension of personal and societal dangers. This role, according to the predominant understanding, is a heuristic one. Lacking access to sound empirical information, or the time and cognitive capacity to make sense of it, ordinary people conform their perceptions of risk to the visceral reactions that putatively dangerous activities evoke. These snap judgments might serve individuals better than nothing, the conventional account suggests. But they don't serve individuals nearly as well as the type of considered, reflective assessment for which they are a substitute. A substantial body of writing in the field of risk perception documents the numerous ways in which affect-driven risk appraisals lead ordinary people, and their popularly accountable representatives, to take positions inimical to society's well-being. The remedy, according to this work, is to shield law from the distorting influence of emotion, primarily by delegating regulatory power to politically insulated experts, who can evaluate the costs and benefits of asserted hazards (nuclear power, genetically modified foods, handguns, etc.) in a deliberate and reasoned fashion.

My goal in this Article is to challenge this position. I don't mean to raise any question about the demonstrated centrality of emotions to risk perception, but only about the prevailing interpretation of it. The conclusion that emotional appraisals are irrational is integral, I'll argue, to a model of risk perception that sees the positions people take toward putatively dangerous activities as reflecting their implicit (and usually skewed) weighing of instrumental costs and benefits. I will lay emphasis instead on an account that sees risk perceptions as embodying individuals' cultural evaluations of the meanings expressed by society's decision to tolerate or abate particular risks. This model of risk perception, I'll argue, suggests that emotion functions not as a heuristic substitute for considered appraisals of information but rather as a perceptive faculty uniquely suited to discerning what stance toward risk best coheres with a person's values. Without the power this affective capacity supplies, it would be impossible for individuals to form rational cultural evaluations of risk. This account suggests that it would also be a mistake to seal off risk regulation from the influence of affect-driven risk appraisals or to assume that affect-driven appraisals cannot themselves be influenced by education and deliberation.

I will develop this argument in three steps. I will begin, in Part I, by describing three theories of risk perception, two of which treat emotion as essential to the cognition of risk. In Part II, I will canvass empirical findings that bear on these alternative understandings of how emotion contributes to risk perception. Finally, in Part III, I will examine what is at stake as a normative and prescriptive matter in the contest between these two conceptions of emotion in risk regulation.

I. Three Theories of Risk Perception, Two Conceptions of Emotion

The profound impact of emotion on risk perception cannot be seriously disputed. Distinct emotional states — from fear to dread to anger to disgust and distinct emotional phenomena — from affective orientations to symbolic associations and imagery have been found to explain perceptions of the dangerousness of all manner of activities and things — from pesticides to mobile phones, from red meat consumption to cigarette smoking.

More amenable to dispute, however, is exactly why emotions exert this influence. Obviously, emotions work in conjunction with more discrete mechanisms of cognition in some fashion. But which ones and how? To sharpen the assessment of the evidence that bears on these questions, I will now sketch out three alternative models of risk perception — the rational weigher, the irrational weigher, and the cultural evaluator theories — and their respective accounts of what (if anything) emotions contribute to the cognition of risk.

A. The Rational Weigher Theory: Emotion as Byproduct

Based on the premises of neoclassical economics, the rational weigher theory asserts that individuals, over time and in aggregate, process information about risky undertakings in a way that maximizes their expected utility. The decision whether to accept hazardous occupations in exchange for higher wages, to engage in unhealthy forms of recreation in exchange for hedonic pleasure, to accept intrusive regulation to mitigate threats to national security or the environment, all turn on a utilitarian balancing of costs and benefits.

On this theory, emotions don't make any contribution to the cognition of risk. They enter into the process, if they do at all, only as reactive byproducts of individuals' processing of information: if a risk appears high relative to benefits, individuals will likely experience a negative emotion (perhaps fear, dread, or anger), whereas if the risk appears low, they will likely experience a positive one (such as hope or relief).

B. The Irrational Weigher Theory: Emotions as Bias

The irrational weigher theory asserts that individuals lack the capacity to process information that maximizes their expected utility. Because of constraints on information, time, and computational power, ordinary individuals must resort to heuristic substitutes for considered analysis; those heuristics, moreover, invariably cause individuals' evaluations of risks to err in substantial and recurring ways. Much of contemporary social psychology and behavioral economics has been dedicated to cataloging the myriad distortions — from the "availability cascades" to "probability neglect" to "overconfidence bias" to "status quo bias" that systematically skew risk perceptions, particularly those of the lay public.

For the irrational weigher theory, the contribution that emotion makes to risk perception is, in the first instance, a heuristic one. Individuals rely on their visceral, affective reactions to compensate for the limits on their ability to engage in more considered assessments. More specifically, irrational weigher theorists have identified emotion or affect as a central component of "System 1 reasoning," which is "fast, automatic, effortless, associative, and often emotionally charged," as opposed to "System 2 reasoning," which is "slower, serial, effortful, and deliberately controlled" and typically involves "execution of learned rules." System 1 is clearly adaptive in the main — heuristic reasoning furnishes guidance when lack of time, information, and cognitive ability make more systematic forms of reasoning infeasible — but it remains obviously "error prone" in comparison to the "more deliberative [and] calculative" System 2. . . .

C. The Cultural Evaluator Theory: Emotion as Expressive Perception

Finally there's the cultural evaluator theory of risk perception. This model rests on a view of rational agency that sees individuals as concerned not merely with maximizing their welfare in some narrow consequentialist sense, but also with adopting stances toward states of affairs that appropriately express the values that define their identities. Often when an individual is assessing what position to take on a putatively dangerous activity, she is, on this account, not weighing (rationally or irrationally) her expected utility but rather evaluating the social meaning of that activity. Against the background of cultural norms (particularly contested ones), would the law's designation of that activity as inimical to society's well-being affirm her values or denigrate them?

Like the irrational weigher theory, the cultural evaluator theory treats emotions as entering into the cognition of risk. But it offers a very different account of how—one firmly aligned with the position that sees emotions as constituents of reason. . . .

This account of emotion doesn't see its function as a heuristic one. That is, emotions don't just enable a person to latch onto a position in the absence of time to acquire and reflect on information. Rather, as a distinctive faculty of cognition, emotions perform a unique role in enabling her to identify the stance that is expressively rational for someone with her commitments. Without the contribution that emotion makes to her powers of expressive perception, she would be lacking this vital incident of rational agency, no matter how much information, no matter how much time, and no matter how much computational acumen she possessed.

II. Empirical Evidence

So far, I have outlined three theories of risk perception and the corresponding accounts of emotion they support. I now want to assess how well these theories fit the growing empirical literature on emotion and risk perception.

A. The Cognitive Priority of Emotion to Risk Perception

Among the most important empirical studies on emotion and risk perception are those that demonstrate the cognitive priority of the former. Rather than conform their emotional appraisals of a putatively dangerous activity (say, nuclear power generation) to their assessment of its risks, individuals conform their assessments of its risks to their emotional appraisals. . . . [These studies] are equally compatible with both the cultural evaluator theory's conception of emotion as expressive perception and the irrational weigher theory's conception of emotion as bias.

B. The Effects of Emotion on Information Processing

Another class of studies purports to identify particular characteristics of individuals' risk perceptions that are plausibly viewed as evidence of the impact of emotion on information processing. Studies of this sort, however, also fail to resolve decisively the dispute between emotion as bias and emotion as expressive perception.

One feature of risk perception said to bear the signature of emotion is the unwillingness of individuals to adjust their decisions about the acceptability of risks to changes in information about their probability. System 2 reasoning requires not only that people form unbiased assessments of the magnitude of risks and benefits, but also that they appropriately combine them to determine the expected utility of forgoing or forbearing them. That doesn't happen when people are emotional. Instead they fail to discount a potential harm by its improbability—the phenomenon of "probability neglect"—because "when intense emotions are engaged, people tend to focus on the adverse outcome, not on its likelihood." By the same token, when people "anticipate a loss of what [they] now have, [they] can become genuinely afraid, in a way that greatly exceeds [their] feelings of pleasurable anticipation when [they] look forward to some supplement to what [they] now have." The result is "status quo" bias, the disposition to refrain from action that entails some risks but that nonetheless has a positive expected value. Alternatively, positive emotions—such as hope or pride—can lead to an "overconfidence bias" that induces people to underestimate risks associated with behavior they value.

But an alternative explanation, one in keeping with the cultural evaluator theory, is that individuals' decisions to forgo or forbear risks is based not on the expected utility of those actions but on their social meanings, which are unlikely to be tied in any systematic way to the actuarial magnitude of those risks. The individualist, for example, who continues to worry more about being rendered defenseless than about being shot as the risks of insufficient gun control appear to increase might "not so much [be] afraid of dying as afraid of death without honor." Similarly, for the person who values an activity—say, smoking—precisely because she subscribes to an ethic that prizes the "authenticity of impulse and risk," a cultivated disposition to discount the likelihood of personal harm may be integral to the very form of life that activity helps her to experience. For such persons, moreover, the very idea of conforming their attitudes toward a risk to the results of a cost-benefit calculus might bear a meaning that denigrates their values. . . .

Another supposed sign of the influence of emotion on information processing is the responsiveness of individual risk perceptions to the vividness of information. The irrational weigher theory treats this as further evidence that emotions warp reasoned analysis. Emotionally gripping depictions of harm (e.g., news coverage of a terrorist attack), it is said, are more salient than emotionally sterile ones (e.g., stories about the consequences of global warming). Accordingly, they are more likely to be noticed and recalled, generating the distorted estimation of risks associated with the "availability effect."

But again the cultural evaluator model offers an alternative explanation that fits the data just as well, if not better. The impact of vivid information on risk perceptions is conditional on individuals' cultural worldviews. Shown news of a school shooting spree, egalitarians and communitarians fix on the horrifying image of dead children and revise upward their assessment of the risks of private gun ownership. What captures the attention of hierarchical and individualistic persons, however, is the tragic inability of school personnel to cut the massacre short because they were forbidden by law to bring their own guns onto school premises — a dreaded outcome that causes them to revise upward their assessment of the risk of gun control. Likewise, terrorism risks loom larger than global warming risks only in the imagination of hierarchs [who stress the value of hierarchy and authority] not in the imagination of egalitarians — and in the mind of individualists, neither is particularly worrisome. Because all persons of all cultural persuasions have a stake in forming an evaluation of the incident that appropriately expresses their values, there's no reason to view anyone's response to the vividness of the story as biased rather than rationally informed by emotion.

A similar conclusion can be drawn about one last feature of risk perceptions often presented as evidence of the biasing effect of emotion. This is the tendency of public risk perceptions to reinforce and feed on themselves. Irrational weigher theorists depict this phenomenon as a form of "hysteria" or "mass panic." They link it to emotion by identifying the cause as "highly vivid cases . . . that receive concentrated media attention" resulting in a distorting "interplay between anxiety, fear, and subjective probabilities."

The problem with this argument is that the power of social influence to amplify perceptions of risk is also known to be highly conditional on individuals' cultural orientations. The view that nuclear power is dangerous and that global warming is a serious threat is uniformly held by egalitarians, but almost uniformly rejected by hierarchs and individualists. . . .

C. Emotion and Systematic Reasoning: Substitutes or Complements?

The experiments I have examined to this point show that emotion matters for risk perception, but they don't address whether emotion is functioning as bias or as a form of expressive perception. A third type arguably does both.

This research relates to how information and emotion interact. The irrational weigher theory treats emotion as an heuristic, System 1 substitute for more considered, System 2 information processing. It follows from this that the situation in which a person is likely to rely most decisively on emotion is when she must form an instantaneous judgment about a risk about which she has little or no information. As people obtain more information on, and have more time to reflect about, a novel risk, their judgments should be less affective or emotional. In this sense, then, the irrational weigher theory hypothesizes a negative interaction between information and emotion.

The cultural evaluator theory suggests something different. According to that theory, emotion enables a person to form an attitude about risk that appropriately expresses her values. Emotion can't reliably perform that function, however, if a person lacks sufficient information to form a coherent judgment about whether crediting it would affirm or denigrate her worldview. On this account, then, emotion can be expected to play a bigger role in the judgment of someone who has had access to information and time to reflect on a relatively novel risk than someone who has not. In this sense, the cultural evaluator theory predicts a positive interaction between information and emotional perception of risk.

Paul Slovic, Don Braman, Geoff Cohen, John Gastil, and I conducted an experiment to test these competing hypotheses. We assessed people's perceptions of the risks of nanotechnology. As we expected, the vast majority of our subjects — about 80% — had heard either "little" or "nothing" about this technology before we conducted our study. Nevertheless, close to 90% had an opinion on whether nanotechnology's potential risks would outweigh its potential benefits. Not surprisingly, their affective responses to nanotechnology exerted a strong influence on their perceptions. But consistent with the prediction of the cultural evaluator theory, and inconsistent with that of the irrational weigher theory, the impact of affect relative to other influences (such as gender, race, or ideology) was significantly larger among persons who knew a modest or substantial amount about nanotechnology before the study. Likewise, we found that affect, as well as cultural worldviews, played an even bigger role in explaining variation among subjects who received information about nanotechnology before their views were elicited than in those who did not receive information first. Again, these findings suggest that emotion is not a heuristic substitute for information, but rather a type of evaluative judgment that depends on access to enough information for a person to evaluate the social meaning of a putatively dangerous activity. . . .

Is this study conclusive in the contest between "emotion as bias" and "emotion as expressive perception"? Definitely not. But as the only study that puts the two squarely in conflict, it underscores the importance of resisting the fallacious inference that because emotion does not perform the role assigned to it by the (discredited) rational weigher model, the function it performs must be an irrational one.

III. Normative and Prescriptive Implications

Only the conceptions of emotion associated with the irrational weigher theory and the cultural evaluator theory fit the data on the relationship between emotion and risk perception. I now want to consider what is at stake as a practical matter in the conflict between them. Whether we see emotion as bias or expressive perception, I will argue, has immense normative and prescriptive implications for risk regulation.

A. Expertise — Scientific and Moral

The normative program associated with the irrational weigher theory has two adversaries. One is a largely anti-interventionist stance that counsels that market forces be trusted to set appropriate levels of risk absent manifest externalities, which themselves should be remedied through regulations that "mimic" the risk-benefit tradeoffs reflected in well-functioning markets. If, as the irrational weigher theory asserts, emotions pervade and distort popular beliefs about risk, then there is little reason to assume that the decisions people make about their own welfare furnish a reliable guide for regulation. The other adversary is a fundamentally "populist" regime that favors reliance on highly participatory democratic processes to identify appropriate levels of risk. That strategy, according to irrational weighers, assures convulsive regulatory responsiveness to the alternating currents of myopia and hysteria that animate popular risk perceptions.

In place of these approaches, the irrational weigher theory advocates delegation of regulatory authority to politically insulated, scientifically trained risk experts. These individuals, it is said, have the information and technical acumen necessary to engage in reflective, System 2 reasoning, free of the biasing effects of emotion. By installing experts in independent regulatory agencies with which politicians cannot (easily) interfere and to which courts are obliged to defer, the law inoculates them from the virus of public irrationality.

Contrary to the objections of the defenders of the pro-market and populist strategies, moreover, irrational weigher theorists argue that this essentially depoliticized mechanism for intervening in private decision making need not be viewed as disrespectful of either individual freedom or self-government. Since ordinary people presumably would disown beliefs that are the product of emotional irrationality, regulating them via standards set by independent experts instead conforms their conduct to the preferences they would hold, as individuals and as a society, if they had the cognitive capacity to form considered and rational beliefs. "When people's fears lead them in the wrong directions," Sunstein explains, this form of "libertarian paternalism can provide a valuable corrective."

The cultural evaluator theory suggests a strong critique of this defense of virtual-representation-by-risk-expert. According to the cultural evaluator model, most of the phenomena that the irrational weigher theory attributes to emotionally biased decision making in fact reflect the use of emotion to form expressively rational stances toward risk. If individuals' factual beliefs are expressive of cultural worldviews, then experts who treat those beliefs as "blunders" unentitled to normative respect in a "deliberative democracy" are necessarily shielding regulatory law from citizens' visions of the good society. In fact, it is quite debatable whether risk experts' judgments are as impervious to emotion as irrational weigher theorists believe. But however much more they know than ordinary members of the public about the actuarial magnitudes of various risks, the scientific experts certainly possess no special insight on the cultural values society's laws should express.

It is exactly this mismatch between the sort of technical expertise possessed by risk experts and the emotional expertise needed to connect stances toward risk to citizens' values that informs unease toward "cost-benefit" and related welfarist modes of policymaking. It's not impossible to imagine the law being coherently informed by such methods. What is impossible to imagine, though, is that the policies will adequately engage the difficult expressive questions that risk conflicts inevitably present. If part of what's troubling (to some) about nuclear power is what it would say about our values to leave to future generations the problem of dealing with ever-accumulating and forever-toxic wastes, then how does it help to treat the likelihood that future generations will in fact find a solution as just another variable in the cost-benefit calculus? If part of what disturbs (some) people about gun control is the condition of servility it expresses to cede protection of themselves and their families exclusively to the state, how responsive is it to print out a regression analysis that shows more lives are saved on net than are lost when handguns are banned? A form of policymaking that deliberately excluded the expressive insight uniquely associated with emotional perception would leave a society in a morally disabled posture analogous to the state of impairment experienced by the emotion-free individuals Damasio describes.

Nevertheless, this objection to deferring to scientific risk experts does not commit the cultural evaluator theory to either the pro-market or populist programs of risk regulation. Recognizing that emotions enable persons to perceive expressive value doesn't imply that the insight it imparts can never be challenged. Indeed, the idea that emotions express cognitive evaluations is historically conjoined to the position that emotions can and should be evaluated as true or false, right or wrong, reasonable or unreasonable, in light of the moral correctness of the values those emotions express.

When we appreciate the expressive contribution that emotions make to risk perception, we are equipped to discern issues of justice that never come into focus under welfarist styles of risk assessment. Should a person about to be operated on be entitled to information about the risk that he could contract HIV from an infected surgeon? Why not, if we think of the decision as reflecting only the interest a prospective patient has in calculating the costs and benefits of her treatment options? But what should our answer be if we know that fear of this risk — at least in those who placidly tolerate many larger risks incident to surgery — expresses commitment to a hierarchical worldview that condemns forms of deviance symbolically associated with AIDS? Is it appropriate for a legislature to limit access to guns in order to avoid the risk of shooting accidents or violent crime? The question is at least a more complicated one if we recognize that part of what motivates aversion to these risks is an egalitarian and communitarian cultural style that despises the individualistic connotations of private gun ownership.

Analogous, and equally difficult, questions arise in other areas of law in which emotions figure. No set of procedures or doctrines, in my view, can ever assure that these issues will be resolved in a just way.

But the normative complexity that the cultural evaluator theory injects into risk regulation is by no means a reason to shy away from it. For if emotion does indeed figure in our risk perceptions in the way that that theory implies, we would certainly be fools not to recognize how dependent risk regulation is on moral, as well as scientific, expertise.

NOTES AND QUESTIONS

1. Kahan's focus is on regulation of risky behavior, but it is easy to see how some similar issues might carry over to natural disasters. For example, some people may view society as having a duty to force people to evacuate and assist them in doing so if necessary. Others may view this as an individual choice and hold people responsible for failing to take disaster precautions for themselves. These perceptions in turn may be tied to cultural differences. Should policy makers attempt to avoid these cultural issues where possible, or should they try to bring them out in the open and discuss them? Or should they try to focus as much as possible on saving as many lives as possible (or preventing as much property damage as possible)?

2. Kahan's argument is also relevant to the question of how decision-making authority should be distributed. If accepted, the argument would suggest that experts should play a less central role than some might favor. Could

it also suggest that disaster issues should be decided on the state level, given that cultural differences in the United States are correlated with geography?

3. These disputes about the nature of risk also relate to prioritization, as discussed in the following excerpt. The author also contests the positions taken in the preceding two excerpts about the nature of risk.

CASS R. SUNSTEIN, WHICH RISKS FIRST?[6]

1997 U. CHI. LEGAL F. 101, 103-105, 112-114 (1997)

. . . Some people think that the government should try to maximize the number of total lives saved.[7] If one program would save one hundred lives, and another eighty, the government should (other things being equal) begin with the first program. But other people, referring to pervasive differences between lay and expert evaluations of risk, reject this idea. They say that lay people have more complex, "richer" judgments about which risks are worst and that these judgments should govern regulatory policy. On this view, there is a danger that expert judgments will hide controversial ideas about rationality behind a technocratic smokescreen.

. . . I reject both of these views. A basic assumption is that the American constitutional order is a republic, or a deliberative democracy, in which public representatives are not supposed merely to register existing judgments but "to refine and enlarge the public view."[8] If the issue of risk regulation is seen in these terms, representatives should attend to reflective citizen judgments, but they should not treat those judgments uncritically or accept them regardless of the reasons offered on their behalf. . . . And if we examine the reasons that underlie risk-related judgments, we will conclude that it would be obtuse to say that government should attempt to maximize the number of lives saved, no matter the source and nature of relevant risks. Lives are not fungible with lives; it matters a great deal for what purpose and in what context lives are being put in danger. But it would also be odd to rely entirely on lay judgments, which are frequently based on confusion, ignorance, and selective attention. When those judgments are based on misunderstandings of the facts, they should play no role in policy.

I contend that government should attempt a three-step inquiry. First it should try to estimate *decently-livable life-years saved*, rather than total lives saved. Thus the first step in its analysis should be to see how much aggregate extension of decently-livable years can be brought about by different regulatory initiatives. The second step should incorporate lay judgments to the extent that these are based on reasonable judgments of value rather than factual error or selective attention. In this way, regulators should ask if regulatory priorities should be shifted from the aggregate measure by exploring whether

---

6. Copyright © 1997, University of Chicago. Reprinted by permission of the University of Chicago Legal Forum.

7. This is the tendency in Stephen Breyer, BREAKING THE VICIOUS CIRCLE: TOWARD EFFECTIVE RISK REGULATION (Harvard 1993).

8. Federalist 10 (Madison), *in* Max Beloff ed., THE FEDERALIST 45 (Basil Blackwell 2d ed. 1987).

there are important qualities in the context that call for a shift. The key questions here are:

— Is the risk inequitably distributed?
— Is it especially dreaded?
— Is it run involuntarily?
— How easily can it be controlled by those exposed?

Answers to these questions may call for an adjustment of the first-stage judgment. As we will see, however, the second two questions raise complex issues, for risks are not "voluntary or not" or "uncontrollable or not," but instead come with small or high costs of avoidance. The ordinary criterion of decently-livable life-years should be adjusted upward when the costs of risk avoidance are especially high, and adjusted downward when the costs of risk avoidance are especially low. The third step consists of an incorporation of effects short of mortality, including (but not limited to) morbidity, adverse effects on aesthetics and recreation, and mortality effects for plants and animals. . . .

There is considerable crudeness . . . in the idea of "lives saved" as the regulatory maximand. Of course no program "saves lives"; at best it extends them. Compare two regulations. The first extends the lives of one hundred elderly people, but in doing so, it gives them five additional years, accompanied by considerable pain and distress. The second extends the lives of eighty children, and in doing so, it gives each of them a statistical likelihood of fifty or more years of life. The second policy seems preferable to the first along two important dimensions. *First:* Lives are certainly not fungible, but where regulatory resources are limited and where choices have to be made, it makes sense (other things being equal and as an administrable start) to save as many years as possible. Other things being equal, many years should be chosen over few. *Second:* If government has a choice between preserving lives in a way that ensures decently-livable years and preserving lives in a way that ensures a barely functional and extremely painful continued existence, it should choose the former. To someone who has a choice between death and five years of constant and considerable pain, the latter will probably seem a lot better; but for government regulators, it is preferable to provide five good years rather than five difficult ones if there is a choice. We might conclude, then, that government agencies should shift their attention from "lives saved" to "decently-livable life-years saved." . . .

An especially controversial issue lurks in the background: it is possible that some lives might be considered not decently-livable because of unjust or highly disadvantageous social conditions. Desperately poor people, for example, may lack decent life prospects already, and a small incremental reduction in their health may seem to push them below the relevant "floor." For purposes of regulatory policy, this ought not to be counted. If it did count, regulatory policy would be devoted to the protection of those already well-off and to the neglect of those in desperate conditions; thus one social injustice would be compounded by another. The question is whether the saved years meet a decent floor, and it should be stipulated that this criterion is met by lives filled with extreme difficulty because of social and economic deprivation alone.

NOTES AND QUESTIONS

1. The elderly are often victims of natural disasters, in part because a higher percentage of the elderly are disabled. Sunstein's analysis suggests that this fact should lessen the amount we would be otherwise willing to invest in precautions. In addition, one might want to zone day care centers away from earthquake faults or flood zones, while worrying less about nursing homes. The same argument would hold for hospices. And in conducting rescue operations, we should similarly prioritize the young and give the lowest priority to the elderly. Is this persuasive?

2. For a fuller presentation of Sunstein's views about risk management, *see* Cass R. Sunstein, Risk and Reason: Safety, Law, and the Environment (2002). In general, he is the paradigm advocate of the "irrational weigher" perspective described by Kahan. Which position do you find more convincing?

3. Sunstein's hope that regulators can be insulated from public "irrationality" does not seem to be supported by the empirical evidence. In a study of Superfund (the federal program for cleaning up hazardous waste sites), two economists concluded that, besides the economically rational factors of expected cancer cases versus clean-up costs, regulatory action "is influenced by many additional factors relating both to risk perceptions and the political nature of the community bearing the risks." *See* W. Kip Viscusi & James T. Hamilton, *Are Risk Regulators Rational? Evidence from Hazardous Waste Cleanup Decisions*, 89 Am. Econ. Rev. 1012 (1999).

B. DETERMINING THE APPROPRIATE RESPONSE TO RISKS

Once we have evaluated a risk, the next question is how to respond. How much should we invest in disaster precautions, for example? One approach to risk is based on rules of thumb or margins of safety, such as designing structures to survive a 100-year earthquake or building a levee system based on a "standard storm." The following article considers the pitfalls of this strategy.

Matthew D. Adler, Policy Analysis for Natural Hazards: Some Cautionary Lessons from Environmental Policy Analysis

56 Duke L.J. 1 (2006)

Technological availability or feasibility might be a matter of what is physically possible, given current science and engineering, or rather a matter of norms and practices among some group of actors. It is hard to imagine the first sort of approach having much role in natural hazards policy analysis. Consider levee design: the largest physically possible levee would be hundreds of feet high and massively thick and strong. Surely ACE [the Army Corps of Engineers] should (always!) stop well short of this point in building its levees. "Physical possibility" as a goal in levee design would be absurd, and as a putative constraint would be no constraint at all. Parallel points could be made about the construction of hazard-resistant buildings and structures — both ordinary residential and commercial property and more critical infrastructure. The strongest physically possible building would be absurdly expensive. Technology also comes into play in warnings and evacuations. It is technologically possible to evacuate everyone from Florida and the Gulf Coast for all of hurricane season, or to send a government representative to warn every household in person. But these are not serious policy proposals.

Technological availability in the second, norms and practices sense is more thinkable. For example, seismic codes could be specified with reference to current building practices. New construction could be required to be as protective as some percentile of existing construction.

A different sort of technology-based approach to policy analysis, exemplified by ACE practices, employs specific technological rules of thumb. Until the 1990s, ACE traditionally "added 3 feet of freeboard to the design height of its levees, a principle that became a staple of Corps flood damage reduction studies and projects." This three-feet-of-freeboard rule was, in particular, used when ACE built levees to withstand a one hundred-year flood, rather than to maximize net benefits — which occurred when local communities were willing to subsidize the additional levee construction costs needed to reach the one hundred-year mark, so that the area protected by the levee would not be counted as part of the one hundred-year floodplain for purposes of the National Flood Insurance Program. Adding three feet was "a measure to prevent overtopping caused by higher water . . . than was forecast for the design flood, as some uncertainties may not have been explicitly considered."

Closely related to technology-based policy analysis, and an important tool in current natural hazards decisionmaking, is reliability-based analysis. An excellent example is the approach used by governmental or quasi-governmental bodies in drafting seismic building codes. These bodies typically aim to write codes that will avoid building collapse in the event of any nonextreme earthquake (for example, any earthquake smaller than the 475-year earthquake). The decisional criterion employed by the code drafters is "prevent building collapse in nonextreme earthquakes" rather than "maximize net benefits, including both economic and safety impacts" or "maximize safety benefits." A similar approach has been traditionally used in designing dams, specifically in deciding how low the risk of dam failure (collapse or overtopping) should be. The goal has traditionally been to design the dam so that it will not fail except in an extreme precipitation event. The criterion, here, is "construct the dam so that it will not fail during nonextreme rainfalls" rather than "maximize net benefits," defined inclusively or narrowly.

To sum up: a variety of proxy tests are currently used, or might conceivably be used, by environmental and natural hazards decisionmakers. These are proxy tests insofar as they focus the decisionmaker's attention on some feature of available choices other than their impact on well-being or some of its dimensions. Proxy tests might be technology-based tests (of various kinds), or, a close cousin, reliability tests. Or they might take some other form.

All this is descriptive. But are proxy tests an appropriate policy-analytic tool for environmental or natural hazard regulators? The answer should have a familiar ring: proxy tests are justifiable, if at all, on institutional grounds. And even if proxy tests are justified, their use by administrative agencies simply shifts the locus of welfare-focused, (non-proxy-based) decisionmaking within the governmental process.

To begin, it is clear that proxy tests will, at some rate, select suboptimal policies — policies that are worse than alternatives with respect to overall welfare, equity, and rights. The critical literature on technology-based tests in environmental law makes this point, showing how a requirement that firms employ "feasible" pollution-reducing measures can lead to inefficient overregulation (if, for example, small firms are required to employ high-fixed-cost technologies) or underregulation (if it would be most efficient to reduce pollution beyond the point that is technologically feasible given continued production of the good, for example by shutting down production entirely).

Similar observations can be made about proxy-based criteria for natural hazards policymaking. Consider ACE's three-feet-of-freeboard rule. The rule is meant to provide an extra margin of protection for communities at risk of flooding. But the protection provided by the rule varies from community to community. A recent study by the National Research Council found that the annual probability of flooding in communities protected by levees built to the one hundred-year flood plus three feet of freeboard varied widely, from one in ten thousand to one in one hundred. "[T]his fixed-freeboard approach provided inconsistent degrees of flood protection to different communities and provided substantially different levels of protection in different regions."

A similar point can be made about the incremental protection provided by the three-feet-of-freeboard rule. Absent freeboard, the community will have an annual probability p of flooding; after freeboard, the community will have an annual probability q of flooding. The difference between p and q depends on local hydrology (the shape of the so-called flood-frequency curve) and local hydraulics (the features of the channel in which the flood waters flow). Finally, the variable incremental protection provided by the three-feet-of-freeboard rule has no systematic connection to the benefits of incremental protection — to the amount of property and number of lives at risk.

Or consider the proxy test used to write seismic building codes: ensure that buildings do not collapse except in extreme earthquakes. This maps, roughly, onto a safety-focused test, which says to construct buildings to avoid fatalities except in extreme earthquakes — since fatalities caused by building shaking in earthquakes mainly occur when buildings collapse. But the mapping is not perfect, because some damage to buildings short of collapse may cause fatalities (for example, when ceilings or lights fall on occupants). Further, much economic loss can occur when buildings are shaken without collapsing: direct economic loss by virtue of damaged building components, systems, or contents (which are expensive to replace), indirect economic loss by virtue of business interruption, and other indirect effects.

Recent experience . . . has shown that structural collapses, although spectacular and newsworthy, are by no means the only source of earthquake-related losses. Economic losses also stem from business interruptions; loss of records and computer databases in the service economy; . . . and widespread, noncatastrophic damage to residential and commercial structures throughout the earthquake region. . . . [One] estimate implies that catastrophic building failure, which is what codes and retrofits are designed to prevent, will be responsible for less than one-tenth of California's future bill for direct earthquake losses. In short, "a code-complying building can 'survive' an earthquake (i.e., not collapse and kill people) and still end up a shambles inside and out." Weak welfarism [Adler's preferred ethical approach] surely does not require that all buildings be reinforced to the point of suffering no damage at all in nonextreme earthquakes. But presumably there is some such strengthening beyond the point identified by the no-collapse proxy that would be warranted—in particular, that would have welfare benefits exceeding the costs of the additional strengthening.

Even though proxy-based tests pick out suboptimal policies at some non-zero rate, instructing agencies to employ proxy tests can be optimal if they are sufficiently accurate in tracking overall well-being, equity, and moral rights, and if the decision costs and rate of bureaucratic error under alternative tests is sufficiently high. . . .

Scholars need to think about proxy-based natural hazards tests in similar terms—by looking to the decision costs and bureaucratic error rates associated with these tests, as compared to alternative policy-analytic tests. In some cases, it will pretty clearly emerge that a proxy-based test is unjustifiable. Consider ACE's three-feet-of-freeboard test, used as a factor to ensure that levees built to protect communities from the one hundred-year flood are not overtopped. Determining the flood elevation in a settled area that would occur in the event of the one hundred-year flood entails a complicated, quantitative, model-driven analysis by ACE. Why, then, use a safety factor in calculating levee height, rather than directly calculating the height that achieves some given level of protection (for example, a five percent chance of being overtopped in the one hundred-year flood)? It is very hard to see why the three-feet-of-freeboard rule substantially lowers the decision costs of ACE decisionmaking, or makes it less manipulable. By contrast, the use of no-collapse tests in designing building codes plausibly has substantial institutional advantages as opposed to, for example, cost-benefit analysis. Determining the no-collapse level, by contrast with cost-benefit analysis, does not require determining the lives saved or direct or indirect economic costs avoided by various possible degrees of building strength. So there is some apparent economy in terms of decision and manipulability costs.

NOTES AND QUESTIONS

1. For an enlightening introduction to how engineers think about risk, *see* Henry Petroski, To Engineer Is Human: The Role of Failure in Successful Design (1982). The "three feet of freeboard" rule is an example of what engineers call a margin of safety.

2. As Adler points out, even if proxy rules (or "rules of thumb" regarding safety margins) are imperfect, they may be justified when more precise analysis is difficult, costly, or subject to political manipulation. Many risk analysts, however, believe that the preferred approach should be cost-benefit analysis. We discuss that approach next.

INTRODUCTORY NOTE ON COST-BENEFIT ANALYSIS

A leading approach to risk management is cost-benefit analysis (CBA). You may or may not find cost-benefit analysis an appealing technique, but there can be little question about its practical significance. Shortly after taking office, President Reagan signed Executive Order 12,291, 46 Fed. Reg. 13,193 (1981), aimed at improving the efficiency of informal rule making by executive agencies. Section 2 directed that "major" regulations not be promulgated unless, "taking into account affected industries [and] the condition of the national economy," the potential benefits to society outweigh potential costs, and net benefits are at a maximum. Review of the cost-benefit analysis is conducted by the Office of Management and Budget. In various guises, this requirement has survived succeeding presidents. Even before this regulation was adopted, Congress had already required cost-benefit analysis for flood control projects.

Whether you favor or are hostile toward environmental economics, a basic understanding of cost-benefit analysis is invaluable. The "cost" side of CBA is relatively straightforward, since it normally involves immediate economic impacts that (at least in theory) are readily determined. But the "benefit" side can be more complex. In considering safety issues, a key issue is attaching a monetary value to human life, so that the benefits of a proposed risk reduction can be compared directly with the costs.[9]

If people demand $1,000 in return for being exposed to a one in a thousand risk of death, it is conventional to say that the "value of life" is $1 million. This is a bit misleading, since they probably would not be willing to commit suicide for that amount of money! To express this distinction, economists often speak of the value of a statistical (as opposed to individual) life.

Without worrying right now about the technicalities, we could assign monetary values to different levels of risk by looking at how much consumers are willing to pay for safer products, or how much income workers are willing to give up for safer jobs, or how much travel time people are willing to sacrifice for the safety benefits of driving more slowly. All of these would be different ways of determining the market value of safety.

Controversy continues over the correct way to value life. Some suggest that instead of using a single uniform figure, the government should assign a higher value for some risks such as cancer, but that a lower value should often be used for risks that disproportionately affect the poor. *See* Cass R. Sunstein,

---

9. For an economic critique of how the government currently handles discounting and valuation-of-life issues, *see* Richard L. Revesz & Michael A. Livermore, RETAKING RATIONALITY: HOW COST-BENEFIT ANALYSIS CAN BETTER PROTECT THE ENVIRONMENT AND OUR HEALTH (2008).

Valuing Life: A Plea for Disaggregation, 54 Duke L.J. 385 (2004). As two critics of the Bush administration's approach note, these disputes have a political dimension:

> In 2000, the U.S. Environmental Protection Agency (EPA) published guidelines that set forth the primary means by which it would value human lives, and determined that each life should be valued at $6.3 million (in year/2000 dollars).
>
> The use of this $6.3 million figure for the valuation of a human life was challenged by the Bush Administration. Through the inclusion of alternative benefit calculations in environmental cost-benefit analyses, the Administration introduced four questionable techniques that inappropriately lower the value assigned to human life. Following public outcry, the Administration suspended using techniques that undervalued the lives of the elderly relative to those of younger individuals, but it continued to employ other techniques that undervalue all lives, regardless of age. This anti-regulatory approach systematically underestimates the health benefits of environmental regulations.

Laura J. Lowenstein & Richard L. Revesz, *Anti-Regulation under the Guise of Rational Regulation: The Bush Administration's Approaches to Valuing Human Lives in Environmental Cost-Benefit Analyses,* 34 Envtl. L. Rep. 10954 (2004).

Often, the costs and benefits of a regulatory measure occur at different times. When the costs accrue today but the benefits are in the future, we need some method of taking the time factor into account. The technique used by economists is called discounting. On average, if a certain level of flooding has only a 1 percent annual probability (the "hundred-year flood"), then much of the benefit of a levee or dam to control such floods will be received in the future, so discounting is appropriate.

Here is how discounting works. If $1 invested at compound interest today will produce $2 in five years, we "discount" the $2 at the same interest rate, concluding that the "present value" of $2 receivable in five years is $1 today. Making this adjustment allows us to compare different investments whose payoffs have varying time profiles. Because discounting is closely related to compound interest, it can have powerful effects over long time periods. Because exponential discounting is essentially the reverse of compounding, we might call it an application of "compound *dis*interest" — the longer the period of time, the less interested we are in the same cost or benefit. Like looking into the wrong end of a telescope, discounting makes distant objects look smaller.

Suppose you are a cost-benefit analyst faced with the following question: if society is willing to spend $1 million to save a life today, how much should it spend to save a life in twenty years? During the 1980s, the Office of Management and Budget (OMB) would have said $150,000. Until 1992, it used a 10 percent discount rate to convert future regulatory costs and benefits into their "present value." OMB Circular A–94 at 4 (1972). Since 1992, OMB has used a 7 percent rate, which would change the answer to $260,000 (almost twice the earlier figure). OMB Circular A–94, rev. (1992). For example, suppose that we are considering whether to spend $200,000,000 to improve a flood control system to withstand a Category 4 hurricane, that we expect this to save a thousand lives, and that our best estimate of the likely time until the next

Category 4 hits is twenty years. Then the flood system upgrade is worth doing if we use a 7 percent discount rate, but not if we use a 10 percent rate.

Over longer time periods, the results of changes in discount rates are even more dramatic, as Cass Sunstein explains:

> If an agency chooses a discount rate of 2%, the outcome will be very different from what it would be if an agency were to choose a discount rate of 10%; the benefits calculation will shift dramatically as a result. If a human life is valued at $8 million, and if an agency chooses a 10% discount rate, a life saved 100 years from now is worth only $581. "At a discount rate of 5%, one death next year counts for more than a billion deaths in 500 years."

Cass R. Sunstein, *Cost-Benefit Default Principles*, 99 Mich. L. Rev. 1651, 1711 (2001). As you can see, in dealing with long-lived infrastructure, it will rarely be worthwhile from an economic point of view to worry about fatalities more than a few decades in the future unless the number will be very large or the cost of precautions is very low.

CBA has been quite controversial, especially as applied to health and safety regulations. The following two excerpts provide contrasting perspectives.

Steve P. Calandrillo, Responsible Regulation: A Sensible Cost-Benefit, Risk versus Risk Approach to Federal Health and Safety Regulation[10]

81 B.U. L. Rev. 957 (2001)

Federal health and safety regulations have saved or improved the lives of thousands of Americans, but protecting our citizens from risk entails significant costs. In a world of limited resources, we must spend our regulatory dollars responsibly in order to do the most we can with the money we have. Given the infeasibility of creating a risk-free society, this paper argues that a sensible cost-benefit, risk versus risk approach be taken in the design of U.S. regulatory oversight policy. The goal should always be to further the best interests of the nation, rather than to satisfy the narrow agenda of powerful industry or political forces. This entails designing safety regulations efficiently to maximize society's welfare, choosing the point where their marginal benefits equal their marginal costs — rather than simply asking whether total benefits exceed total costs in the aggregate. Federal regulatory oversight policy should also ask that proposed regulations compare the risks they reduce to the new risks they unintentionally create (substitution risks). Additionally, our citizens should be educated regarding systematic risk misperceptions, and regulatory agencies should make their risk assessments objectively. Moreover, most-likely scenarios must be addressed by responsible regulatory solutions, rather than the current practice of focusing on worst-case estimates. Finally, agencies should publish and justify their regulatory triggers and perform ex-post evaluations of their programs in an attempt to continuously improve the quality of regulatory design.

Efforts by the executive branch, from Presidents Ford, Carter, Reagan and Clinton, have attempted to inject similar common sense into the regulatory

---

10. Copyright © 2001, Boston University Law Review. Reprinted with permission.

oversight process. Unfortunately, the congressional mandates given to government agencies are often silent on the subject of cost-benefit analysis, and recent Supreme Court cases have held that regulatory agencies are not obligated to even consider the costs of their proposals. I will explore several legislative reform bills that are aimed at overriding congressional mandates, but to date, none have been successful.

Finally, this paper will address certain common criticisms to which a marginal cost benefit, risk-risk approach to responsible regulatory reform would be subject. Most notably, the measurement of costs and benefits is not an exact science, and using "willingness to pay" as a marker of individual and social utility has its limitations. Regulatory reform also faces challenges on moral grounds, as scholars openly decry the explicit tradeoff between human lives and financial resources. While these criticisms contain merit, this paper concludes that to ignore a sensible cost-benefit analysis of federal safety regulations is to divert resources from their most beneficial uses and to settle for second best. In a world of scarcity, we must make regulatory tradeoffs as efficiently as possible in order to do the greatest good for the greatest number, and to save the most lives we can. It would be unethical to do anything less. . . .

"We live in a world of limited resources." "We can't place a dollar value on protecting human life or preserving our environment." Neither statement taken independently strikes the reader as particularly controversial—they both seem perfectly reasonable. Yet there is an inherent and unmistakable tension between the two, for no society has unlimited resources to devote to the protection of human health and the creation of a risk-free world. The questions become: Is it possible to balance the common sense concept of scarce public resources with our deep moral aversion to placing a dollar value on saving human lives? And, more importantly, how do we do it?

We would like to be able to protect every citizen from every harm in our society, but most understand this is neither possible nor financially feasible. Federal environmental and safety regulations aimed at preventing harm have yielded tremendous benefits, but they carry staggering costs—on the order of half a trillion dollars annually! However, despite this reality, there is a startling disconnect between common sense notions of maximizing the effect of scarce resources and of actually putting that notion into practice in carrying out U.S. regulatory programs. Hypothetically, would it be worth tens of millions of dollars to save one person's life if President Bush were to tighten arsenic standards in drinking water to the level proposed by President Clinton in his last days in office? Or would that same money be better spent if it could save thousands of lives by providing subsidized food and prenatal care to low-income mothers and free vaccinations to their babies? If we allocated all our resources to preventing accidental deaths in one area, we would have nothing left over to spend to prevent cancer or to provide food, housing or medical care.

To a large degree, the problem is one of public perception. No politician wants to admit that "we can't save that elderly person's life or institute a proposed environmental protection program, because it will simply cost us too much money to do so." Yet, this cost-benefit rationale is inherent in countless personal decisions made every day, from what career to pursue to what city in which to reside. Similarly, in the regulatory arena, fiscal balancing of the costs against the benefits should play a role in responsible decisionmaking. The tradeoff between costs and results is always present, but we are sometimes gripped by a fear that prevents us from acknowledging it openly. This reluctance limits us as a society because it diverts resources from where they are most needed. Even worse, this diversion is not based on a well-articulated reason, but rather on a fear of the repercussions experienced by those who voice such opinions. For instance, can you imagine a Presidential candidate who said on election-day eve, "I want to do the greatest good for the greatest number, and that means I choose not to help you." Not likely.

This paper proposes that given the reality of limited public resources, America must efficiently reformulate its environmental and health regulatory policies in order to save and improve the most lives possible given the accompanying costs. This is not always going to be politically correct. It entails making tough choices and preferencing certain programs and policies over others, which necessarily implies that some causes will be sacrificed for the greater good. But I urge that given our reality, society must consider carefully how best to structure federal regulatory oversight policy — not how to make it perfect. Perfection is dangerous precisely because it cannot ever be achieved. This paper therefore concentrates on how to efficiently formulate government regulations under the constraint of limited resources, in the hope that such an approach will maximize the overall benefits to our society. . . .

[T]his paper outlines an alternative regulatory approach for America, proposing a sensible cost-benefit, risk versus risk approach to easing the tension between scarce public resources and the deontological value of protecting human lives. In analyzing this tradeoff, we as a caring, thoughtful society should require a cost-benefit analysis of all potential government regulation whether it is aimed at making our environment, air, water, food, or workplace safer. I take this cost-benefit notion one step further than most commentators by suggesting that not only should overall costs and benefits of potential programs be evaluated, but that government agencies must act to set the appropriate regulation at the level where marginal benefits equal marginal costs. Setting our regulatory triggers at this point will have a far greater impact on improving overall social welfare than an absolute cost-benefit comparison would. Most everyone in society should favor a form of regulation that maximizes the benefits minus the costs, and not one that merely asks whether the benefits exceed the costs in the aggregate. . . .

While the achievements made possible by executive oversight have been notable, the success of regulatory reform proposals may also implicitly depend upon rewriting the existing legislative mandates given to government agencies by Congress. Often, the relevant statutory authority governing the mission of U.S. regulatory agencies is oblivious to marginal cost-benefit assessments, or it may even prohibit such comparisons outright. For instance, the Occupational Safety and Health Administration ("OSHA") is charged with assuring "so far as possible [that] every working man and woman in the Nation [have] safe and healthful working conditions." This mandate ignores the fact that nothing can ever be made 100% safe, and that extreme safety precautions necessarily entail extreme costs. Instead, the congressional mandates given to federal regulatory bodies should require, or at a minimum, permit cost-benefit and risk-risk trade-offs to be made. Such an approach will empower courts to enforce common sense notions about how to best allocate scarce public resources in order to benefit a greater number of our citizens than we do today. Modifying legislative mandates will also force regulatory decisionmakers to be accountable for the policy choices they make. . . .

Moreover, some have raised serious moral criticisms, openly deriding cost-benefit analysis as incurably insensitive to the intrinsic value of life. . . . This moral resistance also surfaces in the rhetoric of our politicians and in the language of our existing federal regulatory legislation. Our policies often eschew cost-benefit analysis as irresponsible and insensitive to the ultimate goal at hand, and instead opt for a world that should be made as safe as possible — whatever the costs may be.

I am the first to agree that there are serious problems that would make any marginal cost-benefit standard subject to potential manipulation and abuse. But that does not mean we should not try to improve upon what we currently have. The difficulty of measuring these values does not undermine the principle that responsible regulatory programs should focus their efforts where they can save the most lives given limited resources. We as a country would be foolhardy to choose to ignore cost, benefit and risk tradeoffs merely because of the difficulty in their assessment, because we would then be consciously deciding to do something less than the best we can. Thus, despite the valid concerns raised by critics, we must strive to conquer these problems if our ultimate goal is the betterment of society and the maximization of scarce resources.

Finally, we should bear in mind in conducting the foregoing regulatory oversight analysis that it is a matter of common sense that people weigh costs and benefits in making life decisions all the time. American businesses make cost-benefit and cost-effectiveness calculations daily. While individuals are understandably upset by public health and safety decisions that explicitly trade off lives for dollars, no one really wants to spend everything on safety. Policymakers should similarly be able to balance costs, benefits and risks openly in America's regulatory oversight policy. The choice is not between helping all of our citizens or helping none. Given limited resources, the government can only help some. This paper is therefore intended to provoke thought about how responsible, efficient regulatory policy can maximize the number and the value included within that "some."

NOTES AND QUESTIONS

1. The risk of a natural event can often be estimated from the historical record, assuming that the system in question has remained unchanged. The extent and reliability of the historical record may vary, and in some circumstance the system itself may be changing (as with weather events in climate change). In addition, the harm caused by a natural event is partly a function of human siting decisions as well as precaution and response systems, which may be difficult to assess. All of these issues complicate cost-benefit analysis.

2. If cost-benefit analysis is the standard for making a decision, to what extent should courts review the validity of the analysis? Those who seek regulatory rationality advocate sound science, cost-benefit analysis, and careful judicial review. The result may be to improve the quality of regulations and government projects, but it is also likely to decrease their quantity and delay their implementation. Under what circumstances is this a sound strategy?

3. Quite apart from any practical problems with implementing cost-benefit analysis, some authors raise ethical objections to its use in risk management. These objections are the subject of the next article.

FRANK ACKERMAN & LISA HEINZERLING, PRICING THE PRICELESS:
COST-BENEFIT ANALYSIS OF ENVIRONMENTAL PROTECTION

150 U. PA. L. REV. 1553 (2002)[11]

Many analytical approaches to setting environmental standards require some consideration of costs and benefits. Even technology-based regulation, maligned by cost-benefit enthusiasts as the worst form of regulatory excess, typically entails consideration of economic costs. Cost-benefit analysis differs, however, from other analytical approaches in the following respect: it demands that the advantages and disadvantages of a regulatory policy be reduced, as far as possible, to numbers, and then further reduced to dollars and cents. In this feature of cost-benefit analysis lies its doom. Indeed, looking closely at the products of this pricing scheme makes it seem not only a little cold, but a little crazy as well.

Consider the following examples, which we are not making up. They are not the work of a lunatic fringe, but, on the contrary, they reflect the work products of some of the most influential and reputable of today's cost-benefit practitioners. We are not sure whether to laugh or cry; we find it impossible to treat these studies as serious contributions to a rational discussion.

Several years ago, states were in the middle of their litigation against tobacco companies, seeking to recoup the medical expenditures they had incurred as a result of smoking. At that time, W. Kip Viscusi—a professor of law and economics at Harvard and the primary source of the current $6.3 million estimate for the value of a statistical life—undertook research concluding that states, in fact, saved money as the result of smoking by their citizens.[12] Why? Because they died early! They thus saved their states the trouble and expense of providing nursing home care and other services associated with an aging population.

Viscusi didn't stop there. So great, under Viscusi's assumptions, were the financial benefits to the states of their citizens' premature deaths that, he suggested, "cigarette smoking should be subsidized rather than taxed."

---

11. Copyright © 2002, University of Pennsylvania. Reprinted with permission.

12. W. Kip Viscusi, *Cigarette Taxation and the Social Consequences of Smoking* 47 (Nat'l Bureau of Econ. Research, Working Paper No. 4891, 1994), available at http://papers.nber.org/papers/w4891.pdf.

Amazingly, this cynical conclusion has not been swept into the dustbin where it belongs, but instead recently has been revived: the tobacco company Philip Morris commissioned the well-known consulting group Arthur D. Little to examine the financial benefits to the Czech Republic of smoking among Czech citizens. Arthur D. Little International, Inc., found that smoking was a financial boon for the government—partly because, again, it caused citizens to die earlier and thus reduced government expenditure on pensions, housing, and health care. This conclusion relies, so far as we can determine, on perfectly conventional cost-benefit analysis. . . .

Cost-benefit analysis sets out to do for government what the market does for business: add up the benefits of a public policy and compare them to the costs. . . . Development of environmental regulations has almost always involved consideration of economic costs, with or without formal cost-benefit techniques. What is unique to cost-benefit analysis, and far more problematic, is the other side of the balance, the monetary valuation of the benefits of life, health, and nature itself. . . .

What can it mean to say that saving one life is worth $6.3 million? Human life is the ultimate example of a value that is not a commodity and does not have a price. You cannot buy the right to kill someone for $6.3 million, nor for any other price. Most systems of ethical and religious belief maintain that every life is sacred. If analysts calculated the value of life itself by asking people what it is worth to them (the most common method of valuation of other environmental benefits), the answer would be infinite. . . .

The standard response is that a value like $6.3 million is not actually a price on an individual's life or death. Rather, it is a way of expressing the value of small risks of death; for example, it is one million times the value of a one in a million risk. If people are willing to pay $6.30 to avoid a one in a million increase in the risk of death, then the "value of a statistical life" is $6.3 million.

Unfortunately, this explanation fails to resolve the dilemma. It is true that risk (or "statistical life") and life itself are distinct concepts. In practice, however, analysts often ignore the distinction between valuing risk and valuing life. Many regulations reduce risk for a large number of people and avoid actual death for a much smaller number. A complete cost-benefit analysis should, therefore, include valuation of both of these benefits. However, the standard practice is to calculate a value only for "statistical" life and to ignore life itself.

The confusion between the valuation of risk and the valuation of life itself is embedded in current regulatory practice in another way as well. The Office of Management and Budget, which reviews cost-benefit analyses prepared by federal agencies pursuant to executive order, instructs agencies to discount the benefits of life-saving regulations from the moment of avoided death, rather than from the time when the risk of death is reduced. This approach to discounting is plainly inconsistent with the claim that cost-benefit analysis seeks to evaluate risk. When a life-threatening disease, such as cancer, has a long latency period, many years may pass between the time when a risk is imposed and the time of death. If monetary valuations of statistical life represented risk, instead of life, then the value of statistical life would be discounted from the date of a change in risk (typically, when a new regulation is enforced) rather than from the much later date of avoided actual death.

In acknowledging the monetary value of reducing risk, economic analysts have contributed to our growing awareness that life-threatening risk itself—and not just the end result of such risk, death—is an injury. But they have blurred the line between risks and actual deaths, by calculating the value of reduced risk while pretending that they have produced a valuation of life itself. The paradox of monetizing the infinite or immeasurable value of human life has not been resolved; it only has been glossed over.

. . .

Finally, the economic valuation called for by cost-benefit analysis is fundamentally flawed because it demands an enormous volume of consistently updated information, which is beyond the practical capacity of our society to generate.

All attempts at valuation of the environment begin with a problem: the goal is to assign monetary prices to things that have no prices because they are not for sale. One of the great strengths of the market is that it provides so much information about real prices. For any commodity that actually is bought and sold, prices are communicated automatically, almost costlessly, and with constant updates as needed. To create artificial prices for environmental values, economists have to find some way to mimic the operation of the market. Unfortunately, the process is far from automatic, certainly not costless, and has to be repeated every time an updated price is needed. . . .

For the reasons we have discussed, there is nothing objective about the basic premises of cost-benefit analysis. Treating individuals solely as consumers, rather than as citizens with a sense of moral responsibility to the larger society, represents a distinct and highly contestable world view. Likewise, the use of discounting reflects judgments about the nature of environmental risks and citizens' responsibilities toward future generations that are, at a minimum, debatable. Because value-laden premises permeate cost-benefit analysis, the claim that cost-benefit analysis offers an "objective" way to make government decisions is simply bogus.

Furthermore, as we have seen, cost-benefit analysis relies on a byzantine array of approximations, simplifications, and counterfactual hypotheses. Thus, the actual use of cost-benefit analysis inevitably involves countless judgment calls. People with strong, and clashing, partisan positions naturally will advocate that discretion in the application of this methodology be exercised in favor of their positions, further undermining the claim that cost-benefit analysis is objective.

Perhaps the best way to illustrate how little economic analysis has to contribute, objectively, to the fundamental question of how clean and safe we want our environment to be is to refer again to the controversy over cost-benefit analysis of the EPA's regulation of arsenic in drinking water. As Cass Sunstein has recently argued, the available information on the benefits of arsenic reduction supports estimates of net benefits from regulation ranging from less than zero up to $560 million or more.[13] The number of deaths avoided annually by regulation is, according to Sunstein, between zero

---

13. Cass R. Sunstein, *The Arithmetic of Arsenic*, 90 Geo. L.J. 2255 (2002).

and 112. A procedure that allows such an enormous range of different evaluations of a single rule is certainly not the objective, transparent decision rule that its advocates have advertised. . . .

For many of the same reasons, cost-benefit analysis also generally fails to achieve the goal of transparency. Cost-benefit analysis is a complex, resource-intensive, and expert-driven process. It requires a great deal of time and effort to attempt to unpack even the simplest cost-benefit analysis. Few community groups, for example, have access to the kind of scientific and technical expertise that would allow them to evaluate whether, intentionally or unintentionally, the authors of a cost-benefit analysis have unfairly slighted the interests of the community or some of its members. Few members of the public can participate meaningfully in the debates about the use of particular regression analyses or discount rates which are central to the cost-benefit method.

The translation of lives, health, and nature into dollars also renders decision making about the underlying social values less rather than more transparent. As we have discussed, all of the various steps required to reduce a human life to a dollar value are open to debate and subject to uncertainty. However, the specific dollar values kicked out by cost-benefit analysis tend to obscure these underlying issues rather than encourage full public debate about them.

NOTES AND QUESTIONS

1. One question raised by Ackerman and Heinzerling is whether market valuations should be the basis for government policy. Arguably, the government's determination of the public interest might be based on different criteria than those that individuals use to make private choices. Is it rational for people to use different values as voters than as workers or consumers? Is it paternalistic for the government to impose trade-offs (for example, more disaster-resistant structures but higher housing costs) that people would not voluntarily accept in the market?

2. Is it morally offensive to put a dollar value on life? After all, we do make trade-offs between safety and cost all the time. Isn't cost-benefit analysis just a more systematic way of thinking about these trade-offs? Or does the use of cost-benefit analysis depersonalize our approach to these problems?

3. In considering the role of cost-benefit analysis, it is important to ask: compared to what? In terms of the flood control system, for example, some observers might think that use of cost-benefit analysis would increase rather than decrease attention to safety compared with the status quo.

NOTE ON COST-BENEFIT ANALYSIS, CLIMATE CHANGE, AND DISASTER RISKS

Climate change can be considered the granddaddy of all disasters. The question of how much to reduce emissions is not easily answered. Many economists favor gradual emissions reductions for the next few decades, accelerating toward mid-century. Modeling the systemic economic impact of climate change as well as the costs of adaptation and mitigation involves tremendous challenges, particularly if the projection goes out more than a few years.[14] To begin with, the economic model must build on the outputs of climate models, which are themselves uncertain. Then there is the difficulty of forecasting the future trajectory of the economy over future decades. This clearly cannot be done in detail—for example, no forecaster in 1970 would have predicted the explosive growth of personal computers, let alone the Internet, neither of which existed at the time. Even efforts to forecast at a cruder level must rely heavily on the assumption that the future will on average be much like the recent past—for example, that technological progress will continue at something like its current pace, that some unforeseen factor will not cause a population crash, and so forth. The uncertainties go both ways: to the extent that climate change scenarios are based on projections of future emissions, they implicitly make assumptions about future political and economic developments.

There are now about a dozen models that couple climate change predictions to economic analysis. These models differ in a number of dimensions: whether they focus on the energy sector or rely on a broad macroeconomic analysis, the degree to which they analyze localized versus average global impacts, and their treatment of uncertainty. Models also differ in their assessments of the costs of complying with the Kyoto Protocol, with the range running from negligible losses to at least 1 to 2 percent of GDP annually.[15] The models differ in terms of three critical assumptions about the timing of abatement efforts, the types of policy instruments used, and the likelihood of technological innovation.[16] Other relevant factors include the willingness of economic actors to substitute away from high carbon technologies and trends in energy efficiency.[17]

Among the costs of climate change are increased infrastructure costs to respond to potential weather events. The Stern Review, issued at the request of then-Chancellor of the Exchequer Gordon Brown (now prime minister) by economist Sir Nicholas Stern (head of Britain's Government Economic Service), estimates that

> [i]nfrastructure is particularly vulnerable to heavier floods and storms, in part because OECD economies invest around 20% of GDP or roughly $5.5 trillion in fixed capital each year, of which just over one-quarter typically goes into construction ($1.5 trillion—mostly for infrastructure and buildings). The additional costs of adapting this investment to a higher-risk future could be $15-150 billion each year (0.05-0.5% of GDP), with one-third of the costs borne by the US and one-fifth in Japan. This preliminary cost calculation assumes that adaptation requires extra investment of 1-10% to limit future damages from climate change.[18]

---

14. A good overview of modeling issues can be found in J.C. Haurcade et al., *Estimating the Costs of Mitigating Greenhouse Gases, in* Climate Change 1995: Economic and Social Dimensions of Climate Change: Contribution of Working Group III to the Second Assessment Report of the Intergovernmental Panel on Climate Change 263 (James P. Bruce et al. eds., 1996).

15. Jason F. Shogren & Michael A. Toman, *How Much Climate Change Is Too Much?, in* Climate Change Economics and Policy: An RFF Anthology 35, 42 (Michael A. Toman ed., 2001).

16. *Id.*

17. *Id.* at 43.

18. Nicholas Stern, The Stern Review of the Economics of Climate Change 417 (2007).

Stern also reports some very preliminary efforts regarding the cost of adaptation in the developing world:

> The most recent estimates come from the World Bank show the additional costs of adaptation alone as $4-37 billion each year. This includes only the cost of adapting investments to protect them from climate-change risks, and it is important to remember that there will be major impacts that are sure to occur even with adaptation. The World Bank estimate is based on an examination of the current core flows of development finance, combined with very rough estimates of the proportion of those investments that is sensitive to climate risk and the additional cost to reduce that risk to account for climate change (5-20% as a very rough estimate).[19]

Another estimate, covering only the least developed countries and the short term, is over a billion dollars for the most urgently needed adaptation measures.[20] The cost of adaptation may or may not be large in comparison with the total world economy, but that comparison will not be relevant to localities that need billions of dollars worth of expenditures for climate change adaptation. One of the safer predictions about the impact of climate change is that the debate over who will bear those costs is likely to become quite heated.

The Stern Review received widespread attention in concluding that the world should invest approximately 1 percent of its gross domestic product annually to mitigate greenhouse gas emissions in order to avoid much larger economic losses in the future. The Report has been subject to significant criticism of its methodological assumptions, including that the Review "[c]onsistently leans towards . . . assumptions and formulations that emphasize optimistically-low expected costs of mitigation and pessimistically-high expected damages from greenhouse warming."[21]

Central to many of the critiques is that the Stern Review relies on a very low discount rate in estimating future costs and benefits.[22] Nevertheless, Harvard economist Marin Weitzman concludes that Stern is "right for the wrong reasons."[23] In Weitzman's view, Stern may be right that we should spend money to mitigate climate change now in order to insure against "the small chance of a ruinous catastrophe that is difficult to compensate by ordinary savings."[24]

Cost-benefit analysis certainly is not the only approach to decision making about risks — whether as large as climate change or as small as a flooding creek. The following excerpt defends an important alternative approach.

---

19. *Id.* at 502 (footnotes omitted).
20. *Id.*
21. Martin L. Weitzman, *A Review of the Stern Review on the Economics of Climate Change*, 45 J. Econ. Literature 703 (2007).
22. *See id.*, William D. Nordhaus, *A Review of the Stern Review on the Economics of Climate Change*, 45 J. Econ. Literature 686, 686 (2007) ("An examination of the *Review*'s radical revision of the economics of climate change finds . . . that it depends decisively on the assumption of a near-zero time discount rate. . . . The *Review*'s unambiguous conclusions about the need for extreme immediate action will not survive the substitution of assumptions that are consistent with today's marketplace real interest rates and savings rates.").
23. Weitzman, *supra*, n.21 at 723.
24. *Id.* at 705.

Douglas A. Kysar, It Might Have Been: Risk, Precaution and Opportunity Costs

22 J. Land Use & Envtl. L. 1 (2006)

This apparent difference in regulatory attitude between the United States and Europe often is said to emerge from the jurisdictions' contrasting stances toward two policymaking paradigms that compete for acceptance within environmental, health, and safety regulation: One — known as cost-benefit analysis (CBA) and increasingly associated with the United States[25] — strives to enhance social welfare by predicting, weighting, and aggregating all relevant consequences of policy proposals in order to identify those choices that represent welfare-maximizing uses of public resources; the other — associated with the precautionary principle (PP) and the European approach to risk regulation — eschews optimization in favor of more pragmatic forms of decisionmaking. One oft-cited articulation of the PP, for instance, seeks to trigger an incremental process of risk regulation through the simple admonition, "When an activity raises threats of harm to human health or the environment, precautionary measures should be taken even if some cause and effect relationships are not fully established scientifically." . . .

As J.B. Ruhl has observed, "[t]he prevailing schools of environmental policy have described our problem as a series of linear, one-dimensional decisionmaking systems," an approach that assumes "economic conditions can be translated predictably into economic conclusions that call for prescribed economic measures, [and] environmental conditions can be translated predictably into environmental conclusions that call for environmental measures." If indeed these prevailing schools are correct that biophysical and sociolegal systems are well-behaved — such that they follow linear operating rules, map onto normal or Gaussian probability distributions, and exhibit stable equilibrium outcomes — then data gaps and other shortcomings of human knowledge need not be viewed as deeply problematic.

If, on the other hand, these systems are complex — such that they exhibit "behaviors such as feedback, emergence, path dependence, and nonlinearity" — then risk regulators face a fundamentally different task. Not only must they assess and manage risks of an uncertain magnitude, but they must do so within the context of numerous, overlapping dynamic systems, each of which is characterized by such perplexing features as extreme sensitivity to minor variations in condition, "fat tail[ ]" probability distributions [such as the power law distributions discussed earlier in this chapter], and irreducible levels of uncertainty, or chaos. This is a far more intractable problem setting than has tended to be recognized in the risk regulation debate, even by those who critique CBA for its Herculean informational demands. Because complex adaptive systems contain ineliminable uncertainties that cannot be presumed to be insignificant, such systems by their nature are likely to present ill-posed problems — that is, problems whose imperviousness to resolution is not driven

---

25. *See* Cass R. Sunstein, The Cost-benefit State ix (2002) ("Gradually, and in fits and starts, American government is becoming a cost-benefit state.").

by deficiencies in our epistemic position, but rather by features inherent to the problems themselves. . . .

Criticisms of CBA's efforts to grapple with complexity and uncertainty have particular purchase in the case of potentially catastrophic risks. [H]umanity faces a number of threats of uncertain, but possibly monumental consequence, including some threats that might entail the erasure of all life on the planet. In the face of such complete catastrophic threats, conventional approaches to CBA would, first, sum up the total monetary-equivalent worth of the expected human population at the time of potential destruction and, second, discount that number, both for time and for likelihood. The resulting number would, of course, be finite. It might also be quite small, particularly if the anticipated disaster looms far in the future or with minute probability. One could increase the number to reflect a degree of risk aversion, but the result still would be finite and, if cost-benefit analyses of climate change are an indication, not alarmingly large.

The question then arises whether the expectation calculus of CBA is appropriately textured for the type of decision actually being confronted. . . . Put bluntly, either nanotechnology will transform the planet into "gray goo" or it will not. We do not know what the precise probabilities involved are, but given the nature of discontinuity, we do know that the expected utility outcome—the weighted average of these extremes—will not occur. Thus, by displacing context-sensitive discussion of precisely what outcomes are being gambled in favor of what gains and for which winners and losers, the CBA approach tends to understate the challenge posed by long-term catastrophic risks. . . .

In the context of complex, adaptive systems, the deliberate attempt to optimize may not represent simply an imperfect, but useful aid to decision-making, as CBA defenders often assert. Rather, it may represent a solution concept that is poorly matched for the problem tasks at hand. In the face of ill-posed problems, we cannot confidently expect that the errors of CBA will cluster around an "optimal" result—indeed, for such problems the very notion of an optimum eludes meaningful description. The errors of CBA therefore are capable of deviating substantially and unpredictably from decision paths that are easily identified as desirable—if not necessarily optimal—through less formalistic decision procedures. In light of such concerns, proponents of the PP consciously part ways with the technocratic paradigm underlying risk assessment and CBA. Rather than insist on quantification as a predicate to decisionmaking, they instead argue that environmental, health, and safety regulation should become infused with a "culture of humility about the sufficiency and accuracy of existing knowledge."

As it turns out, the United States has enjoyed a long and successful experience with precisely this approach. Despite the current prominence of CBA among U.S. policymakers and academics, much of U.S. environmental law and regulation continues to be based instead on policies and procedures that reflect a precautionary approach. In several key pollution control areas, for instance, the United States has forsaken optimization in favor of a precautionary practice of requiring installation of the best available pollution abatement technology, often with opt-out procedures extended to firms that are able to demonstrate achievement of equal abatement levels using alternative technologies. This simple heuristic—in essence, "do the best you can"—implies great collective commitment to the preservation of human life and the environment without requiring satisfaction of Herculean informational demands by regulators.

Realistic but unquantifiable threats of catastrophic loss present an additional case in which heuristic decisionmaking procedures may prove more pragmatically sensible than deliberate cost-benefit optimization. With regard to climate change, for instance, future generations may reflect with marvel on our present day attempts to meticulously calculate the costs and benefits of greenhouse policies. Such studies typically lead to a conclusion that the economic benefits of continued fossil fuel consumption more than outweigh the physical, agricultural, and ecological costs that would be averted by restricting emissions, at least for the next few decades. Accordingly, the optimal carbon reduction policy under CBA is a rather limited one that should not begin any time soon. The important lesson from complexity theory, again, is that the apparent CBA consensus on climate change may not merely be wrong; it may be wildly wrong. Especially in light of the relatively minor cost associated with implementing most proposed carbon emissions abatement policies, uncertain but potentially catastrophic consequences of anthropogenic greenhouse gas emissions should not simply be reduced to an expectation value and included within cost-benefit calculation. . . .

This "safe minimum standards" approach has long been associated with the PP. One also may think of the "safe minimum standards" approach as resembling the maximin principle from decision theory, which counsels minimization of the maximum possible loss when decisionmakers are faced with policy choices that are characterized by true uncertainty. Most famously discussed by John Rawls in the context of elaborating an egalitarian theory of justice, the maximin principle reflects what would be termed an extreme degree of risk aversion if probabilistic information on outcomes were actually available, given that the principle focuses attention exclusively on the worst case outcome from each possible course of action under inspection. For this reason, the principle has attracted a substantial share of criticism. Nevertheless, at least as a preliminary stance, proponents of the PP believe that an extreme level of risk aversion is appropriate for policymaking that concerns unknown but potentially devastating threats to the global climate, the ozone layer, biodiversity, and other natural systems that are thought to be of fundamental and irreplaceable importance to humanity.

Whether characterized as the PP, the best available technology requirement, the safe minimum standard, or the maximin principle, each of these related decisionmaking techniques reflects an awareness that truly rational risk regulation sometimes requires officials to abandon the quest for optimization in favor of less ambitious, more pragmatically sensible approaches. Of course, the extreme conservatism of these approaches begs the questions of when and how to relax their dictates in favor of more permissive standards. According to many PP supporters, however, fostering such an adaptive approach to risk regulation is precisely the point of the PP—something that the principle's critics seem reluctant to acknowledge. Unlike the optimization framework of CBA, which must resort to awkward analytical devices in the presence of imperfectly characterized risks, the PP's incremental approach reflects great sensitivity to the fact that effective decisionmaking in the face of many problems demands procedural rationality. . . .

This potential deliberative deficit of preferentialism is also evident in Judge Posner's recent use of CBA to suggest that the optimal post-Katrina reconstruction plan for New Orleans is one in which "the historic portions of the city (the French Quarter and the Garden District) might be rebuilt and preserved as a tourist site, much like Colonial Williamsburg, without having to be part of a city." Posner may well be right that the United States should not spend billions of dollars reconstructing New Orleans to its former scale, especially in light of projected sea level rises over the next century from climate change that would transform the city into an island. But the reason for this conclusion is not to be found in a CBA premised on the decontextualized preferences of individuals. Whatever pre-Katrina tourist behavior might suggest (for it is their disposable dollars that presumably are driving the conclusion that only the French Quarter and the Garden District are worth rebuilding), it is an open question whether individuals post-Katrina agree that they have little use for a revival of the Ninth Ward and other poor, racially-segregated areas of the city. To say nothing of the deeper issues of environmental justice raised by the Katrina tragedy, we understate the role of citizenship when we assume that shared experiences do not affect the preferences that we hold and the meanings that we attribute to our social world. . . .

As noted above, the contention of PP proponents that environmental, health, and safety decisionmaking is characterized by abiding uncertainty does not commit them to the extreme conservatism of the maximin approach as a general or permanent response. Rather, the PP is intended to commence a program of risk regulation that is both proportionate to the scope of the perceived threat and capable of being updated and adjusted over time. Proponents of the safe minimum standards approach within environmental economics also tend to qualify their position, arguing that fidelity to safe minimum standards should yield when the costs of precaution become "immoderate" or "unacceptably large." Within the legal literature, Dan Farber similarly allows for departure from his strong "environmental baseline" approach to policymaking "when costs would clearly overwhelm any potential benefits" from precautionary regulation . . .

. . . Even if we know that the PP's more severe implications will need to be relaxed, the principle nevertheless forces societal discussion regarding the normative status of statistical victims, other societies, and future generations. In that regard, the PP's insistence that human health and the environment deserve constant, anticipatory attention serves as a procedural lever for furthering still-nascent attempts to reason through important questions that lie at the "frontiers of justice"—questions about our responsibilities to members of other nations, other generations, and other species. Such an approach therefore aspires not only to be procedurally rational (e.g., in the sense that dynamic, incremental management approaches are demanded in the face of complexity and uncertainty in biophysical and sociolegal systems) but also to be discursively rational (e.g., in the sense that the PP helps to structure and promote collective deliberation regarding decisions for which our existing, individualized preferences are either ill-formed or ill-suited for the decision under inspection). . . .

Today, the precautionary approach is derided by U.S. policy elites as a "mythical concept . . . like a unicorn." Yet if the analysis of the previous Section translates at all smoothly from the individual to the collective context, then the precautionary approach makes a great deal more concrete sense than PP critics appreciate: Even granting the causal optimizer's claim that "risks are on all sides of social situations," that fact alone does not compel the adoption of an optimization standard, such as CBA, in which risks imposed and opportunities foregone are treated as analytically indistinguishable. . . . Instead, something like the "first, do no harm" admonition of Hippocrates may be necessary at the collective level simply for the implicit reminder contained within it, that a political community's actions and decisions carry distinctive moral weight.

NOTES AND QUESTIONS

1. How would Kysar approach a disaster issue such as the appropriate level of hurricane protection for a city such as New Orleans? Would he apply his maximin principle or something different?
2. Protecting New Orleans from hurricanes could be quite expensive, particularly given climate change. Should we abandon the effort and limit ourselves to protecting smaller enclaves such as the French Quarter, as Judge Posner suggests? Consider how this question might be addressed:

   a. By a cost-benefit analyst like Sunstein?
   b. By someone applying the precautionary principle like Kysar?
   c. By a culturally attuned analyst like Kahan?

3. A related question is the role of experts in deciding disaster issues. Should Congress delegate major issues of disaster policy to experts or make them legislatively?

NOTE ON CRITICISMS OF THE PRECAUTIONARY PRINCIPLE

The precautionary principle is controversial. There seem to be three main criticisms. The first is its vagueness. Chris Stone observes that the principle is vague in part because of the nature of international diplomacy. Nevertheless, he finds it "increasingly frustrating that there is no convergence as to what it means, or as to what regions of action (environment, public health) it is supposed to apply."[26] In some formulations, the precautionary principle is seemingly a mandate to halt activities when a sufficient level of risk appears, whereas in others it operates to create a presumption against activities potentially harmful to the environment, placing the burden of proof on the advocates of those activities. But none of these formulations is precise, and Stone

---

26. Christopher D. Stone, Is There a Precautionary Principle?, 31 Envtl. L. Rep. 10790, B (2001).

doubts whether any general rule more specific than "be careful" can be formulated.

A second criticism is that government intervention creates risks of its own.[27] For example, a building code requirement that is designed to limit seismic risks may increase the expense of new housing, leading people to stay in older buildings that are not subject to the code and are highly vulnerable to earthquakes. If the effects of regulation are also uncertain and present unforeseen risks to health and environment, then the precautionary principle seems to turn against itself, suggesting that we should not proceed with environmental regulations until we can pin down their effects. As Sunstein explains,

> There is an obvious difficulty with the precautionary principle: Both regulation and nonregulation will often give rise to risks; if so, the principle would seem to be paralyzing, forbidding stringent regulation, inaction, and everything in between. Consider, for example, the case of genetic engineering of food. The precautionary principle might seem to call for stringent regulation of genetic engineering, on the theory that this technology contains at least some risk of causing ecological harm. But such regulation would also create risks of adverse effects, simply because genetic engineering holds out a prospect of producing ecological and health benefits. The precautionary principle would seem both to require and to forbid stringent regulation of genetic engineering. The same can be said for many activities and processes, such as nuclear power and non-therapeutic cloning, simply because risks are on all sides of the situation.[28]

Adding force to the first criticism, this critique argues that the principle is not only vague but also incoherent, since it always, or at least often, generates conflicting directions.

The third criticism adds a charge of irrationality against the precautionary principle. Sunstein argues that when the precautionary principle "seems to offer guidance," it is "often because of the operation of probability neglect," meaning the cognitive incapacity of individuals to attend to the relevant risks.[29]

Considerable debate surrounds these criticisms. The first criticism, based on the principle's vagueness, has prompted various attempts to give it greater content with reference to avoiding irreversible actions, keeping options open, and providing insurance against dangerous risks.[30] Alternatively, some supporters argue that the principle requires a type of case-by-case, common law development.[31] The second criticism, regarding the existence of risks on both sides of regulatory decisions, is at least partly countered by noting that

---

27. *See* Jonathan H. Adler, *More Sorry Than Safe: Assessing the Precautionary Principle and the Proposed International Safety Protocol*, 35 Tex. Int'l L.J. 194 (2000); Frank B. Cross, *Paradoxical Perils of the Precautionary Principle*, 53 Wash. & Lee L. Rev. 851, 872 (1996).

28. Cass R. Sunstein, *Probability Neglect: Emotions, Worst Cases, and Law*, 11 Yale L.J. 61, 93 (2002).

29. *Id.* at 94. Sunstein further elaborates his critique in Cass R. Sunstein, *Beyond the Precautionary Principle*, 151 U. Pa. L. Rev. 1003 (2003).

30. *See, e.g.,* Stephen Charest, *Bayesian Approaches to the Precautionary Principle*, 12 Duke Envtl. L. & Pol'y F. 265 (2002); Christian Gollier, Bruno Jullien & Nicolas Treich, *Scientific Progress and Irreversibility: An Economic Interpretation of the "Precautionary Principle,"* 75 J. Pub. Econ. 229 (2000); W. David Montgomery & Anne E. Smith, *Global Climate Change and the Precautionary Principle*, 6 Hum. & Ecological Risk Assessment 399 (2000).

31. *See* Stephen Toulmin, *The Case for Cosmic Prudence*, 56 Tenn. L. Rev. 29 (1998).

regulatory decisions may also have unanticipated benefits. The third criticism, as it turns out, may be backwards: a good argument can be made that the precautionary principle is needed to counter defects in the ways people process probability information; rather than being part of the problem of limited human rationality, the precautionary principle may be part of the cure.[32] At this stage, the academic debate is far from settled.

NOTE ON ENVIRONMENTAL IMPACT STATEMENTS, RISK, AND THE "WORST-CASE SCENARIO"

An environmental impact statement (EIS) must be prepared for federal infrastructure projects such as dams and levees, and for projects requiring a federal license, such as nuclear power plants. An EIS does not dictate the substance of regulatory decisions, but it is at least supposed to force the agency to take a "hard look" at the relevant factors.[33]

At one time, mirroring the precautionary principle, agencies were required to deal with such uncertainty by discussing the "worst-case scenario." The history and implementation of this regulation is instructive.

In 1978, the Council on Environmental Quality, the executive agency supervising implementation of the EIS requirement, provided direction to agencies on how to deal with scientific uncertainty.[34] The regulation applied when there were "gaps in relevant information or scientific uncertainty" about a project's environmental impacts.[35] When such information was obtainable at reasonable cost, the agency was instructed to obtain it, but otherwise the agency was told to pursue the following course:

> If (1) the information relevant to adverse impacts is essential to a reasoned choice among alternatives and is not known and the overall costs of obtaining it are exorbitant or (2) the information relevant to adverse impacts is important to the decision and the means to obtain it are not known (e.g. the means for obtaining it are beyond the state of the art) the agency shall weigh the need for the action against the risk and severity of possible adverse impacts were the agency to proceed in the face of uncertainty. If the agency proceeds, it shall include a worst case analysis and an indication of the probability or improbability of its occurrence.[36]

In a 1981 guidance document, CEQ explained this rule as mandating "reasonable projections of the worst possible consequences of a proposed action."[37] As an illustration, CEQ said that where a proposed water quality facility would have an unknown impact on juvenile fish, the EIS must include "the possibility of the loss of the commercial or sport fishery."[38] Note that agencies

---

32. David A. Dana, *A Behavioral Economic Defense of the Precautionary Principle*, 97 Nw. U. L. Rev. 1315 (2003).

33. *See* Robertson v. Methow Valley Citizens Council, 490 U.S. 332 (1989).

34. *See* Edward A. Fitzgerald, *The Rise and Fall of Worst Case Analysis*, 18 U. Dayton L. Rev. 1 (1992).

35. 40 C.F.R. §1502.22 (1991).

36. *Id.* §1502.22(b) (1991).

37. Vicki O. Masterman, *Worst Case Analysis: The Final Chapter?*, 19 Envtl. L. Rep. 10026, at 10027 n.14 (1989).

38. *Id.*

were not directed to avoid taking action in the face of uncertainty, but rather to engage in a balancing test weighing the need for the action against the risk. Worst case analysis was a disclosure requirement, not a decision technique.

Sierra Club v. Sigler[39] was the leading case to apply the worst case requirement. The case involved a controversial proposal to allow oil tankers to operate in an estuary near the Port of Galveston.[40] The EIS concluded that the project would not significantly increase the probability or likely harm of an oil spill.[41] The relevance of oil spills to the decision was unquestioned and the parties agreed that "an analysis of a supertanker oil spill involving a total cargo loss beyond 24 hours after it occurs is beyond the state of the art."[42] The agency had thought this possibility was too remote to warrant discussion. Relying on CEQ's 1981 guidance document, however, the Fifth Circuit held that the EIS was invalid because it "failed to discuss the 'catastrophic impact' of a total cargo loss by a supertanker in the Bay" and the court faulted the agency for failing to consider "that impact and the probability of its occurrence" in deciding to proceed.[43]

The worst-case requirement was criticized as being excessively pessimistic and too intrusive on agency discretion.[44] In 1983, CEQ proposed (but later withdrew) a guidance document that would have required a worst-case analysis only when a risk crossed an "initial threshold of probability" and was reasonably foreseeable but its consequences were uncertain.[45] In the Fifth Circuit's view, the fact that a risk was extremely remote was relevant in assessing its ultimate import for the final decision but not relevant in deciding whether to include a discussion of it as the worst-case scenario.[46] The court hastened to add, however, that "while remoteness of a possible occurrence does not permit disregarding it in such circumstances as these, where a real possibility of the occurrence has been proved and a database for evaluating its consequences established, the Corps need not concern itself with phantasmagoria hypothesized without a firm basis in evidence and the actual circumstances of the contemplated project, or with disasters the likelihood of which is not shown to be significantly increased by the carrying out of the project."[47]

After withdrawing the 1983 proposal, CEQ called for public comment on possible methods of dealing with uncertainty. It received a laundry list of complaints about the worst-case requirement such as "the limitless nature of the task of conjuring the worst possible case," "the lack of expert support for worst-case analysis in the growing field of risk analysis," and the "minimal value of fanciful worst-case analyses to federal decision-makers who must balance a full range of proven competing interests."[48] CEQ then issued a

---

39. Sierra Club v. Sigler, 695 F.2d 957 (5th Cir. 1983).
40. *Id.* at 962.
41. *Id.* at 968.
42. *Id.* at 973.
43. *Id.*
44. *See* Note, *Federal Agency Treatment of Uncertainty in Environmental Impact Statements under the EPA's Amended NEAP Regulation §1502.22: Worst Case Analysis or Risk Threshold?*, 86 Mich. L. Rev. 777, 807-809 (1988).
45. *Id.*
46. *Sigler*, 695 F.2d at 974.
47. *Id.* at 975 n.14.
48. Masterman, *supra*, note 37.

new regulation dealing with uncertainty, replacing the worst-case scenario requirement. The new regulation, which is still in effect, tells agencies that when important information is not available at a reasonable cost, they must include in the EIS

> (1) a statement that such information is incomplete or unavailable; (2) a statement of the relevance of the incomplete or unavailable information to evaluating reasonably foreseeable significant adverse impacts on the human environment; (3) a summary of existing credible scientific evidence which is relevant to evaluating the reasonably foreseeable significant adverse impacts on the human environment; and (4) the agency's evaluation of such impacts based upon theoretical approaches or research methods generally accepted in the scientific community.[49]

The regulations define "reasonably foreseeable" to include impacts "which have catastrophic consequences, even if their probability of occurrence is low, provided that the analysis of the impacts is supported by credible scientific evidence, is not based on pure conjecture, and is within the rule of reason."[50]

It should be noted that, although the new regulation avoids the term "worst case" and calls for a broader discussion of potential risks, it does still call for discussion of low-probability catastrophes. In effect, it defines "worst case" in terms of the rule of reason rather than completely eliminating the worst case requirement.

The Supreme Court upheld this regulation in Robertson v. Methow Valley Citizens Council and held that NEPA does not require a worst-case analysis.[51] In response to a Forest Service decision to allow construction of a private ski resort, the state game department had "voiced a special concern about potential losses to the State's large migratory deer herd, which uses the Methow Valley as a critical winter range and as its migration route."[52] The state agency projected a possible 50 percent reduction in the herd.[53] The Forest Service was more optimistic but admitted that off-site development caused by the project might "noticeably reduce" the herd.[54] Although the court of appeals held that the EIS was invalid because it failed to put forward an explicit worst-case scenario, the Supreme Court held that the CEQ's current regulation was a reasonable interpretation of the statute.[55] Hence, agencies were no longer required to conduct an explicit worst-case analysis after the new regulation went into effect.

PROBLEM ON RISK

The Army Corps of Engineers plans a 300-foot earth fill dam on a California creek, which would create a 3,600-acre lake. (An earth fill dam is made simply by compacting soil, with more sophisticated designs including drainage systems within the dam.) The dam site is located on an inactive fault, but near

---

49. 40 C.F.R. §1502.22(b).
50. *Id.*
51. Robertson v. Methow Valley Citizens Council, 490 U.S. 332 (1989).
52. *Id.* at 342.
53. *Id.*
54. *Id.* at 343.
55. *Id.* at 354-355.

several active faults. The Corps hired a consultant to conduct a "dynamic analysis" of the dam to test the seismic safety of the design. The consultant concluded that the dam was safe. The process involved constructing a model of the dam in a laboratory and subjecting it to simulated earthquakes that would represent "the maximum credible earthquakes" the dam would be required to withstand. The tests were based on the assumption that the fault that could generate earthquakes having the greatest destructive force on the dam was the San Andreas fault, which is twenty miles from the dam and which could generate an earthquake of a magnitude of 8.3 on the Richter Scale. The consultant did not consider a closer fault (only six miles from the dam), because the fault was thought to be too short to generate a major earthquake.

However, a later study showed that the fault was actually about eight times longer than previously believed. Experts believe that the fault is capable of generating an 8.1 earthquake, which would be more destructive for the dam than an 8.3 on the more distant San Andreas fault. The dam is upstream from a small city with a population of 8,000, many of them immigrant agricultural workers on nearby farms.

Assume the following for purposes of this problem:

- There is a 1 percent chance of an 8.1 earthquake on the fault, and such an earthquake would cause the immediate collapse of the dam.
- If an earthquake does take place, that would happen twenty years after the dam is completed,[56] and it would kill 300-400 people because of the short time that would be available for evacuation. Victims probably would be disproportionately elderly or too poor to own cars.
- The dam will produce net present benefits (not taking into account possible losses due to the earthquake risk) of $7 million in excess of its construction cost and the value of the farmland that would be covered by the reservoir.

Should the Corps abandon the dam project or not? What decision standard would you use — cost-benefit analysis, the precautionary principle, or something else?

Whatever your preferred decision standard, explain what decision-making process you would advise. For instance, would you assign the decision to technical experts or allow local residents to vote on the issue? Should the environmental impact statement discuss the effect of a dam collapse in detail? Would you hold public hearings? Should Congress make the decision or the Corps?

---

56. Obviously, this assumption is highly artificial, but it is intended to help you think about the temporal dimension of the problem without having to engage in too much complexity. A real problem would involve a much more complicated projection about the range of possible future times for the earthquake during the life of the dam, the amount of harm at those various future times, and the discounted value of those harms. But let's keep things simple!

7

COMPENSATION AND RISK SPREADING

There are limits to how successfully we can prevent harm from disasters. When harm actually occurs, the next question is compensation. Should we use private insurance, government programs, or the tort system to provide a safety net for victims? This subject intersects with the one in the previous chapter: the prospect of compensation may undermine the motivation of potential victims to invest in increased safety. This chapter considers methods of victim compensation and their pitfalls.

FEMA provides grants and loans to disaster victims to help with recovery. Moreover, many victims have insurance of one kind or another. But the insurance often excludes damages from disasters. For instance, coverage is often limited to wind damage as opposed to flood damage. . . . And after floods, FEMA typically requires localities to upgrade their building codes for rebuilding—but the added expenses are not covered by the typical insurance policy, even if the policy covers "replacement cost." An additional problem is that insurance companies tend to withdraw from the market after catastrophes—so people may be very vulnerable if another big catastrophe hits in the next few years. For all of these reasons, designing a system for compensating catastrophe victims involves significant complications.

The issues discussed in this chapter connect with some of the questions of race and class discussed earlier. Of course, the problem of compensation for catastrophic loss cuts across all groups and income levels. But for those groups whose hold on assets may have been the most tenuous in the first place, the problem of compensation may loom even larger.

We will begin with a survey of compensation methods, including an in-depth discussion of tort law. We will then focus on federal flood insurance and on private insurance, before considering reform proposals in the final part of the chapter.

A. TORT LAW AND OTHER METHODS OF COMPENSATING VICTIMS

Robert L. Rabin & Suzanne A. Bratis,
Financial Compensation for Catastrophic Loss in the United States

Financial Compensation for Victims after Catastrophe
(M. Faure & T. Honlief eds., Springer Verlag 2005)

We have selected for closer examination three distinct illustrations of approaches taken by the U.S. legal system to compensation for financial loss in particularly notable instances: 1) the personal injury and death toll stemming from the terrorist attacks on September 11, 2001; 2) the property damage suffered in the single most costly hurricane in recent U.S. history, Hurricane Andrew; and 3) the profile of recovery in the prototypical mass tort disaster, a commercial airline crash.

A. The September 11 Victim Compensation Fund

In the immediate aftermath of September 11, a no-fault compensation plan was enacted that closely reflected the anxieties and emotions stirred up by the horrendous toll of deaths and injuries occurring on that fateful day. The September 11 Victim Compensation Fund (the Fund), signed into law just eleven days after the terrorist attacks, addressed only personal injury and fatality claims. Losses related to property damage, as well as business losses or interruptions, remained compensable only in tort, if at all. Moreover the Fund was part of a broader legislative scheme, the Air Transportation Safety and System Stabilization Act, offering a package of loans and subsidies to the airlines to avoid a potential collapse of the U.S. commercial air transport system.

Within limits, the Fund was meant to create baseline assurance that victims of physical injury and their survivors would receive benefits.[1] More precisely, the Fund established eligibility for individuals "present at [any of the three crash sites] at the time, or in the immediate aftermath, of the terrorist-related aircraft crashes,"[2] and who "suffered physical harm or death" as a result of the crashes. For this circumscribed class, the Fund provided benefits for both economic and noneconomic losses on a no-fault basis.

In spelling out those benefits, however, the Fund appeared to be far more generous than earlier-enacted no-fault systems in the United States, virtually all of which follow the traditional model established in the early twentieth century for addressing the toll of industrial injuries: workers' compensation schemes. Under workers' compensation, eligible claimants recover medical expenses and a percentage of lost income (generally based on a schedule of awards in cases of permanent disabling conditions and in death benefit cases), subject to a statutory ceiling.

---

1. The description of the Fund and regulations that follows draws in part on an earlier treatment, *see* Robert L. Rabin, *The Quest for Fairness in Compensating Victims of September 11*, 49 Clev. St. L. Rev. 573 (2001).

2. Air Transportation Safety and System Stabilization Act, Pub. L. No. 107-42, 405(b)(2), 115 Stat. 230, 238 (2001) (codified as amended at 49 U.S.C. §40101 (2004)).

By contrast, under the Fund economic loss was defined to include not just medical expenses and loss of present earnings, but "loss of business or employment opportunities to the extent recovery for such loss is allowed under applicable state law" — presumably, a reference to individual, case-by-case tort principles. And noneconomic loss was broadly defined to include "losses for physical and emotional pain, suffering, inconvenience, physical impairment, mental anguish, disfigurement, loss of enjoyment of life, loss of society and companionship, loss of consortium (other than loss of domestic service), hedonic damages, injury to reputation, and all other non-pecuniary losses of any kind or nature." Interestingly, no parallel to the economic loss definition that referenced "[as] allowed under applicable state law" was included in this latter definition of noneconomic loss. Nonetheless, the pervasive influence of the tort perspective of doing individualized justice — disparaged by critics of the tort system, trumpeted by its advocates — was apparent on the face of both provisions.

But there was one substantial qualification to this apparent generosity of spirit. Under traditional tort principles, there is recovery in tort of out-of-pocket expenses even if they have been reimbursed by "collateral" sources such as health and disability insurance. Under the Fund, there is no recovery for these items. Indeed, the restriction on "double recovery," as tort critics would put it, was written in exceedingly broad terms to cover "all collateral sources, including life insurance, pension funds, death benefit programs, and payments by Federal, State, or local governments related to the terrorist-related aircraft crashes. . . ."

Thus, the Fund steered a somewhat uncertain course between collective principles that would emphasize timely compensation and filling the gaps of unmet need, on the one hand, and individualized recovery that would pull in the direction of the tort model, on the other. Before examining this tension in somewhat more detail, however, consider the escape hatch provided in the Act: the prospect of lodging a tort claim instead of proceeding under the Fund.

One can only speculate about why a statutory tort cause of action for claimants was established in the Fund legislation; perhaps in recognition of the fact that some victims with substantial collateral source recoveries — most notably, victims with major life insurance holdings, accrued pension benefits, or accidental death coverage — might well have anticipated no recoverable benefits under the Fund. Or realistically, Congress may have simply recognized that substantial categories of September 11 victims — most clearly, those suffering property damage and psychological harm without accompanying physical injury — were simply not covered by the Fund. Of course, tort, as the default system, would have been available for addressing these claims — how successfully is another matter — without the need for establishing a federal cause of action under the Act. But this would arguably have created the appearance of treating Fund beneficiaries as second-class citizens if they were offered no tort option.

Whatever the case, Congress's ambivalent embrace of tort is highlighted by the title of section 408, which created the federal cause of action: "*Limitation on Air Carrier Liability.*" If Congress was determined to leave tort as an option, it was equally determined to constrain tort along lines familiar to observers of late twentieth-century U.S. tort reform. The Act established a ceiling on tort liability of the air carriers, providing that liability "shall not be in an amount greater than the limits of the liability coverage maintained by the air carrier."[3] In subsequent legislation, this protective cap on liability, linking it to the limits of insurance coverage, was carried over to aircraft manufacturers, property owners in the World Trade Center, airport owners, and governmental entities.

Ceilings aside, exclusive jurisdiction to hear "all actions brought for any claim (including any claim for loss of property, personal injury, or death) resulting from or relating to the terrorist-related aircraft crashes" was located in the federal district court for the Southern District of New York. But no federal common law was created; rather, the court was to apply the substantive law of the state in which the crash occurred. Finally, just to leave no doubt about it, section 408(b)(1) declared that the federal cause of action was to be "the exclusive remedy for damages arising out of the hijacking and subsequent crashes of such flights."

Thus, claimants eligible under the Fund were put to a choice — they had either to elect a claim for benefits under the Fund or to waive their rights and pursue a tort claim. At the same time, for those falling outside the eligibility limits of the Fund — such as those claiming solely economic loss — tort, as circumscribed in the Act, remained available. Interestingly, the tort option provided in the Fund legislation is not found in the traditional workers' compensation model, which precludes recourse to tort altogether (other later-enacted, no-fault schemes vary in this regard). Nonetheless, in its benefit provisions, as indicated, the Fund was far more generous than any other existing no-fault scheme in the United States.

These singular aspects of the Fund were not lost on the Special Master, appointed under the Act, who faced the immediate task of developing a concrete program for determining benefit awards for victims of September 11. His efforts offer an alternative vision of how one might design a no-fault model for future victims of terrorism, or catastrophic loss more broadly conceived.

When the Special Master, Kenneth Feinberg, was appointed on November 26, 2001, his initial task was to promulgate regulations resolving the principal tensions in the Act and filling in some important blanks. He issued a set of draft regulations ("Interim Final Rule") for commentary on December 21, 2001, and subsequently, on March 8, 2002, he issued final regulations ("Final Rule"), spelling out his interpretations of Fund provisions.

Feinberg's reading of the main provisions of the Fund reveals an interesting effort to strike a balance between understanding the Act in traditional no-fault terms that would have emphasized meeting scheduled basic loss of victims, and interpreting the Act in an open-ended fashion that essentially would have offered tort-type, individualized compensation in a no-fault setting. His manner of resolving this tension is evident in the approach taken to the three key substantive benefit provisions already discussed: collateral source offset, economic loss, and noneconomic loss.

---

3. *Id.* §408(a). The amount of insurance coverage was reported to be $1.5 billion per plane. *See* Jim VandeHei & Milo Geyelin, *Economic Impact: Bush Seeks to Limit Liability of Companies Sued as Result of Attacks*, WALL ST. J., Oct. 25, 2001, at A6.

As mentioned earlier, the Act explicitly called for the offset of life insurance and pension benefits. These provisions raised a firestorm of criticism from victims' families (in particular, the well endowed), concerned that they were likely to receive nothing in Fund benefits because of the foresight of the deceased, who it was argued, had earned or set aside funds for just such a contingency as occurred. These protests were sharpened to a fine point by prospective claimants observing that unconstrained tort — the absence of a Fund — would be a superior option, since life insurance and pension benefits traditionally are not offset under the tort system.

The Special Master responded to these criticisms in the Final Rule, by interpreting the Act to allow reduction of the offset to the extent of victims' self-contributions. More generally, Feinberg announced that it would be "very rare" for *any* eligible claimant to receive less than $250,000. It should be noted that neither of these interpretive moves is grounded in the language of the act.

Rather, the Special Master's actions reflected a fundamental philosophical difference buried in the esoteric legal language of collateral offset. On the one hand, a need-based approach to compensation would point to full offset of all collateral sources, as the Act appeared to require, since these outside benefits do contribute to meeting basic needs. On the other hand, under an individual claimant-focused, tort-type inquiry as to the "deserving" status of the victim, offsets arguably would be ignored entirely. In the end, the Special Master arrived at something of a compromise, liberalizing the statute from the victims' perspective by reducing the offset through recognition of victims' contributions and ignoring entirely outside private charity received by Fund-eligible claimants, as well as establishing a quite substantial presumptive minimum recovery.

As indicated, in addressing economic loss the Act appears to be at cross-purposes with the literal terms of the collateral source offset provision, in referring to recovery of "loss of business or employment opportunities" as defined in state tort law. On its face, this would seem to suggest an individualized inquiry in every case into the lifetime earnings prospects of each deceased victim, entirely at odds with the traditional no-fault approach of scheduled benefits.

In the Final Rule, the Special Master again crafted a compromise. Although there is no mention of scheduling in the statute, Feinberg established a grid applicable to the range of potential claimants — a "presumed economic loss" schedule — based on age, size of family, and recent past earnings, along with a presumptive cap applicable to the upper 2 percent of income earners. In devising this strategy, he provided for awards that recognized very considerable future earnings disparities, an announced range of $250,000 to between $3 and $4 million. But at the same time, he rejected an approach that would have recognized entirely open-ended, case-by-case speculation about future earnings prospects.

Although there are exceptions, no-fault schemes typically do not provide for pain and suffering loss, apart from optional or supplemental recourse to tort. In fact, tort law itself, as encapsulated in wrongful death statutes, did not traditionally provide any pain and suffering loss for survivors — that is, loss of companionship. Indeed, many states still do not recognize nonpecuniary loss as compensable to survivors in tort, limiting recovery to economic loss. And some other states, such as California, refuse to recognize pain and suffering of the deceased *victim* prior to death as recoverable in tort.

Nonetheless, the Special Master provided for *scheduled* noneconomic benefit awards under the Fund, for each victim and every surviving eligible family member. In the Interim Final Rule, $250,000 was to be awarded for each victim; a figure that remained unchanged in the Final Rule. With respect to survivors, the Interim Final Rule provided $50,000 for the spouse and each dependent, a figure that was increased to $100,000 each in the Final Rule. Thus, a surviving spouse with two children would receive benefits of $550,000 for noneconomic loss in a claim under the Fund. . . .

B. Compensating Hurricane Damage: Hurricane Andrew

On August 24, 1992, Hurricane Andrew made landfall in the United States. This Category 4 hurricane struck just east of Homestead Air Force Base in Florida, passed through the southern Florida peninsula and moved onto south-central Louisiana. When it hit Florida, the storm had sustained wind speeds of approximately 145 mph, with gusts of at least 175 mph, and storm surges up to 16.9 feet.

Natural events only become "disasters" because of the impact that they have on human settlements. And disaster events are typically ranked relative to one another based on the costs associated with the damage that they cause. When it struck, Hurricane Andrew became the costliest natural disaster in U.S. history, both in terms of the FEMA relief required and total estimates of property damaged. Total property damage was estimated to be more than 25 billion dollars. Florida witnessed 28,066 of its homes destroyed and another 107,380 damaged. 180,000 people were left homeless, 82,000 businesses were destroyed or damaged, 1.4 million residents were left without power and 32,000 acres of farmland were damaged. In addition, twenty-six deaths were found directly attributable to the hurricane's impact and another 39 lives were lost as an indirect result of the storm.

Hurricane Andrew caused $17 billion in insured damage. Homeowner policy holders in Florida submitted 280,000 claims and recovered over $11 billion or 65% of total insured losses resulting from Andrew. The other types of insurance coverage triggered by the event included commercial multiperil ($3.767 billion), commercial fire ($1.062 billion), automobile/physical damage ($365 million), mobile-home owners ($204 million), and farm owners ($16 million).

The size of the disaster caught many insurance companies unprepared, which affected the efficiency of claims processing. First, insurers were, themselves, victims of the disaster. Many of the insurers' employees who lived in the south Florida area suffered property damage, making it difficult for them to attend to their business duties and their own home crises. Additionally, the storm damaged office buildings, communications services, and data storage facilities of the insurance companies. This damage created hurdles for efficient operation of business.

There was also simply a dearth of claims adjusters in relation to the magnitude of claims filed. Florida's Department of Insurance streamlined its process of licensing claims adjusters in the days following the storm, enabling insurers to use emergency adjusters to deal with the volume of claims. Some insurers did not take advantage of this emergency provision, and the shortage of adjusters introduced delays in the system. With so many policyholders left homeless or severely in need in the first few days after the storm, these delays resulted in many people having to wait for the temporary living expense funds they needed to pay for basic necessities like food, shelter, and clothing.

In 1992, property insurers in Florida collected $1.5 billion in premiums. They paid out about 10 times that amount to victims of Hurricane Andrew. The costs of the hurricane were greater than any company expected and forced members of the Florida insurance industry to recalculate their risks. In the aftermath of Hurricane Andrew, the landscape of Florida's insurance industry changed dramatically. Before Andrew struck, nearly 300 insurers provided a variety of coverage options to Florida's citizenry. As a result of the losses caused by Andrew, seven small insurers became insolvent, 34 insurers informed Florida's Department of Insurance of their intent to withdraw from the market entirely, and 29 reduced their coverage options in the state. Reinsurers also contributed to the situation. Primary insurers are restricted in the coverage that they can offer by the reinsurance available to them and many reinsurers became reluctant to provide coverage after the events of Hurricane Andrew.

The Florida Legislature responded to the state's insurance crisis by creating the Residential Property and Casualty Joint Underwriting Association and the Florida Hurricane Catastrophe Fund, which are currently of major importance. . . .

The risk of hurricane events occurring in Florida is continuous. If anything, climate change studies indicate that the frequency and severity of such storms will increase in the future. And the potential damage that a storm of Andrew's caliber could inflict today far exceeds the destruction that occurred in 1992. One study estimated that if Hurricane Andrew hit with the same force in the same location today, it would cause close to $70 billion in damage, nearly twice the 1992 figure. As coastal area populations continue to increase and infrastructure continues to grow denser, the potential impact of future hurricanes becomes more devastating.

The catastrophe-response infrastructure of both Florida and FEMA were heavily analyzed in the aftermath of the storm. Since 1992, FEMA has updated the Federal Response Plan twice, attempting to strengthen federal coordination, management, and leadership. Likewise, Florida's insurance industry underwent a major overhaul, along the lines discussed above.

The 2004 summer hurricane season put both the national and the state relief reforms to an unprecedented test. Beginning with Hurricane Charley, the southeast coastal states suffered through four significant hurricanes between August and October. As of late October, 2004, combined state and federal disaster aid for Florida alone reached more than $2 billion.

This cluster of hurricanes will provide a test for Florida's insurance industry, as well as FEMA. Florida's government will be challenged both in its role as a primary catastrophe insurer, through the state's newly formed Citizens Property Insurance Corporation, and as a reinsurer, through the Florida Hurricane Catastrophe Fund. These programs were created by the state in direct response to the lessons learned from Hurricane Andrew. As the state cleans up from Hurricane Charley and its three successors, and Florida's residents begin rebuilding their homes and their lives, onlookers will have the opportunity to assess whether Andrew's lessons were well-heeded.

Whatever the doctrinal limitations, tort is frequently criticized from the broader perspectives of economic efficiency, distribution of risk, and fairness. Certainly from a compensation vantage point, the latter two concerns loom large. Tort only provides compensation: 1) when the *wrongdoing* of a defendant can be established, and 2) when the defendant is *solvent*. . . . These limitations, along with the no-duty rules . . . , mean that it is often the case that victims suffering similar injuries are not treated in a like fashion — and indeed that the disparities are sometimes glaring (ranging from no recovery to millions of dollars for similar accidental injuries or deaths). Thus, both in terms of risk distribution and fairness, it can be argued that tort leaves much to be desired.

Moreover, these limitations spill over into a critique from an economic, deterrence-oriented perspective, as well: No-duty rules, as well as insolvency, that insulate risk generators from bearing the cost of accidents for which they are responsible, translate into inadequate incentives on risk generators to provide safety precautions. In addition, the high administrative cost of shifting losses in tort is frequently invoked as an independent shortcoming of the system — undermining both its deterrence function and its efficacy from a risk-distribution and fairness perspective.[4]

As indicated in the section on insurance, the limitations of tort do not mean that those suffering personal injury loss as a consequence of catastrophic harm go entirely uncompensated.[5] About 85% of the U.S. population is covered to some extent by private health insurance, and Medicare offers public health insurance coverage to those over 65 years of age. The resulting gap in medical coverage — while still fairly substantial — is not as wide as the shortfall in coverage for wage loss. Private disability insurance coverage in the U.S. is quite uncommon, and while state disability and unemployment insurance benefits provide short-term partial relief, they do not fill the gap in cases of longer-term or very serious injuries. On this latter score, the federal SSDI insurance program, as indicated earlier, does offer scheduled benefits — although considerably short of full economic restoration — to those experiencing permanent total disability. In sum, the public welfare schemes in the U.S. leave quite large gaps in coverage for the economic consequences of personal injury, and private insurance sources fill only part of the gap, primarily for those carrying generous health insurance.

With regard to residential and commercial property and casualty loss, private insurance is the avenue of recourse. In the case of residential property, it is likely to be held by homeowners; much less likely to be held by renters.

---

4. It is generally thought that injury victims in tort receive roughly 50% of total expenditures by tort defendants. *See* J. Kakalik & N. Pace, RAND Inst. Civ. Just., Costs and Compensation Paid in Tort Litigation (1985).

5. Indeed, a 1991 study conducted by RAND Institute for Civil Justice found that overall areas of personal injury, payments in tort comprised 11% of total benefits received by accident victims — although the percentage would almost certainly be higher for victims in catastrophic loss cases. D. Hensler et al., RAND Inst. Civ. Just., Compensation for Accidental Injuries in the United States (1991).

There are no general exclusions in the standard policies that would apply to catastrophic loss — just as there is none for third-party liability in the personal injury setting.

NOTES AND QUESTIONS

1. The 9/11 compensation fund has not been seen as a model for compensating for death or injury of disaster victims. Most of the attention regarding disasters such as Katrina has been on compensation for property loss. Should we consider a fund to compensate the families of those who were killed, or was 9/11 a unique event because of its national security dimension? Of course 9/11 was different in other ways: the harm was caused by an identifiable enemy, possible liability by the airlines could have had devastating economic effects, and the families of the victims were often affluent and legally sophisticated.

2. Could the federal government be held liable for defectively designing or constructing the New Orleans flood control system? Could state or local governments be held liable for similar problems with nonfederal levees or for failing to inspect and maintain federal levees? Consider your answers in light of the next three cases.

Paterno v. State of California

113 Cal. App. 4th 998; 6 Cal. Rptr. 3d 854; 2003 (2003)

Morrison, J. The environmental aftermath of the Gold Rush continues to plague California. Hydraulic mining debris caused flooding which led to the building of levees at the confluence of the Yuba and Feather Rivers. Almost a century ago the Linda levee was built with uncompacted mining debris, and the use of that debris caused the levee to collapse on February 20, 1986.

About 3,000 plaintiffs sued the State of California (State), Reclamation District 784 (District) and others not now parties, seeking damages. In Paterno v. State of California (1999), 74 Cal. App. 4th 68 [87 Cal. Rptr. 2d 754] (*Paterno I*), we affirmed a defense jury verdict finding no dangerous condition of public property and reversed an inverse condemnation liability finding against defendants, and remanded for another trial on inverse liability. A new coordination judge (Hon. John J. Golden), conducted a lengthy court trial and issued a defense judgment against sample plaintiffs (collectively, Paterno) who filed this appeal.

Paterno embraces Judge Golden's factual findings, which in his view, create inverse liability on the part of the State as a matter of law. We agree. When a public entity operates a flood control system built by someone else, it accepts liability as if it had planned and built the system itself. A public entity cannot be held liable for failing to upgrade a flood control system to provide additional protection. But the trial court found the levee was built with porous, uncompacted mining debris, in a location which encouraged seepage, leading directly to the failure of the levee, and that long before the failure, feasible cures could have fixed the problems. Use of such technology would not have been an upgrade, but would have ensured the planned flood control capacity was achieved.

(2) Inverse liability stems from the California Constitution and is not dependent on tort or private property principles of fault. California Supreme Court precedent dictates that a landowner should not bear a disproportionate share of the harm directly caused by failure of a flood control project due to an unreasonable plan. Whether the plan is unreasonable is not measured by negligence principles, as in a tort case alleging a dangerous condition of public property, but by balancing a number of specific factors referred to as the *Locklin* factors. (Locklin v. City of Lafayette (1994) 7 Cal. 4th 327 [27 Cal. Rptr. 2d 613, 867 P.2d 724] (*Locklin*).) Based on the facts found by the trial court and application of the *Locklin* factors, we conclude Paterno's damages were directly caused by an unreasonable State plan which resulted in the failure of the Linda levee and the State is liable to pay for Paterno's damages. In large part our conclusion is based on the fact that the levee system benefited all of California and saved billions of dollars, and to require Paterno to bear the cost of the partial failure of that system — a failure caused by construction and operation of an unstable levee — would violate *Locklin*. A basic part of the State's flood plan was to accept existing levees as much as possible, to reduce the cost of an extensive, coordinated, flood control system. The People benefited from that cost-saving feature. However, the record shows the State never tested the Linda levee, or reviewed the records of its construction, to see if it was as strong as the global plans assumed it was, and the State even ignored specific warnings about the levee's weaknesses. In such circumstance, the costs of the levee failure must be deemed part of the deferred costs of the project. We do not separately address an alternate theory that the State is liable because of an inadequate levee inspection plan, although we discuss the lack of any plan to examine the heart of the levee.

Although in some ways the District is a coparticipant with the State in operating the levee, we conclude it is entitled to judgment. The District was responsible for and only for ordinary maintenance and could not alter the structure of the levee, even if it had the financial means to do so.

We will affirm the judgment in favor of the District, reverse the judgment in favor of the State with directions to enter judgment in favor of Paterno, and remand for further proceedings. In making this order, we realize this case is as hoary as Jarndyce v. Jarndyce. We expedited this appeal, and counsel assisted this court by providing much of the record and the briefs in computerized format. We will direct that this case be given priority in the trial court and that all available means to expedite the remaining triable issues be implemented. . . .

In 1904 Yuba County adopted a resolution authorizing construction of a levee known as the Morrison Grade, which became the Linda levee. It was built by men and horses using scrapers to borrow nearby material, mostly mining debris. The trial court found: "In the process, little or no compaction of the material was attempted or achieved. As built, Morrison Grade was highly susceptible to seepage failure because of its siting on top of fifteen feet of porous hydraulic mining debris, the porosity of the material of which it was constructed, and the absence of any compaction of that material during construction." The Linda levee was part of the District, formed in 1908, and incorporated into the SRFCP.

Pursuant to the Grant Report the Corps improved the levee in 1934 and 1940 but the trial court found "the existing levee was incorporated into the finished work" without change. The floods of 1955 sorely tested the SRFCP and exposed many deficiencies, but no problems were revealed in the Linda levee, in particular the south levee on the Yuba between the Southern Pacific Railroad and the E Street Bridge (before the Feather confluence). Although the flood stage *exceeded* design capacity and water came within a foot of the top, it held. In the 1964 flood year the Linda levee was also subjected to higher waters than in 1986, yet held.

In February 1986, a tropical weather system brought much warm rain, which in turn caused snow melt triggering massive flooding in California. For three days the Linda levee held water reaching to 76 feet (U.S. Engineering Datum), but it failed when the water had receded to about 74.3 feet; it is designed to hold up to 80 feet. The State concedes the levee failed at about *half* its designed capacity. The trial court found "the resulting 150 foot gap in the embankment allowed roughly 20,000 acre-feet of water . . . to inundate some 7,000 acres of land situated in the communities of Linda and Olivehurst, lying across the river south of Marysville in a territory which had been protected by the [levee] from flooding for many years. The flooding resulted in damage . . . estimated to be in the range of one hundred million dollars." "By 1986, the value of property protected by the levee . . . was about $409,400,000. There was evidently no general perception that the area was not a safe place for urban development."

. . .

On appeal the State (but not the District) asserts the levee broke due to unforeseeable causes (e.g., "hydro-consolidation") and therefore the State cannot be liable to Paterno. We tend to agree with Paterno that the State has waived this argument. At trial the State objected to the trial court's proposal that it consider the Albers factors, which included foreseeability. Elsewhere at trial the State asserted it "has never contended that foreseeability was an issue in this case, ever." The State appears to be improperly changing its theory on appeal by claiming lack of foreseeability as a defense. But the point is important and raises no new factual issues, so we will address it.

The State misapprehends the role of foreseeability. As Paterno points out, foreseeability plays no role in the causation analysis and is not determinative in the balancing step, only informative. This is not a case involving a dangerous condition of public property, and we are not applying tort or water law standards of liability. We are implementing the constitutional command that the State must compensate landowners when it damages their property. As Paterno points out, "Even if the State failed to appreciate the risk of failure, this is not a defense to proximate cause. In other words, the levee's planned design and construction throughout its life 'endangered the levee in a way not adequately valued by the planners.'" We agree with Paterno's interpretation and the point has been made elsewhere.

The "reasonableness" balanced here is not a negligence standard of care, which might turn on foreseeability, but is "determined by balancing the public benefit and private damage in each case." The causation element is restated with greater precision in terms of 'substantial causation.'"

Thus, while foreseeability may weigh in favor of the landowner, lack of foreseeability does not defeat the claim.

In this case the evidence overwhelmingly shows the failure of the levee was foreseeable. The State says "There were no events that reasonably put the State on notice before Linda levee failed that its capability to safely carry flood flows was or was becoming compromised." Paterno does not argue the State actually foresaw the levee failure. But the State must be charged with knowledge of how the levee was built. It operated the levee for decades and had ample opportunity to examine it. If it chose not to do so for fiscal reasons, that would indicate the loss should be absorbed by the State.

NOTES AND QUESTIONS

1. Could victims of Katrina recover against state or local authorities for negligence in designing or maintaining levees? Consider Bernard v. Thigpen Constr. Co., 702 So. 2d 1387 (La. 1997), and Bernard v. Thigpen Constr. Co., 695 So. 2d 518 (La. Ct. App. 1997), *vacated by* 702 So. 2d 1387 (La. 1997). The appellate court had approved certification of the class injured in the 1995 flood, but then the Louisiana Supreme Court set aside the certification after ruling in another decision that "the existence of individual causation and liability issues as to each potential class member may so predominate over common issues that class certification is inappropriate." Bernard v. Thigpen Construction Co., 702 So. 2d 1387, 1388 (La. 1997). The appellate opinion is more interesting in terms of imagining how plaintiffs could come together as a class following a natural disaster.

2. What about tort actions by FEMA against state and local governments to recover for its expenditures? In United States v. Parish of St. Bernard, 756 F.2d 1116 (5th Cir. 1985), the Fifth Circuit affirmed the district court's grant of summary judgment to various local governments and public entities. FEMA had sued to recover over $100 million from the defendants for non-compliance with the National Flood Insurance Program. The court held that Congress had not expressly authorized a contract theory for a right of action under the NFIP, but the federal government could pursue common-law claims to recover the defendants' NFIP-insured property. The NFIP will be discussed in more detail in the next section.

   Would it be helpful for the federal government to have a cause of action against local governments for negligently maintaining levees or failing to implement measures required by federal law? Would this provide an incentive for improved performance at the local level? Or would it just saddle already battered municipalities with a heavy litigation burden?

3. The next case considers the potential liability of the federal government itself for flood damages. Note that while the California constitution requires compensation whenever the government "damages" property, the federal Constitution does not impose such a requirement. Instead, it merely provides liability when property is deliberately "taken" by the government.

Thus, any recovery for the failure of federal flood control projects must be based on tort rather than on inverse compensation.

UNITED STATES V. JAMES

478 U.S. 597, 106 S. Ct. 3116, 92 L. Ed. 2d 48 (1986)

Justice POWELL delivered the opinion of the Court.

[This litigation arose from serious accidents that occurred in the reservoirs of federal flood control projects in Arkansas and Louisiana. In both accidents, recreational users (water-skiers in Arkansas and a fisherman in Louisiana) of the reservoirs were injured or drowned when they were swept through retaining structures after those structures were opened by the United States Corps of Engineers to control flooding. Separate actions were brought against the United States under the Federal Tort Claims Act. In the Arkansas case, the court held that although Government agents had willfully and maliciously failed to warn of a known danger, the Government was immune from damages under 33 U.S.C. §702c, which provides in part that "[no] liability of any kind shall attach to or rest upon the United States for any damage from or by floods or flood waters at any place." In the Louisiana case, the court similarly granted summary judgment for the United States despite the government's concession that it negligently failed to warn of the danger from the current caused by open gates. In a consolidated appeal, the Court of Appeals reversed the judgments. The Court of Appeals held that Congress had not intended to shield the negligent or wrongful acts of government employees either in the construction or continued operation of flood control projects, including the failure to warn the public of hazards to their use of reservoirs.]

The starting point in statutory interpretation is "the language [of the statute] itself." "[We] assume that the legislative purpose is expressed by the ordinary meaning of the words used." The immunity provision in §702c, enacted as part of the Flood Control Act of 1928, outlines immunity in sweeping terms: "No liability of *any* kind shall attach to or rest upon the United States for *any* damage from or by floods or flood waters at *any* place." It is difficult to imagine broader language.

On its face, this language covers the accidents here. Respondents' injuries occurred as a result of the release of waters from reservoirs that had reached flood stage. Given the nature of the accidents at issue, and given the plain terms of the statute, "it requires some ingenuity to create ambiguity."

Although the Court of Appeals found, for example, that the word "damage" was ambiguous because it might refer only to damage to property and exclude damage to persons, the ordinary meaning of the word carries no such limitation. Damages "have historically been awarded both for injury to property and injury to the person — a fact too well-known to have been overlooked by the Congress. . . . Moreover, Congress' choice of the language "*any* damage" and "liability of *any* kind" further undercuts a narrow construction. (Emphasis added.)

Nor do the terms "flood" and "flood waters" create any uncertainty in the context of accidents such as the ones at issue in these cases. The Act concerns flood control projects designed to carry floodwaters. It is thus clear from §702c's plain language that the terms "flood" and "flood waters" apply to all waters contained in or carried through a federal flood control project for purposes of or related to flood control, as well as to waters that such projects cannot control. As both District Courts found, the waters here clearly fall within the ambit of the statute.

We have repeatedly recognized that "[when] . . . the terms of a statute [are] unambiguous, judicial inquiry is complete, except 'in "rare and exceptional circumstances."'" In the absence of a "clearly expressed legislative intention to the contrary," the language of the statute itself "must ordinarily be regarded as conclusive." Despite respondents' contentions and the reasoning of the Court of Appeals, we do not find that the legislative history of the statute justifies departure from the plain words of the statute. Indeed, on balance we think the legislative history of the Flood Control Act of 1928 *reinforces* the plain language of the immunity provision in §702c.

The Flood Control Act enacted "a comprehensive ten-year program for the entire [Mississippi River] valley, embodying a general bank protection scheme, channel stabilization and river regulation, all involving vast expenditures of public funds." The Act was the Nation's response to the disastrous flood in the Mississippi River Valley in 1927. That flood resulted in the loss of nearly 200 lives and more than $200 million in property damage; almost 700,000 people were left homeless. The flood control system in the Mississippi River Valley in response to this catastrophe was the largest public works project undertaken up to that time in the United States.

It is not surprising, in the light of the devastation wrought by the 1927 flood and the magnitude of Congress' undertaking, that the legislative history of §702c shows a consistent concern for limiting the Federal Government's financial liability to expenditures directly necessary for the construction and operation of the various projects. Numerous statements concerning the immunity provision confirm that it was intended to reaffirm sovereign immunity in such a dangerous and extensive project. The Chairman of the House Rules Committee, in opening the discussion on the rule governing debate on the 1928 Act, stated:

> I want this bill so drafted that it will contain all the safeguards necessary for the Federal Government. If we go down there and furnish protection to these people — and I assume it is a national responsibility — I do not want to have anything left out of the bill that would protect us now and for all time to come. I for one do not want to open up a situation that will cause thousands of lawsuits for damages against the Federal Government in the next 10, 20, or 50 years.

A number of other Congressmen unequivocally stated that the United States should not be liable for any expense other than the direct cost of constructing the project.

These statements show that the sweeping language of §702c was no drafting inadvertence. Congress clearly sought to ensure beyond doubt that sovereign immunity would protect the Government from "any" liability associated with flood control. As the Court of Appeals for the Eighth Circuit explained three decades ago in *National Mfg.*, §702c's language "safeguarded the United States against liability of any kind for damage from or by floods or flood waters in the broadest and most emphatic language." The equally broad and emphatic language found in the legislative history shows that Congress understood what it was saying. We therefore conclude that the legislative history fully supports attributing to the unambiguous words of the statute their ordinary meaning.

Justice STEVENS, with whom Justice MARSHALL and Justice O'CONNOR join, dissenting.

As a part of the major undertaking authorized by the Mississippi Flood Control Act of 1928, Congress directed the Secretary of War and the Chief of Engineers to take special steps to acquire lands that were subject to "overflow and damage" along the banks of the Mississippi River where it was impracticable to construct levees. In the section of the Act containing that specific direction concerning the acquisition of "lands so subjected to overflow and damage," there is a sentence stating that "[no] liability of any kind shall attach to or rest upon the United States for any damage from or by floods or flood waters at any place."

According to the Court, Congress intended by this sentence to immunize the Federal Government from liability for any claim for personal injury, even though Congress provided expressly for compensation for property damage in excess of that required by the Constitution. In my view, neither the plain language of the statute nor the legislative history behind it supports imputing such a perverse design to the Legislature. In my opinion, this provision applies only to property damage, and the judgment below should be affirmed. . . .

It would be regrettable but obligatory for this Court to construe the immunity provision to bar personal injury claims if such was the intent of Congress. But when a critical term in the statute suggests a more limited construction, and when the congressional debates are not only consistent with this construction, but nowhere reveal a recognition, let alone an intention, that the immunity provision would deprive those injured by governmental negligence of any remedy, a narrower interpretation is more faithful to the objective of Congress. It defies belief—and ascribes to the Members of Congress a perverse, even barbaric, intent—to think that they spent days debating the measure of extra-constitutional compensation they would provide riparian landowners but intended—without a single word of dissent—to condemn the widows, orphans, and injured victims of negligent operation of flood control projects to an irrational exclusion from the protection of the subsequently enacted Tort Claims Act.

NOTES AND QUESTIONS

1. What is the most likely reconstruction of Congress's intent in passing the flood immunity provision? Should that matter, given the breadth of the statutory language?
2. Does *James* preclude all federal liability for flooding? For instance, suppose a post office truck runs into a fire hydrant, flooding someone's basement.

Does there have to be a connection with a federal flood control project? Consider the following trial court decision.

In re Katrina Canal Breaches Consolidated Litigation

United States District Court, E.D. Louisiana, 2007, 417 F. Supp. 2d 684 E.D. La. 2007

Duval, District Judge.

[Plaintiffs alleged that the MRGO canal "funneled" the Katrina storm surge into the heart of New Orleans.] Plaintiffs contend that the MRGO [Mississippi River Gulf Outlet] is not a flood control project but an aid to navigation. The nub of the issue before the court is whether the MRGO is a flood control project and whether waters that flow through the MRGO are floodwaters. Moreover, the Court must consider the question as to whether §702c immunizes the Government if the damages would have occurred, in whole or in part, as the result of waters caused by negligent acts in constructing and maintaining the MRGO regardless of the existence of flood control project(s). [The government also contended that it was protected by the "discretionary function" exception to federal tort immunity.] . . .

The Government maintains that the plain language of §702c clearly means that the United States cannot be liable for damages caused by any floodwaters of any kind occurring anywhere. They also contend that certain "levees" that were constructed in conjunction with MRGO constitute projects that would be subject to immunity under §702c. As noted, in the alternative, they contend since the water at issue was not contained by flood control projects, regardless of the source of those waters, it is likewise immune. The Court finds that this wholesale approach to immunity in the context of this motion to dismiss is neither supported by the history of the Flood Control Act of 1928, nor in a fair reading of Central Green Co. v. United States, 531 U.S. 425, 121 S. Ct. 1005, 148 L. Ed. 2d 919 (2001) as the Government contends. . . .

This issue was most recently analyzed in *Central Green*, where the Supreme Court grappled with the breadth of immunity granted under section 702c. In that case, owners of real property sued, inter alia, the United States under the FTCA for damage to their pistachio farm allegedly caused by subsurface and surface water flooding from the Madera Canal, a federal facility leased to the Madera Irrigation District (MID). Plaintiffs sought damages from the United States and MID "alleging that their negligence in the design, construction, and maintenance of the canal had caused subsurface flooding resulting in damage to the orchards and increased operating costs for petitioner. Petitioner did not allege that any physical failure of the dam caused damage to its property."

This canal was part or a "branch" of a vast federal project known as the Central Valley Project ("CVP"), which included flood control projects for the Sacramento and San Joaquin Rivers in California. The various portions of the CVP captures and stores waters of both rivers and many of their tributaries, in some cases generating electric energy in the diversion, and then redirects the later to semiarid land below. As described in *Central Green:*

> The Central Valley basin development envisions, in one sense, an integrated undertaking, but also an aggregate of many subsidiary projects, each of which

is of first magnitude. It consists of thirty-eight major dams and reservoirs bordering the valley floor and scores of smaller ones in headwaters. It contemplates twenty-eight hydropower generating stations. It includes hundreds of miles of main canals, thousands of miles of laterals and drains, electric transmission and feeder lines and substations a vast network of structure for the control and use of water on two million acres of land already irrigated, three million acres of land to be newly irrigated, 380,000 acres in the delta needing protection from intrusions of salt water, and for municipal and miscellaneous purposes including cities, towns, duck clubs and game refuges. These projects are not only widely separated geographically, many of them physically independent in operation, but they are authorized in separate acts from year to year and are to be constructed at different times over a considerable span of years.

. . .

[T]he Supreme Court squarely confronted dicta it had rendered in the first occasion it had to interpret §702c, that being in United States v. James, 478 U.S. 597, 106 S. Ct. 3116, 92 L. Ed. 2d 483 (1986) which had "generated conflicting opinions among the Courts of Appeal." In James, two suits were consolidated to determine whether §702c barred recovery for personal injuries to individuals allegedly caused by the negligence of the United States in its failure to warn of dangers from the release of floodwaters from federal flood control projects. The injuries at issue there were caused by turbulent current generated by unwarned releases of waters from a reservoir after the Army Corps of Engineers had determined that the waters were at "flood stage." Thus, the fact that the injuries were caused by "flood waters" was undisputed.

In *James*, the Supreme Court stated in dicta:

> Nor do the terms "flood" and "flood waters" create any uncertainty in the context of accidents such as the ones at issue in these cases. The Act concerns flood control projects designed to carry floodwaters. It is thus clear from §702c's plain language that the terms "flood" and "flood waters" apply to all waters contained in or carried through a federal flood control project for purposes of or related to flood control, as well as to waters that such projects cannot control.

From that statement, many courts focused on whether the damage related in some manner to a flood control project rather than whether it related to floods or flood waters. The Supreme Court in *Central Green* rejected this dicta, and noted that its holding in *James* was simply that "the phrase 'floods or flood water' is not narrowly confined to those waters that a federal project is unable to control, and that it encompasses waters that are released for flood control purposes when reservoired waters are at flood stage."

Nonetheless, the Supreme Court found that the dismissal of the *Central Green* suit using the *James* rationale was inappropriate and noted that "[t]he holding in *James* also differs from the less attenuated and more fact-specific position advanced by the Government, which would require us to take judicial notice of evidence that the Friant Division of the Central Valley Project and, indeed, the Madera Canal itself can and do serve flood control purposes." Thus the Supreme Court concluded that it could not uphold the Ninth Circuit's dismissal of the suit neither based on the "broad definition" of flood waters as found in *James*, nor by taking notice that the canal in *Central Green* from which the water damage flowed was part of a flood control project.

The Supreme Court then examined the nature of the Central Valley Project as described above. It found that the case raised a difficult issue because the property damage at issue was allegedly caused by continuous or repeated flows occurring over a period of years, rather than by a single, discrete incident. Thus it found that "when damage may have been caused over a period of time in part by flood waters and in part by the routine use of the canal when it contained little more than a trickle," it would be error to grant the Government's motion for judgment on the pleadings. The Court concluded, "Accordingly, in determining whether §702c immunity attaches, courts should consider the character of the waters that cause the relevant damage rather than the relation between that damage and a flood control project." Thus, the concept that the Government might be immune from damage from the effect of some water and not as to other water is recognized in *Central Green*.

In the case at bar, the Government likewise seeks to have this Court dismiss this suit taking judicial notice that there were flood control projects — whether constructed using funds appropriated pursuant to the LVP or to the MRGO — extant and as such, the waters which caused the damage, were flood waters and the United States Government is thus immune. However, this approach ignores the pleadings presented. Plaintiffs are not seeking damages for the failure of the levees or flood projects. Plaintiffs contend that MRGO has absolutely nothing to do with a flood control project. Plaintiffs are seeking damages for the effects of the waters in the MRGO with respect to the decimation of the wetlands over a long period of time which in turn created the hazard which resulted in flooding which plaintiffs maintain could not have been controlled by any flood control project.

Furthermore, the Government's position ignores the fact that even the Supreme Court in *Central Green* opened the possibility of a segregation of damages — those for which the Government would be immune under §702c and those for which immunity would not attach. Indeed, the Government even concurred with this reading at oral argument. . . . Thus, contrary to the Government's contention that *Central Green* broadens the immunity provided by 702c, in reality *Central Green* requires the Court to identify the cause of the damage rather than base a decision on the mere fact that a flood control project was involved. *Central Green* does not directly answer the question of what nexus to a flood control project is required for floodwaters to trigger immunity.

The Government is asking this Court to ignore plaintiffs' pleadings, use Rule 12(b)(1) to rewrite plaintiffs' complaint, find that all of the projects, levees and activities in that area are flood control projects, and as a result, because (1) flood waters caused the damage alleged or (2) because flood waters were not contained by these presumptive flood control projects, find the Government immune as a matter of law. There is intense disagreement as to the scope of the "levees" that were created in the dredging of the MRGO — are these spoil-banks or actual flood control projects? Likewise, there are serious questions as to the relationship between the MRGO and the LVP. If indeed there was coordination, it would appear that this would not subsume the cause of action as demonstrated in *Central Green*. . . . Indeed, this case is very much like that found in *Central Green*; while arguably the immediate cause of the damage was indeed "floodwaters," the causation for such floodwaters force and breadth are alleged to have been the defalcations of the Government with respect to the MRGO.

It is clear that the Federal Tort Claim Act did not eviscerate the immunity found in §702c. However, it is not clear that as a matter of law, should plaintiffs prove their allegations as to damages caused by MRGO and not the failure of the flood control projects, that §702c will prevent a recovery for the damages caused by MRGO. . . .

As noted, plaintiffs have brought this suit pursuant to the FTCA. They have that [*sic*] alleged that the Act of March 29, 1956, Pub L. No. 94-455, 70 Stat. 65 (1956) provided for the MRGO to be built. However, plaintiffs contend that the Corps did not exercise due care during the project's investigation, planning, design, construction (Complaint, ¶¶40-43), maintenance (Complaint ¶¶51-60) and operational phases.

In addition, plaintiffs maintain that the Army Corps violated federal law in the investigation, planning and construction of the MRGO because the River and Harbor Act of 1945 ("RHA") required the Army Corps to give to the Secretary of the Interior, during the course of investigations, information developed by the investigations and also opportunity for consultation regarding plans and proposals. Also, the Fish and Wildlife Coordination Act of 1946 ("FWCA"), also mandated that the Army Corps consult and coordinate with the Department of the Interior, Fish and Wildlife Service and the former Louisiana Department of Wild Life and Fisheries with regard to the MRGO's investigation, planning and design. Plaintiffs have alleged that these requirements were not met and that they require further discovery to support these allegations.

Finally, plaintiffs allege that many of errors which provide the basis for this suit constitute action taken that contravenes the Army Corps' internal engineering policies which again requires discovery.

The Government, as previously noted, contends that the due care exception applies because the "flaws" of which plaintiffs complain are "inherent" in the MRGO and as such are barred as the MRGO is the result of the execution by the Army Corps of various Congressional mandates concerning this navigational aid. With respect to the discretionary function exception, the Government maintains that it complied with the all [*sic*] requirements of the RHA and WFCA and has presented some evidence to that it [*sic*]. Furthermore, it maintains that the actions taken by the Army Corps involved making judgments or choices that implicated social, economic and political policy and as such are not subject to suit under the FTCA. . . .

The discretionary function exception defies precise definition of its contours. . . . In the case at bar, plaintiffs have alleged that by virtue of the Government's failure to adhere to the dictates of the River and Harbor Act of 1945 and the Wildlife and Fisheries Act of 1946 in the construction of MRGO. Based on that allegation, the discretionary function exception is ineffective as the first prong is not met. Dueling affidavits have been filed and sufficient questions have been raised in this regard to find that a Motion to Dismiss would be inappropriate at this juncture solely on that basis.

As to the second prong of the discretionary function exception, the salient issues to consider is whether the Government actor is (1) acting in contravention of its own regulations or standards or (2) exercising a policy choice. Considering the allegations concerning the failure to armor the banks of MRGO, the failure to properly maintain the MRGO, and the on-going nature of this project, the Court finds that there are substantial questions of fact which make a dismissal at this juncture unavailable. The MRGO is not a simple one-time, isolated project. Its history spans more than fifty years and innumerable Congressional reports and authorization bills. The Court cannot accept on the record before it that all actions done by the Corps were based on policy determinations. . . . This issue is one [that] must be examined in discovery. For instance, was the dredging of the MRGO simple maintenance that was improperly done under standard engineering dictates that were used by the Corps? Did the Corps violate any of its own engineering policies when it acted? . . .

Thus, based on this analysis, the Court finds, at a minimum, that plaintiffs' allegations concerning

(1) the failure of the Army Corp[s] to consult with the U.S. Fish and Wildlife Service and the Louisiana Department of Wild Life and Fisheries — and to present these agencies' concerns to Congress about the MRGO alignment and the effect thereof on the wet-lands — as required by statute;

(2) the numerosity of the decisions made in constructing and maintaining the MRGO and the inability on this record to characterize such decisions as being grounded in policy;

(3) the issue of whether there were non-policy based decisions made that failed to comport with standard engineering practices;

raise issues that are inextricably tied to the gravamen of the plaintiffs' cause of action and are not subject to Rule 12(b)(1) treatment. Furthermore, applying *Montez*, it is also clear that the entry of a Rule 12(b)(6) dismissal on that basis is impermissible. This finding is supported by the voluminous exhibits presented by the Army Corps, the affidavits presented by plaintiffs and plaintiffs' request for discovery pursuant to Rule 56(f). The Court intends for discovery to commence upon the entering of a Case Management Order so that these issues can be resolved on a full and complete record.

NOTES AND QUESTIONS

1. The Flood Control Act was passed in a different era, when the federal government was generally immune from liability for negligence. It was also an era when federal involvement in flood control was considered quite extraordinary. Should Congress revisit §702 in light of these changed circumstances? Should the Court have considered these changes in interpreting the existing statute?

2. In Mocklin v. Orleans Levee District, 877 F.2d 427 (5th Cir. 1989), the plaintiffs brought suit against several defendants, including the Army Corps of Engineers, for the wrongful death of their son and sought damages under the Federal Torts Claim Act. The child had drowned when he slipped from a

sand bar caused by the dredging into one of the flotation channels used to prevent further flood damage; the Corps had dredged the lake (Lake Pontchartrain) to make flotation channels during the construction phase of levees. The government's defense relied on §702c. The Court concluded that the child died "from or by" flood water within the meaning of the FCA, because the flotation channel where the plaintiffs' son died contained water related to flood control; the flood channels were "inescapably" part of the flood control project.

3. For other examples of the difficulty of suing the federal government for disaster-related activities, *see* Ames Farms v. United States, 1995 U.S. Dist. LEXIS 9827, 94-1448-Civ-Moreno (S.D. Fla. 1995) (dismissing suit for damages to property as a result of debris placement and removal after Hurricane Andrew); B & D Farms Inc. v. United States, 94-1449-Civ-Marcus (S.D. Fla. Dec. 21, 1994) (dismissing suit for damages to property as a result of debris removal after Hurricane Andrew); Dureiko v. Phillips & Jordan, Inc., 1996 U.S. Dist. LEXIS 22365 (S.D. Fla. 1996) (dismissing suit for damages following a claim against government for negligent supervision of contractor which performed cleanup after Hurricane Andrew); Kirchmann v. United States, 8 F.3d 1273 (8th Cir. 1993) (affirming trial court's ruling that federal government was not liable for negligent supervision of a contractor who failed to safely dispose of hazardous waste in farmland).

B. FLOOD INSURANCE

FEMA has succinctly summarized the basics of federal flood insurance program, which combines insurance, land use management, and public disclosure.

FEDERAL EMERGENCY MANAGEMENT AGENCY,
NATIONAL FLOOD INSURANCE PROGRAM — PROGRAM DESCRIPTION

http://www.fema.gov/library/viewRecord.do?id=1480
(August 1, 2002, July 6, 2009)

Section 1315 of the 1968 Act is a key provision that prohibits FEMA from providing flood insurance unless the community adopts and enforces floodplain management regulations that meet or exceed the floodplain management criteria established in accordance with Section 1361(c) of the Act. These floodplain management criteria are contained in 44 Code of Federal Regulations (CFR) Part 60, Criteria for Land Management and Use. The emphasis of the NFIP floodplain management requirements is directed toward reducing threats to lives and the potential for damages to property in flood-prone areas. Over 19,700 communities presently participate in the NFIP. These include nearly all communities with significant flood hazards.

In addition to providing flood insurance and reducing flood damages through floodplain management regulations, the NFIP identifies and maps the Nation's floodplains. Mapping flood hazards creates broad-based awareness of the flood hazards and provides the data needed for floodplain management programs and to actuarially rate new construction for flood insurance.

When the NFIP was created, the U.S. Congress recognized that insurance for "existing buildings" constructed before a community joined the Program would be prohibitively expensive if the premiums were not subsidized by the Federal Government. Congress also recognized that most of these flood-prone buildings were built by individuals who did not have sufficient knowledge of the flood hazard to make informed decisions. Under the NFIP, "existing buildings" are generally referred to as Pre-FIRM (Flood Insurance Rate Map) buildings. These buildings were built before the flood risk was known and identified on the community's FIRM. Currently about 26 percent of the 4.3 million NFIP policies in force are Pre-FIRM subsidized compared to 70 percent of the policies being subsidized in 1978. . . .

The NFIP would not be able to offer insurance at affordable rates without the existence of risk management (floodplain management) to reduce flood losses. In order to assess and manage the flood risk, a national standard was needed. The U.S. Department of Housing and Urban Development, which initially administered the NFIP before FEMA was created, began its administration of the NFIP by calling on a group of experts to advise the agency as to the best standard to be used as the basis for risk assessment, insurance rating, and floodplain management for the Program. After extensive study and coordination with Federal and State agencies, this group recommended the 1-percent-annual-chance flood (also referred to as the 100-year or "Base Flood") be used as the standard for the NFIP.

The 1-percent-annual-chance flood was chosen on the basis that it provides a higher level of protection while not imposing overly stringent requirements or the burden of excessive costs on property owners. The 1-percent-annual-chance flood (or 100-year flood) represents a magnitude and frequency that has a statistical probability of being equaled or exceeded in any given year, or, stated alternatively, the 100-year flood has a 26 percent (or 1 in 4) chance of occurring over the life of a 30-year mortgage. . . .

Section 1304 of the 1968 Act authorizes the Director of FEMA to establish and carry out "*a national flood insurance program which will enable interested persons to purchase insurance against loss resulting from physical damage to or loss of real property or personal property*" resulting from flood. Flood insurance provides the mechanism by which floodplain occupants are compensated for flood damages. Flood insurance also provides a way for some of the financial burden of flood losses to be removed from taxpayers, such as for Federal disaster assistance and casualty loss deductions under Federal income taxes.

The number of policies in force in the United States has increased from about 95,000 before the Flood Disaster Protection Act of 1973, to 2.2 million in 1989, to over 4.3 million currently. Any property owner of insurable property may purchase flood insurance coverage, provided that the community in which the property is located is participating in the NFIP. The amount of flood insurance coverage in force as of March 31, 2002 is over $606 billion.

NOTES AND QUESTIONS

1. Why does the federal government require local land use planning as a prerequisite for flood insurance? What is the government trying to prevent?
2. Except for properties that existed before the program was created, flood insurance premiums are supposed to be set at market rates, so there should be no federal subsidy. Does the system actually work that way? Consider the following material.

WILLIAM O. JENKINS, JR., FEDERAL EMERGENCY MANAGEMENT AGENCY: OVERSIGHT AND MANAGEMENT OF THE NATIONAL FLOOD INSURANCE PROGRAM

Testimony before the Subcommittee on Housing and Community Opportunity, Committee on Financial Services, U.S. House of Representatives) (Oct. 20, 2005)

As GAO has reported, the NFIP, by design, is not actuarially sound. The program does not collect sufficient premium income to build reserves to meet long-term future expected flood losses, in part because Congress authorized subsidized insurance rates to be made available for some properties. FEMA has generally been successful in keeping the NFIP on a sound financial footing, but the catastrophic flooding events of 2004 (involving four separate hurricanes) required FEMA, as of August 2005, to borrow $300 million from the U.S. Treasury to help pay an estimated $1.8 billion on flood insurance claims. Following Hurricane Katrina in August 2005, legislation was enacted to increase FEMA's borrowing authority from $1.5 billion to $3.5 billion through fiscal year 2008.

Properties that suffer repeated flooding but generally pay subsidized flood insurance rates—so-called repetitive-loss properties—constitute a significant drain on NFIP resources. These properties account for roughly 1 percent of properties insured under the NFIP, but account for 25 percent to 30 percent of all claim losses. The Flood Insurance Reform Act of 2004 established a pilot program requiring owners of repetitive-loss properties to elevate, relocate, or demolish houses, with NFIP bearing some of those costs. Future studies of the NFIP should analyze the progress made to reduce the inventory of subsidized repetitive-loss properties, and determine whether additional regulatory or congressional action is needed.

In 1973 and again in 1994, legislation was enacted requiring the mandatory purchase of NFIP policies by some property owners in high-risk areas. In June 2002, GAO reported that the extent to which lenders were required to enforce mandatory purchase requirements was unknown. While FEMA officials believed that many lenders often were noncompliant, neither side could substantiate its claims regarding compliance.

FEMA did not use a statistically valid method for sampling files to be reviewed in its monitoring and oversight activities. As a result, FEMA cannot project the results of these reviews to determine the overall accuracy of claims settled for specific flood events or assess the overall performance of insurance companies and their adjusters in fulfilling responsibilities for the NFIP—actions necessary for FEMA to have reasonable assurance that program objectives are being achieved. . . .

A key characteristic of the NFIP is the extent to which FEMA must rely on others to achieve the program's goals. FEMA's role is principally one of establishing policies and standards that others generally implement on a day-to-day basis and providing financial and management oversight of those who carry out those day-to-day responsibilities. These responsibilities include ensuring that property owners who are required to purchase flood insurance do so, enforcing flood plain management and building regulations, selling and servicing flood insurance policies, and updating and maintaining the nation's flood maps. In our prior work, we have identified several major challenges facing the NFIP:

- **Reducing losses to the program resulting from policy subsidies and repetitive loss properties.** The program is not actuarially sound because of the number of policies in force that are subsidized — about 29 percent at the time of our 2003 report. As a result of these subsidies, some policy-holders pay premiums that represent about 35-40 percent of the true risk premium. Moreover, at the time of our 2004 report, there were about 49,000 repetitive-loss properties — those with two or more losses of $1,000 or more in a 10-year period — representing about 1 percent of the 4.4 million buildings insured under the program. From 1978 until March 2004, these repetitive-loss properties represented about $4.6 billion in claims payments.
- **Increasing property owner participation in the program.** As little as half of eligible properties may participate in the flood insurance program. Moreover, the extent of noncompliance with the mandatory purchase requirement by affected property owners is unknown.
- **Developing accurate, digital flood maps.** In our report on the NFIP's flood map modernization program, we discussed the multiple uses and benefits of accurate, digitized flood plain maps. However, the NFIP faces a major challenge in working with its contractor and state and local partners of varying technical capabilities and resources to produce accurate, digital flood maps. In developing those maps, we recommended that FEMA develop and implement data standards that will enable FEMA, its contractor, and its state and local partners to identify and use consistent data collection and analysis methods for developing maps for communities with similar flood risk.
- **Providing effective oversight of flood insurance operations.** In the report we are releasing today, we note that FEMA faces a challenge in providing effective oversight of the 95 insurance companies and thousands of insurance agents and claims adjusters who are primarily responsible for the day-to-day process of selling and servicing flood insurance policies.

. . .

The most immediate challenge for the NFIP is processing the flood insurance claims resulting from Hurricanes Katrina and Rita. Already, according to FEMA, the NFIP has received about twice as many claims in 2005 as it did in all of 2004, which was itself a record year. The need for effective communication and consistent and appropriate application of policy provisions will be particularly important in working with anxious policyholders, many of whom have been displaced from their homes. In the longer term, Congress and the NFIP face a complex challenge in assessing potential changes to the program that would improve its financial stability, increase participation in the program by property owners in areas at risk of flooding, reduce the number of repetitive-loss properties in the program, and maintain current and accurate flood plain maps. These issues are complex, interrelated, and are likely to involve trade-offs. For example, increasing premiums to better reflect risk may reduce voluntary participation in the program or encourage those who are required to purchase flood insurance to limit their coverage to the minimum required amount (i.e., the amount of their outstanding mortgage balance). This in turn can increase taxpayer exposure for disaster assistance resulting from flooding. There is no "silver bullet" for improving the current structure and operations of the NFIP. It will require sound data and analysis and the cooperation and participation of many stakeholders.

NOTES AND QUESTIONS

1. Flood insurance presents a tricky set of problems. If it is priced too high, people simply may fail to insure. If it is priced too low, society is in effect subsidizing individuals to build in high-risk areas. Obviously, the solution is to price it "just right"—but finding the right level may not be easy, especially because there is no private market to use as a benchmark.

2. There has been serious criticism of how private insurance companies, which act as agents for the program, conduct business on behalf of the government. In Howell v. State Farm Insurance Companies, Civil Action No. 1:04-CV-01494-BEL, several policyholders filed a class-action suit against eight insurers (including State Farm, Omaha Property and Casualty, and Allstate Insurance). The 2004 lawsuit alleged that the eight insurers used inaccurate and unrealistic pricing data to calculate repair and replacement costs on covered flood losses and that this method of calculating claimants' losses generated artificially low damage estimates and settlement offers. Plaintiffs also alleged that insurers pressured them into signing proof-of-loss statements within sixty days after flooding, even though plaintiffs suspected that adjusters had underestimated scope of the damage; plaintiffs felt that they had no choice but to sign the proof-of-loss statements because they feared that they would lose their chance to claim insurance. Moreover, plaintiffs alleged that compensation of claims adjusters created a conflict of interest between policyholders and adjusters, which denied policyholders contractual benefits.

3. Despite all these failings, the flood control program has had some successes, as the following excerpt discusses.

OLIVER A. HOUCK, RISING WATER:
THE NATIONAL FLOOD INSURANCE PROGRAM AND LOUISIANA

60 Tul. L. Rev. 61-164 (1985)

One of the surprises of this research, notwithstanding its negative findings, has been the extent to which the NFIP, in fact, works. It would be hard to find a program which cuts against more fundamental grains: freedom to choose where to live and build, freedom from government restriction (the federal government, at that), and freedom to maximize a profit from the land, buyer beware. Yet, without a strong economic constituency, this program has managed to survive in Congress and to have evolved at least to the flood-map and local-ordinance phase in thousands of communities. The NFIP is a remarkable phenomenon in American politics—an unpopular, grudgingly accepted program making its modest way. The conclusions and criticisms which follow should be taken in that light. This program undertakes a terribly difficult job. One has to remember that doughnut when looking at the hole.

The first impression one carries away from this research is that Congress, for all of its support for the NFIP, has yet to commit fully to making the NFIP's approach to the flood control problem work. The nation can approach flooding in only a few ways: (1) ignore it, (2) keep the water away from the people, (3) pay the people who get wet, or (4) keep the people away from the water. For one hundred years we tried option (1). As a matter of politics and humanity, (1) is no longer an option; given enough disasters—and flood disasters continue on a rising curve—the nation will respond. Options (2) and (3) represent the historic responses, and they are both attractive. Their difficulty is that they are both expensive, and their spectacularly unsuccessful history proves that they can never solve the problem. One is left with option (4). So is Congress, but with a more than wistful eye on the never-ending dams and levees and politically attractive disaster relief grants of (2) and (3). . . .

Congress appears to have made the reasonable choice of the means available under option (4) to guide development away from floodplains. The NFIP is, to the maximum extent imaginable, a local program. One could scarcely think of a lesser federal presence short of, perhaps, simply mailing the insurance checks. Unfortunately, insurance checks will not avert future losses. Indeed, as predicted early on in the testimony which gave birth to the NFIP, insurance payments can encourage future losses. It is up to FEMA, with congressional support, to make the guided development part work. Congress can do more to provide that support, and FEMA can do considerably more to implement it.

Recommendations for action at the congressional level, while unconstrained by existing legislation, are limited by the art of the possible. Congress is not about to forgo new water project construction, or to withhold future disaster relief, nor should it. It should, however, structure these two programs so that they aid rather than frustrate the NFIP. With regard to water projects, it should require, as a condition for authorization of flood control dams, levees, and other structures, evidence that they be: (1) limited to that protection which could not be afforded by full NFIP compliance, (2) authorized only upon a demonstration that no other means of protection are feasible or prudent, and (3) conditioned, even then, upon binding agreements to discourage new development in surrounding flood-hazard areas. No flood-protection rationale for a structural project should be eligible for inclusion in any cost/benefit ratio absent these showings.

Congress should also examine other federal assistance and disaster relief benefits to flood-prone areas. The 1977 amendments to the NFIP, which permitted federally insured financing of development in nonparticipating communities, should be re-examined and repealed. No compelling argument — other than the profits to be made by individual developers — supports federal facilitation of new floodplain development that will lead to inevitable flood losses. Similarly, the more recent amendments proposed to limit disaster relief to participating communities should be adopted. The motives here are neither punitive nor even fiscal. Federal funds simply should be distributed in a way which maximizes local prevention of local flood losses, and the NFIP presents the means to that end.

Lastly, Congress should mandate a study of the degree to which upstream levees and channelization affect water stages downstream. Information on increased stages is available only from small, isolated watersheds. The analysis which accompanies an individual project goes no further. The cumulative effects of thousands of these projects, in virtually every watershed from Ohio to Montana, are largely unrecognized. Decisionmakers at all levels should be aware of the true costs of local, structural strategies to communities downstream, including, of course, the ultimate downstream community, Louisiana.

Turning to improvements available to FEMA and to local authorities within the existing NFIP, there is no part of the program which could not be better performed. In its most jaundiced light, the Emergency Program lags, the mapping is dubious, and the requirements of even the Regular Program are misunderstood, misapplied, and ignored. The deficiencies noted in this report are not new to FEMA: they confirm findings by the Comptroller General on at least two occasions, as well as an independent survey of the National Science Foundation. What may be new to FEMA is the scale of these deficiencies and, as illustrated in *United States v. Parish of St. Bernard* — and Hurricane Juan — their potential consequences. Rather than repeating these findings in full, two bear mention because of their particular significance to Louisiana: the treatment of coastal high-hazard areas and the adequacy of enforcement.

The effect of the NFIP on coastal development remains, to this observer, quite uncertain. In Louisiana, the program has only recently begun to be applied to coastal areas in a way that reflects actual storm damages. The accuracy of mapping remains contested, and there is virtually no experience by which to measure the success of local ordinances. From a purely analytical perspective, no good reason appears for providing federal assistance of any kind to high-hazard coastal development. There is every chance that, over a life of the structure, it will meet hurricane forces and will come off second best. Coastal high-hazard areas are as dynamic and storm-threatened as the barrier islands, and the same logic which led to legislation barring federal assistance to barrier island development should bar federal assistance in these areas as well. From Louisiana's perspective, coastal prospects look particularly bleak given the phenomenal rate of coastal subsidence, the addition of sea-level rise, and FEMA's reluctance to take either into account. At the least, the structural elevation and storm-proofing requirements for insurance eligibility should reflect the anticipated conditions over the life of the structure. Maps updated at a later time provide no remedy; construction will at that point already be grandfathered into the program. The cure starts only when future conditions are looked squarely in the eye. For much of coastal Louisiana they are a grim sight. However, they are no grimmer than the sight of evacuees.

The last word is reserved for enforcement. It is difficult to speak harshly of the efforts of an agency with so much to oversee and so little means. FEMA's regional staff has been decimated in recent years. Here more than anywhere, the unavoidable question is whether Congress and the administration really want the program to work. If they do, they will need to provide resources for the program on the theory that, over time, the enforcement of realistic ordinances will ultimately save the government money. . . .

The NFIP is not a glamorous program. It is also not an easy program to understand. One tends to approach it, as this researcher did several years ago, with high skepticism. One tends to emerge, or at least this researcher did, with the conviction that, perversely, its implementation is successful in almost inverse proportion to the risk of flooding in a given area. Where the risk is low, compliance is generally good; no one's shoe is pinched. Where the risk is high, however, as in much of South Louisiana, tomorrow's development still overrides next year's inevitable losses. We know this much from the positive side: the program can work. What is still unknown is whether Congress will support the program sufficiently to allow it to work in those very places where making it work is the most difficult, and the most necessary.

NOTES AND QUESTIONS

1. Flood insurance covers property loss, but not loss of life. Should the federal government try to fill that gap?
2. Should the government protect people from the consequences of their own choices? When individuals knowingly build in flood-prone areas, should they be held responsible for the risks they are taking?
3. A recent GAO report criticizes the government's rate-setting methods:

> FEMA's method for setting full-risk rates may not ensure that the rates accurately reflect the actual risk of flood damage. FEMA's model for setting these rates incorporates data on flood risks generated by a hydrologic model that is based on largely the same principles as hazard risk models used by private insurers and other federal agencies. More specifically, FEMA generates rates for flood insurance according to estimates of flood risk and expected flood damage. However, a number of factors may affect the accuracy of rates generated by the process. First, the data that FEMA uses to define flood probabilities are outdated or inaccurate. For example, some of the data used to estimate the probability of flooding have not been updated since the 1980s. Similarly, the claims data used as inputs to the model may be inaccurate because of incomplete claims records and missing data. Further, the maps FEMA uses to set premium rates remain substantially out of date despite recent modernization efforts. In addition, an NFIP policy decision allows certain properties remapped into riskier flood zones to keep their previous lower rates, which, like subsidized rates, do not reflect the actual risk of flooding to the properties and do not generate sufficient premiums to cover expected losses. Moreover, FEMA does not collect data on these

properties — known as grandfathered properties — or measure their financial impact on the program and does not know how many of these properties exist, their exact location, or how much they generate in losses. FEMA's rate-setting process also does not fully take into account ongoing and planned development, long-term trends in erosion, or the effects of global climate change, although private sector models are incorporating some of these factors. Finally, FEMA sets flood insurance rates on a nationwide basis, combining and averaging many topographic factors that are relevant to flood risk, so that these factors are not specifically accounted for in setting rates for individual properties. Moreover, some patterns in historical claims and premium data suggest that NFIP's rates may not accurately reflect differences in flood risk. Collectively, these factors increase the risk that full-risk premiums may be insufficient to cover future losses, adding to concerns about NFIP's financial stability.

Government Accountability Office, *FEMA's Rate-Setting Process Warrants Attention* (GAO-09-12 2008).

4. Should the flood insurance program be abandoned, in favor of reliance on private insurance? You may want to consider that question in light of the next section.

C. PRIVATE INSURANCE

We begin with an excerpt that discusses the impact of Hurricane Katrina on the insurance industry, and some possible legislative solutions. We will then look more carefully at some insurance issues raised by Katrina, before turning in the next section to the question of legislation.

Hurricane Katrina: Insurance Losses and National Capacities for Financing Disaster Risk

Congressional Research Service (Sept. 15, 2005)

[Private] insurer losses from Hurricane Katrina are estimated to be $40-$60 billion. This would make the tropical storm the costliest natural disaster in U.S. history, exceeding Hurricane Andrew in 1992 and the September 2001 terrorist attacks. These insured loss figures include damages caused by storm's landfall in Florida on August 25, 2005, that led to an estimated $600 million to $2 billion in insured losses, as well as dozens of offshore oil and gas platforms reported either lost, damaged, or missing and believed sunk. Total damages are expected to exceed $200 billion, with the federal government expected to spend over $100 billion for response and recovery efforts associated with Hurricane Katrina in Alabama, Florida, Louisiana, Mississippi, and other affected areas. These amounts will exceed the initial cost for recovery from the September 11 terror attacks. . . .

Insured loss estimates are likely to change as the extent of losses becomes better known. Disaster experts and modeling firms expect the numbers to change as more is known about the levels of water contamination and economic losses from business interruption and displacement of residents in New Orleans, Biloxi, Pascagoula, and Gulfport. These figures will also change when more accurate information about the economic costs of interruption of oil supply and exports of commodities such as grain becomes available. Most of the U.S. energy operations are in the Gulf Coast region.

Most insurance market analysts would agree that insurers will be able to pay all Katrina-related claims without triggering insurer insolvencies or market disruption. Despite the severity of damages, insurers are well-equipped to manage the financial impact of a catastrophe of this scale. The U.S. personal lines insurers have benefited from recent favorable market conditions and have built up policyholder surplus for an unexpected event like Katrina. [T]he industry as a whole earned $38.7 billion in net after-tax income in 2004, and policyholder surplus increased by 13.4%, or $46.5 billion, to a record $393.5 billion for the same year. A.M. Best, an insurance rating and information agency, reports that almost all rated companies will be able to meet their commitments. A few individual companies' ratings may, however, be lowered.

Although the insurance industry will emerge largely intact from Hurricane Katrina and is better capitalized now than ever, the industry simply does not have sufficient capital to fund a mega-catastrophe. This fact is not new. Insurers and financial market experts knew after Hurricane Andrew in 1992 that outside capital was needed to supplement industry capacity. Since then, new capital entered the catastrophe insurance market.

Insurers learned important lessons from Hurricane Andrew that prompted them to make changes to both protect the industry's balance sheets and stabilize the property insurance markets in the aftermath of a small-to-moderate hurricane. For example, after Hurricane Andrew, the Florida state legislature worked with insurers and regulators to create a hurricane catastrophe system designed to mitigate losses to the insurance industry and prevent insurers from withdrawing from the Florida insurance market. The Florida Hurricane Catastrophe Fund was created as a reinsurance-like entity funded by a portion of insurance premiums and managed by the Florida State Board of Administration. Florida also began using percentage deductibles tied to the value of homes instead of a dollar amount such as $500 per claim. Florida created a state-regulated insurer of last resort to provide insurance when no company is willing to underwrite disaster risks. These measures saved the property insurance industry from financial disaster after the four major hurricanes in 2004. Neither Louisiana, Mississippi, nor Alabama, however, ha[s] a similar catastrophe fund to compensate hurricane victims at a level comparable to what is available in Florida.

Most insurance analysts predict that Hurricane Katrina will likely result in higher pricing and restricted coverage in the hardest-hit areas. Insurers who specialize in coverage for offshore oil rigs and platforms, for example, have already announced 50% increases in premium prices. In addition, insurance rating agencies are now comparing their insurers' modeled catastrophe exposures to the potential market share exposure to determine the need for rating action. Insurance market analysts note that insurers with accurate loss exposure projections will be able to manage their losses within their capital base. Those that are shown to not have accurate loss exposure projections could suffer a rating downgrade.

When claims adjusters are finally able to assess the hundreds of thousands of damaged structures, they will likely face major challenges in distinguishing the portion of damage attributable to wind or flood. What was the wind damage before the levees broke and flooding began? This is important because wind damages are covered under standard commercial and residential property insurance policies, but floods are not. The central question of when the wind-driven rain or rising floodwater came in and when the wind came in will determine how flood claims are apportioned among the National Flood Insurance Program (NFIP), private insurers, and individuals.

It is quite likely that policyholders who lack federal flood insurance coverage might take advantage of vague policy language in their homeowners insurance policies to argue that the ultimate cause of damage was not flooding, but breaches of the New Orleans levees. Insurers are likely, however, to argue that they did not price the flood risk in the homeowners policy, and hence did not set aside reserves to pay such claims.

Although the purchase of federal flood insurance is mandatory for certain property owners as a condition of eligibility for loans from federally regulated lending institutions, many residents in flood-prone areas impacted by Katrina did not have flood insurance. According to the Insurance Information Institute, only about 30% of homes in Louisiana are protected by flood coverage, and even fewer homeowners in Mississippi and Alabama purchased the coverage. A problem is that, although mortgage lenders required homeowners in flood zones to buy flood coverage, these institutions reportedly have no system in place to ensure that homeowners keep the coverage in force. In addition, banks that provide mortgage loans on property found to be uninsured for flood damage might incur losses should homeowners who cannot afford reconstruction abandon both the property and the mortgage commitment. . . .

The increasing magnitude of both insured and uninsured losses from natural disasters represents an ongoing challenge for both governments and the private sector. Natural disasters typically result in large government outlays for disaster relief assistance, and they place a financial strain on private disaster insurance markets. The federal government alone, facing fiscal constraints to cover the losses to the private sector, will find it costly and challenging to meet long-term disaster related spending. In addition, insurers have been and will continue to be reluctant to cover properties in high-risk areas because of high long-run costs (which translates into high prices for disaster insurance) and low demand for disaster insurance.

Most insurance market analysts note that there is no state in the Union that is not subject to catastrophe exposure, and the current situation suggests that the projected exposures are far greater than the insurance industry is currently prepared to handle. The insurance industry's financial capacity and surplus to underwrite a $100 billion-plus mega-catastrophic event remains in doubt.

NOTES AND QUESTIONS

1. We will discuss in more detail in the next section the problems confronted by the insurance industry in covering catastrophic losses as well as possible policy responses.
2. Floods often involve large numbers of highly correlated losses, which are an unappealing subject for insurance companies. The companies may also be reluctant to offer coverage for flood losses in competition with the federal government's insurance program. Consequently, private insurers generally seek to exclude flood damages from insurance coverage even of "all risks" policies.
3. In theory, individuals should know that their insurance does not cover flooding, but consumer knowledge on this point may be somewhat spotty. Should this affect the insurance company's liability? At a press conference immediately after Katrina, Mississippi State Attorney General Jim Hood stated, "All that the people have left is hope and I'm not going to allow an insurance company to wrongfully take that hope away. Although some insurance companies are trying to do the right thing, I won't allow the others to take advantage of people hurt by Hurricane Katrina." He unsuccessfully attempted to have the courts declare unenforceable contract provisions that exclude from coverage loss or damage caused directly or indirectly by water, whether or not driven by wind. The complaint stated that these provisions should be strictly construed against the insurance companies who drafted the insurance policies and their exclusions. The complaint also stated that the issuance of such insurance policies violates the Mississippi Consumer Protection Act. "I'm hopeful that next week we will be able to stop unscrupulous insurance adjusters from requiring people to sign away their rights to 'flood damage' claims in exchange for a significantly smaller amount which will be used for immediate living expenses. I want to encourage the people to continue to fight and I'll do everything I can to make sure that insurance companies pay what they owe," Hood said. Similar claims were made in private litigation between insurers and their customers, as exemplified by the following case.

LEONARD v. NATIONWIDE MUTUAL INSURANCE CO.

United States Court of Appeals for the Fifth Circuit, 499 F.3d 419 (2007)

EDITH H. JONES, Chief Judge:

This homeowner's policy coverage dispute arose from the destruction wrought by Hurricane Katrina along the Mississippi Gulf Coast. . . .

The Leonards' home lies twelve feet above sea level on the southmost edge of Pascagoula, Mississippi, less than two hundred yards from the Mississippi Sound. Hurricane Katrina battered Pascagoula with torrential rain and sustained winds in excess of one hundred miles per hour. By midday, the storm had driven ashore a formidable tidal wave—also called a storm or tidal surge—that flooded the ground floor of the Leonards' two-story home. . . .

Like most homeowner's policies, the Leonards' policy unambiguously excludes damage caused by water — including flooding — in a broadly worded exemption clause (the "water-damages exclusion"):

> (b) Water or damage caused by water-borne material. Loss resulting from water or water-borne material damage described below is not covered even if other perils contributed, directly or indirectly, to cause the loss. Water and water-borne material damage means:
>   1. flood, surface water, waves, tidal waves, overflow of a body of water, spray from these, whether or not driven by wind. . . .

When the Leonards annually renewed their policy, they received the following notice from Nationwide informing them that flood losses would not be covered, but that additional flood coverage was available upon request:

> *IMPORTANT INFORMATION*
>
> A Message From Your Nationwide Agent:
>
> Your policy does not cover flood loss. You can get protection through the National Flood Insurance Program. If you wish to find out more about this protection, please contact your Nationwide Agent.

The Leonards never purchased additional flood coverage under the federally subsidized National Flood Insurance Program ("NFIP").

3. Concurrent Action by Wind and Water

The prefatory language introducing the water-damages exclusion addresses situations in which damage arises from the synergistic action of a covered peril, e.g., wind, and an excluded peril, e.g., water:

> 1. We do not cover loss to any property resulting directly or indirectly from any of the following. *Such a loss is excluded even if another peril or event contributed concurrently or in any sequence to cause the loss.* . . .

Commonly referred to as an "anticoncurrent-causation clause," or "ACC clause," this prefatory language denies coverage whenever an excluded peril and a covered peril combine to damage a dwelling or personal property. The inundation of the Leonards' home was caused by a concurrently caused peril, i.e., a tidal wave, or storm surge — essentially a massive wall of water — pushed ashore by Hurricane Katrina's winds. Accordingly, argues Nationwide, losses attributable to storm surge-induced flooding are excluded under the ACC clause. The validity of the ACC clause is the key interpretive battleground of this appeal. . . .

Paul Leonard testified that when he first bought his policy in 1989, he asked Nationwide's agent Jay Fletcher whether the Nationwide policy covered hurricane-related losses. According to Leonard, Fletcher responded that all hurricane damage was covered. Fletcher stated in his deposition testimony that he did not recall this conversation; the district court deemed it irrelevant to the case.

Leonard claims he spoke again with Fletcher ten years later to discuss a proposed increase in the wind/hail deductible that Nationwide was insti- tuting on its homeowner's policies. Leonard called Fletcher after seeing advertisements for additional NFIP coverage in the wake of Hurricane Georges, which struck the Mississippi coast in 1998. Fletcher allegedly assured Leonard that he did not need additional flood coverage because Leonard did not live in an area classified Zone A for flood risk by the Federal Emergency Management Agency ("FEMA"). Fletcher purportedly added that his own property was not insured under the NFIP. Leonard does not allege that Fletcher told him the Nationwide policy covered flooding caused by a hurricane; Leonard merely inferred from Fletcher's comments that such coverage existed. . . .

Inspection of the Leonards' residence following the storm revealed modest wind damage. The roof suffered broken shingles and loss of ceramic granules, but its water-tight integrity was not compromised. The non-load-bearing walls of the garage and the garage door were severely damaged; doors in the house and garage had been blown open. Finally, a "golf-ball sized" hole in a ground-floor window was likely caused by a wind-driven projectile.

Water damage, in contrast, was extensive. The Leonards' neighborhood had suffered a seventeen-foot storm surge, causing the entire ground floor of their residence to become inundated under five feet of water blown ashore from the Mississippi Sound. Walls, floors, fixtures, and personal property sustained extensive damage. The second floor of the house remained unscathed.

Nationwide's adjuster evaluated the storm damage and, after applying the Leonards' five hundred dollar deductible, tendered a check for $1,661.17 — the amount determined attributable solely to wind. Nationwide informed the Leonards that damages caused by water and the storm surge's concurrent wind-water action were barred, respectively, by the water-damages exclusion and the ACC clause.

At trial, the Leonards offered expert testimony that the total damages actually exceeded $130,000, but this figure did not apportion damages caused by different perils. The Leonards' wind-specific assessment claimed $47,365.41, including costs for roof replacement and structural repairs to the garage.

The district court found the ACC clause ambiguous, leading it to conclude: "Thus, [the ACC] language does not exclude coverage for different damage, the damage caused by wind, a covered peril, even if the wind damage occurred concurrently or in sequence with the excluded water damage. The wind damage is covered; the water damage is not." The court applied "established Mississippi law" dating from the Hurricane Camille cases and explicitly held that a Mississippi policyholder could parse out and recover for loss due to covered wind damage that combined with excluded water damage in a concurrently caused peril. Consequently, as a matter of Mississippi law, Nationwide's ACC clause is invalid. That such rulings vitally affect Nationwide's rights in subsequent litigation involving its homeowner's policy would seem to be emphasized by the Leonards' determination to render the rulings unassailable on appeal.

Although the district court granted the Leonards only a meager monetary recovery for losses proven to have been caused by wind, it also summarily invalidated the ACC clause, stating that "[t]he provisions of the Nationwide policy that purport to exclude coverage entirely for damages caused by a combination of the effects of water (an excluded loss) and damage caused by the effects of wind (a covered loss) are ambiguous." Contrary to the district court's ruling, Nationwide's ACC clause is not ambiguous, nor does Mississippi law preempt the causation regime the clause applies to hurricane claims.

Eschewing a text-based analysis, the district court opines that the clause does not affect the coverage for other losses (covered losses), i.e., damage caused by wind, that occur at or near the same time. Thus, [the ACC clause] does not exclude coverage for different damage, the damage caused by wind, a covered peril, *even if the wind damage occurred concurrently or in sequence with the excluded water damage.* The wind damage is covered; the water damage is not. This conclusion is unjustifiable when read against the clause's plain language. . . .

The clause unambiguously excludes coverage for water damage "even if another peril" — e.g., wind — "contributed concurrently or in any sequence to cause the loss." The plain language of the policy leaves the district court no interpretive leeway to conclude that recovery can be obtained for wind damage that "occurred concurrently or in sequence with the excluded water damage." Moreover, in the past we have not deemed similar policy language ambiguous. Nationwide's assertion that the district court "simply read the clause out of the contract," is not at all wide of the mark. The clause is not ambiguous.

The fatal flaw in the district court's rationale is its failure to recognize the three discrete categories of damage at issue in this litigation: (1) damage caused exclusively by wind; (2) damage caused exclusively by water; and (3) damage caused by wind "concurrently or in any sequence" with water. The classic example of such a concurrent wind-water peril is the storm-surge flooding that follows on the heels of a hurricane's landfall. The only species of damage covered under the policy is damage caused *exclusively* by wind. But if wind and water synergistically caused the *same* damage, such damage is excluded. Thus, the Leonards' money judgment was based on their roof damages solely caused by wind. Contrary to the court's damage matrix, however, had they also proved that a portion of their property damage was caused by the concurrent or sequential action of water — or any number of other enumerated water-borne perils — the policy clearly disallows recovery.

The district court seemed to fear that enforcement of the policy's concurrent causation exclusion would render *any* recovery for hurricane damage illusory. Observing that the policy denies coverage whenever a "wind-storm[] combined with an excluded cause of loss, e.g., flooding," the court hypothesized that "an insured whose dwelling lost its roof in high winds and at the same time suffered an incursion of even an inch of water could recover nothing. . . ." That fear is unfounded, with regard to the policy's wind-coverage clause. . . . If, for example, a policyholder's roof is blown off in a storm, and rain enters through the opening, the damage is covered. Only if storm-surge flooding — an excluded peril — then inundates the *same* area that the rain damaged is the ensuing loss excluded because the loss was caused concurrently or in sequence by the action of a covered and an excluded peril. The district court's unsupported conclusions that the ACC clause is ambiguous and that the policyholder can parse out the portion of the concurrently caused damage that is attributable to wind contradict the policy language.

Like the district court, the Leonards provide no support for their argument that the ACC clause is ambiguous. Instead, they adopt the district court's reliance on venerable Mississippi authorities regarding proximate causation of damage caused by hurricanes. Because the ACC clause is unambiguous, the Leonards can prevail only if they can demonstrate that the clause is prohibited by Mississippi caselaw, statutory law, or public policy. None of these sources of state law restricts Nationwide's use of the ACC clause to preclude recovery for concurrently caused hurricane losses.

Contrary to the Leonards' contention, Mississippi courts have not conclusively resolved whether an insurance policy may preclude recovery for damages caused by the concurrent action of the wind and water of a hurricane. Accordingly, this court, applying state substantive law, must make an educated "*Erie* guess" as to how the Mississippi Supreme Court would resolve the issue.

The default causation rule in Mississippi regarding damages caused concurrently by a covered and an excluded peril under an insurance policy is that the insured may recover if the covered peril was the "dominant and efficient cause" of the loss. This rule is typically referred to as the doctrine of efficient proximate cause. To recover under the doctrine in the context of a homeowner's policy that covers wind damage but excludes damage by water, "it is sufficient to show that wind [i.e., the covered peril] was the proximate or efficient cause of the loss . . . notwithstanding other factors [i.e., excluded perils like water] contributed. . . ."

The Mississippi Supreme Court frequently employed this default rule in the welter of insurance coverage cases that surfaced in the aftermath of Hurricane Camille. It is also the rule the district court and the Leonards contend must apply here. However, although the Mississippi Supreme Court often premised recovery for policyholders on the application of the efficient proximate cause rule, in actuality, in many of the Camille cases the court did little more than uphold jury findings that the damages suffered by policyholders were caused *exclusively by wind*, not by concurrent wind-water action. Such cases thus do not support the Leonards' argument that the Mississippi default rule in hurricane cases is always to allow recovery for covered damages even if they are concurrent with excluded damages and irrespective of contrary policy language. In fact, the Mississippi Supreme Court intimated in one case that even if a covered peril is the efficient proximate cause of damage, a concurrently contributing cause that is excluded under a homeowner's policy may preclude recovery.

Whatever the effect of the efficient proximate cause doctrine in the Hurricane Camille cases, those decisions do not control the current case because none of the policies they involve contain ACC clauses similar to the one at issue here, nor do those cases purport to enshrine efficient proximate causation as an immutable rule of Mississippi insurance policy interpretation. The Fifth Circuit long ago explicitly recognized that efficient proximate causation does not necessarily control Mississippi contracts for hurricane damage.

Two federal appellate courts and many state and district courts have endorsed using ACC clauses to circumvent default causation rules like efficient proximate cause. A majority of states that have considered the matter enforce ACC exclusion clauses. Only Washington and West Virginia do not allow abrogation of the default rule via an ACC clause. California and North Dakota require efficient proximate causation by statute. . . .

For all these reasons, we conclude that use of an ACC clause to supplant the default causation regime is not forbidden by Mississippi caselaw (including the Camille cases which antedate such clauses), statutory law, or public policy. Because the ACC clause is unambiguous and not otherwise voidable under state law, it must stand. . . .

Finally, the Leonards claim that misrepresentations Fletcher made during two conversations in 1989 and 1999 effected an oral modification of their policy, enabling recovery for all Katrina-related losses. The district court allowed litigation of the question whether Fletcher negligently misrepresented the policy's terms, but found that none of Fletcher's statements "could be reasonably understood to alter the terms of the Nationwide policy," and that any inferences that Paul Leonard drew from the conversations were inconsistent with the policy exclusion for water damage.

The Leonards fail to present an actionable claim of negligent misrepresentation because they cannot prove two of the elements required to show apparent authority. First, Nationwide's conduct in no way indicated that Fletcher was authorized to orally modify policies he sold. The Form HO-23-A has an integration clause specifically disclaiming the agent's ability to do so. . . . Paul Leonard admits to having read the policy. Even had he not, knowledge of the integration clause is imputed to him under state law. Only "[t]hose dealing with agents without notice of restrictions upon the agent's authority have a right to presume that their authority is there."

Second, the Leonards' reliance on Fletcher's statements was objectively unreasonable in light of the policy language clearly excluding water damage, including damage caused by a flood.

NOTES AND QUESTIONS

1. From the point of view of the property owner, whether property is destroyed by wind or water is largely irrelevant. But insurers have not wanted to participate in the market for flood insurance, and exclusions for damages caused by water are their effort to avoid coverage for flood risks. Thus, there is a mismatch between the insured's expectation that insurance will cover major risks and the insurer's desire to manage risk exposure.
2. The issue of "wind versus water" can arise in many different settings. Consider the following factual scenarios:
   - The roof is blown off the house by wind. Some water also entered the house from flooding. It is unclear how much of the flooding was due to wind and how much to rain. Who has the burden of proof, the insured or the insurer?
   - A house is flooded first, but then the roof blows off, so the house would have suffered the same water damage even without the flood. Should the fact that the flooding occurred first relieve the insurer from liability, considering that the same damage would have resulted from wind anyway?
   - Rain first floods a lake, but then wind drives the flood waters against levees, bursting the levees and resulting in water damage to a house. Is the proximate cause wind or water?

4. In addition to the "wind versus water" issues, another frequent insurance issue involves the "ordinance or law" exclusion:

> A typical Ordinance or Law exclusion clause reads: "We do not cover loss . . . resulting in any manner from . . . enforcement of any ordinance or law regulating the construction, reconstruction, maintenance, repair or demolition of buildings or other structures." The insurance industry has articulated several reasons for the exclusion.
>
> Insurance companies most frequently state that the purpose of the exclusion is to prevent an insured from obtaining a "windfall" through the enforcement of a local or state ordinance or law. For example, in Bradford v. Home Insurance Co.,[6] the insured sustained damage to his leaching field. The cost of replacing the field with material similar to the original would have been $1,000. However, a local ordinance required that the insured also install a septic tank at a cost of $2,300. The insurer denied coverage for the cost of the tank based on an Ordinance or Law exclusion in the insured's policy and the court upheld the insurer's decision. Another court articulated the purpose of the exclusion as follows:
>
> > [T]he insurer is required . . . to indemnify the insured for the cost of repairing or replacing a building which was lost or destroyed by fire with materials of like kind and quality, but it is not required to assume repair or replacement costs which would provide the insured with a more structurally valuable building than the one that was damaged or destroyed. . . . The owners of new buildings which conform with state or local building laws are merely reimbursed for costs which they actually incurred. On the other hand, the owner of buildings which do not conform with such laws are not permitted to recover costs which they never assumed in the first place.[7]
>
> Such windfalls, however, are inherent in "replacement cost" policies, which obligate insurers to reimburse the insured for the actual cost of repairs and construction without deducting any amount for depreciation. For example, if an insured needed to replace a damaged roof, the insurer would be liable for the cost of the entire new roof, even if the damaged roof had been ten years old. This begs the question: Why is paying to replace a ten-year-old roof with a new roof less objectionable than paying to replace a home built under an old building code with a home that complies with a current building code?
>
> Insurers also justify the exclusion by stating that they must limit their exposure to the risk of having to pay for costs that are uncertain. Moreover, insurers claim that it is expensive to keep track of, and properly estimate, the impact of building codes. Ironically, uncertainty created the need for insurance in the first place and inspires many homeowners to purchase insurance. The basic purpose of insurance is to pool and distribute the risk of uncertain losses over a large number of people so that an individual will not bear the entire impact of a loss. Who better to evaluate and spread risk than insurance companies?

---

6. 384 A.2d 52 (Me. 1978).
7. Breshears v. Indiana Lumbermens Mut. Ins. Co., 63 Cal. Rptr. 879, 883 (Cal. Ct. App. 1967).

Because insurance companies have the knowledge and ability to pool and spread risk, and because ordinances and laws—e.g., building codes—are enacted for the health, safety, and welfare of the public, the following questions must be asked: Why is coverage of building code upgrades not automatically included in insurance policies? Why have insurance companies fought so ardently to support the exclusions despite the fact that courts have been ambivalent toward the exclusions? The fact that some individuals may benefit from an increase in the value of their property because of an upgrade required by an ordinance or law is unimportant when weighed against the potentially devastating effect the exclusions can have when they are enforced.[8]

2. Apart from the substance of insurance claims, their sheer number may overwhelm the litigation system. Consider the following alternative:

In response to Hurricanes Katrina and Rita and the devastation left in their wake, the AAA has developed AAA Disaster Recovery Claims Resolution Services, a permanent program to address insurance claim disputes quickly and fairly. At present, more than 400 neutrals have agreed to serve at reduced rates on the panel for this special dispute management program. The insurance providers have agreed to pay the AAA's case administration fees and the neutral's compensation and expenses. Information about this program can be found at www.adr.org/sp.asp?id=26808/; www.adr.org/si.asp?id=2025; and adr.org/si.asp?id=2024/(Guide to AAA Disaster Recovery Claims).

The AAA previously helped victims of Hurricanes Andrew and Iniki, the Northridge earthquake, and the Grand Forks flood resolve insurance disputes. However, unlike those temporary programs, the new program is permanent. It will have its own formal set of procedures, available at www.adr.org/sp.asp?id=26802/. Under these procedures, the AAA will assist individuals with their property claims regardless of the amount involved. It will also assist businesses with claims under $75,000. This program will use telephone and in-person mediations to resolve disputes.[9]

D. DESIGNING INSURANCE FOR CATASTROPHIC RISKS

STEPHEN D. SUGARMAN,
ROLES OF GOVERNMENT IN COMPENSATING DISASTER VICTIMS

Issues in Legal Scholarship, http://www.bepress.com/ils/iss10/art1 (2007)

The financial consequences of many of the losses that result from catastrophic events may be ameliorated by the advance purchase of private

---

8. Hugh L. Wood, Jr., Comment *The Insurance Fallout Following Hurricane Andrew: Whether Insurance Companies Are Legally Obligated to Pay for Building Code Upgrades despite the "Ordinance or Law" Exclusion Contained in Most Homeowners Policies*, 48 U. MIAMI L. REV. 949 (1994).

9. *AAA OFFERS New Disaster Recovery Services*, 60-JAN DISP. RES. J. 4 (2005).

insurance that covers the peril in question. Life insurance, health insurance, disability insurance, and accidental death and dismemberment insurance are all examples of privately sold policies that provide compensation for individuals suffering casualty losses to the person. Property insurance (covering fire and all sorts of other perils) is a private mechanism that provides compensation to those who suffer covered losses to physical property (both real property and personal property); and homeowner's insurance, for example, will often pay, not only for the rebuilding or repair of one's home, but also for temporary living costs. Business interruption insurance can serve as at least a partial substitute for temporarily lost income or pay for temporarily higher expenses. And while these sorts of insurance policies are primarily used to cover the risk of individual loss in non-disaster settings, they can indeed come into play in the event of a disaster. Yet, one problem with private insurance solutions is that there is sometimes no private insurance available for certain types of catastrophic risks to which people are subject. Indeed, it is precisely the dramatically large event that leads to widespread disastrous consequences that is frequently specifically excluded from certain standard private insurance policies. For example, the destruction of one's home or other buildings is generally not covered by ordinary property insurance (or homeowners') policies if the harm is caused by things like war, nuclear radiation, floods, and, at least in some places, earthquakes.

Sometimes those catastrophic risks may be specially insured against through privately purchased policies that are narrowly tailored to specific potentially catastrophic events (although sometimes the availability of these private policies requires governmental intervention, as discussed later). But often, no private insurance market exists for these risks. While this insurance unavailability might be viewed as a market failure, there are usually understandable reasons why insurers won't underwrite certain risks. First of all, they find themselves unable to sensibly price the insurance, both because the precipitating event too infrequently occurs and when it does the amount of harm it will cause is not really predictable. Moreover, it is especially worrying to insurers that the catastrophe might occur markedly earlier than expected, so that not enough premiums would yet have been accumulated, thereby putting an insurer at risk of insolvency. Even if the timing and scale of the risk were reasonably predictable, however, insuring against infrequent disasters would require a long accumulation and investment of premium income in a way that is not altogether attractive to insurers (and re-insurers who might be enticed to spread the risk beyond the insurer who initially sold coverage to its customers). Among other things, U.S. tax law rules discourage insurance lines that involve premium collection without payouts, even if funds are set aside for eventual losses. Besides, when the gigantic-loss event finally occurs, insurers could be swamped by the claims-handling process, having to rely on out-of-area and/or inexperienced staff who are likely to be more costly and less efficient. As a result, catastrophic risk coverage might simply be an unattractive product for mainstream insurers to offer.

Two common reasons why underwriters typically don't cover certain risks are also relevant in the disaster setting. One is moral hazard, by which I mean that the insured may do something (or fail to do something) that precipitates the insurable event or the level of its consequences. The other is adverse selection, by which I mean the insurer is not easily able to screen out, or charge more to, those customers with higher than average risks. For example, suppose that a lot of people don't take care of their property in a way to minimize the risk of landslide damage and that insurers cannot monitor this failure to take sufficient precautions. Then, not only are landslide damage claims likely to be larger than predicted, but also insurers may find it infeasible to charge different premiums to those who are more and less at risk, thereby forcing them to set premiums at a rate that discourages purchase by responsible owners. In such a setting, especially given the possibility of enormous landslide claims made by lots of customers in one location, who are all harmed by a single major storm, insurers may prefer simply to exclude this risk.

Not all insurance against catastrophic harm is subject to this sort of exclusion, however. For example, "major medical" insurance is designed to cover personally catastrophic risks that would cause the insured to need a great deal of expensive medical care. And this sort of health insurance generally will cover medical costs incurred in connection with any sort of societal disaster. One reason for the availability of this coverage is that, even a major disaster is not likely to cause a large share of any insurer's customer base to file claims.

So, too, large amounts of life insurance are generally available for purchase and proceeds of the policy are normally payable regardless of whether the person died from a societal catastrophe or not. To be sure, in some policies some causes of death are excluded from coverage. These may include suicide for a moderate period of time after the policy is obtained, as well as death from sky diving, bungee jumping, and other specifically listed perils — i.e., what are viewed as extraordinarily dangerous activities that the insured party voluntarily undertakes. But deaths from earthquakes, floods, or terrorism, for example, are generally covered by standard life insurance policies. Again, even a major earthquake is likely to kill only a small share of any one life insurer's clients, and the amount of the insurance payout has been specified (and specifically priced) in advance. . . .

As noted already, sometimes the private insurance market by itself will not provide insurance coverage for the consequences of certain disasters. In that case, government might act, either by becoming an insurer itself and offering (or even mandating purchase of) the missing coverage or by working with insurers to get (or force) them to provide the coverage.

The latter could involve getting each insurer of similar risks (e.g. property insurers) to take on its "fair share" of the target risk (like earthquakes). Or it could involve creating of [sic] a fund paid for by insurers (presumably from extra premiums collected from its customers) that covers the target risk (like earthquakes). Alternatively, government may become the actual insurer of the risk (like earthquakes) although even there government might yet enlist private insurers in the roles of selling the product, collecting the premiums, and perhaps even processing the claims were the covered risk to occur.

The regime supervised by California's current California Earthquake Authority is one example of how government can get involved with creating a market for insurance coverage for a risk that is not covered by nearly all basic property insurance policies sold in California. A somewhat different role is played by the state of Florida under the Florida Hurricane Catastrophe Fund that was created in 1993 in the wake of Hurricane Andrew. The National Flood Insurance Program is an example of how the federal government stepped in to create coverage for a risk that private insurers were generally unwilling to underwrite on their own. Recent governmental interventions designed to assure the availability of insurance against the consequences of terrorism (most importantly, a temporary agreement by the federal government to pay for a share of covered losses) is yet another. These schemes are all aimed at physical property damage. Although not now in place, it is imaginable that, with the help of government, the insurance industry could provide property insurance against the full range of natural disasters.

An important issue confronting any such arrangement — either a comprehensive scheme or one aimed at a specific disaster risk — is the premium structure. Is the government-arranged scheme, on average, charging the equivalent of "market" rates, or are taxpayers subsidizing those who buy the insurance? A justification for subsidy might be the otherwise low-income status of the victims. A second-best sort of justification might be that, if, after the disaster, political realities would require government to come in with taxpayer money and help out anyway, it might be socially desirable to get at least some contribution in advance from those who are specifically at risk.

Additional critical pricing issues are (1) whether individual or classes of buyers will be charged differently because they run different risks, and (2) to what extent will underwriting investigations be carried out and underwriting conditions be attached so as to promote efficient precautions by those who are at risk. Failure to differentiate among insureds in the way a private market would results in subsidies. To be sure, sometimes these seeming subsidies are justified because price classification is simply too costly to engage in. Other times, failure to discriminate in pricing may reflect a positive choice to favor certain parties who are at risk, such as low (or high) income people. In any event, the absence of actuarially sensible risk-related premiums can discourage both insurance companies and certain property owners from participating, and it can cause some people to incur risks they would not run were their insurance costs actuarially fair.

SEAN HECHT,
CLIMATE CHANGE AND THE TRANSFORMATION OF RISK: INSURANCE MATTERS

55 UCLA L. Rev. 1559 (2008)

Some insurance industry leaders have noted that the industry has a significant financial stake in climate change, and some have asserted that the insurance sector can and should play an active role in solving our society's climate change-related problems. This awareness has encouraged significant recent activity among insurance companies to attempt to assess and to react to climate change. Trevor Maynard, Manager of Emerging Risks for the massive surplus insurer Lloyd's of London, has stated that "[c]limate change is already affecting the global insurance industry," and has argued that "[a]ll aspects of an insurer's balance sheet, its liabilities, capital requirements and assets may be affected." And a report issued recently by the major financial services firm Ernst and Young identified climate change as the "top insurance risk in 2008," noting that it is a "long-term issue with broad-reaching implications that will significantly impact the industry." . . .

Climate change will affect, and in some cases is already affecting, most major types of insurance products. First, insurers will feel the impact of climate change on property and casualty insurance, where the insurer bears the risk of a loss suffered directly by the policyholder. These property and casualty claims include not only damage to insured property as a direct result of weather, but also claims for business interruptions and other consequences of weather-induced events. Second, health and life insurers will face increasing costs. Third, insurers will face claims based on liability insurance, where the insurer pays for legal claims brought by third parties against the policyholder. Depending on the risk involved, all these types of insurance may be particularly affected by climate change-related losses or present unique opportunities to encourage the mitigation of such losses. And insurers will face challenges to insurability that may deeply impact the industry's ability to spread risk. This Part will discuss the impact that climate change is likely to have on both loss trends and insurability.

The direct risks to insurers from climate change are primarily catastrophe related. Catastrophes are the single largest threat to insurer solvency. Catastrophes, defined by the American Academy of Actuaries as "infrequent events that cause severe loss, injury or property damage to a large population of exposures," pose a unique, complex, and significant set of risks to insurer solvency. Catastrophes—particularly catastrophes that are stochastic in nature, such as severe weather events, earthquakes, or terrorism—pose challenges of risk magnitude, uncertainty, and correlation, "complicat[ing] the fundamental actuarial and pricing processes that underlie well-functioning insurance markets." Weather-related catastrophes have disrupted insurance markets in the past—for example, after Hurricane Andrew in 1992, and after the 2005 hurricane season in the Gulf of Mexico—and are likely to do so again in the future. According to a 2007 Congressional Research Service report, "[m]ost insurance market analysts note that there is no state in the Union that is not subject to catastrophe exposure, and the current state of affairs suggests that the exposures are far greater than the insurance industry is now currently prepared to handle." And there is significant evidence that climate change will increase both the risks borne by insurers from catastrophic events and the uncertainties associated with these risks. These risks include both first-party risk (the risk of loss by an insured) and third-party risk (the risk that an insured's actions will result in losses to others). In addition, climate change may significantly affect risks and uncertainties from other, noncatastrophic insured losses.

A. Climate Change and Insurance Losses

Insurers' underwriting is affected directly by the risks to which their policyholders are exposed. The insurance industry recognizes that "[f]or many industries, [weather] is the greatest risk to earnings: a risk that cannot be prevented, avoided or isolated." Swiss Re, a surplus insurer that has been aggressive in identifying climate change as a major risk to businesses internationally, has noted that "[v]ariable weather affects supply and demand in almost every industry: evidently in such sectors as energy or agriculture; more subtly, but still significantly, in others, for example retail, clothing, or entertainment." According to a researcher for leading surplus insurer Lloyd's of London, "[c]limate change is already affecting the global insurance industry. There are clear trends in past climate data that have translated into trends in insurance claims," including rising sea levels and consequent storm surges and longer and more frequent forest fires. Since an estimated $3 trillion of the U.S.'s $11 trillion economy is directly affected by weather, it is essential that the insurance industry retain the capacity to buffer businesses' exposure to weather-related losses. . . .

Extreme weather trends will deeply affect the insurance industry. Swiss Re has noted that "extreme events [are] expected to increase both in frequency and severity due to climate change." The Association of British Insurers also believes that climate change has caused extreme weather trends, noting that "climate change is making it likely that storm surges will occur more frequently, and that they will be more destructive when they do." And Lloyd's of London has expressed concerns about the effects of climate change on weather volatility, and on the implications that uncertainties surrounding these effects may have on insurability. Accordingly, some insurers have developed products to meet the "increasing demand for protection against adverse weather" and weather volatility due to climate change.

Unexpected catastrophe losses have already rocked the sector. Researchers Howard Kunreuther and Erwann Michel-Kerjan note that some insurers were taken by surprise at the size of losses from Hurricane Andrew and the Northridge earthquake in 1992 and 1994, respectively. "[F]ollowing Hurricane Andrew, many insurers only marketed coverage against wind damage in Florida because they were required to do so and state insurance pools were formed to limit their risk. In California, insurers refused to renew homeowners' earthquake policies after the 1994 Northridge earthquake, and in their place the California Earthquake Authority was formed by the state in 1996 with funds from insurers and reinsurers." In 2003, natural catastrophes worldwide caused $15 billion in insured losses ($8 billion of which were caused by storms). In 2005, Hurricane Katrina and other weather catastrophes caused insured losses of almost $80 billion worldwide, causing some companies' payouts to exceed insurance premiums. According to a recent report, "Louisiana property insurer losses following Hurricane Katrina were $3 billion more than all premiums collected in the state for the preceding 22 years [and] Lloyd's posted . . . a loss of $180 million in 2005 which equates to $1.12 paid out for ever[y] $1.00 in premium revenues, thanks largely to hurricane losses."

Whether or not current weather patterns already reflect climate change's impacts, insured losses from catastrophic weather events are increasing and are expected to continue to increase. According to a recent study, socioeconomic factors, including the "degree of urbanization and value at risk," "directly influence the level of economic losses due to weather-related events." These factors, in synergy with changing weather patterns, are likely to affect the insurance industry's covered losses significantly over time. And aside from extreme weather events, other adverse effects of climate change should concern the insurance industry because of their potential costs. As insurers' costs rise, the premium levels necessary for an insurer to make a profit rise, shrinking the potential market for the insurance. If costs are high enough, there will be no price point that satisfies both the insurer and the consumer, and there will be no market for the insurance, rendering the risk effectively uninsurable.

Climate change-related risks are likely to affect all major insurance types: property/casualty, health, life, and liability. Property and casualty insurance lines are likely to be affected by climate change, even aside from extreme weather. For example, coastal and sea-level property losses due to flooding from a higher sea level are expected. According to the Intergovernmental Panel on Climate Change, "[m]any millions more people are projected to be flooded every year due to sea-level rise by the 2080s." A report commissioned by the Association of British Insurers predicts that if no action to mitigate climate change is taken, the annual losses from coastal flooding in England and Wales "could increase by between £1.0 billion and £13.5 billion by the end of the century." In addition, property-damaging wildfires may increase in number and in intensity, in part because of climate change-related droughts, changes in wind and vegetation patterns, lightning strike increases, and reduced moisture content in vegetation. As an example of wildfires' potential cost to the insurance industry, one 1991 wildfire that reached the urban Oakland and Berkeley areas in northern California caused $2.4 billion in insured losses, including the loss of 3,400 buildings and 2,000 cars. Swiss Re and Lloyd's of London believe that climate change may have increased the magnitude of losses from the Oakland-Berkeley fire and other wildfires.

. . .

Because of the potential for large losses associated with a single event and other correlated losses, all these climate change-related risks deeply affect the reinsurance industry. Retail insurers transfer large amounts of risk to large companies that specialize in reinsurance and surplus insurance, such as Lloyd's, Swiss Re, and Munich Re. Often, those insurers serve as the primary insurers for risks that are seen as uninsurable by smaller insurers, both because of the deep access to capital that the surplus insurers enjoy and because the surplus insurers are subject to less regulation since they are typically nonadmitted in jurisdictions, such as U.S. states, that maintain strict regulatory requirements on underwriting.

In all, the changing climate is likely to have a wide-ranging and deep impact on the insurance industry. The attention that insurers—including large international insurers such as Swiss Re, Munich Re, AIG, and Lloyds of London, and an increasing number of domestic insurers—have placed on climate change is itself evidence that the industry expects climate change to transform its business practices. [FN93]

B. Climate Change and Insurability of Risks

Climate change presents significant risks to insurability. These risks, in turn, may limit the insurance industry's ability to continue to grow and to be profitable in those insurance lines affected by climate-related risk, unless insurers adapt to the changing conditions — itself a challenge because of the uncertainties inherent in climate change-related risk. Reinsurers will be affected disproportionately, since they bear such a high proportion of catastrophic risk. But innovations in capital markets and the reinsurance industry may enable the insurance sector to continue to manage risks effectively.

1. Climate Change's Threat to Insurability: Uncertainty, Potential for Losses High Enough to Threaten Solvency, and Correlated Risks

Climate change presents a particularly challenging type of risk for insurers because its effects may impact the insurability of a significant number of risks across various insurance product lines. This is especially true to the considerable extent that climate change-related losses are catastrophe-related. . . .

First, climate change's relationship to global weather patterns increases the potential for losses so large that they threaten the solvency of insurers as more severe weather becomes more common and overall variability of conditions increases.

Second, uncertainties in assessing climate change's impacts are high, affecting property and casualty, business interruption, health, and liability insurance, among others. As a result, where a risk has significant ambiguous components, insurers are both more likely to charge a significantly higher premium and more likely to avoid insuring the risk entirely than where a risk is more well-defined. Current catastrophe models, epidemiological assessments, and litigation risk models are likely not adequate to predict future risks.

Third, it is likely that many climate change-related risks are correlated, creating a skewed risk pool and exacerbating the risk of extremely large losses, and that some of these risks are not well-distributed across existing insureds. Severe weather-related losses, in particular, raise these issues, as does sea-level rise.

Finally, as a result of insurers' uncertainty aversion and need to protect against extremely large losses from single or related events, it is not clear that insurers will be willing to insure against some climate change-related risks at a price that policyholders are willing to pay.

Thus, many of the basic criteria of insurability are threatened by climate change. Moreover, the higher the magnitude of climate change in store for the Earth, the greater each of these challenges becomes. There is remarkable uncertainty about conditions around the globe at levels of future global warming that are considered extreme but possible even as soon as 2100.

2. Implications for the Insurance Industry of Climate Change's Threat to Insurability

Under these conditions, climate change poses a potential threat to the stability of the insurance industry over the next several decades if insurers do not take the necessary steps to adapt. One clear consequence of this situation is that insurers should be motivated to conduct research to help to better understand climate change's likely impacts. Insurers are already doing this. But it is less clear that insurers will work hard to adapt their basic products to a world in which the climate is changing. Uncertainty aversion and the possibility of enormous losses can motivate insurers either to attempt to create a business model that addresses climate change-related risk, or alternatively to withdraw from markets entirely.

This latter course of action unfortunately may be the most likely course of action for many insurers, at least in the short term. Insurers often will react to unanticipated losses or to significant changes in risk profile or uncertainty by limiting their underwriting. Regulated insurers, who have relatively less ability to price novel risks at a comfortable premium, are more likely to react this way than nonadmitted insurers such as large reinsurance companies. But even nonadmitted insurers have difficulty assuming risks that are too uncertain or novel, or that cannot be priced at a level that is marketable. So, for example, even large surplus insurers withdrew from the pollution insurance market in 1984 when they judged underwriting environmental liability insurance at marketable rates untenable. Similar problems occurred in the reinsurance market after the insurance industry grossly underestimated potential losses from Hurricane Andrew in 1992.

Climate change is likely to result in a combination of unanticipated losses and increased uncertainty that could create a similar, or even greater, potential for contraction of the insurance industry's overall coverage. But in the long run, such contraction will hurt the industry, and so innovative insurers will be looking for ways to make risks insurable.

Climate change should also provide an incentive for the insurance industry to work to reduce our society's overall greenhouse gas emissions. The difference between the more pessimistic end of the predicted climate spectrum in the future and the more optimistic end — the difference between the real chance of a scenario where "an entirely new planet is coming into being, one largely unrecognizable from the Earth we know today" — and the likelihood of a more manageable set of societal risks will involve dramatic cuts in greenhouse gas (GHG) production worldwide. To the extent that climate change's impacts can be limited, they will be more predictable and thus more insurable, creating business opportunities for insurers.

Climate change thus poses a challenge to the insurance industry's long-term stability, if insurers do not adapt. But taking action to address climate change will better enable the industry to manage its future successfully. This appears to be a primary motivation for the engagement of companies such as Lloyds, Munich Re, and Swiss Re in research, lobbying, and public education about climate change. These initiatives reflect the reality that the entire industry could be harmed by the increasing uncertainty that climate change will bring.

3. The Role of Reinsurance and Other Risk Transfer Instruments in Helping Insurers Cope with Climate Change

Insurers' ability to cope with the dramatic and significant risks posed and exacerbated by climate change is dependent in large part on their ability to transfer risk to reinsurers or other parties. Reinsurance and other vehicles that allow insurers to spread their own risk play a crucial role in allowing insurers to take on risks of large losses. These vehicles allow insurers to reduce both their average loss and maximum possible loss, increasing their capacity to cover risks. In an era in which catastrophe exposure is growing and the limits of insurability of catastrophic loss coverage may be increasingly uncertain, reduction of insurers' average and maximum losses will be even more central to future insurability of these risks.

Unfortunately, the reinsurance market has historically faced challenges covering catastrophic losses. Some losses strain the reinsurance market's liquidity and functionality. As a result, limitations on reinsurance capacity have limited the catastrophe insurance market. Companies and individuals exposed to catastrophe risk have had to turn to other avenues to preserve their capital and reduce this risk. Insurers and other financial institutions are looking to alternative risk-spreading instruments in order to accomplish this goal. Insurance-linked securities (ILSs) and "special-purpose vehicles" are the chief instruments being developed and implemented for this purpose. These instruments allow insurers and other companies to hedge climate risk. They include catastrophe bonds, industry loss warranties, weather derivatives, and "sidecar" companies whose purpose is to issue securities that hedge insurers' and reinsurers' risk. These instruments all allow an insurer or reinsurer to obtain access to capital if a specified set of conditions arises (for example, low rainfall, high temperatures, or a storm of a particular size making landfall). The sellers of the securities are, in essence, betting that the condition will not happen; they receive a premium that they are entitled to keep in the event that the condition is not met. If the condition is met, the sellers agree to pay a much higher, specified amount to the purchaser. Major reinsurers are developing these products. Their market has increased dramatically over the past few years, though it has not yet reached the level that researchers believe will be necessary to sustain a robust catastrophe insurance market.

The huge amount of risk held by a comparatively small number of reinsurers may explain why those companies have been the most proactive in addressing climate risks. Moreover, because reinsurers also often act as non-admitted insurers, they may be doubly exposed to these risks to the extent they act as primary insurers of significant risks associated with climate change.

In short, the success of reinsurance and similar vehicles in allowing insurers and large businesses to spread catastrophic risks will be essential to our society's ability to address climate change. Because insurers rely on risk-spreading instruments to manage their own exposure to high-magnitude or correlated losses, the supply of insurance for catastrophic events depends on the availability of these instruments.

ROBERT L. RABIN & SUZANNE A. BRATIS,
FINANCIAL COMPENSATION FOR CATASTROPHIC LOSS IN THE UNITED STATES

Financial Compensation for Victims after Catastrophe
(M. Faure & T. Honlief eds., Springer Verlag 2005)

The Terrorism Risk Insurance Act of 2002 (TRIA) exemplifies the federal government assuming the role of excess liability insurer, in effect providing a cap on the losses for which the private insurance industry will be responsible in the event of a major act of terrorism.

In terms of insurance losses, the terrorist attacks on the World Trade Center and Pentagon on September 11, 2001, rank as the most costly catastrophe in U.S. history. This is without reference to the personal injury claims compensated under the Victim Compensation Fund, totaling nearly $7 billion, discussed in a separate section of this report. By the middle of October 2003, private insurance companies had received 35,094 claims related to the September 11 attacks on the World Trade Center alone, representing a total of $19.07 billion, including massive numbers of personal property and business interruption claims (the latter including claims for lost income and expenses related to restarting or reinvigorating affected businesses). Workers compensation claims paid by the industry came to 5,660. These aggregate costs far exceeded past terrorism-related damage claims in the U.S.

In the aftermath of the attacks, even before massive numbers of claims began to be filed, the U.S. Congress was faced with widespread concern about the solvency of the American insurance industry. On November 26, 2002, President George W. Bush signed into law the Terrorism Risk Insurance Act of 2002. TRIA was created to ensure the continuing availability of insurance for terrorism risk. Its goals encompassed both protecting the American public, by ensuring continued insurance coverage, and protecting the insurance industry as it rebuilt after the losses caused by September 11. The Act created a mechanism by which the federal government and private insurance providers would share the burden of property and casualty losses resulting from any future terrorist attacks.

Essentially, all commercial insurers doing business within the U.S are required to participate in the program. Under the Act's provisions, insurers are required to make available coverage for insured losses resulting from acts of terrorism in all of their commercial property and casualty insurance policies. The coverage cannot differ materially from the terms, amounts, and other limitations of policies written to cover losses arising from nonterrorist causes. In addition to the continued availability of coverage, insurers must inform policyholders of the premium charged for coverage and the federal share of compensation provided for under the Act.

In return for such actions on the part of insurers, the federal government assumes a percentage of an insurer's losses from compensating claims arising from terrorist acts. Each insurer is responsible for a deductible amount. But once that threshold is reached, federal funds are used to reimburse the insurer 90% of the insured losses in excess of the deductible. Importantly, the Act imposes a $100-billion annual industry-aggregate limit on federal reimbursements.

The program's reimbursement provision is triggered only by the occurrence of an "act of terrorism." To qualify, an event must meet a three-part definition, in addition to a threshold dollar amount of $5 million. The act must: (1) be "a violent act or an act that is dangerous to human life, property or infrastructure"; (2) result in damage within the U.S. (or outside of the United States in the case of air carriers, vessels, and U.S. missions), committed by one or more individuals, on behalf of foreign interests, in an "effort to coerce the civilian population of the United States or to influence the policy or affect the conduct of the United States Government by coercion"; and (3) be certified as an "act of terrorism" by the secretary of the treasury in concurrence with the secretary of state and the attorney general. Reimbursement of the insured (including the federal contribution), and risk management administration, remains in the hands of the private insurer.

In addition to providing for reimbursement, the act also contains provisions for managing litigation arising out of certified acts of terrorism. Once an act of terrorism is certified, the Act creates an exclusive federal cause of action and remedy for property damage, personal injury, or death arising out of or relating to the terrorist act. The federal cause of action preempts certain state law claims and provides for the consolidation of all civil claims. Additionally, the Act provides that punitive damages awarded in actions for property damage, personal injury, or death are not to be counted as "insured losses" and are not paid under the Program. Finally, the United States is provided the right of subrogation with respect to any payment made by the United States under the Program.

The provisions of the Act make it clear that Congress did not intend the program to be a primary source of compensation. Compensation provided for by other federal programs cannot be duplicated by funds from the Program. For example, disaster relief provided under FEMA or benefit awards under the September 11th Victim Compensation Fund must be deducted from the total amount otherwise payable under TRIA. Moreover, the TRIA program is a stopgap measure. The Act expires in 2005 [but was later renewed] and the deductible amount attributed to the insurers increases annually until that point to reduce the total amount of losses subject to federal reimbursement.

RAWLE O. KING, HURRICANE KATRINA: INSURANCE LOSSES
AND NATIONAL CAPACITIES FOR FINANCING DISASTER RISKS

Congressional Budget Office (January 31, 2008)

Catastrophe-insured losses in 2005 totaled $66.1 billion from 24 disasters. Estimated insured losses from Katrina alone were $43.6 billion stemming from 1.75 million claims. Despite the severity of storm damages, Hurricane Katrina and other catastrophes in 2005 did not threaten the solvency and claims-paying ability of the property/casualty (p/c) insurance industry. Insurers benefitted from favorable market conditions during the last three years and experienced significant growth in policyholder surplus. Insurers, in fact, earned record profits in each of the last three years—2004-2006. . . .

Although the insurance industry has emerged largely intact from Hurricane Katrina and is better capitalized now than ever, it simply does not have sufficient capital to pay for a mega-catastrophe. This fact is not new. Insurers and financial market experts knew after Hurricane Andrew in 1992 that outside capital was needed to supplement industry capacity.

As Members of Congress explore ways to respond to the increasing risk and uninsured losses from tropical storms, earthquakes, and disruptive and costly inland flooding, they may be called upon to consider federal policy alternatives to build national capabilities for disaster risk management. Among measures that might be explored are various legislative proposals to pre-fund the cost of disasters with insurance or capital market instruments (risk securitization). . . .

All federal disaster insurance/reinsurance bills, including TRIA, share one feature: they seek to improve the nation's ability to finance catastrophe risk through insurance, as opposed to increased direct spending for federal disaster assistance. Their justification has been based on the argument that such initiatives will: (1) enhance the current catastrophe funding system; (2) make property insurance more available and affordable in high-risk areas; (3) promote the funding of research studies (i.e., earthquake science, actuarial science, economics, and finance) on disaster insurance issues; and (4) expand our knowledge and understanding of the scientific and financial aspects of natural hazards. In addition, proponents of federal disaster insurance have argued that such a scheme would reduce dependence on "free" disaster assistance and support efficient risk management by households and businesses.

Opponents to federal intervention in catastrophe insurance markets believe there is sufficient private sector capacity and federal intervention would only crowd out private capital for insuring disasters and stifle innovative catastrophe risk financing through insurance. . . .

Citing the development of new financial instruments to fund catastrophe coverage and expanded reinsurance capacity, critics of public insurance systems say there is no need for a federal insurance program at this time. They insist that such programs would shield the private sector from loss while creating sizable taxpayer- financed subsidies that undermine private-sector incentives for efficient risk management. Moreover, it has been argued that these programs would encourage population growth and development in high-risk, hurricane-prone areas that should not be developed, and would allow insurers to "cherry pick" the best risks and send the federal government the poor risks. . . .

Historically, Congress has been reluctant to enact federal disaster insurance legislation because of a lack of consensus on what will work, and concerns about adequate provisions for mitigation and avoidance of unnecessary government intrusion into markets being adequately served by private sector financial entities. Congressional reluctance to establish a federal disaster insurance program has been based on the recognition that such a program would conflict with sociological, economic, and actuarial principles that emphasize the "true" cost of government programs (the opportunity cost of the funds), the forgone benefits of a competitive insurance marketplace (e.g., cost efficiency and rate competition), and the absence of consumer choice (the ability to decide whether to purchase coverage).

The federal government has played an important role in the U.S. economic system by assuming risks that the private sector either will not undertake at any price, or will accept but at a price so high that most potential beneficiaries will not purchase the coverage. For example, government risk-bearing now occurs in environmental disasters, nuclear-plant accidents, toxic waste dumps, and flooding. Establishing an explicit federal disaster insurance system to ameliorate the potential damages to homes and commercial buildings stemming from natural disasters would represent another government risk-bearing program—one that could expose taxpayers to funding demands if program revenues fail to cover costs, or if returns are lower than expected. Nevertheless, supporters of a federal disaster insurance program argue that it would be justified by the national scope of the Hurricane Katrina disaster, and by the inability of the private insurance industry to handle future high payouts from a mega-catastrophic event without federal government involvement.

As Members of the 110th Congress explore long-term ways to respond to Hurricane Katrina, consideration might be given to whether there is a need to improve the nation's ability to finance catastrophic risk and, if so, how. Previous Congresses responded to similar concerns by considering legislation to create a federal catastrophe reinsurance program for residential property. Despite broad support for several bills over the past few years, Congress did not authorize a federal reinsurance program until the enactment of the Terrorism Risk Insurance Act of 2002.

Finally, most observers would agree that for the very highest layers of catastrophe risk, the government (and consequently the taxpayer) is now, by default, the insurer of last resort. In the 110th Congress, any one of a number of policy options could be pursued, and will likely be influenced by whether it can be shown that potential losses from Hurricane Katrina are beyond the capacity of private markets to diversify natural hazard risks. Members will likely be grappling with several policy questions. For example, will reinsurance and securitization be enough to maintain insurance solvency after a mega-catastrophic hurricane or earthquake? How can the various funding sources available for catastrophe insurance be expanded and refined to cope with a catastrophic hurricane? Finally, what role, if any, should the federal government play in catastrophe insurance?

NOTES AND QUESTIONS

1. There have been some important changes in catastrophic risk insurance since Hurricane Andrew first showed the potential scale of losses:
   - *Hurricane Insurance Deductibles.* Seventeen states (Alabama, Connecticut, Florida, Georgia, Hawaii, Louisiana, Maine, Maryland, Massachusetts, Mississippi, New Jersey, New York, North Carolina, Rhode Island, South Carolina, Texas, and Virginia) and the District of Columbia require property owners to pay hurricane or windstorm deductibles from 1 percent to 15 percent of the insured value of the property, depending on the type of home (e.g., mobile homes carry a higher percentage deductible) and where the property is located, rather than traditional dollar deductibles used for other types of claims, such as fire damage and theft. Higher deductibles have also been imposed for wind damage. These deductibles allow private insurers to shift the risk onto homeowners.
   - *Capital Market for Catastrophe Securities.* Starting in the late 1980s, insurers, reinsurers, and investment banks began offering catastrophe securities (sometimes known as insurance-linked securities, or ILS) that transfer risk of natural calamities to the capital market. These securities sell because they offer unusually high returns and because the rates of return are not correlated with returns in the stock and bond markets.

- *Building Codes and Construction Standards.* In hurricane-prone areas, home insurance rates are now linked to new building codes and structural standards based on a building's ability to withstand wind damage. Following Hurricane Andrew, the Insurance Institute for Property Loss Reduction (IIPLR) launched a study to develop better wind and seismic building codes so structures could better withstand the force of storms and earthquakes. This led to the Building Code Effectiveness Grading Schedule (BCEGS), which takes into account many factors such as the skill of building inspectors and the budgets of communities. The Florida legislature requires insurers to take into account the BCEGS system when pricing rates.
- *Flourishing of Catastrophe Simulation Modeling after Hurricane Andrew.* These models allow insurers to better predict future windstorm losses based on current demographics and construction methods than reliance on historical data. However, the damage forecasts from these models are often wrong by many orders of magnitude.

2. Federal disaster insurance legislation has been introduced in the 110th Congress that would:
   - establish a commission on catastrophic disaster risk and insurance — H.R. 537 (Meek); H.R. 3644 (Shays); S. 292 (Nelson); S. 928 (Nelson); S. 2286 (Dodd);
   - establish a federal program to provide reinsurance to improve the availability of homeowners' insurance — H.R. 91 (Grown-Waite); H.R. 330 (Brown-Waite); S. 928 (Nelson)
   - establish a state-run nonprofit corporation to allow states to pool catastrophic risks and transfer it directly to investors in the capital markets — H.R. 3355 (Klein); S. 2310 (Clinton);
   - establish a federal program to provide reinsurance for state natural catastrophe insurance programs to help the United States better manage and insure risks of large-scale natural disasters — H.R. 91;
   - change U.S. tax law to allow insurers to accumulate catastrophe reserves on a tax-preferred basis — H.R. 164 (Jindal); S. 926 (Nelson);
   - amend the Internal Revenue Code to create tax-exempt catastrophe savings accounts — H.R. 1787 (Feeney); S. 927 (Nelson); and
   - amend the Internal Revenue Code to allow individual taxpayers in certain hurricane disaster areas a tax credit for 50 percent of their homeowner insurance premiums, up to $250 annually.

3. For more in-depth coverage of these issues, *see* Howard Kunreuther & Richard J. Roth, Sr., Paying the Price: The Status and Role of Insurance against Natural Disasters in the United States (1998).

RECOVERING FROM DISASTER

After a disaster has occurred, the task becomes rebuilding. A city on its knees must confront a host of questions: How much of the old city should be restored? How should land uses be changed from residential to other uses? How can redevelopment be effective and fair at the same time? How can a city minimize the risk of future devastation? This chapter confronts some of those issues.

A. THE BASICS OF RECOVERY

Following hurricanes Ike and Gustav in 2008, the Government Accountability Office (GAO) conducted a survey of past disaster recovery efforts. The survey identified several actions that state and local governments can take as they struggle to pick up the pieces. Because every disaster has its own characteristics, and because communities have different resources, the GAO notes that its recommendations must always be tailored to individual circumstances.

GOVERNMENT ACCOUNTABILITY OFFICE, DISASTER RECOVERY: PAST EXPERIENCES
OFFER INSIGHTS FOR RECOVERING FROM HURRICANES IKE AND GUSTAV
AND OTHER RECENT NATURAL DISASTERS

http://www.gao.gov/new.items/d081120.pdf (Sept. 2008)

While the federal government provides significant financial assistance after major disasters, state and local governments play the lead role in disaster recovery. In our review of past disasters, we have identified several actions — both short- and long-term — that state and local governments can take as they prepare to recover after a major disaster. . . .

First, state and local governments have created clear, implementable, and timely recovery plans. Such plans, which the federal government has both funded and helped communities develop, can provide a roadmap for the recovery process. In the aftermath of a disaster, a recovery plan provides state and local governments with a valuable tool to document and communicate recovery goals, decisions, and priorities. In our review of recovery plans we have identified certain shared characteristics. Specifically, these plans (1) identify clear goals for recovery, (2) include detailed information to facilitate implementation, and (3) are established in a timely manner. For example, within 6 months of the 1995 earthquake that hit Kobe, Japan, the city completed a plan that helped Kobe prioritize and fund recovery projects. The plan also established a basis for subsequent governmental evaluations of the recovery's progress. . . .

With the uncertainty that can exist after major disasters, the inclusion of detailed implementation information in recovery plans can help communities realize their recovery goals. Implementable recovery plans specify objectives and tasks, clarify roles and responsibilities, and identify potential funding sources. Approximately 3 months after the 1997 Red River flood, the city of Grand Forks approved a recovery plan with these characteristics that helped the city take action towards achieving recovery.

. . .

Second, state and local governments have strengthened certain capacities — including having financial resources and technical know-how — to effectively take advantage of federal assistance. . . .

After a major disaster, state and local governments may not have adequate financial capacity to perform many short- and long-term recovery activities, such as continuing government operations and paying for rebuilding projects. The widespread destruction caused by major disasters can impose significant unbudgeted expenses while at the same time decimate the local tax base. Further, federal disaster programs often require state and local governments to match a portion of the assistance they receive, which may pose an additional financial burden. . . .

When recovering from past disasters, some local governments successfully used loans and special taxes to enhance their financial capacity. For example, after the 1997 Red River flood, the state-owned Bank of North Dakota provided a $44 million line of credit to the city of Grand Forks, North Dakota, which the city used to meet FEMA matching requirements. . . .

Another way to augment local financial capacity is to raise revenue through temporary taxes that local governments can target according to their recovery needs. After the 1989 Loma Prieta earthquake, voters in Santa Cruz County took steps to provide additional financial capacity to affected localities. The county implemented a tax increment, called "Measure E," about 1 year after the disaster, which increased the county sales tax by ½ cent for 6 years. The proceeds were targeted to damaged areas within the county based on an allocation approved by voters. Measure E generated approximately $12 million for the city of Santa Cruz, $15 million for the city of Watsonville, and $17 million for unincorporated areas of Santa Cruz County. . . .

Affected jurisdictions have also enhanced their technical capacity to navigate federal disaster programs. For example, after the 2005 Gulf Coast hurricanes, FEMA and Mississippi state officials used federal funding to obtain an on-line accounting system that tracked and facilitated the sharing of operational documents, thereby reducing the burden on applicants of meeting FEMA Public Assistance grant requirements.

Third, federal, state, and local governments focused on strategies that successfully fostered business recovery after a disaster. Small businesses are vital to a community's economic health, yet are especially vulnerable to disasters because they often lack resources to sustain financial loss and have less capacity to withstand market changes. We found that some local governments developed strategies to help small businesses survive the disaster and keep them within the community. For example, by creating temporary locations for businesses, the city of Santa Cruz, California, provided businesses that suffered physical damage during the Loma Prieta earthquake with the means to continue operating. The city of Los Angeles provided technical assistance to counsel businesses on how to adapt to the changed market realities after the Northridge earthquake. The city of Grand Forks offered business loans which provided incentives to remain within the community. Further, tax incentives targeted to businesses and projects consistent with long-term recovery goals can provide another tool to help affected businesses recover. . . .

The federal government has used tax incentives to stimulate business recovery after major disasters. . . . The Congress created tax incentives after the 2005 hurricanes through the Gulf Opportunity Zone Act of 2005 in part to promote business recovery. Following those hurricanes, affected state governments were responsible for allocating four tax incentives, including a $14.9 billion tax-exempt private activity bond authority to assist business recovery. These bonds allowed businesses to borrow funds at lower interest rates than would have otherwise been available because investors purchasing the bonds are not required to pay taxes on the interest they earn on the bonds. The Gulf Coast states exercising this authority are using the tax-exempt private activity bonds for a wide range of purposes to support different businesses, including manufacturing facilities, utilities, medical offices, mortgage companies, hotels, and retail facilities. . . .

Finally, federal, state, and local governments have looked for ways to adopt a comprehensive approach to combating fraud, waste, and abuse. The influx of financial assistance available to victims after a major disaster provides increased opportunities for fraud, waste, and abuse. Specifically, disaster victims are at increased risk for contractor fraud. To address this issue after the 1997 Red River flood, the city of Grand Forks, North Dakota established a credentialing program that issued special photo identifications to contractors who passed licensing and criminal checks. Residents were advised to check for these credentials as they hired contractors to rebuild. Also at risk for fraud, waste, and abuse are federal and state disaster assistance programs. The need to quickly provide assistance to victims puts assistance payments at risk to fraudulent applicants who try to obtain benefits that they are not entitled to receive. . . . [W]ith a framework that prevents, detects, and monitors issues of fraud, waste, and abuse, government programs should not have to make a choice between the speedy delivery of disaster recovery assistance and effective fraud protection. . . .

While receiving millions of dollars in federal assistance, state and local governments bear the main responsibility for helping communities cope with the destruction left in the wake of major disasters. Now that the wind and storm surge from Hurricanes Ike and Gustav have passed, . . . state and local governments face a myriad of decisions regarding the short- and long-term recovery of their communities. We have seen that actions taken shortly after a major disaster and during the early stages of the recovery process can have a significant impact on the success of a community's long-term recovery. Accordingly, this is a critical time for communities affected by these major disasters.

B. NEXT STEPS: REDUCING VULNERABILITY AND INCREASING RESILIENCE

When recovering from disaster, it is not just enough to build back what previously existed. The goal is to build something better—a community that is safer and more sustainable. In the passage below, planning experts Anna Schwab and David J. Brower establish some principles for building resilience at the local level and discuss ways in which municipalities can use their basic police powers to make communities less vulnerable.

Anna K. Schwab & David J. Brower, Increasing Resilience
to Natural Hazards: Obstacles and Opportunities
for Local Governments under the Disaster
Mitigation Act of 2000

Losing Ground: A Nation on Edge, 281, 283-301
(John Nolon & Daniel Rodriguez eds., 2007)

Fortunately, local communities have at their disposal many ways to increase resilience, methods that fall well within the police power delegated to units of local government from their respective states. In the effort to become more resilient to the impacts of natural hazards, communities should adhere to a few basic principles, both to ease the process in terms of efficiency and to increase the political feasibility and overall effectiveness of mitigation measures that are adopted to reduce vulnerability.

The first such principle for successful resilience building involves awareness and acceptance. Community members must be aware of the natural hazards they face, and must accept that they are capable of and responsible for addressing their hazard risks. . . .

The second principle necessary for true resilience is an articulation of values among the citizenry and elected officials. A "mitigation ethic" must be infused into community policies and integrated into the mainstream of community decision making, so that hazard resilience is addressed as an important and valid concern worthy of public attention. . . .

A third principle for building resilience at the local level involves full public engagement in the process of mitigation planning and goal formulation. Although public participation can be a bulky and time-consuming activity (the process of notification, solicitation, and incorporation of citizen response is a major undertaking), the end result is worthwhile. . . .

The fourth major principle that should guide communities seeking hazard resilience is a willingness to invest in the community's capacity for developing and carrying out mitigation policies and programs. There are many components to a community's capacity to engage in mitigation, including:

- *fiscal capability* (the ability to fund or to seek funding for mitigation projects and activities);
- *technical capability* (the ability to carry out hazard identification and vulnerability analyses to produce accurate information regarding where and to what extend hazards are likely to impact the community);
- *legal capability* (the ability and willingness to use the local police power to enact necessary land use and other regulations that restrict the use of hazardous lands for building purposes while respecting the rights of private property owners to realize their investment-backed expectations);
- *institutional capacity* (the ability to create the institutional framework or to designate responsible positions within the existing institutional framework to implement and sustain mitigation policies); and
- *political capacity* (the willpower to propose and carry out enduring mitigation strategies notwithstanding the shortened horizon of some elected positions).

Capacity building [implies] that the knowledge base necessary to plan for and implement hazard mitigation measures must primarily reside within the community itself. . . . Of course, consultants often play a vital role in mitigation programming at the local level. . . . Yet while consultants (for a price) can perform many of the activities involved in generating and analyzing important background data, the real action of devising strategies, adopting goals and implementing policies must be carried out by those with a lasting stake in the ultimate resilience of the community.

Action Strategies for Local Governments

Broadly speaking, there are five interrelated approaches to reducing vulnerability at the local level. Within these categories is a wide selection of specific mitigation strategies and actions, many if not all of which are well within the police power of local governments. . . . [I]n general terms mitigation techniques can be classified as follows

- structural engineering projects
- hazard avoidance
- property protection
- environmental preservation
- education and outreach

. . .

Structural Engineering Projects

Structural mitigation projects are intended to lessen the impact of a hazard by modifying the environment or by interfering with the natural progression of the hazard event. As mentioned earlier, large-scale armoring against nature is expensive (usually beyond what local government acting alone can afford) and may encourage development in unsafe areas. . . .

On a smaller scale (at the community level), structural projects are usually designed by engineers and managed or maintained by public works staff, and include such necessary actions as the construction and maintenance of storm sewers and drainage infrastructure. In most states, storm drainage is provided by counties and municipalities as one of the services required to maintain healthy and safe living conditions. The spending power of local governments allows public monies to be directed to these essential services, and the power of acquisition allows local governments to purchase or condemn land and rights-of-way for stormwater management. . . .

Hazard Avoidance

Over the long term, the most straightforward and cost-effective strategy to minimize or prevent damages and losses from natural hazards is to guide development away from hazard-prone areas. In other words, we attempt to avoid disasters altogether by removing people and property from where the built environment intersects with the hazard event. The most direct way of achieving avoidance objectives is through acquisition of hazard areas, accompanied by demolition or relocation of hazard-prone structures when homes and businesses are present. A second means of hazard avoidance involves land use planning and regulation, including the enactment of zoning and subdivision ordinances. A third method to bring about hazard avoidance invokes the local jurisdiction's powers of spending and taxation. . . . The hazard avoidance approach is most appropriate when alternative locations within the community are available for development. Communities that are at or close to build-out have more limited options for hazard avoidance, although encouraging higher density building and in-fill development in safe locations can help alleviate the constraints imposed by a scarcity of land.

Acquisition and Relocation

Enabling legislation typically empowers local governments to acquire and hold property for public purpose. By acquiring lands in hazard-prone areas, a community can ensure that the land will be put only to those uses that are compatible with the nature of the hazard risk. Picnic shelters and ball fields, for instance, are more appropriate uses of land in the floodplain than homes and businesses. Although acquisition is typically one of the most expensive mitigation tactics, in the long run it is often less expensive to acquire and demolish a building than to repeatedly provide for its reconstruction.

While the power of eminent domain is a necessary tool for acquiring land for certain community needs (schools and road rights-of-way are typical uses of condemnation), it is rarely invoked for hazard mitigation purposes. More common is the acquisition of land from a willing seller. Owners of properties that have experienced repetitive losses and who face probable future flooding are often very willing to sell, so long as the benefits are explained fully, and a viable alternative is made available to them.

On the downside, since title to the property is transferred to the public domain, acquisition may remove properties entirely or in part from the local government's property tax rolls, depending upon the type of acquisition program used. However, the cost of losing tax revenues from these properties is often lower compared to the cost of providing services to properties in hazard areas and the periodic costs of rescue and recovery from disasters. Another disadvantage with acquisition projects in some communities, particularly in rural or impoverished areas, is that the local government becomes the responsible party with respect to maintaining and preserving the acquired land as open space in perpetuity. However, local governments may transfer title to acquired land to other government agencies or to a nonprofit agency, such as a conservation or environmental organization. . . .

Communities have used various methods to fund acquisitions using local financial resources, including bond referendums, taxes and fees, or partnerships with nonprofit organizations. However, the vast majority of buy-out programs are financed with federal funds, such as the Hazard Mitigation Grant Program and the Pre-Disaster Mitigation program administered by the Federal Emergency Management Agency (FEMA). Counties and municipalities have also made use of Community Development Block Grant funds from the U.S. Department of Housing and Urban Development, which are available for projects that benefit low- and moderate-income persons by removing slum and blighted conditions, or that address conditions of urgent need.

Reuse of acquired properties varies according to individual communities' needs and the location and condition of the purchased land. Local governments have created public parks, incorporated land into open space systems, and let the land revert to its natural vegetative state as experimental or communal gardens. Some communities have built picnic shelters, tennis courts, ball fields, and bicycle or jogging paths on acquired land to encourage public uses. Acquisition has also been used to increase floodplain storage capacity, preserve wetlands, maritime forest, estuaries and other natural habitats, and protect aquifer recharge zones and riparian buffers. . . .

Land Use Regulation

Local governments are authorized under the police power to regulate the use of private property to safeguard the physical environment, to encourage economic development, and to protect the public's health and safety. . . . Through various land use regulatory powers, a local government can control the amount, timing, density, quality, and location of new development. All these characteristics of growth are determinants of local vulnerability to natural hazards. . . .

Zoning is the traditional and nearly ubiquitous tool available to local governments to control the use of land. Some communities have made good use of their zoning ordinances for mitigation purposes by delineating hazard areas on the local zoning map. The corresponding text of the ordinance may designate these areas for low-intensity uses such as recreation, open space, conservation, or agriculture. Zoning can also be used to prohibit environmentally hazardous uses, such as junkyards and chemical storage facilities in areas vulnerable to flooding or earthquake. A zoning ordinance may encourage development in safe areas, by allowing greater density in hazard-free zones.

When a community uses the local zoning ordinance as a hazard mitigation tool, the phrasing of its nonconforming use provisions is critical. The rules must be very clear as to whether or not reconstruction will be allowed if buildings are severely damaged or destroyed by a storm or other natural hazard event. Some states have enacted legislation that prohibits restoration in high-hazard zones if damage is assessed at more than 50 percent of a structure's pre-storm value. . . .

Subdivision ordinances control land that is being divided into parcels for sale by establishing standards for infrastructure and lot layout. Subdivision regulations are used to prevent new construction on land that is not suitable for development, and to ensure that infrastructure is provided to adequately support the development. In terms of their effectiveness for hazard mitigation purposes, studies have shown that subdivision controls, although more widely used than zoning, are not well tied to hazard mitigation aims. However, the opportunity to reduce vulnerability can be realized with a well thought out subdivision ordinance that requires careful consideration of the specific topography of proposed development sites during the regulatory review process. . . .

Local Spending Policies

The power to spend municipal funds can strengthen community resilience when spending is carried out as part of a comprehensive public facility and land management policy that includes hazard mitigation as a specific purpose. When making decisions about expenditures for new facilities such as schools, fire stations, sewer treatment plants and other public necessities, local governments can choose to locate these critical facilities in areas with lowered risk of damage from natural hazards. Careful siting can protect lifelines during a disaster, reduce public outlays for repair, and minimize the time and expense for reconstruction following a hazard event. Local governments can also use capital improvement and maintenance programs to prescribe standards for the design and construction of new public facilities with hazard mitigation components, or to retrofit existing public structures. Although many local communities nationwide have taken a proactive approach to safeguarding publicly owned structures, there is a persistent disincentive to protect critical facilities from natural hazards because the damage costs are typically passed on to the federal government through various disaster assistance programs.

. . . [L]ocal governments can also use their spending power to discourage private development in hazardous areas, while directing new growth to designated nonhazard areas. By limiting the availability of public services such as roads, schools, utility lines, and other supporting infrastructure, the municipality can steer development appropriately. However, studies indicate that jurisdictions tend to ignore their own capital programs, and that policies designed to locate public facilities outside of hazard areas to discourage growth do not alter the basic spatial pattern of development. Furthermore, capital improvement programs are generally ineffective for controlling development in communities that have already reached [their capacity for] build-out, or where private developers are able to provide the infrastructure necessary to support new construction. . . .

Local Taxation and Fee Policies

The power of taxation can have a profound impact on the pattern of development in a community. By assessing differential tax rates in certain districts, the local government can influence which lands are relatively affordable to develop. The community can then direct growth to desirable, safe areas, while providing disincentives for developers to build on lands identified as hazardous. . . .

While few communities use their real property taxation policies to manipulate land use patterns for mitigation purposes, local governments have made use of other types of tax incentives to influence design and construction practices. Tax abatements can encourage homeowners and developers to integrate mitigation measures into new structures and to retrofit existing properties, much like tax credits and allowances have been used to encourage the construction of energy efficient homes and office buildings. Tax incentives have been applied to storm proofing, flood proofing, wind strengthening, and seismic retrofitting, among other hardening construction techniques. Tax abatements can also take the form of permit fee waivers for structures built with mitigation features, or discounted construction fees for retrofitting. Waivers of sales taxes on building materials to strengthen or retrofit homes and businesses have also been used as incentive for mitigation. The village of South Holland, Illinois, has a rebate program to help property owners fund retrofitting projects to protect against surface and subsurface flooding. If a project is approved, installed, and inspected, the village will reimburse the owner 25% of the cost up to $2500. About 650 flood-proofing and sewer backup protection projects have been completed under the program. Perhaps not surprisingly, local contractors have become some of the best agents to publicize the program.

Impact fees and special assessments are often levied against property owners to more equitably distribute the financial burden of development to those who directly benefit. Special assessments can be used for mitigation purposes to raise revenue for specific improvements, such as a flood retention pond, or to fund ongoing services such as maintenance of stormwater management systems. These charges do not usually discourage development in the assessment district, but they do transfer some of the cost of living or doing business in a hazard-prone area to those who choose to do so. . . .

Property Protection

In a perfect world, communities would be built in locations that are never exposed to the impacts of natural hazards. Hazard avoidance, however, is an impractical approach to mitigation in areas where development is warranted on economic grounds, where hazard risk is uniformly experienced across the jurisdiction, or where the hazard area itself is integral to the community's identity. In these places, the most appropriate strategy to reduce potential disaster losses is to strengthen buildings and facilities so that they are able to withstand hazard impacts.

Property protection involves physical or structural measures applied to individual buildings and facilities to make them more resilient to identified hazard impacts. . . .

Elevation is one of the most widely used property protection techniques and has successfully reduced future flood losses while keeping neighborhoods intact in communities nationwide. Elevation involves raising the lowest habitable floor above the 100-year or base flood elevation (BFE). Alternatively, elevation entails raising critical components of a building above expected flood levels, including, for example, the [heating, ventilating, and air conditioning], electrical circuitry or other systems that can be damaged by contact with water. . . .

Flood-proofing techniques can provide protection to certain types of buildings. Although the [National Flood Insurance Plan] does not allow flood proofing of new residential structures because of the potential catastrophic nature of damage if flood-proofing measures fail, it is a reasonable mitigation tool for some other types of buildings. Nonresidential buildings can be constructed to withstand anticipated flood forces, and in some instances, older buildings can be retrofitted with flood-proof materials.

Seismic retrofit programs can be cost-effective approaches to reducing earthquake vulnerability. The objective is to make buildings and infrastructure resistant to the effects of ground shaking and liquefaction [of underlying soils]. Both structural and nonstructural retrofit techniques can be adopted to minimize casualties and reduce damages. Low-cost techniques include securing suspended ceilings, bolting bookcases to the walls, or fastening heavy equipment like computers to prevent injury to occupants during earthquake tremors. While these techniques are well accepted in recognized earthquake risk zones, the challenge has been to make seismic preparedness and retrofitting a higher public priority in moderate-risk communities.

. . . [T]he most effective way to promote structural mitigation is through the creation, implementation, and enforcement of *building codes* that reflect adequate standards of protection for specific hazard risks.

Strict compliance with the letter as well as the spirit of the building code is especially critical in the aftermath of a disaster. It is understandable that residents and property owners want to rebuild their homes and businesses as quickly as possible following a hurricane or other large-scale event. There is often considerable political pressure on building officials in the post-disaster environment to expedite or circumvent the permitting process. However, the urge to return to normalcy must not be indulged at the sacrifice of public health and safety. Nor should the rebuilding process take place so quickly that valuable mitigation opportunities are lost.

Some local jurisdictions have moratoria that can be activated during a state of emergency following a natural hazard event. Moratoria provide local officials the time needed to assess the extent of site-specified hazard impacts and to re-map high-hazard areas to reflect actual damages. Moratoria can also help local decision makers set priorities for response and long term recovery efforts and to consider mitigation measures to reduce the risk of future disasters. Moratoria are often used to prevent property owners from rebuilding damaged structures before an acquisition program can be put in motion, or to activate new regulations for elevation and other property protection measures.

The town of Nags Head, located on the hurricane prone Outer Banks of North Carolina, has building moratoria of various lengths that can be activated following a disaster. An initial, 48-hour moratorium goes into effect immediately. Replacement of destroyed structures is halted for 30 days. In the meantime, planners and the Board of Commissioners may adjust the zoning code to reflect new inlets or eroded areas or to incorporate mitigation standards.

All replacement construction must comply with the new ordinances established during the 30-day moratorium. Building permits issued prior to the storm are revoked for at least 30 days. These moratoria have proved useful to local officials in the post-disaster phase to restructure the regulatory regime according to damage actually sustained and newly identified hazard risks.

Environmental Preservation

Termed "ecological infrastructure and natural capital," . . . a community's wetlands, hillsides, shorelines, floodplains, riparian areas, forests, and habitats can provide important and cost-effective natural services and benefits, not the least of which is hazard mitigation. A sustainability approach to natural hazards understands that frequently the most effective way to reduce vulnerability of people and property is to preserve a healthy, well-functioning ecosystem.

Many communities have initiatives to protect and manage these critical ecosystems. Soil conservation and steep slope preservation measures typically place restrictions on the grading of hillsides and prohibit development on landslide-prone slopes. Oceanfront setbacks establish a minimum distance between the existing shoreline and the buildable portion of a lot. Dune preservation laws help protect development against storm surge flooding by restricting pedestrian and vehicular access, and by prohibiting the leveling or lowering of dunes for visual access. Wetland protection and restoration can be effective for stormwater management and floodwater retention. These and other measures are implemented through regulation, acquisition, incentives for private landowners, or partnerships with nonprofit conservation and land trust agencies.

The effectiveness of environmental protection measures for hazard mitigation purposes varies widely, but in general, these measures are most successful when used in concert with state and federal management programs. . . .

Education and Outreach

The key to an effective, long-term initiative that instills a "mitigation ethic" often depends on community consciousness. As citizens, public officials, planners, developers, builders, emergency managers, and school children learn about the nature and consequences of hazards, they can also learn about the steps that can be taken to minimize injuries, damage and economic losses. An array of innovative approaches to foster community support for hazard mitigation and disaster preparedness is available to local government's intent on generating a well-informed citizenry. Hazard mapping, disclosure laws, disaster warning, and public awareness campaigns are some of the more commonly used measures to disseminate information to citizens about their hazard risks. . . .

Financing Local Mitigation Strategies

Local elected officials must balance many competing interests when allocating limited local resources. Highly visible problems, such as roads, schools, housing, and health care often grab the immediate attention of constituents. During periods of economic downturn, high unemployment, and restricted federal aid, local government coffers are strained while the need for government services increases. However, many local governing boards have come to realize that money invested in hazard mitigation activities can protect the community's tax base, saving millions of dollars in property damage by reducing losses from inevitable natural hazards. The economic value of mitigation is particularly evident in communities that have carried out acquisition projects involving repetitive flood structures. Although the initial outlays are steep, it has proven to be a cost-effective strategy over the long term to remove families from flood-hazard properties. Keeping businesses open, residents in their homes, and basic services operating following an emergency results in economic security and social stability for local communities.

State and federal aid is a large part of many local governments' revenue stream. Grants and other aid programs help local governments meet specific needs, including emergency preparedness, disaster recovery, and hazard mitigation. States that experience multiple disaster declarations have been able to funnel money to local governments to carry out large mitigation projects, such as massive buyouts of repetitively flooded structures and elevations of homes in entire neighborhoods.

While outside sources of funding pay for the bulk of large-scale mitigation projects, many creative local governments are becoming more self-reliant when it comes to financing mitigation activities. Local governments have used capital improvement funding, taxes and special assessments, utility fees, municipal bonds, regulatory fees, and other methods of raising revenue to pay for mitigation. . . . Some of the most effective mitigation strategies may require no additional money at all, just a shift in thinking, particularly with regard to land use planning and growth management.

NOTES AND QUESTIONS

1. As Schwab and Brower make clear, local planning is an essential part of hazard mitigation. Some federal laws encourage (and sometimes require) states, tribes, and local governments to develop mitigation strategies to address many types of natural hazards. Examples include the Coastal Zone Management Act, the Community Rating System of the National Flood Insurance Program, the Safe Drinking Water Act, and the Water Resources Planning Act. In addition, many federal programs, such as the National Landslide Hazards Mitigation Strategy, recommend closer partnerships between states and their local governments, where most mitigation necessarily occurs.

2. More specifically, the Disaster Mitigation Act of 2000, U.S.C. §5112 et seq., sometimes called DMA2K, encourages states and local governments to identify natural hazards in their areas and develop plans to reduce the risk. State and local governments that have an approved mitigation plan are eligible to receive increased financial assistance under the Hazard Mitigation Grant Program. Although approved plans need only account for natural disasters, FEMA encourages plans to address "manmade hazards" too.

   State mitigation plans require significant public involvement and must address five basic elements: (1) a description of the planning process;

(2) an assessment of the risks faced; (3) a strategy for reducing risks; (4) coordination; and (5) maintenance.

Local mitigation plans are similar to state plans. One difference is that local plans must also incorporate multijurisdictional plans to allow local governments to work together to address large regional hazards. The process of creating local and multijurisdictional plans will typically include members of communities, businesses, universities, public agencies, and nonprofit organizations. *See* Patricia E. Salkin, *Sustainability at the Edge: The Opportunity and Responsibility of Local Governments to Effectively Plan for Natural Disaster Mitigation, in* LOSING GROUND: A NATION ON EDGE 125 (John Nolon & Daniel Rodriguez eds., 2007).

C. A COMMON SNAG: LAND ACQUISITION

After a major disaster, it is common for a municipality to acquire land for reasons of safety or redevelopment. Officials generally prefer voluntary "buyouts" or other arms-length transactions. They are often faster and, of course, more politically acceptable. But sometimes voluntary transactions are not possible, either because of "holdout" problems or because owners cannot be located. Is it appropriate for local government to use eminent domain to acquire property from current landowners and then turn it over to developers for reuse? Consider the opinions in the following case.

KELO v. CITY OF NEW LONDON

545 U.S. 469, 125 S. Ct. 2655, 162 L. Ed. 2d 439 (2005)

Justice STEVENS delivered the opinion of the Court.

In 2000, the city of New London approved a development plan that, in the words of the Supreme Court of Connecticut, was "projected to create in excess of 1,000 jobs, to increase tax and other revenues, and to revitalize an economically distressed city, including its downtown and waterfront areas." In assembling the land needed for this project, the city's development agent has purchased property from willing sellers and proposes to use the power of eminent domain to acquire the remainder of the property from unwilling owners in exchange for just compensation. The question presented is whether the city's proposed disposition of this property qualifies as a "public use" within the meaning of the Takings Clause of the Fifth Amendment to the Constitution. . . .

Two polar propositions are perfectly clear. On the one hand, it has long been accepted that the sovereign may not take the property of A for the sole purpose of transferring it to another private party B, even though A is paid just compensation. On the other hand, it is equally clear that a State may transfer property from one private party to another if future "use by the public" is the purpose of the taking; the condemnation of land for a railroad with common-carrier duties is a familiar example. Neither of these propositions, however, determines the disposition of this case.

As for the first proposition, the City would no doubt be forbidden from taking petitioners' land for the purpose of conferring a private benefit on a particular private party. Nor would the City be allowed to take property under the mere pretext of a public purpose, when its actual purpose was to bestow a private benefit. The takings before us, however, would be executed pursuant to a "carefully considered" development plan. The trial judge and all the members of the Supreme Court of Connecticut agreed that there was no evidence of an illegitimate purpose in this case.

On the other hand, this is not a case in which the City is planning to open the condemned land — at least not in its entirety — to use by the general public. Nor will the private lessees of the land in any sense be required to operate like common carriers, making their services available to all comers. But although such a projected use would be sufficient to satisfy the public use requirement, this "Court long ago rejected any literal requirement that condemned property be put into use for the general public." Indeed, while many state courts in the mid-19th century endorsed "use by the public" as the proper definition of public use, that narrow view steadily eroded over time. Not only was the "use by the public" test difficult to administer (e.g., what proportion of the public need have access to the property? at what price?), but it proved to be impractical given the diverse and always evolving needs of society. Accordingly, when this Court began applying the Fifth Amendment to the States at the close of the 19th century, it embraced the broader and more natural interpretation of public use as "public purpose." Thus, in a case upholding a mining company's use of an aerial bucket line to transport ore over property it did not own, Justice Holmes' opinion for the Court stressed "the inadequacy of use by the general public as a universal test." We have repeatedly and consistently rejected that narrow test ever since.

The disposition of this case therefore turns on the question whether the City's development plan serves a "public purpose." Without exception, our cases have defined that concept broadly, reflecting our longstanding policy of deference to legislative judgments in this field.

In Berman v. Parker, 348 U.S. 26 (1954), this Court upheld a redevelopment plan targeting a blighted area of Washington, D.C., in which most of the housing for the area's 5,000 inhabitants was beyond repair. Under the plan, the area would be condemned and part of it utilized for the construction of streets, schools, and other public facilities. The remainder of the land would be leased or sold to private parties for the purpose of redevelopment, including the construction of low-cost housing.

The owner of a department store located in the area challenged the condemnation, pointing out that his store was not itself blighted and arguing that the creation of a "better balanced, more attractive community" was not a valid public use. Writing for a unanimous Court, Justice Douglas refused to evaluate this claim in isolation, deferring instead to the legislative and agency judgment that the area "must be planned as a whole" for the plan to be successful. The Court explained that "community redevelopment programs need not, by force of the Constitution, be on a piecemeal basis — lot by lot, building by building." The public use underlying the taking was unequivocally affirmed:

> We do not sit to determine whether a particular housing project is or is not desirable. The concept of the public welfare is broad and inclusive. . . . The

values it represents are spiritual as well as physical, aesthetic as well as monetary. It is within the power of the legislature to determine that the community should be beautiful as well as healthy, spacious as well as clean, well-balanced as well as carefully patrolled. In the present case, the Congress and its authorized agencies have made determinations that take into account a wide variety of values. It is not for us to reappraise them. If those who govern the District of Columbia decide that the Nation's Capital should be beautiful as well as sanitary, there is nothing in the Fifth Amendment that stands in the way.

In Hawaii Housing Authority v. Midkiff, 467 U.S. 229 (1984), the Court considered a Hawaii statute whereby fee title was taken from lessors and transferred to lessees (for just compensation) in order to reduce the concentration of land ownership. We unanimously upheld the statute and rejected the Ninth Circuit's view that it was "a naked attempt on the part of the state of Hawaii to take the property of A and transfer it to B solely for B's private use and benefit." Reaffirming *Berman*'s deferential approach to legislative judgments in this field, we concluded that the State's purpose of eliminating the "social and economic evils of a land oligopoly" qualified as a valid public use. Our opinion also rejected the contention that the mere fact that the State immediately transferred the properties to private individuals upon condemnation somehow diminished the public character of the taking. "[I]t is only the taking's purpose, and not its mechanics," we explained, that matters in determining public use. . . .

Viewed as a whole, our jurisprudence has recognized that the needs of society have varied between different parts of the Nation, just as they have evolved over time in response to changed circumstances. Our earliest cases in particular embodied a strong theme of federalism, emphasizing the "great respect" that we owe to state legislatures and state courts in discerning local public needs. For more than a century, our public use jurisprudence has wisely eschewed rigid formulas and intrusive scrutiny in favor of affording legislatures broad latitude in determining what public needs justify the use of the takings power.

Those who govern the City were not confronted with the need to remove blight in the Fort Trumbull area, but their determination that the area was sufficiently distressed to justify a program of economic rejuvenation is entitled to our deference. The City has carefully formulated an economic development plan that it believes will provide appreciable benefits to the community, including — but by no means limited to — new jobs and increased tax revenue. As with other exercises in urban planning and development, the City is endeavoring to coordinate a variety of commercial, residential, and recreational uses of land, with the hope that they will form a whole greater than the sum of its parts. To effectuate this plan, the City has invoked a state statute that specifically authorizes the use of eminent domain to promote economic development. Given the comprehensive character of the plan, the thorough deliberation that preceded its adoption, and the limited scope of our review, it is appropriate for us, as it was in *Berman*, to resolve the challenges of the individual owners, not on a piecemeal basis, but rather in light of the entire plan. Because that plan unquestionably serves a public purpose, the takings challenged here satisfy the public use requirement of the Fifth Amendment.

To avoid this result, petitioners urge us to adopt a new bright-line rule that economic development does not qualify as a public use. Putting aside the unpersuasive suggestion that the City's plan will provide only purely economic benefits, neither precedent nor logic supports petitioners' proposal. Promoting economic development is a traditional and long accepted function of government. There is, moreover, no principled way of distinguishing economic development from the other public purposes that we have recognized. . . . It would be incongruous to hold that the City's interest in the economic benefits to be derived from the development of the Fort Trumbull area has less of a public character than any of those other interests. Clearly, there is no basis for exempting economic development from our traditionally broad understanding of public purpose.

It is further argued that without a bright-line rule nothing would stop a city from transferring citizen A's property to citizen B for the sole reason that citizen B will put the property to a more productive use and thus pay more taxes. Such a one-to-one transfer of property, executed outside the confines of an integrated development plan, is not presented in this case. While such an unusual exercise of government power would certainly raise a suspicion that a private purpose was afoot, the hypothetical cases posited by petitioners can be confronted if and when they arise. They do not warrant the crafting of an artificial restriction on the concept of public use.

Alternatively, petitioners maintain that for takings of this kind we should require a "reasonable certainty" that the expected public benefits will actually accrue. Such a rule, however, would represent an even greater departure from our precedent. "When the legislature's purpose is legitimate and its means are not irrational, our cases make clear that empirical debates over the wisdom of takings — no less than debates over the wisdom of other kinds of socioeconomic legislation — are not to be carried out in the federal courts." *Midkiff.* . . . The disadvantages of a heightened form of review are especially pronounced in this type of case. Orderly implementation of a comprehensive redevelopment plan obviously requires that the legal rights of all interested parties be established before new construction can be commenced. A constitutional rule that required postponement of the judicial approval of every condemnation until the likelihood of success of the plan had been assured would unquestionably impose a significant impediment to the successful consummation of many such plans.

Justice KENNEDY, concurring.

A court applying rational-basis review under the Public Use Clause should strike down a taking that, by a clear showing, is intended to favor a particular private party, with only incidental or pretextual public benefits, just as a court applying rational-basis review under the Equal Protection Clause must strike down a government classification that is clearly intended to injure a particular class of private parties, with only incidental or pretextual public justifications.

A court confronted with a plausible accusation of impermissible favoritism to private parties should treat the objection as a serious one and review the record to see if it has merit, though with the presumption that the government's actions were reasonable and intended to serve a public purpose. Here, the trial court conducted a careful and extensive inquiry into "whether, in fact, the development plan is of primary benefit to . . . the developer [i.e., Corcoran Jennison], and private businesses which may eventually locate in the plan area [e.g., Pfizer], and in that regard, only of incidental benefit to the city." . . . Even the dissenting justices on the Connecticut Supreme Court agreed that respondents' development plan was intended to revitalize the local economy, not to serve the interests of Pfizer, Corcoran Jennison, or any other private party. This case, then, survives the meaningful rational basis review that in my view is required under the Public Use Clause.

Petitioners and their *amici* argue that any taking justified by the promotion of economic development must be treated by the courts as *per se* invalid, or at least presumptively invalid. Petitioners overstate the need for such a rule, however, by making the incorrect assumption that review under *Berman* and *Midkiff* imposes no meaningful judicial limits on the government's power to condemn any property it likes. A broad *per se* rule or a strong presumption of invalidity, furthermore, would prohibit a large number of government takings that have the purpose and expected effect of conferring substantial benefits on the public at large and so do not offend the Public Use Clause.

My agreement with the Court that a presumption of invalidity is not warranted for economic development takings in general, or for the particular takings at issue in this case, does not foreclose the possibility that a more stringent standard of review than that announced in [earlier cases] might be appropriate for a more narrowly drawn category of takings. There may be private transfers in which the risk of undetected impermissible favoritism of private parties is so acute that a presumption (rebuttable or otherwise) of invalidity is warranted under the Public Use Clause. This demanding level of scrutiny, however, is not required simply because the purpose of the taking is economic development.

This is not the occasion for conjecture as to what sort of cases might justify a more demanding standard, but it is appropriate to underscore aspects of the instant case that convince me no departure from [precedent] is appropriate here. This taking occurred in the context of a comprehensive development plan meant to address a serious city-wide depression, and the projected economic benefits of the project cannot be characterized as *de minimis*. The identity of most of the private beneficiaries were unknown at the time the city formulated its plans. The city complied with elaborate procedural requirements that facilitate review of the record and inquiry into the city's purposes. In sum, while there may be categories of cases in which the transfers are so suspicious, or the procedures employed so prone to abuse, or the purported benefits are so trivial or implausible, that courts should presume an impermissible private purpose, no such circumstances are present in this case.

Justice O'CONNOR, with whom Chief Justice REHNQUIST, Justice SCALIA, and Justice THOMAS join, dissenting.

This case returns us for the first time in over 20 years to the hard question of when a purportedly "public purpose" taking meets the public use requirement. It presents an issue of first impression: Are economic development takings constitutional? I would hold that they are not. We are guided by two precedents about the taking of real property by eminent domain. . . .

The Court's holdings in *Berman* and *Midkiff* were true to the principle underlying the Public Use Clause. In both those cases, the extraordinary, pre-condemnation use of the targeted property inflicted affirmative harm on society—in *Berman* through blight resulting from extreme poverty and in *Midkiff* through oligopoly resulting from extreme wealth. And in both cases, the relevant legislative body had found that eliminating the existing property use was necessary to remedy the harm. Thus a public purpose was realized when the harmful use was eliminated. Because each taking *directly* achieved a public benefit, it did not matter that the property was turned over to private use. Here, in contrast, New London does not claim that Susette Kelo's and Wilhelmina Dery's well-maintained homes are the source of any social harm. Indeed, it could not so claim without adopting the absurd argument that any single-family home that might be razed to make way for an apartment building, or any church that might be replaced with a retail store, or any small business that might be more lucrative if it were instead part of a national franchise, is inherently harmful to society and thus within the government's power to condemn.

In moving away from our decisions sanctioning the condemnation of harmful property use, the Court today significantly expands the meaning of public use. It holds that the sovereign may take private property currently put to ordinary private use, and give it over for new, ordinary private use, so long as the new use is predicted to generate some secondary benefit for the public—such as increased tax revenue, more jobs, maybe even aesthetic pleasure. But nearly any lawful use of real private property can be said to generate some incidental benefit to the public. Thus, if predicted (or even guaranteed) positive side-effects are enough to render transfer from one private party to another constitutional, then the words "for public use" do not realistically exclude *any* takings, and thus do not exert any constraint on the eminent domain power. . . .

Any property may now be taken for the benefit of another private party, but the fallout from this decision will not be random. The beneficiaries are likely to be those citizens with disproportionate influence and power in the political process, including large corporations and development firms. As for the victims, the government now has license to transfer property from those with fewer resources to those with more. The Founders cannot have intended this perverse result. "[T]hat alone is a *just* government," wrote James Madison, "which *impartially* secures to every man, whatever is his *own*."

Justice THOMAS, dissenting.
The most natural reading of the [Takings] Clause is that it allows the government to take property only if the government owns, or the public has a legal right to use, the property, as opposed to taking it for any public purpose or necessity whatsoever. At the time of the founding, dictionaries primarily defined the noun "use" as "[t]he act of employing any thing to any purpose." 2 S. Johnson, A Dictionary of the English Language 2194 (4th ed. 1773) (hereinafter Johnson). The term "use," moreover, "is from the Latin *utor*, which means "to use, make use of, avail one's self of, employ, apply, enjoy, etc." J. Lewis, Law of Eminent Domain §165, p. 224, n.4 (1888) (hereinafter

Lewis). When the government takes property and gives it to a private individual, and the public has no right to use the property, it strains language to say that the public is "employing" the property, regardless of the incidental benefits that might accrue to the public from the private use. The term "public use," then, means that either the government or its citizens as a whole must actually "employ" the taken property. . . .

Our current Public Use Clause jurisprudence, as the Court notes, has rejected this natural reading of the Clause. The Court adopted its modern reading blindly, with little discussion of the Clause's history and original meaning, in two distinct lines of cases: first, in cases adopting the "public purpose" interpretation of the Clause, and second, in cases deferring to legislatures' judgments regarding what constitutes a valid public purpose. Those questionable cases converged in the boundlessly broad and deferential conception of "public use" adopted by this Court in *Berman* and *Midkiff*, cases that take center stage in the Court's opinion. The weakness of those two lines of cases, and consequently *Berman* and *Midkiff*, fatally undermines the doctrinal foundations of the Court's decision. Today's questionable application of these cases is further proof that the "public purpose" standard is not susceptible of principled application. This Court's reliance by rote on this standard is ill advised and should be reconsidered. . . .

The Court relies almost exclusively on this Court's prior cases to derive today's far-reaching, and dangerous, result. . . . When faced with a clash of constitutional principle and a line of unreasoned cases wholly divorced from the text, history, and structure of our founding document, we should not hesitate to resolve the tension in favor of the Constitution's original meaning.

NOTES AND QUESTIONS

1. Justice Thomas noted in his dissent that "[o]ver 97 percent of the individuals forcibly removed from their homes by the 'slum-clearance' project upheld by this Court in *Berman* were black." Of course, if economic development programs are successful, the beneficiaries from increased employment and better-funded government services might also be poor and minority. How, if at all, should the Court take into account potential racial and class dimensions of the problem?
2. Are you persuaded by Justice O'Connor's effort to distinguish prior cases (including the *Midkiff* decision, which she authored)? Under her proposed approach, how would efforts to assemble land for new development fare in a city that had been destroyed in a flood or earthquake? What would it take to satisfy the test suggested by Justice Kennedy in his concurrence?
3. There is serious political opposition to the use of eminent domain for private development. After *Kelo*, forty-two states enacted legal reforms to limit the state use of eminent domain in response to that decision. In 2006, barely a year after Hurricane Katrina, citizens of Louisiana approved two amendments to the state constitution in response to *Kelo*. *See* 2006 La. Acts 851 (amending La. Const. art. I, §§ 4(B), 21(A), and adding art. VI, §21(D)); 2006 La. Acts 859 (adding La. Const. art. I, §4(H)). The amendments

put limits on the state's ability to transfer expropriated property and restricted the state's eminent domain power to traditional public uses such as transportation, flood control, and the construction of public buildings. One provision holds that neither "economic development" nor "any incidental benefit to the public" can be considered in assessing a state's "public purpose." *See* La. Const. art. I, §4(B). Law professor Frank Alexander argues that these restrictions slowed recovery efforts in New Orleans by making it harder to condemn damaged structures that had been abandoned by their owners. (Although Louisiana allows expropriation to eradicate blight, the meaning of that term is often debated and disputes cause delay.) *See* Frank S. Alexander, *Louisiana Land Reform in the Storm's Aftermath*, 53 Loy. L. Rev. 727 (2007).

D. LEARNING FROM THE RECENT PAST

Perhaps the best way to understand how law and politics affect disaster recovery is to see them in action. In the months following Hurricane Katrina, the New Orleans *Times-Picayune* ran a special series on how other cities had responded to sudden catastrophes. *See* Special Editions, *Ruin & Recovery*, Times-Picayune (New Orleans), 2005, http://www.nola.com/speced/ruinandrecovery (Aug. 1, 2009). Two events addressed in that series were the recovery of Kobe, Japan, after the Great Hanshin earthquake of 1995, and the recovery of Grand Forks, North Dakota, after the Mississippi River floods of 1997. Consider these two examples below. Following that, consider the rebuilding of New Orleans after Hurricane Katrina, which is offered as a third example.

1. KOBE, JAPAN

Jed Horne, Carving a Better City

Times-Picayune (New Orleans), Nov. 13, 2005, A1

Three months after the [Great Hanshin Earthquake of January 17, 1995]—the only [natural disaster] to have devastated a modern city as completely as Katrina wrecked New Orleans—Japan's sixth-largest city was still in ruins. Hundreds of acres of a once teeming metropolis had been reduced to rubble. Gas and water service was spotty. Roads and public transportation had collapsed, as had the morale of hundreds of thousands of evacuees still fighting for space in trailer-like emergency housing. . . .

Ten years later, one can stand on Flower Road across from Kobe's city hall and have no clue that a little after dawn on a frigid January morning in 1995, the building's fifth floor pancaked and suddenly became the fourth floor. Hulking office towers broke ranks and lurched into the street. A walk past the busy casbah of shops in the shadow of the elevated Hanshin Expressway near Kobe's eastern boundary offers no hint that hundreds of yards of the elevated superhighway shuddered on massive concrete columns and crashed sideways onto the ground. The port has repaired its caved-in wharves and the towering derricks that pluck shipping containers the size of small houses from freighter decks. Electrified trains come and go with clockwork precision over track that coiled like concertina wire during the quake. The screams of the elderly echo only in the memory of those who tried to free them from shattered cottages before they burned to death. A decade after the Great Hanshin Disaster killed 6,400 people — 90 percent of them in the 20 seconds the quake lasted — and charred hundreds of acres of once densely urban landscape, Kobe largely has healed. The skyline is studded with glistening new apartment towers. Low-rise neighborhoods have been replotted with wider, straighter streets and housing has been rebuilt with fireproof materials.

The comeback attests to what Lawrence Vale [of the Massachusetts Institute of Technology] calls the "resilience" of cities, and it is a mighty if not quite unstoppable force. Urban resilience brought back London after the blitz and downtown New York after Sept. 11. It restored Mexico City, a colossus, after the pulverizing 1985 earthquake, and smaller cities — Tulsa, [Oklahoma], Grand Forks, [North Dakota] — after terrible floods. . . .

The quake, which registered 7.3 on the Richter scale, damaged hundreds of thousands of buildings and destroyed 79,283 Kobe housing units, a figure roughly identical to estimates of New Orleans' eventual loss [after Hurricane Katrina].

About 300,000 victims of the earthquake took refuge in schoolhouses, gymnasiums and other makeshift shelters under deteriorating conditions as vile as the post-Katrina Superdome. Trapped there for weeks, they were then assigned, in some cases for years, to trailer camps.

Immediate Moratorium

The quake struck at 5:46 a.m. and within the hour Mayor Kazutoshi Sasayama had been picked up at his home by the vice mayor, his right-hand man and political heir apparent. In the 45 minutes it took to weave their way through streets not choked by fallen buildings and jumbled cars and buses, Sasayama tried to assess the damage. . . .

"Forty-five minutes of direct observation gave him enough information to start in on the whole thing," said Haruo Hayashi, a Kyoto University professor who specializes in earthquake mitigation. From the destruction he witnessed first-hand, Sasayama could roughly estimate the destruction he had not gotten close enough to see. In his head he adjusted the master plan accordingly, Hayashi said. . . .

Sasayama's first and most aggressive step[ ] in rebuilding Kobe was to impose a moratorium on rebuilding anything at all. The goal was simple: to prevent Kobe from following in the footsteps of post–World War II Tokyo and winding up with endless miles of shantytowns cobbled together by homeowners guided only by urgent need, limited resources and no central planning. . . . Sophisticated members of the Kobe intelligentsia, Hayashi among them, understood what Sasayama was up to and took heart in his tough stance as an early sign that Kobe was going to come back and come back better. But the grassroots political repercussions were toxic. The government was accused of exploiting the disaster to ram through a redesign of Kobe that otherwise would have been politically impossible. Planners were dubbed kajibadorobo by critics, using a Japanese term that translates more or less as "thieves at the scene of a fire." The vice mayor was undone by the intense hostility, which also took the form of lawsuits to stop City Hall. He committed suicide on the first anniversary of the quake. Sasayama rode out the firestorm and two years later was rewarded for the recovery's slowly emerging promise with an overwhelming re-election margin.

Strong Planning

For Sadaharu Ueno, who owned his home but, like many Japanese, not the land underneath it, being denied permission to rebuild seemed like being stripped of his only material asset of real worth. . . .

Ueno and his wife lived in their car for a day or two until they could get to a daughter's place in Osaka. They were eventually able to secure temporary housing in a box about the size of a shipping container set up by Ueno's employer, a manufacturer of metal processing machinery. It was their home for five years and far from [the Rokkomichi district, where they used to live]. But Ueno stayed in touch with old neighbors through their machizukuri kyo-gikai, or town-building organization. In due course the group, like others throughout Kobe, would demand — and get — a role in the process that led to the redevelopment of the area from a warren of traditional one- and two-story houses vulnerable to both quakes and fire, into a cluster of high-rise towers. They surround a small, well-tended park and playground popular with skateboarding adolescents, small children and mothers.

Ironically, the park was one of the features of the redevelopment most bitterly opposed by the machizukuri. The government held its ground, insisting that open space was a life-saving necessity in the event of a future quake and fire: a place of refuge for victims and a staging ground for recovery. . . .

Some of Ueno's neighbors gave up on Rokkomichi and moved away before the elaborate $840 million reconstruction plans could be implemented through a mix of public and private funding. But by riding herd on the government as a member of the machizukuri organization and refusing to relinquish his rights as a stakeholder in the community — albeit the lowly rights of a mere tenant — Ueno eventually secured compensation in the form of a rent-subsidized two-bedroom apartment on the fifth floor of one of the towers. It's a decent place, but not as big as the house destroyed in the earthquake, and the subsidy lasts for only five years. After that, the Uenos are on their own. . . .

Moving Quickly

Mayor Sasayama's planners had raced furiously to create a vision for Kobe's recovery in time for their funding request to be included in the national budget.

They were ably assisted by other professionals. Kazuyoshi Ohnishi, an architect and professor at Kobe University, mustered 1,000 student volunteers and within weeks they had completed a building-by-building assessment of the damage. . . . Tokyo responded with $58 billion, chiefly to repair infrastructure throughout the prefecture centered around Kobe, in the first three years after the quake. In seeking money to rebuild burned-out cityscapes, Kobe proposed "land readjustments," a mechanism in place since the end of World War II that encouraged replacing narrow winding streets and wooden houses with wider avenues and fewer structures, all of them built with fire-resistant materials. . . .

Some properties were expropriated outright to make room for the improved street grid, and most lots were trimmed. The tradeoff was the higher property values that would be realized in a better-built community, city officials argued. All told, 11 ravaged neighborhoods were subjected to the land-readjustment process. In Rokkomichi and two other more drastically overhauled communities, the government built the new housing—mostly high-rise condominiums—and moved residents into them. To generate additional money, they added floors over and above what was needed to accommodate the original population. The extra space was sold on the open market to offset construction costs. . . .

Kobe's grand plan cost Rokkomichi some of its residents. As the plans made their way through the Japanese legislature, the residents with the most at stake in their outcome were kept in the dark for months, an interval during which many of them gave up. Today, only a third of the original community abides in Rokkomichi. The rest are newcomers. . . .

The earthquake response required different thinking, Tarumi came to realize. Neighborhoods were not just about bricks and mortar and money. Their vigor and resilience hinged on flesh-and-blood people, many of whom—including Ueno and even a pillar of the business establishment like Kusuba—were turning up at City Hall to wave placards in the faces of Tarumi's staff as the bureaucrats arrived at work. Eventually, the government not only yielded to community input but came to see positive value in formalizing relations with the machizukuri organizations. . . .

But Tarumi makes no apologies for the goals of the planning process: the mix of earthquake- and fire-proof towers and low-rise structures that replaced the rickety traditional neighborhoods all across Kobe, 110,000 units of public and private housing that were created in short order. Not only was haste necessary to secure funding in the upcoming fiscal year, Tarumi saw himself in a race against the dangerous hodge-podge that would result if homeowners simply rebuilt what they had lost, with gaping holes left by those who chose not to return. Kobe needed a guiding vision of its future both to mitigate future earthquake disaster and the equally costly economic blight that had set in when planning principles were ignored. The alternative was chaos and further degradation as already traumatized communities came back partially or not at all. . . .

Opposed to Handouts

Unlike FEMA in the United States, the central government apparatus responsible for emergency management in Japan is philosophically opposed to direct handouts. While Kobe's postquake infrastructure was being upgraded, private business and individual householders were accorded tax breaks and temporary exemptions, but otherwise left to fend for themselves. Eighty percent of Kobe's 2,000 small-to-medium-size businesses failed. . . .

Eventually funded to the tune of $9 billion by the central government, a Special Fund for the Great Hanshin Disaster was used to provide low-interest loans to Kobe city government, which in turn passed along some of the money in the form of rent subsidies, aid to the elderly and handicapped, and the like. At heart, these were violations of the ban on direct subsidies to quake victims, but the central government had the good sense to look the other away.

Still Recovering

[While Kobe's recovery is impressive, there is below the surface a more complicated reality.] The port, for example, has not come all the way back and schemes to reorient Kobe's economy toward tourism, robotics and information technology remain nascent. At the local level, Nagata, to cite just one laggard community, has not rebounded to its prequake vitality.

Private-sector investment has been inattentive to the needs of the working poor and instead has followed well-to-do residents to the east end of the city, closer to Osaka, epicenter of the megalopolis of 15 million to 20 million people that includes Kobe and provides a source of work for many of its residents.

Nagata's population is still off by almost 20 percent. Huge apartment towers have gone up along the edges of the community, but many apartments are empty, as are a goodly number of storefronts in the enormous triple-decker shopping plaza that replaced the Taisho Suji arcade, a covered street market that became an inferno after the quake.

Kobe remains . . . vulnerable to another quake . . . but no one seriously proposed abandoning the city. The consensus that immediately prevailed within the governing class was to rebuild, not as it was but as it needed to be to assure greater public safety in the future.

NOTES AND QUESTIONS

1. Kobe is one of the most-studied examples of urban recovery in disaster literature. The take-home lesson is often said to be that successful recovery depends on fast action and decisive leadership. In what ways did those elements benefit Kobe's recovery? In what ways did they create barriers and hardship?

2. Jed Horne writes that after the Hanshin earthquake demolished Kobe, "no one seriously proposed abandoning the city." Should that option have been on the table? If so, how should the decision whether to abandon or rebuild have been reached? Would a cost-benefit approach to the question be helpful? *See* Robert W. Hahn, *The Economics of Rebuilding Cities: Reflections after Katrina*, THE ECONOMISTS' VOICE, Vol. 2 (2005), No. 4, Article 1, http://www. bepress.com/ev/vol2/iss4/art1 (arguing that cost-benefit analysis provides a starting point for deciding whether to abandon a city after it has been destroyed by "nature (or an enemy)").

3. The truth is that after a major city is ruined by catastrophe, whether natural or manmade, it is almost always rebuilt. Lawrence J. Vale & Thomas J. Campanella, *Introduction: The Cities Rise Again, in* THE RESILIENT CITY: HOW MODERN CITIES RECOVER FROM DISASTER 3, 4 (Lawrence J. Vale & Thomas J. Campanella eds., 2005) (offering first-century Pompeii as an exception to the rule). After the San Francisco earthquake and fire of 1906, city leaders sought to quell debates about development in an earthquake zone by

downplaying the role of the earthquake and instead emphasizing the more destructive role played by the ensuing fires. That the earthquake *caused* the fires was a point, it was hoped, many outside investors would miss. *See generally*, PHILIP L. FRADKIN, THE GREAT EARTHQUAKE AND FIRESTORMS OF 1906: HOW SAN FRANCISCO NEARLY DESTROYED ITSELF (2005). Today it is much the same. When, in 1993, Hurricane Andrew walloped Dade County, Florida, politicians clamored to provide an $8 billion aid package to resurrect damaged communities; no one seriously considered letting it all go. The question of whether to rebuild will surface again in the discussion of New Orleans.

2. GRAND FORKS, NORTH DAKOTA

GORDON RUSSELL, RISING FROM THE TIDE

TIMES-PICAYUNE (New Orleans), Dec. 11, 2005, A1

Michael Brown had been one of the lucky ones, or so it seemed, when his house, at the south end of town, escaped major damage in the catastrophic Red River flood that swamped the city of Grand Forks in April 1997.

But three years later, the shadow of a wrecking ball hung over Brown's home, which stood in the way of an ambitious flood-control project that was supposed to protect the Grand Forks region from future calamity. Brown no longer felt lucky. He was angry, and he was not alone. Deciding it was time to put up or shut up, Brown, a gynecologist with a busy practice, ran for mayor and won.

Now, more than eight years after the disaster that forever altered Grand Forks and its little sister across the Red River — East Grand Forks, Minn. — Brown is a changed man. With the benefit of hindsight, he sees the buyouts as necessary, even though they spelled doom for more than 1,000 homes, including his.

In a sense, Brown's story is the story of Grand Forks. In moving from disaster to cleanup to rebuilding to recovery, the community ran the emotional gamut from dismay to grief to anger to acceptance.

The years after the flood were marked by a series of wrenching decisions and debates — in particular, over which neighborhoods and homes to protect and which to condemn. Bad feelings boiled over.

But today, most residents and city leaders will say their cities are better places than they were before the flood. After an initial dip estimated at 10 percent, the population of the two towns is the same as it was in1997. And though they all wish the flood had never occurred, residents say the flood brought with it an odd kind of opportunity, a way to correct some of the mistakes of the past.

That hasn't smoothed away all the scar tissue, however. Many business owners and residents are still trying to dig out from under post-flood debt. The new system of levees and floodwalls, once targeted for completion in 2004, won't be finished until the spring of 2007 at the earliest. Only in the past year or two has flood recovery ceased to be Topic No. 1 on the civic agenda. . . .

Unprecedented until Now

The Grand Forks catastrophe entered the record books as the worst flood to befall an American city — until Katrina. Eighty percent of the city was inundated with muddy, sewage-laced water. Nearly every resident was evacuated, most by car, a few by boat or helicopter. Fires raged out of control, with firefighters powerless to stop them.

When the foul waters receded, the tribulation didn't end. In the weeks after the flood, residents wept as they mucked out their ruined homes, tossing treasured mementos, moldy drywall and busted appliances onto the curbs. Evacuees stayed where they could: in impromptu shelters, in distant hotel rooms, on borrowed sofas. As the Gulf Coast holds its collective breath during hurricane season, so does Grand Forks in the spring, particularly when spring follows a brutal winter.

The winter of 1996-97 was one of those. In North Dakota, blizzards are given names, the last of which — Hannah — arrived April 4 and dumped 6 inches of ice and snow, adding to a considerable base piled up by the previous seven storms.

The flood danger in the Grand Cities owes to several factors: The Red River flows north, toward Canada. It freezes in wintertime, and as the thaw arrives, the river tends to back up because the ice farther north — downstream — takes longer to melt. Making matters worse, the channel is shallow, and the surrounding country, actually a prehistoric lake bed, is pancake flat: perfect for widespread flooding. In April 1997, the question facing Grand Forks was not whether the river would flood, but how high the water would get. The National Weather Service called for the river to crest at 49 feet, more than 30 feet above its normal level but still within the capacity of the city's levee system. Sandbagging raised the levee to 52 feet, a reasonable margin of safety, it seemed.

Unfortunately, the forecasts were wrong. The water eventually topped 54 feet. . . .

The levee at Lincoln Park, a neighborhood nestled in a Red River oxbow, was the first to be overtopped, and the river lapped at the rooftops before spreading through the rest of the city. Normally about 110 yards wide, the Red soon measured 22 miles across in places. Officials hurriedly built backup levees of clay and gravel, with varying success. The electricity was ordered shut off in an attempt to prevent fires, but a massive blaze flared up anyway, destroying 11 downtown buildings.

[Despite the damage, there were no fatalities.] Nearly everyone evacuated in advance of the rising waters, and the few who didn't were promptly rescued.

Swift Federal Response

As the water receded and residents began to filter back into town, the basic outlines of Grand Forks' recovery took shape.

The federal response was generally praised. FEMA officials arrived right away. . . . The U.S. Small Business Administration also was on the scene quickly. . . .

Less than two months after the disaster, the [U.S. Army] Corps of Engineers proposed a series of new flood-protection plans for the two towns. Engineers from both municipalities did the same. And days later, Congress had approved a $5.6 billion aid bill for the region that included money for buyouts, business loans, new infrastructure and other needs. . . . Most residents and observers credit the area's political leadership, as well as the federal agencies themselves, for the early successes. Standing out in particular: the mayor of Grand Forks, Pat Owens, a 5-foot dynamo who became a media darling, though she would fail to retain the affection of her constituents. . . .

The congressional delegations of the two affected states banded together to create a unified front in Washington. They were aided, many locals believe, by a downturn in the news cycle that put Grand Forks' plight at the top of the national agenda, if only temporarily.

Tackling Tough Questions

Owens quickly named three of her top administrators — the city engineer, the director of community development and the finance director — to be co-chairmen of the recovery. The "tri-chairs" had broad power, though their recommendations were ultimately subject to approval by politicians. The central questions facing them were . . . : Where should we rebuild? What areas, if any, should be written off? Where should our new flood-protection system go, and how strong must it be? How should we spend our aid?

[O]ne of the first priorities was to inspect homes for damage and determine whether they met the federal threshold of "substantial damage." [U]nder the National Flood Insurance Program, which FEMA administers, a home in the flood plain that sustains 50 percent damage cannot be fixed or rebuilt unless it is raised above the flood level.

In the Grand Cities, about 1,300 homes and businesses were placed in that category. Because of the area's topography and local construction styles, it was rarely practical for an owner to try to raise such a home above flood level, an option available to more New Orleans homeowners given the lack of basements here.

Generally, Grand Cities officials refused to issue building permits to owners of such structures. Instead, they offered voluntary buyouts using federal grant money. If a home was deemed eligible, the city offered the owner a price based on the preflood tax assessment.

In several neighborhoods, the decisions were relatively easy. The hardest-hit section of Grand Forks was Lincoln Park, where at least 300 homes had been inundated to the rooftops. Homes near the river in the Central Park and Riverside Park neighborhoods also were candidates.

Across the river, three low-lying neighborhoods were similarly swamped: The Point, at the confluence of the Red and the Red Lake rivers; Sherlock Park; and Griggs Park. Homeowners in these areas were offered buyouts as well, although East Grand Forks used private appraisers rather than tax assessments to estimate fair market value.

On both sides of the river, any settlement a homeowner had received from flood insurance was subtracted from the buyout offer.

That policy was controversial. Owners who had carried insurance kvetched that they were being penalized in getting the same payout as the uninsured, despite having paid premiums, sometimes for years. . . .

Still, in both cities, the first phase of buyouts went relatively smoothly. The ban on renovation left many homeowners holding title to useless property. They weren't happy about it, but the decision was an easy one: Take the money and run. Four months after the flood, the city had already begun acquiring ruined homes.

"We moved pretty quick, and most of that was attributable to the fact that people wanted to get on with their lives," said Karl Lindquist, city attorney for East Grand Forks.

Even if most homeowners thought the buyouts fair, the disaster left many of them impaired financially. . . .

Most of the worst-hit areas contained old, low-priced housing stock. Lincoln Park, for instance, was dominated by young families and older couples in or near retirement. Homes often sold for as little as $40,000, and many residents held small mortgages, or none at all. But the newer homes in farther-flung subdivisions that were available after the flood often carried price tags of $110,000 and up.

Homeowners were forced to bridge the gap. In many cases, they had savings or could borrow from family members, but for many middle-aged couples, that meant making tough choices—and some retirements got postponed.

Both cities offered a similar program that took some, but not all, of the sting out of the deal. Anyone who bought a home within the city limits of either town got a $10,000 loan, forgivable after five years if the homeowner stayed in place.

Seeing the need for affordable housing, Grand Forks officials got into the development business directly, with a two-phase subdivision known as Congressional in the western part of town, across Interstate 29. By building on smaller lots and leveraging federal money to drive down costs, they were able to sell new homes for as little as $90,000.

Buyouts Extended

It wasn't only those who were bought out who had to make adjustments. Many of those outside the buyout areas were often faced with the unpleasant task of having to renovate a partially damaged home, often without the benefit of an insurance check.

City officials soon extended buyouts beyond the condemned areas. Eventually, anyone whose home was substantially damaged—regardless of the condition of the surrounding area, and whether or not the home lay in the 100-year-flood plain—could sell to the city.

Grand Forks, which had received $171 million in federal block grants, used that money rather than FEMA hazard- mitigation grants to buy the properties in later phases. The reason: Properties bought with block-grant money could eventually be redeveloped, whereas FEMA-financed buyouts required the city to leave the lot fallow.

The last phase of the buyout program was the most contentious because it involved purchasing about 300 properties, many barely damaged, that stood in the way of, or outside, the proposed flood-protection system. . . .

Meanwhile, the city's engineer, Ken Vein, and the Corps of Engineers were in basic agreement that the new levee system had to be located well to the west of the river to create a larger flood plain, but the plan would have condemned a large swath of the city, including many of its oldest neighborhoods. A similar arrangement was conceived on the less-populated east bank, but it was less controversial because fewer homes were affected.

The flood was caused by the inability to push enough water through the constricted channel between Grand Forks and East Grand Forks, a passage that, during the flood, carried nearly as much water as the Mississippi River. Any solution had to allow for greater flow; the easiest way to achieve that was to make the area between the levees wider. . . .

Though knocking down the town's riverside neighborhoods was an unpleasant prospect, it's not as if Grand Forks had no place to grow. [T]he prairie to the west of Grand Forks is an all but limitless expanse of cheap land less prone to flooding. The city could easily expand in that direction, and it has.

But Vein's original plan, which he called "very conservative" from an engineering standpoint, was seen as draconian, and it was quickly shot down. The corps, which ultimately would have to approve and largely finance most of the flood-protection system, was a tougher foe for those who wanted to see more of the city saved. . . .

The corps eventually signed on to a plan that included an intertwined mix of levees and L-shaped floodwalls that allowed the corps to build in places closer to the river and save homes. . . .

The plan was finalized in 2000, when the corps and the two cities signed a pact settling the levee footprints and each party's responsibilities. The project's total cost was $403 million. When it's complete, residents of the two towns will no longer be required to carry flood insurance policies.

Vein, a modest and self-effacing man, said he thinks the revised plan that grew out of the sometimes-heated discussions is superior to the ones he and the corps initially proposed.

"A conservative engineer is going to say, 'Let's move the whole city west,'" he said. "But I think there is a balance. I think it (the final plan) is a far better plan." Even if the levee plan was eventually made more palatable, the whole process was endlessly picked apart by citizens still reeling from the flood.

Some people thought Mayor Owens had turned over too much policy-making power to administrators such as Vein, who, while their professional credentials were unquestioned, were less versed in politics. The anger manifested itself in various ways. Whereas preflood City Council meetings had often drawn a handful of spectators, sometimes-seething crowds of more than 1,000 jammed the council's temporary meeting rooms in an auditorium at the University of North Dakota on the town's western fringe. . . . Ultimately, there was a fairly spectacular political bloodletting, at least by the sober standards of North Dakota.

Rebuilding Controversies

The fallout wasn't completely attributable to the buyout program. Many people were struggling to repair and rebuild, and they saw some of the plans put forward by city leaders as boondoggles. . . .

[T]he city pumped tens of millions of dollars into its stately brick-and-brownstone downtown, which had suffered from blight before the flood and fire. . . .

The city offered to sell buildings to retailers and restaurateurs at deep discounts, and then gave buyers renovation grants to boot. Many store owners also took advantage of low-interest SBA loans.

The city also spent millions on a two-building office complex known as the Corporate Center. The city-owned buildings were slow to fill, and though one is almost fully leased, the other still has a high vacancy rate, although O'Leary said rents have covered the cost of the buildings. . . .

Today the city's downtown is more vibrant than most older cities, and more attractive than the seedy place it was before the flood, most say. Still, though, there are missing teeth in the cityscape where buildings used to stand. . . .

Today, though, much of the bad feeling [about political decisions made during the recovery] seems to have washed away, owing in part to a palpable sense of shared sacrifice that appears to have helped the cities weather devastation and recovery.

Locals noted that High Plains folk are a hardy breed, and they help one another out. . . .

The collectivist mindset owes in part to Grand Forks' homogeneity. Light-hearted insults about the relative merits of Swedish or Norwegian ancestry are about the closest thing to ethnic tension in Grand Forks, where nearly everyone is not only white but also Lutheran.

Today, even sometime critics of the regime in place during the flood . . . now say the group made tough but fair decisions. . . .

"The leadership style you need to direct a recovery is not always a leadership style that makes everyone happy," Vein said. "If you try to do a recovery by consensus, nobody will agree and nothing will happen. So you do what's right, and it may not be popular."

NOTES AND QUESTIONS

1. Notice the influential roles played by Mayor Pat Owens and the congressional delegations of North Dakota and Minnesota. Their skills and cooperation were essential in attracting positive media attention and in bringing federal dollars to their states. To what degree should a city's ability to recover from disaster depend on the skills and connections of its political representatives? Is that relationship inevitable, or would it be possible to design a national relief strategy that is less dependent on the identities of individual politicians?

2. The buyout program in Grand Forks illustrates the difficulty in designing a compensation program that is at once effective, fair, and forward-looking. To be an effective tool for redevelopment, a program has to include a large portion of owners, including, it would seem, owners who chose to under-insure. Including the underinsured will seem unfair to neighboring owners who did insure but who are eligible for no larger benefit. As for being forward-looking, what message does a community send by aiding flooded homeowners who are underinsured? Note also that the city chose to use federal community block grant money for some buyouts rather than FEMA money so that recipients could rebuild on the flood-prone land. Was this a good idea? One explanation for the city's choices is the belief that to succeed

politically, any buyout plan must have broad appeal. And broad appeal requires balancing and compromise. In your estimation, how well did the city do?

3. NEW ORLEANS, LOUISIANA

The story of New Orleans' recovery after Hurricane Katrina is still being written. And that story, or course, has many perspectives. Below is a small sample of some of those perspectives—one concerned with the city's geographic footprint, one concerned with racial and economic identity, and the last concerned with demographic and economic indicators.

RICHARD CAMPANELLA, BIENVILLE'S DILEMMA: A HISTORICAL GEOGRAPHY
OF NEW ORLEANS

351-354 (2008)

Various philosophies have emerged on the rebuilding of New Orleans, each with its own logic, passion, experts, and dogma. But all can be boiled down to a simple line on a map, separating areas recommended for rebuilding from those deemed best returned to nature. Where people locate their build/no-build line says as much about them—and how they view and weigh science, economics, social, and humanistic values—as it says about the geographical future of New Orleans.

One philosophy recommends the total abandonment of the metropolis. Its advocates essentially draw the build/no-build line at the metropolis' upper boundary . . . or above [the northern shore of Lake Pontchartrain, whose southern shore forms the upper boundary of new Orleans]. St. Louis University geologist Timothy M. Kusky first voiced the "abandonist" philosophy in a *Boston Globe* editorial entitled "Time to Move to Higher Ground" which later earned him a national audience on CBS *60 Minutes*. He readily acknowledged:

> New Orleans is one of America's great historic cities, and our *emotional response* to the disaster is to rebuild it grander and greater than before. However this may not be the *most rational* or *scientifically sound* response and could lead to *even greater human catastrophe* and *financial loss* in the future.

Abandonists like Kusky tend to be pragmatic and fiscally conservative; for them it is a rational question of hard science, hard dollars, and body counts. In making their case, they cite only the gloomiest scientific data on subsidence, coastal erosion, and sea-level rise, and dismiss humanist and cultural arguments as "emotional" or "nostalgic." Abandonists almost always have nothing to lose personally if the city does disappear, and feel no obligation to propose financial compensation plans for those who do. They are loathed in New Orleans, but occupy a seat at the table in the national discourse.

At the opposite end are those who advocate maintaining the urban footprint at all costs. Unlike abandonists, "maintainers" see this as primarily a humanist and cultural question, rather than a scientific or engineering one. To be against maintaining all neighborhoods is to be against people and against culture—worse yet, against *certain* peoples and *certain* cultures.

Maintainers tend to be passionate, oftentimes angry, and for good reason: many are flood victims and have everything to lose if the build/no-build line crosses their homes. If a levee can be built well enough to protect *them*, they reason, why not extend it around *us?* Among the most outspoken maintainers are social activists who interpret any postdiluvian adjustment to the urban perimeter as a conspiracy of "politically conservative, economically neoliberal power elites" who "are doing everything in their power to prevent (working-class African Americans) from returning." Ignoring scientific data and fiscal constraints, maintainers push the build/no-build line beyond the rural fringes of St. Bernard Parish, even all the way to the Gulf of Mexico.

In between fall the "concessionists," usually aficionados of the city, particularly its historical heart, and often residents of its unflooded sections. Concessionists struggle to balance troubling scientific data with treasured social and cultural resources. Their answer: concede certain low-lying modern subdivisions to nature — areas which, incidentally, they never found structurally appealing in the first place — and increase population density and flood protection in the higher, historically significant areas. Concessionists argue that, in the long run, this would reduce costs, minimize grief, protect the environment, and save lives. Concessionists sometimes failed to recognize, however, that footprint shrinkage itself costs money, in the form of fair and immediate compensation to homeowners.

Sensitive to accusations of elitism, concessionists soften their message with careful wordsmithing and confusing maps. They place their build/no-build line somewhere between those of the abandonists and the maintainers — sometimes near the Industrial Canal [east of the city's core] and the lakefront, usually to the exclusion of the distant, charmless, low-lying subdivisions of New Orleans East [a mainly African American part of the city]. Concessionists enjoy widespread support among many educated professionals who live on high ground, but encounter fierce resistance among maintainers, who often accuse them [of] being, at best, unrealistic utopian dreamers, and at worst, elitist, classist, racist land-grabbers.

Reports that rural, isolated lower Plaquemines Parish — home to only 14,000 people, or 2 percent of the region's population — may not receive full funding for levee maintenance seems to have spawned a fourth philosophy: push the build/no-build line down just past Belle Chasse, the only major community in upper Plaquemines Parish that adjoins the metropolitan area. Advocates include city dwellers, both concessionists and maintainers, who stand to benefit from the abandonment of lower Plaquemines because it would clear the path for aggressive coastal restoration while reducing the price tag on their own protection. Let the sediment-laden waters of the Mississippi River replenish those eroding marshes, they might contend; we need to restore them to buffer the metropolis against storm surges. What about the rural peoples who have called those marshes home for over a century? Well, as geologist Kusky put it in his now-famous abandonist editorial, it's "time to move to higher ground."

Thus, social, cultural, and humanistic values, plus a sense of personal investment, tend to push the build/no-build line in a downriver direction, while scientific and financial values nudge the line upriver. What to make of all this?

First, even the most ardent lovers of New Orleans should refrain from loathing the abandonists. After all, concessionists (and those maintainers willing to sacrifice lower Plaquemines) are essentially making the same abandonist arguments that earned Kusky the enduring hatred of many New Orleanians. They're just applying them below different lines on the map.

Second, we should probably only pencil in whatever build/no-build lines we draw, because we may well wish to change them if the going gets rough. Others have. Illinois Republican Rep. J. Dennis Hastert was among the first to hint at abandonment when he said rebuilding New Orleans "doesn't make sense to me. And it's a question that certainly we should ask." Shaken by angry responses, he later clarified his statement: "I am not advocating that the city be abandoned or relocated. . . ." Wallace, Roberts & Todd, a design firm hired to advise the [Bring New Orleans Back] Commission, at first professed a bold maintainer philosophy ("If you plan on shrinkage, shrinkage is what you'll get") but ended up recommending concessions in their final report to the Commission. Even Kusky softened his abandonist advice and suggested the possibility of "newer, higher, stronger seawalls" for "the business and historic parts of the city."

I, too, as a geographer with both physical and cultural interests, have grappled with my concessionist recommendations when confronted by the tragic personal stories of individuals who desperately want to maintain the world they once knew and loved. Should another hurricane of the magnitude of Katrina strike New Orleans, we may see build/no-build lines erased and redrawn *en masse:* maintainers may become concessionists, concessionists may be willing to concede more, and abandonists will increase their ranks.

Finally, beware of those who claim to speak solely "for science," or "for the people." This is a complicated, interdisciplinary dilemma. The social scientist needs to be at the table as much as the physical scientist; the humanist deserves a voice as much as the economist; the poor renter of a shotgun house should be heard as much as the rich owner of a mansion. We should acknowledge that a tangle of personal, cultural, financial, nostalgic, emotional, practical, and scientific factors underlie which philosophy — abandon, maintain, or concede — we uphold for the future of New Orleans, and that *this is OK; this is acceptable.*

Postscript: Who Prevailed?

[Mayor Ray Nagin of New Orleans,] supported by most flooded homeowners and a vociferous cadre of local officials, opted for a politically safe *laissez-faire* repopulation and rebuilding policy. Abetting their victory, more through passivity than active support, was the federal government: FEMA's revised Advisory Base Flood Elevation maps, released in 2006, continued to make flood insurance available to heavily flooded areas, thus encouraging their rebuilding. And no federal buy-out plan promised compensation to homeowners and business owners who would be forced off their land in a concessionist (eminent domain) mandate coming from city, state, or federal levels. No sane person "concedes" his or her major life investment without fair compensation.

The apparent outcome: *Let people return and rebuild as they can and as they wish, and we'll act on the patterns as they fall in place.* The maintainers prevailed in drawing the build/no-build line along the existing, pre-Katrina urban edge (though the possibility of a lower-Plaquemines concession remains). Whether that line gets erased and redrawn again—by concessionists or by abandonists—will be determined by the insurance industry, by mortgage companies, by property values, by federal intervention, by disappointed residents forced to re-address their initial post-Katrina rebuilding stance, and ultimately, by nature.

Mtanguliza Sanyika, Katrina and the Condition of Black New Orleans: The Struggle for Justice, Equity, and Democracy

Race, Place and Environmental Justice after Hurricane Katrina: Struggles to Reclaim, Rebuild, and Revitalize New Orleans and the Gulf Coast, 87, 104-110 (Robert D. Bullard & Beverly Wright eds., 2009)

Since Katrina in August 2005 . . . a number of key and highly visible public issues have surfaced that were simmering before and after Katrina. The recovery, rebuilding, and revitalization of the city are the dominant public policy concerns three years after the storm and flood. The levee repair can't be trusted, schools are still troubled, health care remains inadequate, street violence continues, contract decisions and jobs for locals are questionable, the prisons are overcrowded with black youth, and political control of City Hall remains tenuous. It is beyond the scope of this chapter to adequately treat all of the issues, but there are at least seven that are sometimes less obvious and require additional analysis and public debate by all sectors.

First, there is no consensus among the stakeholders about the future of the city. One of the first rules of recovery after a disaster is development of a consensus on a vision for the future. That never happened in New Orleans because the elites attempted to impose their vision of a smaller, whiter, richer city on the body politic. The black citizenry was not consulted, has never agreed to this vision, and thus does not trust the motives of the elites. . . .

This lack of consensus initially set the recovery back by at least nine to twelve months. Furthermore, the capacity to manage a recovery may be in direct proportion to the presence or absence of a consensus among the body politic. There is no shortage of recovery plans; what is missing is the citywide plan that reflects the vision of the majority African American population. While the formal planning process has momentarily helped to define a vision, evidence suggests that the elites continue to challenge perceived black and/or public interests.

Recent elite-backed efforts reveal a fundamental difference in vision between the business and power elites and the many citizens regarding what is the public good and the desired future of the city. . . . New Orleans remains a city without an agreed-upon vision and is divided by race and class divisions that may not be resolved anytime soon. Dialogue is difficult because of the elite's inability to accept power sharing with the black and working-class majority.

A second issue is the crystallization of the public housing crisis, and the uncertain future of its residents. Before Katrina, 14,000 families occupied public housing in the city. Since Katrina, virtually all of the public housing projects have remained closed, although they only sustained first-floor water damage, with no apparent structural damage. [The U.S. Department of Housing and Urban Development] has proclaimed its intent to reopen approximately 2,100 of its total of 5,000 units, and to demolish the St. Bernard, C.W. Peete, Magnolia, and Lafitte projects. . . . Allegedly, mixed-income developments will replace the former units, but this remains to be seen. . . .

A fourth and highly contentious issue was the development of the recovery plan and strategy for both neighborhood-specific plans/projects and citywide infrastructure repair. Unfortunately, the federal dollars for the recovery were sent not to the city but instead to an appointed state-created entity, the Louisiana Recovery Authority (LRA), which has emerged as the "heavyweight" in the recovery effort with direct control of more than $10 billion of the federal recovery funding, which has been poorly administered. Residents have encountered nightmarish problems in applying for and receiving LRA funds for their home repair.

The City Council initiated a neighborhood planning process—the Lambert Advisory plans—primarily in the "wet" or more devastated (and predominantly black) neighborhoods of the city to support and facilitate the initiatives taken by residents to plan for their neighborhood recovery. FEMA chose not to fund the City Council planning initiative, and the LRA then pursued independent funding of its own planning citywide and neighborhood planning initiative through the Greater New Orleans Foundation (GNOF) and the Rockefeller Foundation. More important, decision making, coordination, and resource allocation were potentially housed in this collaborative, and the projects of the wet neighborhoods might be delayed until the dry neighborhoods have completed their process.

Many felt the plan would dilute the power of the mayor and council. Many on the council in effect constitute a shadow government. In part, this conclusion was based on both public and private statements of the LRA/GNOF operatives that suggested a lack of confidence in the ability of either this mayoral administration or the City Council to effectively manage the recovery effort. This intervention by the LRA/GNOF collaborative has led to the suspicion that the elites were once again attempting to exert control over elected officials and dilute black interests. A broad perception in the black community was that at stake was a determination of which neighborhoods were viable, or the resurfacing of the footprint reduction proposal, or the capture of the federal infrastructure dollars for the private sector's desired development projects. Whatever the original intent, or the intended motives, the LRA/GNOF process morphed into the Unified New Orleans Plan (UNOP), which was in fundamental conflict with the neighborhood dynamics of the City Council's Lambert Advisory plans and projects. This conflict resulted in enormous confusion and further racial and class animosity, some of which remains to this day.

A fifth issue is related to the implementation of the recovery strategy that resulted from the planning initiatives after the completion and acceptance of the Lambert Advisory neighborhood plans by the City Council and LRA. In June 2007, the city also adopted a required parish-wide plan, the Orleans Parish Strategic Recovery and Revitalization Plan (OPSRRP). The parish plan was to be a synthesis of the GNOF/UNOP citywide and neighborhood plans and the

Lambert Advisory plans and projects for the wet neighborhoods, and the LRA-backed UNOP citywide, infrastructure, and neighborhood plans. The OPSRRP was to be implemented by the newly created Office of Recovery and Development Administration (ORDA), headed by a nationally recognized planner, Dr. Ed Blakely.

The AALP had invited Dr. Blakely and other prominent African American planners to visit New Orleans on three occasions and assess its potential for recovery and rebuilding. These scoping visits and assessments provided Dr. Blakely with the opportunity to observe the damage firsthand and conclude that all of New Orleans could be rebuilt and that footprint reduction was unnecessary. Eventually these assessment visits led to Mayor [Ray] Nagin's decision to retain Dr. Blakely as the executive director of the recovery effort. . . .

The implementation plan for the OPSRRP divides the city's Katrina-impacted neighborhoods into three categories based on level of damage and treatment required. It then prioritizes 17 target development zones, with the Lower Ninth Ward, [New Orleans East], and Gentilly [near the geographic center of the city] at the top of the list. Initial funding from the LRA of $117 million has been committed along with about $294 million from other disaster loan waiver payments for projects in the neighborhoods and the city.

There is tension regarding what percentage of the disaster funds should be allocated citywide and what percentage should be allocated to the neighborhoods. There is also tension about the appropriate roles and capacity of the newly reconstituted New Orleans Redevelopment Agency (NORA) in property transfer and property development versus the appropriate roles of the ORDA. . . .

A sixth major issue is the tension between indigenous workers and the immigrant Hispanic workers who have been brought in by contractors under highly questionable circumstances.

Unfortunately, local contractors have exploited Hispanic workers, many of whom are undocumented workers simply seeking a better life for themselves and their families. That economic interest often clashes with the interests of African American stakeholders who have been excluded from the rebuilding workforce.

The working and housing conditions that are often accepted by immigrant workers are unacceptable to indigenous African Americans, who know that U.S. labor laws and regulations are being significantly violated by such avaricious contractors. The 2006 report of the Advancement Project suggests avenues for intervention in the interests of both indigenous African Americans and immigrant workers (Advancement Project and National Immigrants Law Center 2006). It is in the interests of blacks, Latinos, and all progressive and human-centered peoples to support enforcement of worker protections and the right of black workers to access jobs in the rebuilding of New Orleans.

A seventh and final issue is the capacity of some return of residents to the city after three years. There are many residents in the diaspora who have now settled in their adopted city and may choose not to return. Rents in [New Orleans] are out of control and are beyond the reach of most low-income citizens in the diaspora. Since public housing developments are being demolished and gentrification has not abated, there are serious problems of affordability of the city to its former residents. For instance, a two-bedroom apartment that formerly rented for $450 a month now goes for $750; a three-bedroom apartment formerly renting for $700 to $800 a month now goes for $1,200 to $1,300 a month. Home prices have also jumped by as much as 25 to 30 percent in some areas of the city.

These seven issues are not intended to be exhaustive but only indicative of day-to-day problems in the post-disaster rebuilding environment. New issues and problems are certain to arise as we attempt to recover, rebuild, and recalibrate the relationship between the citizens, government, business, and other stakeholders.

Conclusions

New Orleans has been traditionally regarded as the Big Easy, a place to come to relax, forget your cares, and indulge in the sensuous and celebratory pleasures of life such as food, music, and dance and letting the good times roll, "Laissez les bontemps rouler." To others, it is also the most African city in North America with a human-centered ease of life, a colorful expressiveness, a comfortable blend of the sacred and the secular, and respect for ancestral tradition and values. New Orleanians are accustomed to this dual coexistence but remain acutely aware of the burden of a deep, racially based class schism between the haves and the have-nots. The pre-Katrina socioeconomic statistics were numbing — two-thirds of African American households in the city led a day-to-day marginal existence on the edge of constant economic disaster. Katrina exposed the level and depth of the disastrous and marginal condition of the most vulnerable segments of the black community.

Katrina taught us that under such circumstances, government cannot be relied on exclusively to protect us or rescue us from disastrous conditions. Perhaps the neglect and abandonment by the federal government is a stark reminder that we as citizens must accept the responsibility to organize our resources to do some things for ourselves, in addition to the continuous battle to force government accountability. . . .

We all must join the struggle to make New Orleans more just, equitable, democratic, and sustainable for its Katrina victims of all races and ethnicities and genders. The world is watching how we respond to the deepest internal contradictions of the modern-day city in contemporary American history. Our claim to democracy may rest in the balance.

NOTES AND QUESTIONS

1. Ed Blakely, an expert in planning and public redevelopment, served as an adviser both to New York City after the 9/11 attacks and to the city of Kobe, Japan, after the Great Hanshin earthquake. As the preceding essay notes, he also served as Executive Director of Recovery Management for the City of New Orleans from January 2007 to May 2009. An iron-willed and outspoken figure, Blakely's tenure was often marked with controversy and questions about his effectiveness. *See, e.g.,* Stephanie Grace, Opinion, *Blakely and Nagin Are Two of a Kind*, TIMES-PICAYUNE (New Orleans), May 11, 2009, B5.

2. Louisiana used millions of dollars in special federal Community Development Block Grants and tax credits to develop programs to rebuild the housing stock. These included two programs to promote the repair of large and small rental properties, and one, known as the Road Home program, to compensate homeowners for the costs of rebuilding. Although these programs greatly accelerated the rebuilding process, they have been criticized for not doing enough for the city's vulnerable populations. Because of funding limitations, the rental repair programs were only able to support the repair of less than one-third of the 82,000 rental units lost to hurricanes Katrina and Rita. PolicyLink, "A Long Way Home: The State of Housing Recovery in Louisiana," 6 (2008), www.policylink.org (December. 1, 2008). As for homeowners, nearly three-quarters of Road Home applicants had gaps between the received rebuilding resources and the actual costs of repair. The average shortfall for African Americans ($39,082) was roughly $8,000 more than it was for Whites ($30,863). *Id.* at 42. In the Lower-Ninth Ward, which was almost entirely African American, the gap between a household's average damage estimate and the average government grant exceeded $75,000. *Id.* at 47. The reason for the inequality is that the formula for grant awards was based on a home's prestorm value rather than the cost of repair. Because homes in African American neighborhoods had lower prestorm values (on average), their owners received less even when repair costs were similar to those in other neighborhoods.

3. Some residents had feared that after Katrina New Orleans would lose its African American identity. But two years after the storm, the city's racial profile was pretty close to what it was before the storm. According to estimates from the U.S. Census Bureau, "the proportion of the New Orleans population that is African American fell from 66.7 percent in 2000 to 60.2 percent in 2007. The proportion of the city's population that is Asian increased from 2.3 percent in 2000 to 3.0 percent in 2007 and the proportion that is Hispanic (of any race) increased from 3.1 percent to 4.5 percent." Allison Plyer & Joy Bonaguro, Demographic Profiles of New Orleans & the Metro Area, May 21, 2009, http://www.gnocdc.org/ 2007Demographics/index.html (June 17, 2009). Demographers expect the percentage of African Americans and Hispanics to continue growing at a gradual rate. *See* Michelle Krupa, "Black, Hispanic Numbers Jump," TIMES-PICAYUNE (New Orleans), May 14, 2009, at A1.

EPILOGUE

"So how's New Orleans doing?" This is the question a local gets asked every time he or she ventures out of the state — often by a waiter, a hotel clerk, or a cabin-mate on the plane. Crafting a succinct answer is hard, but one might start with the statistical data. Since 2005 the Brookings Institution has kept a "New Orleans Index," a database designed to track the city's progress in terms of population growth, economic development, and other characteristics. Below is an excerpt from a New Orleans Index report issued four years after the storm. (Later updates can be found at www.brookings.edu.)

METROPOLITAN POLICY PROGRAM AT BROOKINGS,
THE NEW ORLEANS INDEX: TRACKING THE RECOVERY
OF NEW ORLEANS AND THE METRO AREA (AUG. 2009)

---

https://gnocdc.s3.amazonaws.com/NOLAIndex/NOLAIndex.pdf
(Aug. 26, 2009)

Population Trends

- [In 2009], population growth picked up pace in the city of New Orleans, reaching 76.4 percent of pre-Katrina residences actively receiving mail, a 4.3 percentage point increase from [August 2008]. . . . From August 2008 to June 2009, Orleans Parish [where New Orleans is located] added 8,577 active residences compared with 5,345 added from August 2007 to June 2008. The New Orleans metro area is now home to nearly 90 percent of the pre-Katrina number of households receiving mail. . . .
- While growth in households has increased since August 2008, growth in school enrollment across the metro area has slowed, suggesting that recent arrivals to the metro area are likely singles and childless couples.

Economy Trends

- The New Orleans metro area continues to weather the national recession relatively well, only losing 0.9 percent of total jobs since last June compared to a 4.1 percent loss for the nation. Industry sectors with the largest declines nationally since June 2008 — including construction and manufacturing — shed relatively few jobs in the New Orleans metro [area] and represented a relatively small portion of the region's overall economy. Of those sectors with more than 50,000 jobs in the region, only professional and business services suffered severe job losses (down 3.5 percent). . . .
- New Orleans sales tax revenue declined in April and May 2009 for the first time since 2006, reflecting the national decline in consumer spending.
- General cargo handled at the Port of New Orleans was down 19 percent in 2008, signaling the effects of not only a national, but a global recession. In 2007, 7.4 million short tons of general cargo passed through the port, compared to only 5.9 million in 2008.

Housing Trends

- The market for single family homes across the metro area cooled in 2009, with sales volumes and average prices down markedly from one year earlier. The total number of homes sold in the metro area fell to 686 in May 2009, down 23 percent from one year earlier and nearly half the number sold in May 2006 and May 2007. . . .
- In its fourth year of disaster recovery, the pace of home reconstruction and new construction has slowed in New Orleans.
- As of June 2009, the Road Home program has disbursed $7.95 billion in grants to 124,219 underinsured homeowners, the vast majority of whom will rebuild. As the Road Home transitions to a new contractor, only 8,635 applicants remain — half of whom are still demonstrating their eligibility.
- Orleans and [neighboring] St. Bernard parishes continue to have very high numbers of vacant and blighted residences, though these numbers

have declined in the fourth year of recovery. . . . [A]s of March 2009, the share of unoccupied residential addresses in Orleans and St. Bernard, at 31 and 53 percent respectively, exceeds other cities also grappling with excess land and buildings. In absolute numbers, New Orleans has 65,888 unoccupied residential addresses—nearly as many as Detroit. In St. Bernard, 14,372 residences are unoccupied.

- Many essential service workers [such as those in food service, health care support, and retails sales] in the New Orleans area cannot afford the fair market rents of an apartment in the region.

Infrastructure Trends

- FEMA has obligated an additional $900 million for infrastructure repairs in Louisiana since [July 2008], bringing the total to nearly $7.8 billion, of which 58 percent has been paid to localities. Nearly four years after Katrina, total funding approved for disaster recovery is still on the rise—particularly in hard hit parishes where damage is so extensive that local governments are overwhelmed trying to document it all.
- New Orleans remains vulnerable to storm-related flooding—but how vulnerable is currently unknown. The Army Corps of Engineers continues work on the Hurricane and Storm Damage Risk Reduction System that is intended to provide protection from a storm surge that has a 1 percent chance of occurring any given year. However, Katrina was a 0.25 percent [or "400-year"] storm, stronger than the level of protection for which the system currently under construction is designed. Because no regularly-updated indicators exist on land loss, coastal restoration, and mitigation of flood risk due to human engineering, tracking recovery in this realm is challenging.

NOTES AND QUESTIONS

1. Aside from a strengthened levee system, the most enduring legacy of the New Orleans recovery could be the reform of the city's notoriously dysfunctional school system. Before Katrina, Louisiana's public schools ranked at the bottom of federal government surveys; and the schools in Orleans Parish, which encompasses New Orleans, ranked second-to-last among the state parishes. The city's school system was overwhelmingly poor and nearly all African American. The system suffered decaying buildings and unexplained budget deficits. Education officials were indicted for bribery and theft. New school superintendents, each promising to bring integrity and control to the troubled district, came and went like the coastal breeze.

   In 2005 Katrina washed that system away, along with many of the classrooms and playing fields. As Paul Tough wrote in the *New York Times Magazine,*

   > What is being built in its place is an educational landscape unlike any other, a radical experiment in reform. More than half of the city's public-school students are now being educated in charter schools, publicly financed but privately run, and most of the rest are enrolled in schools run by an unusually decentralized and rapidly changing school district. From across the country, and in increasing numbers, hundreds of ambitious, idealistic

young educators . . . have descended on New Orleans, determined to take advantage of the opportunity not just to innovate and reinvent but also to prove to the rest of the country that an entire city of children in the demographic generally considered the hardest to educate — poor African American kids — can achieve high levels of academic success.

Paul Tough, *A Teachable Moment*, N.Y. Times Mag., Aug. 17, 2008, at 30.

Only time will tell. For now the New Orleans system "is a bewildering tangle of interlocking organizational structures administering 86 public schools." *Id.* The system is divided into two school districts, the Orleans Parish School District, which now oversees the schools with satisfactory performance, and the state's Recovery School District, which oversees schools ranked as "failing." The large majority of the city's schools fall into the latter category, including thirty-three charter schools.

Many parents complain that the arrangement locks in the same educational inequalities that existed before the storm. For instance, most traditional and charter schools in the Orleans Parish School District admit students on the basis of test scores and writing samples, in some cases giving preference to residents in more affluent neighborhoods nearby. In contrast, traditional and charter schools in the Recovery School District admit anyone regardless of performance. In addition, whereas traditional schools in either district provide services for a wide range of disabilities, charter schools — because of their smaller size — do not.

For more on the legal issues surrounding education reform in New Orleans, see Danielle Holley-Walker, *The Accountability Cycle: The Recovery School District Act and New Orleans' Charter Schools*, 40 Conn. L. Rev. 125 (2007); Anna Williams Shavers, *Katrina's Children: Revealing the Broken Promise of Education*, 31 T. Marshall L. Rev. 499 (2006).

2. Health care was another city service thrown into turmoil after the storm. Almost four years after the storm, an article in *The Economist* described it this way:

> [T]hough the number of chronically sick in the city has risen sharply, medical services remain in tatters. Only 57% of the city's medical facilities have reopened, and tens of thousands of records have been lost. . . . Charity Hospital, the main refuge for the poor and uninsured for more than 250 years, is shuttered and surrounded by wire fencing. . . . Last month a group of citizens launched a legal appeal for it to be reopened, claiming that corrupt officials are using it as an excuse to get access to federal relief funds. But the owners of the building want to sell it.
>
> The Lindy Boggs Medical Centre [in New Orleans' Mid-City neighborhood] became a symbol of the struggle for survival in the hot, dank days after the flood. A day after the levees broke, the generators in the hospital failed, knocking out ventilators, transfusion machines and fresh water supplies. Nineteen patients died. The hospital is now to become a shopping centre.[1]

---

1. More recently, developers announced that the Boggs medical facility may, instead, be converted to a nursing home. Kate Moran, *Boggs Medical Center May Become a Nursing Home*, Times-Picayune (New Orleans), June 4, 2009, http://www.nola.com/news/index.ssf/2009/06/boggs_medical_center_may_becom.html (Aug. 26, 2009).

Even in hospitals that are functioning again, medical staff are in short supply and treatment has become riskier.

New Orleans: City of Sickness, The Economist, May 14, 2009, at 40.

Experts are also concerned about the lack of mental health services. In New Orleans, reports of mental illness are on the rise; rates of depression have tripled since 2006 and suicide rates have doubled. *Id.* Yet, as this book goes to print, there is no public hospital in the New Orleans city limits that provides inpatient services for the mentally ill. For more on the state of mental health services in New Orleans, see the excellent series of articles titled "Asylum after the Storm," which appeared in the *Washington Times*: Audrey Hudson et al., *Mentally Ill Struggle in Post-Katrina New Orleans*, Wash. Times, Aug. 3, 2009, A1; Audrey Hudson, *Mental Illness Tidal Wave*, Wash. Times, Aug. 4, 2009, at A1; Audrey Hudson, *Clash of Solutions from Powers That Be*, Wash. Times, Aug. 5, 2009, at A1.

3. To sum up, although much progress has been made in New Orleans, there is still more work to do. On the eve of the fourth anniversary of Katrina, the New Orleans *Times-Picayune* published this editorial on its front page, addressed to President Barack Obama:

Dear Mr. President,

Tomorrow we will mark the fourth anniversary of Hurricane Katrina, which claimed the lives of more than 1,400 Louisianians and nearly killed a great American city. . . .

We know you don't lack passion for our community and its recovery. Though you haven't been here as president, as a senator you visited five times after Katrina. We remember well the fervor of your speech at Tulane University on your last visit, a year and a half ago.

"I promise you that when I'm in the White House, I will commit myself every day to keeping up Washington's end of the bargain," you said then. "This will be a priority of my presidency. And I will make it clear to members of my administration that their responsibilities don't end in places like the 9th Ward; they begin in places like the 9th Ward."

We await the fulfillment of many of these promises. We are grateful for the federal aid that has flowed our way, including $14.7 billion in improvements to levees and drainage and other storm protection measures. . . .

But much remains to be done.

The wetlands and barrier islands that are the first defense of Louisiana's energy coast must be restored if we are to survive long term.

Flood protection on a massive scale, the ultimate rampart the Netherlands saw fit to build, should be our model as well, a vital safeguard against a Category 5 storm and its surge. Such a substantial commitment, you told our reporters last week, "remains a strong goal." For us and for the nation, it's a vital necessity.

The economic revitalization of a new medical facility to replace the destroyed Charity Hospital would give New Orleans a shot in the arm it desperately needs. We urge you to see to it that the stalled project moves forward.

Our community is resilient and hard-working. Together with volunteers from around the country, we are striving to make this a better place than it was before the storm, with renovated houses, vastly improved schools and a unique culture that's as vibrant as ever.

But there's no substitute for the focus, the energy, the commitment that a president alone can bestow. There's no substitute for you, as president, seeing our recovery and its halting progress with your own eyes, for taking time to walk in our shoes. So we ask you to bring your considerable intellect, your problem-solving ability, your influence to bear. When a president pays attention, so does the nation.

Editorial, *We're Counting on You, Mr. President*, TIMES-PICAYUNE (New Orleans), Aug. 28, 2009, at A1. On October 15, 2009, Barack Obama made his first visit to New Orleans as President of the United States.

E. PROBLEM

Below is a problem designed to encourage you to think more about the many issues and diverse interests involved in rebuilding a city. The facts are fictional, but they are based on accounts of real hurricanes that have hit the United States in the last twenty-five years. The problem may be used as a class exercise in which students act as advocates for particular interest groups, or, more simply, as a launch pad for more general classroom discussion.

RISING FROM THE RUBBLE: THE CITY OF WILD PALMS

Wild Palms is a coastal city of about 100,000 people, located on the Gulf of Mexico. Incorporated in the 1800s, Wild Palms is known for its beach resorts, good fishing, and historical Spanish and Caribbean architecture. The city is also occasionally visited by tropical storms and hurricanes.

A month ago in August (let us imagine), Wild Palms was raked by Hurricane Addie, a Category 4 storm with winds near 140 mph and a surge of more than eighteen feet. Twenty people died in the storm and hundreds more were injured. Addie's winds flattened buildings throughout the city, including schools, houses of worship, and tens of thousands of homes. Because of high insurance rates, at least one-third of the damaged households were not insured for wind damage. In one of the most dramatic events, storm winds demolished a privately owned mobile home park on the outskirts of town. The facility provided housing for more than 300 agricultural laborers and their families. Nearly all park residents were Latino with household earnings at or below the federal poverty line. This agricultural workforce is essential to the farm economy of the surrounding county, which provides almost a quarter of the nation's tomatoes, green beans, and squash. Many farm operators are concerned that worker housing will not be replaced in time for the upcoming winter harvest.

In addition, Hurricane Addie's eighteen-foot surge flooded several square miles of low coastal land. Among the areas worst hit was the city's East Side neighborhood, a working-class, traditionally African American neighborhood filled with handsome century-old architecture. East Side was sliding into disrepair even before the storm, and some privately wonder if it is even worth bringing back. Despite federal requirements, officials estimate that a quarter of damaged homes lacked flood insurance.

Addie was one of the most powerful storms known to have hit this part of the coast. Experts loosely describe it as a "400-year storm," that is, a storm that has a 0.25 percent chance of striking in any given year. (As a comparison, Hurricane Katrina is considered a 400-year storm.)

The city is really struggling. Most small businesses have yet to reopen. The local university closed its classrooms and dormitories for the semester, leaving thousands of students in limbo. The nearby Air Force base—an important source of employment that was already slated to close down—now says it will accelerate its departure. And the major league baseball team that had kept its spring training camp in Wild Palms (thus generating tourism and national publicity) recently announced plans to permanently move its facilities to another Southern city.

Officials in Wild Palms estimate that its population has dropped from 100,000 to about 70,000. The city's morale is falling rapidly. "It's so ugly here, it's hard to get anyone to think about tomorrow," one resident told a Washington journalist. "There isn't a leaf left. There isn't a bird in the sky."

To address rebuilding efforts, the mayor of Wild Palms has planned several meetings of government and civic leaders. Although nearly everyone wants a safer and more resilient city, the course is not clear. The city will always be prone to violent storms. And in an era of accelerated climate change, no one can accurately predict the effects of future sea level rise or the cycle and intensity of future tropical storms.

Imagine you represent one of the three parties below. How would you address the following issues and questions?

1. The Mayor's Office
2. The Wild Palms Chamber of Commerce, a nonprofit organization interested in promoting local and regional business and development
3. Disaster Justice Now!, a local nonprofit organization promoting the interests of poor communities and communities of color

Rebuilding Homes. Wild Palms hopes to benefit from a package of federal Community Development Block Grants that will be given to the state and used to help rebuild devastated areas. (Though many owners had insurance, such coverage is usually not enough to completely rebuild a home.) As a first step, Congress has asked the state and the city of Wild Palms to propose a detailed plan for how the money will be managed and spent. Although funds for the city are expected to be significant, everyone understands there will not be enough to satisfy every need. Priorities must be set. If the money is spread broadly, but too thin, there is a chance that no group will be able to successfully rebound. The mayor has assembled a meeting of government and civic leaders to address the following fundamental questions.

1. How should individual grants be allocated? Should they be available to owners of homes, owners of rental units, the owner of the mobile home park? In what proportions? What about vacation homes? Should uninsured owners be eligible?

2. How should an individual grant amount be determined? Should calculations be based on prestorm value, the cost of rebuilding, financial need, or some other factor(s)?

3. How should the grants be used? In addition to rebuilding, some propose that owners be allowed to sell their damaged property to the city or state in exchange for grant money; recipients could then use the funds to relocate to a safer part of town. If adopted, should this buyout program be limited to owners who plan to relocate *within* the city? Or should it apply to those relocating outside the city? What about those relocating outside the state?

Increasing Resilience. In the short time after the storm, the city's mayor has become a quasi-expert in the history of municipal disaster recovery. She is particularly inspired by the recovery of Kobe, Japan. With that in mind, the mayor immediately imposed a building moratorium in Wild Palms, which is to remain in effect until officials decide what to do. The mayor has assembled a meeting of government and civic leaders to address the following questions related to disaster mitigation.

1. What new building code should be imposed and how should it be enforced? Some experts recommend a code similar to the state-of-the-art regulations of Florida's Miami-Dade County. That code requires special "hurricane clips" that fasten a house's roof to the frame and insists that a roof's surface be attached with screws rather than nails. In addition, the code mandates storm shutters and glass that can withstand winds of up to 146 mph. But the requirements are expensive and can increase building costs by more than 33 percent. Assuming the city adopts a new code, when should it be required? The traditional "50% Rule" holds that any structure with damage amounting to 50 percent or more must comply with an updated code. But this leaves out many buildings. In addition, avoidance of compliance is common. In New Orleans many homeowners were able to circumvent new rules by convincing sympathetic officials to assess their damages at 49 percent.

2. What should the city's new footprint look like? With a smaller population, keeping the old footprint might result in a city that is too spread out. Providing services such as police and fire protection to outlying areas might become too costly. Some city planners warn of a "jack-o'-lantern effect" in which residential streets are dotted intermittently with blighted properties, like the missing teeth of a Halloween pumpkin. On the other hand, people are attached to their communities and benefit significantly from the social relationships they have nurtured over the years, including those linked by culture, geography, religion, commerce, and recreation. For many people,

the largest asset they own is the residential lot in their neighborhood. Assuming a smaller footprint is desirable, how should the new contours be implemented? Should the city prevent rebuilding in some neighborhoods? Would that be constitutional under Lucas v. South Carolina Coastal Council (Chapter 2)? Or should the city use targeted investment and economic incentives to encourage people to develop in desired areas? For a city strapped for cash, how can that be accomplished?

3. How long should the city's building moratorium remain in effect? Residents are understandably anxious to rebuild their lives. Some argue that the moratorium has already discouraged many evacuees from moving back. Should the mayor now lift the moratorium entirely? Should the mayor lift the moratorium in some areas, but retain it in the more vulnerable areas, such as East Side or the site of the demolished mobile home park? At what point does a moratorium in such circumstances become a regulatory taking? *See* Tahoe-Sierra Preservation Council, Inc. v. Tahoe Regional Planning Agency, 535 U.S. 302 (2002) (thirty-two-month moratorium in Lake Tahoe Basin while scientists studied environmental effects of development was not a per se taking).

Revitalizing the Economy. One of the most controversial issues involves the East Side neighborhood. Residents have been adamant about rebuilding their community. Various historic preservation groups also support this effort. The area is obviously prone to dangerous flooding, but civil engineers say it could be made much safer if new houses were built on raised foundations and artificial barriers were created to protect especially vulnerable parts of the neighborhood.

In contrast, the mayor is wondering if it might be more sensible to buy out East Side residences, clear the area, and build a waterfront park that could be used year-round for public events, festivals and other activities. The park would be designed to absorb the shock of a storm surge and to drain invading water away from residential communities. The park could be partially funded by selling three-quarters of the reclaimed land to a private developer for use as a high-rise resort with a hotel and casino. The plan would not only move East Side residents out of harm's way, the mayor reasons, but also revitalize the city's threatened economy.

East Side residents, of course, oppose the plan. They claim that the mayor is just trying to oust the community from a valuable swath of land. They believe that such an expropriation would amount to an unconstitutional taking under the federal constitution. But to be absolutely sure, an East Side advocacy group is working to add an amendment to the state constitution, patterned after the post-*Kelo* amendment adopted in Louisiana. The amendment would limit the state's use of expropriation to traditional public purposes and hold that enhanced tax revenues or economic development could not be considered in determining "public use."

Is expropriation a good idea? What are the alternatives? Could the mayor's plan survive a challenge under *Kelo*? What are the long-term implications of the proposed amendment to the state constitution?

CHAPTER 9

INTERNATIONAL DISASTER LAW AND POLICY

In many ways, disasters occurring within the United States are not so different from those occurring in other countries. Both sets are driven by a combination of environmental hazards, human development, and human vulnerabilities. Reducing the risk, responding to victims, and reimagining the future all pose enormous political and psychological challenges. Every country, when planning for or responding to disaster must find the right balance between local rule and national rule, autonomy and order, fairness and efficiency.

But two factors set many foreign disasters apart: intensity and complexity. This is particularly so in poorer countries. By intensity, we mean the power with which a disaster disables a country's political and economic institutions, its access to natural resources, and its morale. When hurricanes Katrina and Rita ripped through the Gulf Coast, lives and property were lost and a city fell to its knees, but the United States as a whole carried on almost as before. In terms of our Gross Domestic Product, those storms were barely a blip on the radar screen. But when a cyclone swamps half of Bangladesh, or an earthquake shatters a Pakistani city, tens of thousands of lives can be lost; in terms of economic development, such countries can be set back months or even years. In addition, things get much more complex. Many developing countries, for instance, have inefficient or even dysfunctional political institutions. Because they are poor, they must rely much more on outside aid (from other countries and outside organizations), which brings along its own bureaucracies. Add to this extreme differences in wealth, strong religious and ethnic tensions, and (in some cases) antidemocratic political institutions, and you have a witch's cauldron of logistical issues.

This chapter gives you a brief look at the legal and political elements associated with disaster in the international context, paying special attention to issues in developing countries. We will first look at the distribution of disaster risk around the world. We will then look at the combination of causes, primarily ecological exposure and social vulnerability. Next, we will introduce some of the most important international agreements relevant to disaster risk, including incentives for better planning and agreements addressing discrimination. Finally, we conclude with a discussion exercise that hopes to pull together many concepts presented in this chapter as well as in the rest of the book.

A. THE GEOGRAPHY OF DISASTER

UNITED NATIONS INTERNATIONAL STRATEGY FOR DISASTER REDUCTION,
GLOBAL ASSESSMENT REPORT ON DISASTER RISK REDUCTION

Chapter 1, 3-12 (2009), http://www.preventionweb.net/english/hyogo/gar/
report/index.php?id=9413

In 2008, numerous major disasters provided a stark reminder of the massive concentrations of disaster risk that threaten human development gains across the world. In May, the tropical cyclone Nargis caused an estimated 140,000 mortalities in Myanmar, primarily due to a storm surge in the low-lying, densely populated Irrawaddy River delta.

In May, China's most powerful earthquake since 1976 affected Sichuan and parts of Chongqing, Gansu, Hubei, Shaanxi and Yunnan killing at least 87,556 people, injuring more than 365,000 and affecting more than 60 million people in ten provinces and regions. An estimated 5.36 million buildings collapsed and more than 21 million buildings were damaged. . . .

Also in August 2008, the Kosi River in Bihar, India, broke through an embankment and changed its course 120 km eastwards, rendering useless more than 300 km of flood defences that had been built to protect towns and villages. Flowing into supposedly flood safe areas, the river affected 3.3 million people in 1,598 villages located in 15 districts. It was characterized as the worst flood in the area for 50 years, prompting the Prime Minister of India, Manmohan Singh, to declare a "national calamity" on 28th August.

Internationally reported disaster loss is heavily concentrated in a small number of infrequently occurring events. Between January 1975 and October 2008 and excluding epidemics, the International Emergency Disasters Database EMDAT recorded 8,866 events killing 2,283,767 people. Of these, 23 mega-disasters . . . killed 1,786,084 people, mainly in developing countries. In other words, 0.26% of the events accounted for 78.2% of the mortality.

In the same period, recorded economic losses were US$1,527.6 billion. [Twenty-five] mega-disasters . . . represented only 0.28% of the events, yet accounted for 40% of that loss, mainly in developed countries. Of the ten disasters with the highest death tolls since 1975, no fewer than half . . . have occurred in the five year period between 2003 and 2008. [L]ikewise . . . four of the ten disasters with the highest economic losses occurred in the same period.

Nationally reported disaster loss is similarly highly concentrated. Losses reported between 1970 and 2007 at the local government level in a sample of 12 Asian and Latin American countries showed that 84% of the mortality and 75% of the destroyed housing was concentrated in only 0.7% of the loss reports. Destruction in the housing sector usually accounts for a significant proportion of direct economic loss in disasters.

At whatever scale disaster losses are viewed, therefore, mortality and direct economic loss appear to be highly concentrated geographically and associated with a very small number of hazard events. These are areas where major concentrations of vulnerable people and economic assets are exposed to very severe hazards. . . .

In contrast, and at whatever scale disaster losses are viewed, wide regions are exposed to more frequently occurring low-intensity losses. These widespread low-intensity losses are associated with other risk impacts such as a large number of affected people and damage to housing and local infrastructure, but not to major mortality or destruction of economic assets. For example, 99.3% of local loss reports in the 12 countries mentioned accounted for only 16% of the mortality but 51% of housing damage. These losses are pervasive in both space and time. In the country sample, 82% of local government areas reported disaster losses at least once between 1970 and 2007, 48% reported disaster losses six or more times and there was an average of nine local loss reports per day. . . .

The fact that disasters have a disproportionate impact on the poor in developing countries has been highlighted in research for at least 30 years. . . .

This Report confirms that poorer countries have disproportionately higher mortality and economic loss risks, given similar levels of hazard exposure. For example, globally, high-income countries account for 39% of the exposure to tropical cyclones but only 1% of the mortality risk. Low-income countries represent 13% of the exposure but no less than 81% of the mortality risk.

For example, gross domestic product (GDP) per capita in Japan is US$31,267 compared to US$5,137 in the Philippines, and Japan has a human development index of 0.953 compared to 0.771 in the Philippines. Japan also has about 1.4 times as many people exposed to tropical cyclones than the Philippines. However, if affected by a cyclone of the same magnitude, mortality in the Philippines would be 17 times higher than that in Japan.

Countries with small and vulnerable economies, such as many Small Island Developing States and Land-Locked Developing Countries not only suffer higher relative levels of economic loss, with respect to the size of their GDPs. They also have a particularly low resilience to loss, meaning that disaster losses can lead to major setbacks in economic development. The countries with the highest economic vulnerability to natural hazards and the lowest resilience are also those with very low participation in world markets and low export diversification.

At the local level, there is also empirical evidence to show that poor areas suffer disproportionately high levels of damage in disasters and that this is related to factors such as unsafe housing. Case study evidence from particular cities also shows that both disaster occurrence and loss are associated with processes that increase the hazard exposure of the poor—for example, the expansion of informal settlements in hazard prone areas. . . .

Disaster risk is now widely recognized as an integral part of a wider con-stellation of risks related to food and energy insecurity, financial and economic instability, global climate change, environmental degradation, disease and epidemics, conflict and extreme poverty. . . .

[R]eports by the United Nations Department for Social and Economic Affairs and by the World Economic Forum have argued that different kinds of risk now form an interlocked system, implying that impacts in one sphere spill over into other areas, and that actions to reduce one risk may imply trade-offs in reducing others. The [Fourth Assessment Report of the U.N. Intergovernmental Panel on Climate Change in 2007] dispelled any remaining doubt that climate change is a catastrophic threat on a global scale.

These interlinkages are becoming increasingly visible. In 2008, successive global crises hit the headlines as the prices of grain and energy sources fluctu-ated wildly and the global financial system threatened to collapse, all in the context of ongoing concerns about global climate change, conflict, security and extreme poverty. These systemic risks now pose a very serious threat to global security and sustainability. Ongoing disaster losses undermine resil-ience to other kinds of threats, while major impacts in mega-disasters can trigger reactions in other risk spheres.

The way disaster risk is magnified by other kinds of global risk, and in turn feeds back into them, can be illustrated by a hypothetical but plausible example. If global climate change magnifies the severity of drought in a key grain producing region causing harvest failure, this could feed back into speculative increases in food prices. The most affected will not only be those living in the region but poor households in other parts of the world who spend a large proportion of their income on food. Faced with chronic food insecurity and with their resilience undermined by other hazards such as poor health or conflict, poor rural households may then migrate to urban areas. In many towns and cities across developing countries migration from rural areas is absorbed through the growth of informal settlements in areas prone to hazards such as floods. Flood risk in turn may also be further mag-nified by climate change.

Other examples of the interlocked nature of risk include the increase of oil prices when hurricanes threaten the Gulf of Mexico at the same time as conflict threatens oil production in Nigeria. As the credit crisis in developed countries is pushing economies into recession, the construction boom in the Persian Gulf is faltering, leading to a decrease in remittances from migrant workers to relatives in the Indian sub-continent. This in turn may lead to decreasing economic resilience in poor households in that region, increased rural-urban migration and subsequent increases in the population exposed to weather-related hazards in cities.

The linkages between disaster risk, poverty and climate change, described above, form a particularly tightly interlocked group of global challenges, in which impacts in any one sphere spill over into the other two and which have to be addressed in a way that recognizes their inter-connectedness.

	Year	Country	Disaster	Fatalities
Disasters with more than 10,000 fatalities, January 1975 – June 2008[4]	1983	Ethiopia	Ethiopian drought	300,000
	1976	China	Tangshan earthquake	242,000
	2004	South Indian Ocean	Indian Ocean tsunami	226,408
	1983	Sudan	Sudan drought	150,000
(Highlighting denotes disasters within the five-year period, 2003–2008.)	1991	Bangladesh	Cyclone Gorky	138,866
	2008	Myanmar	Cyclone Nargis	133,655
	1981	Mozambique	Southern Mozambique drought	100,000
Source: EMDAT; Analysis by ISDR, 2008 (data as of September 2008)	2008	China	Sichuan earthquake	87,476
	2005	India, Pakistan	Kashmir earthquake	73,338
	2003	Europe	European heat wave	56,809
	1990	Iran	Manjil-Rudbar earthquake	40,000
	1999	Venezuela	Vargas floods	30,000
	2003	Iran	Bam earthquake	26,796
	1978	Iran	Tabas earthquake	25,000
	1988	Soviet Union	Spitak earthquake	25,000
	1976	Guatemala	The Guatemala earthquake	23,000
	1985	Colombia	Nevado Del Ruiz volcano	21,800
	2001	India	Gujarat earthquake	20,005
	1999	Turkey	Izmit earthquake	17,127
	1998	Honduras	Hurricane Mitch	14,600
	1977	India	Andhra Pradesh cyclone	14,204
	1985	Bangladesh	Bangladesh cyclone	10,000
	1975	China	Haicheng earthquake	10,000

Reprinted from UNISDR, Global Assessment Report on Disaster Risk Reduction (2009).

	Year	Country	Hazard	Total loss (billion US$)
Disasters leading to losses of more than US$ 10 billion, January 1975 – June 2008	2005	United States of America	Hurricane Katrina	125
	1995	Japan	Kobe earthquake	100
	2008	China	Sichuan earthquake	30
	1998	China	Yangtze flood	30
(Highlighting denotes disasters within the five-year period, 2003–2008.)	2004	Japan	Chuetsu earthquake	28
	1992	United States of America	Hurricane Andrew	26.5
	1980	Italy	Irpinia earthquake	20
Source: EMDAT; Analysis by ISDR, 2008 (data as of September 2008)	2004	United States of America	Hurricane Ivan	18
	1997	Indonesia	Wild fires	17
	1994	United States of America	Northridge earthquake	16.5
	2005	United States of America	Hurricane Charley	16
	2004	United States of America	Hurricane Rita	16
	1995	Democratic People's Republic of Korea	Korea floods	15
	2005	United States of America	Hurricane Wilma	14.3
	1999	Taiwan (China)	Chichi earthquake	14.1
	1988	Soviet Union	Spitak earthquake	14
	1994	China	China drought	13.8
	1991	China	Eastern China floods	13.6
	1996	China	Yellow River flood	12.6
	2007	Japan	Niigataken Chuetsu-oki earthquake	12.5
	1993	United States of America	Great Midwest flood	12
	2002	Germany	River Elbe floods	11.7
	2004	United States of America	Hurricane Frances	11
	1991	Japan	Typhoon Mireille	10
	1995	United States of America	Major west coast wind storm	10

Reprinted from UNISDR, Global Assessment Report on Disaster Risk Reduction (2009).

NOTES AND QUESTION

1. Sometimes maps help us visualize concepts in new ways. The map below is called a "density equalizing map," or "cartogram." Through calculated distortion, it shows the proportion of people affected by disasters from 1975 to 2004 in terms of "resized" territorial space. (In this case, being "affected" includes requiring emergency assistance for basic survival or catching a disease not usually found in the area.) Does this cartogram persuade you to see disaster risk in a different way? What role should geographic and economic distribution of risk play in shaping disaster policy? For more cartograms on a variety of topics, *see* http://www.worldmapper.org.

Affected by Disaster

Source: Social and Spatial Inequalities Group, University of Sheffield, and Mark Newman, University of Michigan.

B. ECOLOGY AND EXPOSURE

JANET ABRAMOVITZ, UNNATURAL DISASTERS

Worldwatch Paper 158, Worldwatch Institute, 5-12 (2001),
http://www.worldwatch.org/node/832

Just as not every natural disturbance is a disaster, not every disaster is completely natural. We have altered so many natural systems so dramatically that their ability to bounce back from disturbance has been greatly diminished. Deforestation impairs watersheds, raises the risk of fires, and contributes to climate change. Destruction of coastal wetlands, dunes, and mangroves eliminates nature's shock absorbers for coastal storms. Such human-made changes end up making naturally vulnerable areas — such as hillsides, rivers, coastal zones, and low-lying islands — even more vulnerable to extreme weather events.

Droughts, and the famines that often follow, may be the most widely understood — if underreported — example of an unnatural disaster. They are triggered partly by global climate variability (both natural and human-induced) and partly by resource mismanagement such as deforestation, over-grazing, and the overtapping of rivers and wells for irrigation. Considered slow-onset events, droughts are not as well reported as rapid-onset events like storms and floods, nor are they usually included in disaster-related financial loss data. Yet they affect major portions of Africa and Asia and are projected to continue worsening in the coming years as a result of climate change. According to data prepared by the Centre for Research on the Epidemiology of Disasters and published in the World Disasters Report, droughts and famines accounted for 42 percent of disaster-related deaths between 1991 and 2000. . . .

Human settlements, too, have become less resilient as we put more structures, more economic activity, and more people in vulnerable places. Our usual approach to natural disturbances is to try to prevent them through short-sighted strategies using methods that all too often exacerbate them. Dams and levees, for example, change the flow of rivers and can increase the frequency and severity of floods and droughts.

China's Yangtze River dramatically shows the consequences of the loss of healthy ecosystems. The flooding in 1998 caused more than 4,000 deaths, affected 223 million people, inundated 25 million hectares of cropland, and cost well over $36 billion. Heavy summer rains are common in southern and central China, and flooding often ensues. But in 1998, as the floodwater continued to rise, it became clear that other factors besides heavy rains were at play. One influence was the extensive deforestation that had left many steep hillsides bare. Indeed, in the past few decades 85 percent of the forest cover in the Yangtze basin has been cleared by logging and agriculture. The loss of forests, which normally intercept rainfall and allow it to be absorbed by the soil, permitted water to rush across the land, carrying valuable topsoil with it. As the runoff raced across the denuded landscape, it caused floods.

In addition, the Yangtze's natural flood controls had been undermined by numerous dams and levees, and a large proportion of the basin's wetlands and lakes, which usually act as natural "sponges," had been filled in or drained. The areas previously left open to give floodwaters a place to go have filled instead with waves of human settlements. All these changes reduced the capacity of the Yangtze's watershed to absorb rain, and greatly increased the speed and severity of the resulting runoff. . . .

Paradoxically, clearing natural forests also exacerbates drought in dry years by allowing the soil to dry out more quickly. Such droughts helped fuel the record-breaking fires in Indonesia and Brazil in 1997-98. These massive fires occurred in tropical forests that are normally too moist to burn. But when fragmented by logging and agricultural clearing, the forests dried to the point where fires set deliberately to clear land were quickly able to spread out of control. In Indonesia, industrial timber and palm oil plantation owners took advantage of a severe El Niño drought to expand their areas and in 1997-98 burned at least 9.8 million hectares, an area the size of South Korea.

The smoke and haze from Indonesia's fires choked neighboring countries, affecting about 70 million people. The economic damage to the region has been conservatively estimated at about $9.3 billion. Schools, airports, and businesses were shut down. Many crops were lost to the drought and fires, and the haze impaired the pollination of other crops and wild plants, the ecological repercussions of which will unfold for many years. If harm to fisheries, biodiversity, orangutans, and long-term health were included, the damage figure would be far higher. . . .

In South Africa, the spread of non-native vegetation (including pine and wattle trees) has greatly increased the incidence of intense and dangerous fires. The invasives are also hijacking precious water resources—some 7 percent of the annual surface water flow—and displacing globally unique native plant communities. Alien plants already cover some 10 million hectares—about 8 percent of the vast nation. A serious effort is under way in South Africa to stop the spread of invasive species, which, unless checked, are predicted to double in area in the next 20 years.

In contrast to the human-made unnatural disasters that should be prevented but are not, considerable effort is spent trying to stop natural disturbances that are actually beneficial. The result is disasters of unnatural proportions. . . .

[For instance,] a common response to floods is to try to prevent them by controlling rivers. But contrary to popular belief, containing a river in embankments, dams, channels, reservoirs, and other structures does not reduce flooding. Instead, it dramatically increases the rate of flow, and causes even worse flooding downstream. The Rhine River, for example, is cut off from 90 percent of its original floodplain in its upper reaches, and flows twice as fast as it did before the modifications. Flooding in the basin has grown significantly more frequent and severe due to increased urbanization, river engineering, and poor floodplain management. . . .

On the other side of the globe, Bangladesh suffered its most extensive flood of the century in the summer of 1998, when two thirds of the country was inundated for months. Annual floods are a natural and beneficial cycle in this low-lying coastal nation, which encircles the meandering deltas of the Ganges, Brahmaputra, and Meghna Rivers. The people of Bangladesh have long adapted their housing, land use patterns, and economic activities to these "barsha" or beneficial floods. However, 1998 brought a "bonna" or devastating flood. Floodwaters reached near-record levels and did not recede for months. All told, 1,300 people died, 31 million people were left temporarily homeless, and 16,000 kilometers of roads were heavily damaged. Overall damage estimates exceed $3.4 billion—or 10 percent of the nation's GDP.

A number of factors precipitated Bangladesh's bonna flood. Heavy rainfall upriver in the Himalayas of north India and Nepal, some of which fell on heavily logged areas, exacerbated the disaster, as did the runoff from extensive development upstream that helped clog the region's rivers and floodplains with silt and mud. In the future, climate change will make Bangladesh even more vulnerable, as rising sea levels are projected to submerge 20 percent of the nation's land area and increased extreme rainfall and cyclone activity could bring more flooding. This problem will be made worse because large expanses of stabilizing mangroves have been removed from shores in recent years to make way for shrimp ponds, exposing the coast to more inundation.

Further, a major reason that so much of Bangladesh was submerged for so long was that extensive embankments built in the last 10 years as part of the nation's Flood Action Plan actually prevented the drainage of water, because water that topped the embankment during the flood's peak could not drain as the river water receded. . . . While the Bangladeshi peasants look at most floods as beneficial, engineers and donors tend to see all flooding as a problem to be solved by technical measures. As [one] researcher . . . has noted, "when it comes to perception of floods and their danger, few heed the wisdom of villagers, even though it is they who have to (mostly) live with the flood."

C. SOCIAL VULNERABILITY

ROBERT R.M. VERCHICK, FACING CATASTROPHE: ENVIRONMENTAL ACTION FOR A POST-KATRINA WORLD

(2010) (FORTHCOMING)

[In developing countries,] the relatively poor and the socially excluded endure special burdens. As in industrialized countries, poverty and bigotry push settlements into cheap and dangerous areas like flood plains or landfills. The grass huts and tin-roof shanties that tens of millions of people call home provide little protection. Disaster aggravates engrained patterns of discriminatory treatment. In southern India, after the Asian Tsunami, human rights advocates reported widespread discrimination against lower-caste *dalits*, in the distribution of supplies, the removal of bodies, and the availability of shelters.

Women and girls also face disproportionate harm. Poring over international surveys, one confronts the alarming fact that in the developing world women and girls are much more likely to die during naturally triggered disasters. The Asian Tsunami [of 2004] claimed the lives of twice as many women than men in two hard-hit districts in the Indian state Tamil Nadu. In one district of Sri Lanka, women and girls accounted for 80 percent of fatalities. In both the 2005 Kashmir Earthquake and India's 1993 Latur Earthquake, many more women died than men. The disparity is attributable to many factors. As primary care-givers, women are more likely to be home during a disaster; and these homes are often poorly constructed or in a vulnerable area. Women are usually the first ones to search for missing family members, exposing themselves to hammering rains, mudslides, and other perils. Sometimes women are constrained by social norms. During the Asian Tsunami many women drown[ed] because they were "ashamed" to run to shore after waves ripped away parts of their clothing. In some cultures women and girls are not taught to swim.

On May 3, 2008, a cyclone called Nargis tore through the Irawaddy Delta of Myanmar, a low-lying coastal nation roughly the size of Texas. The delta is laced with hundreds of rivers and tributaries and rarely rises above ten feet above sea level. Communities living on those muddy flats were pulverized. The

United Nations estimates that 2.4 million people were severely affected by the cyclone and that 1.4 million people were left in immediate need of food, water, shelter, and medical care. Weeks after the storm, local officials estimated that 134,000 people had died or were missing, a figure that comports with early estimates by the Red Cross. It is possible the death toll was much higher, as Myanmar (which is also known as Burma) is run by a military dictatorship that is notorious for secrecy and a myriad of human rights abuses.

The events of the storm, which played out in news reports around the world, offer a shocking glimpse at yet another category of people especially vulnerable to natural hazards: citizens of oppressive, non-democratic regimes that simply don't care. Myanmar's military government, for instance, had never bothered to draft a disaster relief plan for a major cyclone although the threat was well known. And even after India's meteorological department notified Burmese officials of the cyclone's approach two days in advance, the government did little to warn its citizens on the Irrawaddy. In the aftermath, Myanmar denied access to international aid workers and frustrated attempts to deliver supplies into the region, at one point leading the United States to accuse the government of "criminal neglect."

But there were also powerful aspects of ethnicity and class in this story, which were nearly ignored in America's mainstream media. Myanmar has more than 100 different ethnic groups and sub-groups within its borders, making it one of the most ethnically diverse populations in South East Asia. The largest minority group, the Karens, live mainly on the Irrawaddy Delta where the cyclone hit. The Karens have suffered persecution from the governing junta since the country's early days of independence more than a half century ago.

After the storm, there were many reports of government officials hording supplies or selling them to victims at inflated prices. Some journalists described soldiers forcing survivors into hard labor, forcing them to "break up large boulders into pieces of rock for road construction" for less than a dollar a day. Those in the area reported that Karens, in particular, were being discriminated against. Human rights workers cited unconfirmed reports that boatmen helping with the evacuation were taking ethnic Burmese from the delta but leaving Karens behind. Such reports are consistent with a historic pattern of discrimination against Karens by the Burmese government, which includes violent attacks, property seizures, and forced labor. Some human rights observers believed such discrimination was "really the root of the [aid distribution] problem." This can be seen as an extension of political and ethnic oppression that had been occurring for decades, just as violence toward blacks during America's [Great Mississippi River Flood of 1927] can be seen as an extension of generations of continued government-supported racial oppression.

Discriminatory abuse appeared to have spilled over against other ethnic groups on the delta, including the Mon, Muslim Indians, aboriginal groups, and even the ethnic Burmese. A relatively wealthy class of Chinese landowners on the delta feared the government would use the evacuation as an opportunity to seize their land. Hardship . . . affects some [groups] more acutely because of past discrimination and other violations of human rights. For instance, millions of storm survivors were left homeless and denied interim shelter by even their own government. The homeless crisis in Myanmar thus equals the scale of the Asian Tsunami in 2004. But the tragedy is compounded by the fact that before the cyclone, an estimated one million people were *already* internally displaced — most of them, members of ethnic minorities — whose homes had been seized or destroyed by soldiers in "counterinsurgency" efforts or to make way for dams, oil pipelines, and mining operations. In the half-century before the storm, some delta communities had relocated more than 100 times — often at the point of a gun.

Children were particularly harmed. The United Nation's Children's Fund (UNICEF) estimates that 40 percent of those who died in the cyclone and accompanying floods were children. Those children lucky enough to survive faced another set of struggles. Because of small body size, many were at special risk to disease and starvation. Children are also at much higher risk of pro-tracted trauma and psychological problems, especially those who lost parents or other family members. Some independent relief centers, like those operated by UNICEF, provided "child-friendly" programs in which children played and made drawings as a means of coping with loss and trauma. Hundreds, perhaps even thousands, of children were separated from their parents during the storm or, perhaps, orphaned. They now face the prospects of living in dour state-run orphanages or, worse, being swept up in the global slave trade. Myanmar has long been a "source country" for human trafficking, including domestic servitude, bonded labor, and forced prostitution. Less than two weeks after the cyclone, the United Nations had already reported an incident of two "brokers" entering a relief center in Yangon (also known as Rangoon) and trying to recruit orphaned children. The pair was arrested, but in the wake of the storm, the trend of child abductions and trafficking appeared likely to increase.

The earthquake that shook China's Sichuan province in 2008 occurred in the same month as Cyclone Nargis. In contrast to that painful fiasco, Chinese leaders generally won praise for the efficiency and relative transparency of their relief efforts. Still, one can find evidence of distributional unfairness. As in Myanmar — or, for that matter, the United States — social problems that exist before a catastrophe are thrown into sharp relief when all hell breaks loose.

With a magnitude of 7.9, the Sichuan Earthquake was the strongest earth-quake China had seen in thirty years. It killed more than 70,000 people and left almost 5 million homeless. After the quake, tours of affected communities revealed the poor had suffered most. In some poorer villages, where homes are made of cheap material and families live on $100 per month, nearly every building lay in ruins. As is common, most residents in these communities lacked insurance. Although China's central government set aside $772 million for relief aid, many villagers reasonably feared there would not be enough to go around. "The government has never helped us," said one villager to an American news service, "We don't trust that they will help us now." Before the earthquake, government statistics showed that 2.1 million people in Sichuan province lived in poverty. Weeks after the quake, the Chinese govern-ment reported that an additional 1.4 million farmers in 4,000 villages had fallen into poverty because of the destruction.

In Beijing political circles, class is a sensitive topic. President Hu Jintao had based much of his public legitimacy on efforts to shrink China's widening economic gap, which is most noticeable when comparing urban and rural populations. Days after the earthquake an article in the *Wall Street Journal* contrasted two areas in the strike zone. In one, a rural village called Yinhua, [b]oulders loosed by [the] quake, some as big as vans, littered the main road . . . along with the vehicles they knocked over or crushed." Nearly every home was destroyed. Meanwhile, roughly 55 miles away in Sichuan's capital city, Chengdu, conditions were very different. "The glitzy new office towers and hotels . . . were still standing and largely intact. The city suffered relatively little in [the] quake, despite its proximity to the epicenter."

The collapse of nearly 7,000 school buildings in Sichuan heaped more attention on China's economic inequality. At least 10,000 children perished in school buildings that many believe were poorly constructed and out of compliance with building codes. Thousands of enraged parents demanded government inquiries and protested what they called "tofu buildings." Many parents were "especially upset that some schools for poor students crumbled into rubble even though government offices and more elite schools not far away survived the May 12 quake largely intact." Public outcry over such disparities appeared to knock the Chinese leadership on its heels. They were, after all in the midst of preparing for Beijing's much-anticipated [2008 Summer] Olympic Games, which, with its "Water Cube" and stylish stadium, would prove to be one of the most expensive and lavish celebrations the world had ever seen. Weeks after the quake, Chinese officials were seen buying the silence of angry parents who had lost children in the calamity, offering them anywhere from $5,600 to $8,800 in cash in exchange for a signed promise to avoid protests and "maintain social order."

NOTES AND QUESTIONS

1. The social vulnerabilities described in Myanmar and China are made worse by the lack of government transparency, democratic processes, and civil liberties. How do such features help vulnerable populations in times of disaster? To what degree should values such as transparency or autonomy be limited by the need for efficiency and quick response? Who should decide that balance?

2. In the aftermath of Cyclone Nargis, news reports generally praised the swift and generous response of the international community, while properly condemning Myanmar's callous government. Although the Burmese junta bears ultimate responsibility for the government's repression, corruption, and mismanagement, some observers have suggested that the international community made matters worse by restricting foreign aid except in times of catastrophic emergency. Soon after the Myanmar disaster, a well-respected, nonpartisan think tank called the International Crisis Group offered this view:

   > Twenty years of aid restrictions — which see Myanmar receiving twenty times less assistance per capita than other least-developed countries — have

weakened, not strengthened, the forces for change. Bringing about peace and democracy will require visionary leaders at all levels, backed by strong organisations, who can manage the transition and provide effective governance. These are not common attributes of an isolated and impoverished society. As the country's socio-economic crisis deepens and its human resources and administrative capacity decline, it will become harder and harder for any government to turn the situation around.

INTERNATIONAL CRISIS GROUP, BURMA/MYANMAR AFTER NARGIS: TIME TO NORMALISE AID RELATIONS (Asia Report No. 161), Oct. 20, 2008, at i, http://www.crisisgroup. org/home/index.cfm?id=5734 (Aug. 25, 2009). What responsibility do nations have to address social vulnerabilities within foreign countries *before* disaster strikes? What is the best way to accomplish this? Do you agree with the view expressed above?

D. INTERNATIONAL LAW AND INTERNATIONAL AID

1. THE HYOGO FRAMEWORK AND MITIGATION PROJECTS

In January 2005, government officials from around the globe met in Kobe, Japan, to discuss disaster preparation and response. By an odd coincidence, only days before, an enormous earthquake off the west coast of Sumatra had triggered the devastating Asian tsunami that battered the coasts of eleven countries and killed more than 225,000 people. At that international meeting, called the World Conference on Disaster Reduction, all member states of the United Nations agreed to reduce disaster loss by strengthening the resilience of nations and communities at risk. One product of the conference, reported widely by the press, was a plan to establish an international early warning system to identify coastal storms and tsunamis in time for people to evacuate. A related and even more ambitious product was an international framework intended to guide the world's disaster initiatives through 2015. The document was called the Hyogo Framework, named after the prefecture, or political district, in which Kobe is located. An excerpt from this document is reprinted below.

HYOGO FRAMEWORK FOR ACTION 2005-2015:
BUILDING THE RESILIENCE OF NATIONS AND COMMUNITIES TO DISASTERS

(A/CONF.206/6)

I. Preamble

. . .

A. Challenges Posed by Disasters

. . .

There is now international acknowledgement that efforts to reduce disaster risks must be systematically integrated into policies, plans and programmes for sustainable development and poverty reduction, and supported through bilateral, regional and international cooperation, including partnerships. Sustainable development, poverty reduction, good governance and disaster risk reduction are mutually supportive objectives, and in order to meet the challenges ahead, accelerated efforts must be made to build the necessary capacities at the community and national levels to manage and reduce risk. . . .

III. Priorities for Action 2005-2015

A. General Considerations

In determining appropriate action to achieve the expected outcome and strategic goals, the Conference reaffirms that the following general considerations will be taken into account: . . .

(b) Taking into account the importance of international cooperation and partnerships, each State has the primary responsibility for its own sustainable development and for taking effective measures to reduce disaster risk. . . .

(c) An integrated, multi-hazard approach to disaster risk reduction should be factored into policies, planning and programming. . . .

(d) A gender perspective should be integrated into all disaster risk management policies. . . .

(e) Cultural diversity, age, and vulnerable groups should be taken into account when planning for disaster risk reduction, as appropriate;

(f) Both communities and local authorities should be empowered to manage and reduce disaster risk by having access to the necessary information, resources and authority to implement actions for disaster risk reduction;

(g) Disaster-prone developing countries, especially least developed countries and small island developing States, warrant particular attention in view of their higher vulnerability and risk levels, which often greatly exceed their capacity to respond to and recover from disasters;

. . .

B. Priorities for Action

. . .

The Conference has adopted the following five priorities for action:

1. Ensure that disaster risk reduction is a national and a local priority with a strong institutional basis for implementation

. . .

Key activities:

(i) National institutional and legislative frameworks

(a) Support the creation and strengthening of national integrated disaster risk reduction mechanisms, such as multi sectoral national platforms, with designated responsibilities at the national through to the local levels to facilitate coordination across sectors. . . .

(b) Integrate risk reduction, as appropriate, into development policies and planning at all levels of government, including in poverty reduction strategies and sectors and multi sector policies and plans. . . .

(d) Recognize the importance and specificity of local risk patterns and trends, decentralize responsibilities and resources for disaster risk reduction to relevant sub-national or local authorities, as appropriate.

(ii) Resources

(e) Assess existing human resource capacities for disaster risk reduction at all levels and develop capacity-building plans and programmes for meeting ongoing and future requirements. . . .

(g) Governments should demonstrate the strong political determination required to promote and integrate disaster risk reduction into development programming.

(iii) Community participation

(h) Promote community participation in disaster risk reduction through the adoption of specific policies, the promotion of networking, the strategic management of volunteer resources, the attribution of roles and responsibilities, and the delegation and provision of the necessary authority and resources.

2. Identify, assess and monitor disaster risks and enhance early warning

. . .

Key activities:

(i) National and local risk assessments

(a) Develop, update periodically and widely disseminate risk maps and related information to decision-makers, the general public and communities at risk in an appropriate format. . . .

(ii) Early warning

. . .

(d) Develop early warning systems that are people centered, in particular systems whose warnings are timely and understandable to those at risk, which take into account the demographic, gender, cultural and livelihood characteristics of the target audiences, including guidance on how to act upon warnings, and that support effective operations by disaster managers and other decision makers.

(iii) Capacity

(i) Support the development and sustainability of the infrastructure and scientific, technological, technical and institutional capacities needed to research, observe, analyse, map and where possible forecast natural and related hazards, vulnerabilities and disaster impacts. . . .

(iv) Regional and emerging risks

. . .

(n) Cooperate regionally and internationally, as appropriate, to assess and monitor regional and trans-boundary hazards, and exchange information and provide early warnings through appropriate arrangements, such as, *inter alia*, those relating to the management of river basins. . . .

3. Use knowledge, innovation and education to build a culture of safety and resilience at all levels

. . .

Key activities:

(i) Information management and exchange

(a) Provide easily understandable information on disaster risks and protection options, especially to citizens in high-risk areas, to encourage and enable people to take action to reduce risks and build resilience. . . .

(ii) Education and training

(h) Promote the inclusion of disaster risk reduction knowledge in relevant sections of school curricula at all levels and the use of other formal and informal channels to reach youth and children. . . .

(i) Promote the implementation of local risk assessment and disaster preparedness programmes in schools and institutions of higher education. . . .

(m) Ensure equal access to appropriate training and educational opportunities for women and vulnerable constituencies; promote gender and cultural sensitivity training as integral components of education and training for disaster risk reduction.

(iii) Research

(n) Develop improved methods for predictive multi-risk assessments and socioeconomic cost—benefit analysis of risk reduction actions at all levels; incorporate these methods into decision-making processes at regional, national and local levels.

. . .

4. Reduce the underlying risk factors

Key activities:

(i) Environmental and natural resource management

(a) Encourage the sustainable use and management of ecosystems, including through better land-use planning and development activities to reduce risk and vulnerabilities.

(b) Implement integrated environmental and natural resource management approaches that incorporate disaster risk reduction, including structural and non-structural measures, such as integrated flood management and appropriate management of fragile ecosystems.

(c) Promote the integration of risk reduction associated with existing climate variability and future climate change into strategies for the reduction of disaster risk and adaptation to climate change, which would include the clear identification of climate-related disaster risks, the design of specific risk reduction measures and an improved and routine use of climate risk information by planners, engineers and other decision-makers.

(ii) Social and economic development practices

(d) Promote food security as an important factor in ensuring the resilience of communities to hazards, particularly in areas prone to drought, flood, cyclones and other hazards that can weaken agriculture-based livelihoods. . . .

(f) Protect and strengthen critical public facilities and physical infrastructure, particularly schools, clinics, hospitals, water and power plants, communications and transport lifelines, disaster warning and management centres, and culturally important lands and structures through proper design, retrofitting and re-building, in order to render them adequately resilient to hazards.

(g) Strengthen the implementation of social safety-net mechanisms to assist the poor, the elderly and the disabled, and other populations affected by disasters. Enhance recovery schemes including psycho-social training programmes in order to mitigate the psychological damage of vulnerable populations, particularly children, in the aftermath of disasters. . . .

(j) Promote diversified income options for populations in high-risk areas to reduce their vulnerability to hazards, and ensure that their income and assets are not undermined by development policy and processes that increase their vulnerability to disasters. . . .

(iii) Land-use planning and other technical measures

(n) Incorporate disaster risk assessments into the urban planning and management of disaster-prone human settlements, in particular highly populated areas and quickly urbanizing settlements. . . .

(q) Incorporate disaster risk assessment into rural development planning and management, in particular with regard to mountain and coastal flood plain areas. . . .

5. Strengthen disaster preparedness for effective response at all levels . . .
Key activities:
. . .

(d) Prepare or review and periodically update disaster preparedness and contingency plans and policies at all levels, with a particular focus on the most vulnerable areas and groups. Promote regular disaster preparedness exercises, including evacuation drills, with a view to ensuring rapid and effective disaster response and access to essential food and non-food relief supplies, as appropriate, to local needs.
. . .

IV. Implementation and Follow-Up

States, within the bounds of their financial capabilities, regional and international organizations, through appropriate multilateral, regional and bilateral coordination mechanisms, should . . .

(a) Mobilize the appropriate resources and capabilities of relevant national, regional and international bodies, including the United Nations system;

(b) Provide for and support, through bilateral and multilateral channels, the implementation of this Framework for Action in disaster-prone developing countries, including through financial and technical assistance, addressing debt sustainability, technology transfer on mutually agreed terms, and public–private partnerships, and encourage North–South and South–South cooperation;

(c) Mainstream disaster risk reduction measures appropriately into multilateral and bilateral development assistance programmes including those related to poverty reduction, natural resource management, urban development and adaptation to climate change;

(d) Provide adequate voluntary financial contributions to the United Nations Trust Fund for Disaster Reduction, in the effort to ensure the adequate support for the follow-up activities to this Framework for Action.

NOTES AND QUESTIONS

1. Although the Hyogo Framework was not the first international agreement to address disaster mitigation, it is the most comprehensive. For instance, the Yokohama Strategy for a Safer World: Guidelines for Natural Disaster Prevention, Preparedness and Mitigation and its Plan of Action (1994) established many of the principles expanded upon at Hyogo. The Agenda for Humanitarian Action adopted by the International Conference of the Red

Cross and Red Crescent in December 2003 set forth goals and actions to "reduce the risk and impact of disasters and improve preparedness and response mechanisms."

Many international environmental agreements also address disaster risk. The U.N. Convention to Combat Desertification in Those Countries Experiencing Serious Drought and/or Desertification, Particularly in Africa, adopted in 1994, specifically targeted issues of water scarcity. The U.N. Millennium Declaration of 2000 listed among its key objectives, "[p]rotecting the vulnerable" and "[p]rotecting our common environment"; the parties also resolved to "intensify cooperation to reduce the number and effects of natural and man-made disasters." The Johannesburg Plan of Implementation of the World Summit on Sustainable Development, held in 2002, urged that "[a]n integrated, multi-hazard, inclusive approach to address vulnerability, risk, assessment and disaster management, including prevention, mitigation, preparedness, response and recovery, is an essential element of a safer world in the 21st century." The Johannesburg Plan also requested the Intergovernmental Panel on Climate Change (IPCC) to "improve techniques and methodologies for assessing the effects of climate change, and encourage the continuing assessment of those adverse effects." Similarly, the U.N. General Assembly has encouraged the IPCC to continue to assess the adverse effects of climate change on the socioeconomic and natural disaster reduction systems of developing countries.

2. The Hyogo Framework emphasizes the broad interdisciplinary nature of disaster planning and response. Note the attention paid to scale of government (federalism), identity and culture, poverty, land use planning, environmental protection, risk analysis, and education. The document also emphasizes systemic integration — the idea that disaster policies should be "mainstreamed" into more general initiatives having to do with economic development, environmental protection, land use planning, scientific research, and other concerns. What are the challenges in mainstreaming disaster policy in this way? Why not encourage a nation or the international community to concentrate on a *single* initiative or agreement that would address disaster mitigation in all aspects?

3. Another obvious, but less prominent, theme is the need for resources: information, technology, training, and of course, money. Many of the resources needed for disaster mitigation and the inevitable emergency response are simply beyond reach in places such as Haiti, Bangladesh, or Pakistan. For this reason, the Hyogo Framework urges wealthier nations to offer "financial and technical assistance" to poorer countries and to provide "adequate voluntary financial contributions" to the United Nations disaster reduction fund. But charity is a weak foundation for long-term development efforts such as this. How would you persuade a wealthy government to invest in disaster mitigation for developing countries? Could such investment be justified in terms of national or economic security? Is there something recipient nations could offer in return?

4. As of 2007, more than thirty-eight countries have established "national platforms" for implementing Hyogo's strategic goals. More than 100 countries now have some agency or other body responsible for implementing and

monitoring progress toward these goals. Hyogo-inspired risk reduction strategies have already been designed or implemented in the Andes region, Central America, the Caribbean, the Pacific, Asia, Africa, and Europe. In earthquake-prone Kazakhstan, for instance, the U.N. Development Programme is helping to incorporate disaster response information in grade school curricula as a way of building resilience in poorer communities. Nigeria, whose people sometimes endure heavy rains and dangerous floods, has integrated risk reduction into its regional planning budgets and antipoverty initiatives. In Vietnam, a special partnership of government offices, private donors, and NGOs is promoting disaster management for the country's storm-swept jungles and shores; the effort focuses on *both* lifting villagers out of poverty *and* protecting river basins, swamps, and coastal beaches.

For more information on the Hyogo Framework and its implementation, see U.N. International Strategy for Disaster Reduction, Report of the Secretary General, Implementation of the International Strategy for Disaster, Risk Reduction, Sept. 5, 2007, www.unisdr.org (Dec. 1, 2008); U.N. International Strategy for Disaster Reduction, Linking Disaster Risk Reduction and Poverty Reduction: Good Practices and Lessons Learned, 2008, www.unisdr.org (Dec. 1, 2008); and U.N. International Strategy for Disaster Reduction, Hyogo Framework for Action 2005-2015: Building the Resilience of Nations and Communities to Disasters, (undated), www.unisdr.org (Dec. 1, 2008).

5. To see how disaster mitigation unfolds on the ground, read the following case study from Gaibandha, a remote part of Bangladesh located at the confluence of the Tista and Brahmaputra rivers. The project was implemented by a nonprofit organization called Practical Action and funded by the British government.

**U.N. International Strategy for Disaster Reduction,
Linking Disaster Risk Reduction and Poverty Reduction:
Good Practices and Lessons Learned**

---

www.unisdr.org (2008)

Gaibandha District is located in northern Bangladesh at the confluence of two major rivers: Tista and Brahmaputra. This location makes the area vulnerable to disasters, due to flooding and river erosion. Frequent disasters make life in the area much more difficult than in the rest of country, depriving residents of land, employment opportunities and basic services.

As a result, local populations live below subsistence level. They often have to live where there are minimal or no basic services, such as safe water, sanitation, health and education. Communications are extremely poor. The remoteness of the district and the complexity of its problems result in a high degree of social marginalization, child labour, exploitation, child marriage, early pregnancies and violation of human rights. Women and children are the most vulnerable, as men migrate in large numbers in search of employment and livelihood security.

To cope with their situation of both extreme poverty and disaster risk, the communities generally depend on external relief and rehabilitation after a disaster. Vulnerable community members are also forced to engage in indentured labour for their survival.

The 20,000 households targeted by the project were a highly disadvantaged segment of the community. After losing their lands and shelters permanently in the river, the communities relocated to the flood protection embankment where there were no basic services, employment opportunities or secure livelihood options. The project's comprehensive approaches have helped them secure access to income and basic services such as shelter, health, education and food. Highly diversified and alternative risk reduction strategies and income opportunities have been explored throughout the command areas (over 1,600 km^2) with proven results and visible impacts on the communities' lives and livelihoods. The project beneficiaries now have a range of innovative mechanisms to cope sustainably with disaster risk and poverty, which has significantly reduced migration.

To help manage and minimize disaster risk, the project has developed participatory technologies all over the command areas and in the district. The major risk reduction and livelihood strategies are:

- Providing access to improve livelihood knowledge, skills and information through capacity building training and demonstrations of off-farm and on-farm based technologies.
- Developing infrastructure services and facilities such as multi-purpose shelters, cluster villages, community clinics, schools, safe water and sanitation.
- Establishing community-based early warning and rapid evacuation systems.
- Ensuring better access to common property resources, and to social, civil and political rights.

The project works directly with the communities to reduce poverty, disaster risk and vulnerability, by building capacity through technological and social interventions. The interventions include:

- Flood-friendly agriculture, fisheries and livestock resource management.
- Flood-resistant housing and multi-purpose shelter development.
- Alternative income generation through light engineering training.
- Small enterprise development through small businesses, and agro-processing for added value (which has created better access to common property resources, ensuring legal rights).
- Influencing policy makers to recognize successful practices for national and international dissemination.

In combining disaster risk reduction with poverty reduction, the project has used comprehensive disaster risk reduction strategies, shifting relief-dependent attitudes towards long-term disaster risk reduction, management and planning. Additionally, the project worked to motivate local, national and international agencies to mainstream disaster issues into development practices for the sake of effective and long-term sustainable solutions. In a nutshell, the project has demonstrated a number of ways to help communities reduce their vulnerability to disasters, which also help them overcome chronic poverty and social problems. It has also developed people's capacity to cope with frequent natural hazards, and to adapt to climate change. . . .

The project can be described as good practice because it has developed a very effective risk reduction and management model, as well as a number of innovative pro-poor-based natural resource management technologies. These technologies were designed for wider impact on the poor and naturally disadvantaged communities not only in the project areas, but also in other districts and regions.

The project also developed innovative ideas and models on risk reduction and management, climate change adaptation and natural resource management issues. Innovative ideas included:

- The development of a model cluster village to resettle communities displaced by river erosion.
- The development of multi-purpose shelters to accommodate affected communities hit by flood disasters.
- The establishment of a community-based rapid evacuation system to minimize community risk and vulnerability.
- The development of unique, low-cost and pro-poor technologies such as agricultural production on barren sand bars, floating gardens and cage aquaculture.
- Improved access of marginalized people to basic rights (health, education, sanitation and legal rights), particularly for women and children.

All the above ideas, innovations, knowledge and learning strongly motivated community members, policy makers, development practitioners, donors and other stakeholders both at the local, national and international levels. The project also influenced the development of a new policy for poor people living on the edge of mighty rivers in Bangladesh.

The project was shared at a number of international forums to influence policy makers and development practitioners in building awareness of climate change issues. These included World Water Week 2007 and the House of Lords event for the Oxfam "Make Poverty History" campaign in the United Kingdom, as well as other events at Sheffield University (UK), the British parliament, the German and Belgian parliaments, and the Plenary Meeting of the Asia-Pacific Forum for Environment and Development (APFED) in China. . . .

The project has initiated a very comprehensive disaster risk and poverty reduction strategy, aiming to develop a sustainable model for replication in other parts of Bangladesh, particularly among disadvantaged communities living on the edge of mighty rivers. Replication could be easily achieved in other parts of the country with a tiny amendment to national policy, and channeling of national and donor funding to relevant development initiatives.

2. PROTECTING AGAINST DISCRIMINATION

Of international agreements important to disaster management, many focus on human rights. These include the International Covenant on Civil and Political Rights, the Convention on the Elimination of All Forms of Racial Discrimination (CERD), and the Protocol Relating to the Status of Refugees, all of which the United States has ratified. Other relevant treaties, but which the United States has not ratified, include the International Covenant on Economic, Social and Cultural Rights; the Convention on the Elimination of All Forms of Discrimination against Women (CEDAW); and the Convention on the Rights of the Child. For the most part these agreements were not written with disaster management specifically in mind. And although aggrieved individuals have the right to issue complaints with the United Nations, none of these conventions creates individual rights legally enforceable in the traditional sense. Consider these excerpted provisions of two important antidiscrimination agreements, CERD and CEDAW.

INTERNATIONAL CONVENTION ON THE ELIMINATION OF ALL FORMS OF RACIAL DISCRIMINATION

660 U.N.T.S. 195 (1965)

Article 1

1. In this Convention, the term "racial discrimination" shall mean any distinction, exclusion, restriction or preference based on race, color, descent, or national or ethnic origin which has the purpose or effect of nullifying or impairing the recognition, enjoyment or exercise, on an equal footing, of human rights and fundamental freedoms in the political, economic, social, cultural or any other field of public life.

2. This Convention shall not apply to distinctions, exclusions, restrictions or preferences made by a State Party to this Convention between citizens and non-citizens.

3. Nothing in this Convention may be interpreted as affecting in any way the legal provisions of States Parties concerning nationality, citizenship or naturalization, provided that such provisions do not discriminate against any particular nationality.

. . .

Article 2

1. States Parties condemn racial discrimination and undertake to pursue by all appropriate means and without delay a policy of eliminating racial discrimination in all its forms and promoting understanding among all races . . .

Article 5

In compliance with the fundamental obligations laid down in article 2 of this Convention, States Parties undertake to prohibit and to eliminate racial discrimination in all its forms and to guarantee the right of everyone, without distinction as to race, colour, or national or ethnic origin, to equality before the law, notably in the enjoyment of the following rights:

(a) The right to equal treatment before the tribunals and all other organs administering justice;

(b) The right to security of person and protection by the State against violence or bodily harm, whether inflicted by government officials or by any individual group or institution;

(c) Political rights, in particular the right to participate in elections — to vote and to stand for election — on the basis of universal and equal suffrage, to take part in the Government as well as in the conduct of public affairs at any level and to have equal access to public service;

(d) Other civil rights, in particular:
   (i) The right to freedom of movement and residence within the border of the State;
   (ii) The right to leave any country, including one's own, and to return to one's country;
   (iii) The right to nationality;
   (iv) The right to marriage and choice of spouse;
   (v) The right to own property alone as well as in association with others;
   (vi) The right to inherit;
   (vii) The right to freedom of thought, conscience and religion;
   (viii) The right to freedom of opinion and expression;
   (ix) The right to freedom of peaceful assembly and association;

(e) Economic, social and cultural rights, in particular:
   (i) The rights to work, to free choice of employment, to just and favourable conditions of work, to protection against unemployment, to equal pay for equal work, to just and favourable remuneration;
   (ii) The right to form and join trade unions;
   (iii) The right to housing;
   (iv) The right to public health, medical care, social security and social services;
   (v) The right to education and training;
   (vi) The right to equal participation in cultural activities;

(f) The right of access to any place or service intended for use by the general public, such as transport, hotels, restaurants, cafes, theatres and parks. . . .

Convention on the Elimination of All Forms of Discrimination Against Women

1249 U.N.T.S. 13 (1979)

Article 1

For the purposes of the present Convention, the term "discrimination against women" shall mean any distinction, exclusion or restriction made on the basis of sex which has the effect or purpose of impairing or nullifying the recognition, enjoyment or exercise by women, irrespective of their marital status, on a basis of equality of men and women, of human rights and fundamental freedoms in the political, economic, social, cultural, civil or any other field.

Article 2

States Parties condemn discrimination against women in all its forms, agree to pursue by all appropriate means and without delay a policy of eliminating discrimination against women. . . .

Article 3

States Parties shall take in all fields, in particular in the political, social, economic and cultural fields, all appropriate measures, including legislation, to ensure the full development and advancement of women, for the purpose of guaranteeing them the exercise and enjoyment of human rights and fundamental freedoms on a basis of equality with men.

Article 4

1. Adoption by States Parties of temporary special measures aimed at accelerating de facto equality between men and women shall not be considered discrimination as defined in the present Convention . . .

2. Adoption by States Parties of special measures, including those measures contained in the present Convention, aimed at protecting maternity shall not be considered discriminatory. . . .

Article 5

States Parties shall take all appropriate measures:

(a) To modify the social and cultural patterns of conduct of men and women, with a view to achieving the elimination of prejudices and customary and all other practices which are based on the idea of the inferiority or the superiority of either of the sexes or on stereotyped roles for men and women;

(b) To ensure that family education includes a proper understanding of maternity as a social function and the recognition of the common responsibility of men and women in the upbringing and development of their children, it being understood that the interest of the children is the primordial consideration in all cases.

Article 6

States Parties shall take all appropriate measures, including legislation, to suppress all forms of traffic in women and exploitation of prostitution of women.

Article 7

States Parties shall take all appropriate measures to eliminate discrimination against women in the political and public life of the country and, in particular, shall ensure to women, on equal terms with men, the right:

(a) To vote in all elections and public referenda and to be eligible for election to all publicly elected bodies;

(b) To participate in the formulation of government policy and the implementation thereof and to hold public office and perform all public functions at all levels of government;

(c) To participate in non-governmental organizations and associations concerned with the public and political life of the country.

. . .

Article 11

1. States Parties shall take all appropriate measures to eliminate discrimination against women in the field of employment in order to ensure, on a basis of equality of men and women, the same rights, in particular:

(a) The right to work as an inalienable right of all human beings;

(b) The right to the same employment opportunities, including the application of the same criteria for selection in matters of employment;

(c) The right to free choice of profession and employment . . .

(d) The right to equal remuneration, including benefits, and to equal treatment in respect of work of equal value . . .

(f) The right to protection of health and to safety in working conditions, including the safeguarding of the function of reproduction.

. . .

Article 12

1. States Parties shall take all appropriate measures to eliminate discrimination against women in the field of health care in order to ensure, on a basis of equality of men and women, access to health care services, including those related to family planning.

2. Notwithstanding the provisions of paragraph I of this article, States Parties shall ensure to women appropriate services in connection with pregnancy, confinement and the post-natal period, granting free services where necessary, as well as adequate nutrition during pregnancy and lactation.

Article 13

States Parties shall take all appropriate measures to eliminate discrimination against women in other areas of economic and social life in order to ensure, on a basis of equality of men and women, the same rights, in particular:

(a) The right to family benefits;

(b) The right to bank loans, mortgages and other forms of financial credit;

(c) The right to participate in recreational activities, sports and all aspects of cultural life.

Article 14

1. States Parties shall take into account the particular problems faced by rural women and the significant roles which rural women play in the economic survival of their families, including their work in the non-monetized sectors of the economy, and shall take all appropriate measures to ensure the application of the provisions of the present Convention to women in rural areas.

2. States Parties shall take all appropriate measures to eliminate discrimination against women in rural areas in order to ensure, on a basis of equality of

men and women, that they participate in and benefit from rural development and, in particular, shall ensure to such women the right:

(a) To participate in the elaboration and implementation of development planning at all levels;

(b) To have access to adequate health care facilities, including information, counselling and services in family planning;

(c) To benefit directly from social security programmes;

(d) To obtain all types of training and education, formal and non-formal, including that relating to functional literacy, as well as, inter alia, the benefit of all community and extension services, in order to increase their technical proficiency;

(e) To organize self-help groups and co-operatives in order to obtain equal access to economic opportunities through employment or self employment;

(f) To participate in all community activities;

(g) To have access to agricultural credit and loans, marketing facilities, appropriate technology and equal treatment in land and agrarian reform as well as in land resettlement schemes;

(h) To enjoy adequate living conditions, particularly in relation to housing, sanitation, electricity and water supply, transport and communications.

NOTES AND QUESTIONS

1. CERD and CEDAW are among the treaties most often invoked by critics of disaster relief efforts around the world. Why do you suppose this is so? Is it because of the prominence of discrimination issues in times of disaster, or because of the lack of more forceful treaties dealing with disaster in general?

2. Recall the descriptions of Cyclone Nargis, the Sichuan earthquake, and other disasters recounted in the excerpt by Professor Verchick earlier in this chapter. What possible violations of CERD or CEDAW do you see in those accounts? Myanmar ratified CEDAW in 1997 (with some stated reservations), but has not ratified CERD. China ratified CEDAW in 1980, and CERD in 1981. Keep these treaties in mind when we present a description of the 2004 Asian tsunami later in this chapter.

3. PROTECTING INTERNALLY DISPLACED PERSONS

Days after Hurricane Katrina, when it became clear that the two million residents who had fled their homes would not be returning for a while, Americans wondered what to call them. Some news organizations referred to them as "refugees." But many Louisianans resented that term. They pointed out, correctly, that in legal parlance the word *refugee* refers to a person who has fled to another country, not just crossed a state line. Given the government's insensitive response to their rescue, calling them "refugees" reinforced the view that individuals—many of whom were urban, poor, and Black—were not part of the "real" America. So the press and the public settled instead on "evacuees," or "storm victims," or in casual conversation, "Katrina people."

What many did not know is that the United Nations had already established a phrase to describe people who have been forced to flee their homes, for reasons of armed conflict or disaster, but who remain in their country. It calls them "internally displaced persons," or "IDPs." Although numbers are wildly uncertain, experts believe there are roughly 24 million IDPs in the world at any given time. Most are probably displaced for reasons of war or other violent conflict. But disasters, both natural and man made, contribute significantly to the problem, as in Ethiopia (drought), Pakistan (earthquake), India (flood), and China (earthquake). As we saw in the example of Myanmar after Cyclone Nargis, the internally displaced are at special risk of being neglected or mistreated for reasons of ethnicity, sex, age, or other characteristics.

International law offers no special protections to IDPs as it does to international refugees. Moreover, the United Nations scatters responsibility for IDP issues across many agencies, making comprehensive solutions more difficult. The United Nations, however, has endorsed a document called the Guiding Principles on Internal Displacement, assembled at the request of then-U.N. Secretary-General Boutros Boutros-Ghali in 1992. U.N. Office of the High Commissioner for Human Rights, GUIDING PRINCIPLES ON INTERNAL DISPLACEMENT, www.unhchr.ch (Dec. 1, 2008). Like the Hyogo Framework, the Guiding Principles are another attempt to reduce risk by attacking oppression and set a sensible foundation for future legal development. Though not binding, they are said to reflect "international human rights and humanitarian law and analogous refugee law." Francis M. Deng, INTRODUCTORY NOTE BY THE REPRESENTATIVE OF THE SECRETARY-GENERAL ON INTERNALLY DISPLACED PERSONS, U.N. Office for the Coordination of Humanitarian Affairs (undated), www.reliefweb.int (Dec. 28, 2008). Some provisions concerning physical security and the right to travel, for instance, are drawn from the Covenant on Civil and Political Rights, to which the United States is a party. The Guiding Principles detail, in thirty principles, the guarantees that nations owe to IDPs in all three phases of internal displacement: the predisplacement phase, the phase of actual displacement, and the phase of return or resettlement.

GUIDING PRINCIPLES ON INTERNAL DISPLACEMENT

U.N. Doc. E/CN.4/1998/53/Add.2 (1998)

Introduction: Scope and Purpose

1. These Guiding Principles address the specific needs of internally displaced persons worldwide. They identify rights and guarantees relevant to the protection of persons from forced displacement and to their protection and assistance during displacement as well as during return or resettlement and reintegration.

2. For the purposes of these Principles, internally displaced persons are persons or groups of persons who have been forced or obliged to flee or to leave their homes or places of habitual residence, in particular as a result of

or in order to avoid the effects of armed conflict, situations of generalized violence, violations of human rights or natural or human-made disasters, and who have not crossed an internationally recognized State border. . . .

Section I — General Principles

Principle 1

1. Internally displaced persons shall enjoy, in full equality, the same rights and freedoms under international and domestic law as do other persons in their country. They shall not be discriminated against in the enjoyment of any rights and freedoms on the ground that they are internally displaced. . . .

Principle 2

1. These Principles shall be observed by all authorities, groups and persons irrespective of their legal status and applied without any adverse distinction. . . .

Principle 3

1. National authorities have the primary duty and responsibility to provide protection and humanitarian assistance to internally displaced persons within their jurisdiction.

2. Internally displaced persons have the right to request and to receive protection and humanitarian assistance from these authorities. They shall not be persecuted or punished for making such a request.

Principle 4

1. These Principles shall be applied without discrimination of any kind, such as race, color, sex, language, religion or belief, political or other opinion, national, ethnic or social origin, legal or social status, age, disability, property, birth, or on any other similar criteria.

2. Certain internally displaced persons, such as children, especially unaccompanied minors, expectant mothers, mothers with young children, female heads of household, persons with disabilities and elderly persons, shall be entitled to protection and assistance required by their condition and to treatment which takes into account their special needs.

Section II — Principles Relating to Protection from Displacement

Principle 5

All authorities and international actors shall respect and ensure respect for their obligations under international law, including human rights and humanitarian law, in all circumstances, so as to prevent and avoid conditions that might lead to displacement of persons.

Principle 6

1. Every human being shall have the right to be protected against being arbitrarily displaced from his or her home or place of habitual residence.

2. The prohibition of arbitrary displacement includes displacement:

(a) When it is based on policies of apartheid, "ethnic cleansing" or similar practices aimed at/or resulting in altering the ethnic, religious or racial composition of the affected population; . . .

(c) In cases of large-scale development projects, which are not justi-fied by compelling and overriding public interests;

(d) In cases of disasters, unless the safety and health of those affected requires their evacuation; . . .

3. Displacement shall last no longer than required by the circumstances.

Principle 7

1. Prior to any decision requiring the displacement of persons, the author-ities concerned shall ensure that all feasible alternatives are explored in order to avoid displacement altogether. Where no alternatives exist, all measures shall be taken to minimize displacement and its adverse effects.

2. The authorities undertaking such displacement shall ensure, to the greatest practicable extent, that proper accommodation is provided to the displaced persons, that such displacements are effected in satisfactory condi-tions of safety, nutrition, health and hygiene, and that members of the same family are not separated. . . .

Principle 8

Displacement shall not be carried out in a manner that violates the rights to life, dignity, liberty and security of those affected.

Principle 9

States are under a particular obligation to protect against the displacement of indigenous peoples, minorities, peasants, pastoralists and other groups with a special dependency on and attachment to their lands.

Section III — Principles Relating to Protection During Displacement

Principle 10

1. Every human being has the inherent right to life which shall be pro-tected by law. No one shall be arbitrarily deprived of his or her life. . . .

Principle 11

1. Every human being has the right to dignity and physical, mental and moral integrity.

2. Internally displaced persons, whether or not their liberty has been restricted, shall be protected in particular against:

(a) Rape, mutilation, torture, cruel, inhuman or degrading treatment or punishment, and other outrages upon personal dignity, such as acts of gender-specific violence, forced prostitution and any form of indecent assault;

(b) Slavery or any contemporary form of slavery, such as sale into marriage, sexual exploitation, or forced labour of children; and

(c) Acts of violence intended to spread terror among internally dis-placed persons. Threats and incitement to commit any of the foregoing acts shall be prohibited.

Principle 12

1. Every human being has the right to liberty and security of person. No one shall be subjected to arbitrary arrest or detention.

2. To give effect to this right for internally displaced persons, they shall not be interned in or confined to a camp. If in exceptional circumstances such internment or confinement is absolutely necessary, it shall not last longer than required by the circumstances.

3. Internally displaced persons shall be protected from discriminatory arrest and detention as a result of their displacement. . . .

Principle 14

1. Every internally displaced person has the right to liberty of movement and freedom to choose his or her residence.

2. In particular, internally displaced persons have the right to move freely in and out of camps or other settlements.

Principle 15

Internally displaced persons have:

(a) The right to seek safety in another part of the country;
(b) The right to leave their country;
(c) The right to seek asylum in another country; and
(d) The right to be protected against forcible return to or resettlement in any place where their life, safety, liberty and/or health would be at risk.

Principle 16

1. All internally displaced persons have the right to know the fate and whereabouts of missing relatives.

2. The authorities concerned shall endeavour to establish the fate and whereabouts of internally displaced persons reported missing. . . . They shall inform the next of kin on the progress of the investigation and notify them of any result.

3. The authorities concerned shall endeavour to collect and identify the mortal remains of those deceased, prevent their despoliation or mutilation, and facilitate the return of those remains to the next of kin or dispose of them respectfully. . . .

Principle 17

1. Every human being has the right to respect of his or her family life.

2. To give effect to this right for internally displaced persons, family members who wish to remain together shall be allowed to do so.

3. Families which are separated by displacement should be reunited as quickly as possible. All appropriate steps shall be taken to expedite the reunion of such families, particularly when children are involved. The responsible authorities shall facilitate inquiries made by family members and encourage and cooperate with the work of humanitarian organizations engaged in the task of family reunification.

4. Members of internally displaced families whose personal liberty has been restricted by internment or confinement in camps shall have the right to remain together.

Principle 18

1. All internally displaced persons have the right to an adequate standard of living.

2. At the minimum, regardless of the circumstances, and without discrimination, competent authorities shall provide internally displaced persons with and ensure safe access to:

(a) Essential food and potable water;
(b) Basic shelter and housing;
(c) Appropriate clothing; and
(d) Essential medical services and sanitation.

3. Special efforts should be made to ensure the full participation of women in the planning and distribution of these basic supplies.

Principle 19

1. All wounded and sick internally displaced persons as well as those with disabilities shall receive to the fullest extent practicable and with the least possible delay, the medical care and attention they require, without distinction on any grounds other than medical ones. . . .

2. Special attention should be paid to the health needs of women, including access to female health care providers and services, such as reproductive health care, as well as appropriate counselling for victims of sexual and other abuses.

3. Special attention should also be given to the prevention of contagious and infectious diseases, including AIDS, among internally displaced persons.

Principle 20

1. Every human being has the right to recognition everywhere as a person before the law.

2. To give effect to this right for internally displaced persons, the authorities concerned shall issue to them all documents necessary for the enjoyment and exercise of their legal rights, such as passports, personal identification documents, birth certificates and marriage certificates. In particular, the authorities shall facilitate the issuance of new documents or the replacement of documents lost in the course of displacement, without imposing unreasonable conditions, such as requiring the return to one's area of habitual residence . . . .

Principle 21

1. No one shall be arbitrarily deprived of property and possessions.

2. The property and possessions of internally displaced persons shall in all circumstances be protected, in particular, against the following acts:

(a) Pillage; [and]
(b) Direct or indiscriminate attacks or other acts of violence; . . .

3. Property and possessions left behind by internally displaced persons should be protected against destruction and arbitrary and illegal appropriation, occupation or use. . . .

Principle 22

1. Internally displaced persons, whether or not they are living in camps, shall not be discriminated against as a result of their displacement in the enjoyment of the following rights:

(a) The rights to freedom of thought, conscience, religion or belief, opinion and expression; . . .

(d) The right to vote and to participate in governmental and public affairs, including the right to have access to the means necessary to exercise this right; and

(e) The right to communicate in a language they understand.

Principle 23

1. Every human being has the right to education.

2. To give effect to this right for internally displaced persons, the authorities concerned shall ensure that such persons, in particular displaced children, receive education which shall be free and compulsory at the primary level. . . .

Section IV—Principles Relating to Humanitarian Assistance

Principle 24

1. All humanitarian assistance shall be carried out in accordance with the principles of humanity and impartiality and without discrimination. . . .

Principle 25

1. The primary duty and responsibility for providing humanitarian assistance to internally displaced persons lies with national authorities.

2. International humanitarian organizations and other appropriate actors have the right to offer their services in support of the internally displaced. Such an offer shall not be regarded as an unfriendly act or an interference in a State's internal affairs and shall be considered in good faith. . . .

3. All authorities concerned shall grant and facilitate the free passage of humanitarian assistance and grant persons engaged in the provision of such assistance rapid and unimpeded access to the internally displaced.

Principle 26

Persons engaged in humanitarian assistance, their transport and supplies shall be respected and protected. They shall not be the object of attack or other acts of violence. . . .

Section V—Principles Relating to Return, Resettlement and Reintegration

Principle 28

1. Competent authorities have the primary duty and responsibility to establish conditions, as well as provide the means, which allow internally displaced persons to return voluntarily, in safety and with dignity, to their homes or places of habitual residence, or to resettle voluntarily in another part of the country. Such authorities shall endeavour to facilitate the reintegration of returned or resettled internally displaced persons.

2. Special efforts should be made to ensure the full participation of internally displaced persons in the planning and management of their return or resettlement and reintegration.

Principle 29

1. Internally displaced persons who have returned to their homes or places of habitual residence or who have resettled in another part of the country shall not be discriminated against as a result of their having been displaced. They

shall have the right to participate fully and equally in public affairs at all levels and have equal access to public services.

2. Competent authorities have the duty and responsibility to assist returned and/or resettled internally displaced persons to recover, to the extent possible, their property and possessions which they left behind or were dispossessed of upon their displacement. When recovery of such property and possessions is not possible, competent authorities shall provide or assist these persons in obtaining appropriate compensation or another form of just reparation. . . .

NOTES AND QUESTIONS

1. At first glance, the Guiding Principles seem straightforward, but there is mischief in the details. How would you answer the following questions?

   a. The Guiding Principles forbid "discrimination of any kind" and say that families have the "right to remain together" when housed in camps. Should a country like Pakistan (to pick just one example) be able to segregate relief camps by sex in order to comport with religious custom or to protect women from abuse or violence? Should India be able to segregate relief camps by religious caste for similar reasons?

   b. The Guiding Principles emphasize the needs of women and children. Principle 19, for instance, says "special attention should be paid to the health needs of women, including access to female health care providers and services, such as reproductive health care." What does that access include? Birth control (with or without a partner's consent)? Reversal of a tubal ligation (for women wishing to become pregnant again after losing a child)? Abortion? Principle 4 says children should be provided "assistance . . . which takes into account their special needs." This includes appropriate schooling (Principle 23). Are children entitled to child counseling? Organized recreational activities? Education in their native language? Special education for those with mental or physical disabilities?

   c. Principle 4 says all provisions will be applied without discrimination based on "legal . . . status." Does this prevent a country from checking the identification papers of IDPs before providing them with transportation or relief services? Suppose a country finds within its relief camps illegal residents seeking services. May these persons be legally deported? If so, what is the chance illegal residents will seek the aid that the Guiding Principles say they are entitled to? After Hurricane Gustav hit the Texas coast in 2008, some legal aid workers reported that U.S. immigration officials were checking the residency documents of evacuees returning to their home cities. Is this a violation of Principle 4? How about Principles 28 and 29?

   d. Principle 29 requires state officials to assist IDPs in recovering their property and possessions, or, where recovery is impossible, assist IDPs with "appropriate compensation" or "just reparation." What does that mean? If the government is partly responsible for the failure of a levee or a dam, does that mean the dispossessed are owed compensation? Is that a reversal of sovereign immunity? If not, what practical effect does Principle 29 have?

If your class has trouble reaching consensus, don't worry. At this point none of the questions has been definitively resolved. The debates will continue.

2. Following hurricanes Katrina and Rita in 2005, some human rights experts argued that the U.S. federal government and some state governments had violated several of the Guiding Principles. *See, e.g.,* Lolita Buckner Inniss, *A Domestic Right of Return? Race, Rights, and Residency in New Orleans in the Aftermath of Hurricane Katrina,* 27 B.C. THIRD WORLD L.J. 325, 368-369 (2007); Frederic L. Kirgis, "Hurricane Katrina and Internally Displaced Persons," American Society of International Law, Sept. 21, 2005, http://www.asil.org/insights050921.cfm (July 1, 2009).

Some experts claimed that the U.S. response to Hurricane Katrina, by allowing a disproportionate burden to fall upon African Americans, had also violated CERD. In 2008, a UN treaty committee agreed and urged U.S. officials to afford displaced residents a greater say in decisions affecting their ability to return to New Orleans, including decisions about the future of public housing. U.N. COMMITTEE ON THE ELIMINATION OF ALL FORMS OF RACIAL DISCRIMINATION, CONSIDERATION OF REPORTS SUBMITTED BY STATES PARTIES UNDER ARTICLE 9 OF THE CONVENTION, MAY 8, 2008, http://www.universalhumanrightsindex.org/documents/824/1310/document/en/text.html (July 1, 2009). American officials immediately downplayed the significance of the committee's report and suggested it was misinformed. (Though standing behind the report's conclusion, committee members would later concede they had not visited New Orleans.) *See* David Hammer, *Critics Admit They Didn't Visit, Research Post-Katrina New Orleans,* TIMES-PICAYUNE, March 5, 2008, http://blog.nola.com/updates/2008/03/critics_admit_they_didnt_visit.html (July 1, 2009).

As already pointed out, the United States has not agreed to the Guiding Principles on Internally Displaced Persons, and in any event the agreement is unenforceable. The United States is a party to CERD, but that agreement is not enforceable either. What, then, is the value of calling attention to suspected violations of international agreements such as these? What if the alleged violator is *not* a global power? How does that change the calculus?

3. Critics fault the Guiding Principles for their lack of binding effect. Bahame Tom Nyanduga, a Special Rapporteur for the African Commission on Human and Peoples' Rights, has called the absence of binding protection for IDPs "a grave lacuna in international law." Bahame Tom Nyanduga, THE CHALLENGE OF INTERNAL DISPLACEMENT IN AFRICA, FORCED MIGRATION REVIEW 21, 58 (September 2004).

Despite that omission, the Guiding Principles are gaining some traction and are presumably making a difference in people's lives. Several U.N. entities — such as the U.N. Development Programme, the High Commissioner for Human Rights, and UNICEF — have incorporated the Guiding Principles into their actions and policies. U.N. treaty bodies, which monitor the implementation of U.N. human rights conventions, have referred to the Guiding Principles in their observations of member states. A few countries — including Burundi, Colombia, the Philippines, Sri Lanka, and Uganda — have integrated some of the principles into their national policies.

Although the U.S government does not recognize the Guiding Principles as law, the U.S. Agency for International Development (USAID) explicitly uses the principles to guide foreign assistance efforts in regions of disaster or war. Take a look at this excerpt from USAID's statement on IPDs.

U.S. Agency for International Development, USAID Assistance to Internally Displaced Persons

http://www.usaid.gov/policy/ads/200/200mbc.pdf, 1-3 (Oct. 2004)

At least 25 million people are uprooted within the borders of their own countries by armed conflict, generalized violence, persecution, and natural and human-caused disasters. The plight of these internally displaced persons (IDPs) in some 52 countries is a pressing humanitarian, human rights, development, and political challenge for the global community. . . .

The U.S. Agency for International Development (USAID) recognizes that the 25 million people displaced within their own countries are a pressing humanitarian, human rights, development, and political challenge for the global community. There are nearly twice as many internally displaced persons (IDPs) as the 13 million civilians classified as refugees who have crossed international frontiers, thereby gaining protection under international laws.

USAID's interest in internal displacement is driven by humanitarian and development concerns as well as political and security considerations. Involuntary displacement can lead to disaffection that could be exploited to threaten regional stability. The National Security Strategy of the United States, issued in 2002, elevated the importance of development, citing it — along with defense and diplomacy — as a fundamental element of U.S. security.

Since IDPs remain within the territorial jurisdiction of their own countries, the primary responsibility for their welfare and protection lies with the respective governing authorities. The international community should provide assistance and support to ensure this responsibility is being fulfilled. USAID advocates that IDPs should be granted the full security and protection provided for under applicable norms of international human rights law, international humanitarian law, and national law. Population displacement can endure for a few days, several years, or even decades, creating a wide range of needs. Basic protection for at-risk populations requires attention during the immediate humanitarian response to population displacement as well as during the longer-term transition toward development and stability.

The inclusion of a comprehensive response to the problem of internal displacement in the broader USAID strategy is a priority. This reflects the growing understanding of how population displacement can negatively affect stability and development prospects. USAID is committed to a long-term perspective that promotes durable solutions and eventual self-reliance for displaced persons, reinforcing the principle that internal displacement is an Agency-wide concern.

With its strong operational presence in the field, USAID will address the broad array of needs confronting all phases of displacement, ranging from emergency relief to transitional aid to long-term development assistance. The transitional phase is critical, requiring the coordinated efforts of all partners to develop a comprehensive strategy that facilitates IDP resettlement and reintegration. The ultimate goal is to enable IDPs to become fully productive contributors to economic and social progress in their local communities.

USAID will serve as the U.S. Government's lead coordinator on internal displacement to ensure a coherent response from the U.S. Government and the international community. The Agency will work closely with the U.S. Department of State and other U.S. Government entities, U.N. agencies, international organizations, nongovernmental organizations (NGOs), host governments, and local institutions in affected countries. As part of its advocacy role, USAID promotes

- lifesaving humanitarian access to needy populations
- information sharing to forge common understanding of the problems and build consensus on policy and strategic approaches
- the protection of IDPs during all phases of displacement
- accountability and evaluation of programs
- wider international recognition of the U.N. Guiding Principles on Internal Displacement as a useful framework for dealing with internal displacement

Internal population displacement and the factors that cause it pose difficult challenges and present complex legal and sovereignty issues. The availability of resources, security, and humanitarian access will affect the scale of assistance and protection that USAID and the international community can provide. USAID will review these challenging issues on a regular basis to develop and update effective strategies.

NOTES AND QUESTION

1. In this statement, USAID says it promotes "wider international recognition" of the Guiding Principles as a policy framework. Why, then, has the U.S. government not recognized the application of those principles on American soil? What specific provisions, if any, do you think the government objects to?

E. PULLING IT ALL TOGETHER

As a way of synthesizing the many issues in this chapter — geographic distribution, ecological exposure, social vulnerability, and international law — we ask you to review this last case study of one of the most devastating and broad-scaled catastrophes of the last half-century: the 2004 Asian tsunami.

ACTION AID INTERNATIONAL, TSUNAMI RESPONSE: A HUMAN RIGHTS ASSESSMENT

www.reliefweb.int/rw/RWFiles2006.nsf/FilesByRWDocUNIDFileName/SODA-6LM2SS-tsunami_HR01.pdf/$File/tsunami_HR01.pdf (January 2006)

The December 2004 tsunami unleashed loss and destruction of horrific magnitude in 12 countries in Asia and Africa. One year after the tragedy, despite the tremendous efforts of local, national and international agencies, the rehabilitation and reconstruction process is fraught with difficulties.

Even though all the affected countries have ratified international human rights instruments, they are failing to meet these standards in post-tsunami relief and rehabilitation work. Allegations of human rights violations in tsunami-affected areas are rampant. These include discrimination in aid distribution, forced relocation, arbitrary arrests and sexual and gender-based violence. One year on, tsunami reconstruction efforts are plagued with serious delays and have not been given the priority they warrant. . . .

Inadequate response and a lack of consideration for the human rights of victims creates a human-induced tragedy that exacerbates the plight of those already suffering the effects of a disaster brought on by natural causes. Therefore, individual states, international agencies including the UN and its programmes, civil society and the private sector, must redouble efforts towards the realisation of human rights worldwide, including rights to disaster-preparedness and disaster-response. Indeed this is essential if we are to reduce the loss of life, human suffering and homelessness resulting from disasters in the future. It is only through national and international cooperation based on human rights standards that people uprooted and at risk as a result of devastating natural disasters can be effectively protected. This report is a significant contribution. It assesses the status of post-tsunami reconstruction and clearly highlights multiple human rights violations in Indonesia, Thailand, Sri Lanka, India and the Maldives. It makes the demand for human rights standards in resettlement and reconstruction all the more urgent. Non-discriminatory access to relief and rehabilitation, mechanisms to ensure transparency and accountability, and provision for the active participation of survivors are fundamental, while all efforts must take into account the special needs and concerns of women. . . .

Land

The right to land is one of the most contentious issues to have arisen in the wake of the tsunami. Across the region there are cases of conflict between communities who have historically lived along the coastline and government departments, major land-owners and developers. With coastal land at a premium for tourism and sea areas coveted by industrial fishing companies, the governments of India, Sri Lanka, Indonesia and Thailand are discouraging— and even preventing—people from returning to their original land and fishing areas. In some cases governments have made compensation contingent on people relinquishing their rights to coastal land. In other cases, governments have failed to compensate local residents and farmers for land that has become uninhabitable or barren due to sea water. Survivors from Kuala Bubon in West Aceh, Indonesia, are still awaiting compensation for lost land and earnings, despite repeated promises from the chief of Indonesia's National Land Agency.

Buffer Zones

An aspect of government policy that has caused great hardship to tsunami survivors has been the imposition of "buffer zones" preventing people from rebuilding homes along the coast. India, Indonesia, Sri Lanka, Thailand and the Maldives have all created restricted areas or islands, supposedly to mitigate the impact of future storms or tsunamis. With moving inland often a precondition for receiving a new house, poorer families are left with little choice but to relocate. . . .

In India, the "coastal regulation zone" (CRZ), in existence since 1991, restricts dwellings and other residential activity within 500 metres of the high-tide line. Post-tsunami, the government declared its intention to enforce this regulation rigorously. This generated a huge outcry from fishing communities along the coast of Tamil Nadu as it would have meant relocating several hundreds of villages. Not only would it prevent fishing communities from earning a living but it would deny their customary rights to land by the sea. For a number of those surveyed, renewed enforcement of the CRZ would mean relinquishing legal tenure for coastal land and properties to the state under the guise of safety concerns. After an intense three-month campaign by fisher people's organizations, the government of Tamil Nadu has recently amended legislation, accepting their right to remain close to the sea but withholding benefits from those who choose to do so. People are now allowed to rebuild and repair houses within 200 metres of the hightide line but they must pay for it themselves. On the other hand, if they choose to move more than 200 metres from the hightide line, they are eligible to receive a new house from the government. In the case of Manginpudi Beach village in Andhra Pradesh, residents have been forcibly relocated two kilometres away from their original village, making way for new tourist resorts. The government promised to allocate new land to them and build them new homes, but to date residents have no information as to when these will be ready.

In Sri Lanka, in response to popular pressure in the run-up to presidential elections, the 100-200 metre "buffer zone" established in the aftermath of the tsunami was reduced to 35 metres in the south and west, and 50 metres in the east. In Jaffna in the north it remains at 100 metres. Throughout 2005, the Sri Lankan buffer zone led to confusion and concern among families living in temporary camps who did not know when or whether they would be able to rebuild on the site of their old homes.

In the Maldives, the government is seeking to implement a "safe island" programme which will lead to the displacement of more people. The programme's stated aims are to develop a few islands as economically and socially sustainable. The government argues that this will enable cost-effective delivery of services and will provide protection from natural and other disasters. It will also, according to the government, divert the influx of migrants to its capital, Male. This plan, in existence since 1998, is now being funded by the European Union, World Bank, United Nations Development Programme (UNDP) and others through a trust fund managed by the government in collaboration with the UNDP. At present the entire population of three islands . . . and part of the population of a further 10 islands, are being relocated to other islands. People are left with no choice but to move as it is a precondition of housing and livelihood rehabilitation. Those affected by this programme have expressed their doubts about the safety rationale of the government and ask why the populations of more than 180 islands in similar circumstances (in terms of elevation, topography, proximity of homes to the sea) are not also being moved.

. . .

Land for Permanent Housing

One of the main reasons for slow progress on permanent housing is the paucity of land. In several cases, government agencies have been slow to acquire land from private parties or have been reluctant to pay the market price. In two areas of Prakasham in Andhra Pradesh, India, a local NGO had taken on responsibility for the construction of permanent housing but the price quoted to purchase the 2.5 acres of land needed was considered by the government to be extremely high. Progress has now stalled and there is confusion over who will bear the cost. Residents doubt whether the plan will go ahead.

In Iraimandurai, Tamil Nadu, India, residents have had to give up their rights to their coastal land in order to be eligible for government land and a house farther from the sea. Although many were unhappy about relinquishing their land rights, they felt there was no other option if they were to receive help. The relocation will damage their livelihoods and increase other costs, including the cost of transport for children to get to school. Residents also feel it will mean the loss of social networks and their sense of community.

Housing

The human right to adequate housing cannot be interpreted as merely being the right to four walls and a roof. The concept of adequacy in relation to the right to housing is understood as adequacy of privacy, space, security, lighting and ventilation, basic infrastructure and location with regard to work and basic facilities.

Temporary Housing

One of the most appalling facts in post-tsunami rehabilitation is that a year on from the disaster a large number of people are still living in temporary shelters and some even in tents. There are also many living in damaged houses. Living conditions in all these forms of shelter are uniformly poor.

In Indonesia, official sources confirmed in September 2005 that more than 470,000 people were living as internally displaced people in temporary shelters or with relatives. In the Maldives, the number of internally displaced people stands at more than 11,000. Of these some 5,200 are living in temporary shelters. The rest are living with their friends and relatives, either because temporary shelter was not available or because they refused it as they found the living conditions unacceptable. . . .

In India, temporary housing consists of one-room structures, irrespective of family size. At all sites, women and men have complained about the inadequate size of the shelters, which range from 2.4×3.0 metres to 3.6×4.5 metres and house between four and seven people each. . . .

Temporary shelters provided by the government in . . . the Maldives are 4.9×7.6 meters each. . . . Most shelters house two families (nine to twelve people in total). . . . Lack of privacy and sleeping space is a particular concern for women and adolescent girls. . . . Children of all ages and both sexes sleep together, making the younger ones, particularly girls, vulnerable to abuse.

Livelihood

The right to earn a living is fundamental. It provides people with the power to control their lives with dignity. Estimations from the [United Nations] and the World Bank suggest the loss of livelihoods in India alone post-tsunami was US$700 million. In Indonesia, unemployment has risen by more than 30 per cent since the tsunami. The loss of earning capacity not only affects household income but contributes to the psychological depression that often follows a disaster.

In Andhra Pradesh, India, fishermen complain that, despite compensation and aid they have received, they are still unable to cope with the loss of income because of a change in sea patterns after the tsunami. Most of their former fishing sites are no longer remunerative. They no longer have a fixed place for fishing and have to hunt out new locations. Generally their catch is lower or different, resulting in lower income. . . .

In Thailand, migrant workers are protected by the 1998 Labour Protection Act, which deals with issues including the minimum wage, overtime wages, working hours and holidays. Since the tsunami, local landlords and factories will only employ migrant workers on the condition that they forgo their rights under this Act. In tsunami-affected areas of Thailand, most migrant workers have been found to be receiving less than the legal minimum wage or are compelled to work more than the stipulated 48-hour week. Many migrant workers are being cheated out of their wages with the money "disappearing" between the employer and the middleman.

Our field research shows that government response to the massive loss of livelihoods is far from satisfactory. Employment initiatives by government have only begun in a third of villages surveyed; none have begun in Indonesia and India. Where employment generation has begun, workers are often brought in from outside the area, rather than using local people who need the work and have a vested interest in the quick reconstruction of their environment. . . .

Women

Women the world over tend to have more responsibility for looking after children, providing food and running a home than men. In a post-disaster situation, when support systems—including physical infrastructure—break down, women bear the additional burden. Indeed, they are often the ones leading the recovery process in their families and communities. In responding to the tsunami, governments have, once again, largely neglected the particular needs of women. Women have not been included in decision-making regarding damage assessment, allocation of plots, land surveys or design of shelters and permanent houses. Orphaned girls, single women, women heading their households and women who are elderly, disabled or part of minority and vulnerable communities remain the most neglected.

Relief Distribution

Immediately after the tsunami, aid was often distributed in places and ways that were more accessible to men. It was a struggle for women to be recognized as heads of households and receive their dues. Only in a very few cases was special attention given to the needs of single women, including widows. In all countries, compensation was almost always handed out to male members of the family who did not necessarily share it with the women.

In Sri Lanka, women who owned land in their own names prior to the tsunami, particularly Muslim women who had received property as part of their dowry, have raised concerns that they are not considered eligible for compensation. Even in cases where the original house or land was in the woman's name, the government deposits compensation payments in the name of the man. Banks in the northeast of Sri Lanka reportedly asked women to sign a letter relinquishing their rights to the house and land to their husbands in order to facilitate compensation payments. . . .

Water and Sanitation

The absence of proper sanitation facilities is a serious cause for concern. Not only are people's rights to adequate housing violated but also their right to health. And there are grave implications for women's mobility and security. One of the most common complaints across all countries was the inadequacy of toilets. . . .

In both Sri Lanka and India [, for instance,] women complain that toilets built close to temporary shelters lack water or that they have to walk long distances to use toilet facilities. The absence of proper street lighting in most resettlement camps makes it unsafe for women walking to the toilets. . . .

Reproductive Rights

The notion of a woman's body as a site of her spouse's and his family's reproductive demands is an old one. In India, in families who lost children in the tsunami, women are under great pressure to replace dead offspring. The fact that many women had previously been convinced to go through sterilization operations makes the situation all the more tragic. Scores of women flocked to health centers in search of the "miracle" — a reversal of tubectomy, known in medical terminology as "recanalization." . . .

Relief camps all over Asia report an almost complete lack of healthcare services for expectant women and mothers with newborn babies. Government relief measures have also completely ignored the needs of menstruating women and girls. In Tamil Nadu in India most families received only dhotis and saris (outer clothing), but no undergarments or sanitary napkins for women. . . .

Violence

Violence against women was manifest soon after the tsunami struck and included shocking reports of women being pulled out of the water and then raped. Vulnerability to sexual violence increases manifold under camp conditions where toilet facilities and living quarters are forced out into the public domain. . . .

In Thailand, women immigrant labourers have reported the increased risk of being drawn into human trafficking and say that they regularly face sexual violence, including rape by employment agents. Women report that difficult camp conditions, trauma and unemployment are contributing to increased alcoholism among men. This often results in increased violence in the home. In Beureugang in West Aceh, [Indonesia,] women living in government temporary settlements have explained that husbands who are not working are more likely to inflict psychological and physical abuse.

Livelihoods

Women's concerns have once again largely been ignored in schemes to restore livelihoods. In spite of their obvious contribution to both fishing and agriculture, women are rarely recognised as fisherfolk or farmers; and therefore when schemes of livelihood restoration are taken up, they rarely involve women. While fishermen in India carry out the visibly strenuous and danger-ous task of deep-sea fishing, once the fish is offloaded, women take over com-pletely. Little has been done to compensate women in the fishing community who perform important tasks such as cleaning, drying and selling the fish catch. Women from fishing communities who were widowed by the tsunami and therefore lost access to the catch that their husbands would have normally brought in, have not been considered in government livelihood programmes.

Discrimination

. . .

Discrimination is evident in all countries [affected by the tsunami] and has been a major factor in impeding people's access to relief and rehabilitation post-tsunami.

For dalits (members of the "lowest" caste) in India, discrimination that existed before the tsunami increased afterwards when they were even more vulnerable. . . .

In the Andamans [a chain of islands in the Indian Ocean] there is evidence that compensation has been hijacked by local political groups. Residents com-plain that people have received compensation on the basis of party political affiliation rather than need. . . .

[In Thailand,] discrimination by the state has severely affected the rights of . . . Mokens or sea gypsies. In a temple in Phang Nga, while everyone else received large relief packages, Moken families were given a box of milk or canned sardines. Mokens were also denied help by the government as many are not Thai citizens. . . .

Some religious foundations in Thailand have made it a precondition of help that Mokens must change their religion and participate in the religious activities of the foundation. In other places, religious foundations will only help those who paste a sticker displaying a religious symbol in front of their tent or house.

F. EXERCISE

In preparation for a future cyclone or another tsunami, imagine that India decides to develop a disaster response strategy using the U.N. Guiding Principles on Internal Displacement as an important policy framework. Since India is also a party to CERD and CEDAW, it wants its disaster response strategy to comply with these agreements too. As a first step, India's national Ministry of Home Affairs agrees to collaborate with the Indian state of Andhra Pradesh to develop practical strategies for protecting the socially and economically vulnerable.

Located on India's southeastern coast, Andhra Pradesh is known for its rich agricultural lands and busy fishing villages. Its 600-mile coastline is the second longest in India. (Gujarat has the longest.) Andhra Pradesh is also one of India's most populous states, with nearly 76 million people, mostly Hindu with a small minority (about 15%) of Christians and Muslims.

Since Andhra Pradesh was so heavily damaged during the Asian Tsunami, it is hoped that the region will be a source of lessons for the future. Local citizens' organizations are also being invited to collaborate. Recently, USAID has expressed an interest in helping to plan and modestly fund parts of the project.

A small meeting has been called to lay out the possibilities and address some fundamental concerns.

The participants are

1. a representative from India's Ministry of Home Affairs,
2. a representative from the state government of Andhra Pradesh,
3. a representative from the Kattumaram Fishing Project, a nongovernmental organization that promotes the interests of rural fisherfolk in Andhra Pradesh,
4. a representative of the Many Hands Network, a nongovernmental organization that promotes the interests of rural women in southern India, and
5. a representative from USAID.

The questions to be discussed are the following:

1. What are the most important aspects of the Guiding Principles? That is, what values provide the "framework" on which the state's policy should be based?
2. What reforms or improvements are most needed to promote those values? Try to agree on the top three reforms.
3. How should compliance with the reforms be enforced? What level of government should be responsible for implementation? For enforcement? For evaluation?
4. How should the reforms be funded?

Choose a role and divide into groups to address these questions. Be prepared to report on the results.

TABLE OF CASES

*Principal case decisions reproduced
or excerpted are noted by italic font.*

TABLE OF AUTHORITIES

Books and Treatises

Barry, John M., Rising Tide: The Great Mississippi Flood of 1927 and How It Changed America (1998), 192

Beck, Ulrich, Risk Society: Toward a New Modernity (1986), 204

Blaikie, Piers, Cannon, Terry, Davis, Ian & Wisner, Ben, At Risk: Natural Hazards, People's Vulnerability and Disasters (1994), 217

Breyer, Stephen, Breaking the Vicious Circle: Toward Effective Risk Regulation (1993), 263

Bullard, Robert D., Dumping in Dixie: Race, Class and Environmental Quality (3d ed. 2000), 224

Burby, Raymond J., Cooperating With Nature (1998), 40

Calvino, Italo. Invisible Cities (1972), 1

Campanella, Richard, Bienville's Dilemma: A Historical Geography of New Orleans (2008), 375-378

Cawardine, William, The Pullman Strike (1973), 120

Center for Progressive Reform, An Unnatural Disaster: The Aftermath of Hurricane Katrina (2005), 204, 223, 224

Chomsky, Noam, Language and Mind (enlarged ed. 1972), 152

Cohen, Joel, How Many People Can the Earth Support? (1995), 208

Cross, Terry L. et al., Towards a Culturally Competent System of Care, Volume I: A Monograph of Effective Services for Minority Children Who Are Severely Emotionally Disturbed (1989), 226

Ehrlich, Paul & Ehrlich, Anne, The Population Explosion (1990), 208

Farber, Dan, Lincoln's Constitution (2003), 83

Federalist 10 (Madison), The Federalist 45 (Max Beloff, ed. 1987), 263

Fradkin, Philip L., The Great Earthquake And Firestorms Of 1906: How San Francisco Nearly Destroyed Itself (2005), 369

Hensler, D., et al., RAND Inst. Civ. Just., Compensation for Accidental Injuries in the United States (1991), 298

Holland, John H., Emergence: From Chaos to Order (1998), 154

Hollander, Jack M., The Real Environmental Crisis: Why Poverty, Not Affluence, Is the Environment's Number One Enemy (2003), 213

Hurston, Zora Neal, Their Eyes Were Watching God (2006; 1st ed. 1937), 203

Johnson, Steven, Emergence: The Connected Lives of Ants, Brains, Cities, and Software (2001), 154

Kakalik, J. & Pace, N., RAND Inst. Civ. Just., Costs and Compensation Paid in Tort Litigation (1985), 298

King, Elizabeth M. & Mason, Andrew D., Engendering Development — Through Gender Equality in Rights, Resources, and Voice (2001), 233

Klinenberg, Eric, Heat Wave: A Social Autopsy Of Disaster In Chicago (2002), 233

Kunreuther, Howard and Roth, Richard J., Sr., Paying the Price: The Status and Role of Insurance Against Natural Disasters in the United States (1998), 343

Lemann, Nicholas, The Promised Land: The Great Black Migration and How It Changed America (1991), 192

Lipsey, Richard G. & Steiner, Peter O., Economics (5th ed., 1978), 243

Margolis, Howard, Dealing With Risk: Why the Public and the Experts Disagree on Environmental Issues (1996), 253, 254

Perry, Ronald W. & E.L. Quarantelli, eds. What is a Disaster? New Answers to Old Questions (2005), 3

ProAct, The Role Of Environmental Management And Eco-Engineering In Disaster Risk Reduction And Climate Change Adaptation (2008), 58

Randle, Timothy J. et al., Geomorphology and River Hydraulics Of The Teton River Upstream Of Teton Dam, Teton River, Idaho (2000), 67

Revesz, Richard L. & Livermore, Michael A., Retaking Rationality: How Cost-Benefit Analysis Can Better Protect the Environment and our Health (2008), 269

Rubin, Claire B., ed., Emergency Management: The American Experience 1900-2005 (2007), 90

Schroeder, Manfred, Fractals, Chaos, Power Laws: Minutes from an Infinite Paradise (1991), 250

Schumpeter, Joseph A., Capitalism, Socialism and Democracy (1975) (1st ed. 1942), 226

Sphere Project Handbook: Humanitarian Charter and Minimum Standards in Disaster Response (2004), 212-213

Stern, Nicholas, The Stern Review Of The Economics Of Climate Change (2007), 279, 280

Sunstein, Cass R., Risk And Reason: Safety, Law, and the Environment (2002), 265

Sunstein, Cass R., The Cost-Benefit State (2002), 281

Thomas, Gordon & Witts, Max Morgan, The San Francisco Earthquake (1971), 40

Verchick, Robert R.M., Facing Catastrophe: Environmental Action for a Post-Katrina World (forthcoming, 2010), 54, 55-57, 399-402

Warren, Robert Penn, All the King's Men (1996; 1st ed. 1946), 247

Weart, Spencer, The Discovery of Global Warming (2003), 208

Yonder, Ayse, Akcar, Sengul & Gopalan, Prema, Women's Participation in Disaster Relief and Recovery (2005), 233

Articles

AAA Offers New Disaster Recovery Services, 60-JAN Dispute Res. J. 4 (2005), 329

Abbott, Ernest B., Representing Local Governments in Catastrophic Events: DHS/FEMA Response and Recovery Issues, 37 Urb. Law. 467 (2005), 93

Abbott, Ernest B., et al, State, Local, and First Responder Issues. Hurricane Katrina Task Force Subcommittee Report, 2006, published by the ABA Standing Committee on Law and National Security, the ABA Section of State and Government, and the ABA Section of Administrative Law & Regulatory Practice, 161-63

Abramovitz, Janet, Unnatural Disasters, Worldwatch Paper, 158, Worldwatch Institute, 5-12 (2001), www.worldwatch.org/node/832, 396-399

Ackerman, Frank & Heinzerling, Lisa, Pricing The Priceless: Cost-Benefit Analysis Of Environmental Protection, 150 U. Pa. L. Rev. 1553 (2002), 275-278

Adler, Jonathan H., More Sorry Than Safe: Assessing the Precautionary Principle and the Proposed International Safety Protocol, 35 Tex. Int'l L.J. 194 (2000), 286

Adler, Matthew, D., Policy Analysis for Natural Hazards: Some Cautionary Lessons From Environmental Policy Analysis, 56 Duke L.J. 1 (2006), 265-268

Aguirre, B.E., Dialectics of Vulnerability and Resilience, 14 Geo. J. on Poverty L. & Pol'y 39, 41-45 (2007), 217-19

Alexander, Frank S., Louisiana Land Reforming the Storm's Aftermath, 53 Loy. L. Rev. 727 (2007), 364

Alexandre, Michèle, Navigating the Topography of Inequality Post-Disaster: A Propose for Remedying Past Geographic Segregation during Rebuilding, in Law and Recovery From Disaster: Hurricane Katrina 19 (Robin Paul Malloy, ed., 2009), 226, 236

Alford, Roger, Flood-Prone Appalachian Town Seeks Higher Ground, Miami Herald (June 17, 2009), 37

Aloisi, Silvia, Italy Quake Exposes Poor Building Standards, Reuters, Apr. 7, 2009, (available at http://www.alertnet.org/thenews/newsdesk/L7932819.htm), 69

Annas, George J., Blinded by Bioterrorism: Public Health and Liberty in the 21st Century, 13 Health Matrix 33, 58 (2003), 167

Apt, Jay et al., Electricity: Protecting Essential Services, in Seeds of Disaster, Roots Of Response: How Private Action Can Reduce Public Vulnerability 211-212 (Philip E. Auerswald et al., eds., 2006), 17

Auerswald, Philip E., Complexity and Interdependence, in Seeds of Disaster, Roots Of Response: How Private Action Can Reduce Public Vulnerability 157 (Philip E. Auerswald, et al., eds., 2006), 15, 17, 22

Auerswald, Philip E. et al., Where Private Efficiency Meets Public Vulnerability: The Critical Infrastructure, in Seeds of Disaster, Roots Of Response: How Private Action Can Reduce Public Vulnerability 3, 9 (Philip E. Auerswald et al., eds., 2006), 21

Balcius, James & Liang, Bryan A., Public Health Law & Military Medical Assets: Legal Issues in Federalizing National Guard Personnel, 18 Annals Health L. 35 (2009), 111

Bankoff, Greg, The Tale of the Three Pigs: Taking Another Look at Vulnerability in the Light of the Indian Ocean Tsunami and Hurricane Katrina, http://understandingkatrina.ssrc.org/bankoff (Dec. 12, 2005), 212

Barnes, Julian E. & Walsh, Kenneth T., A Uniform Response?, U.S. News & World Rep., Oct. 3, 2005, at 28, 126

Barron, David J. & Lederman, Martin S., The Commander in Chief at the Lowest Ebb — A Constitutional History, 121 Harv. L. Rev. 941 (2008), 83

Bassett, Debra Lyn, Place, Disasters, and Disabilities, in Law and Recovery From Disaster: Hurricane Katrina 51 (Robin Paul Malloy, ed., 2009), 236

Bea, Keith, Disaster Evacuation and Displacement Policy: Issues for Congress (Sept. 2, 2005) (CRS Order Code RS22235), 151

Bennett, Dan, Note, The Domestic Role of the Military in America: Why Modifying or Repealing the Posse Comitatus Act Would Be a Mistake, 10 Lewis & Clark L. Rev. 935 (2006), 114

Bolin, Robert & Stanford, Lois, The Northridge Earthquake: Community-Based Approaches to Unmet Recovery Needs, 22 Disasters 21 (1998), 229

Borden, Kevin A. & Cutter, Susan L., Spatial Patterns of Natural Hazards Mortality in the United States, Int'l J. Health Geographics 7:64 (2008), 24

Braine, Theresa, Was 2005 the Year of Natural Disasters?, 84:1 Bull. World Health Org. 4 (Jan. 2006), 204-07

Brandt-Erichsen, Svend et al., EPA Proposes Regulating Greenhouse Gases under Clean Air Act: Hearing in Seattle on May 21, 2009, Marten Law Group Environmental News, April 17, 2009, www.martenlaw.com/news/?20090417-epa-proposes-regulating-ghg, 73

Branscomb, Lewis M. & Michel-Kerjan, Erwann O., Public-Private Collaboration on a National and International Scale, in Seeds of Disaster, Roots Of Response: How Private Action Can Reduce Public Vulnerability 395 (Philip E. Auerswald et al., eds., 2006), 19

Brook, Brian C., Note, Federalizing the First Responders to Acts of Terrorism via the Militia Clauses, 54 Duke L. J. 999 (2005), 81

Byrnes, P. D., Lowry, W.J. & Bondurant, E.J. II, Product Shortages, Allocation and the Antitrust Laws, 20 Antitrust Bull. 713 (1975), 244

Calandrillo, Steve P., Responsible Regulation: A Sensible Cost-Benefit, Risk Versus Risk Approach to Federal Health and Safety Regulation, 81 B.U. L. Rev. 957 (2001), 271-274

Carey, Christopher, Cities Look to Flood Plains for Jobs, Growth, Tax Dollars, St. Louis Post-Dispatch, July 29, 2003, at A1, 35

Charest, Stephen, Bayesian Approaches to the Precautionary Principle, 12 Duke Envtl. L. & Pol'y F. 265 (2002), 286

Chen, Jim, Law among the Ruins, in Law and Recovery From Disaster: Hurricane Katrina 1(Robin Paul Malloy ed., 2009), 209

Chen, Jim, Of Agriculture's First Disobedience and Its Fruit, 48 Vand. L. Rev. 1261 (1995), 192

Chen, Jim, The Nature of the Public Utility: Infrastructure, the Market, and the Law, 98 NW. U. L. Rev. 1617 (2004), 179

Congressional Research Service, Hurricane Katrina, Insurance Losses and National Capacities for Finance Disaster Risk, http://fpc.state.gov/documents/organization/53683.pdf (Sept. 15, 2005), 319-321

Costanza, Robert et al., The Value of the World's Ecosystem Services and Natural Capital, Nature, vol. 387 (May 15, 1997), 54

Cross, Frank B., Paradoxical Perils of the Precautionary Principle, 53 Wash & Lee L. Rev. 851, 872 (1996), 286

Cunningham, Michael T., The Military's Involvement in Law Enforcement: The Threat Is Not What You Think, 26 Seattle U. L. Rev. 699 (2003), 114, 115

Cutter, Susan L., The Geography of Social Vulnerability: Race, Class, and Catastrophe, http://understandingkatrina.ssrc.org/Cutter (Sept. 23, 2005), 214-16

Dana, David, A., A Behavioral Economic Defense of the Precautionary Principle, 97 NW. U. L. Rev. 1315 (2003), 287

Daniels, Brigham, Emerging Commons and Tragic Institutions, 37 Envtl. L. 515 (2007), 63

Danielsen, Finn et al., The Asian Tsunami: A Protective Role for Coastal Vegetation, 310 Science 643 (2005), 57

Davidson, Lee, Shaken to Pieces, Desert News, April 25, 2006, 70

Dean, Cornelia, Some Experts Say It's Time to Evacuate the Coast (for Good), N.Y. Times, Oct, 4, 2005, 37

DeBianchi, Jessica, Military Law: Winds of Change—Examining the Present-Day Propriety of the Posse Comitatus Act after Hurricane Katrina, 17 U. Fla. J.L. & Pub. Pol'y 473 (2006), 114

Dixon, Philip M., Weiner, Jacob, Mitchell-Olds, Thomas & Woodley, Robert, Bootstrapping the Gini Coefficient of Inequality, 68 Ecology 1548 (1988), 212

Dodman, David, et al., Urban Development and Intensive and Extensive Risk (2008), (available at http://www.preventionweb.net/english/hyogo/gar/background-papers), 24

Donahue, John D. & Zeckhauser, Richard J., Sharing the Watch, in Seeds of Disaster, Roots Of Response: How Private Action Can Reduce Public Vulnerability 429 (Philip E. Auerswald et al., eds., 2006), 21

Donato, Katharine & Hakimzadeh, Shirin, The Changing Face of the Gulf Coast: Immigration to Louisiana, Mississippi, and Alabama, http://www.migrationinformation.org/Feature/display.cfm?id=368 (Jan. 1, 2006), 237

Dougherty, Candidus, "Necessity Hath No Law": Executive Power and the Posse Comitatus Act, 31 Campbell L. Rev. 1 (2008), 83

Dougherty, Candidus, While the Government Fiddled Around, The Big Easy Drowned: How the Posse Comitatus Act Became the Government's Alibi for the Hurricane Katrina Disaster, 29 N. Ill. U. L. Rev. 117, 146 (2008), 112

Duhart, Olympia & Rodriguez-Dod, Eloisa C., Legislation and Criminalization Impacting Renters Displaced by Katrina, in Law and Recovery From Disaster: Hurricane Katrina 1, 3 (Robin Paul Malloy, ed., 2009), 225, 236

Eastman, John C., Restoring the "General" to the General Welfare Clause, 4 Chap. L. Rev. 63 (2001), 80.

Editorial, We're Counting on You, Mr. President, Times-Picayune, Aug. 28, 2009, at A1, 387

Enarson, Elaine, Women and Girls Last? Averting the Second Post-Katrina Disaster, http://understandingkatrina.ssrc.org/Enarson (Nov. 15, 2005), 231-232

Engdahl, David E., Soldiers, Riots and Revolution: The Law and History of Military Troops in Civil Disorders, 57 Iowa L. Rev. 1 (1971), 108

Farber, Daniel A., Disaster Law and Inequality, 25 Law & Ineq. 297 (2007), 231, 233

Farber, Daniel A., Probabilities Behaving Badly: Complexity Theory and Environmental Uncertainty, 37 U.C. Davis L. Rev. 145 (2003), 160

Farber, Daniel A., Stretching the Margins: The Geographic Nexus in Environmental Law, 48 Stan. L. Rev. 1247 (1996), 208

Feinstein, Jack, Managing Reliability in Electric Power Companies, in Seeds of Disaster, Roots Of Response: How Private Action Can Reduce Public Vulnerability 164, 178 (Philip E. Auerswald et al., eds., 2006), 14, 16

Felicetti, Gary & Luce, John, The Posse Comitatus Act: Setting the Record Straight on 124 Years of Mischief and Misunderstanding Before Any More Damage Is Done, 175 Mil. L. Rev. 86 (2003), 113

Fitzgerald, Edward A., The Rise and Fall of Worst Case Analysis, 18 U. Dayton L. Rev. 1 (1992), 287

Foley, Meraiah, Death Toll in Australian Fire Climbs to 131, N.Y. Times, Feb. 8, 2009, at A8, 46

Frickel, Scott, Our Toxic Gumbo: Recipe for a Politics of Environmental Knowledge, http://understandingkatrina.ssrc.org/frickel (Oct. 6, 2005), 204

Furman, H.W.C., Restrictions upon Use of the Army Imposed by the Posse Comitatus Act, 27 Mil. L. Rev. 85 (1960), 108

Fussell, Elizabeth, Leaving New Orleans: Social Stratification, Networks, and Hurricane Evacuation, http://understandingkatrina.ssrc.org/Fussell (Sept. 26, 2005), 240

Gabe, Thomas, Falk, Gene & McCarty, Maggie, Hurricane Katrina: Social-Demographic Characteristics of Impacted Areas (Nov. 4, 2005) (CRS Order Code RL33141), 223, 233-35

Gardina, Jackie, Toward Military Rule? A Critique of Executive Discretion to Use the Military in Domestic Emergencies, 91 Marq. L. Rev. 1027(2008), 129

Gauna, Eileen, Katrina and Environmental Injustice, http://jurist.law.pitt.edu/forumy/2005/10/katrina-and-environmental-injustice.php (Oct. 10, 2005), 224

Gigerenzer, Rerd, Dread Risk, September 11, and Fatal Traffic Accidents, 15 Psych. Sci. 286 (2004), 254

Gilette, Clayton P. & Krier, James E., Risk, Court, and Agencies, 138 U. Pa. L. Rev. 1027 (1990), 251-253

Gilligan, Matthew J., Opening the Gate? An Analysis of Military Law Enforcement Authority over Civilian Lawbreakers On and Off the Federal Installation, 161 Mil. L. Rev. 1 (1999), 118

Gilman, Nils, What Katrina Teaches about the Meaning of Racism, http://understandingkatrina.ssrc.org/Gilman (Sept. 14, 2005), 221

Gollier, Christian, Jullien, Bruno & Treich, Nicolas, Scientific Progress and Irreversibility: An Economic Interpretation of the "Precautionary Principle," 75 J. Pub. Econ. 229 (2000), 286

Grace, Stephanie, Blakely and Nagin, Are Two of a Kind, Opinion, Times-Picayune, May 11, 2009, at B5, 381

Grace, Stephanie, Defiant Rumsfeld Left City to Suffer, Times-Picayune, May 21, 2009, 122

Greenberger, Michael, Yes, Virginia, the President Can Deploy Federal Troops to Prevent the Loss of a Major American City from a Devastating Natural Catastrophe, 26 Miss. C. L. Rev. 107 (2006), 128

Griffin, Stephen M., Stop Federalism Before It Kills Again: Reflections on Hurricane Katrina, 21 St. John's J. Legal Comment 527 (2007), 83, 88

Gude, Patricia, et al., Potential for Future Development on Fire-Prone Lands, J. Forestry, 106(4) 198 (June 2008), 42, 45, 46, 47

Hahn, Robert W., The Economics of Rebuilding Cities: Reflections after Katrina, The Economists' Voice Vol. 2 [2005], No. 4, Article 1 at http://www.bepress.com/ev/vol2/iss4/art1, 368

Hammer, David, Critics Admit They Didn't Visit, Research Post-Katrina New Orleans, Times-Picayune, March 5, 2008, http://blog.nola.com/updates/2008/03/critics_admit_they_didnt_visit.html, 424

Hammond, Matthew C., The Posse Comitatus Act: A Principle in Need of Renewal, 75 Wash. U. L.Q. 953 (1997), 117

Haurcade, J.C. et al., Estimating the Costs of Mitigating Greenhouse Gases, in Climate Change 1995: Economic and Social Dimensions Of Climate Change: Contribution of Working Group III to the Second Assessment Report of the Intergovernmental Panel on Climate Change 263 (James P. Bruce et al. eds., 1996), 279

Hausrath, Katherine, Tough Love: Should We Analyze Federal Emergency Management Agency Disaster Planning under the National Environmental Policy Act?, 13 Hastings W. NW. J. Envtl. L. & Pol'y 161 (2007), 63

Hecht, Sean, Climate Change and the Transformation of Risk: Insurance Matters, 55 UCLA L. Rev. 1559 (2008), 332-338

Hill, Barry T., U.S. Gen. Accounting Office, Fire Management: Lessons Learned From the Cerro Grande (Los Alamos) Fire And Actions Needed To Reduce Risks 1 (2000), 6

Hodge, Jr., James G. & Anderson, Evan D., Principles and Practice of Legal Triage during Public Health Emergencies, 64 N.Y.U. Ann. Surv. Am. L. 249 (2008), 167

Hogue, Henry B., Federal Emergency Management and Homeland Security Organization: Historical Developments and Legislative Options 20-21 (CRS Report for Congress, Order Code RL33369, June 1, 2006), 133

Low, Patrick, Trade and the Environment: What Worries the Developing Countries?, 23 Envtl. L. 705 (1993), 213

Lowenstein, Laura J. & Revesz, Richard L., Anti-Regulation under the Guise of Rational Regulation: The Bush Administration's Approaches to Valuing Human Lives in Environmental Cost-Benefit Analyses, 34 Envtl. L. Rep. 10954 (2004), 270

Luntz, Taryn, Draft Executive Order Aims to Curb Floodplain Development, N.Y. Times, July 21, 2009, (available at http://www.nytimes.com/gwire/2009/07/21/21greenwire-draft-executive-order-aims-to-curbfloodplain-64438.html), 33

Lytton, Christopher H., America's Borders and Civil Liberties in a Post — September 11th World, 12 J. Trasnat'l L. & Pol'y 197 (2003), 114

Margolis, Howard, A New Account of Expert/Lay Conflicts of Risk Intuition, 8 Duke Envtl. L. & Pol'y F. 115 (1997), 254

Massey, Douglas S. & Espinosa, Kristin, What's Driving Mexico-US Migration?: A Theoretical, Empirical and Policy Analysis, 102 Am. J. Sociology 939 (1997), 240

Masterman, Vickie O., Worst Case Analysis: The Final Chapter?, 19 Envtl. L. Rep. 10026 (1989), 287, 288

Mazzetti, Mark & Johnston, David, BushWeighed Using Military in U.S. Arrests, N.Y. Times, July 25, 2009, at A1, 83

Mazzone, Jason, The Commandeerer in Chief, 83 Notre Dame L. Rev. 265 (2007), 81

Mazzone, Jason, The Security Constitution, 53 UCLA Law Rev. 29 (2005), 80

McGarvey, Joe & Wilhelm, John D., National Association of Regulatory Utility Commissioners/National Regulatory Research Institute, 2003 Survey on Critical Infrastructure Security 3-4 (available at nrri.org/pubs/multiutility/04-01pdf), 14

Metropolitan Policy Program at Brookings, The New Orleans Index: Tracking the Recovery of New Orleans and the Metro Area (Aug. 2009), https://gnocdc.s3.amazonaws.com/NOLAIndex/NOLAIndex.pdf, 383-384

Montgomery, David W. & Smith, Anne E., Global Climate Change and the Precautionary Principle, 6 Hum. & Ecological Risk Assessment 399 (2000), 286

Montgomery, David W., Baron, Robert A. & Weinkopf, Mary K., Potential Effects of Proposed Price Gouging Legislation on the Cost and Severity of Gas Supply Interruptions, 3 J. Compet. L. & Econ.357 (2007), 244

Moss, Mitchell et al., The Stafford Act and Priorities for Reform, 6 J. Homeland Security & Emergency Mgmt. 8-9 (2009), 154, 193-98

Nathan, Richard P. & Luncy, Marc, Who's in Charge? Who Should Be? The Role of the Federal Government in Megadisasters: Based on Lessons from Hurricane Katrina (June 2, 2009), available at http://www.rockinst.org/pdf/disaster_recovery/gulfgov/gulfgov_reports/2009-06-02-Whos_in_Charge.PDF, 193

National Fair Housing Alliance, No Home for the Holidays: Report on Housing Discrimination Against Hurricane Katrina Survivors (Dec. 20, 2005) (available at http://newreconstruction.civilrights.org/NFHAKatrinaDiscriminationReport.pdf), 225

Nelson, Arthur C. & Lane, Robert E., The Next 100 Million, Planning Magazine 73(1): 4 (2007), 10

Nickelsburg, Stephen M., Note, Mere Volunteers? The Promise and Limits of Community-Based Environmental Protection, 84 Va. L. Rev. 1371 (1998), 208

Noll, Roger G. & Krier, James E., Some Implications of Cognitive Psychology for Risk Regulation, 19 J. Legal Stud. 747 (1990), 253

Nordhaus, William D., A Review of the Stern Review on the Economics of Climate Change, 45 J. Econ. Literature 686 (2007), 280

Note, Federal Agency Treatment of Uncertainty in Environmental Impact Statements under the EPA's Amended NEAP Regulation §1502.22: Worst Case Analysis or Risk Threshold?, 86 Mich. L. Rev. 777 (1988), 288

Rose, Carol M., The Story of Lucas: Environmental Land Use Regulation Between Developers and the Deep Blue Sea, in Richard J. Lazarus & Oliver A. Houck, Environmental Law Stories 268-269 (2005), 53

Russell, Gordon, Rising From the Tide, Times-Picayune, Dec. 11, 2005, A1, 369-374

Ryan, Erin, Federalism and the Tug of War Within: Seeking Checks and Balance in the Interjurisdictional Gray Area, 66 Md. L. Rev. 503, 522-536 (2007), 84-87

Salkin, Patricia E., Sustainability at the Edge: The Opportunity and Responsibility of Local Governments to Effectively Plan for Natural Disaster Mitigation, in Losing Ground: A Nation on Edge 125 (John Nolon & Daniel Rodriguez, eds., 2007), 357

Salzman, Jim, A Field of Green? The Past and Future Ecosystem Services, 21. 2 J. Land Use & Envtl. L. 133 (Spring 2006), 22

Sanyika, Mtanguliza, Katrina and The Condition Of Black New Orleans: The Struggle For Justice, Equity, and Democracy, in Race, Place and Environmental Justice After Hurricane Katrina: Struggles To Reclaim, Rebuild, And Revitalize New Orleans And The Gulf Coast, 87 (Robert D. Bullard & Beverly Wright eds., 2009), 378-381

Schulman, Paul R. & Roe, Emery, Managing for Reliability in an Age of Terrorism, in Seeds of Disaster, Roots Of Response: How Private Action Can Reduce Public Vulnerability 132-133 (Philip E. Auerswald et al., eds., 2006), 17,18

Schwab, Anna K., & Brower, David J., Increasing Resilience To Natural Hazards: Obstacles And Opportunities For Local Governments Under The Disaster Mitigation Act Of 2000, in Losing Ground: A Nation On Edge, 281, 283-301 (John Nolon & Daniel Rodriguez, eds., 2007), 348-356

Schwartz, John. Army Corps Admits Flaws in New Orleans Levees, N.Y. Times, June 1, 2006, 64

Serota, James I., Monopoly Pricing in a Time of Shortage, 33 Loy. U. Chi. L.J. 791 (2002), 244

Shavers, Anna Williams, Katrina's Children: Revealing the Broken Promise of Education, 31 T. Marshall L. Rev. 499 (2006), 385

Shipley, Sara, Unprecedented Growth in the Flood Plain Brings Riches and Risks: Business Grows on Land under Water 10 Years Ago, St. Louis Post-Dispatch, July 27, 2003, at A1, 34, 35

Shogren, Jason F. & Toman, Michael A., How Much Climate Change Is Too Much?, in Climate Change Economics and Policy: An RFF Anthology 35 (Michael A. Toman, ed., 2001), 279

The Sichuan Earthquake: Salt in Their Wounds, Economist, May 16, 2009, at 48, 69

Skarbeck, David, Market Failure and Natural Disasters: A Reexamination of Anti-Gouging Laws, 37 Pub. Contract L. J. 771 (2008), 244

Slovic, Fischhoff & Lichtenstein, Facts and Fears: Understanding Perceived Risk, in Societal Risk Assessment: How Safe is Safe Enough? (R. Schwing & W. Albers, Jr., eds. 1980), 251

Slovic, Paul, Perception of Risk, 236 Science 280 (1987), 251

Smith, Neil, There's No Such Thing as a Natural Disaster, http://understanding katrina.ssrc.org/Smith (Sept. 26, 2005), 207

Smith, Rebecca K., War on Wildfire: The U.S. Forest Service's Fire Suppression Policy and Its Legal, Scientific, and Political Context, 15 U. Balt. J. Envtl. L. 25, 38 (2007), 59

Soil Science Society of America, Wetlands Restoration Not a Panacea for Louisiana Coast, Science Daily (Sept. 30, 2008), (available at http://www.sciencedaily.com/releases/2008/09/080924190637.htm), 57

Sonner, Scott, Floods Prompt Review of Canals, Hayward Daily Rev., April 5, 2008, 68

van der Vink, G., et al., Why the United States Is Becoming More Vulnerable to Natural Disasters, EOS, Transactions, American Geophysical Union 79(3) 533 (Nov. 1998), 25

Van Heerden, Ivar L., et al. The Failure of the New Orleans Levee System During Hurricane Katrina (Dec. 18, 2006), available at http://www.publichealth. hurricane.lsu.edu/teamla.htm, 2

Viscusi, W. Kip, Cigarette Taxation and the Social Consequences of Smoking 47 (Nat'l Bureau of Econ. Research, Working Paper No. 4891, 1994), available at http://papers.nber.org/papers/w4891.pdf, 275

Viscusi, W. Kip & Hamilton, James T., Are Risk Regulators Rational? Evidence from Hazardous Waste Cleanup Decisions, 89 Am. Econ. Rev. 1012 (1999), 265

Vladeck, Stephen I., Note, Emergency Power and the Militia Acts, 114 Yale L.J. 149(2004), 80, 119

Vladeck, Stephen I., The Domestic Commander in Chief, 29 Cardozo L. Rev. 1091 (2008), 80, 82

Wald, Matthew L., The Blackout: What Went Wrong; Experts Asking Why Problems Spread So Far, N.Y. Times, August 16, 2003, at A1, 16.

Wasem, Ruth Ellen, Katrina-Related Immigration Issues and Legislation (Sept. 19, 2005) (CRS Order Code RL33091), 237-240

Weiss, Debra Cassens, Will Swine Flu Merit Quarantines? If So, New Laws Give States Authority, ABA Journal, Apr. 27, 2009, available at http://www.abajournal. com/news/will_swine_flu_merit_quarantines_if_so_new_laws_give_states_ authority/, 166

Weitzman, Martin L., A Review of the Stern Review on the Economics of Climate Change, 45 J. Econ. Literature 703 (2007), 280

Wellner, Alison Stein, The Mobility Myth, Reason Online, April 2006, (available at http://www.reason.com/news/show/33288.html), 25

Wildman, Terry, Cleco Faces the Beast, available at http://tdworld.com/katrina_ reflections_supp/Cleco-Katrina-reflection, 182

Wines, Michael, To Protect an Ancient City, China Moves to Raze It, N.Y. Times, May 27, 2009, 71

Winthrop, Jim, The Oklahoma City Bombing: Immediate Response Authority and Other Military Assistance to Civil Authority (MAC), Army Law, July 1997, 94, 126

Wishnie, Lauren, Fire and Federalism: A Forest Fire Is Always an Emergency, 17 N.Y.U. Envtl. L.J. 1006 (2008), 46

Wood, Hugh L., Jr., Note, The Insurance Fallout Following Hurricane Andrew: Whether Insurance Companies Are Legally Obligated to Pay For Building Code Upgrades Despite The "Ordinance Or Law" Exclusion Contained In Most Homeowners Policies, 48 U. Miami L. Rev. 949 (1994), 329

Zeichner, Lee M., Private Sector Integration, in American Bar Association, Hurricane Katrina Task Force Subcommittee Report 33 (Feb. 2006), 179

Zocchetti, David. Public Disclosure of Information by Emergency Services Agencies: A Post—September 11 Paradigm Shift, in A Legal Guide to Homeland Security And Emergency Management for State and Local Governments 1, 4-7 (Ernest B. Abbott & Otto J. Hetzel eds., 2005), 20

Congressional Reports

H.R. Rep. No. 97-71, Part II, 97th Cong., 1st Sess. 4 (1981) (citing 1 William Blackstone, Commentaries *343-44), reprinted in 1981 U.S.C.C.A.N. 1781, 108

H.R. Rep. No. 106-710, at 175 (2000) (Conf. Rep.), 6

Legislative Proceedings

Federal Emergency Management Agency: Oversight and Management of the National Flood Insurance Program: Hearing before the Subcommittee on Housing and Community Opportunity of the House Committee on Financial Services (Oct. 20, 2005) (statement of William O. Jenkins, Jr., Director, Homeland Security and Justice Issues), http://128.32.29.133/disastersSearch.php?search=oversight+and+management, 313-315

Hurricane Katrina: The Role of the Governors in Managing the Catastrophe: Hearing before the S. Comm. on Homeland Sec. and Governmental Affairs, 109th Cong. 25 (2006) (statement of Kathleen Blanco, Gov., State of Louisiana), 115

Introduction of the Pets Evacuation and Transportation Standards (PETS) Act of 2005, 151 Cong. Rec. E1943, E1943 (Sept. 22, 2005) (statement of Rep. Tom Lantos, D-Cal.), 99

Federal Statutes

2003 Healthy Forests Restoration Act (HFRA), Pub. L. No. 108-148, 117 Stat. 1887 (2003) (codified at 16 U.S.C. §§ 6501-6591(2003)), 45

Air Transportation Safety and System Stabilization Act, Pub. L. No. 107-42, 405(b)(2), 115 Stat. 230, 238 (2001) (codified as amended at 49 U.S.C. §40101 (2004)), 292

American Clean Energy and Security Act, H.R. 2454, 111th Cong. (2009), 73

Disaster Mitigation Act of 2000, Pub. L. No. 106-390, 114 Stat. 1552 §322 (codified at 42 U.S.C. §5165), 77, 101, 348-357

Federal Coastal Zone Management Act of 1972, 16 U.S.C. §§ 1455-1456, 53, 78

Federal Tort Claims Act, 28 U.S.C. §2680, 93, 303

Homeland Security Act of 2002, Pub. L. No. 107-296, 116 Stat. 2135 (codified at 6 U.S.C. §§ 101-557), 132, 133

Pet Evacuation and Transportation Standards Act of 2006, Pub. L. No. 109-308, 120 Stat. 1725 §2 (codified at 42 U.S.C. §5196), 77, 99

Posse Comitatus Act, 18 U.S.C. §1385, 107-129

Post-Katrina Emergency Management Reform Act of 2006, Pub. L. No. 109-295, §§ 689b(b)-689c, 120 Stat. 1394, 1449 (2006), codified at 6 U.S.C. §§ 774-775, at 133, 134, 135, 146, 154, 186, 198, 240

Public Health Security and Bioterrorism Preparedness and Response Act of 2002, Pub. L. No. 107-188, §102, 116 Stat. 594, 599-603, at 106

Public Health Services Act, 42 U.S.C. §§ 201-300hh-11, 104-106

Robert T. Stafford Disaster Relief and Emergency Assistance Act, 42 U.S.C. §§ 5121-5208 (2009), 90 et. seq.

Water Resources Development Act of 2007, Pub. L. No. 110-114, 121 Stat. 1041, 1290 (codified at 33 U.S.C. §3303), 66

Weapons of Mass Destruction Act, 50 U.S.C. §§ 2301-2368 (2008), 104

Web-based Materials

Department of Homeland Security, Critical Infrastructure Sector Partnership, (available at http://www.dhs.gov/xprevprot/partnerships/editorial_0206.shtm), 21

Disasters and the Law Database (University of California — Berkeley School of Law), http://www.law.berkeley.edu/library/dynamic/disasters, 5

Disaster Research Center (University of Delaware), http://www.udel.edu/DRC, 5

Envision Utah, http://www.envisionutah.org/envisionprocess.phtml, 35

Miscellaneous Documents

PolicyLink, A Long Way Home: The State of Housing Recovery in Louisiana, 6 (2008), www.policylink.org, 382

Proposed Endangerment and Cause or Contribute Findings for Greenhouse Gases under Section 202(a) of the Clean Air Act, 74 Fed. Reg. 18886-01 (Apr. 24, 2009), 73

Report of the Second Assembly of the Gilbert F. White National Flood Policy Forum, Floodplain Management 2050 xi (2007), 10, 23, 25, 28-32, 33, 34, 35, 38

Save the Children, The Disaster Decade: Lessons Unlearned for the U.S. (June 2009), available at ://www.savethechildren.org/programs/us-literacy-and-nutrition/disaster-decade-lessons.html), 100

Seed, R.B. et al., Investigation of the Performance of the New Orleans Flood Protection Systems in Hurricane Katrina on August 29, 2005 (Final Report), July 31, 2006, (available at http://works.bepress.com/rmoss/17), 2, 64

Social and Spatial Inequalities Group, University of Sheffield, and Mark Newman, University of Michigan, http://worldmapper.org, 396

Sorooshian, Soroosh, Presentation to Straw Bale Forum, Hat Ranch, Williams, A. Z., Climate Variability, Water Resources, and Urban Growth in the Southwest (July 16, 2008), 72

Statement on Signing the Department of Homeland Security Appropriations Act, 2007, 42 Weekly Comp. Pres. Doc. 1742 (Oct. 4, 2006), 135

Stene, Eric A., The Teton Basin Project (Bureau of Reclamation History Program 1995) (available at http://www.usbr.gov/dataweb/html/teton.html), 67

Stockholm Declaration, Report of the United Nations Conference on the Human Environment, U.N. Doc. A/Conf.48/14, 11 I.L.M. 1416, 1416 (1972), 213

United Nations, 2009 Global Assessment Report on Disaster Risk Reduction: Risk And Poverty in a Changing Climate 5 (2009), 9, 23-24, 59-62

United Nations International Strategy for Disaster Reduction, 2005 Disasters in Numbers, http://www.unisdr.org/disaster-statistics/pdf/2005-disaster-in-numbers.pdf, 9

United Nations International Strategy For Disaster Reduction, Linking Disaster Risk Reduction And Poverty Reduction: Good Practices And Lessons Learned, 2008, www.unisdr.org, 409-411

United Nations International Strategy For Disaster Reduction, Report Of The Secretary General, Implementation Of The International Strategy For Disaster, Risk Reduction, Sept. 5, 2007, www.unisdr.org, 409

United Nations, World Population to Increase by 2.6 Billion over Next 45 Years with All Growth Occurring in Less Developed Countries, Press Release, Feb. 24, 2005, (available at http://www.un.org/News/Press/docs/2005/pop918.doc.htm), 23

Unreinforced Masonry Buildings (URMs), www.seattle.gov/dpd/Emergency/UnreinforcedMasonryBuildings/default.asp, 70

U.S. Agency For International Development, USAID Assistance To Internally Displaced Persons, http://www.usaid.gov/policy/ads/200/200mbc.pdf (Oct. 2004), 425-426

U.S. Army Corps of Engineers, Performance Evaluation of the New Orleans And Southeast Louisiana Hurricane Protection System: Final Report of the Interagency Performance Evaluation Task Force, Vol. I (June2009), I-3, available at ipet.wes.army.mil, 3

U.S.-Canada Power System Outage Task Force, Final Report on the August 14, 2003 Blackout in the United States and Canada: Causes and Recommendations 5 (2004), (available at http://www.nerc.com/filez/blackout.html), 16

GLOSSARY OF ACRONYMS

ASFPM	Association of State Floodplain Managers
ASPHEP	Assistant Secretary for Public Health Emergency Preparedness
BCEGS	Building Code Effectiveness Grading Schedule
BNOB	Bring New Orleans Back Committee
CCF	Climate Change Futures
CDBG	Community Development Block Grant
CDC	Centers for Disease Control
CEA	California Earthquake Authority
CI/KR	Critical Infrastructure and Key Resources
CLIVAR	Climate Variability and Predictability World Climate Research Programme
COP	Conference of Parties (Montreal, post-Kyoto)
DCN	Cuban National Civil Defense
DED	Deferred Enforced Departure
DHS	Department of Homeland Security
DOD	Department of Defense
EMAC	Emergency Management Assistance Compact
ENSO	El Niño/Southern Oscillation
ESF	Emergency Support Functions
EVD	Extended Voluntary Departure
FCA	Flood Control Act
FCO	Federal Coordinating Officer
FEMA	Federal Emergency Management Agency
FERC	Federal Energy Regulatory Commission
FHWA	Federal Highway Administration
FTA	Federal Transit Administration
GAO	Government Accountability Office
GDP	Gross Domestic Product
GHG	Greenhouse Gas
HANO	Housing Authority of New Orleans
HHS	Health and Human Services
HMGP	Hazard Mitigation Grant Program
HSC	Homeland Security Council
HSOC	Homeland Security Operations Center

HUD	Housing and Urban Development
ICODS	Interagency Committee on Dam Safety
ICS	Incident Command System
IDP	Internally Displaced Persons
IHP	Individual Housing Program
IIMG	Interagency Incident Management Group
IIPL	Insurance Institute for Property Loss Reduction
ILS	Insurance-Linked Securities
INA	Immigration and Nationality Act
INS	Incidents of National Significance
INV	Cuban National Housing Institute
IPCC	Intergovernmental Panel on Climate Change
IPF	Cuban Institute of Physical Planning
JFO	Joint Field Office
MRE	Meals Ready to Eat
MSEHPA	Model State Emergency Health Powers Act
MSHA	Mine Safety and Health Administration (Dept. of Labor)
MSPHA	Model State Public Health Act
NAO	North Atlantic Oscillation
NAS	National Academy of Sciences
NDSP	National Dam Safety Program
NDSRB	National Dam Safety Review Board
NFIP	National Flood Insurance Program
NHC	National Hurricane Center
NID	National Inventory of Dams
NIMS	National Incident Management System
NPRA	National Preparedness and Response Authority
NRCS	Natural Resources Conservation Service (Dept. of Agriculture)
NRF	National Response Framework
NRF-CIA	National Response Framework's Catastrophic Incident Annex
NRP	National Response Plan
O&M	Operation and Maintenance Procedures (Army Corps of Engineers)
PAHO	Pan American Health Organization
PETS	Pet Evacuation and Transportation Standards Act
PFO	Principal Federal Official
PML	Probable Maximum Losses
RRCC	Regional Response Coordination Center
SAD	State Active Duty
SARS	Severe Acute Respiratory Syndrome
SNS	Strategic National Stockpile
SPR	Strategic Petroleum Reserve
SREMAC	Southern Regional Emergency Management Assistance Compact
SRFCP	Sacramento River Flood Control Project
SSA	Social Security Act
TFAH	Trust for America's Health
TPA	Temporary Protected Status
TRIA	Terrorism Risk Insurance Act of 2002
UNFCCC	United Nations Framework Convention on Climate Change
WHO	World Health Organization
WRDA	Water Resources Development Act

INDEX